AF446814

The Early Modern Atlantic Economy

This book throws new light on the interlocking commercial relationships of the Atlantic trading world during the centuries ending with the American and French revolutions. Grouped under four themes – the role of merchants and their connections; the development of trades; imperial economies; and colonial working societies – and written by an international team of thirteen celebrated economic historians, these essays add to our knowledge and understanding of the transatlantic economy. Contributions range from studies of individual businessmen, labour patterns, port cities and branches of trade, to comparative studies of trading nations. They consider the role of the British and French empires as well as the imperial endeavours of other European powers in the Atlantic, drawing attention to the wider implications. This book throws new light on commerce and the early modern Atlantic economy, and will be a valuable resource for economic historians at all levels.

JOHN J. MCCUSKER is Ewing Halsell Distinguished Professor of American History and Professor of Economics at Trinity University, San Antonio, Texas. His recent books include *Essays in the Economic History of the Atlantic World* (1997), *How Much is That in Real Money? A Historical Price Index for Use as a Deflator of Money Values in the Economy of the United States* (1992, revised edn, 2000), and *The Beginnings of Commercial and Financial Journalism: The Commodity Price Currents, Exchange Rate Currents, and Money Currents of Early Modern Europe* (with Cora Gravesteijn, 1991).

KENNETH MORGAN is Professor of History at Brunel University, London. His recent publications include *Fritz Reiner, Maestro and Martinet* (2001), *Slavery and Servitude in North America, 1607–1800* (2000), *Slavery, Atlantic Trade and the British Economy, 1660–1800* (2000), *The Birth of Industrial Britain: Economic Change, 1750–1850* (1999), and *Bristol and the Atlantic Trade in the Eighteenth Century* (1993).

The Early Modern Atlantic Economy

Edited by

John J. McCusker

and

Kenneth Morgan

CAMBRIDGE UNIVERSITY PRESS

PUBLISHED BY THE PRESS SYNDICATE OF THE UNIVERSITY OF CAMBRIDGE
The Pitt Building, Trumpington Street, Cambridge, United Kingdom

CAMBRIDGE UNIVERSITY PRESS
The Edinburgh Building, Cambridge CB2 2RU, UK   www.cup.cam.ac.uk
40 West 20th Street, New York, NY 10011–4211, USA   www.cup.org
10 Stamford Road, Oakleigh, Melbourne 3166, Australia
Ruiz de Alarcón 13, 28014 Madrid, Spain

First published 2000

Printed in the United Kingdom at the University Press, Cambridge

Typeset in Plantin 10/12pt [VN]

A catalogue record for this book is available from the British Library

Library of Congress Cataloguing in Publication data

The early modern Atlantic economy/edited by John J. McCusker
    and Kenneth Morgan.
        p.   cm.
    ISBN 0 521 78249 X
1. Great Britain – colonies – commerce – history – 18th century.
2. Great Britain – commerce – America – history – 18th century.
3. America – commerce – Great Britain – history – 18th century.
4. France – colonies – commerce – history – 17th century.
5. France – commerce – America – history – 17th century.
6. America – commerce – France – history – 17th century.   I. McCusker,
John J.   II. Morgan, Kenneth.

HF3093.E2 2000
382'.09182'1–dc21   00–028924

ISBN 0521 78249X hardback

Contents

Figures

Tables

Abbreviations

Act of . . . References in this format to English (and, later, British) laws can be traced in [Great Britain, Laws and Statutes], *The Statutes of the Realm. Printed from Original Records and Authentic Manuscripts*, ed. Alexander Luders et al. (London, 1810–1828) (for the years prior to 1714, with the exception of 1642–1660); *Acts and Ordinances of the Interregnum, 1642–1660*, ed. C. H. Firth and R. S. Raith, 3 vols. (London, 1911); *The Statutes at Large of Great Britain*, ed. Danby Pickering, 46 vols. (Cambridge, 1762–1807) (for the period from 1714 to 1806); and *The Statutes of the United Kingdom of Great Britain and Ireland*, ed. Thomas Edlyne Tomlins et al., 29 vols. (London, 1804–1869) (for the years after 1806)

Add. MSS	Additional Manuscripts, in the Department of Manuscripts, British Library (BL), London
Adm	Admiralty Records, in the Public Record Office (PRO), London
ADM, Vannes	Archives Départmentales, du Morbihan, Vannes
AHR	*American Historical Review*
AN	Archives Nationales, Paris
AN-CAOM	Archives Nationales, Aix-en-Provence
AO	Exchequer and Audit Department Records, in the Public Record Office (PRO), London
BL	British Library (formerly the British Museum Library), London
BT	Board of Trade Records, in the Public Record Office (PRO), London
C	Records of the Chancery, in the Public Record Office (PRO), London
CHS	Connecticut Historical Society, Hartford
CLRO	City of London Records Office
CO	Colonial Office Records, in the Public Record Office (PRO), London

CPD	*Parliamentary Debates*. 621 vols. (London, 1804–1908) First series
Customs	Board of Customs and Excise Records, in the Public Record Office (PRO), London
DAR	Daughters of the American Revolution
DP	Dropmore Papers in the British Library (BL), London
E	Records of the Exchequer, in the Public Record Office (PRO), London
EcHR	*Economic History Review*
FO	Foreign Office Records, in the Public Record Office (PRO), London
HC	House of Commons
HCA	High Court of Admiralty Records, in the Public Record Office (PRO), London
HLP	House of Lords Sessional Papers
HLRO	House of Lords Record Office, London
HSP	The Historical Society of Pennsylvania, Philadelphia
JEcH	*Journal of Economic History*
JHC	*The Journals of the House of Commons*, in progress, 1742 to date
JIH	*Journal of Interdisciplinary History*
KB	Records of the Court of King's Bench, in the Public Record Office (PRO), London
Lambert	[Great Britain, Parliament, House of Commons] *House of Commons Sessional Papers of the Eighteenth Century*. Edited by Sheila Lambert. 147 vols. Wilmington, Del., 1975
LC	Library of Congress, Washington, D.C.
MM	*Mariner's Mirror: The Journal of the Society for Nautical Research*
MHS	Massachusetts Historical Society, Boston
McCusker, *Rum and the American Revolution*	John J. McCusker, *Rum and the American Revolution: The Rum Trade and the Balance of Payments of the Thirteen Continental Colonies, 1650–1775*, 2 vols. New York, 1989
McCusker and Menard, *Economy of British America*	John J. McCusker and Russell R. Menard, *The Economy of British America, 1607–1789*, 2nd edn Chapel Hill, N.C., 1991
MMWIPM	Minutes of the Meetings of the West India Planters and Merchants, West India Committee

	Records, University of the West Indies Library, St Augustine, Trinidad
NOSL	Naval Office Shipping List(s)
NEHGS	New England Historic Genealogical Society, Boston, Massachusetts
NRO, B-H(K) Coll.	Northamptonshire Record Office, Bateman–Hanbury (Kelmarsh) Collection
NYHS	New York Historical Society
PP	Parliamentary Papers
POE	Port of entry
Price, *Tobacco in Atlantic Trade*	Jacob M. Price, *Tobacco in Atlantic Trade: the Chesapeake, London and Glasgow 1675–1775.* Aldershot, 1995
Price, *The Atlantic Frontier*	Jacob M. Price, *The Atlantic Frontier of the Thirteen American Colonies and States: Essays in Eighteenth Century Commercial and Social History.* Aldershot, 1996
Price, *Overseas Trade and Traders*	Jacob M. Price, *Overseas Trade and Traders: Essays on Some Commercial, Financial and Political Challenges Facing British Atlantic Merchants, 1660–1775.* Aldershot, 1996
PC	Privy Council Registers, in the Public Record Office (PRO), London
PRO	Public Record Office Documents, in the Public Record Office (PRO), London
PROB	Prerogative Court of Canterbury Records, in the Public Record Office (PRO), London
SHC	Southern Historical Collection, University of North Carolina, Chapel Hill
SP	State Paper Office Records, in the Public Record Office (PRO), London
Stevens Trans.	Benjamin Franklin Stevens, Transcripts of Manuscripts in the Archives of England, France, Holland, and Spain Relating to America, 1763–83, Manuscript Division, Library of Congress (LC), Washington, D.C.
T	Treasury Office Records, in the Public Record Office (PRO), London
WMQ	*William and Mary Quarterly*

Contributors

LOIS GREEN CARR Maryland State Archives, Annapolis

FRANÇOIS CROUZET University of Paris IV-The Sorbonne

LOUIS M. CULLEN Trinity College, Dublin

RICHARD S. DUNN University of Pennsylvania

STANLEY L. ENGERMAN University of Rochester

DAVID HANCOCK University of Michigan

PETER MATHIAS Downing College, Cambridge

JOHN J. McCUSKER Trinity University, San Antonio, Texas

RUSSELL R. MENARD University of Minnesota

KENNETH MORGAN Brunel University, London

PATRICK K. O'BRIEN London School of Economics

HENRY ROSEVEARE King's College, London

CAROLE SHAMMAS University of Southern California

To Jacob M. Price

Introduction

John J. McCusker and Kenneth Morgan

As European countries began to expand overseas in the early modern period, transatlantic enterprise became an important conduit for business connections, international migration, the transfer of capital and the establishment of settler societies around the Atlantic littoral. Merchants in European ports established contacts with their counterparts, as well as factors and agents, in port cities in North America, the West Indies and coastal west Africa. They developed complex credit networks and business techniques suited to particular lines of trade. Ships plied the Atlantic sailing routes with cargoes of provisions and manufactured goods destined for markets in Africa and the New World and tropical produce picked up in the Americas for sale in Europe. Some vessels also took on board human cargoes such as European emigrants and African slaves.

This transatlantic commercial activity began as a relatively small-scale affair in the sixteenth century, gathered momentum in the seventeenth century and reached its apogee over the following hundred years. It was in the eighteenth century, at the end of the early modern period, that the integrated transatlantic economy attained its fullest articulation with communication channels that bridged the Atlantic successfully, thanks to growth in the circulation of business news, the organization of fleets, convoys and packets, and the cutting of transit time on various shipping routes. The sheer scope and complexity of the major Atlantic trades and the impact on Europe and New World settler societies of the products, trade and profits growing from this commerce meant that this 'great wheel of circulation' was an integral part of the development of western European societies in the early modern period.[1]

This collection of essays provides a fresh set of explorations connected to the broad theme of transatlantic enterprise, in its social, demographic and economic ramifications, in the hope that new light can be thrown on

---

[1] The phrase is quoted from the title of Russell R. Menard, 'The great wheel of circulation', *Reviews in American History*, 6 (1978), 435–8. On the mechanisms at work in integrating the British empire, see Ian K. Steele, *The English Atlantic, 1675–1740: an Exploration of Communication and Continuity* (Oxford, 1986).

the interlocking commercial relationships of the Atlantic trading world during the centuries ending with the American and French revolutions. Grouped under four themes – the role of merchants and their connections, the development of trades, imperial economies and colonial working societies – an international team of historians here presents a series of studies that add to our knowledge and interpretation of the transatlantic economy. Most of the chapters concentrate on the British and French empires, but all have wider implications and some explicitly contain references to the imperial endeavours of other European powers in the Atlantic. Contributions range from studies of individual businessmen, labour patterns, ports and branches of trade to comparative studies of trading nations. Some are based on detailed archival research; others distil thoughts on general themes that fall within the overall remit of the book. All, it is hoped, illuminate the operation of the early modern Atlantic economy.

The chapters offered here are also intended to honour the work of Jacob M. Price, the leading historian in recent decades of the transatlantic economy in the seventeenth and eighteenth centuries. Professor Price's mastery of the sources available for this scholarly field is widely known, as is his expertise in the commercial history of the tobacco trade and the external sectors of the British and American economies in the early modern period. He has demonstrated his ability to make highly effective use of the material he has researched during a long scholarly career, and has been a wise and generous counsellor to others who have entered the field. His great study *France and the Chesapeake: a History of the French Tobacco Monopoly 1674–1791, and of its Relationship to the British and American Tobacco Trades* (2 vols., Ann Arbor, 1973), almost a French *thèse* in its range and scope, stands as his *magnum opus*.[2] But Jacob Price is also well known for his *Capital and Credit in British Overseas Trade: the View from the Chesapeake, 1700–1776* (1980), for *Perry of London: a Family and a Firm on the Seaborne Frontier, 1615–1753* (1992), and for a regular flow of learned articles.[3] Recently, he has provided a summation of many strands

---

[2] For a detailed, appreciative appraisal of this book see Elizabeth Fox-Genovese and Eugene D. Genovese, *Fruits of Merchant Capital: Slavery and Bourgeois Property in the Rise and Expansion of Capitalism* (Oxford, 1983), ch. 3.

[3] Jacob M. Price has published three volumes of collected articles: *Tobacco in Atlantic Trade: the Chesapeake, London and Glasgow 1675–1775*; *The Atlantic Frontier of the Thirteen American Colonies and States: Essays in Eighteenth Century Commercial and Social History*; and *Overseas Trade and Traders: Essays on Some Commercial, Financial and Political Challenges facing British Atlantic Merchants, 1660–1775*. The last volume includes (pp. xi–xiv) a chronological list of his articles on economic history, 1954–96. References below to Price's individual articles cite their place in these volumes rather than their original publication details. Because the volumes contain facsimile reprints of the articles, pagination is not continuous and so they are cited here by individual chapters.

developed in his articles in a chapter for *The Oxford History of the British Empire*.[4] The essays in the volume at hand are offered in Professor Price's honour by fellow historians in his field who have gained by his scholarship, friendship and sage counsel and who consider that the best compliment that they can pay to his work is to offer new studies that explore the themes to which he has devoted his scholarly energies.

The role of merchants and their connections

The book opens with two contributions – one general in scope, the other more specifically located in time – dealing with the role of merchants and their connections in the Atlantic economy of early modern Europe and America. Peter Mathias sets the scene with some broad reflections on the interconnections between kinship, risk and credit in the seventeenth and eighteenth centuries. Operating in a high-risk trading environment that revolved around personal contacts, merchants needed to make use of kinship networks for entry into business and to further commercial alliances between families, often through marriage. But these direct personal relationships could be difficult to secure because of demographic uncertainty. The range of technical expertise needed by businessmen grew ever more complex. As the Atlantic economy burgeoned and more and more merchants needed to trade with those with whom they had no direct personal acquaintance, credit standing and creditworthiness became of paramount importance in establishing and sustaining commercial ties. Jacob Price has demonstrated this in many of his publications, notably in his study of Joshua Johnson, a member of an Annapolis trading house who was sent to London a few years before the outbreak of the American War of Independence.[5] Mathias underscores the general significance of these credit arrangements when he suggests that 'capital and credit requirements were much higher in relation to turn-over than in more recent times of faster, more assured communications' (p. 22).

Little public information was available on the creditworthiness of businessmen, and so the knowledge of personal character and trustworthiness built up over the course of individual commercial transactions was crucial

---

[4] Jacob M. Price, 'The imperial economy, 1700–1776', in P. J. Marshall, ed., *The Oxford History of the British Empire*. Vol. II: *The Eighteenth Century* (Oxford, 1998), pp. 78–104. Price has also written studies dealing with methodological issues in history: see his 'Party, purpose, and pattern: Sir Lewis Namier and his critics', *Journal of British Studies*, 1 (1961), 71–93, and Val R. Lorwin and Jacob M. Price, eds., *The Dimensions of the Past: Materials, Problems, and Opportunities for Quantitative Work in History* (New Haven, 1972).

[5] Jacob M. Price, 'Joshua Johnson in London, 1771–1775: credit and commercial organization in the British Chesapeake trade', in his *Tobacco in Atlantic Trade*, ch. 8, adapted in his edition of *Joshua Johnson's Letterbook, 1771–1774: Letters from a Merchant in London to his Partners in Maryland*, London Record Society, 15 (1979).

to maintaining a well-run business. Reputation and trust could disappear where credit was over-extended, debts accumulated and liquidity problems arose; but they remained the bedrock of sound commercial dealings in a time of unlimited liability. The risk of dealing with unknown individuals helps to explain why groups such as Quakers, Jews and Scots traders kept much of their business to their own kind. As Price has shown in his own work, the intricate family and business links among Quaker merchants and shippers provided a firm foundation for trading in a reasonably secure way.[6] Mathias indicates that moral obligation often lay at the bottom of commercial relationships, with a form of 'moral credit' being accorded by businessmen to those who had helped them. What mattered more than anything for substantial merchants in transatlantic trade was recognition of their credit standing. Because they were faced with frequent interruptions to shipping lanes through war on the high seas, as well as the normal ups and downs of the business cycle, the knowledge that a particular merchant with whom they had dealt stood in good credit was the crucial indicator for continuing business.

Kenneth Morgan looks more specifically at the role of merchants in a significant branch of transatlantic trade. He argues that, owing to the high risks of foreign trade, business networks in the British export trade to North America became more closely intertwined in the second half of the eighteenth century, a time when such commerce experienced considerable growth despite fluctuations caused by war, non-importation agreements in some American colonies, and seasonal and yearly fluctuations in the demand for goods. He finds that commodities were dispatched with greater precision as the market for them grew more complex. American merchants visited British ports frequently during the American revolutionary period, gathering detailed information on manufactured goods for export. At the same time British merchants made their way to North America, acquiring direct knowledge of business conditions there. In addition to establishing this greater depth of personal knowledge acquired by merchants who inspected export goods and their production processes, Morgan also suggests that transatlantic business networks in the export trade were stimulated in other ways: by the dissemination of a more varied range of samples and business documents (such as pattern books, textile samples and privately printed sheets listing the prices and quality of goods); by the growth of direct correspondence between American merchants and inland agents and manufacturers in Britain; by greater sophistication in financing commerce (notably the complex credit

---

[6] Jacob M. Price, 'The great Quaker business families of eighteenth century London: the rise and fall of a sectarian patriciate' and 'English Quaker merchants and the war at sea, 1689–1783', in his *Overseas Trade and Traders*, chs. 3 and 4.

mechanisms adopted); and by links forged between merchants, agents, suppliers and manufacturers on both sides of the Atlantic in order to coordinate the demand for goods (especially textiles) destined for North American markets in relation to their colour, price, variety and finishing.

The development of trades

Jacob Price's work includes articles dealing with the role of British ports in oceanic trade and with the careers of individual merchant houses.[7] It is therefore fitting that the first two contributions in the section on the development of trades follow this approach to mercantile history. In one, Henry Roseveare investigates the power struggle in the port of London in the mid-eighteenth century. In the other, Louis M. Cullen traces the career of an Irishman who had an intricate business involvement in *ancien régime* France.

Roseveare's chapter extends his investigations into the internal history of the port of London in the early modern period – a much neglected subject.[8] He looks at the acquisition of quays and wharves along the River Thames as indicators of the complex, competitive strategies of the port's users, and suggests that this had important repercussions for most overseas sectors of commerce flowing in and out of the metropolis, and for the American and West Indian trades in particular. By the 1740s a powerful coalition of London's banking, insurance and commercial leaders were dissatisfied with the wharfingers' cartel, which had monopolized control of the legal quays since 1695. Their complaints about extortion by the wharfingers exposed the operating deficiencies of the port of London some fifty years before major new docks were built there. Appreciation of these internal difficulties in port organization provides a useful corrective to historians who are reluctant to concede that London's commercial hegemony of British ports was eroded by the rise of the west coast outports during the eighteenth century.[9]

---

[7] For example, 'The rise of Glasgow in the Chesapeake tobacco trade', in *Tobacco in Atlantic Trade*, ch. 1, and 'Competition between ports in British long distance trade, c. 1660–1800', in Augustín Guimera and Dolores Romero, eds., *Puertos y sistemas portuarios (siglos XVI–XX). Actas del coloquio internacional el sistema portuario español* (Madrid, 1996), pp. 19–36.

[8] See Henry Roseveare, '"Wiggins' Key" revisited: trade and shipping in the later seventeenth century port of London', *Journal of Transport History*, 3rd series, 16 (1995), 1–20; '"The damned combination": the port of London and the wharfingers' cartel of 1695', *The London Journal*, 21 (1996), 97–111; and 'The eighteenth-century port of London reconsidered', in Guimera and Romero, eds., *Puertos y sistemas portuarios*, pp. 37–52.

[9] For example, Christopher J. French, '"Crowded with traders and a great commerce": London's domination of English overseas trade, 1700–1775', *The London Journal*, 17 (1992), 27–35.

London also appears in Cullen's study, but this time as a financial centre for the remittance and transference of bills of exchange. Thomas Sutton, the subject of Cullen's chapter, illustrates the wide-ranging networks of influence and business acquaintance tapped by someone who was both an Irish businessman and a French courtier. Sutton belonged to an Irish business circle based in Dublin, London, Paris, Bordeaux, Saint-Malo and Cadiz; to an Irish official and courtier group in France in professions such as the navy, army and the church; and to a circle based partly in Lorient and partly in Saint-Malo, with intermarriage between the French and the Irish. In its intricate portrayal of these overlapping connections and the way in which they facilitated Sutton's interest in French economic, military and naval power, this study examines connections reminiscent of the far-flung but different business links that Jacob Price traced for the Russells, Lees and Clerks in Britain, Maryland and India in the eighteenth and nineteenth centuries.[10] Roseveare's and Cullen's chapters are merely the first steps in what one hopes will be a fuller scholarly investigation over the next generation of the overseas commercial residence and networks of British, Irish and American businessmen in the age of enlightenment.

The best recent book dealing with the far-flung networks of British merchants with transatlantic interests has been David Hancock's *Citizens of the World: London Merchants and the Integration of the British Atlantic Community, 1735–1785* (1995). In his contribution to this volume, Hancock shifts his focus from an interlocking group of mainly Scots merchants making their fortunes in London to the widespread commercial networks of traders dealing in Madeira wine. Charting the changes in the production of Madeira from a simple table wine in 1700 to a complex, highly processed drink by 1800, he traces the expansion in the volume of wine leaving Funchal in the eighteenth century, the shifts in global markets for Madeira wine and, especially, the impact of this drink on consumption in North America, where it found its largest market. Hancock rightly refers to the growth in the production and consumption of Madeira wine as 'a revolution in the trade' in the eighteenth century. His most significant contribution is to demonstrate how Madeira merchants effected this transformation. They managed their North American business through personal contacts in selling, conducted conversations with customers about the taste and colour of the product, coordinated services for their customers by drawing on expertise from around the world and, most importantly, marketed the product by adjusting packaging, devising connoisseur terminology and adopting

[10] Jacob M. Price, 'One family's empire: the Russell–Lee–Clerk connection in Maryland, Britain, and India, 1707–1857', in his *Tobacco in Atlantic Trade*, ch. 9.

luxury pricing. By these means, Madeira merchants 'built a commercial system in which the gains from trade flowed across imperial boundaries' (p. 153).[11]

Broad treatments of trade development feature in the contributions by Russell R. Menard and Carole Shammas. Menard takes a comparative look at the difference in sugar cultivation methods in Barbados and Brazil in the seventeenth century. In the former, sugar was processed at the plantation's own mill; in the latter, a dispersed system of production was common, with sugar-cane grown by small farmers and then taken to large mills for processing. The difference in organizational methods arose from changes in labour supply, access to credit and different legal codes. Barbadians had enough slaves to permit sugar cultivation throughout half the island by 1665; they had access to credit and could legally collect debts with the backing of local courts. There was thus no need for a dispersed system of production. Brazilians, on the contrary, had a good supply of slaves, mainly from Portuguese vessels arriving from Angola, but available credit to buy them was restricted and the law did not permit creditors to seize equipment, livestock and slaves in lieu of payment. For these economic and legal reasons, a more dispersed mode of sugar cultivation persisted in Brazil for a long time. But such a system created a class of producers – the *lavradores de cana* – who could not be displaced when the Brazilian sugar industry ultimately centralized.

This comparative framework also informs Shammas's discussion, which focuses on the role of plantation goods in early modern European consumption. She criticizes the notion that domestic markets and European durable and semi-durable goods were more significant in widening and boosting consumption than imports, and considers that analysing foreign trade in relation to gross domestic product plays down its real significance for demand because most of the world's people did not live in nation state economies in the early modern period. Her view is that the colonies altered the infrastructure and the political economy of western Europe. The demand in Europe for tropical groceries – sugar, tea, tobacco, cocoa, chocolate – plus cotton textiles grew rapidly and extensively in the centuries between 1500 and 1800 as a result of consumer demand rather than government planning. The growth of plantation complexes for growing tropical crops, such as those discussed by Menard for Brazil and Barbados, amounted to an agricultural revolution that makes the early modern innovations in wheat farming such as mixed husbandry, new systems of rotation, and soil amendments pale in comparison. This is a vigorous counterblast to historians who regard early

---

[11] See also David Hancock, 'Commerce and conversation in the eighteenth-century Atlantic: the invention of Madeira wine', *JIH*, 29 (1998), 197–220.

modern European consumption as primarily the result of the increase of home demand in growing domestic markets.

This section concludes with John J. McCusker's wide-ranging consideration of the time when distilled alcoholic beverages began to be consumed extensively in the Atlantic world. Focusing on the century and a half between *c.* 1650 and the American Revolution, McCusker charts the technological improvements in distilling and the concomitant growth in the trade in sugar from the western hemisphere that increased the availability of spirits in western Europe and lowered their price. Distilling became an industry only after 1600. Commercial distilleries, able to cut the cost of raw materials and production and, thus, to charge lower prices, spread throughout France, the Netherlands, the German states and Great Britain. In the Caribbean Anglo-American businessmen benefited not just from the production and sale of sugar and its byproducts to the British Isles but also, because of the islands' substantial trade with New England, from the French ban on all distilling in its colonies. By the 1770s and 1780s the demand for spirits was substantial. For some residents of Great Britain annual consumption of spirits amounted on an average to perhaps nine litres per year while among the white settlers in British North America it was almost sixteen. McCusker's chapter, examining the production of spirits within the broad parameters of an imperial trading framework, suggests that a study of distilled spirits consumption might provide a foundation for comparative work looking at the growth of distilling and sugar refining in the early modern world, with reference to their technologies, capital and labour inputs and entrepreneurial changes.[12]

Imperial economies

A trio of papers follows, all investigating the nature of imperial economies. Stanley L. Engerman offers a broad comparative overview of the settlement patterns and long-term development of the French and British empires in the Americas in the seventeenth and eighteenth centuries.[13] Patrick K. O'Brien and François Crouzet both examine features of the British imperial economy during the interruptions to normal trading practices and shipping lanes during the wars with revolutionary and Napoleonic France.

[12] For a recent study of changes in the business of sugar refining, see Kenneth Morgan, 'Sugar refining in Bristol', in Kristine Bruland and Patrick O'Brien, eds., *From Family Firms to Corporate Capitalism: Essays in Business and Industrial History in Honour of Peter Mathias* (Oxford, 1998), pp. 139–69.

[13] The North American context of French overseas enterprise has recently been evaluated in Marc Egnal, *New World Economies: the Growth of the Thirteen Colonies and Early Canada* (New York, 1998).

Engerman's theme is the greater impact of Great Britain's colonial empire on its industrialization than was the case with France and its colonies. Both France and Britain followed mercantilist policies towards their colonies; the Atlantic empires of both countries flourished until the 1780s; and there were similarities in the economic performance of both nations. The chief distinction, according to Engerman, lay in the comparative performances of the West Indian trade sector of the two countries after 1783. British West India commerce, despite setbacks, recovered significantly thereafter, as did trade relations between Great Britain and the United States.[14] But the loss of land and reduction of sugar cultivation in Saint-Domingue as a result of the massive slave revolt of 1791 was calamitous. The French West India trade never recovered. During the decades around the turn of the nineteenth century when, if it had flourished, it could have contributed more significantly to French industrialization, Saint-Domingue was moribund.

O'Brien examines Britain's monetary policy and foreign commerce during the French revolutionary and Napoleonic wars, a period when, as he reminds us, commerce in the English Channel and the Atlantic ocean was so precarious that nearly 11,000 British merchant ships were lost to enemy marauders. Concerned with evaluating a contemporary critique that accused the government, the Bank of England and the mercantile community of mishandling the nation's credit and monetary system at a time of threat to national security, he shows that this viewpoint owes more to rhetoric than to fact. In O'Brien's analysis, the exceptional demands of the wartime dislocation of trade are seen as demanding a flexible and expansionary monetary policy. This was implemented in 1797 when, after a run on the Bank of England's gold reserve, the government suspended specie payments and allowed itself and the Bank to pursue a non-convertible currency policy. As crises occurred in the British trading economy – one between 1805 and 1808, another in the years 1810–12 – flexible supplies of credit from banks and other financial intermediaries made it possible for British merchants and manufacturers to stockpile goods whenever the enemy interrupted the flow of commodities to Europe and the Americas, or whenever France or the United States threatened to cut off supplies of foodstuffs and industrial raw materials. O'Brien robustly defends his argument that monetary policy from 1797 to 1815 was 'functional for the security of the realm and efficient for the growth and stability of Britain's wartime economy' (p. 257).

---

[14] See in this regard John J. McCusker, 'The economy of the British West Indies, 1763–1790: growth, stagnation, or decline?' in his *Essays in the Economic History of the Atlantic World* (London, 1997), pp. 310–30.

Crouzet focuses on a segment of the same period as O'Brien, but his detailed case study of a mini-crisis in the imperial economy in the years 1803–7 ranges more widely than might at first be apparent, given his stated chronological limits. The general framework consists of the liberal commercial policy that Britain pursued towards neutral countries between 1794 and 1807 that enabled the United States, in particular, to compete effectively with British re-exported goods to Europe by sending products from the French, Dutch and Spanish colonies in the Caribbean via American ports to European destinations. From 1799 onwards the British sugar trade was affected badly as American vessels sold foreign sugar on the Continent while British stocks of sugar accumulated in home ports and British sugar prices fell. Other sectors of Britain's imperial economy were also harmed by American competition in the oceanic carrying trade, notably the supply of foodstuffs to the West Indies and in the trade in East India piece goods from India to Europe.

Crouzet is the first historian to examine this commercial crisis in the depth that the rich documentation available deserves, and he fully demonstrates the seriousness of the crisis as discussed in parliamentary committees in 1806–7. Since the crisis in those years was very much tied to overproduction of sugar in the British Caribbean, it would be interesting to take the argument a step further to see to what extent this crisis in imperial trade bore on the abolition of the British slave trade, which was prominent in parliamentary debates at this time.[15] The crisis was resolved in 1808 when Britain eliminated American competition in the colonial carrying trade by restricting neutral trade under orders in council of 1807.

Colonial working societies

Transatlantic enterprise was possible only through the productive efforts of white and black settlers, free and unfree, in the Americas; without their labour, the rise in the volume and value of commodities sent eastwards across the Atlantic would not have occurred. Price's work has focused more on the mechanics and significance of merchant communities, trade and international finance than on labour patterns. But much of his output has concentrated on the Chesapeake tobacco colonies and he has also investigated general patterns of socio-economic development in early

---

[15] For different views on the connection between the crisis in the West Indian sugar economy *c.* 1805–7 and the abolition of the British slave trade see Eric Williams, *Capitalism and Slavery* (London, 1944), pp. 149–50, 152; Roger Anstey, 'Capitalism and slavery: a critique', *EcHR*, 2nd series, 21 (1968), 307–20; and Seymour Drescher, *Econocide: British Slavery in the Era of Abolition* (Pittsburgh, 1977).

North America,[16] so the final two contributions fit well into his broad scholarly interests. In this section entitled 'Colonial working societies', Lois Green Carr evaluates the standard of living for emigrants to the eighteenth-century Chesapeake, while Richard S. Dunn continues his work on the history of slave plantation communities at Mount Airy, Virginia, and Mesopotamia, Jamaica. In his essay he considers slave labour patterns in Mount Airy's transition in the early nineteenth century from mainly tobacco cultivation to grain production, a phenomenon that had begun some decades earlier in Maryland.[17]

Carr's findings for the standard of living enjoyed by British immigrants in the Chesapeake are different from the conclusions she arrived at for a similar group in the seventeenth century. In an earlier piece she argued that seventeenth-century British emigrants to the Chesapeake faced a shorter life in North America and less physical comfort than in England, but that indentured servants – a sizeable proportion of emigrants – could improve their status after freedom by acquiring land and gaining greater control over their lives.[18] For the eighteenth century, the picture is different: immigrants to the Chesapeake had a better life expectancy after arrival than in the seventeenth century, but opportunities to acquire land or improve their lot in life had diminished. These immigrants married later in the Chesapeake than was common in English society but they enjoyed more years of married life than their seventeenth-century emigrant counterparts. In setting down some general markers for further work on this topic – one beset by fragmentary sources – Carr concludes that

[o]n the whole . . . eighteenth-century British immigrants did not suffer the severe decline in life's comforts and changes in habits that seventeenth-century immigrants had. True, for the most the housing was inferior to that of England in permanence and size, and many, especially among the poor, sacrificed some household conveniences. But the big loss for these later immigrants lay elsewhere – in decreasing opportunities to acquire land and participate in local decision-making (p. 337).

Dunn completes the volume with a case study of the Tayloe family's organization of their slave labour force at Mount Airy in the early nineteenth century. Faced with a situation where less labour was needed for

<hr>

[16] For example, 'Quantifying colonial America', *JIH*, 6 (1976), 701–9; 'Trade and commerce: the British colonies', in Jacob E. Cooke, ed., *Encyclopedia of the North American Colonies*, 3 vols. (New York, 1993), I, pp. 511–32; and 'The transatlantic economy', in *The Atlantic Frontier*, ch. 1.

[17] The transition is covered in Paul G. E. Clemens, *The Atlantic Economy and Colonial Maryland's Eastern Shore: from Tobacco to Grain* (Ithaca, N.Y., 1980).

[18] Lois Green Carr, 'Emigration and the standard of living: the seventeenth-century Chesapeake', *JEcH*, 52 (1992), 271–91.

tending grain and livestock than had been required for growing tobacco, the Tayloes adopted management practices that squeezed the maximum productivity out of their workforce. Keeping workers busy by constantly shifting their work assignments, coordinating the work of field labourers with artisans to meet the varying demands of the estate's annual work cycle, attempting to get the right mixture of slaves working on each site – these were some of the management strategies pursued. The Tayloes found jobs for almost all of their potentially surplus slaves and sold only those who did not fit into the system. Dunn characterizes Tayloe as someone who 'made the difficult transition from tobacco culture to mixed agriculture in an aggressively entrepreneurial style' (p. 362), and notes that the productivity of slaves at Mount Airy exceeded that found elsewhere in the Chesapeake.

Conclusion

By focusing on the labour of slaves in the Chesapeake, Dunn returns us full circle from the end product of transatlantic enterprise, namely the consumption of American commodities in European markets, to the beginning of the cycle, which was the production of goods in North America for export across the Atlantic. In tracing the business networks, credit practices, organization of production, distribution of commodities, comparative economic performance of European Atlantic empires and living standards and labour patterns of white and black settlers in North America, the essays in this volume seek to encompass the range of historical interests found in the work of Jacob Price and to suggest the state of the debates on the impact of transatlantic enterprise in the early modern period. They have also provided new research findings and pointers to future investigations in this field. They are offered here as a summation of where we have reached in looking at the Atlantic trading world in its formative and mature years, and they provide an agenda for future historians to follow up. If any of those historians assemble and analyse their material with the depth, care and incisiveness of Jacob Price's scholarly work, they will furnish the historical profession with solid studies of lasting significance.

Part I

The role of merchants and their connections

1 Risk, credit and kinship in early modern enterprise

Peter Mathias

This contribution to a volume honouring Jacob Price and celebrating his work takes as its themes risk, credit and kinship in the early modern period, exploring the ways in which they interacted to condition business strategies and the day-to-day conduct of business. It seeks to survey and assess generally rather than to add to research.[1] Considerations about kinship, credit, risk and the avoidance of risk have suffused all of Jacob Price's investigations into transatlantic trade and finance in the seventeenth and eighteenth centuries, either explicitly or as a structural feature of the context. Indeed, because uncertainty and risk were almost universally present to so much greater an extent in 'normal' trading activities in that period than in conducting equivalent transactions in the twentieth century they conditioned the operation of the business system in an elemental way. Nor can risk be easily distinguished from uncertainty in the commonly assumed modern conceptual sense – where risk can supposedly be quantified (a precondition for commercial insurance) and uncertainty not. Many categories of risk had uncertainties also built into them and were in large measure open ended. Focusing attention on avoiding or minimizing risk may imply taking too negative or too defensive a view about the conduct of business in this period. It takes for granted other aspects of business which are emphasized in the literature of entrepreneurship in historical settings – the motivations of businessmen for expanding the scale of their operations, increasing their profits, pioneering innovations, making their personal fortunes, enhancing their social status with the accumulation of wealth. But one set of determinants does

---

[1] This chapter draws on, and adds to, my paper 'Strategies for reducing risk by entrepreneurs in the early modern period', in C. Lesger and L. Noordegraaf, eds., *Entrepreneurs and Entrepreneurship in Early Modern Times: Merchants and Industrialists within the Orbit of the Dutch Staplemarket*, Hollandse Historische Reeks, 24 (The Hague, 1995). For the general debate see O. E. Williamson, *Markets and Hierarchies* (New York, 1975); J. March and H. Simon, *Organisations* (Oxford, 1958); W. Reddy, *The Rise of Market Culture* (Cambridge, 1989); A. Godley and O. Westall, eds., *Business History and Business Culture* (Manchester, 1996).

not exclude the other. Entrepreneurship had to be exercised within the parameters of high risk, which made demands of their own, while different phases in the evolution of a business, different stages in a person's business career and different circumstances at a particular point of time would determine varied responses. This was particularly the case in circumstances of intense, occasional short-term fluctuations in trade and financial liquidity.

The central theme argued in the following pages is that the context of risk emphasized the importance of face-to-face personal relationships and kinship in business, in particular concerning access to credit.[2] Within the general parameter the family matrix was so often central to the operations of business, whether in structural relationships (patterns of ownership, succession, the identification of ownership with management authority and the like) or in everyday dealings.[3] A major dimension of such a matrix was demographic – and the demographic dynamic added risks and uncertainties of its own, as well as opportunities, which could not be anticipated. These demographic indeterminacies – as with economic and financial indeterminacies – are often subsumed and articulated (in the terms in which they were perceived) as 'luck'. The greater the degree of indeterminacy in a situation, the greater the role often put down to 'luck' – which is acknowledging the same reality through different perceptions and articulations. Demographic dynamics for the family firm were then very different from what they were in the later nineteenth and twentieth centuries. The hazards of survivability were much greater (compounded when in a tropical setting). This produced early – and unexpected – succession to ownership, unexpected windfalls from legacies, lower probabilities for direct succession through male heirs (or daughters) in a family firm. Higher demographic risks also enhance the importance of wider kinship relations in partnership successions, the role of widows and the propensity for re-marriage. The rights of patrimony and the normal legal provision for nominating kin to succession in a partnership con-

---

[2] J. Scott, *Social Network Analysis* (London, 1991); M. Casson and M. B. Rose, eds., *Institutions and the Evolution of Modern Business* (special issue, *Business History*, London, 1993). The introduction to the latter volume states that 'one of the consequences of making the institutional environment endogenous would be that networks and their social underpinnings would move from the periphery to the core of institutional theory' (p. 6). See especially in the same volume Casson, 'Institutional economics and business history: a way forward', where he notes that 'Transaction costs reflect a lack of trust between the people concerned' (pp. 151–2).

[3] S. R. H. Jones, 'Transaction costs and the theory of the firm', in Casson and Rose, eds., *Institutions and the Evolution of Modern Business*, pp. 9–25; P. Dasgupta, 'Trust as a commodity', in D. Gambetta, ed., *Trust: Making and Breaking Cooperative Relations* (New York, 1988), pp. 49–72; A. Etzioni, *The Moral Dimension: towards a New Economics* (New York, 1988); F. Fukuyama, *Trust* (London, 1995).

solidated the matrix, where demographic success permitted. The provision of capital and credit (more long-term capital than normal trade credit, except in emergencies) was another vital nexus linking kinship, and trusted personal connections, with the operation of business.

Such interpersonal and interkinship relationships are integrally linked with the context of high risk within which business had perforce to be conducted. One dimension of high risk derived from natural hazards of various kinds – the improving but still greatly limited control over nature: slow communications and the uncertainties imposed by storm, calm, flood, drought or frost. Technological weaknesses reinforced such natural hazards and, for the most part, had to be accommodated to the dictates of nature rather than being able to overcome them. The operation of the business system also created endogenous risks, apart from those consequent upon a hostile nature and a limited technology. Legal, institutional and political processes imposed great uncertainties, long delays and high costs. The most elemental 'law and order' precondition for the successful conduct of most legitimate business – the physical security of property and assets, a peaceful, well-ordered environment where commercial transactions could take place in a context of defined legal rules – was often lacking in many European as well as non-European settings, on occasion if not more permanently. More frequently, war created risks in international shipping and commerce. These various categories of risk can be elaborated at length but the general conclusion – even, perhaps, constituting a general law – would be that the weaker the institutional context, from a wide variety of sources of risk and uncertainty, then the higher the premium to be placed on individual dealings with known individuals, personal trust and the kinship nexus. As the common phrase puts it: 'blood is thicker than water'.

Wealth in the parents of a businessman and in his kinship group more widely, together with wealth brought by his wife and her family, could cover a multitude of risks. Very few great fortunes were created in a single generation by the efforts of a single man of business. Modest capital at least, and modest personal connections, were usually preconditions for success and overcoming the initial risks of establishing a business. The hazards of setting up in business were minimized by following one's father in trade or being introduced into a partnership by patrimony. Following in the shoes of one's father, or other relative, directly offered knowledge of the trade, connections with established clients, customers and suppliers, with the confidence and trust that continuity of dealing over earlier years had built up. In general, access to a prosperous business or professional career depended greatly upon family wealth and connections, despite well-publicized individual instances to the contrary. The fame of such exceptions correlated with their infrequency, compounded by much mythologizing on the poor-boy-made-good theme, which also has to be discounted. Where direct succession to the family firm did not happen, entry into an allied trade, or another partnership with personal links, could bring many of the same advantages. Young men were often taught the trade, following their schooling, by being placed with the firm of a family friend, living under his roof for a year or so. Membership of an elite trading or city company, preeminently the East India Company, could usually be contrived by powerful established members for a kinsman, if not secured by outright nomination as with an ordinary commercial or professional partnership.

Potentially lucrative business positions commanded high apprenticeship or acceptance fees which imposed high barriers to entry, as with the main trading companies with monopoly privileges, major brewers and distillers and more generally wherever large capital and potentially high returns were in question. Such fees could run up to £500–1,000 in the mid- and late eighteenth century, but provided a privileged entrée to a lucrative commercial world.[4] Even with high fees a personal introduction would be a prerequisite for acceptance. In all these ways parental wealth and influence could secure a privileged position for sons beginning a new career. At issue was not just the means of learning the trade in question, with the relevant technical skills, but of gaining access to the insider's world of personal contacts, confidential relationships, personal trust and status in the trade. This was not the only ladder to potential success but it was much the easiest and the fastest. In a context of high risk privileged access was at a premium. Given prevailing demographic patterns (provided that he took care to survive) the son could stand to inherit at an early age or be invited into the firm of an uncle or a cousin without male heirs. The demographic lottery could also yield unexpected legacies with extensive failures in the direct line of succession. Maintaining close links with kin on the side of both parents was thus elementary prudence.

The demographic odds also offered opportunity to the able apprentice who had demonstrated his talents as a salaried clerk or manager.[5] Apart from the possibility of working his way into the partnership (usually by way of a loan from an existing partner, at interest, but paid off by instalments saved from his salary), the salaried clerk who found himself in a strategic position running the business might even aspire to the possibil-

---

[4] R. Campbell, *The London Tradesman* (1749); see, for example, in brewing Peter Mathias, *The Brewing Industry in England, 1700–1830* (Cambridge, 1959).

[5] This sequence was played out in the relations between the Thrale family, with no male heirs, and the salaried manager of the large brewery in London, John Perkins. See Mathias, *The Brewing Industry*.

ity of marrying his master's daughter, or (it had been known) his master's widow. High talent in non-kin could also be rewarded where male heirs did not wish to take on the trade or were considered unsuitable. Where a business was important to a family's fortunes and extensive capital was engaged, practical considerations sometimes challenged the dictates of kinship. High risk and the safeguarding of capital, together with the income flows, produced important incentives to consolidate the operation of business with kinship links – and not only over the question of succession. Clearly, this has been the case in many walks of life, not least in the expansion and consolidation of landed estates, where dynastic alliances have traditionally constituted an essential strategy. Kings and princes, nobles and commoners have followed this motivation, jointly pursuing wealth, power and dynastic advantage.

Everything that has been said about discounting risk when setting up in business by choosing one's parents wisely relates in equal measure – and with greater choice – to the businessman's own marriage and this, of course, when he was young was far from being independent of his family's status. Marriage often cemented alliances between families with close business interests, while being arranged informally and remaining dependent on the personal consent of the two parties, despite family pressures. Such a marriage contract usually reflected a carefully estimated reciprocity, not cast only in terms of capital sums in down payment for a dowry and a wife's portion but including presumptions about the prospective earning power and inheritance of the bridegroom. Unless on marriage the wife's capital (or the widow's assets) was legally separated and administered on her behalf through a trust, as with an unmarried heiress, then her assets became her husband's. In the normal lottery of marriage, before the days of Married Women's Property Acts giving statutory protection, the husband won the jackpot. Past, present and future thus converged in the making of such alliances.

Where capital values and earning power derived from a business these considerations of personal ownership and control operated with much greater effect than when the assets were in land and property or in government stock (the 'Funds' in English parlance). To yield a continuing stream of income and to maintain their capital value all assets required skills in management, but the required degree of active management and the skills involved varied widely between different categories of assets. Minimal expertise and supervision, but honesty in administration by trustees or those with powers of attorney, was demanded by assets in the Funds. Freehold property required maintenance and effective supervision of tenants, but arrangements could be made to organize this, usually through local solicitors or land agents. Such services were widely available for both town and country. In the case of business assets, however, the case was more complicated. Effective management skills, technical expertise in the case of productive enterprise, application and honesty were paramount if the income stream from profits was to be preserved and the capital value of the assets which produced the income maintained, let alone enhanced. In the words of Samuel Johnson's famous comment on the sale of the Thrale brewery to Messrs. Barclay and Perkins: 'What can misses do with a brew-house? Lands are fitter for daughters than trade.'[6]

Daily attendance and supervision were required, just to maintain routine business and accounting, but the supervision of a salaried clerk on the spot could not supply the initiatives or the decisions which were the reality of doing business, as distinct from fulfilling its routine functions. This was not just a question of honesty, in a context where the opportunities for deception were manifold, but raised wider issues of decision-making, risk-taking, investment decisions and incentives. If a salaried clerk or manager with the necessary abilities found himself with such responsibilities he would want a share of the profits, which meant participating in the equity capital of the business as a partner – in short, moving from salaried manager to part owner. Where assets were in trade the elderly partner could hope to pull out by transferring his assets into land and property or the Funds without significant loss, if trading conditions were favourable. Most trading assets (stock, good commerical debts owing, perhaps some shares of ships) could be realized in a short time, if they were not taken over by existing or incoming partners. This is doubtless one reason for the relative absence of family dynasties in trade.

In the case of manufacturing realizing assets was not so easy. More capital was embodied in fixed assets, such as buildings, plant and equipment, which had to be utilized with specific skills and experience if the potential stream of income which they could yield was to be achieved. Without a certain level of technical knowledge, for example, being cheated was always a danger. A manufacturing enterprise also required associated trading skills and financial skills, in the absence of which similar risks applied. It was therefore that much more risky for an outsider to buy the business outright and take it over as a going concern. The greater the scale of operations and the larger the sum required then the greater the risk and the higher the odds against a successful outright sale. Such assets (whether tangible or in business connections) quickly deteriorate when unused. Hence the double incentive for selling to existing partners or negotiating partnership rights with an existing manager who had the necessary skills but lacked capital. The ageing owner without suitable

[6] Peter Mathias, *The Transformation of England: Essays in the Economic and Social History of England in the Eighteenth Century* (London, 1979).

male kin in the next generation had the confidence of preserving income and capital values while the ambitions of the lucky manager were satisfied, as his commitment to the firm combined with his own advancement and that of his family. The existence of a daughter created an opportunity for consolidating dynastic and business continuity in the next generation by a new alliance between kin and firm, with similar double advantages.

An equivalent route for advancement beckoned the impecunious clerk in a trading concern. If honest, capable and possessing book-keeping skills he might become a supercargo, acting as agent for the principals in trade. Considerable responsibilities would fall to him overseas when quick decisions had to be taken in the light of the actual market conditions prevailing when a ship arrived in port. Original instructions might not be able to be carried out profitably, while waiting for new instructions might well prove the worst option possible. Where principals were weeks or months away from taking decisions, the man on the spot was in the best position for taking advantage of any turn in the market. Opportunities would often present themselves for a supercargo to trade a little on his own account (and he might be able to command a modest space on a ship for this), from which small beginnings greater gains might follow. An offer of advancement might well follow the demonstration of such honesty and ability.

Credit

The role of credit in the operation of business and its relationship with risk is so fundamental that it merits a specific discussion. Many sorts of risk impinged upon a business by way of making extra demands for credit, in different forms. Risks, as we have seen, were inherent in the context of nature, climate and technology. Storm and shipwreck were endemic at sea, as were delays in the fulfilment of transactions. Ships could wait for weeks at the quayside for full loading (inland transport and production could also be held up by many kinds of natural hazard). The inherent logistics of inland transport by barge and wagon curtailed efficiency, compounded by delays (which meant higher costs) beyond these intrinsic parameters. Ships could wait for days or more for a favourable wind to clear the Thames estuary or the Downs or the Bristol Channel. Customs clearance could be time consuming; quayside spaces or warehousing capacity could be stretched when delays in making port led to a bunching of arrivals.

When shipping was controlled in a convoy system, as sometimes happened in wartime, such delays were compounded as the convoy assembled, followed by further delays from slow sailing and changes of route.

Even after an effective insurance market developed for ships and cargoes in the early eighteenth century the recoverable costs did not compensate for all the forms of loss, such as the consequences of delayed transactions and the payment of claims. Seasonal interruptions to agricultural, industrial, mining, construction, shipping and trading activities were endemic. Export markets (and also the home market) were subject to cyclical variations – affecting returns by way of price movements as well as changes in volume. Where industrial production was scattered over different sites, with different processes utilizing artisan technology taking place in different localities, delays in fulfilling orders could be inordinate. In a sense speculative trading was inevitable given the decoupling between taking commercial decisions and the information on which they had been based, even if consignments were only dispatched according to firm orders. Market conditions could change between the time of placing an order and the arrival of the ship carrying the goods. The same was true on a lesser scale for the commercial time gap between London and the provinces. A week might be required for commercial intelligence between Britain and the North Sea littoral. Returns from a trading venture to the eastern Baltic from Britain would take half a year, a full year possibly for the transatlantic trades and two years to India, south-east Asia and the far east. Inland bills were normally payable at twenty-eight days, with equivalent extensions for maturity according to the distance of trading areas. Even discounting the risks of non-payment, destruction or damage, the uncertainties resulting from delays and enforced changes in prices meant that capital and credit requirements were much higher in relation to turnover than in more recent times of faster, more assured communications. Margins could also be finer as such efficiencies increased. Extra credit needs arose where such delays proved longer than anticipated. Because so much capital was locked up in stocks of raw materials, goods being made and goods in the course of distribution – in all of which mercantile credit was paramount – the efficient control of stocks was central to business efficiency and the minimizing of risk from over-extended credit. Procedures for recovering debt, beyond the 'protesting' of bills of exchange, could be uncertain and protracted, with the certainty of high legal costs. Debt recovery in a foreign country compounded all these difficulties. The Crown of Virginia Act of 1663, for example, made it 'almost impossible' for a British creditor to use the local courts to collect from a debtor who had moved to the colony.[7]

---

[7] Jacob M. Price, *Perry of London: a Family and a Firm on the Seaborne Frontier, 1615–1753* (Cambridge, Mass., 1992), pp. 81–2. The Colonial Debts Act subsequently reversed the situation when 'land, houses, chattels and slaves of planter debtors became liable for the satisfaction of debts'. The process could still prove protracted and expensive.

The centrality of credit is amply documented. The Perrys usually bought at eighteen months' credit and, in turn, for goods exported in adventures to America at least twelve months' credit had to be offered, with a retail mark up of 100 per cent or more.[8] Large planters in Virginia had the leverage to command extended credit from importing merchants, but middling planter consignees could be held on a short credit leash.[9] The credit chain stretched from the merchant supplying raw materials on credit to 'putters-out' and manufacturers in England right through to upcountry store owners in the Chesapeake and other colonies: 'the real cost involved in the long credit offered by the export merchant rested in turn upon the long credits available from the wholesaler'.[10] Twelve months' credit was usual in the domestic trades in England. Those who agreed to six months' credit 'keep constantly giving orders and send up bills when it suits them, or are not drawn upon for the full balance perhaps for 2 or 3 years, the accompt remaining open, it may be said that almost every country shopkeeper has credit for a year, if not more'.[11] Credit facilities have long been acknowledged as the key to developments in the trade and the development of the West Indian slave economy. As a Liverpool slave trader put it, the right sort of credit 'made the wheel turn'.[12] 'First place must be given to credit' in the development of Virginia and Maryland repeats the assertion.[13]

Good credit, access to credit and access to cash to meet the unexpected, unanticipatable emergency were keys to survival in this commercial world beset with risk and uncertainty. In normal trading conditions discounting bills of exchange with a banker would enable a businessman to get returns in cash without holdings bills to maturity. He might also take advantage of short-term ledger credits from suppliers – in ordinary

[8] *Ibid.*, p. 49.   [9] *Ibid.*, pp. 66–7.

[10] Jacob M. Price, *Capital and Credit in British Overseas Trade: the View from the Chesapeake, 1700–1776* (Cambridge, Mass., 1980), pp. 124, 143, 192. Chapter 7 is entitled 'The significance of credit'.

[11] *The Tradesman's Directory* (London, 1756), pp. 54–5.

[12] Jacob M. Price, 'Credit in the slave trade and plantation economies', in *The Atlantic Frontier*, ch. 5.

[13] Jacob M. Price, 'Glasgow in the Chesapeake tobacco trade', in *ibid.*, ch. 1. See also Jacob M. Price, *France and the Chesapeake: a History of the French Tobacco Monopoly, 1674–1791, and of its Relationship to the British and American Tobacco Trades*, 2 vols. (Ann Arbor, 1973), p. 733; Richard Pares, 'A London West-India merchant house, 1740–1769', in Richard Pares and A. J. P. Taylor, eds., *Essays Presented to Sir Lewis Namier* (London, 1956), pp. 45–50; Richard B. Sheridan, 'The commercial and financial organisation of the British slave trade, 1750–1807', *EcHR*, 11 (1958), 249–63; Rosemary E. Ommer, ed., *Merchant Credit and Labour Shortage in Historical Perspective* (Fredericton, 1990); Jacob M. Price, ed., *Joshua Johnson's Letterbook, 1771–1774: Letters from a Merchant in London to his Partners in Maryland*, London Record Society, 15 (1979); Jacob M. Price, 'Transaction costs: a note on merchant credit and the origin of private trade', in James D. Tracy, ed., *The Political Economy of Merchant Empires* (Cambridge, 1991), pp. 276–97.

circumstances mercantile credit could offer great flexibility. In certain circumstances a 'float' of short-term credit could also be rolled over, or renewed, rather than liquidated at term to form – in effect by overdraft and doubtless at 5 per cent per annum – longer-term credit requirements. The need for such extensions of credit, however, could prove to be hazardous when credit was tight and where commercial and financial confidence had lapsed, propelling a rush for liquidity. Then merchants, bankers and lenders in general would demand to get back into cash to protect their own positions and the demands for liquidity being made on them by their own creditors. Short-term loans would be called in, bills presented for payment at their legal limits, further discounts refused or accepted only at a high cost because of the rise in the discount rate (to the legal limit) which such contractions in multiple but interlinked credit markets would bring. Such contractions operated in common trading areas – with particular sensitivity between Amsterdam and London – apart from the linkages in internal markets. The integration of regional and local credit centres with London progressed rapidly with the development after the mid-eighteenth century of a network of country banks, all having correspondent banks in the capital.

A business could require extra short-term credit urgently in such a situation, just when its normal sources were adding to the pressure with demands for repayment. Mercantile assets (whether stocks or commercial credits awaiting maturity) would probably not be negotiable in such a commercial or financial crisis, or marketable only at an unacceptable discount. The enforced realization of such assets in a short-term liquidity crisis would invite disaster. On the other hand, holding a large reserve in cash against such an eventuality imposed high costs: apart from the necessary marginal cash 'float' to cover ordinary dealings such financial resources would be earning a return if left in the business or invested in the Funds.

Where, in such circumstances, could the owner or partner in a business turn for accommodation? The context, universally, was of personal, unlimited liability, which meant that no line could be drawn between the debts of the business and the private and personal assets of the owners. Family savings and assets would normally be the main recourse, together with help from trusted close confidants – such as the long-known family attorney or those long associated in trade. Those offering assistance would need to know that the need for accommodation arose from crisis market conditions facing the firm rather than from speculative overtrading or fraudulent dealings. A personal relationship developing personal trust was required to produce such confidence.[14] This has been well put for the Dutch context:

Merchants were pre-occupied with risk and reputation because they were preoccupied with continuity . . . It was a question of faith, of conscience, of trust and reputation. Those were essential values in trade. A merchant was dependent on others and it was often difficult to know whether a person was trustworthy. One had to go by reputation . . . people made a clear distinction between 'us' and 'them' between 'friends' and 'strangers'. Everyone who did not belong to the circle of . . . friends was a stranger of whom one could not be completely sure.[15]

The most extreme form of risk in lending would be an unsecured 'note of hand' – meaning that such a debt might well not be recoverable in law – so that personal trust was absolute and the only assurance for repayment was the honouring of the borrower's word. Security would normally be taken to cover a loan and the commonest form of security – many times more extensive than holdings in government stock – was freehold land and property. When unencumbered by existing mortgages this was the cheapest and the most reliable way of raising cash. The mortgage market was well organized, easily tappable through attorneys, and offered interest rates only about a percentage point over the return on government stock. Hence freehold property owned by the businessman needing more liquidity, or by members of his family or his wife's family, could be pledged. Kinship, by creating a bond of personal confidence, provided a crucial base for lending of last resort for a relative over-extended in business. Wider kinship linkages, with extensive cousinhoods, where close association and mutual trust prevailed, also provided a genealogical nexus for such assistance.[16] This has been extensively documented for Jewish, Quaker, Scottish and other minority groups in business (not least by Jacob Price), but there is every reason to suppose that this was a universal characteristic of the linkage between kinship and enterprise.[17] The wider the operative kinship network – where relationships remained active – the more extensive this safety net could be: many cousins could ensure survival through a temporary business depression or money panic.

[14] N. Nohria and R. G. Eccles, eds., *Networks and Organisations: Structure, Form and Action* (Boston, 1992); Grahame Thompson, Jennifer Frances, Rosalind Lecacic and Jeremy Mitchell, eds., *Markets, Hierarchies and Networks: the Coordination of Social Life* (London, 1993).

[15] L. Kooijmans, 'Risk and reputation in the mentality of merchants in the early modern period', in Lesger and Noordegraaf, eds., *Entrepreneurs and Entrepreneurship in Early Modern Times*, pp. 27, 32.

[16] A. W. Sleeswijk, 'Social ties and commercial transactions of an eighteenth century French merchant', in *ibid.*, pp. 203–12. This documents the kinship networks in the Dutch–Bordeaux wine trade, reinforced by membership of the Walloon church in Bordeaux.

[17] Price, *France and the Chesapeake*, pp. 596–8 (for cousinhoods in the Whitehaven tobacco trade); Price, 'Joshua Johnson in London, 1771–5' and 'Buchanan and Simson, 1759–1763', in his *Tobacco in Atlantic Trade*, ch. 8, pp. 155–6 (the Hanbury cousinhood), ch. 6, pp. 15–16.

Apart from unencumbered land and property the next most marketable category of asset which could be realized was a holding in the Funds (total holdings of British government stock were over £50 million in 1730, £80 million by 1750 and £600 million in 1810). Such holdings were realizable: the elemental condition and supreme asset of a permanent funded debt was that its holdings were always negotiable, commanding a market, even if at a discount from the purchase price. The exceptional circumstances of Charles II's 'stop of the Exchequer' in 1672, which immediately froze public credit, were never repeated; and nor could they have been if the state was to be financially viable in the British context (where levels of taxation were determined in Parliament and where the Bank of England rather than the government controlled the money supply). Military, political and commercial crises could depress the price of government stock, particularly when large new loans were being marketed in wartime, and this would make the sale of such assets for cash more expensive; but holdings in the Funds were a major recourse for a businessman whose kin had savings in this form.

The operation of the usury laws, which put a ceiling on rates of interest (in the eighteenth century 6 per cent per annum before 1714 and 5 per cent thereafter), affected such capital and credit transactions. The 'real' rate of interest on government stock was not affected because the legal basis was deemed to be that on the stock 'at par' – the par price being 100 and the formal return being usually $3\frac{1}{2}$ per cent or 3 per cent. The actual return to the lender depended on the current price of government stock on the market: if this was 50 then the capital would be yielding 7 per cent or 6 per cent. Normal interpersonal loans would be at 5 per cent per annum – borrowed in pounds, repaid in guineas – at the maximum allowed under the usury laws. For the lender taking security for a loan, due care was needed to ensure a safety margin between the cash handed over and the realizable value of the asset (in case the security had to be realized in less favourable market conditions should the borrower default on the loan). Creditors asked to liquidate their holdings in the Funds might require that repayment of their capital at the end of the loan take the form of replacing the same 'par value' of stock as had been realized to provide the loan originally. If the price of the Funds had fallen in the interim the capital cost of replacement would be higher so that the borrower would, in effect, be paying at a higher rate than the usury law maximum (i.e. 5 per cent per annum plus any loss on the capital transaction). This, however, was within the legal rules.

The mode of operation of the usury law itself increased the intensity of disruption in credit markets and hence the risk facing borrowers on those occasions when the market rate of interest was driven above 5 per cent per annum. With commercial interest rates for discounting bills, as well as personal loans, being legally pegged at that point some lenders moved out of the discount market looking for better returns in government stock or even in Amsterdam. Discounts therefore had to be rationed by quantity rather than by price. This increased the rate of interest in the discount market, which itself generalized the panic among those seeking accommodation and fearful of being denied. Such occasions were relatively rare and short lived – at times, usually in war, of acute commercial and financial pressures – but they made the search for credit more difficult just when such accommodation was most needed.

Apart from the occasional need for short-term credit in an emergency, longer-term borrowing might also be needed – for example, when a business was being established or when a major investment had to be undertaken, making capital demands beyond the limit which could be met from annual profits. Here, again, the same logic applied, with kin being a usual recourse, often associated where the context allowed by extending a partnership to bring in equity capital. Long-term personal lending, at the standard fixed interest rate, was also widespread outside the kinship group, where a bond of personal trust could be sustained.

Despite such various exigencies it might well prove that, in times of temporary commercial constraint, customers could not repay outstanding commercial debts when the normal credit period had transpired. This could happen on both sides – with the failure of debtors to honour their credit limits preventing repayments in turn to commercial creditors when bills of exchange on the firm matured. Where this happened, providing that the business was essentially sound – and, in some circumstances, even if it was not – little use would be served by protesting the bills or taking legal action to foreclose on loans. If recoverable at all, an enforced sale of the commercial assets of a trading business at such impropitious times might realize only a few pence in the pound and with long delays. Industrial assets might well be even less saleable. Only the lawyers would profit from such a decision to invoke the law. Better to hold on – letting short-term credit continue into long-term at 5 per cent per annum, and with security if possible. As well as obliging in this way, establishing such a 'moral' credit balance might be put to good use in later circumstances. The sense of reciprocal obligations extending over time could be finely tuned. While a customer was under such a loan or credit tie, of course, he would find it difficult to seek keener prices from alternative suppliers.

Credit, and access to credit, was thus the key to successful trading, and had been so for centuries. The pervasiveness of credit in the medieval economy has been amply documented: doubtless credit is coeval with commerce itself.[18] A financial structure of growing complexity and soph-istication articulated ever greater and more complex credit needs and credit flows in the seventeenth and eighteenth centuries. The universality of credit, as an integral constituent of commercial dealings rather than an applied lubricant, was such that to identify the growth of commercial and industrial capitalism as the triumph of the 'cash nexus' in a 'money economy' is a perverse interpretation. Monetization was a complex pro-cess as it spread into many relationships, but this trend marched hand in hand with the elaboration of credit, not as a substitute for credit. Indeed, one rule for success might be 'let him owe', provided the lender was sure of the standing of the debtor and that payment eventually would be secure. Prudence and consideration ran together, and the moral obliga-tion thus created could be useful in the future.

Creditworthiness

Access to credit, as a precondition for business operations, had as its Janus-face creditworthiness. Again, the context of high risk and a limited institutional structure conditioned the mode of operation. Very little knowledge was available: no credit ratings, no published accounts and no professional auditing, while bank dealings were a highly personal affair. Beyond the charmed circle of partners and their private ledgers (to which the ordinary clerks in the counting house would not have access) all was rumour and hearsay. Law provided an outer envelope within which the business system operated, but personal trust and confidence, personal standing and personal introductions were of the essence. A prominent Glasgow tobacco merchant wrote that at the local level in Virginia in 1766 'it is in dependence on the labour, industry and honesty of many [small planters], not of their real property that they get goods on credit from different storekeepers', although larger loans were normally secured on bonds at 5–6 per cent per annum interest.[19] A man's personal reputation in business was all. Published homilies abounded about trustworthiness and personal character bringing their due reward, accompanied by down-side scare stories that a rake's progress of personal extravagance, the pursuit of pleasure, vice and irresponsible behaviour would surely lead to nemesis for the person and his business conjoined. Contemporary litera-ture – fiction, drama and pedagogic – abounds with such moral tales. At

---

[18] See J. Day, *The Medieval Market Economy* (Oxford, 1987); R. H. Britnell and B. M. S. Campbell, *A Commercialising Economy: England, 1086–1300* (Manchester, 1995); J. Kermode, 'Money and credit in the fifteenth century', *Business History Review*, 65 (1991), 475–501; P. Nightingale, 'Monetary circulation and mercantile credit in later medieval England', *EcHR*, 43 (1990), 560–75.

[19] Price, *Capital and Credit in British Overseas Trade*, p. 125, and *The Atlantic Frontier*, ch. 5.

the heart of this truth lay personal trust and the need to maintain the respect of one's fellows. In formal terms this was endowed with Christian obligations, following in medieval theological and moral traditions (with oaths normally sworn on the Bible), but broadened in secular dealings in the seventeenth century to cover general contractual obligations in civil society (taking up a later philosophical position).[20] Such conceptual and moral premises, when translated into the context of business dealings, rested upon more elemental empirical foundations. Personal trust was in its nature reciprocal and forward looking, usually with the implications that a transaction was not to be seen as unique, isolated, one off, but potentially as part of a sequence. To gain personal trust and establish confidence, dealings needed to be honest, confidentiality respected, commitments fulfilled, agreements and promises kept, pledges redeemed. Reciprocal honesty was a precondition for on-going business relations. As an observer put the point in 1717:

To support and maintain a man's private credit, 'tis absolutely necessary that the world have a fixed opinion of the honesty and integrity, as well as ability of a person . . . indeed a readiness and willingness to perform one's engagements is such a fundamental of credit, that all the affluence of money and the most immense riches are of no consequence if there be ground for the least suspicion of disingenuity.[21]

Parallels drawn between a lady's honour and the maintenance of creditworthiness in a business were commonplace, with the assumption that once personal credibility had been forfeited it could never be regained. Such respectability could not be asserted, bought or acquired in the short run. Reputation, standing, status in the trade depended on the perceptions of others. It was other people, upon whom he depended in trade, rather than the businessman himself, who created his respectability by according him status, and such credibility had to be built up over time and won by performance as well as words. There was no distinction to be made between the firm and the person in this respect, as there was none in law. Continuity was itself important as a demonstration of survivability – with continuity over the cycle of business booms and depressions. The sobriquet of 'the Old Bank', for example, sent its own message.

With continuity went roots: respectability could be confirmed by accepting positions of voluntary office – itself a mark of trust within one's community. In minority-group communities such appointments would be virtually elective by the seniors of the community. In trusts and

---

²⁰ A. B. Seligman, 'The changing pre-contractual frame of modern society', in *The Responsive Community* (Winter 1995–6, Washington, D.C.), pp. 28–40.
²¹ A. A. Sykes, *A Letter to a Friend . . .* (London, 1717).

charities appointments were offered by existing trustees – all a mark of social and personal standing. This dynamic operated at virtually all levels of 'respectable' society – from village level upwards. The word 'friend', widely in use in the eighteenth century when referring to a trusted personal acquaintance or collaborator in business (not just within the Quaker community as the formal mode of address to fellow Quakers) is resonant with the implications of personal trust and the obligations which friendship entailed. In business the assumption would be that mutual dealings had established a bond of reciprocity, a presumption of good will and willingness to help. Personal and business considerations would not be separated. A request to oblige would be made in the personal confidence that previous obligations fulfilled on the other side had established a moral credit balance in the ledger of personal dealings which could be drawn on, an expression of the matrix of personal trust and obligation upon which successful business dealings always rested.

Interest has revived recently in non-market modes of transaction and the ways in which considerations other than the naked economic calculus of price and quality become integrated with such dealings. The spectrum between gift exchange, barter and purely economic considerations is a wide one. Avner Offer has recently called this the 'economy of regard'.[22] The reality is not so much that these were alternative motivations and mechanisms for exchange to impersonal market transactions, but how market mechanisms were integrated with such other considerations and (in the circumstances of the context under discussion here) necessarily complementary, if markets were to operate effectively. As well as requiring a framework of law and public regulation, together with a set of market rules for governing the niceties of market dealings, a further dimension of what can most easily be described as 'moral' obligation upon participants was also present. Of course, taking a past, present and future time frame into consideration, 'moral' conduct brought material advantage as personal trust built up such confidence, and confidence encouraged business. As emphasized above, the higher the level of risk and uncertainty the greater the premium on such personal qualities and their recognition in the market. The classical economic theory of the market took such considerations largely for granted, at least to the point of not seeking to integrate them conceptually into a formal model. 'The neoclassical paradigm "neglects social influence on economic decision-making", whereas historical research seems to indicate their overriding importance in early-modern

---

[22] Avner Offer, 'Between the gift and the market: the economy of regard', *EcHR* (1997), 450–76.

merchant rationality.'[23] The same was true of the political requirements for an effective market – another precondition for the market economy which was seldom articulated in formal terms. The platitudes of contemporary commentators about personal probity nevertheless rested upon a truth of profound significance for success in business, when rooted in its institutional context.

Accepting the obligations of reciprocity, as an underlying principle, provided the common denominator for the rules of conduct in so many instances, even if the actuality of reciprocity and its modes could be subtle, delicate and oblique as well as direct. Reciprocity remained a fundamental feature of interpersonal relationships. Obligations of friendship in the business context – where business dealings were the main focus of transactions – impinged indirectly on a dynamic which could become complex.[24] If businessman A had bonds of trust and mutual confidence with businessman B, then A could recommend a third party C, in whom he placed his own personal confidence, to B – with B having an obligation through his friendship with A to oblige C, provided that this was within the limits of prudence and reasonableness (in his view). A, for his part, would not wish to put his friendship with B under strain by seeking an 'unreasonable' favour on behalf of C. C then had the obligation of dealing honourably with B or risking his friendship with A, who had intermediated on his behalf. Networks of mutual trust and obligation were built up on such personal recommendations to mutual advantage. Of course, the chain of personal trust might be broken if obligations were not fulfilled, and this could then ramify through the network as the reverse dynamic took hold. The ramifications of such relationships spread widely beyond the purely commercial nexus.

Credit, clearly, was fundamental in such a matrix – a precondition for its operation – and a means of attaining mutually advantageous results. In Jacob Price's words,

Most contemporary correspondence reveals that merchants fully understood the uses of credit in creating a business clientele . . . credit could also be a highly rational, mutually advantageous relationship for both clear-sighted lenders and intelligent borrowers.[25]

But social, and even political, obligations often lay behind the granting of credit, by family and kin, by patrons to clients, by merchants to members of the social and power elite to whom they might be beholden, actually or potentially in past, present or future. These non-economic imperatives,

---

[23] Sleeswijk, 'Social ties and commercial transactions', p. 211. A subsection of the text is entitled 'The social embeddedness of merchant behaviour' (pp. 203–4).
[24] See in Scott, *Social Network Analysis*.
[25] Price, *Capital and Credit in British Overseas Trade*, p. 16.

in a society held together by interpersonal dealings, might well be at the expense of economic rationality, narrowly considered. Professor Lawrence Fontaine has written with great perception of those credit relations in French provincial society in the eighteenth century. She sees credit 'not so much part of a money market but concerned with social obligations and power over men' – apart from credit transactions between merchants.[26] Effective commercial transactions, even in the most market-orientated contexts, still operated within the matrix of personal trust and reputation – the congenial aspect of this being social reciprocation, but the dark side fear of adverse material consequences. A correspondent pleading with John Norton in 1772 not to refuse a bill of exchange wrote, 'I should look upon it as so fatal a stab to the reputation of a trader that I should never be able to recover it.'[27] John Norton himself wrote 'when once my credit is lost all is lost with me'.[28] More positively came the recognition of 'something that may not improperly be called a commercial friendship . . . which takes its rise from a long correspondence and is established by a punctual and steady integrity on both sides'.[29] Thus the command of credit in times of commercial pressure may have been of more strategic importance than technical and administrative skills and this, in turn, depended on personal reputation, inspiring mutual trust, which had grown up over a long period, and was demonstrably proof against adversity.[30] 'The commercial ideal of honour – and hence of trust', writes Professor Fontaine, 'was initially constructed to guard against the twin fears of personal insolvency and collective bankruptcy: it functioned simultaneously as a safeguard against risk and as a framework for a mutually supportive society.'[31]

Minority groups – religious minority groups or communities of different nationals in an alien setting – offer the clearest examples of the importance of kin, closely associated other families and the personally known networks of individuals for the operation of business. The main concern here is not the long-argued debate about the role of different theologies and their associated value systems as a motivating force for business success, whether Jewish, Calvinist or other variants of Protestantism in the European context such as the Huguenot, Quaker or

26 Lawrence Fontaine, 'Antonio and Shylock: an essay on credit and trust in eighteenth-century France' (given as the Tawney Memorial Lecture at the Economic History Society Conference in Lancaster, 1996).
27 W. Reynolds to J. Norton, 28 November 1772, in Frances Norton Mason, ed., *John Norton & Sons: Merchants of London and Virginia* (Newton Abbot, 1968), p. xvi.
28 John Norton to J. H. Norton, 16 February 1773, *ibid.*, p. xvii.
29 R. Corbin (planter) to Osgood Hanbury (merchant), 13 June 1758, *ibid.*, pp. xvi–xvii.
30 Robert A. East, 'The business entrepreneur in a changing colonial economy, 1763–1795', *JEcH* (Supplement), 6 (1946), 22–3.
31 Fontaine, 'Antonio and Shylock'.

Unitarian. Such attributes do not seem to have had an exclusive specificity to any one theology – minority groups identified with different religions acquired such characteristics, while secular motivational norms of entrepreneurship could become integral with religious values almost independently of the underlying theology. Many aspects of the behaviour of a minority group in business are not exceptional or *sui generis*, although often more visible, more clearly identified and better documented than with non-minority groups in the same area of business. The degree of articulation of minority groups varied greatly with context, ranging from formal 'ghetto' status (with personal freedom, terms of settlement, range of permitted business operations, legal privileges current within a defined area and the like being subject to legal authorization by state or monarch) to a self-imposed separateness conditioned by race, religion, national and cultural identity, reinforced by reciprocal alienation on the part of other social groups.[32] But many of what are often taken as the key characteristics of minority group business behaviour and which gave cumulative resilience and self-reinforcing economic strength were not specific to a minority group role but a more general response to context. The commonest attributes – often cast in terms of accusations – are those of being clannish, secretive, doing business where practicable, lending and borrowing within the kinship group or a magic circle of coreligionists or fellow nationals, consolidating business interests with kinship links. This traditional charge of maintaining a 'commonwealth within themselves' was a universal attribute of minority groups in business, most clearly visible to competitors or would-be suppliers and customers outside the group in question, who were doubtless parties to alternative networks themselves. Apart from providing a basis for normative values, legitimizing the lives and work of fellow sectarians, religion provided the matrix for the coherence of the community in the sense of social organization, and the basis for networking. The social matrix of religion therefore became of great significance in the establishment of communities of personal trust, through membership of churches (membership of a particular church congregation could provide a focus for such consolidation), chapels, Quaker meetings and synagogues.

To the extent that hostility and alienation were projected against

---

[32] See, for example, Andrew Pettegree, *Foreign Protestant Communities in 16th Century London* (Oxford, 1986); P. W. Klein, 'Little London: British merchants in Rotterdam during the 17th and 18th centuries', in D. C. Coleman and Peter Mathias, eds., *Enterprise and History: Essays in Honour of Charles Wilson* (Cambridge, 1984); D. J. Ormrod, 'The Atlantic economy and the protestant capitalist international, 1651–1775', *Historical Research*, 66 (1993), 197–208; H. Pohl, 'Die Portugiesen in Antwerpen, 1567–1698', *Vierteljahrschrift fur Social- und Wirtschaftsgeschichte*, 63 (1977); C. H. Yungblub, *Strangers Settled amongst Us* (London, 1996).

minority groups, all the forces in the context of business which have been identified as increasing risk were maximized, and encouraged the consolidation and internal coherence of the minority group in question. An 'alien' merchant coming to a foreign country would find the church at which his fellow countrymen and fellow sectarians worshipped his own natural focus. Apart from worship he could participate in social intercourse in his own language. Information networking as well as business collaboration were advantageous attributes of active participation. Virtually all the Dutch merchants in London in the early modern period worshipped at their own Dutch church in Austin Friars. The Scottish Presbyterian community at Veere, near Middelberg, was the mirror image on a smaller scale. Marriage partners were also potentially to be found within the same communities linked by a common faith, as social relationships endorsed the religious. Where a minority group had an international nexus as with the Quakers in transatlantic commerce or the Huguenots or – preeminently – the Jewish Sephardic communities more widely, a confidential information network had high value for all those with access. Non-local connections along the trade routes gave great strength.

Financial independence and strength were a necessary basis for the security of minority groups in a hostile environment. For the poorest members of the group there would be no public welfare. Private charity had strings attached which might threaten religious independence. At a higher level minorities would be excluded from the spoils of office. Fixed assets in land and property (where allowed) could also be more at risk, because less easily transferred or realized than financial assets, which could provide a better basis for current income. Some attributes of the context of high risk, that is to say, applied more forcibly to minority groups identified and segregated by religion, race or nationality. Equally, money lending, banking and finance were the most confidential of dealings with the highest premiums on personal trust and individual wealth. Personal family wealth with accumulation through the continuity of generations (if the hazards of genealogical discontinuity could be avoided – and a wide cousinhood could help with that) meant that well-established kinship groups enjoyed the benefits of cumulative advantage. These may well have been particularly important in banking, exemplified in Jewish and Quaker circles, although, as Jacob Price has shown, the family continuity and strength in banking and brewing of London Quaker families did not lead to their continuing as practising members of the sect – rather the reverse.[33] The dynamics of assimilation as against the surviv-

---

[33] Jacob M. Price, 'The great Quaker business families of 18th century London', in his *Overseas Trade and Traders*, ch. 3.

ing identities of minority groups are complex. The greater the alienation and hostility of the host environment, the greater the degree of separateness in the identity of the minority group by race, nationality and religion – with interacting influences – then the greater tended to be its continuity. Where conditions of high risk survive, whether by location and context or by the nature of the business, we see surviving the modes of business which were almost universal in the period under discussion in these pages, which Jacob Price has made his own.

2 Business networks in the British export trade to North America, 1750–1800

Kenneth Morgan

This chapter offers an analysis of business networks in the British export trade to North America in the second half of the eighteenth century, a significant yet relatively understudied topic in transatlantic commercial enterprise. A framework for the discussion is provided by selected aggregate data plus some comments on the changing role of British exports between 1750 and 1800. Valuations based on 'official' prices in customs ledgers provide a good index of trade volume. These show that English exports to North America more than trebled in value from £256,000 in 1700–1 to £971,000 in 1750–1, when they accounted for 10.6 per cent of total exports. British exports to North America more than doubled in value from £2,649,000 in 1772–3 to £5,700,000 in 1797–8, when they comprised 31.2 per cent of exports. The lure of markets in North America was particularly important for British textile industries. By the 1790s anything between a third and a half of the exports in Britain's fastest growing industry – cotton – were dispatched to the United States of America. By the turn of the nineteenth century, 40 per cent of British wool textile exports were similarly sent to North American markets.[1]

This growth of exports to North America reflected the 'empire of goods' that bound together Britain and its American colonies before the War of Independence, and the continuing commercial links between

This chapter was presented as a paper at the Economic History Society Conference, University of Lancaster, April 1996; at the Fifth Anglo-American Conference of Business Historians, University of Glasgow, July 1997; and at a Maritime History seminar at the University of Exeter, June 1999. My thanks are due to Robin Pearson, John J. McCusker and H. E. S. Fisher for inviting me to present a paper on these occasions; to John Smail for fruitful dialogue on the marketing of eighteenth-century British exports; to the archives cited below for permission to cite their manuscript collections; and to Brunel University for the funding that made it possible to undertake this research.

[1] Phyllis Deane and W. A. Cole, *British Economic Growth, 1688–1959,* 2nd edn (Cambridge, 1967), p. 87; Michael M. Edwards, *The Growth of the British Cotton Trade, 1780–1815* (Manchester, 1967), p. 243; François Crouzet, *Britain Ascendant: Comparative Studies in Franco-British Economic History* (Cambridge, 1990), ch. 6; Ralph Davis, *The Industrial Revolution and British Overseas Trade* (Leicester, 1979), p. 19.

Britain and the United States after 1783. It was an Atlantic extension of the consumer revolution of eighteenth-century Britain. Lying behind the rise in the value of this trade was a widening array of export commodities in the second half of the eighteenth century. In that period the variety of textiles, hardware and metalware available for export expanded; the types of imported merchandise advertised in colonial American newspapers increased significantly; and a great expansion of shops occurred in American towns and ports. North American consumers also wanted a wide selection of manufactured goods.[2] Demand for British manufactured wares arose from very rapid population growth in North America (an increase from 275,000 people in 1700 to 5.3 million in 1800) coupled with rising living standards and changing tastes among the white population, where the per capita income of white settlers rose at an annual rate of between 0.3 and 0.6 per cent during the eighteenth century – a figure comparable to growth rates in Britain at the time.[3] American consumption of British manufactures was helped by the relative weakness of homespun industry that resulted from restrictive imperial legislation (before 1776) plus high labour costs, relatively scarce capital and raw material shortages in textiles in North America.[4]

---

[2] Neil McKendrick, 'The consumer revolution of eighteenth-century England', in Neil McKendrick, John Brewer and J. H. Plumb, *The Birth of a Consumer Society: the Commercialisation of Eighteenth-Century England* (London, 1983), pp. 1–33; T. H. Breen, 'An empire of goods: the anglicization of colonial America, 1690–1776', *Journal of British Studies*, 25 (1986), 467–99; T. H. Breen, '"Baubles of Britain": the American and consumer revolutions of the eighteenth century', *Past and Present*, no. 119 (1988), 73–104; Thomas M. Doerflinger, 'Farmers and dry goods in the Philadelphia market area, 1750–1800', in Ronald Hoffman, John J. McCusker, Russell R. Menard and Peter J. Albert, eds., *The Economy of Early America: the Revolutionary Period, 1763–1790* (Charlottesville, Va., 1988), pp. 166–95; Edwards, *Growth of the British Cotton Trade*, pp. 49–50; Richard L. Bushman, 'Shopping and advertising in colonial America', in Cary Carson, Ronald Hoffman and Peter J. Albert, eds., *Of Consuming Interests: the Style of Life in the Eighteenth Century* (Charlottesville, Va., 1994), pp. 233–51; John Smail, *Merchants, Markets and Manufacture: the English Wool Textile Industry in the Eighteenth Century* (Basingstoke, 1999), pp. 6, 42. For a critique of the concept of a consumer revolution see John Styles, 'Manufacturing, consumption and design in eighteenth-century England', in John Brewer and Roy Porter, eds., *Consumption and the World of Goods* (London, 1993). Perceptive commentary on North American consumption of British manufactured goods can be found in Carole Shammas, *The Pre-Industrial Consumer in England and America* (Oxford, 1990), pp. 266–90, and Ann Smart Martin, 'Makers, buyers, and users: consumerism as a material culture framework', *Winterthur Portfolio*, 28 (1993), 141–57.

[3] US Department of Commerce, Bureau of the Census, *Historical Statistics of the United States: Colonial Times to 1970*, 2 vols. (Washington, D.C., 1975), I, series A 6–8, p. 8, series Z 1–19, p. 1168; McCusker and Menard, *Economy of British America*, pp. 55–60, 268.

[4] See, for example, McCusker and Menard, *Economy of British America*, ch. 15; Adrienne D. Hood, 'The material world of cloth: production and use in eighteenth-century rural Pennsylvania', *WMQ*, 3rd series, 53 (1996), 43–66.

The growth of British exports in the second half of the eighteenth century also stemmed from changing economic conditions in Britain and overseas markets. It reflected the incentive provided for manufacturers in Yorkshire, Lancashire and the Midlands to increase the productivity of textiles, metalware and hardware through extra employment, the division of labour and improved commercial organization at a time when British manufactured exports needed to diversify to avoid declining European markets and when exports, rather than agricultural incomes, were becoming a major stimulus to British manufacturing.[5] By the period 1780–1801, exports were contributing significantly to British economic growth and accounted for 19.3 per cent of the incremental increase to gross national product in Britain over the period. In the same period recent estimates have shown that between 50 and 79 per cent of additional industrial production was exported from Britain.[6] The United States market, as the figures cited above demonstrate, played a vital role in this acceleration of British exports in the last two decades of the eighteenth century – a time that coincided with the onset of industrialization in the domestic economy.[7]

An investigation of the commercial networks that sustained the transatlantic commerce in exports should enable us to identify the main features of business organization in the trade and how they altered in the second half of the eighteenth century. It can throw light on the impact of the American Revolution on the Atlantic economy – particularly the extent to which this was a watershed in British commercial history – by illustrating how one important branch of Anglo-American trade was rebuilt fairly rapidly after hostilities ended. In so doing, some sugges-

---

[5] Patrick O'Brien, 'Agriculture and the home market for English industry, 1660–1820', *English Historical Review*, 100 (1985), 773–800; Ralph Davis, 'English foreign trade, 1700–1774', *EcHR*, 2nd series, 15 (1962–3), 102–3; Jacob M. Price, 'Colonial trade and British economic development, 1660–1775', *Lex et Scientia: the International Journal of Law and Science*, 14 (1978), 106–26, reprinted in Price's *Overseas Trade and Traders*, ch. 1; P. K. O'Brien and S. L. Engerman, 'Exports and the growth of the British economy from the Glorious Revolution to the Peace of Amiens', in Barbara L. Solow, ed., *Slavery and the Rise of the Atlantic System* (Cambridge, 1991), pp. 177–209; S. D. Smith, 'British exports to colonial North America and the mercantilist fallacy', *Business History*, 37 (1995), 45–63, and 'The market for manufactures in the thirteen continental colonies, 1698–1776', *EcHR*, 2nd series, 51 (1998), 676–708; Kenneth Morgan, 'Atlantic trade and British economic growth in the eighteenth century', in Peter Mathias and John A. Davis, eds., *The Nature of Industrialization: International Trade and British Economic Growth from the Eighteenth Century to the Present Day* (Oxford, 1996), pp. 27–8.

[6] N. F. R. Crafts, 'British economic growth, 1700–1831: a review of the evidence', *EcHR*, 2nd series, 36 (1983), table 8, 197; Crouzet, *Britain Ascendant*, pp. 237–8, 330; Javier Cuenca Esteban, 'The rising share of British industrial exports in industrial output, 1700–1851', *JEcH*, 57 (1997), 879–906.

[7] Kenneth Morgan, *Slavery, Atlantic Trade and the British Economy, 1660–1800* (Cambridge, 2000), ch. 5.

tions can be put forward about why French merchants failed to compete successfully in supplying manufactured exports to the newly independent United States. The analysis also indicates how business institutions contributed to economic development in the early industrial revolution. My focus will be on the business strategies of merchants, manufacturers, agents and suppliers in the British ports and inland centres and on their American merchant correspondents. The main sources drawn upon are merchants' letterbooks, account books, travel journals and printed literature. The discussion is not intended to suggest that the business developments highlighted were confined to transatlantic trade. Many of them were no doubt replicated in the British export trade to European markets in the eighteenth century – a topic ripe for new research and analysis.[8]

To understand business networks in the export trade, one first needs to grasp several contextual matters. The most important is that the export trade operated under conditions of considerable risk. The rapid growth of exports to North America in the second half of the eighteenth century did not follow a consistent upward trend. There were many peaks and troughs, occasioned by interruptions to trade from non-importation boycotts in the years 1765–6, 1768–70 and 1774–6, when Philadelphia, New York, Boston and Charleston were closed for long stretches of time to British vessels. These interruptions to commerce recurred in the American War of Independence, when all legal British trade to the North American mainland ceased apart from voyages to New York City and Philadelphia while they were under British military control. Additionally, the trade itself was one in which it was essential for commercial success that goods arrived on time in season. Spring goods were shipped in the New Year to reach America in February and March. Autumn goods were sent out in June and July to arrive at their markets before the end of September. Export wares that did not arrive to meet these seasonal requirements proved difficult to sell. At the British end of the trade, a relatively small number of commercial houses at the ports controlled exports, and dispatched goods to hundreds of merchants in North America. The trade was heavily dependent on the expertise and solvency of these large British export firms and on the ability of their American correspondents to pay promptly for goods received.[9]

---

[8] Available studies on the marketing of British exports to Europe in the eighteenth century include Edwards, *The Growth of the British Cotton Trade*; Trevor Fawcett, 'Argonauts and commercial travellers: the foreign marketing of Norwich stuffs in the later eighteenth century', *Textile History*, 16 (1995), 151–82, and Smail, *Merchants, Markets and Manufacture*.

[9] Thomas M. Doerflinger, *A Vigorous Spirit of Enterprise: Merchants and Economic Development in Revolutionary Philadelphia* (Chapel Hill, N.C., 1986), pp. 87–8; Doerflinger, 'Farmers and dry goods,' p. 168.

Unfortunately, a boom-and-bust character was the norm in the export trade, with frequent instances of chronic gluts of goods in North America and overstretching of credit to many small American importers, leading to indebtedness for many participants.[10] Business failures in the export trade at London and other British ports produced waves of shock in Britain and North America – notably during the financial crises of 1772 and 1793 – and affected the credit standing of those in trade. Merchant bankruptcy was a common phenomenon in the aftermath of speculative booms.[11] Besides these problems, merchants' invoices show long lists of an incredible variety of goods, which made accurate ordering and supply of wares difficult.[12] Clearly, successful merchants needed to reduce these risks in a highly competitive commercial world. It is not surprising, therefore, that business links between British and American merchants, suppliers and agents in the hinterland of British ports, and manufacturers became more closely intertwined during the second half of the eighteenth century, leading, as we shall see, to a more fully developed Anglo-American commercial world and to important changes in the conduct, speed and precision with which goods were handled.

[10] The best discussion of fluctuations in the dry goods trade is Doerflinger, *A Vigorous Spirit of Enterprise*, pp. 85–97.

[11] For instance HSP, Thomas Clifford, Jr to John Clifford, 10 July 1784, Pemberton papers: Clifford correspondence, vol. VII; Van Pelt Library, Special collections, University of Pennsylvania, Philadelphia, Samuel Wetherill & Sons to Brondram, Templeman & Jaques, 25 May 1793, Samuel Wetherill & Sons letterbook (1789–1828), Wetherill papers; NYHS, New York City, Lynch & Stoughton to John Kirwan & Sons, 5 June 1793, Lynch & Stoughton letterbook (1791–4). See also Jacob M. Price, *Capital and Credit in British Overseas Trade: the View from the Chesapeake, 1700–1776* (Cambridge, Mass., 1980), ch. 7; Richard B. Sheridan, 'The British credit crisis of 1772 and the American colonies', *JEcH*, 20 (1960), 161–86; Julian Hoppit, 'Financial crises in eighteenth-century England', *EcHR*, 2nd series, 29 (1986), 39–58; Julian Hoppit, *Risk and Failure in English Business, 1700–1800* (Cambridge, 1987), pp. 99–102, 130–9.

[12] See, for example, the invoices in Philip L. White, *The Beekmans of New York in Politics and Commerce, 1647–1870*, 3 vols. (New York, 1956), III, pp. 1404–11; Frances Norton Mason, ed., *John Norton & Sons: Merchants of London and Virginia* (Richmond, Va., 1937), pp. 72–3, 119–21, 124–6, 146–7, 151–2, 190–2, 211–12, 218–19, 329–31, 354–5, 357–9; W. W. Abbot and Dorothy Twohig, eds., *The Papers of George Washington: Colonial Series*, 10 vols. (Charlottesville, Va., 1983–95), VII, pp. 22–9, 124–30, 191–9, 288–95, 353–7, 419–23, 471–5; HSP, Jones & Wister invoice book (1759–62); Pennsylvania State Archives, Harrisburg, Robert Usher invoice book (1759–61); DAR Library, Hudson, New York, Memorandum of sundries to be shipped by Messrs. Champion & Dickason . . . 8 April 1784, Thomas Jenkins letterbook (1782–5); New York State Library, Albany, invoices in David Vanderheyden invoice book (1763–9); William L. Clements Library, University of Michigan, Ann Arbor, James Douglas account book (1784–92), fos. 2, 129, 134–7; Baker Library, Harvard University Business School, foreign invoices (1757–74), Samuel Abbot papers, box 12.

I

One noticeable change in the business networks in the Anglo-American export trade was the rise in the number of American merchants visiting English ports and manufacturing centres specifically with a view to gaining up-to-date knowledge of the range, colour and price of goods available for export and their production processes. We are familiar, through much research, with the industrial espionage of European agents coming to Britain in the early industrial revolution,[13] and recently there has been discussion of similar missions by Americans coming to Britain in the early nineteenth century.[14] Less well-known is the rise in tours of British ports and manufactories by American merchants, especially at the time of the War of Independence. This was a phenomenon partly caused by political circumstances, for some of these traders were Quakers, and hence pacifists, who spent time living in England during the Revolution; in addition, of course, there were strong transatlantic links among the Religious Society of Friends. But it was also caused by curiosity at the commercial and economic growth of Britain and by the urge to make money: these travellers often visited Britain to increase their knowledge of economic conditions and trade for the time when the American revolutionary war came to an end.

I edited the travel journals of one such visitor, the young Jabez Maud Fisher, son of a wealthy Philadelphia Quaker merchant, who was sent by his father to the British Isles in 1775. There he undertook a comprehensive tour of over three years making contacts with Quaker merchants and manufacturers, seeing various technological processes at work in industry, visiting warehouses, gaining first-hand acquaintance with the range and supply networks for metalware, hardware and textiles, and keeping a detailed notebook on the best commercial contacts for British exports and inland centres for the eventual resumption of his father's dry goods trade between Philadelphia and Britain. Fisher visited Coalbrookdale, copper works at Swansea and Neath, the White Cloth Hall at Leeds, the industrial centres of Sheffield, Birmingham and Manchester, burgeoning ports such as Liverpool and Port Glasgow, and Cornish copper and tin

---

[13] See, for example, Gabriel Jars, *Voyages métallurgiques*, 3 vols. (Paris, 1781); F. de St Fond, *Voyages en Angleterre . . .* (Paris, 1797); S. G. Lindberg, ed., *Bengt Ferrner: Resa in Europa, En Astronom, Industriespion och Teaterhabitue Genom Denmark, Tyskland, Holland, England och Italien, 1758–1762* (Uppsala, 1956); Jean Chevalier, 'La mission de Gabriel Jars dans les mines et les usines Britannique en 1764', *Transactions of the Newcomen Society*, 26 (1947–9), 57–66; M. W. Flinn, 'The travel diaries of Swedish engineers of the eighteenth century as sources of technological history', *Transactions of the Newcomen Society*, 31 (1957–9), 95–106.

[14] David J. Jeremy, 'Transatlantic industrial espionage in the early nineteenth century: barriers and penetrations', *Textile History*, 26 (1995), 95–122.

mines. He contacted merchants and manufacturers in London, the chief provincial ports and in inland towns such as Nottingham, Lancaster, Leeds and the other cities mentioned above. He kept detailed notes on the price, quality and variety of manufactured goods for export and the credit terms offered.[15]

Samuel Rowland Fisher, the brother of Jabez, made tours of Britain in 1767–8 and 1783–4. On his first visit he ordered goods from Newcastle, Leeds and Lancaster and bought camblets at Durham, all to be sent to London for dispatch by the firm of Harford & Powell to his father's firm, Joshua Fisher & Sons, in Philadelphia. His notebook from the tour lists the goods and prices available at different British towns.[16] On his second tour, just after the end of the revolutionary war, he called to see hosiery manufacturers at Nottingham; Manchester products in London warehouses; gloves at Worcester; linen and cotton wares at Manchester; the goods and prices at glass warehouses in Warrington; and he also checked the manufactured wares on offer at the semi-annual Bristol fair. He was impressed with the sheer number of woollen and worsted articles manufactured in and around Leeds. He commented on the low price of manufactured wares at Sheffield, and noted that hosiery manufactured at Nottingham was generally of a higher price and quality than that made at Leicester.[17]

The Philadelphia Quaker merchant John Warder was another visitor to Britain around the same time. He undertook a tour of the north of England in 1773 and made a later trip to commercial centres in Britain during the War of Independence. Some examples of his business enquiries in 1776 and 1777 illustrate his keen grasp of the economic conditions that could be tapped by American merchants when transatlantic trade resumed. He visited Josiah Wedgwood's potteries and asked for the different kinds and prices of wares made there and the expense of delivering goods to Liverpool, Bristol and London so that he could judge the best port for mercantile contacts; he also enquired after the credit on wares and the discounts available for cash payment. He looked into the organization of the nail trade in the Midlands, since that was a branch of commerce in which Americans participated fully before 1776. He took an excursion through the manufacturing centres of the north of England, noting the lack of available labour in Manchester and the reduction in the

[15] Kenneth Morgan, ed., *An American Quaker in the British Isles: the Travel Journals of Jabez Maud Fisher, 1775–1779* (Oxford, 1992).

[16] HSP, Samuel Rowland Fisher journals (1767–8).

[17] HSP, Samuel Rowland Fisher journals (1783–4), entries for 15 September, 23 and 26 October, 5, 7 and 15 November, 1 December 1783. Microfilm copies of the two journals kept by Samuel Rowland Fisher are available at the Religious Society of Friends Library, London.

quantity of woollens at Leeds in 1777 compared with four years earlier – attributable to the loss of North American markets. While in England, Warder corresponded with Quaker businessmen such as Mildred & Roberts, merchants of London in the Chesapeake trade; Frank, Tuckett & Waring, merchants and factors of Bristol; Robert and Nathaniel Hyde, check and fustian manufacturers and merchants of Manchester; Benjamin Bower, merchant of Manchester; William Rathbone, a large West India and American merchant of Liverpool; and Rawlinson & Chorley, another Liverpool merchant firm. These were some of the major English businessmen with interests in exports to North America.[18]

The Fisher brothers and John Warder were just three out of many Americans undertaking such tours with specific commercial considerations in mind. Other examples include the residence in London in the early 1770s of Joshua Johnson, partner in the Annapolis merchant firm of Wallace, Davidson & Johnson, and the visit to England of the prominent Charleston merchant Henry Laurens in 1772. Both Johnson and Laurens spent their time finding out about suppliers of goods, credit terms and discounts offered, and the general progress of the English economy.[19] In 1764 Josiah Trumbull, the son of a leading Connecticut merchant, travelled to England, where he visited and commented on manufacturing works and trade conditions in Manchester and Birmingham, all the while taking note of the quality and price of goods intended for American markets.[20] In the early 1770s a New York firm sent a partner to London to travel through the manufacturing districts two or three times a year to inspect goods before they were shipped and to establish connections to send them from London or any of the outports to New York.[21] The American manufacturer Joshua Gilpin made tours from Philadelphia throughout the British Isles in the mid-1790s, investigating industrial developments, internal improvements and mechanical devices.[22] Other Philadelphia merchants made similar trips to Britain gathering business

[18] HSP, John Warder to Jacob Watson, 27 August 1776, 21 May 1777, and to Josiah Wedgwood, 4 June 1777, John Warder letterbooks (1776–8).

[19] Jacob M. Price, ed., *Joshua Johnson's Letterbook, 1771–1774: Letters from a Merchant in London to his Partners in Maryland*, London Record Society, 15 (1979); Henry Laurens to James Laurens, 6 February 1772, in Philip M. Hamer, George C. Rogers and David R. Chesnutt, eds., *The Papers of Henry Laurens*, 13 vols. (Columbia, S.C., 1968–   ), VIII, p. 177.

[20] CHS, Jos. Trumbull to Jonathan Trumbull, Sr, 17 June 1764, Jonathan Trumbull, Sr papers, box 2.

[21] Baker Library, Abraham Lott & Co. to Samuel Abbot, 24 February 1773, Samuel Abbot papers, box 2.

[22] Pennsylvania State Archives, Joshua Gilpin journals (1795–1801). This material is discussed in Harold B. Hancock and Norman B. Wilkinson, 'Joshua Gilpin: an American manufacturer in England and Wales, 1795–1801', parts 1 and 2, *Transactions of the Newcomen Society*, 32 (1959–60), 15–26, and 33 (1960–1), 57–66.

information, and some joined mercantile houses there.[23] Immediately after the Revolution Wallace, Johnson & Muir of Annapolis sent a merchant partner to London, with the intention that he visit all the capital manufacturing towns to form plans to have goods on the proper terms.[24] Around the same time Thomas Blount of North Carolina undertook a similar businessman's tour of English ports and industrial towns. He found Liverpool to be better suited to his firm's trade than any other port in England because it was near 'many capital manufacturing towns' and had lower commission and brokerage charges than London.[25] Other Americans who were not businessmen also toured Britain in the American revolutionary era, and they were similarly fascinated by the economic progress they witnessed.[26]

This transatlantic traffic was not just a one-way affair. British merchants also made their way to North America. John Glover, for instance, inspected manufactured goods at Leeds before setting out for North America to do business for Harrisons & Ansley of London in the linen trade.[27] John Oseland, a member of a Bristol merchant partnership, visited Philadelphia and New York on business to determine the nature of the markets for exports there.[28] In 1769 Nathaniel Hyde, partner in a Manchester textile business, paid a business trip to New York.[29] In 1771

[23] See for instance HSP, Henry Drinker diary (Am. 057); HSP, Richard Vaux diaries (1779–82); HSP, Samuel Shoemaker diary (1783–5); HSP, James Renwick to Andrew Clow, 24 December 1784, papers of Andrew Clow and David Cay, Gratz Collection; HSP, Pemberton papers: Clifford letterbooks; HSP, Robert Philips to Philips, Cramond & Co., 7 April 1790, Cramond, Philips & Co. correspondence; LC, Manuscripts division, Samuel Smith to John Smith, 5 September 1772, Samuel Smith letterbooks (1772–4), Samuel Smith papers, box 7; Staffordshire Record Office, Stafford, George Philips to George Wood at Thomas Greg & Co., 20 December 1793, Records of J. & N. Philips & Co. (D 644/1/16); 'Memoir of Thomas Gilpin', *Pennsylvania Magazine of History and Biography*, 49 (1925), 289–328.

[24] Maryland Historical Society, Baltimore, circular letter dated 20 December 1784, and Wallace, Johnson & Muir to Overton Cosby, 29 April 1785, Wallace, Johnson & Muir letterbook (1784–5).

[25] Thomas Blount to John Gray Blount, 25 August, 26 September 1785, in Alice Barnwell Keith, ed., *The John Gray Blount Papers*, 2 vols. (Raleigh, N.C., 1952, 1959), I, pp. 209, 219–20.

[26] For instance Religious Society of Friends Library, London, Thomas Parke journals (1771–2); Indiana University, Bloomington, Jonathan Williams, 'Journal of a Journey with Dr Franklin, Inglehouse and Canton to Manchester, Sheffield and Birmingham, 18–27 May 1771'. Both of these sources are available on microfilm at the American Philosophical Society Library, Philadelphia. Williams's tour is summarized in William B. Willcox, ed., *The Papers of Benjamin Franklin*, 32 vols. (New Haven, 1976), XVIII, pp. 113–16.

[27] LC, Samuel Elam to Stephen Collins, 1 January 1774, Stephen Collins papers, vol. XVII.

[28] HSP, James & Drinker to Freeman & Oseland, 2 July 1760, James & Drinker letterbook (1759–62).

[29] Florence M. Montgomery, *Textiles in America 1650–1870. Dictionary Based on Original Documents: Prints and Paintings, Commercial Records, American Merchants' Papers, Shopkeepers' Advertisements, and Pattern Books with Original Swatches of Cloth* . . . (New York, 1984), p. 400.

an agreement was made between two merchants from Leeds and one from Burnley, a Leeds dyer, a Leeds stuff maker and another stuff maker who was to act as their agent in North America.[30] In the 1770s and 1780s one finds examples of a Leeds merchant visiting Philadelphia to try to sell woollens; two members of another Leeds firm travelling with goods for sale to Philadelphia and North Carolina; a member of a Birmingham firm offering samples of goods on two trips to New York and Philadelphia; another trader, from Bristol and Birmingham, going to Boston with a pattern book of ribbons; a Scottish merchant setting up trade in New York; and a merchant connected with firms in Annapolis and London in printed calico manufacture calling on the Browns of Providence, Rhode Island, with patterns of printed textiles that could be selected and ordered.[31] Other businessmen visited North America on missions to tap the market there for British manufactured goods: one example was Henry Wansey, a Salisbury clothier, who spent some time in Philadelphia and New York in 1794, looking at trade conditions in those ports, and who also inspected the American woollen industry.[32] There seems little doubt that these examples 'were just the visible links of a far larger mercantile chain' of British merchants visiting the United States and, in some cases, setting up in trade there in the 1790s.[33]

The movement of merchants between Britain and America represented an attempt at more aggressive marketing techniques than had been the norm earlier in the export trade. These strategies have been examined for trade in the 1780s between British ports and Philadelphia, the largest city and biggest port in the new United States. Instead of allowing their American correspondents to assume title to the goods they exported, a number of British firms began to ship off large cargoes on their own account, and often dispatched young partners to Philadelphia to solicit business. Moreover, some British adventurers purchased goods on credit,

[30] West Yorkshire Archives Service, Leeds, Articles of agreement for an American factor, 1771, CA 1/p. 44; Smail, *Merchants, Markets and Manufacture*, p. 91.
[31] LC, Stephen Collins to Samuel Elam, 29 December 1770, Stephen Collins letterbook (1760–73), and Charles Startin to Stephen Collins, 2 December 1785, *ibid.*, vols. XXX and LVII; HSP, William Pollard to Ely Hill, 16 March 1774, William Pollard letterbook (1772–4); HSP, James & Drinker to Thomas Pearsall, 25 February 1764, James & Drinker letterbook (1762–4); NEHGS, Boston, Henry Bromfield to Thomas Bromfield, 20 September 1771, Henry Bromfield letterbook (1771–2); W. T. Baxter, *The House of Hancock: Business in Boston 1724–1775* (Cambridge, Mass., 1945), p. 246; Florence M. Montgomery, '"Fortunes to be Acquired": textiles in 18th-century Rhode Island', *Rhode Island History*, 31 (1972), 56; Eileen Elizabeth Cox, 'A study of the diary of Robert Mercer, merchant in New York, 1770 to 1774' (University of Stirling M.Litt. thesis, 1982).
[32] David J. Jeremy, ed., *Henry Wansey and his American Journal, 1794*, Memoirs of the American Philosophical Society, 82 (Philadelphia, 1970).
[33] John R. Killick, 'Bolton Ogden & Co.: a case study in Anglo-American trade, 1790–1850', *Business History Review*, 48 (1974), 506.

took them to Philadelphia, rented a store and sold the wares on their own account.[34] After 1790 Yorkshire woollen merchants and manufacturers often sent out agents or partners to the United States. This helped to quicken the pace of sales and to provide closer supervision of the composition of woollen shipments for different markets at a time when Yorkshire woollens were dispatched in abundance to North America.[35]

In addition, a number of merchants left Britain for substantial periods of time to conduct business in North America and some Americans came to British ports to set up in trade. Scottish factors in the Chesapeake, keeping well-stocked supplies of dry goods throughout the tobacco growing areas, are among the best known of these migrants.[36] But one also finds a cosmopolitan element of British merchants in Philadelphia, New York, Baltimore, Charleston and Boston, and Americans settling at Bristol, Liverpool and London. While these migrants criss-crossing the Atlantic were a minority of merchants in specific ports, they took with them knowledge of the range of goods best suited for shipment across the ocean and a keen eye for the best marketing techniques.[37]

II

A second business development helping to sustain the trade was the dissemination of a more varied range of samples and business documents. Separated by the Atlantic Ocean and operating under relatively slow communications – business information could only travel, via letters, as fast as ships could sail – British and American merchants found that the competitive nature of the export trade necessitated fuller, more varied business documents than the traditional method of sending letters in duplicate or triplicate to ensure safe arrival. There was a marked trend towards sending correspondents pattern books of manufacturers' goods,

[34] Doerflinger, *Vigorous Spirit of Enterprise*, p. 245.

[35] Herbert Heaton, 'Yorkshire cloth traders in the United States, 1770–1840', *The Thoresby Miscellany*, vol. II: *Publications of the Thoresby Society*, 37, 1941 (Leeds, 1945), pp. 241–3; D. T. Jenkins and K. G. Ponting, *The British Wool Textile Industry 1770–1914* (London, 1982), pp. 58–9. For an example of Birmingham merchant manufacturers with partners in Philadelphia in the 1790s, see PRO, C12/246/25.

[36] T. M. Devine, *The Tobacco Lords: a Study of the Tobacco Merchants of Glasgow and their Trading Activities, c. 1740–1790* (Edinburgh, 1975); William R. Brock, *Scotus Americanus: a Survey of Sources for Links between Scotland and America in the Eighteenth Century* (Edinburgh, 1982).

[37] W. E. Minchinton, 'The merchants of Bristol in the eighteenth century', in *Sociétés et groupes sociaux en Aquitaine et en Angleterre. Fédérations Historiques du Sud-ouest* (Bordeaux, 1979), p. 189; South Caroliniana Library, Columbia, S.C., Ball Family papers; William L. Sachse, *The Colonial American in Britain* (Madison, 1956); H. V. Bowen, *Elites, Enterprise and the Making of the British Overseas Empire 1688–1775* (London, 1996), pp. 109–10.

samples of textiles, printed sheets with prices and ranges of commodities, and printed partnership papers when a new firm was set up or when partners changed. The changes of partnership recorded formally on printed sheets were significant in a commercial world dependent very much on business reputation and trust. To reassure American customers, such documents sometimes mentioned that the new partner had a thorough knowledge of various British manufactures.[38] One example of the printed papers relating to partnership changes came with the announcement in 1795 that Thomas Gould was leaving his partners Harrison, Ansley & Co. of Bread Street, London, to carry on the same business under the firm of Thomas Gould & Co. of Cheapside, the only differences being that the new concern declined to purchase goods on commission and intended to deal in a range of cotton goods. At the same time, the papers announced, the firm of Nathaniel and Joseph Gould & Co. would continue their usual trade at Manchester in fustians, dimities and Irish linens. At the bottom of the printed sheet was appended the articles manufactured by the Goulds and suitable for the American market – muslinets; quiltings, 28 to 30 inches wide; corded dimities, all patterns and prices; ginghams; half ell jeans; satinets; thicksets; velverets; and so on.[39]

Samples and pattern cards were already being sent overseas in the Yorkshire worsted industry by the 1730s, in the Birmingham 'toy' trades by the 1750s, and in the Norwich textile trade by the early 1760s.[40] But they were used much more frequently thereafter, even if not in a systematic fashion.[41] The Philadelphia merchant Stephen Collins, for instance, corresponded with Bristolians who furnished him with a printed sheet of prices of Bristol crown window glass and glass bottles for sale, and with a Leeds merchant who sent a sample set of patterns of articles he could provide with reference to quality, finishing and colour. William Birkbeck & Co. of Settle, in the Pennines, manufacturers of woollen stuffs and merchants, sent samples of hardens – a coarse fabric made from the hards of flax or hemp – in the hope that they would suit the Philadelphia

---

[38] NYHS, printed sheet dated 1 July 1772, Cruger miscellaneous papers.

[39] LC, printed statement of Thomas Gould addressed to Zaccheus Collins, 2 November 1795, Stephen Collins papers, vol. LXXXVIII. For other examples, see Birmingham Central Reference Library, printed circular for Ketland, Cotterill & Son, 1 July 1795, Scholefield, Goodman & Sons papers; Houghton Library, Harvard University, Champion & Hayley to Nathaniel Holmes, 16 March 1754, Brown papers, vol. VI; HSP, Oates & Wilson to John Clifford, 1 January 1790, Pemberton papers: Clifford correspondence, vol. IX (1788–90); CHS, Alexander Champion & George Hayley to Trumbull, Fitch & Trumbull, 1 February 1766, and Lane, Son & Fraser to Jonathan Trumbull, 14 May 1766, Jonathan Trumbull, Sr, papers, box 2.

[40] Styles, 'Manufacturing, consumption and design', p. 532 and n. 23; Ursula Priestley, ed., *The Letters of Philip Stannard, Norwich Textile Manufacturer (1751–1763)* (Norfolk Record Society, 57, Cambridge, 1994), p. 9.

[41] Smail, *Merchants, Markets and Manufacture*, p. 83.

market.[42] Joshua Johnson, a junior partner in an Annapolis merchant house resident in London, sent a set of patterns from a London linen drapery house to his senior partners in Maryland.[43] One can find other instances of samples and patterns sent by English merchants to America, and of memoranda of the type, quality and price of goods available from London for the Boston market, from Manchester for Providence, Rhode Island, and from London for consumption in Connecticut.[44] In the Yorkshire woollen trade, pattern cards were used frequently in the North American market in the 1780s and 1790s.[45] American merchants were anxious to receive these documents quickly because they competed with other traders in the same ports who also received pattern books, and there was much to be gained from being first with a sample of the fashions that could be ordered for the next season.[46] American merchants sometimes reciprocated by sending orders to British textile houses with pieces of coloured cloth attached to indicate precisely the colour and texture they wanted.[47]

Sending samples reduced the problems of trading by distance by enabling American merchants to see the colour and feel the quality of material on offer, especially textiles. Pattern cards or books were equally important in this regard. They comprised numbered swatches in panels that unfolded, allowing a large number of swatches to be viewed simultaneously. The patterns were pasted on paper in a small compass with the prices annexed and the number of yards for piece goods.[48] British mer-

[42] LC, Thomas & Richard Lee to Stephen Collins, 24 February 1785; Lucas, Pater & Coathupe to Stephen Collins, 16 May 1790; Smithson, Rayner & Richie to Stephen Collins, 10 September 1794, Stephen Collins papers, vols. XXI, XLVIII–XLXIX; Baker Library, William Birkbeck & Co. to Reynell & Coates, 2 August 1774, Reynell & Coates papers, vol. I folder 3; Morgan, ed., *An American Quaker in the British Isles*, p. 290.

[43] Price, ed., *Joshua Johnson's letterbook*, p. 8.

[44] Baker Library, many letters and memoranda in Samuel Abbot's London letter and memorandum book (1758–75); Massachusetts Historical Society, Boston, Jonathan Jackson to George Brown, 27 June 1766, Jonathan Jackson letterbook (1765–74); John Carter Brown Library, Providence, Rhode Island, Nathaniel & Falk Phillips & Co. to Brown & Benson, 11 February 1791, Brown papers, P-E9, vol. III; CHS, Samuel Sparrow to Col. Jonathan Trumbull, 28 March 1750, Jonathan Trumbull, Sr, papers, box 1.

[45] Smail, *Merchants, Markets and Manufacture*, p. 115.

[46] NEHGS, Henry Bromfield to Joseph Flight, 29 August 1771, Henry Bromfield letterbook (1771–2).

[47] PRO, C114/103, William Wistar to David and Daniel Glover, 14 December 1795, and James Parsons, Jr, to David and Daniel Glover, 16 August 1796, Glover invoice book (1789–1805).

[48] NEHGS, Jonathan Jackson to George Brown, 27 June 1766, Jonathan Jackson letterbook (1765–74); Winterthur Museum, Delaware, Manchester pattern books and Norwich pattern books, *c.* 1750–1800, the Joseph Downs collection of manuscripts and printed ephemera; and similar pattern books cited in Montgomery, *Textiles in America*, pp. 399–400.

chants sending pattern cards usually required their American counterparts to select a number from the card for the goods they wanted. Thus,
for instance, a New York or Philadelphia merchant could order broadcloths from Leeds by citing the prices he would pay and the number of
the pattern.[49] One British firm trading in cotton goods noted that all
sorts of their goods dyed in the piece could be supplied in any colour by
referring to the colour of any of the pattern cards on counterparts preserved, or by enclosing in a letter a pattern of any different colours
wanted.[50] By doing so, Americans could expect to receive British manufactured wares with exact attention to colour and price.[51] American
merchants could show the pattern book to their customers over a wide
catchment area; indeed, one Boston merchant in 1771 distributed the
pattern book he received not just to customers in and around his own
city but to customers in New York City and Philadelphia as well.[52] A
Yorkshire trader visiting Boston with a set of patterns of woollen goods
was willing to loan the book to various Boston merchants.[53] By these
means, the latest fashions could be seen at first hand in North America.[54]
Sometimes, of course, matters went awry: if the colours of cloth sent to
American ports failed to match those ordered from the pattern book,
they could prove unsaleable.[55]

These innovations were underpinned by fuller and speedier avenues of
information available to merchants in the second half of the eighteenth
century: extensive newspaper advertising of their wares and premises in
both the British and American press; much circulation of commercial
news via *Lloyd's List*, the London commodity price current, the London

---

[49] HSP, John Hadfield & Sons to Andrew Clow, 4 April 1785, Andrew Clow business
correspondence, box 12, Claude W. Unger Collection; HSP, James & Drinker to [?],
1 September 1756, James & Drinker letterbook (1756–9); Winterthur Museum, Daniel
Wistar to Benjamin & John Bower, 4 November 1767, and to Samuel Elam, 17 November 1767, Daniel Wistar order book (1762–8), Wistar Family papers, box 5, Joseph
Downs Collection; PRO, C114/103, James Parsons & Sons to David and Daniel Glover,
1 January 1790, Glover invoice book (1789–1805). Cf. Styles, 'Manufacturing, consumption and design'.
[50] Baker Library, Gideon Bickerdike to Reynell & Coates, 22 August 1774, Reynell &
Coates papers, vol. I, folder 3.
[51] Baker Library, Samuel Elam to Samuel Abbot & Co., 27 September 1773, Abbot foreign
letters, Sundry (1773), Samuel Abbot papers, box 5, file 1C; LC, Samuel Elam to
Stephen Collins, 27 September 1773, Stephen Collins papers, vol. XVI.
[52] NEHGS, Henry Bromfield to Joseph Flight, 29 August 1771, Henry Bromfield letterbook (1771–2).
[53] Baker Library, 'A List of Manufactures exported by Samuel Elam of Leeds, August
1771', List of goods from abroad, 1767–71, Samuel Abbot papers, box 5, file 3.
[54] Bucks County Historical Society, Doylestown, Pa., Kuhn & Risberg to Cruger, Lidiard &
Mullat, 19 October 1783, Kuhn & Risberg letterbook (1779–85).
[55] HSP, James & Drinker to David Barclay & Sons, 1 July 1760, and to Samuel & Thomas
Fludyer, 2 July 1760, James & Drinker letterbook (1759–62).

exchange rate current, and the talk at London and colonial coffee houses; details of cargoes, goods and prices in customs bills of entry and commercial and financial newspapers; the efficiency of the packet service from Falmouth to North America from the late 1770s onwards; and knowledge of American money and coins of account from British subscriptions to John Wright's *American Negociator*.[56]

III

The third characteristic of business networks in the Anglo-American export trade was the growth of direct correspondence between American merchants and inland agents and manufacturers in Britain. Before *c.* 1750 this was uncommon; inland traders mainly gained their knowledge of American markets and commodity requirements from British merchants.[57] But by the 1750s and 1760s American merchants were writing directly to Birmingham 'toy' manufacturers and the latter were forwarding letters from British export merchants to their American correspondents.[58] This change in business practice continued thereafter, as direct links were maintained between American merchants and businessmen in inland Britain. Not all merchants availed themselves of this means of commercial communication; but a sufficient number did so for this to be identified as another innovation in the marketing of transatlantic goods. In the 1760s and 1770s, William Pollard dispatched many letters from Philadelphia to woollen merchants and manufacturers in and around Halifax, with detailed instructions on the goods he wanted and with specific instructions about sending broadcloths, naps, duffils and bearskins. He sent similar instructions about metalware to Birmingham manufacturers, and also wrote to businessmen in Nottingham and

---

[56] On these developments, see Ian K. Steele, *The English Atlantic 1675–1740: an Exploration of Communication and Community* (New York, 1986); John J. McCusker, 'European bills of entry and marine lists: early commercial publications and the origins of the business press', *Harvard Library Bulletin*, 21 (1983), 209–55 and 316–39, reprinted as *European Bills of Entry and Marine Lists: Early Commercial Publications and the Origins of the Business Press* (Cambridge, Mass., 1985); John J. McCusker, 'The business press in England before 1775', *The Library: Transactions of the Bibliographical Society*, 6th series, 8 (1986), 205–31, reprinted in his *Essays in the Economic History of the Atlantic World* (London, 1997), pp. 145–76; John J. McCusker and Cora Gravesteijn, *The Beginnings of Commercial and Financial Journalism: the Commodity Price Currents, Exchange Rate Currents, and Money Currents of Early Modern Europe* (Amsterdam, 1991); and Jacob M. Price, 'Who cared about the colonies? The impact of the Thirteen Colonies on British society and politics, circa 1714–1775', in Bernard Bailyn and Philip D. Morgan, eds., *Strangers within the Realm: Cultural Margins of the First British Empire* (Chapel Hill, N.C., 1991), pp. 395–436, reprinted in Price's *The Atlantic Frontier*, ch. 6.

[57] Price, *Capital and Credit in British Overseas Trade*, esp. ch. 6.

[58] Kenneth Morgan, *Bristol and the Atlantic Trade in the Eighteenth Century* (Cambridge, 1993), p. 109.

Manchester.[59] One Philadelphia merchant firm requested linen checks, cotton hollands and dyed jeans from a Manchester manufacturer.[60] Another corresponded directly with manufacturers in Warrington, Cheshire.[61] Yet another, Stephen Collins, a substantial importer of dry goods, received letters from traders in Birmingham, Nottingham and Leeds.[62] In the 1790s, Abraham Varick of New York wrote directly for goods to Sheffield, Manchester, Leeds and Birmingham.[63] In 1770 Robert and Nathaniel Hyde wrote from Manchester to Samuel Abbot in Boston that they would only export to America the goods they manufactured, and that they could offer their correspondents better terms than were available at the ports. In 1777 the same firm sent a batch of twenty letters soliciting business from Philadelphia firms.[64] A good many of these commercial connections reflect the emergence of merchant-manufacturers in the industrial regions of provincial England in the second half of the eighteenth century.[65]

There were good commercial reasons for such correspondence. American merchants who placed orders where goods were manufactured had their wares finished and packaged with careful attention.[66] Quite simply, articles were better purchased on the spot where they were made.[67] This was important, given that American consumers were very particular in their choice of goods and in view of the problems that could beset packaging and the inland supply of goods in England over long distances.[68] In the Yorkshire woollen industry, a major supplier of exports to North America, so many candidates for American custom were scattered

---

[59] See many letters in Columbia University, Rare Books and Manuscripts Division, William Pollard letterbook (1764–8), Montgomery collection, MS 151; and HSP, William Pollard letterbook (1772–4). Pollard's business career is discussed in Smail, *Merchants, Markets and Manufacture*, pp. 79–85.

[60] HSP, Willing & Morris to Robert Hibbert, 25 October 1754, Willing & Morris letterbook (1754–61).

[61] LC, John Lownes to Samuel Fothergill and Thomas Merrick, n.d., John Lownes letterbook (1760–9).

[62] For example LC, Samuel Elam to Stephen Collins, 13 February 1772; Nathaniel & Robert Denison to Stephen Collins, 10 June 1772; and John Goodall to Stephen Collins, 20 January 1772; Stephen Collins papers, vols. XIII and XIV.

[63] NYHS, Abraham Varick order book (1791–8).

[64] Baker Library, Robert & Nathaniel Hyde to Samuel Abbot, 1 January 1770, foreign letters and accounts, 1757–87, Samuel Abbot papers, box 5; LC, Robert & Nathaniel Hyde & Co. to Stephen Collins *et al.*, 3 November 1777, Stephen Collins papers, vol. XXI. For the range of goods exported by the Hydes, see Montgomery, *Textiles in America*, p. 400.

[65] Stanley D. Chapman, *Merchant Enterprise in Britain: from the Industrial Revolution to World War I* (Cambridge, 1992), p. 61.

[66] LC, Samuel Elam to Stephen Collins, 5 March 1774, Stephen Collins papers, vol. XVII.

[67] LC, Welch, Wilkinson & Startin to Stephen Collins, 2 December 1771, *ibid.*, vol. XIII.

[68] NEHGS, Henry Bromfield to Edmund Halliday, 26 March 1772, Henry Bromfield letterbook (1771–2); Morgan, *Bristol and the Atlantic Trade*, pp. 120–2.

around the West Riding that they had to perform well and obtain good supplies of quality cloth to keep overseas orders flowing in, and so they favoured direct correspondence with American merchants for relaying detailed commercial information, without using merchants based in British ports as intermediaries. This method of marketing had the added advantage of cutting out reliance on middlemen such as warehousemen in the ports.[69] One Manchester firm emphasized to a Boston correspondent in 1761 that a great saving was possible by having goods immediately from the place they were manufactured at and shipped at the nearest port without land carriage or intermediate profits or commissions.[70] Direct correspondence between American merchants and British manufacturers was one way of integrating the internal domestic market in Britain to international consumption centres for manufactured products; and this was consolidated, in many cases, by the visits of American businessmen to inland centres of industry described above.

IV

The fourth business development associated with the Anglo-American export trade consisted of greater sophistication in the financing of trade. Commercial enterprise in the early modern era was founded on a bedrock of credit.[71] British overseas trade, accordingly, was conducted mainly on commercial credit rather than on borrowing by bond or from banks.[72] As the export trade burgeoned, lengthening of credit became a necessity to attract custom. By the late eighteenth century, British merchants allowed their American correspondents anything up to nine, twelve or (occasionally) eighteen months' credit on goods they ordered.[73] These long credits were one of the main advantages that the United States derived from Britain; they were usually more generous than those provided by European merchants, and were a major reason why Americans still largely looked to Britain for manufactured goods after the War of Independence despite their capacity as an independent nation to trade

[69] LC, Zaccheus Collins to Smithson, Rayner & Richie, 10 December 1794, Stephen Collins letterbook (1794–1801), Stephen Collins papers, vol. LXIX; Smail, *Merchants, Markets and Manufacture*, pp. 79–86.

[70] NEHGS, Hyde & Hamilton to Thomas Hancock, 20 February 1761, Thomas Hancock foreign letters (1728–64), Hancock collection, box 7.

[71] This is brought out in Mathias, 'Risk, credit and kinship', p. 15 above, and Nuala Zahedieh, 'Credit, risk and reputation in late seventeenth-century colonial trade', in Olaf Uwe Janzen, ed., *Merchant Organization and Maritime Trade in the North Atlantic, 1660–1815*, Research in Maritime History, 15 (St John's, Newfoundland, 1998), pp. 53–74.

[72] Price, *Capital and Credit in British Overseas Trade*, chs. 4–6.

[73] *Ibid.*; Morgan, *Bristol and the Atlantic Trade*, pp. 110–11.

worldwide.[74] Thus the French usually wanted cash payment for goods on delivery rather than extending credit, while the British found it easy to resume correspondence with American merchants with whom they had traded before the Revolution.[75] In 1785 a New York merchant noted that British shippers had commanded three-quarters of the transatlantic export trade since the peace, and as long as they gave credits of nine and twelve months they would receive orders from every American state 'as few other countries shew disposition to trust us and without European credits, the Importations must be confined, as the Capitals are too slender to enable our doing much'.[76] Credit terms varied from season to season, but in years of cheap credit even retail shopkeepers and merchants' apprentices in North America were encouraged by British merchants to become importers.[77]

Extensive credit and an oversupply of goods could cause problems in payment from North America. Boston merchants had to gather remittances from many customers scattered throughout Massachusetts and parts of Connecticut, New Hampshire and Maine.[78] Importers in New York needed sufficient time to allow country retailers to pay up; most of these businessmen had small capital and found it difficult to settle accounts punctually.[79] Most of the dry goods sold in South Carolina were generally paid for only once a year.[80] Some Philadelphia merchants had to collect money and bills from customers living anything between 50 and 300 miles away in the countryside; it was not merely the distance that made payments difficult to collect but the lack of circulating cash for country shopkeepers to pay merchants in the city.[81] In desperation one New York merchant told a merchant in Hull

how, in what manner, or at what period we poor Americans shall be able to make returns for the bountifull, astonishing remittances of Dry Goods poured in & arriving daily the Almighty only knows. Our Warehouses from one end of the

---

[74] Edwards, *The Growth of the British Cotton Trade*, p. 65; PRO, FO5/6, Consular Reports: Phineas Bond to Lord Grenville, 23 November 1794.

[75] Crouzet, *Britain Ascendant*, pp. 319–20; Peter P. Hill, *French Perceptions of the Early American Republic, 1783–1793* (Philadelphia, 1988), pp. 50, 67 (a reference suggested to me by Jeremy Black).

[76] Doerflinger, *Vigorous Spirit of Enterprise*, p. 173; NYHS, Lynch & Stoughton to Bire, Overman & Co., 17 February 1785 (quotation), Lynch & Stoughton letterbook (1783–7).

[77] Hagley Museum and Library, Eleutherian Mills, Delaware, David Cay to Andrew Clow, 31 May 1789, Andrew Clow & Co. papers (1784–1836), box 2.

[78] Baxter, *The House of Hancock*, pp. 188–9.

[79] NYHS, Lynch & Stoughton to Francis Bire, 10 April 1784, Lynch & Stoughton letterbook (1783–7).

[80] Austin & Laurens to Gidney Clarke, 25 August 1756, in Hamer *et al.*, eds., *Laurens Papers*, II, p. 296.

[81] Columbia University, William Pollard to Christopher Rawson, 20 September 1766, William Pollard letterbook (1764–8).

Continent to the other seem a pile of Riches, which the resource of this country cannot answer for in many years to come. Every Market is stocked with a very indifferent prospect of Sales & still less of recoveries.'[82]

Such a tale of woe was echoed in many other mercantile complaints when a glut of goods arrived at North American ports.[83]

But long credits also caused problems for suppliers of goods in Britain; they needed regular cash payments for their workers' wages and for payment for materials.[84] Overproduction of goods for America, notably just after the resumption of regular trade in 1783 and 1784, led to a shock to credit and to manufacturers being very cautious about delivering goods for other than ready money.[85] Drapers, for instance, could suffer from the extensive credit given by London merchants to overseas customers when they themselves were buying on short credit: all too often the merchants were slow to settle accounts with suppliers.[86] Indeed, the American Revolution gave a great shock to credit. Capital, it was said in 1785, commanded less credit than before and Birmingham manufacturers needed quick payment for goods to cover their costs.[87] In 1785 a London firm lamented the squeeze on credit for 'the trading part of the kingdom' in Atlantic commerce: tradesmen and manufacturers were not in a position to extend their credits and 'the Wealth of Croesus would be insufficient for the Trade'.[88] The export trade, especially after 1783, was therefore one that combined extensive credit between British and American merchants, but also pressures for rapid cash settlements between British exporters and their suppliers, with discounts offered by the latter for payment in ready money. The fact that suppliers of manufactured goods for export were scattered widely throughout the hinterland of ports and beyond meant that coordination of payments between merchants, manufacturers and distributors was a time-consuming affair.[89]

[82] NYHS, Lynch & Stoughton to Francis Bire, 3 November 1784, Lynch & Stoughton letterbook (1783–7).

[83] For instance, Duke University Library, Durham, N.C., Hogg & Clayton to Smith, Strachan & Co., 26 July 1764, Hogg & Clayton letterbook and accounts (1762–71); SHC, George Nelson to Messrs Lamberts, 14 January 1790, George Nelson letterbook (1784–98); LC, Harrison, Ansley & Co. to Stephen Collins, 1 August 1785, Stephen Collins papers, vol. XXIX.

[84] LC, Nathaniel & Robert Denison to Stephen Collins, 1 November 1785, Stephen Collins papers, vol. XXX; Morgan, *Bristol and the Atlantic Trade*, pp. 115–16.

[85] LC, [?] to Stephen Collins, 29 September 1784, Stephen Collins papers, vol. XXVII.

[86] LC, Harrison Ansley & Co. to Stephen Collins, 26 February 1785, *ibid.*

[87] LC, Capper, Startin & Co. to Stephen Collins, 29 September 1785, *ibid.*, vol. XXX.

[88] Rhode Island Historical Society, Providence, Rhode Island, Champion & Dickason to Moses Brown, 10 August 1785, Moses Brown papers, box for 1760–85.

[89] Morgan, *Bristol and the Atlantic Trade*, ch. 4; M. M. Schofield, 'The Virginia trade of the firm of Sparling and Bolden, of Liverpool, 1788–99', *Transactions of the Historic Society of Lancashire and Cheshire*, 116 (1964), 117–65.

The complexity of the credit and cash requirements of Atlantic trade led British exporters to offer incentives to American merchants for prompt payment. One big London firm trading in linens and East India goods allowed twelve months' credit for goods in their own immediate branch of business and nine months for products bought on commission. As an encouragement for their correspondents to pay promptly, they allowed a discount at the rate of 6 per cent per annum. But there was a penalty of interest at 5 per cent per annum for exceeding the credit period.[90] Another London merchant house allowed twelve months' credit, with a discount of 5 per cent per annum for earlier payment and a 5 per cent annual interest rate for failing to settle balances on time.[91] Inland traders were sometimes more generous in their discounts. One Wakefield woollen firm allowed twelve months' credit on their wares, but offered a 10 per cent discount for early payment.[92] The Leeds firm Elam & Buck, which was very active in trade with North America, had the same terms for their woollen exports. They added that they would pass bills at thirty days' sight to credit as soon as they were accepted.[93] A Nottingham merchant and manufacturer sold hosiery and breeches to a merchant based in Weathersfield, Connecticut, at a 20 per cent discount on London prices.[94] Birmingham traders offered substantial discounts – 35 to 45 per cent on gilt buttons, 40 per cent on silver-plated lacquer, 12.5 per cent on hard metal, and between 5 and 15 per cent on other goods.[95] After the American Revolution some Bristol merchants offered a 7.5 per cent discount for the export of glassware paid with ready money and a 10 per cent discount for Queensware (or, in the latter case, 5 per cent if paid within six months). They also received discounts from 10 to 20 per cent from Birmingham manufacturers for buying goods for export for cash payment.[96] These various conditions for credit, with appropriate discounts, indicate the incentives given by British inland traders and merchants to American correspondents in a very competitive trade.

[90] MHS, Harrison, Ansley & Co. to Governor Hancock, 26 April 1784, Hancock papers; Baker Library, Harrison & Ansley to Samuel Abbot, 29 May 1769, foreign letters and accounts, Samuel Abbot papers, box 5.

[91] NYHS, John Roberts to Reynell & Coates, 6 August 1774, Samuel Coates papers. Cf. similar terms in HSP, Neate & Pigou to Richard Waln, Jr, 19 April 1763, Richard Waln papers.

[92] HSP, John & Jeremiah Naylor & Co. to Andrew Clow, 29 March 1790, Unger Collection: Clow business correspondence.

[93] NYHS, Elam & Buck to Reynell & Coates, 8 September 1777, Samuel Coates papers; R. G. Wilson, *Gentlemen Merchants: the Merchant Community in Leeds, 1700–1830* (Manchester, 1971), appendix B, p. 243.

[94] CHS, Peter Verstille to John Olds, 18 August 1770, Peter Verstille letterbook (1765–74).

[95] CHS, Jos. Trumbull to Jonathan Trumbull, Sr, 17 June 1764, Jonathan Trumbull, Sr, papers, box 2.

[96] Morgan, *Bristol and the Atlantic Trade*, pp. 108–9.

V

The final significant business development in the Anglo-American export trade, though not the least, was the links forged between merchants, agents, suppliers and manufacturers to coordinate the demand for goods for specific American markets in relation to their colour, price, variety and finishing. This was especially significant in textiles, the most prominent branch of British exports after 1783.[97] British merchants here gained another advantage over their European competitors, as few goods came from the Continent to the United States immediately after 1783 because 'little knowledge . . . has been observed in calculating the proper articles fit for the respective States, as they differ in their Importations proportionable to their Climate which has seldom been considered in Europe'.[98] Cultural and linguistic problems were as significant in this regard as purely economic differences. The French, it was claimed, were 'not only ignorant of the Taste in patterns, and the quality of the Goods that suits our Countrymen, but all the Dictionaries of the World could not translate the names of the goods ordered'.[99]

In an impressionistic manner, the intricacy of demand for exports for specific North American markets can be sensed from comments made by Philadelphia merchants. One informed a Nottingham hosier that green, yellow, blue and white mittens were not worth half price in the Quaker city, where more subdued colours of grey and brown were required. Another noted that sheetings made in Barnsley were thinner than those made at Knaresborough and would therefore not suit the Philadelphia market. He requested dyed jeans and pillows from a Manchester firm, to be 'all neat drabs, doves and Leads, No Olives' and gave instructions to 'be particular with the colours of those as the Sale depends upon them'. Others requested purple ground calicoes that were 'newest & most fashionable'; cotton handkerchiefs that were 'light & fancy Grounds' with no black grounds 'nor any with black borders nor purple borders'; and silks and cotton thicksets in drab colours suitable for Quaker customers.[100]

---

[97] Crouzet, *Britain Ascendant*, ch. 6.

[98] NYHS, Lynch & Stoughton to Francis Bowers, 7 October 1784, Lynch & Stoughton letterbook (1783–7).

[99] James B. Hedges, *Browns of Providence Plantations: Colonial Years* (Cambridge, Mass., 1952), p. 253.

[100] LC, Stephen Collins to Nathaniel & Robert Denison, 25 November 1772, Stephen Collins letterbook (1760–73), Stephen Collins papers, vol. LVII; HSP, Samuel Rowland Fisher journals, 6 November 1783 and order dated 22 December 1767; HSP, List of goods ordered by James & Drinker from William Neate of London, 17 December 1756, James & Drinker letterbook (1756–9); Winterthur Museum, Order to Williams & Bellamy, Miles & Wistar order book (1771–4) and order to Peel, Yates & Co., 1 July 1785, Wistar family order book (1784–9).

The complexity of the demand for particular colours of textiles led some Philadelphians to order woollens that were not illustrated on pattern cards and to send colours to show what they meant by 'doves, leads, brown, blues'.[101]

Specific lines and colours of goods were required by different ports and their hinterland customers in North America: unassorted goods sent at random prices would not sell.[102] Americans frequently requested bold colours for calico-printed cottons and, though there was only a limited range of patterns, British textile printers varied those available by printing on various backgrounds.[103] Complaints by Americans reveal the intricacy of the demand for particular types of textiles, especially with regard to colours, patterns, texture, length of cloth and finishing. Thus a report from Baltimore noted that 6/4 cloths were much better consumed there than narrow cloths of the same firmness.[104] William Pollard, writing from New York, took to task a Yorkshire supplier for being inattentive in dyeing shalloons: the browns were all one colour and should have been varied and the lack of light coloured pieces among the cloth would be a great detriment to the sale.[105] A Philadelphia merchant ordering broadcloths from a Leeds woollen firm noted tersely, 'let those be thin Cloths fit for Women's cloaks & exactly to pattern'.[106] A Boston merchant, opening a package of silks from London, noted with displeasure that they were 'such colours as would not sell here to the end of time'.[107] Another Bostonian was displeased to receive camblets from London contrary to his memorandum: the only lengths that would sell there, he stated, were 33- or 42-yard pieces.[108] 'It is requisite you should be very attentive to the Colors ordered', a Philadelphia merchant partnership advised a Leeds woollen merchant firm, 'this being a material point to us, likewise to the finishing of the broad Cloths which must be Manufactured firm, the

---

[101] HSP, James & Drinker to Samuel & Thomas Fludyer, 2 July 1760, James & Drinker letterbook (1759–62), and Henry Drinker to Pigou & Booth, 30 October 1773, Henry Drinker foreign letters (1772–85).

[102] HSP, William Pollard to John Ramsden, 20 December 1773, William Pollard letterbook (1772–4).

[103] S. D. Chapman and S. Chassagne, *European Textile Printers of the Eighteenth Century: a Study of Peel and Oberkampf* (London, 1981), pp. 81–2.

[104] LC, Robert & Alexander McKim to Stephen Collins, 16 November 1784, Stephen Collins papers, vol. XXVIII.

[105] Columbia University, William Pollard to Thomas Swaine, 12 October 1767, William Pollard letterbook (1764–8).

[106] Winterthur Museum, order to Samuel & Emanuel Elam, 24 November 1763, Daniel Wistar order book (1762–8), Wistar family papers.

[107] NEHGS, John Hancock to Barnards & Harrison, 24 June 1765, John Hancock letterbook (1762–83).

[108] Baker Library, Samuel Abbot to Trecothick & Thomlinson, 3 September 1765, Samuel Abbot's London letterbook (1758–65), Samuel Abbot papers, vol. XXXA.

Threads must be well cover'd & the dressing be very smooth so as to feel soft & silky. The Coatings must be stout & well cover'd.'[109] Advertisements in North American newspapers convey fully the emphasis on particular types and colours of goods required by American customers.[110]

Before the American Revolution stores in the Chesapeake, often operated by Scottish factors, were quite specific in the goods they wanted from Britain. Storekeepers knew they needed to keep a well-sorted inventory of goods to attract and retain customers.[111] One such factor, Alexander Henderson of Occoquan, wanted his store well supplied with dry goods; he frequently sent back to Scotland schemes of goods he required. These were to be complied with if good profits were to be made by outdoing rival Glasgow stores in Virginia. In particular, Henderson requested all the trimmings to be ordered for different cloths: the sale of such items was futile without the proper trimmings. He also requested that a supplier of sowing, stitching and shoemaker's thread should comply exactly with the list sent and 'not at his pleasure mix green yellow & other Colors' with them.[112] A superintending factor for the Glasgow-based Cuninghame partners, based at Falmouth, Virginia, requested that his storekeeper at Fauquier, Virginia, should make out a particular scheme of goods divided into

general heads, such as linen, woollens, hats, sadlery etc. Under each of these the quality and price of the most minute article must be precisely specified. Avoid putting two or three articles together or listing two articles in one line as one of them may be overlooked and not sent.[113]

Attention to colour and finishing of goods was very important for trading with the American market because consumers there were attuned to fashions already popular in Britain, and they took great care in selecting quality goods even among items produced relatively cheaply and in

---

[109] PRO, C114/103, Wistar & Aston to David & Daniel Glover, 1 January 1791, Glover invoice book (1789–1805).

[110] Examples can be found in Alfred Coxe Prime, *Arts and Crafts in Philadelphia, Maryland, and South Carolina: Gleanings from Newspapers*, 2 vols. (Topsfield, Mass., 1929, 1932), covering 1721–1800; George Francis Dow, *Arts and Crafts in New England, 1704–1775: Gleanings from Boston Newspapers* (Topsfield, Mass., 1927); and Rita Susswein Gottesman, *Arts and Crafts in New York: Advertisements and News Items from New York City Newspapers* (New York, 1938, 1954), covering 1726–99.

[111] Lois Green Carr and Lorena S. Walsh, 'Changing lifestyles and consumer behavior in the colonial Chesapeake', in Carson *et al.*, eds., *Of Consuming Interests*, p. 108.

[112] Alexandria Public Library, Alexandria, Va., Alexander Henderson to John Glassford, 7 August 1758, 20 September 1762, and 'A scheme of goods for Colchester store, 1763', Alexander Henderson letterbook (1758–65). A xerox copy of this MS is available at the Mitchell Library, Glasgow.

[113] James Robinson to John Turner, 22 April 1769, in T. M. Devine, ed., *A Scottish Firm in Virginia 1767–1777: W. Cuninghame and Co.* (Scottish History Society, 4th series, 20, Edinburgh, 1984), p. 12.

bulk.[114] Such purchasing reflected a growing American desire not just for fashion in terms of up-to-date merchandise but for fashion in the sense of refinement.[115] Some articles sold entirely on account of their novelty or fashion.[116] Americans had acquired a taste for fashionable wares from Britain; but goods that were out of date in, say, Bristol would be unfashionable in Philadelphia, too.[117] Already by 1750 secondhand goods were difficult to sell in the Chesapeake and even stockings, shoes, hats and other ready-made goods were 'slighted'.[118] Thus some American merchants did not keep a large stock of exported wares on hand because if they did not sell quickly they could become unsaleable and be remaindered by cheaper, better imported goods.[119] The fussiness of American importers of textiles is illustrated in a Boston merchant's remark that

people here are very particular in the choice of cloths, they burn & scrape to see if the thread is even, round & fine & choose those that are mellow & well dress'd, with a good Gloss upon them. These qualities are what will recommend them, & no regard is paid to the Maker's name.[120]

Similar comments along these lines frequently appear in mercantile correspondence. In the 1760s William Pollard told a Halifax supplier that his durants were spoiled in dressing and looked more like goods off a tenter than out of a press; he also criticized callimancoes for not being as pressed as they should be, adding 'goods that come here must be finished in the best manner'.[121] He wanted shalloons and callimancoes from the West Riding of Yorkshire sent as good as they were from London, noting that the latter had better finishing.[122] This attention to quality was presumably absorbed by inland manufacturers in Britain even though they were producing substantial amounts of goods rapidly; one Leeds firm in

[114] HSP, John Clifford to Dowell, Gardner & Dowell, 14 June 1786, Clifford letterbook (1773–89), Clifford correspondence, vol. XXIX, Pemberton papers; HSP, Chaloner & White to Richard Ware, 20 April 1784, and to Edward Doughty, 19 May 1784, Chaloner & White letterbook (1782–4).

[115] Bushman, 'Shopping and advertising', p. 243. For the display of eighteenth-century imported textiles, see Florence M. Montgomery, 'Furnishing textiles at the John Brown House, Providence, Rhode Island', *Antiques*, 101 (1972), 496–502.

[116] MHS, Jonathan Jackson to Thomas Bromfield, 24 March 1766, Jonathan Jackson letterbook (1765–74).

[117] HSP, John Clifford to Dowell, Gardner & Dowell, 14 June 1786, Clifford letterbook (1773–89), Clifford correspondence, vol. XXIX, Pemberton papers.

[118] Carr and Walsh, 'Changing lifestyles and consumer behavior', p. 109.

[119] SHC, George Nelson to Samuel Bellamy, 8 March 1791, George Nelson letterbook (1784–98).

[120] NEHGS, Henry Bromfield to Edmund Halliday, 26 March 1772, Henry Bromfield letterbook (1771–2).

[121] Columbia University, William Pollard to John Woolmer, 18 August 1764, William Pollard letterbook (1764–8).

[122] Columbia University, William Pollard to John Swire, 4 February 1765, *ibid.*

the 1790s assured a merchant in Providence that they dressed and finished coatings, plains, narrow cloth and kerseymeres under their own eyes,
and knew 'the necessary mode of finishing' for the American market.[123]

British merchants in the export trade also had to compete keenly over
prices. By the 1760s, the cost of British manufactures was so well known
in North America that when an article was overcharged it lay unsold for a
long while.[124] American merchants also knew the difference in prices for
similar goods available at different places in Britain. William Pollard
noted that the coarse sort of spotted swanskins were regularly in demand
in Philadelphia, but that they were best made in Bristol and came cheaper
from there than from Yorkshire.[125] Similarly, he claimed that a parcel of
durants was higher by at least 2s. to 2s. 6d. from Yorkshire than from
London, added to which there was no comparison in the finishing: 'your
pink & Scarlet dont seem as if they been in a press at all, & shou'd have
been press'd & Gloss'd as much as possible'.[126] A merchant in Salem,
Massachusetts, comparing prices for exports from London and Bristol,
found the former exceeded the latter by anything from 10 to 30 per
cent.[127] A keen eye was also cast over price differences between different
merchants in individual ports.[128] American traders who enquired from
what part of Britain they could best be supplied in a particular branch of
goods found they could make 'a handsome profit'.[129] All these considerations – colour, texture, price, quality – were important in giving British
exporters a competitive edge over French suppliers of goods to the United
States in the late eighteenth century.[130]

VI

The five business developments in the Anglo-American export trade
outlined in this chapter had a significant impact on business organization
in early industrial Britain. The proliferation of transatlantic visits by

[123] John Carter Brown Library, Richard Sisson to Brown & Benson, 4 November 1793,
Brown papers, P-E9, vol. IV.
[124] MHS, Jonathan Jackson to DeBerdt, Burkitt & Sayre, 30 May 1767, Jonathan Jackson
letterbook (1765–74).
[125] Columbia University, William Pollard to Christopher Rawson, 20 September 1767,
William Pollard letterbook (1764–8).
[126] Columbia University, William Pollard to John Hamerton, 28 August 1764, *ibid.*
[127] James Duncan Phillips Library, Essex Institute, Salem, Mass., Samuel Curwen to
Hayley & Hopkins, 25 October 1771, Samuel Curwen papers.
[128] Jonathan Jackson to DeBerdt, Burkitt & Sayre, 9 May 1768, in Kenneth Wiggins Porter,
The Jacksons and the Lees: Two Generations of Massachusetts Merchants, 2 vols. (Cambridge, Mass., 1937), 1, pp. 203–4.
[129] HSP, Chaloner & White to Edward Doughty, 19 May 1784, Chaloner & White
letterbook (1782–4).
[130] Hill, *French Perceptions of the Early American Republic*, pp. 49, 58–60.

merchants either to North America or to Britain after the mid-1760s is not just attributable to the random survival of documents for that period; it reflected the greater involvement in the trade of a range of businessmen. The close links forged between American merchants and British manufacturers and merchants, with personnel sent to and fro across the Atlantic to gain direct knowledge of the varied export wares on offer and to see, on the spot, the best way of gauging price and quality in relation to diverse consumer tastes, point to a growing interdependence of businessmen in the export trade. Greater use of samples and printed documents, especially pattern cards, helped to overcome the risks caused by distance in a trade where attention to fashion, colour and texture of goods, notably textiles, was crucial for sales in discerning, competitive, volatile markets. The rise in direct correspondence between American merchants and manufacturers and British manufacturers and inland merchants was one way of integrating the domestic market in Britain with international flows of manufactured products; it gave entrepreneurs in the north and the Midlands a significant role in retailing wares overseas; and this was consolidated, in some cases, by the visits of American businessmen to inland centres of British industry described above.

The combination of flexible, extensive credit offered by British merchants to their American counterparts plus the need for quick cash settlements with suppliers in Britain meant that successful export firms were at the forefront of the financial requirements of a modernizing economy, and were adjusting to the greater cash and credit needs generated by increased manufacturing perhaps better than some European competitors. Close coordination of the colour, design, quality and finishing of consumer products between British and American merchants, manufacturers and suppliers suggests that the range of goods available for overseas markets was extended and developed by fierce commercial competition, and that product diversification and a high turnover of goods was stimulated by the growth of transatlantic business networks rather than being the sole result of productivity induced by technical innovation. In short, a case can be made for the continuity of Anglo-American merchant endeavours after the American Revolution, but at a higher level of intensity, and for evolving business networks in the trade helping to produce productivity gains, qualitative economic change and deeper retail networks in the British economy in the late eighteenth century. These features of the export trade in British manufactured goods have recently been highlighted in a study of the Yorkshire woollen industry in the eighteenth century.[131] I have shown

---

[131] Smail, *Merchants, Markets and Manufacture*.

here that they have broader application to other aspects of the export trade in the second half of that century. The transatlantic links addressed in this chapter suggest that it might be preferable to analyse the growth of aggregate demand in relation to Britain's early industrialization, produced by a combination of domestic and external factors, rather than resorting to the traditional distinction between home and foreign demand as triggers for economic development.

Part II

The development of trades

3 Property versus commerce in the mid-eighteenth-century port of London

Henry Roseveare

London's demonstrable ascendancy in the international trade of eighteenth-century England seems to have been sufficiently overwhelming to silence any twentieth-century doubts about its inevitability and the decline of its share in England's trade, from about three-quarters of its value at the beginning of the century to about two-thirds in the 1770s, can be dismissed as a comparatively minor statistical adjustment to a variety of healthy exogenous factors – such as the vigorous growth of transatlantic trade and the benign conjunctures which favoured the rising fortunes of Bristol, Liverpool and Glasgow. London, it seems agreed, was in possession of sufficiently strong institutional and resource endowments for its trading supremacy to survive the intermittent inconveniences of war, recession or changing fashions of demand.[1]

Among those institutional endowments one must unquestionably include the port of London – but upon what basis? How clearly is the role of the port conceived by economic historians? How fully are its functions

This contribution is a by-product of work still in progress on the history of the port of London, *c.* 1660–1800, funded by the Economic and Social Research Council, grant ref. R000231566.

[1] The eighteenth-century port of London's international trade has been placed in perspective by C. J. French in '"Crowded with traders and great commerce": London's domination of English overseas trade, 1700–1775', *The London Journal*, 17 (1992), 27–35; and 'London's overseas trade with Europe 1700–1775', *Journal of European Economic History*, 23 (1994), 475–501. His earlier article, 'Productivity in the Atlantic shipping industry: a quantitative study', *JIH*, 17 (1987), 613–38, also has useful hints on the comparative efficiencies of London and other Atlantic ports which question the verdict of P. J. Cain and A. G. Hopkins that 'in general it is mistaken to see the "rise of the outports" as a gain made at London's expense' – 'Gentlemanly capitalism and British expansion overseas I. The old colonial system, 1688–1850', *EcHR*, 2nd series, 39 (1986), 519, n. 96. Kenneth Morgan, *Bristol and the Atlantic Trade in the Eighteenth Century* (Cambridge, 1993) fully evaluates the changing balance of advantage between London, Bristol, Liverpool and Glasgow, but the clearest recognition of London's eighteenth-century deficiencies remains Rupert C. Jarvis's 'The metamorphosis of the Port of London', *The London Journal*, 3 (1977), 55–72.

understood? Is it assumed to have operated impartially and cost-effectively for all the sectors it served – and, if not, what scale of diseconomies in London should be added to the normal tariff of transaction costs which all ports incur? These questions have not been systematically pressed, let alone answered, and this chapter will certainly fail to do more than place a question mark against the issue; but it seems appropriate to raise the matter in connection with the work of a historian who, particularly in his edition of *Joshua Johnson's Letterbook, 1771–1774* and in *Perry of London*, has done so much to bring into focus the realities of mercantile life in eighteenth-century London. It is the latter study which provides a specific point of departure for this chapter.

I

A seemingly minor but none the less intriguing feature of *Perry of London* is the Perrys' brief interest in two of the twenty odd 'legal quays' of the port of London. Chester's quay and Brewer's quay were, as Professor Price has shown,[2] significant components of the port, accounting for only about 8 per cent of the wharves' frontage to the Thames but, with their proximity to the Custom House, strategically well sited for the efficient handling of London's dutiable trade. Chester's quay, indeed, was uniquely singled out by name in the 1662 Statute of Frauds as the first quay west of the Tower of London at which any importing vessels might legally unload.[3]

The Perrys' interest in these properties was comparatively short lived. Chester's quay had been purchased from Nicholas Lechmere in May 1697 and was held in thirds by Micaiah I (1641–1721), his son Richard IV (d. 1720) and his partner Thomas Lane (d. 1710). After the death of Lane's widow, the residual Lane share duly passed through the hands of Richard IV to his son Micajah III (1695–1753) but the declining fortunes of the Perrys appear to have enforced the sale of title in 1735.[4] Purchased by a fellow merchant, Bartholomew Clarke, for £9,500, Chester's quay had passed, with Clarke's daughter, into the hands of the des Bouverie family by the 1750s, together with the adjoining Brewer's quay.[5] Both wharves were to remain there until the interests of

---

[2] Jacob M. Price, *Perry of London: a Family and a Firm on the Seaborne Frontier, 1615–1753* (Cambridge, Mass., 1992), p. 24.

[3] Act of 14 Car. II. c.11, §i. *Statutes of the Realm* (1810–28), vol. V, p. 393.

[4] Price, *Perry of London*, p. 80; PRO, C54/5539 mm. 34–5 – indenture of sale, 15 October 1735.

[5] Mary Clarke (1701–39) married Jacob des Bouverie (later Viscount Folkestone) in January 1723. Their eldest son, William (1725–76), was created earl of Radnor in 1765 but Mary's inheritance, of Delapré abbey, Northamptonshire, and the wharves passed to

all the old legal quays were bought out by the Treasury in 1805. By then the annual gross profits of the combined leases of Brewer's and Chester's were put at £5,057 and the owner was awarded total compensation of £26,594. 9s.[6]

It is probably futile to speculate about the wharves' monetary value to the Perrys. For Brewer's quay an improved rental of nearly £800 per annum was anticipated in 1728 when the existing tenancy lease would fall in, but in 1720 Richard Perry's will valued it at a mere £150 per annum.[7] An improved rental of £700 for Chester's quay would not be unrealistic and by the mid-eighteenth century the combined rental of the two quays was indeed authoritatively estimated at £1,500 per annum.[8] However, one might reasonably infer from the terms of Richard Perry's will and the 1735 sale that the Perrys never derived the fullest financial potential from their possession of these two well-sited wharves. There are none the less grounds for suggesting that both the ownership and the management of London's legal quays offered other advantages which, while less easily measured than rentals or capital values, could be of considerable commercial value and ultimately of importance for London's international trade in the eighteenth century. By acquiring interests in these Thamesside properties the Perrys were in fact participating in a complex, competitive strategy which was only open to the most powerful of players and which had major significance for most overseas sectors, and for American and West Indian interests in particular.

One can convey something of this point by citing the identity and importance of some of the Perrys' wharf-owning and wharf-leasing neighbours. Perhaps first in importance and certainly in timing was Sir Josiah Child who, in the wake of the fire of London, had quickly built up a combination of long leaseholds and a freehold interest in three contiguous wharves between Billingsgate and London bridge – Hammond's, Botolph and Lyon quays.[9] By 1695 he was able to obtain a rental of £1,350 per annum on a four-year tenancy of all three and very shortly before his death

---

her second son the Hon. Edward Bouverie (1738–1810), MP for Salisbury (1761–71) and Northampton (1790–1810).

[6] CLRO box 223B, Sessions papers – valuations 1799–1810. These record the London juries' compensation awards to freeholders and tenants of the old legal quays for compulsory purchase and loss of trade under the terms of the Acts 'For making Wet Docks, etc' of 1800 and 'For the Further Improvement of the Port of London' of 1803, Act of 39 and 40 Geo. III. c.47 §cx and 43 Geo. III c.124 §viii.

[7] Price, *Perry of London*, p. 26; PRO, PROB 11/574.

[8] NRO, B-H(K) Coll., no. 558 'Account of the Rents of all the Free Wharfs' (*c.* 1755). This notes that Brewer's quay had recently been rebuilt.

[9] PRO, PC 2/60, 383; PC 2/61, 91, 112, 124–5. In July 1668 Child was obliged to appeal to the Privy Council for protection against the Lord Mayor and Court of Aldermen, who objected to his rebuilding plans for the three wharves.

in 1699 a fourteen-year lease was agreed at £1,600 per annum.[10] Not surprisingly, Child's group – collectively known as 'Botolph's' – enjoyed a major share of East India Company business long after the demise of its distinguished governor,[11] and his descendants continued to hold Lyon quay until late in the eighteenth century. Possibly his example was infectious, for other governors of the East India Company were to show a keen interest in the legal quays. Alderman Sir John Fleet, lord mayor of London in 1692–3, Member of Parliament for the City, who served four terms as governor of the Company between 1694 and 1708,[12] had acquired possession of two contiguous quays and adjacent warehousing by 1692.[13] Sabb's dock, with a mere 30 feet of frontage to the river, was one of the smallest in the port but Bear quay, with its important corn market, was a major acquisition which Sir John and then his son James continued to manage actively until 1718. At this point the family of Sir John Thompson (lord mayor of London 1736–7, governor of the Russia Company, a director of the South Sea Company and for four terms director of the Bank of England)[14] entered briefly into the port's history as part owner of the Bear quay and Sabb's dock leases before Sir John passed his interest to his son-in-law, Sir William St Quintin.[15] St Quintin was to find himself rubbing shoulders with another aldermanic part owner, the wealthy brewer Sir Crisp Gascoyne (1700–61) who became lord mayor in 1752. Meanwhile the tenancy of the Botolph and Lyon quays was passing through the hands of Sir Edward Bellamy[16] between 1731 and 1733 to Sir Joseph Eyles and his family,[17] who managed them together until 1747.

[10] Chancery, Town Depositions, PRO, C24/1309 (evidence of Peter Delamotte, Jr, 6 March 1711).

[11] Chancery, Masters' Exhibits, PRO, C110/49 (part 1) bundle 9 – 'India Account from March 1723 to March 1724'.

[12] See W. Foster, 'Sir John Fleet', *English Historical Review*, 51 (1936), 681–5.

[13] Guildhall Library, London: Land Tax Assessments.

[14] A. B. Beaven, *The Aldermen of the City of London*, 2 vols. (London, 1908–13) I, pp. 68, 86; II, pp. 125, 196, 279.

[15] Sir William St Quintin, 4th Bt (1699/1700?–1770) succeeded his uncle in the baronetcy in 1723 and married Rebecca, the daughter and heiress of Sir John Thompson in 1724. He was MP for Thirsk, 1722–7. G. E. Cokayne, *Complete Baronetage*, 6 vols. (London, 1900–9); R. Sedgwick, *The House of Commons, 1715–1754*, 2 vols. (London, 1970) II, p. 405.

[16] Edward Bellamy (d. 1749), alderman 1723, sheriff 1724, Knight 1727, lord mayor 1734–5, director of the Bank of England 1723–6, 1727–9, deputy governor 1729–31, governor 1731–3. In the general election of 1741 he came sixth in the poll for the City of London seats, behind his Whig colleague Micajah Perry. Beaven, *Aldermen*, I, pp. 31, 68, 227, 252, 259, 280; II, pp. 125, 130.

[17] Sir Joseph Eyles (*c*. 1690–1740), fourth son of Sir Francis Eyles, 1st Bt, was brother of Sir John Eyles (1683–1745), MP for the City of London and lord mayor of London, director of the East India Company, of the Bank of England and of the South Sea Company. Joseph, knighted 1724, was likewise MP (1722–40), a director of the East India Company, of the Bank of England and the London Assurance. Sedgwick, *The House of*

The bare record of these powerful men – senior aldermen, Members of Parliament, directors and governors of the nation's major corporations – is enough to confirm that at the height of their prosperity as the City's leading tobacco importers the Perrys were not alone in seeking advantage in the control of the legal quays. But what were those advantages, and how could they be realized?

II

The key to a possible answer lies jointly with Sir Josiah Child and Sir John Fleet. The former was the supporting sponsor and the latter was the leading actor in a remarkable stratagem which, in July 1695, completely transformed the management of the port of London and determined its character until the close of the eighteenth century. The story has been told in more detail elsewhere[18] but its essential feature was a joint agreement by the hitherto rival occupants of the legal quays to pool their resources, form a joint stock company and confront London's merchants with a cartel.[19] The inducements were compelling. Faced with a substantial diminution of London's trade during the Nine Years' War the wharfingers had entered upon very lean times and, competing desperately for business, had found themselves nearly powerless to resist the merchants' downward pressure on their fees. Yet, individually or collectively, their monopoly of handling all dutiable trade through London had been guaranteed by the 1660 Act for Tonnage & Poundage and by the 1662 Statute of Frauds which, with a few minor exceptions, restricted the legal transit of goods, in or out, to the so-called 'free quays' or 'legal quays', named and measured out by the Exchequer Commissions of 1559 and 1667.[20] Appreciation of the potentialities of this monopoly evidently began to dawn upon the hard-pressed wharfingers, some of whom had been allegedly coerced to

Commons, 1715–54, II, pp. 20–2. Joseph married Sarah, daughter of Sir Jeffrey Jeffreys, a leading tobacco merchant of the early 1690s, for whose career see Jacob M. Price, *The Tobacco Adventure to Russia: Enterprise, Politics, and Diplomacy in the Quest for a Northern Market for English Colonial Tobacco, 1676–1722*. American Philosophical Society, *Transactions*, new series, 51, part 1 (Philadelphia, 1961), pp. 13, 14, 30, 32, 64, 110, and *Perry of London*, pp. 54–5.

[18] See my article, ' "The Damned Combination": the port of London and the wharfingers' cartel of 1695', *The London Journal*, 21 (1996), 97–111.

[19] The evidence was brought to light by the very lengthy Chancery cases of *Fleet, and others* v. *Ashton*, and *Ashton* v. *Fleet*; see Town Depositions, PRO, C24/1309, C24/1315 and C24/1317; for a subsequent House of Lords appeal, with a summary account, see BL, 'Legal Tracts 1721–1726' (BL 509.k.17 [2 & 2*]).

[20] For the Commission of 1559 and a description of the wharves see Brian Dietz, ed., *The Port and Trade of Early Elizabethan London: Documents* (London Record Society, 1972), pp. 156–67; for that of 1667 see John Strype's 1720 edition of Stow's *Survey of London*, book V, pp. 281–4 or almost any eighteenth-century manual of Customs regulations.

condone customs evasion by their dictatorial clients. In a preliminary calculation the scheme's planners conjectured that, collectively organized, the wharfingers' economies in labour, equipment, bad debts, theft and competitive bidding would be worth over £12,000 per annum,[21] a figure which at that date was nearly equivalent to the total rentals of the quays. Some of these savings, they acknowledged, would have to be returned in selective discounts to their principal clients in the great trading corporations – the Royal African Company, the Levant Company and – above all – the East India Company. Child's approval and Fleet's leadership clearly indicate the paramount influence of that company's interests on the formation of this twenty-one-year agreement, but the attractive possibilities of discrimination and cost-cutting on behalf of any favoured merchants clearly extended to many other sectors.

The precise terms of agreement between the twelve principal individuals and partnerships which currently leased or owned the twenty-one legal quays in 1695 were secret and were concluded by deed poll under the supervision of John Asgill[22] in a format which avoided public enrolment. However, it was not long before the merchants of London were aware of significant changes in their treatment at the wharves. No longer were they courted for their custom; no longer were they permitted extended credit of six months to a year on their wharfage and warehousing bills. An importing captain's conventional freedom to select which wharfinger he preferred was curtailed: he must take the wharf to which the cartel's managers directed him and he must make exclusive use of the cartel's small fleet of lighters rather than any of the other five hundred on the river. Above all, there was a marked change of tone in the treatment of merchants and shippers alike. The former competitive servility of the wharfingers, accentuated by the much scarcer business of the Nine Years' War, had given way to a collective arrogance and indifference from which delay, loss and serious accidents had accrued.

Such, in essence, were the charges brought to a head in 1705 with a concerted campaign by embittered London merchants. A petition signed by 294 of them was presented to the House of Commons on 9 January[23] and followed up later in the year by a fifty-five-page pamphlet, *The Case of the Traders of London As it now stands since the Copartnership of the Wharfingers*.[24] This set out in some detail the complaints of merchants, masters of ships and other traders against 'the insufferable treatment they daily meet

---

[21] See '"The Damned Combination"' and sources cited.

[22] John Asgill (1659–1738), the lawyer and Land Bank projector.

[23] *JHC*, XIV, 473, 475.

[24] Guildhall Library, A8.4, No. 68. For the wharfingers' one-page reply, 'The Case of the Wharfingers, Proprietors and Farmers of the Free Keys of the Port of London' (1705) see University of London, Goldsmiths' Library, 4235, no. 115.

with from the wharfingers since their confederacy', but also went on to narrate with commendable accuracy the recent history of relations between national government, the city corporation and the legal quays. They recalled the statutory indictment of the wharfingers which had been incorporated in the Additional Act for the Rebuilding of the City of London in 1670.[25] Citing 'great exactions' levied on the post-fire wharves it had provided sanction for a fixed table of wharfage and cranage rates to be authorized by the king in council. The actual task of drawing up a tariff was assigned by the Privy Council to the Court of Aldermen in April 1674, which in turn deputed it to a committee of its members[26] but, on pursuing their research from the council registers to the Repertories of the City, the authors of the pamphlet found, as does the modern researcher, that the matter had quietly foundered. True, a comprehensive tariff of charges had been devised and imposed for some of the minor wharves which lined the Thames above London bridge and the rebuilt borders of the Fleet river at Blackfriars,[27] but in the face of detailed representations from the legal quays and slipshod counter-representations from the merchants, the aldermanic committee had failed to adjudicate decisively between their two competing tariffs – that of the merchants recommending rather imprecise rates half as generous as those of the wharfingers.[28]

The consequences of this failure were to be profound for it meant that until the 1790s there was to be no officially authorized tariff in place to govern charges at the London waterside for such essential services as wharfage, cranage or lighterage. However, complete anarchy and unbridled extortion were averted. The wharfingers' carefully worked out tariff of charges, itemized by commodity and by bag, bale, barrel or butt, was evidently a fairly realistic one which gradually acquired the legitimacy of convention. It was still thought to be operative as a benchmark in the 1790s when the whole subject was aired before the House of Commons' select committee of inquiry into 'providing sufficient accommodation for the increased trade and shipping of the Port of London'.[29] But in 1705 it was speciously plausible for *The Case of the Traders* and the petition to Parliament to allege that the wharfingers 'have advanced the Rates of

---

[25] 22 Car. II. c.11, §21, §26.

[26] CLRO, Repertories of the Court of Aldermen, Repertory 79, fos. 125, 172, 196 (5 March, 7 April, 5 May 1674).

[27] Privy Council Registers, PRO, PC. 2/64, fo. 210 'Wharfage and cranage rates at Brooks Wharf, adjoining Queenhithe', 1 May 1674; PC2/65 fos. 191–4, rates for Bridewell dock and Fleet river from Thames to Holborn bridge, 21 April 1676.

[28] The two lists of rates are set out in *The Case of the Traders*, 14–30, 32–48.

[29] See HC, Lambert, CII, 211 (evidence of Edward Ogle) and appendix Eee. I have published a selection from these tariffs in '"Wiggins' Key" revisited: trade and shipping in the later seventeenth-century port of London', *Journal of Transport History*, 16 (1995), 7.

Wharfage, and Rents of their Warehouses; and may further advance them to what they please'.

Apart from some figures drawn from the 1640s and 1650s, *The Case of the Traders* failed to produce much hard evidence for such a charge and, after fierce lobbying by both sides, the petitioners' campaign before the House of Commons select committee of January 1705 ran into the sands of an indefinite adjournment. Indeed, the campaign as a whole is possibly more significant for its promotion by Sir Gilbert Heathcote, Whig Member of Parliament for the City of London and director of the Bank of England, than for the substance of its argument.[30] Heathcote had a genuine grievance against the wharfingers: he had twice sought damages for losses to his cargoes and was to take a successful case against Sir John Fleet before Queen's Bench in September 1705.[31] But of more importance is his championship of the largely Whig 'New East India Company' interest against the 'Old' East India Company led by the Tory Sir John Fleet[32] and, knowing the pervasive violence of this contest, at its height between 1693 and 1709, it is tempting to attribute some of the motivation for the merchants' confrontation with the wharfingers to this more immediate conflict. Ownership or management of the legal quays was, unquestionably, a valuable card to play in the struggle for commercial and political advantage.

Whether the Perrys saw their investment in this light does not appear from the evidence, and for some time after 1714 there is nothing much to indicate that naked political partisanship was the decisive factor in conflicts over the management of the port of London. However, commercial partisanship is another matter. It is clear enough that a cartel formed under the auspices of the East India Company and, committed as it was to favouring the great joint stock or regulated companies, might be open to objections from smaller or less overtly organized commercial interests. And so it proves. By the 1740s the grievances of London's West Indian and American merchants against the wharfingers' management of the port had reached a critical point, marked by an impressive coalition of London's banking, insurance and commercial leaders.

III

The evidence for this crisis is peculiarly elusive and is supported almost solely by documents surviving among the private papers of a single

---

[30] For Heathcote's parliamentary career see Sedgwick, *The House of Commons, 1715–54*, II, p. 123.

[31] The case was sufficiently interesting to secure a record in *The English Reports*, XXI (1902), 889 and XXII (1902), 883.

[32] The conflict of interests is assessed by Henry Horwitz in 'The East India trade, the politicians, and the constitution: 1689–1702', *Journal of British Studies*, 17 (1978), 1–18.

wharf-owner, William Hanbury of Kelmarsh.[33] Belonging to a junior branch of this prolific family, William does not appear to have been close to his more eminent and prosperous Quaker kinsmen, John, Osgood or Capel Hanbury. Nevertheless, his marriage to Sarah Western was an auspicious one which not only brought him in touch with the first Viscount Bateman (his wife's uncle) but gave him control of one half of Dice key, sited centrally in the port. Leased in the 1660s and bought in the 1680s by Thomas Western, the greatest ironmaster of his day,[34] the 3,400 square feet of this quay, with its seventeen warehouses, six cellars and three cranes, had passed down to Western's great-granddaughter Sarah and her Bateman kinsmen, with whom Hanbury actively managed it until his death in 1768. By then his antiquarian interests and a natural anxiety to maximize the inheritance had led him to compile a very full documentary collection on the legal quays which is invaluable to the historian and crucial to much which follows.[35]

Yet there is one item absent from the Hanbury files the existence of which elsewhere has been briefly noted by Professor Price. This is a Chancery case of 1742,[36] notable for Micajah Perry's leading position among the petitioners, all of whom are either past or present wharf-owners, wharf-managers or their executors. However, the significance of their suit against Richard Nutt's widow is considerably greater than would appear from its substance. Ostensibly, the petition merely sought to silence the litigious and bankrupt widow and recover outstanding claims against her late wine-cooper husband. But, as the petition goes on to claim, there was a substantial element of conspiracy in the widow's refusal of responsibility for her husband's debts, and behind her obduracy lay an alleged confederacy of certain named men, among whom one is intrigued to recognize some proven opponents of the wharfingers' cartel.[37]

In suits of this kind it was standard form to make such allegations of conspiracy, but on this occasion there are good grounds for taking them at face value for, in effect, by forcing the wharf interests to sue for relief the respondent and her backers had achieved by low cunning what Sir Gilbert

---

[33] For the Hanburys see A. Audrey Locke, *The Hanbury Family*, 2 vols. (1916), and for the Kelmarsh branch see vol. I, ch. IV. William Hanbury (1704–68) stood unsuccessfully for Parliament in 1748, but could count many MPs among his acquaintances. He was succeeded by his only son, William (1748–1807), who inherited the Bateman estate of Shobdon Court, Herefordshire, from his mother.

[34] For a condensed biography of Western, see J. R. Woodhead, *The Rulers of London 1660–1689* (London and Middlesex Archaeological Society, 1965), p. 174.

[35] NRO, B-H(K) Coll. contains nearly 380 bundles and files relating to the port of London.

[36] Chancery Pleadings, PRO, C11/1607/29 cited in Price, *Perry of London*, pp. 25, 151.

[37] Among those allegedly conspiring were Joseph Broad and Samuel Davenport, who in 1711 and after had given evidence unfavourable to the cartel in the prolonged suits of Joseph Ashton.

Heathcote had failed to achieve by frontal assault in 1705 – the full exposure of the cartel's identity, with its owners and managers fully named and its terms of formation fully dated and explained. The irksome secrecy of the original deed poll had now been breached: a joint stock co-partnership, renewed for fourteen years from 29 September 1730, had been publicly exposed and there could be no further doubts about the cartel's existence and no further mystery about its responsible participants. Hoist by their own petard, as it were, this suit by the controlling interests of the legal quays had handed their opponents an easy but useful victory. However, it was sufficient neither to thwart a successive renewal of the joint stock in 1744 nor to render unnecessary the formidable campaign against the wharfingers which was mobilized in 1746–7.

According to the material in the Hanbury collection, the opening shots in the campaign were a formal representation to the Treasury, backed up later by a reasoned petition of London merchants addressed to the Commissioners of Customs.[38] The undated memorial to the Treasury, of which no trace seems to survive in Treasury records,[39] reviewed the late-seventeenth-century foundation of the current legal quays and argued for their physical inadequacy. 'The Trade of this Kingdom hath been greatly increased and more especially that of this Great port of London.' As a consequence, shipping was constricted, goods were delayed and markets were lost – circumstances which were exploited by the wharfingers' conspiracy to raise charges and obstruct litigation. Like the petitioners of 1705, those of 1746 drew attention to the sheer slipperiness of the cartel – 'not a Corporate Body, having no Charter, Patent or Common Seal . . . it is difficult to contend with them at Law' and 'their ill practices are not to be Defeated without very great Trouble and Expence'. Nevertheless, the memorialists had a remedy: let the legal quays be opened up and enlarged; let the extensive area adjoining the Tower of London's eastern flanks (known as Iron Gate Stairs), which the memorialists had succeeded in purchasing, be enfranchised as a new 'legal quay'. In return, they 'do humbly propose to take such Rates only for Wharfage and Lighters as have heretofore Accustomed [sic], and without any Regard to such late advanced Rates and prices'.

The transparent self-seeking of this proposal was more than offset by the subsequent petition of the merchants. Also undated, and nowhere

---

[38] NRO, B-H(K) Coll. nos. 547 and 549.
[39] PRO, Treasury Minute Books (T29/30 and T29/31), Treasury board papers (T1/315–26) and Treasury outletters (Customs) T11/22–4 for the period between 1744 and 1750 have been searched carefully but unsuccessfully for some acknowledgement of the merchants' petition. I am grateful to Dr Nicholas Cox of the Public Record Office, Kew, for confirmation that Treasury records of the late 1740s suffered losses from damp and decay.

acknowledged in the surviving records of the Customs Commissioners,[40] their statement of grievances was evidently framed as an itemized indictment of the wharfingers, whose record of extortion was now set out in all its petty detail. The merchants alluded to the wharfage for German linen in 'Bremen packs': once handled for 3s. per pack and 1s. 6d. per half-pack but 'about ten years ago' altered to 2s. 6d. for packs and half-packs alike. They cited 'Russia yarn', once charged at 1s. 6d. per ton but 'about Eleven years ago' charged on the bale of 4 to 5 cwt. Then there was Gum Seneca 'which used to be 8d. p. Cask wharfage and Lighterage, was abt. 3 years ago advanced to 1s. p. Cask which is an advance of 4d per Cask'. But, above all, they stressed sugar and tobacco. Re-exports of the former, once paying 9d. per hogshead for wharfage, 'was in the year 1745 raised to 1s. per hogshead'. As for tobacco, the question was more complicated, for the Virginia hogshead must be distinguished from the Maryland, 'as the Maryland hhds bear no proportion to a true medium' and the wharfingers were unjustified in taking weights of the latter to justify a doubling of charges. 'Tobacco that paid only 6d. per hhd wharfage and lighterage Inwards and the same outwards was in the year 1744 advanced to 1s. p. hhd inwards and 8d. p.hhd outwards. This advance is 8d. upon a hhd.' Yet even Maryland hogsheads had gained only 150 or 200 lb as a result of tighter packing 'and can no ways Justify the advance of wharfage in any Degree, much less in attempting to make it double w[hat] it was before'. Admittedly, 'the wharfingers may say they have agreed with some of the Hambro merchants for the Bremen Packs, and in the Tobaccos with some of the Virginia Merchants, which may be true, But nothing of this kind can justify the Imposition'.

At this point one might pause briefly to ponder the commercial significance of what the petitioners alleged. What scale of burden did increases of 3d. per hogshead on sugar and 8d. per hogshead on tobacco re-exports represent? There can be little dispute that, as percentages, additions of one-third and two-thirds respectively seem onerous and in the aggregate of several thousand hogsheads must constitute a significant addition to transport costs. Yet, on closer inspection, wharf charges of any kind generally amount to a negligible component in the transaction costs borne by the importing merchant. Dwarfed by customs, insurance and freight (to say nothing of commission and brokerage), charges of 9d., 12d. or even 1s. 8d. per hogshead dwindle into insignificance. In a

---

[40] Very few of the routine working papers of the Customs headquarters survived the fire of 1814, and the miscellaneous volumes which have been preserved have yielded nothing relevant to this matter. See R. C. Jarvis, 'Critical historical introduction' to Elizabeth E. Hoon, *The Organization of the English Customs System, 1696–1786* (reprint, Newton Abbot, 1968), pp. vii–xxvii. Edward Carson, *The Ancient and Rightful Customs* (London, 1972), appendix A, has a helpful listing of surviving Customs and Excise records.

convenient example taken from 1737[41] the itemized charges on a single hogshead of Maryland tobacco, carried to London and sold there, total £20 12s. (of which customs represents 82 per cent and freight 8.5 per cent) and the specific wharfage component is too small to be separately noted. Indeed, of all the petty charges for which the wharf-managers were directly responsible it is not wharfage or lighterage which was most lucrative or bore most heavily: it was warehousing. If the importer chose to store his hogsheads upon the legal quays – and many did – he carried rentals which, depending on the size or convenience of the premises, could vary between 5s. and 18s. per week. For sugar the early eighteenth-century warehousing rate appears to have been standardized at 3d. per hogshead per week, and the duration of that burden was entirely at the discretion of the merchant. Robert Heysham, a West India merchant and Member of Parliament for the City of London (well-known to Micajah Perry and Professor Price),[42] dealt extensively with the wharfingers' cartel and imported some 5,400 hogsheads of sugar in the seven years 1710–16. The duration of his warehousing rentals varied with market conditions, from as much as 13.3 weeks in 1710 to as little as 2.2 weeks in 1714, but averaged 6.5 weeks overall. For almost every consignment of Heysham's sugars it is the warehousing component which greatly exceeds the wharfage and lighterage.[43] The same was undoubtedly true for tobacco, and was a point which the wharfingers were apt to stress in their own defence. It was not they but the dilatory merchant who encumbered the waterside with uncollected cargoes, creating costly confusion and unnecessary damage.

However, this is to miss the essential point of the petitioners' complaint. It was not so much the quantitative burden of the wharfingers' imposition as the arbitrariness of it which grated. The wharfingers had no legal basis for their original charges, let alone for their recent increases. Yet, secure in their statutory monopoly and emboldened by their confederacy, they rode roughshod over the unprotected merchant:

The Method which the Wharfingers take with those who refuse to come into any agreement, to pay an Advanced Rate on any Species of Merchandize, is very Short, and peremptory, and is another Evidence of their power, for they use no other Ceremony, But go directly to the merchant when his ship is to be reported, and tell him That unless he will pay the advanced Rate, his Goods shall not be

---

[41] James F. Shepherd and Gary M. Walton, *Shipping, Maritime Trade and the Economic Development of Colonial North America* (Cambridge, 1972), table 4.3, p. 56.

[42] Price, *Perry of London*, pp. 72–3.

[43] My evidence is drawn from the posthumous investigation of Heysham's obligations to the wharfingers' cartel undertaken by the Court of Chancery in 1728–9, PRO, C38/402. The case, with its Bills and Answers, is to be found under the names of *Lateward et al.* v. *Edward Dodd and William Robinson Lytton* (Heysham's executors) in C11/1761/24.

Landed, which is making use of a power in itself unlawfull, to Countenance a more unlawfull practice afterwards.

The merchants went on to indict the overcrowding and inefficient management of the wharves, where cargoes might take double the statutory limit of twenty days to unload and where, packed like sardines, vessels might be partially unloaded and then left untended while some favoured client was given preference. The cost to the merchant was probably matched by the cost to the revenue, in tide-waiters' attendance and 'pilfering and plundering of Goods, from the dark Avenues & Cartways that lead into Thames Street, as daily Experience can Testify'. From this allegation it was easy to pass on to a concluding statement of support for the Treasury memorialists, agreeing in the attractiveness of the Tower wharf site, guarded by high walls and conveniently near the king's garrison.

The only helpful clue to the dating of these representations is Hanbury's copy of 'Queries sent by the Commissioners of the Customs to the Petitioners', signed by William Wood, the long-serving secretary to the Customs Commissioners (1742–65) and dated '11th Feb 1746'. This reads plausibly like a genuine, formal minute of the board, noting the reception of the memorial to the Treasury and the petition of the merchants, summarizing their case and then posing three challenges: that the petitioners should lay before the board their proof for the growth of London's trade in recent years; for the wharfingers' alleged combination and their recent increases in charges; and for the original wharfage rates prevailing on the legal quays at their inception and at ten, twenty and thirty years past.

Whether taken literally as a minute of February 1746 (stated in new style) or of February 1747 (in old style) there is no corroboration of this debate to be found in surviving official records at either of these dates. But Hanbury's collection is convincingly completed with an interesting little booklet, with marbled covers, endorsed: 'Draft of Answer to the Commrs Querys'.[44] It is notable less for its detailed repetition of the merchants' grievances, already set out to the Commissioners, than for its scholarly recension of the arguments last published in 1705 by *The Case of the Traders* and for its gleeful reference to the Chancery suit of 1742. The latter, it rejoiced, had exposed the identity of the partnership and confirmed the merchant community's suspicion of a covert collusion in the raising of charges and the control of lighterage. As for the former, the research published in 1705 was again invoked to explain the historic failure of the City and Privy Council to establish fixed rates as required by the Rebuilding Act of 1670.

---

[44] NRO, B-H(K) Coll. no. 551.

However, this draft 'Answer' fails to provide more than anecdotal evidence for the recent growth of London's trade – it merely gestures towards the shipping packed three deep at the quays – and it confessed that it had been found 'too difficult' to procure hard evidence for increased charges at ten, twenty or thirty years past. Yet, unembarrassed by this abject admission, the 'Answer' returned to the charge of crippling increases in charges, particularly upon sugar and tobacco, which were now more emphatically underlined as the principal victims of the cartel's mismanagement. Repeating the earlier figures, the 'Answer' stressed

These articles are in the most considerable Branches of Trade, and Two of them, vizt. the Tobacco and Sugar, are the first for the Employment of Shipping and are the most frequent at the Waterside, which of course makes the advance so much the more Beneficial to the Wharfingers and more essentially affecting to Trade.

IV

Any doubts about the motivating interests behind these protests are removed by the identities of their sponsors. The memorial to the Treasury had been signed by Jonathan Forward, William Whitaker, John Philpot 'of London, Merchants' and by Joseph Goodman, Esq.; the petition of the merchants was subscribed by 151 individuals or partnerships. Taken together they represent a remarkable concentration of London's banking, insurance and commercial leaders, the latter strongly coloured by involvement in Atlantic trades in general and with tobacco in particular.

This last point can be quickly established by reference to a source often cited to good effect by Professor Price,[45] namely a Treasury list of tobacco bonds outstanding in the port of London which, by its nature, provides a good index of the comparative volume and value of trade by individual merchants. In October 1747 thirty-one merchants (among a total of forty-four) were listed as those carrying the largest obligations for duty.

All but those whose names are asterisked were signatories to either the memorial or the petition. Responsible for over 81 per cent of London's obligations to the Treasury in 1747 they are clearly a preponderant representation of the American tobacco interests of their day. Jonathan Forward is, of course, well known as the leading and long-standing contractor for the transport of felons to America,[46] but the tobacco trade

---

[45] See, for example, Jacob M. Price and Paul G. E. Clemens, 'A revolution of scale in overseas trade: British firms in the Chesapeake trade, 1675–1775', in Price, *Tobacco in Atlantic Trade*, ch. 3, or Price, *Perry of London*, p. 99.

[46] Abbot E. Smith, *Colonists in Bondage: White Servitude and Convict Labor in America, 1607–1776* (Chapel Hill, N.C., 1947), pp. 113, 366; Treasury payments to Forward on this account may be traced throughout the calendars, e.g. *Calendar of Treasury Books and Papers*, 1731–4 (1898) and 1735–8 (1900).

Table 3.1. *From 'An Account of all Tobacco Bonds standing out in the Port of London, Oct. 24th, 1747'*

Name	Debt outstanding in £s.	% of London total	% of total for Britain
John Hanbury	68,698.86	14.43	8.79
John Philpot	45,379.89	9.53	5.81
John Buchanan	41,921.15	8.81	5.36
John Moorey	25,161.86	5.29	3.22
William Black*	20,476.40	4.30	2.62
Jonathan Forward	20,367.00	4.28	2.61
Joseph Adams	19,619.75	4.12	2.51
George Buchanan	16,841.06	3.54	2.16
Richard Oswald*	15,411.69	3.24	1.97
William Whitaker	15,354.80	3.23	1.97
Edward Athawes*	14,414.28	3.03	1.84
John Sydenham	14,111.11	2.96	1.81
Thomas Flowerdew	14,091.73	2.96	1.80
William Bowden	13,843.72	2.91	1.77
James Buchanan	13,353.41	2.81	1.71
Lawrence Williams*	11,879.82	2.50	1.52
Humphrey Bell	10,975.63	2.31	1.40
Christopher Smyth	10,246.40	2.15	1.31
Thomas Reynolds	8,802.22	1.85	1.13
William Hunt	7,448.06	1.56	0.95
Sir Theodore Janssen	6,404.90	1.35	0.82
Edward Hunt	6,297.82	1.32	0.81
Jacob Berry	4,821.38	1.01	0.62
Jeremiah Smith	4,633.33	0.97	0.59
Benjamin Horrocks*	4,263.53	0.90	0.55
William Anderson	4,221.60	0.89	0.54
William Tover	3,917.81	0.82	0.50
Isaac Levy*	3,777.77	0.79	0.48
Andrew Reid	3,452.43	0.73	0.44
John Maynard	3,396.43	0.71	0.43
Richard Molineaux	2,951.97	0.62	0.38
Total	456,537.81	95.91	58.43
Total for London	476,029.33		
Total for Britain	781,400.51		

Source: PRO, T1/326 fos. 110–14.

seems to have become his major preoccupation and in the early 1750s both he and John Philpot were to seek the Treasury's indulgence for their large, outstanding debts on tobacco bonds.[47]

Yet even Forward's prominence is overshadowed by that of some other signatories to the petition. Alphabetically listed, names such as Charles Boehm, Merrick Burrell, Abel Fonnereau, Silvanus Grove, John Hanbury, William Hunt, Sir Theodore Janssen, and Gerard and Joshua Van Neck are likely to attract immediate recognition as major figures in the business life of mid-eighteenth-century England, while in the list as a whole only 11 of the 151 entries fail to be registered somewhere in the business or biographical directories of the period.[48] Forty-two were known participants in the tobacco trade at some point in their careers,[49] and although many are unhelpfully recorded merely as 'merchant' one may identify at least seven as specialists in German or Hamburg trade, five with connections to New England and four as 'Turkey' merchants.

More striking, perhaps, is the presence of as many as thirteen signatories who were directors of either the Royal Exchange Assurance or the London Assurance[50] which, between them, accounted for most of the fire and shipping insurance business of the times. Their concern with the costly and overcrowded conditions of the legal quays can be readily understood, and throughout the decades leading up to the decisive reforms of the 1790s the insurance companies were to be persistent advocates for the enlargement and modernization of the port of London. The presence of six present or future directors of the Bank of England and three directors of the South Sea Company[51] is also of major significance, adding substantial weight to the force of the petition. The appearance of five directors of the

[47] See Treasury outletters, Customs, PRO, T11/23, fos. 409, 440; T11/24, fos. 33, 116.

[48] I have consulted all the period's London directories, available in the British Library and the Guildhall Library, for which see P. J. Atkins, *The Directories of London, 1677–1977* (London, 1990). *The Gentleman's Magazine* and its obituaries have provided additional identifications.

[49] I am indebted to correspondence with Jacob M. Price for the identification of many of these and, of course, to his *France and the Chesapeake* and 'The last phase of the Virginia–London consignment trade: James Buchanan & Co., 1758–1768', in Price, *Tobacco in Atlantic Trade*, ch. 7.

[50] See Barry Supple, *The Royal Exchange Assurance: a History of British Insurance 1720–1970* (London, 1970); B. Drew, *The London Assurance: a Second Chronicle* (London, 1949). Guildhall Library, MS. 8726, II lists the directorate of the London Assurance 1720–65. The Royal Exchange directors among the petitioners were Josiah Bullock, George Fitzgerald, Jr, Tilman Henckell, William Hunt, John Johnson, Ralph Knox, Thomas Sikes and Breanffe Stonehewer; the London Assurance directors were Sylvanus Grove, Godhard Hagen, John Henniker, Thomas Lane and John Thomlinson.

[51] The current or future Bank of England directors who signed the petition were Charles Boehm, Merrick Burrell, Benjamin Mee, William Hunt, Sir Theodore Janssen, and James Sperling; the South Sea Company directors were Joseph Adams, Alexander Coutts and Richard Jackson.

East India Company[52] is perhaps less to be expected for, as the history of the cartel has shown, John Company (as the East India Company was also known) had long been a sponsor and beneficiary of its operations, and until the internal history of the mid-eighteenth-century Company is better understood their posture must remain unexplained.

V

At this point it would be timely to recall who the wharfingers and wharf-owners were who faced this formidable onslaught. Among the latter, so far as they can be identified, there had been little further change since the late seventeenth century. Four or five wharves remained in the institutional hands which had held them since the Restoration or before – the Corporation of the City, the cordwainers, the fishmongers and the vintners livery companies held one apiece and the title to Custom House quay had finally passed from the control of the Cope family to the crown.[53] Sir Josiah Child's leases and titles were now held by his son, the first earl Tylney (1680–1750) and the former Perry wharves, inherited by Mary Clarke (1701–39), were about to pass from her husband, Jacob des Bouverie, Viscount Folkestone (1694–1761), to their second son, the Hon. Edward Bouverie (1738–1810). Fresh wharf continued its long descent through several hands towards its unwise purchase by David Garrick in 1776;[54] the shorter descent of Dice quay from Thomas Western to William Hanbury and Richard Bateman has already been noted. Meanwhile, in the one instance where wharves had been both owned and managed by a professional wharfinger and lighterman – Gaunt's and Cox's quays near London bridge – the will of William Clapham in 1730 had bequeathed the title to the son of his wife's niece by her first husband.[55] By this intricate descent William Skrine (1721–83), son of a wealthy Bath physician and later Member of Parliament for Callington, became proprietor of premises and business which, in 1805, the Treasury had to buy out for nearly £43,000.[56]

---

[52] Richard Chauncey, John Dorrien, Abel Fonnereau, Samuel Harrison and William Pomeroy (whose death in October 1747 helps limit the probable date of the petition).

[53] For the chequered history of Custom House quay, see T. F. Reddaway, 'The London Custom House 1666–1740', *London Topographical Record*, 21 (1958), 1–25.

[54] See Guildhall Library, MS 535 and MS 23,770 for the lengthy schedule of deeds, 1401–1807. Garrick invested in a £15,000 mortgage on the quay but the debtor absconded to the far east.

[55] PRO, PROB11/639 (William Clapham's will of 6 July 1730). The Clapham family's acquisition of Cox's quay and Gaunt's (or Grant's) quay is fully documented in Guildhall Library MS 14,008. For William Skrine (1721–83) see Sir Lewis Namier and John Brooke, eds., *The House of Commons 1754–1790*, 3 vols. (London, 1964), III, p. 443.

[56] For the adjudication on this test case, see *The Times*, law report for 13 May 1805.

Without pursuing every record of title, these examples are enough to indicate that mid-eighteenth-century wharf-owners were not likely to be intimately involved in the day-to-day conduct of trade – although the 1760s were to reveal that, as Members of Parliament, several of them would tenaciously defend their vested interest. But in terms of the politics of commerce, their significance is much less than that of their tenants, the wharf-managers who actually controlled the business of the quays.

Among these the 1740s had seen the beginning of an important process of amalgamation in the management of wharves and lighters which was to characterize the port of London throughout the second half of the eighteenth century. While it had not been uncommon for groups of three contiguous wharves among the twenty-one to be jointly leased and managed, in the late seventeenth century there now began a process of consolidation which placed five, six or more wharves in the hands of one individual or partnership. The Delamotte family, whose association with the legal quays went back beyond the 1680s,[57] were managing five contiguous wharves in the early 1740s, and it is interesting to observe the manner in which Thomas Dinely (a director and later governor of the London Assurance between 1721 and his death in 1777) acquired the management, first of Brewer's quay in 1732 and then of Josiah Child's group of three by 1747. By this date the young Barrington Buggin, shipbroker and East India Company ship's husband,[58] was just beginning the process which, by 1778, put him in managerial control of no fewer than nine. Other major wharfingers of the mid-century were Richard and William Lateward who took over Dinely's group in 1749 and managed a total of eleven wharves by 1758.

Yet, while consolidation characterized the wharf management of the period, a very different process typifies the pattern of vested interest in the leaseholds of the quays. Like the shipping in which so many wharfingers took small shares, the leases became speculative investments held in eighths, or tenths or sixteenths, and while the natural processes of divided inheritances, debt and enforced sales had for long tended to fracture leasehold interests into smaller and smaller holdings one may discern by mid-century a calculated practice of subleasing and covert shareholding which put the wharves into many more hands. Thus in his will of 1764[59] William Lateward bequeathed a mere one-sixteenth share in the leases of Botolph quay (owned by the City) and of Lyon quay (owned by the earl

---

[57] Peter Delamotte, Jr, giving evidence in 1711 at the age of thirty-nine, claimed to have known many of his fellow wharfingers since boyhood. Chancery, Town Depositions PRO, C24/1309.

[58] For information and speculation about Buggin and 'Buggin's turn' see Brian Dietz in *MM* 78 (1992), 330–1, and my subsequent comment in *MM*, 79 (1993), 96–7.

[59] PRO, PROB11/928.

Tylney), while in 1774 Thomas Dinely left a one-eighth interest in these identical leases.[60] On Bear quay and Sabb's dock the lease shared by Sir Crisp Gascoyne, Sir William St Quintin and three others was to be sublet in 1756 to two wharfingers who, in turn, distributed shares to concealed sleeping partners in eighths.[61] Barrington Buggin, while disposing of substantial stock market wealth in 1789, was to bequeath only a one-tenth share of a leasehold in Hammond's quay.[62]

Thus, the interests vested in the profitability of the wharves were considerably more numerous and complex than the patterns of wharf ownership or wharf management might suggest, and it is not easy to believe that the men guilty of what the petitioners alleged could have formed a distinctive or united phalanx. Some, remarkably, were the petitioners' colleagues. Dinely, as already noted, was partnered in the directorate of London Assurance by Silvanus Grove, a Virginia merchant and director of the New Pennsylvania Company, as well as by John Henniker, Thomas Lane and John Thomlinson, New England merchants who all signed the petition. Solomon Ashley (Member of Parliament for Bridport, 1734–41), who managed Galley quay between 1747 and his death in 1775, was a director of the Royal African Company as was John Boddicott who, in partnership with Richard Boddicott and Thomas Bethel, managed four wharves between 1746 and 1756. They, too, had their colleagues among the ship brokers and insurers who figure among the petitioners. Indeed, had Micajah Perry been able to retain his title to Brewer's and Chester's quays into the late 1740s he would have found himself confronted by Robert Cary, another of the leading tobacco merchants of his generation, who signed the petition and who succeeded Perry as Virginia's financial agent in London.[63]

All in all, the wharf interests seem considerably less impressive than the men who now challenged them. About the stature of Sir Theodore Janssen and the two Van Necks little need be said, but it is worth weighing the importance of other signatories, such as William Hunt – a director of the Bank of England since 1728, deputy governor and governor between 1747 and 1752, or of his fellow directors, Merrick Burrell, Benjamin Mee and Charles Boehm. Two of them – Hunt and Mee – are among the eight directors of the Royal Exchange Assurance who form such a notable group in the petition. The young Edward Forster, a future governor of the Royal Exchange Assurance, partner in a banking house and for thirty years governor of the Russia Company, is among them. There are also men about whom we would know little but for the researches of Professor

<hr>

[60] PRO, PROB11/1036.
[61] PRO, Chancery Pleadings, C12/1002/2 (10 September 1761).
[62] PRO, PROB11/1185.   [63] For Cary see Price, *Perry of London*, pp. 84–5.

Price. The Buchanans, James, George and John, are here as are such central figures in *France and the Chesapeake* as James Douglas (William Law's purchasing agent in the 1720s) and George Fitzgerald (Jr) who was playing a crucial role in the facilitation of English tobacco exports to France despite the outbreak of war in 1744. His presence in the petition, together with his Van Neck associates, might be regarded as highly significant as a portent of those commercial interests which suffered most from the costliness of the port's mismanagement.

Professor Price has somewhere expressed his scepticism about the importance to be attached to petitions and their signatories,[64] and a campaign of protest such as this, which has left so little trace in the official records of the day, may seem to merit little attention. Yet, viewing the preoccupations of the Treasury and the Customs Commission throughout the years 1744 to 1750 – with a great continental war, with a Jacobite rebellion and its aftermath and with endemic problems of smuggling – it is not difficult to understand why an internal dispute between wharfingers and a segment of their clientele might fail to be officially registered. Furthermore, it could be argued that the merchant-petitioners' campaign had been misdirected. Unlike their predecessors in 1705 or their successors in 1765 the petitioners of 1746–7 did not choose to approach the House of Commons, although several of their number had sat, or were sitting, in the House.[65] Instead, by addressing themselves solely to the Commissioners of Customs they had sadly miscalculated, for it is evident that successive boards of Customs Commissioners were very well disposed towards the cartel, seeing in its unitary organization of the port an efficient ally against fraud.[66] As for the legal quays surrounding them to left and right, Customs officers found them more convenient to superintend than the scattered 'sufferance wharves' down river or those which lined the southern shore. Thus, when asked to comment on the memorialists' case for an extension of the legal quays down river they dismissed it with almost frivolous contempt.[67] It was impracticable, they argued; Customs officers would have to trudge round the Tower, often at night, 'a

---

[64] See Jacob M. Price, 'Who cared about the colonies? The impact of the thirteen colonies on British society and politics, circa 1714–1775', in Bernard Bailyn and Philip D. Morgan, eds., *Strangers within the Realm: Cultural Margins of the First British Empire* (Chapel Hill, N.C., 1991), pp. 405–6.

[65] See for example Merrick Burrell, Sir Theodore Janssen, Richard Jackson and John Thomlinson.

[66] Several senior Customs officials were to confirm this view in their evidence to the Chancery case of *Fleet, & Co.* v. *Ashton*, but allegations that the cartel had bribed the Customs Board with lavish dinners also surfaced in the evidence: see '"The Damned Combination"'. Successive boards of Customs were to remain obstinately favourable to the cartel until the 1760s.

[67] NRO, B-H(K) Coll. no. 552.

long and dangerous circuit' to a remote area where they would be beyond reach of help and advice. Furthermore, it would require many additional officers: an allegation well calculated to ensure the Treasury's veto. And so it proved. The campaign of 1746–7 ended inconclusively, tobacco duties were raised, and it was left to a subsequent generation to dislodge the property interests vested in control of the legal quays.

Nevertheless, the objectivity of the petitioners' case and the weight of their collective standing were not inferior to those of the interests which, in the mid-1790s, persuaded Pitt the Younger to set up the House of Commons' select committee of inquiry into the requirements of the port of London. By that date, it is true, the sheer volume of shipping crowding into the Pool of London was probably 150 per cent up on the figures for the mid-century,[68] and the scale of the West Indian sugar imports in value and volume dwarfed that of mid-century tobacco.[69] Yet it can hardly be denied that the grievances of the 1740s represented a significant and timely comment on the port of London's deficiencies – deficiencies which mattered to London's eighteenth-century merchants in general, to its Atlantic merchants in particular and which should certainly be pondered seriously by their twentieth-century historians.

[68] The 1796 Report from the select committee of inquiry into increased trade and shipping of the port of London found the number of overseas ships entering the port in 1794 to be 117 per cent up on 1751 and their tonnage to have increased by nearly 165 per cent. Lambert, CII, p. v.

[69] London's sugar imports in the early 1790s were averaging about 1,250,000 cwt per annum while its tobacco imports in 1745–9 averaged under 215,000 cwt. See Morgan, *Bristol and the Atlantic Trade*, pp. 155, 190.

4 Irish businessman and French courtier: the career of Thomas Sutton, comte de Clonard, *c.* 1722–1782

Louis M. Cullen

Thomas Sutton, comte de Clonard, though his death was lamented in a letter to the foreign minister, Vergennes, by the playwright/*brasseur d'affaires* Pierre Augustin Caron de Beaumarchais,[1] has long remained in the shadows, variously described as English, Scottish or even Dutch. He was, however, leader of the private interest in the French East India Company which, after the Company's suspension in 1769, organized a successful private trade to the East Indies. Like the English East India Company, the French Company, closely involved in matters of high policy and public finance, had became a battleground for conflict between rival political interests. Sutton also linked trade in the Indian Ocean to slaving voyages from the east coast of Africa (he was, though as a secondary interest, a plantation owner in Saint-Domingue). He had mining interests in Spain, and in wartime engaged in ambitious privateering ventures. In the Seven Years War and afterwards in the ill-fated Guyana (Cayenne) plantation venture, he had close ties with the duke of Choiseul (Etienne-François Choiseul), the dominant French politician (variously war minister, navy minister and foreign minister) from 1757 to 1770; and he had ties with all naval ministers, from the 1750s to his death in 1782.

An internecine struggle in the 1760s in the French East India Company was in essence one between a still largely unstudied Choiseul circle represented by Sutton and his man of straw, the banker Isaac Panchaud,[2] and an interest for which the Paris banker Jacques Necker and the abbé

---

[1] R. Bigo, *La caisse d'escompte et les origines de la banque de France* (Paris, 1927), p. 40

[2] Panchaud's role has been exaggerated, notably by Herbert Luthy in *La banque protestante en France de la révocation de l'Edit de Nantes jusqu'à la Révolution* (Paris, 1959–61). See also L. M. Cullen, 'Luthy's *La banque protestante*: a reassessment', *Bulletin du centre d'histoire des espaces atlantiques*, new series, 5 (1990), 229–63.

Terray were spokesmen. This interest opposed Choiseul's maritime perspective, and though ultimately accepting book-keeping economies in French finances, resisted reforms in internal or external trade or in the real economy.

The Lamaignère and Delaye papers survived only because after the bankruptcy (unconnected to Sutton's affairs) of the Delaye house, they ended up in the amirauté de Vannes archives through legal complications arising from the prize shares in one of Sutton's final – and most ambitious – privateering ventures in 1780. Without them we would know little about Sutton's affairs.[3] Lamaignère and Delaye had become agents in Le Havre for Sutton at the time of the Guyana venture and latter from 1773 in the Indian Ocean; at a time of renewed likelihood of war they also opened a house in Lorient from 1776.[4]

Sutton's high politics, the story of the second or Turgot *caisse d'escompte* of 1776, and his relations with Beaumarchais, the government's agent in its dealings with the Americans, remain unclear. He was by nature secretive. As war approached, all he would convey to Antoine Delaye in May 1778 was the fact of 'my almost continuous absence for some time on account of important business'.[5] Delaye had already lamented in 1776 that 'you know that M. de Clonard is secretive and speaks of his business to no one'.[6] At the height of his political intrigue in 1772 one of the Delaye nephews was advised by their uncle that as Sutton could lodge him 'that is essential in order to know all the people in Paris who cross his doorstep'.[7]

Sutton's first known tie with the East India Company – or with France – was in a contract where he was still described as 'de Wexford' which he signed in person with a Lorient merchant in 1748, to supply the company

---

[3] Sutton himself was never a bankrupt. The conclusion in some rough notes by Thomas La Croix, former archivist in Vannes (ADM, Vannes, II J 32) that 'au moment de la révolution, Closnard est mort, laissant un passif considérable qui a entrainé la faillite des Delayes' is incorrect on several grounds, though a mistake easily made in a cursory look at the huge and badly organized Lamaignère and Delaye papers and the odd circumstances of their survival in the *amirauté* archives. On the Delaye bankruptcy, see ADM, Vannes, E2441, grand livre 1784. The Clonard succession owed 48,447 livres (ADM, Vannes, E2412; the répertoire suggests that the volume number is E2413). See also *nomination d'arbitres* 8 July 1785 in AN, minutier central, étude XXVI, 737.

[4] Lamaignère, a native of Bayonne, had resided in Portugal, as did two nephews Antoine and Joseph Arnaud who joined him in Le Havre in 1768.

[5] ADM, Vannes, E2375, 13 May 1778.

[6] ADM, Vannes, Lamaignère and Delaye papers, E2366, 12 January 1776, Antoine Delaye to Lamaignère. The collection is a substantial corpus, E2340–445. As the folders are not always clearly numbered and several are often contained in a single loosely bound packet, some mixing up of items has at times made it difficult to identify with confidence the exact chronological divide between folders, and where this seems to have happened the two relevant reference numbers are given.

[7] ADM, Vannes, E2365/6, 27 April 1772, Cadiz, Lamaignère to Joseph Arnaud Delaye.

with salt beef from Ireland.[8] It was but a step forward from his little-known peacetime trade into elusive but better-documented wartime commitments. In February 1759, on orders from the Ministry of the Marine communicated by his compatriot the maréchal comte de Thomond, he returned to Ireland on board one of his own vessels to complete 'a tour of all the provinces and forts in the kingdom'. On his return to France in May 1759, he saw Choiseul, who ordered him to remain in Paris 'until further orders, saying that I could be useful'. He had already provided some pilots to the Ministry and came back with three more. His other vessel, one of 150 tons, was still in Brest in 1760 'in order to conceal from the public and from the pilots their intended purpose'.[9] His Irish voyage had been covered by a passport. In 1760 he was in receipt of two passports for trade with Ireland, and the fact that one of the vessels, ostensibly trading with Wexford, a port with little foreign trade, received a further passport in March suggests that trade was a cover for deeper purposes.[10] A year later an agreement existed with the government for Sutton to fit out two of the king's vessels as privateers.[11] A vessel captained by his brother was active in the Channel in early 1762,[12] and probably one of the vessels was in the squadron commanded by the chevalier de Ternay which later in the year occupied St John's, Newfoundland.[13] A proposal for the creation of a new Irish regiment by recruitment among Irish fishermen on the Newfoundland fishery (which annually engaged up to 5,000 Irishmen), which would bear the title *Royale Marine Irlandaise* or *Royal Irlandais* and be commanded by his brother, had already been put to Choiseul,[14] and must have been one of the several objectives of the chevalier de Ternay's squadron. Of the 334 Irishmen brought back, few had a taste for military

[8] Archives du port, Lorient, East India Company archives, I P4, fo. 87 verso, Paris, 4 September 1748.

[9] Archives de la guerre, Paris, A¹3568, 'Extrait de la lettre de M. Clonard à Monsieur le duc de Choiseul écrite à Versailles ce 24 Septembre 1760'.

[10] AN, F²40, fos. 348, 351, 26 January, 16 March 1760. As the archives of the amirauté de Saint-Pol de Leon, which include the port of Brest, were destroyed in a bombing raid in the Second World War, Sutton's privateering vessels and the movement of his vessels generally from Brest cannot be studied.

[11] AN, Marine B²371, fos. 79, 113, Versailles, to Hocquart, 7, 21 September 1761.

[12] A letter by [Jean-Baptiste] de Clonard, 11 January 1762, reports on a cruise. Archives de la guerre, Paris, A¹3623.

[13] W. H. Fyers, 'The loss and recapture of St. John's in 1762', *Journal of the Society for Army Historical Research*, 11 (1932), 187. I am indebted to Mr Leo Moakler of St John's, Newfoundland for this reference. See also Archives de la guerre, Paris, A¹3628, De Clonard, 16 October 1762.

[14] AN–CAOM, C7229. 'Soumission que fait O'Kennelly lieutenant colonel et capitaine de Lally'. The only date given is 1762, but it is clearly from early in the year. The proposal is set out again and more specifically and probably more accurately in 1763 by Thomas Sutton himself. AN, Marine B³557, De Clonard to Choiseul, 24 January 1763.

or naval service (a mere twenty-six), but at Sutton's prompting forty-nine put their names forward to go to Cayenne.[15]

Sutton first became prominent in the East India Company in 1764 when it became a front issue in French politics; he, Francis de Rothe, a fellow Wexford man at the centre of Company affairs, and Magon de la Balue, the Paris banking representative of the Saint-Malo and Cadiz trading family, presented a common front in a group which favoured sweeping reform in the eastern trade.[16] Necker, prominent in defending the existing status of the Company in 1764, backed by conservative interests in the Company, became a syndic of the Company in the following year. Necker's and Terray's rise in the directorial and syndical ranks of the Company as spokesmen of the anti-Choiseul group[17] parallels the countervailing rise on the opposing side of Sutton, a very active director judging from the frequency of his signature among his fellow directors on Company orders, and that of his henchman Panchaud.

I

Dying at about sixty years of age, according to his burial entry in the parish registers of Angoulême on 15 September 1782,[18] Sutton would have been born in 1722. He married Phyllis Masterson of Castletown, county Wexford, on 18 April 1742, and the children as late as 1757 were also born in Wexford.[19] The Mastersons and Talbots were the only two Catholic families which succeeded in holding on to large properties in the county. This background, and family links by the marriage of Sutton's brother Jean-Baptiste to a Talbot (likewise intermarried into the Mastersons) enhanced the local standing of the Suttons. The family were probably distantly connected, through the Wexford family Colclough,[20] to the

---

[15] AN, Marine B³557, fos. 188, 190–1, 196–206, 208, 210–14, 217–19, 227–9, 232, 234, 24 January–16 March 1763, from Hocquart, and the two Clonards, to Choiseul.

[16] Accounts vary somewhat in detail between 'Lettre d'un actionnaire à un autre actionnaire', 1770, in *Mémoires concernant l'administration des finances sous le ministère de monsieur l'abbé Terrai, contrôleur général* (London, 1776), p. 306; Luthy, *La banque protestante*, vol. II, p. 384; and Haudrère, *La compagnie française des Indes au xviii siècle, 1719–1795* (Paris, 1989), pp. 1110–1. Letters from the Company in Paris to Rothe in Lorient in 1763–4 also provide some detail. Archives du port, Lorient, East India Company records,1P297/16. The preceding year's politics in the company are described in detail in Haudrère, *La compagnie française des Indes*, pp. 1087–90.

[17] The 'Lettre à Monsieur Necker', 1780, attributes Necker's rise to public prominence to his role within the Company (p. 6).

[18] Archives départementales de la Charente, Angoulême, parish of Saint-Paul, E16/11. He died on 13 September.

[19] AN, minutier central, étude XXVI, 714, 8 May 1783. See also pedigrees of the Suttons, Talbots, Mastersons and Byrnes, in Genealogical Office, Dublin, MSS 162, 168, 179.

[20] AN, étude XC, 367, 24 December 1750, referring to will of 24 June 1743.

London Irish house of the first and second George Fitzgeralds, uncle and later his heir and nephew who held the tobacco contract which features so prominently in Jacob Price's *France and the Chesapeake*. The Talbot ties ensured access, through the Talbots' relative the catholic peer Lord Shrewsbury, even to the English government: *c.* 1779 Lord North commented on an 'overture . . . so direct, precise and important and comes from a person [De Clonard] so united with the French ministry and particularly with Mr De Sartine that I think it right to lay it immediately before your Majesty and to communicate it to Cabinet'.[21] Like the Tooles, another Wexford family of relatives (a young Toole described as nephew flits through Sutton documents and East India Company records in the early 1760s), the Suttons conformed to the pattern of Irish military service families. Thomas had a brother as a *capitaine de brûlot*; four sons entered naval and military service (one was a colonel and one a captain in military service; two seamen sons at the time of their deaths were captain and ensign respectively).[22]

Sutton first appeared on the stage of business history in 1745, in a curious affair when two Portuguese treasure ships had been brought into Cork by British privateers (one of them, incidentally, captained by a Talbot) with a bullion cargo worth about half the annual value of Irish export trade. He was one of the agents of the second George Fitzgerald in attempting to buy speculatively, with the help of sweet words and alcohol, the prize shares of the crews of the privateers.[23] Three years later his contract with the East India Company in Paris provides the first clue to his future French role. Sutton's permanent residence there dates from mid-1757, when he was still known as Thomas Sutton; later in the year he assumed the style of De Clonard, and *lettres de naturalité* and of *reconnaissance de noblesse* in 1763 seem to have consecrated social standing and recognition of wartime service alike.[24] At that time, too, he was involved

---

[21] J. Fortescue, *The Correspondence of King George III* (1778–9) (London, 1928), vol. IV, p. 550. I am indebted to my student Eugene Coyle for this reference.

[22] Sutton's brother was captain of one of the vessels to transport goods and men to Guyana. *Capitaine de brûlot* meant in fact a commercial captain who became captain of naval ventures and acquired naval rank; his later life was spent in the East India Company or private voyages to the East Indies, and he died at Madagascar in 1778.

[23] PRO, Exchequer bills and answers, E112/1225, no. 3044, depositions of Lodwick Funk and Thomas Comyn. George Fitzgerald's involvement can be traced in E112/1223, nos. 2983 and 2998 and E112/1225, no. 3027.

[24] 'Lettres de naturalité avec reconnaissance d'ancienne noblesse', November 1763, from Chérin, 191 in Haudrère, *La compagnie française des Indes*, pp. 1095–6. Sutton arrived in Brest on a small Guernsey privateer by July 1757, and by September he was already well enough established for the Ministry of the Marine, in turning down a transatlantic proposal from him as too sensitive, to do so 'quelque confiance qu'on puisse prendre du Sieur Sutton personnellement' (Service historique de la marine, Archives du port de Brest, IE 153, fos. 59, 263, Ministry of the Marine to the intendant of the port, 15 July, 14 September 1757).

in Choiseul's settlement project in Cayenne in 1762–4, helping to move the settlers, troops and supplies,[25] including flour and beef, to the Lamaignère firm in Le Havre, for whom he was 'le plus honnête correspondent que je connaisse'.[26] After 1763–4, Sutton's ties with Lamaignère were desultory until 1769.

II

When the East India Company was suspended in 1769, and private trade to the east became possible, Sutton had need of an agent to act for him in the ports, a trust which Lamaignère and the nephews who joined him in 1768–9 welcomed as it gave them the prospect of enlarging their rather slight business. Sutton's position was helped by the high status of Francis de Rothe, a fellow Wexford man, who had been head of French trade in Canton for twenty years, and who had returned to take charge of the East India Company port of Lorient in the course of the Seven Years' War. In 1763 Choiseul, with his plans for the navy's future in mind, then offered Rothe the post of intendant of Brest, France's major naval port.[27] The health grounds pleaded by Rothe for declining Choiseul's offer were probably genuine, as he also ceased to be a director of the East India Company; however, he remained an associate of Sutton's financial and mining speculations in the 1760s and also became an active backer of Sutton's new projects in private trade. Moreover, he may crucially have put to the Ministry of the Marine the idea of selling vessels for East Indian voyages to private individuals, and through the 1770s his association with Sutton can be regularly documented. Sutton disliked having bills drawn on him (which would make public the scale of his commitments), and bills by Lamaignère and Delaye were drawn on either Panchaud or Rothe.

Sutton was a member of two large circles. The first was an Irish business one based on Dublin, London, Paris, Bordeaux, Saint-Malo and Cadiz. The marriage in London in 1771 of a Sutton daughter to Andrew French, a well-connected Irishman from County Galway, was a key element in this circle, cementing the ties already existing with another Galway house, that of Isidore Lynch, in London, as was the marriage of another daughter to a nephew of the childless Daniel McCarthy, one of Bordeaux's major merchants, in 1777. The marriages corresponded with the strategy of private trade with the east, and the importance of

[25] AN, Marine B² 372, fo. 673, king's orders, 26 April 1763. On the colony, see B. Cherubini, 'Les acadiens en Guyane française, des colons exemplaires pour une colonisation en dilettante', *Bulletin du centre d'histoire des espaces atlantiques*, new series, 5 (1990), 157–96.
[26] ADM, Vannes, E2373, letterbook 1763–68, 7 June 1764.
[27] Rothe's widow's letter in 1781 to De Castries in AN-CAOM E358; Rothe to Poissonière, 4 December [1763], Archives du Port, Lorient, East India Company records, IP 297/16, no. 93.

Bordeaux as a supply centre for the East Indiamen. In the proposed general contract with the Ministry of the Marine, Bordeaux was, despite some opposition to the idea, Sutton's preferred supply base. He had also purchased land in the nearby Landes, engaging in reclamation (as did Beaumarchais).

The status of this network was enhanced by its ties with a second group, an Irish official and courtier mafia, whose influence peaked at this time. The Lally affair itself, the *cause célèbre* in which Lally, the Irishman who commanded the French forces in India, was scapegoated for its loss in the Seven Years' War, highlighted the high place of the Irish in French society and politics. Lally apart, the two McNamaras in the navy, the maréchal comte de Thomond, the Rothe–Sutton–Darcy circle in the East India Company, and the courtier Dillons variously in the army and in the church represented its pinnacle (symbolically, it is no accident that the recognizedly best account of French aristocratic social *mœurs* was by Lucy Dillon, niece of the celebrated archbishop Dillon, successively of Toulouse and Narbonne). Sutton's large-scale mining venture in Spain in the late 1760s drew in some of the French aristocracy,[28] and a daughter married an Auvergne marquis in 1771. Choiseul's relative, C.-G. Praslin (comte de Choiseul, later duc de Praslin), who became foreign minister when Choiseul vacated the office in 1761 (and succeeded him as minister of the marine in 1766), had an Irish wife. Fittingly in 1780 Sutton arranged a magnificent dinner for General Dillon and his entourage aboard his most ambitious privateering vessel, itself named after one of its sponsors, the king's brother, the comte d'Artois.

Sutton belonged to a further – or third – circle, in part a Lorient one (especially from the early 1760s to his death in 1776 the house of René Foucaud), in part a Saint-Malo one, both through the Magons, and other Saint-Malo ties created by Rothe's marriage to a Hay, from a Saint-Malo Irish family. Sutton, associated with this circle and somewhat more distantly with the Bayonne (and Choiseul) figure of Laborde, banker and merchant, represented an interest in the ports with a stake in the Company quite distinct from the Paris courtier interest, which put metropolitan and domestic political concerns before maritime ones. The new ideas of the circle should not be exaggerated (though the backing for a *caisse d'escompte* in 1769 and again in 1776 was important, and Sutton, described as a 'homme de grand mérite', knew Anne-Robert-Jacques Turgot,[29] the econ-

---

[28] They can be followed from documents in AN, Minutier central, étude XXVI. Chaussinand de Nogaret's 'A propos d'une entreprise française en Espagne au XVIIIe siècle: les sociétaires de la compagnie de Guadalcanal', *Revue d'histoire économique et sociale*, 20 (1973), 185–200 is based mainly on them.

[29] Archives des affaires étrangères, Correspondance politique Angleterre, 508, fos. 13–14, Garnier to de Reyneval, 6 January 1775 (in code).

omist and celebrated reforming *contrôleur-général* of 1774–6). With calculation, they exploited the good will of politicians. As goods and troops had to be transported to support French military stations in the east they were able to have ceded to them on highly advantageous terms the unused vessels of what had been a semi-state company.

III

Sutton's underlying interests from the start were Choiseul's, of associating economic and military and naval power. In this sense he becomes a vehicle for understanding the role of Choiseul and the divisions in French policy in the wake of the Seven Years War. That in turn involves understanding the reasons for the rapid and otherwise puzzling rise of Necker in the 1760s. To explain the phenomenon Luthy, without any real evidence, cast Necker in a dominating role in the foreign exchanges between London and Paris which made him indispensable for economic reasons to the East India Company. However, Necker's business house had a marginal place in the foreign exchanges; he was simply a buyer, once he secured contracts, of bills to service them, not a house made essential to those in political power by its hold on the foreign exchange market. His rising political position, not his stake in the exchanges, for instance, gained him a role in supplying silver to the East India Company: he could acquire this only through a circle in which the Magons and Labordes, both houses with a large business stake in silver-rich Cadiz, were major figures.

Some of the ideas set in motion by the embarrassment of the Company were extreme, favouring a total freedom of trade with the east. That illustrates how central its plight was to the debate on reform in a highly regulated society, just as for those who opposed deregulation in French economic life, the East India Company was unavoidably part of the whole which had to be defended against economic libertarianism. If disestablished, the company could be replaced by private trade with the east, which would also transport the men and supplies needed by a Ministry of the Marine, whose role in the east had been revamped by Choiseul and Praslin to favour defence rather than expensive state-financed colonization. It was less the threat of war with England than the place of defence as a priority in overall policy that caused the downfall of Choiseul in December 1770. Terray's ascent to the office of *contrôleur général* in 1769 reflected the advance of the opposing faction in the political struggle. Significantly, in the wake of Praslin's departure from the Ministry of the Marine at the same time as his cousin, Terray briefly held the post in the first days of 1771.

If Necker was part of a front supporting the status quo at large, he also came in the late 1760s to enjoy as a banker the political favour of managing the foreign exchange business of the ever-more indebted French East India Company. However, *pace* Luthy, it was Panchaud, not Necker, who was close to the exchange business with London, and as a partner in what had been the house of Selwyn & Foley. Selwyn had returned to England in 1765, and Panchaud, who then became a partner, was soon sole survivor.[30] The role of both Necker and Panchaud was to help to handle paper between London and Paris, in Necker's case on the company account, in Panchaud's case on the account of Sutton and his London associates. London was central to the conduct of all French trade with the east, either on the Company's account or on any alternative basis of trading, whether private or reincorporated, as France had little export trade in the orient and hence needed to remit through London. Bourdieu & Chollet, Necker's agents in London, in the late 1760s purchased in London bills on India on the Company account, and paid for them in long-dated paper on Paris. Such a mass of unorthodox paper issued in 1768–9 was easily identified, and precisely because it was long dated, it overhung the market. Sutton's business interests in India, on the other hand, when they began to engage in the trade from 1769, drew bills on London to the order of English residents in India who were desperate to remit their profits to London, and Sutton and his associates then transferred funds to London by purchases of short-trade bills over the intervening eighteen months to discharge the liabilities maturing in 1771 and later in the hands of their London agents. Technically this was a much superior operation. It used the normal exchange market (instead of flooding it, as Bourdieu & Chollet had, with an uncommon, little-wanted, easily identified paper, which, given its long term, and the disrepute of the Company, had been hard to sell and quickly sank to a large discount); and hence it did not advertise the size of the dealings involved. Offering in London as means of payment for bills on India an unorthodox paper on Paris, the Necker circuit were not able to take advantage of the desperation of wealthholders in India to transfer money to London, whereas after 1769 the private interests through their agents in India maximized their advantage by offering bills on London at long dates (a somewhat disadvantageous arangement for the wealthholders who had little bargaining power, but a highly beneficial one to the French trading interest which received funds in India immediately and only later needed to buy short-dated paper in Paris to transfer resources to London to honour the bills when they matured). In other words, the English in India lent French private interests the resources they required for the eastern trade, whereas

---

[30] Archives des affaires étrangères, Correspondance politique Angleterre, 477, fo. 427, to Rochefort, Versailles, 29 March 1768. Panchaud resided in the same house as Foley, and at an earlier date Selwyn. See *ibid.*, fo. 383, details of capitation, 1763–7.

the ineffective Necker circle had given the French Company bills which matured in India at a much later date, and which had been purchased by creating expensive and damaging liabilities on Paris. The success of the new private operations is shown in the fact that the private trade, quite large in its peak years, was conducted in the 1770s without any noticeable exchange strains.

Choiseul was aware of the inept handling of the Necker transactions, which could be seen as a contribution of the order of £1 million to the financing of English trade with the east.[31] In any event this could only have been a once-off operation, not a regular method of financing trade, and it actually hastened rather than put off a decision on the future of the Company. Panchaud later alleged that Necker and Bourdieu & Chollet took advantage of the depreciation of the paper to have agents buy it up at a low price on their own account, thus making a further personal profit. However, the charge is not central to the technical issues. The whole operation was a highly inefficient way of handling exchange transactions. Moreoever, they had created a situation in which paper was thrown on the market: had they not had their own cover agents to buy it up at a discount, others would have emerged to do precisely the same thing (in that sense it raised the same technical questions as the *reconnaissances du Canada*, the paper issued before the loss of Canada to its American creditors by the French government, and later the subject of protracted diplomatic negotiations. This was bought up at a heavy discount by Panchaud and some of Sutton's London associates, though not on Sutton's account).

IV

One of the interests of Panchaud and Sutton was the creation of a *caisse d'escompte* or discounting bank. Essentially, the large debt of the French East India Company, if taken over by the bank, would be akin to a loan to the state (it would save the state from having to assume responsibility for the debt), and would thus serve technically as the backing for credit creation by the bank. Laborde, who had set up a *caisse* in 1767, offered in March 1769 to take over the debt of the Company.[32] This itself seems to have been an outcome of proposals by merchants in the ports to put up funds to pay off the Company's debts and to open the trade to the east.[33] Thus, in essence, the divide in 1769 was between a court interest which wanted the Company to continue (or, after it was suspended, wanted the

---

[31] PRO, SP78, 277, fo. 175, Harcourt, 22 March 1769.
[32] PRO, SP78, 277, fos. 158–60, Harcourt, 15 March 1769.
[33] *Glasgow Journal*, 3–10 March 1768. See also 25 February–3 March 1768.

suspension removed) and a broader interest, part political and part mercantile, which sought a freer trade, and the creation of a *caisse d'escompte* in support of trade. Necker and Terray were effectively spokesmen for a court group which favoured less radical change in economic life and perhaps genuinely thought private trade impossible.

Even the British ambassador, Harcourt, in reporting events in March 1769 identified the possibilities of either a revamped company or of deregulation which if 'the trade is to be laid open, he considered a wild scheme'.[34] Panchaud's role was less as leader of the opposition, than as the person who at the general assembly of the Company read out a memorial setting out (very ineffectively, one source later recalled) the arguments against continuing the Company.[35] Three meetings in March/ April underlined how intractable the problems were, and the more so as a majority of shareholders in early April had declined to guarantee a new loan, the price of keeping the Company afloat, out of the Company's revenue. As a result a positive decision to wind up the Company seemed certain, although, as Harcourt observed, such a step ran counter to the wishes of a majority of the *actionnaires*.[36] The Conseil decided in July on its termination and the establishment of a *caisse d'escompte*: 'Mr Panchaud . . . and one Monsieur Clonart [sic], it is supposed will be put at the head of this new caisse'.[37] Writers were employed by the government to illustrate that the Company trade was ruinous to the public.[38] However, in another of the many palace *révolutions* in French decision-making, the expected *arrêt* which finally appeared on 13 August merely suspended the privileges of the Company. Walpole reported from the British mission that Necker's reading out of a memorial at the assembly on 8 August was the decisive factor, though, as noted by Walpole, expressed more 'in the free thought and language of a republican (Mr Necker is a Genevois) than the modesty of a subject of the king of France'.[39] The earlier writers were now contradicted by other pamphlets, notably by the 'Réponse au mémoire de M. l'abbé Morellet sur la Compagnie des Indes – imprimé en exécution de la délibération de messieurs les actionnaires prise dans

---

[34] PRO, London, SP78, 277, fo. 212, Harcourt, 28 March 1769.

[35] Paris letter of 28 July in *Glasgow Journal*, 10–17 August 1769. It refers to assemblies on 14 and 29 March.

[36] PRO, SP78, 278, fos. 223–5, Harcourt, 26 July 1769. In this he seems to be correct: press reports suggested a vote by three to one in favour of continuing the Company. *Glasgow Journal*, 6–13 April 1769. See also Haudrère, *La compagnie française des Indes*, p. 1116.

[37] PRO, SP78, 278, fos. 223–5, Harcourt, 26 July 1769.

[38] PRO, SP78, 278, fo. 216, Walpole, 20 July 1769. The struggle was reported in Britain. The Morellet pamphlet, which set out views which were akin to those of Choiseul, was summarized in some detail in the *Scots Magazine* for August 1769. The news is given also in *Glasgow Journal*, 17–24 August 1769.

[39] PRO, SP78, 278, fos. 233–6, 9 August 1769, Walpole; also fos. 258–9, Walpole.

l'assemblée générale du 8 Aout'.[40] Necker's strength lay not in the intrinsic appeal of his arguments but in the gathering strength of the anti-Choiseul interest within and outside the Company, working on the conservative and timid majority of *actionnaires*.

French politics was dominated by a power struggle on the interrelated issues, partly of efficiently financing France's huge national debt, and partly of the associated questions of real reform and foreign policy. It was also a conflict between those who saw things in continental terms and those who saw the future in naval strength, in the reduction of expensive land-based commitments in the east and in a backing for an unencumbered private trade through institutions like a *caisse* or bank. In the East India Company, the questions were inextricably linked: the problem of Company indebtedness had to be faced, and alternatives to continuing the Company raised questions, variously libertarian or closely related to foreign policy. If the Company was suspended, a key practical problem was how to ensure the carriage of supplies and troops to French settlements in the east, and also in Choiseulian terms to guarantee the availability of large vessels which could be quickly adapted for naval needs in wartime. An understanding that the state would buy the vessels back in the event of war, and even more pressingly, as the fate of the Company was not sealed until 1773, in the event of the Company being reconstituted, was essential if private investment was to be forthcoming. Rothe's widow later claimed that the policy of alliance between state and private interests originated with her husband, and a proposal on these lines may in fact go back to a proposal put to the Company itself as far back as 1768.[41] Throughout 1770 Sutton was in contact with the Ministry of the Marine with a view to drawing up a general contract for the traffic to the east. There were high hopes of its adoption, and Lamaignère and Delaye would manage the traffic. Despite the presence of a faction which would like to have re-established the Company, the hopes of a deal seemed bright to the Sutton interest as Terray was 'seeking economies'.[42]

This stage in developments itself was close to the suspension in February 1770 of the payment of *billets* (promissory notes) and of *rescriptions* (treasury receipts) drawn on the tax farmers. This has sometimes been represented as an attack both on Choiseul and on Choiseul's banker

---

[40] On the writing, see also an interesting summary by P. Haudrère, 'Un texte satirique inédit sur la suppression de la compagnie française des Indes en 1769', *Information historique*, 40 (1978), 117–19; also Haudrère, *La compagnie française des Indes*, pp. 1126–32.

[41] AN, Colonies E358, Widow Rothe to de Castries, 18 September 1781; Rothe to De Boynes, 30 November 1772.

[42] ADM, Vannes, E2365 or E2366, 8 January 1770.

friends Magon and Laborde. However, it was more obviously a result of the gravity of the fiscal crisis at that time, worsened by the serious harvest failure which with a scissors-like effect both depressed revenue and increased outlays. Suspension of *rescriptions* did not create a problem for Magon as court banker: technically, it helped him as it freed him from the obligation to honour them. The problem arose for Magon and others alike in other or private business in which they held *rescriptions* not as liabilities which they had to honour but as assets (which were now by a stroke of the pen reduced to mere interest-bearing documents). The real dilemma for private houses was to create a cash flow to replace now-frozen *rescriptions*, payment of which would have been expected at or after the end of March. According to Antoine Delaye, when the news of the suspension broke, and Magon de la Balue was about to announce the suspension of his payments, 'Monsieur de Clonard formed a plan of preventing the suspension of the house of Magon; if he failed, it would have brought down a hundred houses and all the Paris bankers'. Sutton called on Magon de la Balue and, on an assurance from him that he was in good standing with Laborde, then saw Laborde to get his backing. Magon de la Balue needed support to cover a gap between 2 million livres in liquid assets and 6 million in liabilities. Laborde also had been affected by having taken *rescriptions* at Terray's request (a circumstance sometimes overlooked in accounts of the crisis) in 1769 to cover immediate military expenditure to the amount of one and half million livres:[43] this was a large sum, but on the scale of Laborde's business not a crushing one. The efforts to shore up Magon were confirmed immediately by Harcourt, the British ambassador.[44] Clonard was said by Delaye to have earned the thanks of Terray himself.[45] The commercial houses of Magon and of Laborde continued normally. The relations between the Saint-Malo house and the Paris house of Magon de la Balue were unruffled even in the first months of 1770,[46] and Laborde continued his banking and commodity affairs. However, inevitably, business conditions got worse, and the Paris nephew in March wrote that 'there have been many failures which will lead to the collapse of others. I have fears for an important house here. In the end I believe that all the banks will go to the devil.'[47]

---

[43] AN, Laborde papers, 2AQ 26¹, 5 March 1773.
[44] PRO, SP78, 278, fos. 93–4, 22 February 1770, Harcourt.
[45] ADM, Vannes, E2365, Delaye, Paris, 25 February 1770.
[46] Arch. Dep. d'Ille-et-Vilaine, Rennes, Magon de la Balue papers, II J46, letter book 69–1771.
[47] ADM, Vannes, E2365/E2366, 11 March 1770, Delaye, Paris.

V

Somewhat surprisingly if the saving of money was the sole consideration, and despite the grim fiscal prospects which were to result in the suspension of payment of public effects in February, by the end of January 1770 Terray wished to relaunch the company.[48] Ominously – as the Ministry of the Marine would be all the more central to negotiations if the Company were wound up – there had been been a rumour earlier in the month that Terray had been appointed minister of the marine. However, in the wake of two protracted meetings of the shareholders in January and April, hopes of a contract were still not dashed. Indeed, Clonard's role in supporting the credit of Magon de la Balue was seen as securing the continuation of the good will of Praslin, the minister of the marine, and Antoine Delaye's confidence at the end of February was high. Clonard was tied up in negotiations all through the remainder of April and May: there were contacts with Choiseul, Praslin, Dubucq (chief clerk in the Ministry of the Marine) and apparently also with Terray.[49] A visit to Bordeaux scheduled for May was deferred, reflecting the critical stage of the negotiations which were now at the stage of spelling out actual freight rates to the Indian Ocean and minimum size of contracts for the vessels. The number of vessels under the proposed contract was reduced from ten to six; this would help to eliminate any opposition to private trade from officers of the marine[50] (who might be put on the reserve if the business was entirely in private hands); and the confident opinion was expressed that 'the affair can not fail to take place'. In a temporary ascendancy regained by the Praslin–Choiseul interest in the obscure and complex French politics of the year, an administration was set up for the French possessions by the Conseil, with three administrators, one of them Clonard, the others the sympathetic figures of De Bray and La Rochette (the latter already an investor in Clonard's biggest mining venture). This body, it was emphasized within the Lamaignère–Delaye family, would be under the tutelage of Praslin as minister of the marine, not under the *contrôleur général* who was left only with the liquidation of the company: 'this office will be in charge of all expeditions, supplies and dispatches; the same directors or administrators will likewise sign the permissions for vessels wishing to go to the Indies'. There was elation in reporting that 'Monsieur de Clonard will I believe be the person who will be principally in charge and who will mostly see the minister'.[51] No time was

---

48 *Ibid.*, 22 January 1770, in Portuguese, Lamaignère, Paris.
49 ADM, E2365/6. Choiseul had deputed the matter to Praslin, Delaye, Paris, 12 May 1770.
50 ADM, E 2365/6, Paris, 21 May 1770. This letter is particularly informative.
51 ADM, Vannes, E2365/6, 6 July 1770.

being lost: Foucaud from Lorient was already in Paris to arrange for the purchase of four ships, two for Bengal, two for China, in transactions costing 5 million livres.[52] The worsening relations with England were regarded as helping progress, and on 28 September it was expected that the contract would be signed on 3 October.[53] That it was not signed, pointed to another change in the wind. The decisive loss of momentum foreshadowed, several months ahead, the fall of Choiseul in December, and the Falklands crisis simply provided the excuse for a final push against him. Terray even became briefly minister of the marine,[54] an essential emergency step in ensuring with Praslin's removal, that the loyal Choiseulian allies in the Ministry were silenced. Within a week the new administration of the Indies was revoked, and by the end of January, according to family reports 'Monsieur de Clonard begins to despair of the negotiations'.[55]

With de Boynes taking Terray's place as minister of the marine, prospects for negotiation improved again.[56] In any event, even for the Terray interest, though committed to reviving the Company, in the short term, contracts to private interests were unavoidable. With apparently brighter prospects in May and June, the idea of the uncle going to the east as agent of the project emerged. By the outset of December from Clonard's assurances, it was possible to write that 'from some words he said to me earlier, I believe that our affair will be more important that we were counting on'.[57] So confident was Lamaignère that the partnership between him and his elder nephew for both of them to go east was drawn up in the same month.[58]

At this stage the proposal for a company gathered speed again in public rumour,[59] and the issue seems to have been in essence who would control it. At the end of the month, with Clonard retaining only 'a glimmer of hope', Praslin spent an afternoon closeted with him in his house.[60] These contacts were part of a rearguard action and it was reported a few weeks later that 'talk of the company is no longer so

---

[52] ADM, Vannes, E2365/6, 24, 25 July 1770.

[53] ADM, Vannes, E2365/6, 21 September, 28 September 1770.

[54] ADM, Vannes, E2365/6, 5 January 1771. Ironically, and very inaccurately, the letter was optimistic on the strength of Clonard's knowing Terray: 'je croye que c'est une bonne affaire pour nous parce qu'ils sont amys et certainement j'aime mieux que ce soit luy que tout autre'.

[55] ADM, Vannes, E2365/6, 21 January 1771. This is significantly earlier than the date suggested by Haudrère of March 1771 (*La compagnie française des Indes*, p. 1140).

[56] ADM, Vannes, E2365/6, 23 April 1771.

[57] ADM, Vannes, E2365/6, 4 December 1771, Lamaignère.

[58] ADM, Vannes, E2410/2411, acte de société, Paris, December 1771.

[59] ADM, Vannes, E2365/6, Delaye, 25 December 1771.

[60] ADM, Vannes, E2365/6, 10 December 1771, Lamaignère. The wavering in policy is reflected in the nuances in the correspondence over time.

warm. Those involved in the affair will submit a new proposal to the minister in three days.'[61] In the seesaw about a company, a proposal now emerged of a company providing free trade as far as the Isles de France and Bourbon in the Indian Ocean (an old idea of Choiseul's from the mid-1760s) and a company monopoly only beyond that point. Moreover, the company would now not be a courtier company, as the Clonard interest would be represented among the directors. The proposal in this form was attributed in London news to Clonard:

advices by the last French mail informs us that the Comte de Clonard, an Irish gentleman ennobled in that kingdom, has lately submitted a scheme to the inspection of the Duke d'Aiguillon, by which the re-establishment of the French East India Company to its former splendour and importance is proposed in a manner equally facile and eligible,[62]

and Lamaignère writing in 1773 from Port Louis and hence commenting on news that was already six or more months old that a new company had been 'accepted' with Clonard, Panchaud and De Roche (Rochette?) among the directors, declared that: 'if that is true it may prove a great stroke for us'.[63] For Lamaignère a company with open trade to the Indian Ocean provided everything; for the others already engaged and, by 1772, on a very large scale in trade – successfully – as far afield as China, it meant little unless they were to enjoy the direction of it. The new company failed to draw in enough subscriptions,[64] probably as much because of politics as of economics. Who the real victors were in the struggle is not immediately clear; however, even if no new company was floated, one of the consequences of the struggle was to kill off the prospect of a *caisse d'escompte*, a result which accorded with the

[61] ADM, Vannes, E2365/6, 31 December 1771, Lamaignère.

[62] *Edinburgh Advertiser*, 4–8 September 1772. It is not perfectly clear whether this proposal was afoot as early as June 1772 or was a counterblast to an earlier one. *Edinburgh Advertiser*, 26–30 June 1772. The British embassy reported on it at dates in October 1772, and March 1773. PRO, SP78, vol. 286, fos. 99, 100, 21 October 1772; vol. 287, fos. 58–60, 93, 17 February, 3 March 1773, all from St Paul. See also Haudrère, *La compagnie française des Indes*, p. 1142. Especially important is the letter from Harcourt in SP78, vol. 284, fos. 72–6, 7 February 1772, enclosing letter of De Boynes to Law de Lauriston, 18 January 1772. So changeable was De Boynes's policy that Harcourt observed that he had sent eight different circulars to the East Indies.

[63] ADM, Vannes, E2366, Lamaignère, 18 July 1773, Port Louis.

[64] See PRO, SP78, vol. 287, fos. 58–60, 93, 17 Feb., 3 March 1773. The reason is attributed to the success of the private trade by Haudrère, *La compagnie française des Indes*, p. 1142. That, however, misses the point that Sutton and his associates were central to the organisation of the private trade as well as to the idea of a company. The divide seems to have been a political reluctance to accept a company controlled in effect by that interest. Terray had already had to concede that the only company possible in French fiscal circumstances was one in which the trade to the Île de Bourbon and the Île de France was in private hands; that meant that the only remaining question was who would control the company.

ideas of Necker. Necker's peculiar and pompous confidence displayed in the absurd *Eloge de Colbert* in 1773, a defence, by implication, of state control in all demesnes, was a challenge to the libertarian ideas which made possible the appointment of Turgot as a reforming *contrôleur-général* in 1774 and which also were behind the idea of a free-standing *caisse d'escompte*. The directors of a further *caisse* in 1776, made possible by Turgot's backing, would be chosen by election, and Clonard seemed confident of a reassuring outcome.[65]

VI

Thus, despite the Terray commitment to a company, the trade remained private. Its development had begun even before the Company's privilege was suspended. At the outset of 1769 Sutton had already purchased a vessel for a voyage to the Île de France.[66] Rothe and his brother-in-law in 1769 purchased two vessels from the government.[67] This was advantageous for them, but, once suspension was in prospect or achieved, such arrangements were also essential for the government if it was to secure supplies to the settlements in the Indian Ocean. Under de Boynes, the first vessel for the 1772 expeditions was sold to Rothe in late 1771[68] and Foucaud was an active purchaser in 1772.[69] A majority of the ships in 1769–71 were Lorient vessels. In 1772 under an agreement with *armateurs* (ship-owners) negotiated by Rothe, the setting out of twelve vessels was guaranteed, eight for India and onwards to China, four to Bengal.[70] Rothe's aim was that the vessels should get to Canton ahead of the English vessels. From 1772 non-Lorient vessels drew significantly ahead of Lorient in tonnage in the trade.[71] However, outside interests had been drawn in by the Lorient circle itself: in the early years Rothe himself on at least one occasion purchased a quarter share in a Saint-Malo vessel. As early as late 1769 the Magon de la Balue house in Saint-Malo was in touch with Pierre Bernier, a Sutton ally, about the readiness of a friend in

[65] ADM, Vannes, E2375, Sutton to Delaye, Le Havre, 13 April 1776
[66] ADM, Vannes, E2382, letterbook, 1768–77, 4 January 1769, to De Clonard.
[67] Paris letter 23 October in *Glasgow Journal*, 26 October–2 November 1769. See also *Lettre d'un actionnaire à un autre actionnaire*, p. 399.
[68] AN, Colonies E358, copy of letter of Rothe to de Boynes, 5 December, 1772.
[69] AN, Colonies E358, 30 November, 1772, Rothe to de Boynes.
[70] AN, Colonies E358, letter of Rothe to de Castries, 18 September 1781. The letters in E358 bring out the central importance of Rothe. For further details of his importance, see his Inventaire in étude XVII/1052, September 1788, and étude L/665, August–September 1781, correspondence. See also the inventory of Panchaud, étude X /783, 23 August 1789.
[71] Haudrère, *La compagnie française des Indes*, p. 123.

Amiens to invest in trade to China.[72] This picture contradicts the Luthy view of a dominance of Paris houses: the Paris-based Panchaud's first investment on his own account appears to have been in 1775.

By 1773, as a result of the scale of the Sutton–Rothe–Foucaud investment in the Canton route there was already complaint of surplus;[73] and the quantities of tea landed in Lorient by the French vessels compared favourably with other European marts.[74] The years 1772 and 1773 were difficult for the Indies trades at large, reflecting the European financial crisis of 1772 and its immediate aftermath. There was on the other hand a distinct optimism in the autumn of 1774.[75] Far from a shortage of vessels at any time, the complaint by the adventurers, no doubt, a self-interested one (prompted by the politically well-connected faction who made the case for a new company under their control), was of excessive competition and an unregulated market.

The growth of trade to the east opened up other possibilities: apart from a contract to carry supplies and men to the east on government account, and trading ventures to India and China, some of the Sutton vessels developed a triangular pattern, calling on the way back at Mozambique or Zanzibar to load slaves for the West Indies. Despite some misgivings both by the family itself and by Foucaud about a man of Lamaignère's age going to the east, he was on his way by mid-1772. He had reached the Île de France by November, and his nephew Joseph Arnaud Delaye was in the Île de Bourbon by the following May. Trade continued smoothly up to 1778 when the outbreak of war and Lamaignère's death in the same year changed things.

Sutton's interests were now multiple. He himself was a party in ways which are obscure to French assistance to America and to preparations for war. One of his men of affairs, Panchaud, became a director of the *caisse d'escompte* of 1776. Sutton proposed leasing Château Latour in the same year (one of the owners, when Sutton, allegedly on behalf of a friend, had sounded him out for a nine-year lease, was advised that 'this gentleman has the reputation of being very rich, but also of being an intriguer and a projector of great ventures; I think it is necessary to be on

---

[72] Archives Departement d'Ille -et-Vilaine, Rennes, Magon de la Balue papers, IF 1904, letterbook 1769–71, to Pierre Bernier, 15 November 1769.

[73] AN, Colonies E358, 26 September, 23 November 1773, Rothe to De Boynes. The British press said as much a year earlier. *Glasgow Journal*, 5–12 November 1772.

[74] See A. L. Cross, *Eighteenth-century Documents Relating to the Royal Forests, the Sheriffs and Smuggling* (New York, 1928), p. 295, for an account of teas exported to Europe from Canton, 1772–80.

[75] ADM, Vannes, E2366, 14 October 1774, Joseph Delaye, Cape of Good Hope, to Lamaignère.

one's guard with people of this sort').[76] With Panchaud he purchased the Sèvres pottery in 1777, though it was sold in the following year.[77]

Sutton's links with the new naval minister, Sartine, became closer, and he had intriguing direct ties with both the Americans and with the British. Inevitably war led once more to privateering. His contacts with Franklin, personal and by correspondence, appear to have related to this activity.[78] Characteristically, it was privateering on a grand scale in the case of the *Comte d'Artois* in late 1779 (so named in recognition of the interest taken by the king's brother in the venture), which contained not only a large crew but some 400 soldiers under the style of the *légion d'Artois*. Its purpose seems to have been an ambitious one of harrying British trade from near waters to the far side of the Atlantic. This was not a success,[79] though more routine and successful ventures followed. In 1782 with peace in prospect Sutton was readying things for peacetime trade. He was in the Rochefort region from January to September, apart form a brief visit to Paris in late March. He was, as always, projecting things on a grand scale. He was superintending the construction of a fast-sailing vessel, was projecting the construction of another, and was loading two vessels of which one was to carry goods and troops for the Dutch settlement at the Cape, and then to go on into the Indian Ocean and to return with slaves. The technical complexities of the *Comte d'Artois* (the application of prize regulations to landsmen, i.e. soldiers, as opposed to seamen) led him to plan a further visit to Paris to use his influence with de Castries, the minister of the marine. Despite being a victim for two weeks of the great European influenza epidemic of 1782, he proposed first a fortnight's visit to the Landes (he had a reclamation project there) and to his married daughter in Bordeaux. On his way, at Angoulême on 13 September he died, and was buried there. His life and circle remain to study further, in the knowledge that everything that comes to light adds to his political and business importance.

[76] R. Pijassou, *Un grand vignoble de qualité. Le Médoc* (Paris, 1980), vol. I, p. 607.

[77] AN, minutier central, XCI, 1154, 19 August 1777 (ter); XCI, 1154, 20 November 1778. Panchaud was in financial trouble again, and failed a second time in 1779. The outbreak of war meant that Sutton needed funds for his grand projects; in other words while he declined some commitments in 1777 because he had purchased the glass works, in 1778, with war breaking out, he needed funds for his maritime ventures. His approach is hinted at in his letter in ADM, Vannes, E2375, Sutton to Delaye, 8 October 1777.

[78] Barbara B. Oberg, ed., *Papers of Benjamin Franklin*, vol. XXVI (New Haven, 1987), p. 576, n. 7, vol. XXIX (1992), pp. 127, 474–5, vol. XXX (1993), p. 601.

[79] For very useful accounts of the outcome from British sources, see J. De Courcy Ireland, 'Les Suttons de Clonard, marins français', *Contacts*, no. 25 (1985), 31–3; G. Rutherford, 'Ambrose Sutton, chevalier de Clonard', *Irish Sword*, 1 (1952–3), 253–61.

5 'A revolution in the trade': wine distribution and the development of the infrastructure of the Atlantic market economy, 1703–1807

David Hancock

In 1807, Marien Lamar, near the end of his tenure as the United States' consul on Madeira, wrote to a relative in Great Britain who had inquired about their family's prior involvement in the Atlantic wine trade. In response, the ageing American agent waded through nearly an entire century of genealogy and history. His family had at times experienced unrivalled success and, at others, crushing failure. His brother's father-in-law, a Maryland physician and planter named Richard Hill, had fallen on hard times and moved to the island in 1739, hoping to revive his flagging fortunes by earning enough in the wine trade to repay his numerous debts, some of which were owed to Madeira's merchants, and provide for his large family. Sons, brothers and nephews from Maryland and Pennsylvania followed him there during the first ten years of his residence on the island, and more distant kin from Great Britain joined the firm in ensuing decades – all to avail themselves of the opportunity of making a large profit from the beverage that was fast earning a reputation as an Atlantic luxury good. Looking backwards over seventy years, Marien Lamar realized that there had been nothing less than a 'revolution in the trade' and that his family had been part of this transformation.[1] What was this 'revolution in the trade' that the consul and his contemporaries remarked upon time and again, and what was its significance?

---

[1] Marien Lamar to —, 1 December 1807, Newton & Gordon Scrapbook, vol. I, Cossart papers, Suffolk, England. For earlier uses of the phrase, see John Leacock, Sr, to William Leacock, 16 August 1791, Leacock & Sons letterbook 1791–4, fo. 2 and 31 January, 14 April 1800, 20 February, 26 October 1801, Leacock & Leacock letterbook 1799–1802, fos. 107, 131, 227–8, Leacock papers, Casa Branca, Funchal. Britain's consul Thomas Cheap outlines these alterations in a letter to the Board of Trade. According to Cheap, between 1745 and 1765, there occurred 'an increase in the demand for Madeira wines in America, the introduction of the use of them in Great Britain & India', and a call for a 'large quantity' by 'the settlements in India'. On the supply side the growers made 'their own price' (that is, raised them to 'extravagantly high' levels) and insisted on payment of their best wines in bills of exchange drawn on Lisbon and London merchants. PRO, CO388/95, Thomas Cheap to John Pownall, 1 July 1765.

Introduction

When specialists and students of Atlantic history consider the development of metropolitan and colonial economies and societies, they are forced to come to terms with the role of overseas commerce. This is particularly true in the study of the eighteenth-century economy, one of the characteristics of which was the development of global markets. Over the course of just one hundred years, the commodity, labour and capital markets of Europe and European colonies became integrated in what may be called the first global market. Much of the integration took place as European states developed their American colonies, and involved interactions *across* imperial boundaries. The volume of oceanic trade grew enormously, with imports and exports rising to unprecedented levels. The composition and direction of oceanic trade shifted over the course of the century; and this was especially true in the second half, when the kinds and origins of foodstuffs diversified remarkably. Control over many trades changed, in matters of shipping, trading and financing. The demand for commodities grew and evolved, especially in the Americas, and an Atlantic-based, although increasingly global, system emerged.

The trading system that emerged ramified internally into economies around the Atlantic rim. Winifred Rothenberg, to take one recent scholar as an example, has documented the remarkable eighteenth-century convergence of prices of goods and services in the Massachusetts back-country, evidence of the extent of the market as well as of the integration of the hinterland's economy with that of the Atlantic economy.[2] Massachusetts was not unique: homesteaders along the banks of the Ohio River drank Madeira wine, as did merchants' clerks in Canton and Limpao; farm labourers around Lisbon and Seville ate Carolina rice; German families made bread with Pennsylvania wheat flour; Philadelphia ladies wore India cottons.

If the Atlantic trading system is to be more than a mantra recited by contemporary historians in search of a new interpretive paradigm, we need to know with greater specificity how and why that Atlantic world actually worked, and not just at the level of imperial exchange so well reconstructed by previous generations of historians. In understanding the role played by overseas trade in binding together that world, one model has emerged over the course of the past few decades, a model we might call the 'hub and spoke'. The canonical version of this model is the organization and operation of the Atlantic tobacco business. The tobacco trade exhibited a number of salient features. It involved the export of an

[2] Winifred Rothenberg, *From Market-Places to a Market Economy: the Transformation of Rural Massachusetts, 1750–1850* (Chicago, 1992).

agricultural commodity produced in the colonies for the metropolis: by the 1760s and 1770s, some six-sevenths of the Chesapeake's leafy exports were sent to Britain. It was managed and financed from the mother country, largely from London and Glasgow, and to a lesser extent Bristol, Liverpool and Whitehaven. The customers of the traders who imported the product were themselves middlemen, either large contractors in foreign countries or, in Britain, commercial middlemen, tobacco processors and manufacturers. For tobacco importers in England and Scotland, 'distribution' meant sales to a relatively small number of foreign monopolists or British middlemen.[3] The restrictive Navigation Acts and numerous mercantile regulations and the system of marketing together ensured the dominance of the core.

With some modifications, the hub-and-spoke model of transatlantic distribution describes the sugar export trade from America as well. And, although slaves were generally taken directly to America from Africa, the management of the slave trade also follows the same model.[4] But there is another model of eighteenth-century Atlantic commerce exemplified by the Madeira wine trade. In contrast to the tobacco or sugar trades, like the slave trade the Madeira wine trade dealt with an import into the colonies. This is not the core of the difference, however. The significant difference is in the management and distribution of Madeira wine: it was decentralized, opportunistic and specific. Unlike hub-and-spoke trades, it was organized *away from* the metropolis in the regions of production and consumption; we might call it a 'spider-web' trade with lines of correspondence going in every direction. All roads did not lead to London; the bulk of the commodity did not even go to Britain. Madeira wine traders directly connected Copenhagen, Bordeaux, Lisbon, Bengal, Canton, Cape Verde, Bahia, Surinam, St Croix, the thirteen colonies and

[3] The subject of the transatlantic tobacco trade is synonymous with the name of Jacob Price. The best detailed introduction to the material can be found in his 'The rise of Glasgow in the Chesapeake tobacco trade, 1707–1775' and 'The economic growth of the Chesapeake and the European market, 1697–1775' in his *Tobacco in Atlantic Trade*, chs. 1 and 2; *The Tobacco Adventure to Russia: Enterprise, Politics, and Diplomacy in the Quest for a Northern Market for English Colonial Tobacco, 1676–1722* (Philadelphia, 1961); and *France and the Chesapeake: a History of the French Tobacco Monopoly, 1674–1791, and of its Relationship to the British and American Tobacco Trades* (Ann Arbor, 1973).

[4] On the sugar trade, see the many works of Richard Pares, especially 'The London sugar market, 1740–1769', *EcHR*, 2nd series, 9 (1956), 254–70, 'A London West India merchant house', in Richard Pares and A. J. P. Taylor, eds., *Essays Presented to Sir Lewis Namier* (London, 1956), pp. 75–107; McCusker, *Rum and the American Revolution*, pp. 232–4, 402–6, 414. On the slave trade, see K. G. Davies, *The Royal African Company* (London, 1957); James A. Rawley, *The Trans-Atlantic Slave Trade* (New York, 1981); and Joseph Inikori, 'Market structure and the profits of the British African trade', *JEcH*, 41 (1981), 756. For wider applications of the term, see J. H. Parry, *Trade and Dominion: the European Oversea Empires in the Eighteenth Century* (London, 1971), p. 51; and more recently Thomas M. Truxes, *Irish–American Trade, 1660–1783* (Cambridge, 1988), p. 2.

Québec. They responded to the specific opportunities their specific environments presented, often calling on personal ties. In doing so, they responded to actual differences in their customers, suppliers, agents and markets.[5]

This chapter examines the development of the spider-web trade over the course of a slightly extended eighteenth century, from 1703 to 1807, with particular reference to the elaboration of American distribution channels and networks. It looks at four related phenomena that characterized Marien Lamar's trade 'revolution': the shift in the direction of the trade – in the destination of the goods and the residence of the customers, the growth and change in the island's distribution group, the complementary developments in distribution in America, and the way the island distributors managed the trade – the decentralized, opportunistic and specific entrepreneurship that made Madeira wine 'America's wine'.

The dimensions of the trade

At the heart of the trade in Madeira wine was a commodity that was 'invented' between 1703 and 1807. At the beginning of the eighteenth century, Madeira wine was a simple table wine, made from a base of white 'must' (the juice of the grape before fermentation was completed) to which the growers and exporters added varying amounts of red must in order to give it the colour, body, smoothness and flavour consumers desired. Little else was done to the wine. By the beginning of the nineteenth century, Madeira was a complex, highly processed drink increasingly made from single varietals and fortified, agitated, aged, heated and packaged in custom-sized, custom-labelled and custom-decorated containers.[6]

The island's total must production does not appear to have risen much between 1703 and 1807. In 1807, the land under cultivation by large landowners and peasant *velhoes* was essentially what it had been in 1703 and, for that matter, in 1603, although the lands under cultivation at the beginning of the seventeenth century were for the most part planted with sugar-cane. Roughly two-thirds of cultivable land was tilled and planted with vines by the time of the signing of the Methuen treaty of 1703; little was added to the cultivated acreage in the ensuing century. Wine growers either owned land outright, inheriting it from their par-

---

[5] This model appears to have structured the wheat and rice trades from British America, to name just two, as well as the substantial linen trade from Ireland and the English wool trade.

[6] The transformation is detailed in David Hancock, 'Commerce and conversation in the eighteenth-century Atlantic: the invention of Madeira wine', *JIH*, 29 (1998), 197–219.

ents, or more commonly rented it from or worked it for large land-owners. Approximately three-quarters of cultivated land was rented in 1700; nearly the same amount was rented a century later. The number of wine growers remained constant throughout the century. As an agricultural activity, must production fluctuated from year to year, sometimes wildly, depending on weather and pestilence. But there was no change in normal output: in 1807, as in 1703, about 26,000 pipes of wine were harvested.[7]

Nevertheless, as table 5.1 suggests, the volume of wine shipping rose. In the 105 years from 1703 to 1807, the number of ships annually leaving Funchal doubled; and the quantity of wine they took with them tripled. Most of the expansion occurred as a function of the increase in the importance of the Atlantic Wine Islands to the trade of British America and the new United States; the principal export of the islands – wine – rose from seventh in the portfolio of American imports at the end of the colonial era to fourth in the first decade of the nineteenth century.[8] This expansion occurred mainly in the last third of the period – when shipping prices of Madeira wine nearly doubled, ship departures almost tripled and wine exports tripled. Wine that had previously been allocated for local consumption, manufactured into vinegar and brandy, or marked for wastage, had been converted to the export trade.

The exportation of wines from Madeira to America was directly shaped by geography and diplomacy. Transatlantic shipping in general surged during the seventeenth century, and this made the pinch of shipping costs more urgent for British and American shipowners, cargo owners and

[7] According to Noel Cossart, land was owned by landlords (*senhorios*) who only owned the land; it was worked by tenants (*velhoes*) who leased it from the landlords. Two types of tenants existed: *caseiros*, who lived on the land, and generally more affluent *meyros*, who did not. A tenant gave half the crop in lieu of rent, although the landlord had the right to buy the other half if he or she so chose (*Madeira: the Island Vineyard* (London, 1984), p. 13). Total yield figures survive for only twenty-two harvests; they are buried in the correspondences of island merchants. Terminology varied in contemporary descriptions by Madeira's residents. The basic division, as far as wine traders were concerned, was between 'natives' (Portuguese born on the island or elsewhere and resident there) and 'foreigners' (all others). 'Natives' connoted not only tenants (peasants or others) and landowners but also Portuguese merchants. For an example of the usage, see William Bolton to Robert Heysham, 6 May 1712, Graham Blandy, ed., *The Bolton Letters: the Letters of an English Merchant in Madeira, 1701–1714*, vol. II (Funchal, 1960), pp. 62–3.

[8] 'By the end of the colonial period', James F. Shepherd and Gary M. Walton note, trade with Southern Europe and the Wine Islands had grown to 'substantial proportions'. As late as 1768–72, the average annual value of all wine (mainly the wines of Madeira and the Azores) ranked seventh among the principal articles imported into the Thirteen Colonies; by 1802–4, it ranked fourth, behind coffee, sugar and rum. In 1768–72, the annual average value of wine was £1,000; by 1802–4, it was £2,962,039. (Shepherd and Walton, *The Economic Rise of Early America* (Cambridge, 1979), pp. 86–7; and Timothy Pitkin, *A Statistical View of the Commerce of the United States of America* (Hartford, 1816), p. 155).

Table 5.1. *Departures from the island of Madeira, 1727–1807*

Year	Ships	Year	Ships
1727	57	1768	192
1728	202	1769	201
1729	154	1770	176
1730	140	1771	140
1731	152	1772	170
1732	140	1773	204
1733	146	1774	210
1734	149	1775	174
1735	180	1776	125
1736	161	1777	95
1737	152	1778	146
1738	156	1779	102
1739	96	1780	104
1740	118	1781	87
1741	114	1782	132
1742	145	1783	185
1743	143	1784	137
1744	116	1785	160
1745	109	1786	146
1746	105	1787	185
1747	98	1788	188
1748	133	1789	150
1749	157	1790	195
1750	150	1791	240
1751	136	1792	180
1752	135	1793	140
1753	133	1794	158
1754	142	1795	155
1755	115	1796	216
1756	9	1797	180
1757	0	1798	165
1758	91	1799	174
1759	0	1800	203
1760	64	1801	251
1761	79	1802	267
1762	37	1803	234
1763	154	1804	315
1764	186	1805	294
1765	181	1806	266
1766	159	1807	246
1767	197		

Source: Livros dos Entradas (1727–1807) e Saidas (1779–1807), Provedoria e Junta da Real Fazenda, Arquivo Nacional da Torre do Tombo, Lisbon, Portugal.

captains, especially when one of the legs of the voyage was in ballast. As Madeira was 'not much out of the way going down to the West Indies', it came to be regarded as 'generally worth a ship's while in peaceable times (or, in war-time, if a ship of force) to touch' there, as they frequently 'met with some freight' that was of 'great service'. By taking on cargo in Madeira, the owners could recover some of their costs on two-thirds of an outbound voyage from Europe, or on a return inbound voyage to America.[9]

British politicians and diplomats, too, were keen to grant trade preferences to Portugal, as a means of checking the power of France in the field of trade. Madeira wines imported into British America were exempted from duties under the second Navigation Act – the 1663 'Act for the Encouragement of Trade' – which allowed them to pass to America directly without paying crown duty. Their position within the British commercial empire was reinforced by the Anglo–Portuguese commercial treaty negotiated by Paul Methuen in 1703, which allowed Portuguese wines to pass into Britain at a third the tariff charged on French wines, thereby frustrating the intentions of British importers to develop a home market for claret, and of British re-exporters to develop an American market for port (which was then cheaper, but which would still be charged re-export fees).[10]

Thus, the trade winds and Great Britain's growing body of mercantile law encouraged Madeira's distributors to develop their primary market in British America.[11] Anecdotal mention of the ships in the harbour of Funchal in William Bolton's letterbooks suggests that the encouragement worked: more than two-thirds of all shipments in the years 1702–13 left for British America. Of the 545 ship departures Bolton noted, some 48 per cent left for the British West Indies, another 20 per cent left for British North America (New England), and 6 per cent for other parts of America such as Brazil and Curaçao. Other countries and regions imported smaller quantities; for instance, some 3 per cent was shipped

[9] Spence, Leacock & Spence to William Woodmass, 1762, Spence, Leacock & Spence letterbook 1762–5, fo. 23, Leacock papers, Casa Branca, Funchal.
[10] For the 1663 statute, see 15 Car. II, cap. 7, v. Detailed discussion of the exception appears in Charles M. Andrews, *The Colonial Period of American History*. Vol. IV: *England's Commercial and Colonial Policy* (New Haven, 1938), pp. 109–11; and Lawrence A. Harper, *The English Navigation Laws: a Seventeenth Century Experiment in Social Engineering* (New York, 1939), pp. 59–60. On the development of diplomatic and commercial relations, generally, see V. M. Shillington and A. B. Chapman, *The Commercial Relations of England and Portugal* (London, 1919); and H. E. S. Fisher, *The Portugal Trade: a Study of Anglo-Portuguese Commerce, 1700–1770* (London, 1971).
[11] Harper, *English Navigation Laws*; George L. Beer, *The Old Colonial System, 1660–1754*, 2 vols. (New York, 1912); and A. D. Francis, *The Methuens and Portugal, 1691–1708* (Cambridge, 1966).

directly to India, 2 per cent to Portugal, and 8 per cent to England, Scotland and Ireland.[12]

The more or less complete series of *entrada* books listing arrivals into and departures from the port of Funchal begins in 1727 and confirms the importance of British America suggested by Bolton's letters. The *entrada* records do not record outbound cargoes, but they do show ships' destinations and the pattern of Madeira's trade. This trade consisted almost entirely of reshipments of goods brought to Madeira, and Madeira wine.[13] From 1727 to 1738, on the eve of the War of Jenkins' Ear, 70 per cent of all departing ships went to the British West Indies, the British North American colonies, and other European powers' colonies in the Americas. British settlements in the Caribbean always took the greatest share of the wine – never less than a third of it. British colonies to the north took a quarter, directly. The actual imports into North America were probably greater than this, however. The *entradas* usually list only the initial stops of outbound vessels, and many of the pipes listed as destined for the Caribbean were never unloaded there, but held on board and eventually taken to North America. In addition, the *entradas* generally omit the comings and goings of British naval vessels, which did not have to pay duties when entering the harbours of friendly nations, and which left with goods.

War usually retarded transatlantic wine shipping. By the end of the French and Indian War in America and the Seven Years' War in Europe, less than half of Madeira's ships went to British America. The British West Indies' share declined to 23 per cent during 1754–62, and Britain's North American colonies' share declined to 17 per cent in the same period. The Anglo-French conflict of the 1750s and 1760s was especially disruptive to Madeira shipping. Nearly three-quarters of the Madeira

---

[12] For the 1702–13 statistics, see Blandy, *Bolton Letters*, pp. 21–68. There are no letters for 1711, and only those for January 1714 have survived. The 1695–1700 shipping has been similarly analysed in detail by José Manuel Azevedo e Silva in 'A navegação e o comércio vistos do Funchal nos finais do século XVII', in *ACTAS III. Colóquio Internacional de História da Madeira* (Funchal, 1993), 353–82, especially tables II–III, and figs. 1–2, on pp. 363–4 and 381–2. Of the 292 ship departures Bolton noted, 44 per cent left for the British West Indies, another 10 per cent left for British North America (all New England), and 5 per cent for Pernambuco (although four-fifths of the Brazil ships moved on to the Cape of Good Hope, Madagascar and India). In contrast, some 12 per cent of the ships went directly to England and Ireland, and more than 4 per cent to Portugal.

[13] The statistics in this and the paragraphs that follow are culled from the Livros dos Entradas e Saidas, Provedoria e Junta da Real Fazenda, kept at the Arquivo Nacional da Torre do Tombo, Lisbon. They have been previously analysed by João José Abreu De Sousa, *O Movimento do porto do Funchal e a conjuntura da Madeira de 1727 a 1810. Alguns Aspectos* (Funchal, 1989). Maria De Lourdes de Freitas Ferraz has calculated exports from these records from 1780 to 1800: *Dinamismo sócio-económico do Funchal na segunda metade do século XVIII* (Lisbon, 1994). Their calculations, however, are marred by numerous computational errors. More significantly, they group regional areas together in such a way as to hide more than they reveal.

shipping fleet was British or American owned. Not surprisingly, few vessels came to Madeira from Europe, on account of the high freight rates, high seamen's wages, and high insurance premiums induced by the threat of capture or destruction on the high seas. Throughout the war, but especially near the end, the trade from America was 'very inconsiderable' on account of the cost of shipping and especially of American 'vessels being forced into the transport service'.[14]

The Treaty of Paris that was signed in February 1763 ushered in a return to shipping patterns that had prevailed nearly twenty-five years before. The total share of Madeira ships going to British and European possessions in the Americas rose to 76 per cent, slightly more than had prevailed in the years before 1739; but the share going to the British West Indies reached a new all-time high – 43 per cent – and the share going to British North America returned to its pre-war level – 24 per cent. In large measure, this efflorescence emanated from the opening of new lands to the British, in the Caribbean and the parts of America wrung from the Indians in backcountry New York, the lands west of the Appalachians, and the Floridas, as well as from the maintenance of a British standing army in the backcountry.[15]

The years of the American Revolution witnessed a drastic decline in all wine exports to the British Caribbean, in large measure because of the increase in the interruptions to transatlantic communication and in the hazards to transatlantic shipping. According to the *saida* records, which begin in 1779, the British West Indies' share of wine exports fell to 26 per cent during the war years.[16] The share of Britain's thirteen mainland

---

[14] Thomas Newton to Adoniah Schuyler, 22 January 1756, Thomas Newton letterbook, Madeira Wine Company Archives. That the number of ships declined did not necessarily mean that the amount of wine shipped and consumed dropped with it. Especially in the Seven Years' War, 'the number of troops and also the many privateers . . . fitted out from' New York and other large ports was seen to have increased the consumption of Madeira wine. This was especially true after Spain declared war against Britain, Britain prohibited Canary wines from being imported into America, and Portugal declared war against France and Spain. Thomas Newton to Malcolm Campbell, 14 October 1756, Thomas Newton letterbook, Madeira Wine Company Archives; Newton & Gordon to John Provoost, 17 June 1762, to John Tweedy, 27 June 1762, Newton & Gordon letterbooks, vol. III, fos. 2, 10; and Alexander Hamilton to George Spence, 13 December 1758, letterbook of assorted Leacock letters, Casa Branca, Funchal.

[15] Thomas Newton to Newton & Gordon, 27 November 1762, box 3, bundle 1764–5, Cossart & Gordon Papers, Liverpool University Archives, documents the efforts of one officer in the army who 'sold out' and became involved with some of the 'principal Gentlemen' in New York City in 'a grand scheme of trade up in the Back Settlements'. The officer intended 'to do a good deal in the Madeira way'.

[16] A comparison of *entradas* and *saidas* for the years 1779–82 reveals that the share of wine exports taken by British America was somewhat greater than the share of wine ships that went to it, a fact which is attributable to the unusually large purchases of the military. Of the 421 departures in these four years, 16 per cent went to the British West Indies and 13 per cent to mainland British North America.

Table 5.2. *Wine exports from Madeira, 1779–1807 (pipes of 110 gallons)*

	1779	1780	1781	1782	1783	1784	1785	1786	1787	1788	1789	1790	1791	1792	1793
British West Indies	2,239	1,399	2,051	2,606	3,205		2,373	2,249	2,971	3,726	2,285	4,154	4,883	5,001	4,335
13 colonies/United States	369	3,073	2,915	1,903	2,973		1,118	568	1,695	1,961	1,402	2,647	386	1,564	2,550
Other British North America	125	0	0	0	0		0	174	187	252	228	0	0	164	218
European America	1,066	1,489	1,322	1,806	1,724		514	636	397	109	278	676	200	327	181
India, Asia and China	1,210	1,655	710	1,034	2,336		4,051	5,949	3,566	4,586	983	3,733	5,833	926	2,439
Other and none listed	2,524	1,128	895	865	1,067		1,106	307	748	365	259	767	895	918	1,102

	1794	1795	1796	1797	1798	1799	1800	1801	1802	1803	1804	1805	1806	1807
British West Indies	3,659	3,283	5,468	5,149	3,301	4,883	6,076	6,624	6,890	6,303	5,838	8,651	3,288	3,635
13 colonies/United States	3,419	3,035	2,913	2,588	1,485	386	2,307	2,231	2,369	2,927	3,549	2,468	2,342	1,301
Other British North America	195	0	341	448	374	0	165	481	291	122	449	273	49	0
European America	991	354	999	876	963	200	888	849	1,567	166	825	2,857	631	941
India, Asia and China	2,990	7,146	4,638	4,450	5,589	5,833	6,027	4,418	3,652	2,193	4,796	3,382	4,555	3,366
Other and none listed	1,430	820	893	269	363	895	1,468	1,485	2,057	1,418	2,921	2,736	7,780	8,210

Source: Livros dos Saidas (1779–1807), Provedoria e Junta da Real Fazenda, Arquivo Nacional da Torre do Tombo, Lisbon, Portugal.

colonies remained the same, but the pattern was different. All of 1779's shipments to the rebellious Thirteen Colonies, as well as two-thirds of 1780's and 1781's, went to New York City, mostly for the use of the British army and navy stationed there. Most of these shipments were managed by the Scots firm Newton & Gordon. John & James Searle and, to a lesser extent, Lamar, Hill, Bisset & Co., two Madeira firms whose partners had come from America, supplied the rebels.[17] Most colonies imported nothing from Madeira during the war.[18]

To compensate for the loss of the Caribbean markets and disruptions in the North American trade, the distributors turned eastward.[19] Island traders cultivated markets in the Persian Gulf region (Combroon and Bussora), India (Fort William, Fort St George, Bombay and Fort Marlboro) and 'that important branch of our Commerce' China (especially Canton, Limpao and Macao). Conservative firms that had previously been reluctant to enter eastern markets, even during the 1760s when these markets had grown by leaps and bounds, now accepted India contracts and developed consumer bases in that part of the world.

[17] *Saidas* for 1779, 1780 and 1781. In these three years, these three firms shipped a fifth of all island exports, and nearly as much (18.4 per cent) of all exports destined for the Thirteen Colonies. On victualling opportunities, see Newton & Gordon to Francis Newton, 25 April 1779, Newton & Gordon letterbooks, vol. IV, fo. 459. Johnston in Madeira urged both Newton and Gordon in London to waste no time in enlarging 'our acquaintance' in the West India squadron and getting 'good introductions to Navy Agents at seaports', like those William Murdoch of Fergusson & Murdoch was obtaining. On the deals Newton & Gordon struck with the Scotsman Daniel Wier, the British Commissary General stationed in New York, who was a close friend of Newton & Gordon's London correspondents Wilkinson and Gordon, see Newton & Gordon letterbooks, vol. VI, fos. 200, 208; and Daniel Wier letterbook, *passim*, NYHS and HSP. On the supply of American troops by the Hill and Searle firms, see Lewis Pintard's letters, in the Boudinot Papers, American Bible Society, New York City. On the provisioning of New York, generally, see Edward Curtis, *The Organization of the British Army in the American Revolution* (New Haven, 1926); Oscar Barck, *New York City during the War* (New York, 1931); David Syrett, *Shipping and the American War, 1775–1783* (London, 1970); Norman Baker, *Government and Contractors: the British Treasury and War Supplies, 1775–1783* (London, 1971); and Robert M. Dructor, 'The New York commercial community: the revolutionary experience', Ph.D. thesis, University of Pittsburgh (1975), ch. 4.

[18] The cessation of shipping to the thirteen colonies during the war is reflected in the bills of lading of both the Nowlan & Leacock and the Newton & Gordon firms.

[19] Some firms also turned their sights homeward. The west of England became 'more deserving of the attention of a Madeira concern'; as a result of 'the extensive manufactories spreading everywhere along the west coast and interior part of that country, opulence' was making 'rapid strides, and of course drags luxury along attendant'. Newton & Gordon to Thomas Gordon, 12 February 1787, Newton & Gordon letterbooks, vol. IX, fo. 340. See also John Leacock, Sr, to William Leacock, 16 August 1791. The Leacocks enjoyed 'no prospect of deriving any advantage from our friends or connections in America' and therefore directed their 'principal attention to cultivate those we have fixed in England and to render them permanent'. Accordingly, William Leacock paid a visit to Liverpool, Bristol and Bath.

Portuguese merchants were particularly adept at exploiting the new India trade: 'the natives', Joseph Gillis informed his partner Henry Hill in Philadelphia, had 'got much into the spirit of trading' with the subcontinent by 1783 – 'no less than 4,000 pipes having been sent annually to India, for these four years past, and all in Portuguese ships & shipped by Portuguese'. As this trade developed during the war, India, China and other settlements in Asia absorbed roughly 16 per cent of Madeira's exports. They were able to take much more, claimed the more adventurous traders.[20]

For decades, British India had taken some of Madeira's wine. The first record of an official Company purchase of a cargo occurred in 1716, when Joseph Hayward shipped Madeira wine to Fort William (Calcutta) on board the *King William*. Unlike previous cargoes of claret, Florence and mountain wines, Madeira pleased. Acting on favourable reports two years later, the Court of Directors of the East India Company ordered that 100 pipes of Madeira be shipped each year to Fort St George (Madras) and its other factories. Alongside this public trade, there flourished a vigorous private trade: space on each ship was apportioned to each member of the crew (who altogether were granted about 5 per cent of the total cargo space), individual allocations varying with rank; space was also granted to passengers. Given these restrictions on private trade, non-Company merchants who always depended on private imports were never significant players in the India market.[21] After the success of the *King William*, a taste for Madeira spread fairly rapidly. One cellar held up as a model in the 1740s contained four bottles of beer, twelve bottles of claret, and 100 bottles of Madeira.[22] In response to rising demand, a more elaborate system of procurement had evolved by the 1740s. The forts ordered wine from the directors in London, who in turn directed one or two of their ships to stop at the island for wine.[23]

After Clive's victory at the battle of Plassey (1757) and the growth of the East India Company's role in the Moghul imperial structure, the

[20] Joseph Gillis to Henry Hill, 4 April, 6 May, 26 August 1783, letterbook vol. IX, fos. 2, 14–16, John J. Smith's Collection, Hill Family Papers, HSP.

[21] *Fort William–India House Correspondence*, vol. 1, p. 465: Fort William to Court of Directors, 4 February 1750/1; Henry Love, *Vestiges of Old Madras*, vol. II (London, 1913), p. 135, nos. 2–3. As 'private' goods, Madeira wine was probably shipped to the British East Indies before 1716. William Bolton's numerous letters make passing reference to India ships anchoring before Funchal and loading wine. But 1716 marks the date when the directors began making official requests. In addition to the 'public' and 'private' trades, there flourished a 'clandestine' trade as well. I am indebted to Huw Bowen for confirming and clarifying many of these points.

[22] *Madras Dialogues* (1740–5), reprinted in Love, *Vestiges*, II, p. 330.

[23] *Fort William–India House Correspondence*, vol. I, pp. 2, 465; Fort William to Court of Directors, 4 February 1750/1, *Fort William–India House Correspondence*, vol. I, p. 465.

India market increased significantly. The Company began directing three to six Company ships per year to stop at Madeira on their voyage to the subcontinent; other extra India-bound ships came on their own. Whereas India had been a destination for only 0.6 per cent of all ships leaving Funchal in 1727–39, it had become a stop for 2.4 per cent in the aftermath of the Seven Years' war.[24] 'The want of a Madeira ship', which the directors occasionally thought dispensable, laid a Presidency 'under a very great Inconvenience, which is particularly felt by the gentlemen of the Army whose fatigues required that they should be indulged with every refreshment that can be afforded for their relief'. While 'other Wines, as Lisbon & c.', might have been had 'in lieu thereof', the foreigners who imported these wines raised their prices 'in proportion to the Necessity'. 'Immoderate rates' and the fact that Madeira wine was regarded as 'necessary to health' ensured a stop at the island.[25] During the 1760s and 1770s, 'unexpected demand' from the subcontinent was the order of the day and seriously disrupted traditional ways of doing business on Madeira. Superior wines were depleted, for instance, and inferior wines called into service. The London partners of Madeira wine firms jockeyed for the much coveted annual contracts, even if the right to supply was usually granted to those with partners previously or presently on the Court of Directors.[26]

In the decade 1783–93, the share taken by the India, China and Asia settlements (40 per cent of Madeira's exports), as well as by the British West Indies (33 per cent), rose. But the share imported by the former thirteen colonies, now the new United States, fell to 15 per cent of all exports, down from 25 per cent before and during the war. Attempts were made to return to the old familiar track. William Johnston, for one, was optimistic. He tried thwarting attempts by his firm to move into the Bombay trade with a call to return to the Americans: 'In consequence of the peace', he wrote to his partners in London, 'we look forward to America as a principal mart of our produce, and a country whence we may bring commodities to this market with more success than our importation

[24] Fort William to Court of Directors, 4 January 1754, *ibid.*, I, p. 722.
[25] Fort William to Court of Directors, 16 January, 12 November 1761, *ibid.*, vol. III, pp. 289, 358.
[26] Newton & Gordon to Robert & Alexander Maitland, 8 September 1762, to Francis Newton, 14 January, 14 May 1768, 25 January, 29 May 1775, 5 April, 25 August 1777, Newton & Gordon letterbooks, vol. III, fo. 34, vol. IV, fos. 164, 250, vol. V, fos. 436, 575, vol. VI, fos. 208, 265; Newton & Gordon to Thomas Newton, 25 March 1764, box 2, bundle 7, Francis Newton to Newton & Gordon, 14 August 1770, box 5, bundle 1770–1, Cossart & Gordon papers, Liverpool University Archives. In the 1780s, the Portuguese, especially Pedro Jorge Monteiro and Dona Guiomar, along with John Searle and James Ayres, won most of the contracts. In 1786 the Court of Directors began to sell these contracts at public auction.

has of late years been attended with'. In writing to the Bostonian John Rowe several months later, John Leacock suggested that 'the long unhappy contention of late years in America', which deprived Madeirans of 'all communication with the Continent', was the reason his firm had not written in eight years. Leacock hoped that, 'now these obstacles are removed & peace again restored', they would be 'on the same footing . . . as formerly'.[27] Johnston's and Leacock's excuses aside, most firms were reluctant to do much about returning to America. Johnston's partner Thomas Murdoch was more on the mark when he wrote:

we have not entered into a serious consequence with any person on that continent, things there being so little settled and moneys in your hands being so scarce. We have merely, to keep people in mind of our firm, dropt, at different times, a few words to those whose names only we are acquainted with at Philadelphia and Charleston. But our correspondence has been confined to hints, a sort of war of ports, and skirmishes, as was that much mismanaged one which lost Great Britain her colonies.[28]

The French revolutionary wars, which began in 1793 and, as one conflict or another, persisted beyond 1807 through 1815, seem to have had little effect on either old or new trends.[29] Exports to British America and the new United States were a majority (59 per cent) of all Madeira's exports. Exports to the United States continued at a low level (16 per cent) compared to pre-1775 shares, and those to the West Indies continued to be in excess of one-third. Exports to India, Asia and China (28 per cent) continued strong, even if they did not match the large shares of the 1780s, a continuance aided by the 1793 Charter Act which ruled that the Company must allow for up to 3,000 tons of private cargo each year.[30]

The 'dog that didn't bark' in this story is the non-emergence of the British and Portuguese home markets. Portuguese drinkers on the main-

---

[27] William Johnston to Thomas Gordon, 10 March 1783, Newton & Gordon letterbooks, vol. VIII, fo. 13; and John Leacock, Sr, to John Rowe, 30 June 1783, Nowlan & Leacock letterbook, 1781–4, Casa Branca, Funchal.

[28] Newton & Gordon to Thomas Gordon, 24 February 1785, to Hugh Moore, 30 April 1785, 22 March 1786, to James Young, 23 March 1789, to Francis Newton, 10 September 1789, Newton & Gordon Letterbooks, vol. VIII, fos. 381, 447, vol. IX, fo. 179, vol. XII, fos. 13, 133. It was not until 'the establishment of a permanent government, and the return of prosperity & cultivation' as evidenced in the lowering of 'very high prices' in America 'which precluded all probability of gain', that the firms seriously reconsidered their decision.

[29] Nor did the activities of Algerine pirates. Their marauding certainly constricted the work of Spanish merchants and for a time benefited the work of the Portuguese, although eventually the latter came to be pinched by the increase in the costs of marine insurance.

[30] Significant increases in wine exports came with the opening of new islands in the Caribbean, like Saint-Domingue, Martinique, Demerara and Trinidad, to British trade. John Leacock to William Leacock, 13 April 1796, Leacock & Sons Letterbook 1794–7, and 26 October 1801, Leacock & Leacock Letterbook 1799–1802, Leacock Papers.

land never took more than 3 per cent of the island's wine exports, and usually much less.[31] British wine-bibbers never took directly more than 7 per cent. Legal importation of foreign wine into Great Britain grew threefold over the period 1703–1807.[32] Portuguese wine (mainland wines like 'port' wine from Oporto and Carcavelos wine from Lisbon) dominated the market: some 65 per cent of all wine imported into Britain

[31] Portuguese merchants and consumers never developed a trade in or taste for Madeira wine, for many of the same reasons inhibiting British merchants and consumers sketched below.

[32] Elizabeth B. Schumpeter, *English Overseas Trade Statistics, 1697–1808* (Oxford, 1960), tables xvi–xvii. For quantitative discussion in the present study, Schumpeter's tons have been converted into 110-gallon pipes, which were the more common unit in the trade. In cumulating the wine, Schumpeter or her assistant made certain tabulation errors, and her quantities should not to be taken at face value. First, Schumpeter paid no attention to the differences in the capacity of the pipes as they were imported into the country. Nowhere in the Atlantic world was a pipe a pipe, or a ton a ton. The size of a pipe coming from Funchal could be and generally was constructed to be 10 to 20 gallons less than pipes made and shipped from Barbados or New York; the size of a Madeira pipe was also smaller than that of a Portuguese, Spanish and French pipe. Each country had its own capacity regulations and norms. As determined by local law, Antigua pipes were to contain 126 gallons, Barbados, Jamaica, Virginia and New York 120 gallons, India pipes 115 gallons, and Madeira pipes only 110 gallons. Newton & Gordon letterbooks, vol. III, fo. 305, vol. IV, fos. 36, 611, vol. VI, fo. 340, and vol. VIII, fo. 247. Even in London, the more standard volume for a pipe was 110 gallons in 1775. Johnston & Jolly to Newton & Gordon, 5 March 1763, box 3, bundle 1764–5, Newton & Gordon papers, Liverpool University Archives. There is some reason to adopt 126 as the standard, for a Law of 1706/7 (5 Anne, cap. 27, s. 17) mandated that a pipe or butt should contain 126 gallons. But there is no reason to believe that any shipper actually adhered to that standard. A more thorough recumulation would have converted each of the pipes to gallons and then reconverted the total quantity to the more modern English pipes of 126 gallons. Less possible to control for, but still important to be aware of, are two additional considerations: British merchants' chronic under-declaration of commodities which were subject to duties on their importation and over-declaration of goods which would receive bounties or drawbacks upon re-exportation; and the incidence of smuggling, since Schumpeter's figures represent only legal importations, not smuggled wines, which at times may have been significant, especially in the case of French wines early in the century. Despite the problems relating to the determination of quantity, Schumpeter's work still provides a reasonably rough guide to the relative share that Madeira enjoyed as an imported wine and is used here, although the author is undertaking a recalculation.
 As for the value of the wine, Schumpeter's work is more seriously flawed and quite useless. In essence, she relied upon the scale of the prices used by the record-keepers themselves for certain commodities; but, as in the case of all wines, these were merely official prices per unit, fixed late in the late seventeenth and early eighteenth centuries and never or seldom changed. Thus, they do not reflect (even in a gross way) market prices. In the case of certain commodities, like Madeira wine, where the price rose sharply over the course of the century and it became the Atlantic's most expensive wine, official valuations were serious understatements of the actual market value. Given this fact, it is not at all clear that wine imports 'were an insignificant item in the total' value of all imported goods or that, as T. S. Ashton claimed, they constituted 10.8 per cent of Britain's portfolio in 1700 and 2.4 per cent a century later. T. S. Ashton, 'Introduction', in Schumpeter, *English Overseas Trade Statistics*, vol. I. The matter is still unresolved. Fortunately for the present study, the value of wine imports into Britain is of secondary importance to that of their quantity.

came from Portugal proper.[33] Spain and its Canary Islands were the sources of another quarter of imports. All other countries were insignificant players: France sent only 4 per cent in claret, champagne, burgundy and cognac; Madeira 3 per cent; and Germany and Italy each just above 1 per cent.

Several factors worked against the development of the home markets. Ocean currents and wind patterns – natural phenomena that allowed vessels from Europe to sail quickly and safely to the island and on to the Americas – impeded the reverse passage from Funchal to London or Lisbon.[34] It took about as much time to go from Funchal to London directly as it did to go indirectly by way of British America if little time was spent in ports along the way. Madeira distributors warned consumers on the Continent that they had 'seldom or never any vessel direct from this [island] to London'. Port, by contrast, could be transported overland in times of peace through Portugal, Spain and France by wooden wagons or coastwise by small craft.[35] Compounding the problem in Portugal was that alternatives already existed: several locally made wines were produced in greater quantities and retailed at lower prices. Red and white port, white Carcavelos and red Lisbon were all available on the mainland for those who did not drink their own home-made supply.

Island distributors

By comparison with contemporary trading communities of any significance, the group of Madeira distributors was small. Between 1703 and 1807, at least 929 men and women assumed responsibility for buying wine from the growers, processing it, packing it, finding foreign buyers and placing it on board their ships.[36] As the trade grew over the century,

[33] It is possible that mainland figures include those of imports from the Western Islands (the Azores), but there is no mention of the inclusion and one would think that such an important source of Atlantic wine would merit its own separate entry.

[34] Admiralty Office, *Admiralty Weather Manual* (London, 1938), p. 204.

[35] Spence, Leacock & Spence to David Loudon, 14 August 1764, Spence, Leacock & Spence letterbook 1762–5, fo. 158; and Nowlan & Leacock, 19 July 1780, Nowlan & Leacock letterbook 1774–81, fo. 364.

[36] The list of 929 distributors is compiled from several sources. In the *Livros dos entradas e saidas*, one finds the names of the *consignatarios*, the men or women to whom dry goods, fish, flour, rice and the like were consigned for either sale on the island or re-export to Lisbon, Portuguese Africa or Asia, or Brazil and who also managed the export of the wine. These references are not complete: the *entradas* cover only the years 1727–1807, and the *saidas* do not cover even these years; the records for 1733–68 appear to have been destroyed or lost. The problem of missing export records is surmountable, however. Since every wine exporter was involved in importing other goods, the problem is minor – all exporters are included – although some non-exporters may also be included, for not all importers were exporters. More serious are other considerations: first, before 1727, *entradas* do not exist, and *saidas* exist only for 1721–3; and, second, these records usually list only heads of mercantile firms or prominent members. Junior partners or sleeping

the number of merchants in the community rose more than threefold: in 1721, there were 63 exporters; in 1807, 202. New entrants to the community, especially in the last third of the century, transformed the conduct of the trade.

The British and British American Madeira merchants came from the intermediate ranks of their birthplace societies. Most were younger sons, having come from middling families which, if they could help financially at all, provided only for the eldest. Many had already moved from their birthplaces and the farms and villages where they had grown up; some had spent time in large port towns, regional capitals like Dublin, capital cities like Edinburgh, or the great metropolis London; a few had roamed even farther afield.

Walter, Robert and John Scott, who arrived in the late 1720s and early 1730s, were younger sons in one of the borders' larger clans, the Scotts of Berwickshire.[37] Near neighbours, Andrew, Francis and Thomas Newton were also younger sons, in their case the children of an unemployed minister living in Earlston, Berwickshire. Both having fought on the losing side in the 1745 Jacobite rebellion, Andrew Newton fled to Virginia and established himself as a merchant, and Francis Newton sought anonymity in the City of London, where he found work as a clerk in a counting-house for several years and from which he moved to Madeira three years later; with their assistance, their younger brother Thomas on coming of age set himself up as a dry goods merchant, first in London and later New York, until near-bankruptcy in the mid-1750s caused him to join his elder brother Francis in Madeira.[38] John Leacock was even less

senior partners in large firms are not routinely mentioned. The latter is less serious a problem for Portuguese firms, which were always small. Thus, the corps gleaned from the Funchal customs records needs to be augmented. This can be done with miscellaneous information entered into mercantile and governmental records. Yet, even when augmented, the final tally of 929 merchants is only a lower estimate.

[37] Walter Scott was christened on 3 February 1706 and his brother Robert Scott on 11 February 1708, in Duns. They first appear in the *saidas* on 15 December 1728, and 25 August 1729, respectively. *Livros dos saidas*, no. 252, fos. 53, 69, Arquivo Nacional da Torre do Tombo, Lisbon. A younger brother John arrived several years later and took over the management of Robert's business when Robert moved to London in 1736 or 1737. On the Scotts, see PRO, CO137/17 *sub* 29 May 1737; K. G. Davies, ed., *Calendar of State Papers (Colonial): 1737* (London, 1963), vol. XLIII, *sub* 13 October 1737; Walter B. Edgar, ed., *The Letter Book of Robert Pringle*, 2 vols. (Columbia, S.C., 1972), I, p. 29 n. 8, and p. 158; PRO, Will of Walter Scott, dated 12 June 1768, proved 2 July 1776, Will of Robert Scott, dated 11 April 1769, proved 1 June 1771, PROB 11; and Arthur H. Plaisted, *The Manor and Parish Records of Medmenham, Buckinghamshire* (London, 1925), pp. 139–40. John Scott, who eventually settled in York, died intestate in 1775.

[38] Newton & Gordon Scrapbook, vol. I, Cossart papers. In Earlston, Andrew Newton was christened on 3 June 1708, and Francis Newton on 22 March 1713. Thomas Newton is listed in *A Complete Guide* (London, 1749); he died intestate in New York between November 1766 and June 1769. Newton & Gordon 1764–74 ledger, Madeira Wine Company, Funchal. Francis Newton died in London after December 1809. Newton & Gordon letterbooks, vol. XXXII, fo. 168, Cossart papers.

well provided for in childhood: his father died in 1736 and his mother enrolled him in Christ's Hospital, a school for orphans; five years later, the only option open to the penniless 'blue coat' was a seven-year apprenticeship to William Murdoch and John Catanach in their Madeira wine house. That is, his only chance was a long apprenticeship with a friend of a business acquaintance of his father in a land he had never seen.[39]

Some of the distributors were refugees who had left their homelands for religious reasons, like the Huguenot Peter Vallete, Jr, who fled France after the revocation of the Edict of Nantes in 1685, went immediately to England where he was granted naturalization, and subsequently established a business on Madeira, which he plied through the late 1720s, when he permanently settled in New York. Others were refugees for political reasons, like Dominick Sarsfield, Francis Newton and Alexander Gordon of Letterfourie, who had all supported the Stuart Pretenders.[40] And still others, like Richard Hill, were financial refugees, fleeing creditors. 'Necessity, not choice, drove us here', he admitted. His family was 'shunned and neglected on every side', when a series of shipping disasters and bad loans left him 'needy' in Londontown, Maryland, for it was 'no new thing for poverty and contempt to go hand in hand'.[41]

Whatever the conditions that had pushed them out, Madeira's British and American traders were profit seekers. And if they lacked economic opportunities at home or inherited wealth, they possessed the second greatest advantage an eighteenth-century merchant could have: family ties and connections.[42] They drew upon their numerous kith and kin to

---

[39] Leacock's articles of apprenticeship with Catanach (9 March 1741) are in the Leacock papers, Casa Branca, Funchal.

[40] On Vallete (or Vallette, Valette, Valet or Vallet), see *Collections of the New York Historical Society for 1893* (New York, 1894), p. 261; . . . *for 1894*, pp. 300–1; . . . *for 1895*, pp. 132–4; . . . *for 1896*, pp. 346–7. At the time Peter Vallete moved to New York, his brother moved to Jamaica and became a planter. In the late 1720s, Peter Vallete was involved in transporting skilled indentured servants from London to New York. In 1733, as part owner of the *Dolphin*, he was importing from the Isle of Man, Ireland, Madeira and Antigua, and exporting to Ireland; in 1738, he was importing from Ireland and exporting to Madeira. A decade later, he was appointed the manager of the lottery for the College in New York. Isaac N. P. Stokes, ed., *The Iconography of Manhattan Island*, vol. IV (New York, 1922), pp. 510, 601; PRO, CO5/1225. He died in December 1752. *The New-York Post Boy*, 18 December 1752. Dominick Sarsfield, of County Cork, who died in 1767, fled Ireland during the Williamite wars of the 1690s and settled in Madeira. John Burke, *A Genealogical and Heraldic Dictionary of the Landed Gentry*, vol. II (London, 1858), p. 1,062.

[41] John J. Smith, ed., *Letters of Doctor Richard Hill and His Children* (Philadelphia, 1854), pp. 19–22, 36, 56, 83, 90.

[42] The education of the distributors is difficult to ascertain. All were clearly literate and apparently received primary instruction. Some twenty-three received secondary education. Eight attended university. At least two received medical training and worked as doctors – Richard Hill and Thomas Lamar. And three served in the army or navy.

man their counting-houses with partners and clerks, represent them in established markets, introduce them to customers and agents in new markets, and ship their goods.

Overall, the island distribution of the group of 929 wholesalers was nearly evenly split between Portuguese (58 per cent) and non-Portuguese (42 per cent). Merchants of British origin constituted the largest share of the non-Portuguese distributors – 333 (36 per cent of the total). English merchants dominated the British community, with Scots, Irish and British American colonists (later citizens of the new United States), all of whom were of British origin, providing smaller numbers – 7 per cent, 3 per cent and 4 per cent, respectively.

The island's merchant group tripled over the century and, as it did so, the roles played by the different national groups changed. The Portuguese dominated the trade before 1703, but by the 1750s and 1760s the most important traders were the British, and the Americans were gaining in strength, aggressively capturing home markets. Of the 106 ships that departed Funchal for New York, New Jersey, Pennsylvania, Maryland and Virginia in 1750–3, for instance, nearly half were handled by Hill; on a smaller scale, Searle, who had just arrived on the island, was managing all exports to New Jersey. By 1807, the British had regained much of their former shipping clout, but only over certain routes, and the end of the period under study found the British controlling some markets and the Americans holding on to others.

For the most part, the Portuguese were pushed aside as the trade developed. The Portuguese on the island, who never allowed the British to own land and thus produce wine, persisted as the growers. Whether tenants or landlords, each inhabitant sold and shipped on his or her own account, in addition to selling what remained to European or American distributors. But Portuguese distribution is a red herring, for this was almost always small and erratic. The preponderance of the Portuguese in the market (58 per cent of the wholesalers) is thus an illusion, for the bulk of them never shipped more than two or three cargoes. The Portuguese were vineyard owners and workers; in contrast, and with very few exceptions, the sole reason the British were on the island was to trade. Compounding the situation was the insularity of the British in their relationships with the 'natives': they did not normally form business alliances or partnerships with the Portuguese; they did not intermarry; and they did not generally mix socially. Their approach to the hosts did little to break down the divide raised by the barrier to owning land.

In 1721, the earliest year for which there are reliable records, there were sixty-three exporters, of whom nine were British and all but one of the rest were Portuguese. Six years later, at least 160 exporters lived and worked on the island. A substantial British presence really began at mid-century, following the War of Austrian Succession, and that of the Americans can be dated to the heady investment period that followed the close of the Seven Years' War. In the period 1748–74, numerous British and American mercantile small fry swarmed to the island to establish a house, and many a sea captain thought himself capable of becoming a wine merchant. Still, by 1768, when the merchant group had grown to 216, the Portuguese still formed the overwhelming majority of the merchants (80 per cent) and the Britons still less than a sixth. Among the latter, Scots had assumed a fairly strong position, forming more than a third of British residents, and six British Americans had joined their ranks.[43] Continental Europeans had become a presence in the trade: the Danish, Dutch, French and Spanish had all established houses on the island. The greatest changes in the ethnic composition of the merchant body happened towards the end of the period under study. Even though the size of the community fell to 202 merchants in 1807, the British and Americans increased their numbers. Now the market was managed by 126 Portuguese and 67 British and American distributors.

These numbers somewhat understate the strength of the British merchants. As table 5.3 shows, the ten largest merchants of 1727, 6 per cent of the merchants, exported 70 per cent of the wine (6,418 pipes). English exporter Charles Chambers shipped a third of all exports: 3,085 pipes. There was only one Portuguese merchant among the ten largest – Marcos Gônçalves Rocio – the second biggest exporter with 1,137 pipes (13 per cent). All the other large exporters were English. Thus, over half (58 per cent) of Madeira wine exports was managed by nine British men.[44]

In 1768, the top ten merchants still garnered 68 per cent of the trade; they exported 4,699 pipes that year. No one trader dominated as Chambers had at the beginning of the century: the largest merchant, James Denyer, shipped only 13 per cent. The British continued to dominate. Among the ten largest exporters was one Portuguese – Paulo Teixeira Pinto, the sixth largest exporter; he shipped 358 pipes, 5 per cent of the total. The nine Britons of the ten largest exporters in 1768 managed 63

---

[43] The Americans included Marylanders James Jenkins, Thomas Patten and Joseph Gillis, all of Lamar, Hill, Bisset & Co.; New Yorkers John Searle and James Ayres; and another Marylander Henry Cock. The representation of Quakers and Huguenots was exceptionally high, out of all proportion to the general population.

[44] The 1727 statistics are similar to the 1721 statistics. In the earlier year, 67 per cent of all wine exports were handled by three British citizens: the Huguenot Peter Vallete (32 per cent), Richard Miles (28 per cent) and James Pope (7 per cent).

Table 5.3. *Top exporters of wine in Madeira*

Year	Rank	Merchant	Pipes	Share of total export (%)
1727	1	Charles Chambers	3,085	33.7
	2	Marcos Gônçalves Rocio	1,137	12.5
	3	James Pope	559	6.1
	4	Richard Miles	510	5.6
	5	Benjamin Bartlett	304	3.3
	6	Pantaleao Fernandes	291	3.2
	7	Anthony Lynch	194	2.1
	8	John West	169	1.8
	9	William Goddard	96	1.0
	10	John Bisset	76	0.8
1768	1	James Denyer	899	13.0
	2	David Taylor	851	12.3
	3	Thomas Loughnan	606	8.7
	4	James & John Murdoch	405	5.8
	5	James Ayres	368	5.3
	6	Paulo Teixeira Pinto	358	5.2
	7	James Duff	325	4.7
	8	Joseph Gillis	320	4.6
	9	John Searle II	294	4.2
	10	Andrew Donaldson	273	3.9
1807	1	Newton, Gordon, Murdoch & Scott	1,985	11.0
	2	Gordon, Duff & Co.	1,880	10.5
	3	Phelps, Page & Co.	1,548	8.6
	4	Murdoch, Yuille & Wardrop	1,043	5.8
	5	Colson, Smith & Robinson	1,039	5.8
	6	Monteiro & Co.	951	5.3
	7	George & Robert Blackburn	788	4.4
	8	Correia de Franca	768	4.3
	9	Scott & Co.	763	4.2
	10	Christopher & William Lynch	685	3.8

Source: Livros dos Saidas (1727, 1768, & 1807), Provedoria e Junta da Real Fazenda, Arquivo Nacional da Torre do Tombo, Lisbon, Portugal.

per cent of the exports. Among the nine, Scots managed 28 per cent of the exports, and Americans 9 per cent. In 1807, the island's ten largest wine exporters still handled nearly two-thirds of the trade (11,449 pipes, or 64 per cent). Two Portuguese firms – Monteiro & Co. and Correia de Franca – were among the ten, sharing 10 per cent of the trade between them. Eight British firms – four primarily Scottish, three English and one Irish – managed over half of all exports (54 per cent).

Since the Revolution, the British had stopped the advance of the Americans. Henry, Valentine and Robert Cock of Maryland, James

Jenkins of Philadelphia, and George and Thomas Patten of Maryland, American merchants whose firms had mushroomed in the heady days of the 1760s and 1770s, had been folded into British firms. Other firms unravelled in the natural course of family business interests, like the three-generation house of Lamar, Hill, Bisset & Co., when the third generation partners decided to diversify their activities and remain at home in Philadelphia. Still other firms collapsed from financial imprudence, as was the case with the houses managed by John Searle III and John Colpoys, who escaped their creditors in 1798 by fleeing – Searle to the Cape of Good Hope and Colpoys to Ireland – and Searle's cousin the American consul John Marsden Pintard, whose disastrous financial and commercial speculations forced him to close up shop and return to Philadelphia and New York in 1799. In 1807, only six or seven American merchants were at work on the island. Like George Day Welsh, a Philadelphian whose sea captain father had once plied the waters between Philadelphia and Madeira, they often had to ally themselves with British firms.[45]

British and British American dominance was more pronounced in shipping. In 1727, 52 per cent of the ships whose *entradas* and *saidas* included listings for nationality were British ships; 40 per cent were Portuguese. By 1768, some 87 per cent were British; only 5 per cent were Portuguese. By the close of the period under study, the Portuguese had regained their footing, commanding 31 per cent of the fleet. The share of British ships had fallen to 32 per cent. United States ships, which in 1768 had been included in the British total, now assumed the lead, taking 33 per cent in their own bottoms in 1807.[46]

The nationality of the captains of these ships shows a similar pattern. In 1727, fifty-six ships dropped anchor in the road of Funchal and reported the nationality of their masters. Of these, some twenty-two had British captains, and another fourteen had British American captains; only nine had Portuguese captains. Forty years later, when reporting of captains' nationalities is nearly full, some 98 out of 194 ships were steered by British captains, and another 67 by British Americans. At the end of the period, in 1807, in witness to the increasing strength of the Portuguese, Portuguese captains from the Azores, Madeira and mainland constituted 30 per cent of the group, whereas some 32 per cent of all captains hailed from Britain and the same share from the States.

---

[45] Other Americans included Marien Lamar, John Leander Cathcart, Lewis Searle Pintard, William Steinson, William Shaw and Richard Foster.

[46] It is possible that the fall in British-owned shipping was a function of the colouring of British vessels during the Napoleonic wars, that is of British captains disguising their ships by raising the flags of other countries. But no discussion in British distributors' business correspondences documents such a practice on any significant scale.

American customers

The eighteenth century saw the elaboration of a distributional infrastructure in America. This is one of the great, as yet largely untold stories about the economic development of British America and later the United States. Ports were built and expanded; shops and markets were set up; agency relationships were formed; commercial tracts and newspapers were published; roads were built and improved; distributors increased and spread out across the land; and an immense variety of goods were brought from Calcutta, Hamburg, Bristol and Madeira to people in Boston, Lancaster, Savannah and Kingston.[47] The parallel transformative effect was not felt as greatly in Britain at the time, in part because most areas of England began the century with usable riverine and coastal transport systems in place; over the course of the century, the systems were greatly enhanced with the addition of numerous canals, lighthouses and harbours and the dredging and straightening of rivers, and their model was replicated in Scotland and Ireland. But the effect of transport improvements in Britain, while incalculable, was nowhere near so profound as similar changes in America, where few such structures existed at the outset of the period.[48]

[47] Consider the case of Lancaster, Pennsylvania. The town was founded in 1730. It had thirty-eight merchants in 1759, twenty-two merchants in 1770, and twenty-one merchants in 1789. The decline in the number of merchants (who were really little more than shopkeepers) has been attributed to 'the increasingly extensive operations of a handful of large wholesalers and retailers who were able to engross the bulk of the trade of town and country'. Jerome H. Wood, *Conestoga Crossroads: Lancaster, Pennsylvania, 1730–1790* (Harrisburg, 1979), p. 97. What happened in Lancaster occurred in nearly every community in America. Robert L. Meriwether, *The Expansion of South Carolina, 1729–1765* (Kingsport, Tenn., 1940); R. Eugene Harper, *The Transformation of Western Pennsylvania, 1770–1800* (Pittsburgh, 1991); and Ruth L. Higgins, *Expansion in New York* (Columbus, Ohio, 1931). With respect to both speed and cost, significant transformations in the transport of bulk goods over long distances did not occur until after the war of 1812; yet, incremental changes in the building and improvement of roads and canals by chartered corporations and private joint-stock corporations and the introduction of steamboats replacing pole-driven flatboats in 1807 were not insignificant. Charles G. Sellers, *The Market Revolution: Jacksonian America, 1815–1846* (New York, 1991), pp. 342–5; and Ronald Shaw, *Canals for a Nation* (Lexington, Ky., 1990), pp. 1–24.

[48] William Albert, *The Turnpike Road System in England, 1663–1840* (Cambridge, 1972); Eric Pawson, *Transport and Economy: the Turnpike Roads of Eighteenth-Century Britain* (London, 1977); John Armstrong and Philip Bagwell, 'Coastal shipping', in Derek H. Aldcroft and Michael J. Freeman, eds., *Transport in the Industrial Revolution* (Manchester, 1983), pp. 142–76; Theo Barker and Dorian Gerhold, *The Rise and Rise of Road Transport, 1700–1990* (Cambridge, 1993), pp. 8–34; D. F. Harrison, 'Bridges and economic development, 1300–1800', *EcHR*, 2nd ser., 45 (1992), 240–61; and T. C. Barker, 'The beginnings of the canal age in the British Isles', in L. S. Pressnell, ed., *Studies in the Industrial Revolution* (London, 1960), pp. 1–22. Scotland and Ireland witnessed significant improvement in transport services only in the third quarter of the eighteenth century. Jean Lindsay, *The Canals of Scotland* (Newton Abbot, 1968). It might be argued

Of course, this great structural transformation was not the way the situation presented itself to the Madeira wine merchants. Their problem was to sell their wine. In solving that problem, they found a number of individually small, occasion-specific, but highly workable solutions – some less formal and structured, and some more so. In any case, the results belie the model of rude self-sufficiency often applied to America by later historians, and speak to the extent of connections that bound the emerging Atlantic community together.

Madeira wine was the premier beverage imported into the thirteen colonies and the United States throughout the eighteenth century. Between 1700 and 1775, 64 per cent of all wine imported into the area that became the United States came from Madeira.[49] Separation from Great

that if wine was seldom conveyed by road, then the improvement of road transport bears little on the distribution of the commodity. But such was not the case. London, Winchester, Edinburgh and Ayr retailers all suggested that wine retailers in Great Britain preferred road transport to coastwise distribution. On short journeys, it probably saved money. On longer jaunts via common and private carriers it saved more money: it was fast and reliable, and retailers valued the perishability of the commodity and the urgency with which it was desired by the consumer over the higher transport costs. Moreover, wine shipments to British consumers were generally made in small lots to prevent its deterioration and, as a relatively expensive luxury good, to prevent breakage. Only when wine was being re-exported from London to a Glasgow or Liverpool wholesaler in large bulk was coastal transport a desideratum. Almost as a rule, the lightest goods of the highest value often went via road carriers. Contrary to what Armstrong and Bagwell, 'Coastal shipping', p. 143, assert, wine in the eighteenth century was one of these commodities.

[49] During the colonial period, only 10 per cent came from the Canaries, and 7 per cent from the Azores. Wines from the Portuguese mainland, which had dominated the market of England and Wales, comprised only 0.3 per cent, and wines from the Spanish mainland slightly more – 1.3 per cent. Lastly, 'other' wines included French, Italian and those listed simply as 'wines' and constituted 17 per cent; the greatest share of these were of the last. Madeira reigned chief among wines in all years but 1754, 1761, 1762 and 1765.

For some colonies for certain periods, it is possible to reconstitute a wine and spirits portfolio and track the changes in its composition. Given the incompleteness in the coverage of existing records, such agglomeration is not possible for each colony. Yet it is possible to cumulate all entries for wines imported into British America between 1700 and 1775 and obtain a summary statement of colonial consumer preferences. The entries appear in the Naval Office shipping lists, quarterly accounts of all ships entering and leaving colonial ports which were kept by naval officers appointed by the Treasury and resident in the ports. Although they do not contain entries for all approved customs ports, or for all years, or for all quarters in those years when entries have been entered in some quarters, or on occasion certain categories of information, the lists can be combined into a more or less summary report. The following lists at the PRO have been used in the construction of the present tally: New Hampshire (1724–5, 1727, 1742–3, 1745–9, 1751–5, 1757–64, 1766–9), Massachusetts (1716–19, 1752–65), New York (1713–43, 1748, 1751, 1753–5, 1763–4), New Jersey (1723–7, 1733, 1739–41, 1743–51, 1754–5, 1757–9, 1763–4), Virginia (1700–4, 1726–59, 1768–9), and South Carolina (1717–18, 1724, 1731–2, 1734–8, 1752–3, 1757–60, 1762–3, 1766, 1768–72): New Hampshire (CO5/967–8), Massachusetts (CO5/849–51), New York (CO5/1222–8), New Jersey (CO5/975, 1035–6), Virginia (CO5/1446–7), South Carolina (CO510–11), Georgia (CO5/710), and East Florida (CO5/573). Analysis of the Naval Office Shipping Lists for the British West Indian ports provides similar percentages. Jamaica (CO142/15–19), St Christopher (CO243/1/15 and T1/512), Antigua (T1/152) and Grenada (CO106/1).

Britain moderated this trend. In the years for which import data have survived – 1789 to 1806 – Madeira wine fell from 31 per cent of the wines imported into the United States in 1789–90, to 8 per cent in 1805–6, averaging about 11 per cent throughout. Wines from other wine-producing countries, like Spain and France, were now regularly imported: sherry, St Lucar, burgundy and champagne, for instance, came into vogue, once Britain's restrictive mercantile regulations no longer frustrated their entry. Indeed, in half of the years between 1793 and 1807, the quantity of sherry imported exceeded that of Madeira. Nevertheless, despite the greater variety of wines and the stiff competition raised by sherry, Madeira remained the single greatest wine import; given the high market price, its share of the value of all wines was unmatched.[50]

Some colonies and states imported well above the average: 84 per cent of the wine New Yorkers imported in the eighteenth century was Madeira; similarly, 77 per cent of Virginians' wine was Madeira. After the Revolution, some states remained relatively committed to Madeira: 45 per cent and 46 per cent of the wines imported into New York and South Carolina, respectively, were Madeira in 1789–91. The role of New York was doubly important. Not only did its inhabitants acquire a reputation for drinking a lot of the wine, but its merchants also became the leaders in developing a trade with the interior, especially the Northwest Territory. Not all colonies and states took such large amounts. Colonial Massachusetts, for instance, with its flourishing fish trade and its strong ties to southern Europe and the Atlantic wine islands (not just Madeira but also the Azores and Canaries) imported over a third of its wine from the Azores; another eighth came from the Canaries; only a fifth came from Madeira. After the Revolution, just over a fifth of the state's wine imports were still Madeira.[51]

The local competition, wine made from native grapes, was not successfully introduced until 1807.[52] Americans distilled brandy, whiskey and cider and brewed beer, of course, and these were widely drunk, especially

---

[50] All Portuguese wines – port, Lisbon, Madeira and Azores – declined. The greatest increases over the period 1789–1806 occurred with French wines, rising from 2 per cent to 31 per cent. *American State Papers: Documents, Legislative and Executive, of the Congress of the United States*, vol. VII (class IV): *Commerce and Navigation*, vol. I (Washington, D.C., 1832), *passim*. Compared with other wines, re-exports of Madeira wine were high in 1790–1 (70 per cent), 1791–2 (39 per cent) and 1792–3 (21 per cent). After 1793, re-exports of Madeira wine averaged 4 per cent of total wine exports. In 1793–1806, Madeira re-exports constituted 26 per cent of Madeira imports. The figures for values closely parallel those digested by Adam Seybert for net imports for each calendar year between 1795 and 1800. *Statistical Annals* (Philadelphia, 1818), p. 260.
[51] *American State Papers*, pp. 36, 194–203. State-by-state accounts survive only for 1789–91.
[52] Thomas Pinney, *A History of Wine in America: from the Beginning to Prohibition* (Berkeley, 1989), pp. 118–22.

in rural regions. Although it is hard to be precise about such things, they were the drinks most commonly drunk by men and women outside the cities and towns. Since America was, even at the time of the Revolution, more than three-quarters rural, the size of the home-made drinks market was substantial. Cider was usually produced in the home or on the farm. Beer could be produced in the home, but more often was made by a local brewer; only in the last third of the century did it become common to import beer from Wales or the West Country.[53] Nevertheless, in the eighteenth-century American diet, wine was a commonplace. It was not always so. Some wine was stowed on English ships bound for America as early as the 1630s, and some early New England merchants' accounts and letters contain references to the importation of small amounts of wine after 1660.[54] But there were no significant channels for distributing imported wines and spirits before 1700. Unlike England, where a trade in French wines (mainly from Gascony) had flourished from at least the late twelfth century onwards, America had developed only a rudimentary wine distribution system in the port cities and some county seats by 1700. The situation was even ruder in the new and fledgeling inland markets that were springing up after 1700.[55] As a result, while Madeirans encountered competition from French, Italian, Spanish and other Portuguese merchants in London and the outports, as well as from their agents and

[53] On the production of and market for beer and cider, see Sarah F. McMahon, 'A comfortable subsistence: the changing composition of diet in rural New England, 1620–1840', *WMQ*, 42 (1985), 42–3; and Percy W. Bidwell and John I. Falconer, *History of Agriculture in the Northern United States, 1620–1860* (Washington, D.C., 1925), p. 16. Yet, contrast the account provided by Joseph Bennett in 1740, wherein he notes that, while 'no good beer' was to be found anywhere in New England, Madeira wine and rum punches were 'the liquors they drink in common'. 'The history of New England, 1740', MSS Sparks 2, Houghton Library, Harvard University.

[54] On the importation of wine into seventeenth-century Massachusetts, see James Savage ed., *The History of New England from 1630 to 1649, by John Winthrop, Esq.*, vol. II (Boston, 1826), p. 95; *A Volume relating to the Early History of Boston containing the Aspinwall Notarial Records from 1644 to 1651* (Boston, 1903), p. 296; John Josselyn, *An Account of Two Voyages to New-England*, 2nd edn (London, 1675), in *Collections of the Massachusetts Historical Society*, 3rd series, vol. III (Boston, 1833), pp. 213–353. One 1680 partnership agreement between Samuel Shrimpton and Stephen Wesendonck established a firm 'in the trade and secret of making & managing' Rhenish, Canary, French, and Passado wines. Shrimpton was to buy the wines, and Wesendonck to blend and package them (Miscellaneous Bound Manuscripts Additional, Massachusetts Historical Society, Boston). Salem Captain George Corwin's Boston warehouse, for example, contained several pipes of Madeira wine in it at the time of his death in 1685 (George F. Dow, ed., *An Inventory . . . of Captain George Corwin* (Salem, 1910), p. 8). On New York's wine imports, see 'Jacobus Van Cortlandt's shipments from the port of New York, 1699–1702', *New York Historical Society Quarterly Bulletin*, 20 (October 1936), 113–21. By 1700, the revenues of New York depended 'chiefly' on duties on 'Wines at the Maderas' and spirits. Edmund B. O'Callaghan, ed., *Documents relative to the Colonial History of the State of New-York*, vol. IV (Albany, 1854), p. 600.

[55] Margery K. James, *Studies in the Medieval Wine Trade* (Oxford, 1971), ch. 5.

correspondents in inland British market towns, they encountered a largely unexploited commercial field in the Americas. There, the population
was growing by leaps and bounds, and rising incomes were the marvel of
the western world. As for wines, America was a relatively untapped
market.

The earliest distribution channels were individual, informal and irregular. In some cases, individual consumers struck up commercial relationships with wine-trading houses in Madeira.[56] These customers were
usually the wealthiest in their communities. Elite urban merchant families like the Hancocks annually requested two and sometimes four pipes
from Madeira, regardless of price, which they used in their home. They
also ordered a pipe or two of 'the very best Madeira wine' for their friends
and peers: Thomas Hancock, for example, did this in 1759, for Massachusetts' governor; his nephew John Hancock did the same in 1767 for
its treasurer, and two pipes for his friends John and Jonathan Amory,
wealthy Boston merchants who at the time were strangers to Madeira's
distributors. The Hancocks also purchased in bulk for resale: in the same
year that he placed the Amorys' order, John ordered six pipes that he
then resold to several Boston public houses 'where the Best Company
resorts'.[57]

Although they were deployed everywhere in early America, individual
contacts became most important to wine distribution in riverine economies, such as those of Maryland, Virginia and North Carolina, where the
rich and powerful inhabitants lived and worked along major waterways
stretching deep into the interior. If they existed at all, public amenities –
warehouses, stores, inns, ordinaries and fairs – were scattered across the
colony or state, and so provided no easy market point for resale by
overseas traders. More often than not, the Madeirans and their agents
bypassed interior sites and moved along the rivers into the parishes and
counties, focusing their efforts on individual householders and plantation
owners. If and when they pushed beyond city or riverside locations (and
this was seldom), Madeira merchants exploited their ties to back country
people to whom they were bound by religion, such as Maryland Quakers,
or Carolina and New York Huguenots.

Only slightly more elaborated than individual exporters shipping
to individual consumers, and certainly less elite a mechanism, were
wagon-train operators who would take anything for a price, packhorse

---

[56] See, for example, Robert Carter to John Hyde, 26 May 1729, Robert Carter to Micajah
Perry, 2 July 1729, Robert Carter Letterbook, fos. 62, 77, Virginia Historical Society,
Richmond.
[57] John Hancock to Lamar, Hill, Bisset & Co., 20 January, 12 November 1767, Hancock
Papers, Special Collections, Harvard Business School, Boston. After the Revolution,
Lamar, Hill, Bisset & Co. resumed their shipment of two pipes per year.

traders and itinerant pedlars – workers whose employment depended heavily on the improvement of the roads and gradual westward expansion. Their means were often insufficient to purchase and transport whole barrels of wine; but the few surviving lists of goods they sold indicate that a bottle or case of wine was not unheard of among their wares. One pedlar was noticed for carrying two barrels of wine and some rum, as well as coffee and sugar. In the back country communities they serviced, pedlars, packhorsemen and wagoneers sold to consumers outright or to enterprising farmers, who often set up *ad hoc* retail establishments and dispensaries in their own houses and barns. The itinerants allowed such enterprisers to add a glass of wine to their offerings, alongside a dram of whiskey and cider.[58] Slowly, as the population of the back country grew and its economy prospered, their operations took on the look of the well-fixed stores, warehouses and inns, taverns and dram shops of the port towns.[59]

The proliferation of more specialized commercial services in the last third of the eighteenth century had an immense effect on wine distribution in America, as it did on the distribution of almost all consumer goods. At the beginning of the century, most people purchased wines and spirits in a tavern, ordinary or dram shop; by the end of the century, they were just as likely to buy them in a storekeeper's shop or house that doubled as a store. The storekeeper's more structured and formalized

[58] The farmer-retailers bought as readily from local county merchants and wagon-train traders as from packhorse traders and itinerant pedlars. On the wagons, see Wood, *Conestoga Crossroads*, pp. 108–9. The literature on itinerant pedlars is not extensive. See Richard R. Beeman, ed., 'Trade and travel in post-revolutionary Virginia: a diary of an itinerant peddler, 1807–1808', *Virginia Magazine of History and Biography*, 84 (1976), 174–88; Daniel H. Usner, Jr, 'The frontier exchange economy of the lower Mississippi valley in the eighteenth century', *WMQ*, 3rd series, 44 (1987), 165–92; and Daniel B. Thorp, 'Doing business in the backcountry: retail trade in colonial Rowan County, North Carolina', *WMQ*, 3rd series, 48 (1991), 400. Much work remains to be done on the packhorse trade.

[59] On the quite remarkable growth of taverns and dram shops in the towns and counties of Massachusetts, see David Conroy, 'The culture and politics of drink in colonial and revolutionary Massachusetts, 1681–1790', University of Connecticut, Ph.D. thesis (1987), p. 179. On taverns and tavern-keepers generally, also see Kym Rice, *Early American Taverns: for the Entertainment of Friends and Strangers* (Chicago, 1983); Robert Graham, 'The taverns of colonial Philadelphia', *Transactions of the American Philosophical Society*, 43 (1953), 318–25; Peter Thompson, 'A social history of Philadelphia's taverns, 1663–1800', Ph.D. thesis, University of Pennsylvania (1989); Patricia Gibbs, 'Taverns in tidewater Virginia, 1700–1774', AM thesis, College of William and Mary (1968); Anne Hedges, 'Richmond's taverns in the years 1775–1810', AM thesis, University of Richmond (1993); James W. Hosier, 'Travelers' comments on Virginia taverns, ordinaries and other accommodations from 1750 to 1812', AM thesis, University of Richmond (1964); Paton Yoder, 'Tavern regulation in Virginia', *Virginia Magazine of History and Biography*, 87 (1979), 259–78; Gretchen Sorin, 'Tavern fare comestibles in Alexandria, 1770–1810', *Northern Virginia Heritage*, 3 (1981), 3–20.

distribution approach was city centred, and it hinged on the work of an importer. Although the importer could be a ship captain or a Madeira exporter's supercargo, most commonly, an importer of wine and spirits was a merchant, usually a general merchant, who lived and worked in the largest city of the colony or state and enjoyed easy access to the sea.[60] The urban general merchant certainly imported for his own personal use, but the bulk of his purchases were for resale to other distributors – inside the city, to lesser wholesale merchants, general (and, eventually, specialized) retail storekeepers, and the proprietors of inns and their ilk; and, outside the city, to the owners of general stores and drink dispensaries who paid a visit to the city for the purpose of buying wine, spirits and 'other goods too tedious to mention'.[61] As it happened, more storekeepers than liquor-dispensers went to the city to buy from importers; many liquor-dispensers found it cheaper and easier to buy from storekeepers when the latter returned to the back country. In the city, purchasers tasted and selected the drink on site, from the pipe, hogshead or quarter-cask, either on board the ship or in the importer's counting-house, warehouse or dwell-ing-house, as prominent Philadelphians did in the cellar of Henry Hill's house on South Fourth Street. The barrel was broached, the wine tasted and, if satisfactory, bottled, and the bottles carted or carried away. As competition among importer/distributors like Hill accelerated in the last quarter of the century, they began to send their wines to the purchasers in the countryside at the importers' expense. Some firms sent personal representatives to 'go a drumming' up business and when payment was received shipped the wine via wagon. Other more aggressive retailers

[60] Two others grew in importance as sales outlets over the course of the century: the vendue masters of the city or town, and the assignees of a bankrupt. In 1766, for instance, New York had two vendue masters – Nicholas William Stuyvesant, and Moore & Lynsen – whose public auctions were held at their offices, the site of the property being sold, a coffee-house or tavern, or a dock. *New York Mercury*, 9 June 1766. Yet, even if American towns possessed the full panoply of distribution services, not all urban communities were equally attractive for an expeditious, profitable sale of wine. In 'Colonial Philadelphia and its backcountry', *Winterthur Portfolio*, 7 (1972), 168, John F. Walzer argues that as late as 1775 'Philadelphia merchants could still offer lower prices for imports, better prices for exports, better credit terms, a wider selection of imported goods, and greater dispatch in the transaction of business than Baltimore'.

[61] Inns, taverns, ordinaries and general stores spread with remarkable speed, as metropoli-tans, colonials and Indians clashed with the French during the 1750s and 1760s. Wartime food and drink demands were greater than those that could be supplied by ordinary farmers; as a result, more well-equipped, institutionalized dispensaries arose to meet them, in western Virginia, Pennsylvania and New York. The dispensaries remained to serve incoming settlers after the French and Indian War was concluded. Robert D. Mitchell, *Commercialism and Frontier: Perspectives on the Early Shenandoah Valley* (Char-lottesville, 1977), pp. 144–5. See also, more generally, Charles J. Farmer, 'Country stores and frontier exchange systems in southside Virginia during the eighteenth century' (Ph.D. thesis, University of Maryland, 1984), 2 vols.

consigned the wine to the back country retailers instead of requiring payment in advance.[62]

Over the course of the century after 1663, wine marketing and retailing slowly emerged as a principal business. But from England's medieval period and through the first 150 years of American settlement, wine selling was an adjunct to other trades. Merchants who imported wine on their own account or as agents of European entrepreneurs always imported other things as well. They were in the truest sense of the word 'general merchants'. Wine to them was a product, not a business. The *Pennsylvania Gazette*, which commenced publication in December 1728, contained only three wine advertisements in 1729 and 1730, and these hawked only 'fine wines' or 'good wine'; in 1731, one notice announced the sale by the tavern-keeper Mrs Mankin of 'very good Madera wine', and another notice advertised David Evans, another tavern-keeper, offering 'some good Rhenish wine'. Before 1737, only wine, Rhenish or Madeira were advertised. Slowly, gradually, the number of wines at market rose. In 1737, some five different retailers advertised Madeira, red port, Canary and claret; in 1738, one retailer floated Frontignan; and in 1739 one retailer hawked Florence. All of these goods were put up for sale alongside dry goods. The most common distributors of imported wines in the colonies were primarily purveyors of dry goods, perhaps because the wine islands were entrepôts for distributing British cloth to southern Europe. Cloth ships bound from London to America unloaded a portion of their cargo in Madeira and took on wine. As heavy importers of southern European fruit and salt, grocers sometimes dispensed Atlantic wines, but less frequently than dry goods storekeepers. And for obvious reasons, proprietors of inns, taverns and ordinaries distributed wine, although the dispensing of wine was only one of the many services they provided.[63]

Specialized wine traders first appeared in the newspaper advertisements, tax lists and trade directories of Philadelphia, New York, Boston and Charleston in the 1750s and 1760s, but they did not flourish until the fourth quarter of the eighteenth century. In Philadelphia, for example,

[62] Payment could be made in wagon services, barter goods or money cash. The most common form of back country payment to Philadelphia importers was in goods. Trade accounts with customers in the back country were a small fraction of those in the city or in tidewater plantation communities of the south. Wood, in *Conestoga Crossroads*, p. 103, argues that back country merchants considered the inventory, reputation and punctuality of Philadelphia merchants before selecting a house with which to do business.

[63] *The Pennsylvania Gazette*, 12 May 1737 (John Valentine), 16 November 1738 (Evan Morgan). In the first twenty years of its publication (1729–49), some twenty-one wholesalers and retailers advertised Madeira wine in *The Pennsylvania Gazette* on forty-eight separate occasions. The first mention of Madeira appeared on 22 August 1734, when seven pipes were put up at public vendue.

there was no mention of a 'wine shop' as a distinct establishment before mid-century. Not until 1753 does *The Pennsylvania Gazette* describe someone as an owner of a 'wine store': in that year, Samuel Grisley sold 'old choice Madeira wine, by the quarter cask, gallon and quart' and old Malmsey, Lisbon and white wines by the bottle, 'at his wine store, below the Jersey market, where there is a green lamp before the door'. John Mitchell opened a 'Wine, Spirit, Rum and Sugar Store' in Front Street in 1774, and his offerings testify to the greatly expanded range of the specialists: Madeira, claret, port, Lisbon, sherry, mountain, Tenerife, Fayal, Frontignan, French white, hock and red Lisbon wine; Spanish brandy; Shone's, Kenton's and Parker's London porter; Burton and Taunton bottled ale; West India and New England rum; Holland geneva; plus a wide range of oils, teas, sugars, spices and the like. Mitchell the wine merchant sold his wines 'new or old', 'dry or sweet', 'genuine', 'excellent', or 'of the best quality', by the pipe, hogshead, quarter-cask, anchor, gallon or dozen. No mention of a 'wine merchant' occurred before 1772, although that is surely what Grisley was in 1753, as well as William Braventon, who had resided in both London and Portugal and 'acquired much experience in the art and mystery of the wine trade', and who in 1753 announced that he was setting up shop as a 'vintner' (blender) and 'wine cooper' (blender and packager) – professionals that for centuries had combined the work of selling wine with blending and packaging it.[64]

During and after the Revolution, however, wine stores, cellars, merchants, coopers and vintners abound in growing number. Some

[64] *The Pennsylvania Gazette*, 13 September 1753, 26 June 1755. See also 17 May, 21 August 1773, and 11, 12 May (Bache's Wine Store), 23 November (Mitchell's Wine, Spirit, Rum & Sugar Store) 1774. Before 1775, there is no mention of a 'wine shop' or a 'wine cellar' as a retail establishment. Moreover, there is no one who advertises himself as a 'wine merchant' *per se*, although in March 1772 the German Ludwig Kuhn describes himself as a clerk who 'would suit a wine merchant best, as in Europe he has been a considerable time in that trade, as well for himself as others, and consequently is a good judge of wines'. *Pennsylvania Gazette*, 26 March 1772. Benjamin Morgan had advertised his services as a wine cooper as early as 1729. *Ibid.*, 4 March 1729. Similar specialization occurred outside Philadelphia at roughly the same time. Further west, in Lancaster, for instance, the Scot James Burd, who had previously worked as a merchant in Philadelphia, was the first to open a 'Wine Store' in 1759, in concert with his father-in-law Edward Shippen, Sr. There he sold several qualities of Madeira, which he obtained either directly from the Hill firm or indirectly from his brother-in-law Edward Shippen, Jr, and Thomas Willing in Philadelphia, as well as Tenerife and Malaga, in addition to rum, spirits, brandy and sugar. Lily L. Nixon, *James Burd: Frontier Defender, 1726–1793* (Philadelphia, 1941), p. 127; and Wood, Jr, *Conestoga Crossroads*, p. 98. Despite the push for specialization, the combination of retail services persisted, especially in non-urban or undeveloped regions. As late as 1797, the proprietor announced the sale of 'dry and wet goods', at his Spring House store, eight miles from Chestnut Hill on the road to Bethlehem. There, it was declared, 'tavern-keepers may be supplied with wines and liquors warranted free of adulteration on very moderate terms', as well as 'every article suitable for a store'. *Pennsylvania Gazette*, 31 May 1797.

eighty-nine separate individuals and firms placed advertisements relating to wine in the papers between 1775 and 1783. Later on, Clement Biddle's *Philadelphia Directory* of 1791, for instance, notes the presence of eight wine specialists: not only four described as 'wine merchant', including one who had previously worked as a merchant in Madeira, and one described as 'wine merchant and grocer', but also another as 'wine cooper' and two more as 'bottler[s] of liquors' (an occupation with tasks similar to those of a vintner). By 1811, when the *Census Directory* was published, the number had doubled: the city had at least six wine merchants, five wine coopers, five liquor stores where wine was sold, and one proprietor of a bottling cellar.[65]

Managing the Madeira trade

In the 1720s, Madeiran ships regularly set sail only for 'Carolina' (presumably South Carolina and its port of Charleston), Virginia, Pennsylvania (Philadelphia), New York (New York) and Massachusetts (Boston), as well as Barbados, Antigua, St Kitts and Jamaica. One or two ships from Madeira dropped anchor in Connecticut (New London), Rhode Island (Newport) or Bermuda; but these were rare. By the 1800s, ships regularly left the island for all the principal North American ports, plus lesser ones in Maryland (Baltimore), Massachusetts (Salem), Nova Scotia (Halifax), Newfoundland and Quebec. Even greater gains had occurred in the Caribbean. The spread of the trade to nearly every colony or possession in British America was neither random nor haphazard; there was a pattern to it. Madeira firms developed a trade with a few

[65] Clement Biddle, *The Philadelphia Directory* (Philadelphia, 1791); and Anon., *Census Directory for 1811* (Philadelphia, 1811). Doerflinger, *A Vigorous Spirit of Enterprise*, p. 77, sketches the ancillary specialization by region and by commodity at work in Philadelphia's import trading community; the process was fixed by the 1780s. For similar growth in wine specialists in other American towns and cities, see anon., *The Boston Directory* (Boston, 1789); Edward Cotton, *The Boston Directory* (Boston, 1807); William Duncan, *The New York Directory and Register, for the Year 1792* (New York, 1792); *Longworth's American Almanac, New-York Register, and City Directory* (New York, 1807); Eleazer Elizer, *A Directory for 1803* (Charleston, 1803). David Hancock, 'Markets, merchants, and the wider world of Boston's wine, 1700–1775', in Conrad Wright and Katheryn Viens, eds., *Entrepreneurs: the Boston Business Community, 1700–1850* (Boston, 1997), pp. 21–2, 28–33, documents the increase in captains and merchants shipping and trading wine in Boston and Massachusetts. The New York case was the most pronounced. Some 175 enterprisers (vendue masters, merchants, wholesalers, retailers, store owners, specialists like cork-cutters and brokers) advertised the sale of wine in New York City between 1768 and 1775; during the war, 387 individuals advertised. The average number of advertisements placed in New York City newspapers more than doubled from forty-two in the pre-war period to ninety-eight in the war period. The high level of wartime advertising was maintained after the war. Dructor, 'The New York commercial community, p. 170.

customers in a large port town, gradually increased the number of people to whom they shipped in that town, and expanded from that base to other centres in the colony and then to new colonies adjacent. On the North American mainland, firms typically began in one of three or four cities – Boston, New York, Philadelphia or Charleston – or in one of two plantation regions – the Chesapeake or the South Carolina low country.

How did they do this? Their business correspondence reveals four aspects of the way Madeira merchants managed their North American business. The merchants used personal contacts in selling – starting by making relatives and friends customers, eventually appointing agents in America and, as their houses grew, escalating to stationing resident partners there. They maintained regular conversations with their customers about the product – how it should taste and what it should look like. They coordinated multiple products and services for their customers, drawing on expertise and assistance from around the world. And they engaged in a range of marketing activities – adjusting the packaging, devising connoisseur terminology and adopting luxury pricing. In doing these things, the Madeira wine merchants used the established business techniques of their day, and modified them to sell a luxury product to discriminating, often difficult customers across more than 2,500 miles of ocean.

Madeira merchants built their businesses on personal relationships – the element of early modern commercial networks that modern business and social historians are most familiar with. The closest relationships were family, then extended kinship, even looser ethnicity and finally the merest of acquaintance that flowed from past or present proximity. Hardly a week went by in the career of a Madeira wine distributor when he or his correspondents did not make use of these connections. In this, Madeira's merchants were wholly typical of merchants of their day.

Given the extent to which Madeira's trading houses were initially built along family and kinship lines, it is not surprising that deploying familial, kin and ethnic connections was an important means of building a correspondent base. Newton & Gordon's first correspondent in Jamaica was the brother of Alexander Johnston, the Scot who first provided work in London for the Jacobite Francis Newton and later provided the capital to set up Thomas Gordon in business; of the fifty-two correspondents Newton & Gordon attracted over the next ten years, over three-quarters were either friends of their families, friends of Alexander Johnston, or other Scots.

But to succeed, a firm had to move beyond the base of family, kin and ethnic group to more extended personal and business relations. Most mid-sized and large firms realized this. 'Early attachments are always the most lasting', noted one schoolfellow of Thomas Gordon: 'They often reap much happiness in point of society, business or advancement in life'. There was 'vast advantage', for instance, to boys 'being sent to publick school'; certainly, Thomas Gordon's Mercers' School provided him with an introduction to John Corrie, James Plunderleath, Andrew Robertson and Basil Cooper – all subsequent correspondents – in much the same way that John Leacock's Christ's Hospital alumni 'network' funnelled consignments to him.[66]

Later attachments, too, were grist for the mill. After he moved to Madeira in 1756, Thomas Newton wrote a volume of letters with the intent of enlarging the orders of his firm in the New York area. He had no more tie to many of his correspondents than having lived eight years among them. Often he wrote twenty letters a day with the same message. Friendship and acquaintance were primary reasons for his calling on a customer and expecting an order in return. 'I rely on your *friendship* in giving me the preference of what you do this way', he wrote to Anthony Sarly in 1756. From his 'intimate friendship' with Malcolm Campbell, he flattered himself that Campbell would expend his 'utmost endeavours to procure me soon the consignment of a vessel & to speak to all your friends & acquaintances to give me the preference'. 'Old acquaintance' with Dr Robert Knox and 'intimate friendship' with his brother were enough to win an order. Not just any acquaintance would do, of course; some were better than others. Most firms, like Newton & Gordon, were 'ever ambitious of extending . . . connexions with gentlemen of character'. 'Character' often meant having numerous friends and being willing to share them.[67]

Two groups were especially desirable: merchants with correspondents not known to the distributor; and ship captains with contacts among the communities to which they delivered goods. Newton & Gordon, for instance, had long dealt with Alexander Stupart, a captain who annually dropped anchor in Jamaica's waters, and the firm felt it should hire him to visit the island on their behalf, delivering their shipments and gathering new orders; they did not 'know a man better calculated for . . . picking up orders among his friends'. Merchants figured as the other great catch. Thomas Newton had been 'well acquainted' with Mr. Burnett, an attorney in New York, and Burnett 'promised . . . to write to his brother in Antigua to give' the firm the preference. Prior connections sometimes overrode present relationships, as Samuel and David Bean of Jamaica

---

[66] John Corrie to Thomas Gordon, 7 January 1771, box 5, bundle 1770–1, Cossart & Gordon Papers, Liverpool University Archives.

[67] Thomas Newton to Anthony Sarly, 22 January 1756, to Malcolm Campbell, 22 January 1756, to Dr Robert Knox, 23 March 1756, to Evan Cameron, 3 June 1756, Thomas Newton Letterbook, fos. 1, 3, 7, Madeira Wine Company Archives.

informed Newton & Gordon: formerly the Beans had done business with Scott, Pringle & Cheap, but as Gordon was 'an old acquaintance', an early childhood friend from Dumfries, they thought themselves 'obliged to give' Gordon's house 'the preference'.[68]

Merchants even took advantage of the casual contacts that arose naturally in the course of travel, given the island's place in the trade winds and ocean currents. Passengers had to stay somewhere, if their ship was in the harbour for more than a few days, and the flea- and rat-infested vessels stinking of rancid food and human excrement held little allure. In an island essentially Catholic and Portuguese and a town where lodgings were anything but salubrious, they stayed with the British. The imposition on the merchant was not eased by the fact that, in the last half of the century, Madeira was becoming something of an attraction. Transoceanic voyagers came to inquire about the production of the wine, the what were thought to be 'Gothic' practices of Portuguese Catholics, and the drama of the landscape. Beginning in 1748, pamphlets and books describing the community were published. At a time when competition among merchants was increasing, the custom of distributor hospitality became established. The partners and agents overseas who had procured an order from a seaman or traveller would recommend that person and his companions to the distributor, who would house and feed them for the duration of their stay, and chaperone them on their jaunts around the island. Taking care of important customers, such as naval officers, general merchants and ship captains, was just part of doing business; but firms also extended their reach by taking care of prospective purchasers. A house like Newton & Gordon or Leacock & Sons might host as many as twelve visitors at a time, and most of these were not established correspondents.[69]

[68] Malcolm Campbell, to Francis Newton, 27 September 1756, 12 February 1759, Thomas Newton letterbook, fos. 15, 19, 50, Madeira Wine Company Archives; Samuel & David Bean to Newton & Gordon, 15 April 1760, loose letters, Madeira Wine Company Archives; Thomas Gordon to Francis Newton, 8 April, 15 May 1769, vol. IV, fos. 326, 341, Newton & Gordon to Fisher & Berney, 20 April 1789, vol. XI, fo. 41, Newton & Gordon letterbooks.

[69] For instances of hospitality, see *Letters of Doctor Richard Hill*, pp. 51, 63, 123; Gordon Brothers to James Gordon, 27 December 1761, Letterfourie papers, Buckie, Banffshire, Scotland ('6 or 7 people that lodged with me & generally 10 to 12 at dinner'); Newton & Gordon to Thomas Gordon, 20 February 1793 (Mr Span – 'our guest during his stay' – was 'a great man because a very rich man in the commercial world'), Newton & Gordon letterbooks, vol. XV, fo. 64. On top of the 'commercial' and 'social' visitors were the 'medical' visitors, who came in droves towards the end of the century, as the British and American medical community began to popularize the benefits of Madeira's climate to consumptive patients. Unfortunately, the island climate and air generally exacerbated lung problems, and most 'of the invalids who crowd this island . . . and turn many of our houses into hospitals' died there within months of their arrival. Newton & Gordon to Bond & Ryland, 9 April 1770, to Jeffrey & Russell, 1 March 1792, to Allan & Smyth, 5 December 1792, to Thomas Gordon, 15 December 1794, 5 March 1798, Newton & Gordon letterbooks, vol. IV, fos. 464, vol. XIV, fos. 114, 447, vol. XVI, fo. 193, vol. XVIII, fo. 260.

The number of visitors taking advantage of the island's hospitality grew remarkably in the 1790s, and so did the annoyance of the accidental innkeepers. 'Had we a mansion as large as Greenwich Hospital', Thomas Murdoch fumed to Francis Newton, it would have been 'insufficient to accommodate the numerous guests recommended to our attention'. Having company in the house could be 'ruination to our business', thought John Leacock, for the firm could not 'help paying some degree of attention equal to what they would meet with' from other houses. The extra expense and the extraordinary diversion 'which breaks in upon our house & its management of business' were seen as intolerable by those who were willing to speak their minds. Yet the tradition persisted into the nineteenth century, for as long as one merchant adhered to it, all did. The logic remained irrefutable: the 'behaviour & attention' that a merchant like James Murdoch lavished on all who visited him enabled him, 'by his acquaintance, to enlarge & benefit his mercantile connections'.[70]

Madeira merchants did not leave it up to their customers to come or write to them. The partners of firms visited their primary markets on a regular basis 'in order to acquire some more friends in those quarters'. Most mid-sized and large firms sent a partner to America and Britain every two or three years. In 1756, Dr Richard Hill went to America to 'drive all before him', that is, to procure orders from old and new customers and arrange for return consignments, and he stayed for two years. Gedley Clare Burges of Madeira left his sometime partner Robert Jones in London and, with Jones's letters of recommendation in his brief, set out on an elaborate 'visitation of the counties', taking in Liverpool, Dublin, Cork, Waterford and Bristol. Early the next year, his competitor George Spence of Newton & Spence made a similar journey to Scotland to drum up orders. Spence's partner Francis Newton articulated the challenge quite clearly: 'Your principal study', he hectored Spence, 'ought to be to procure orders and consignments.' In 1758, after Francis Newton parted with Spence and aligned himself with Thomas Gordon, Gordon and the London general merchant Alexander Johnston went to Bristol and Liverpool 'to procure a good deal of business' for the new firm. Given the absence of other Madeirans, they met with success. In America, Newton's brother Thomas, the third partner in Newton & Gordon, and the New York merchant John Provoost travelled to various towns in New York and New England to do the same, but with less positive results. There they encountered the likes of John Searle and

<hr>

[70] Thomas Murdoch to Francis Newton, 1 February 1790, Newton & Gordon letterbooks, vol. XII, fo. 218; John Leacock, Jr, to William Leacock, 18 October 1799, 28 October 1800, 29 May 1801, Leacock & Leacock letterbook 1799–1802, fos. 80, 206, 258, Leacock papers.

James Anderson (an agent of Andrew Donaldson), who had just arrived from Madeira and were also scouring the region with the intent of 'procuring an opening to a larger correspondence'. Even personal trips, occasioned by the death of a parent or one's marriage, were turned into vigorous attempts to expand one's portfolio of customers.[71]

As the competition to expand customer lists mounted in the 1750s and 1760s, the firms appointed part-time and later full-time agents in London, Philadelphia and New York. Eventually, they settled their own partners there to monitor commercial developments, and scout out and secure new correspondents. After Francis Newton's arrival in Madeira in 1748, for instance, he relied on his former employer Alexander Johnston to handle London concerns. But, by 1761, there were 'so many partners' of competitors 'residing in London' that Newton & Gordon began to worry. The London-based partners could devote more time and procure more orders than a part-time agent with other interests and commitments. Nearly every firm of size and ambition sent a partner to London eventually; in Newton & Gordon's case, they sent Francis Newton in 1767.[72] But it was not enough to cover only London. American ports needed to be managed personally as well. So in 1758 Newton & Gordon sent Thomas Newton to New York. After he died, Newton & Gordon made John Provoost and later Waddell Cunningham their agents (whom they referred to as 'partners'); at the end of the century, all of their 'transactions in America' went 'more or less through the hands' of their agent Robert Lenox. 'Having partners on the spot' came to be regarded as a *sine qua non* of doing business 'in the Madeira Way'.[73]

Two-way communication in the world of Atlantic commerce built the important ties that bound people together across imperial divides and roisterous waters, and transformed a collection of independent operatives

---

[71] Daniel Henry Smith to James Gordon, 25 July 1774, Letterfourie papers; Francis Newton to George Spence, 9 June 1756, 6 December 1756, 17 February 1757, Newton & Gordon letterbooks, vol. I, fos. 208, 235, 248; Gedley Clare Burgess to Michael Nowlan, 29 July 1756, Burgess & Nowlan letterbook, fo. 23; Thomas Newton to Francis Newton, 31 October, 29 November 1758, 4 September 1759, Thomas Newton letterbook, fos. 44, 46, Madeira Wine Company Archives; Thomas Newton to Newton & Gordon, 10 July 1762, box 8, bundle 1774–5, Cossart & Gordon papers, Liverpool University Archives; and Newton & Gordon to Thomas Newton, 9 June, 3 September 1763, 15 May 1765, Newton & Gordon letterbooks, vol. III, fos. 154, 193, 407.

[72] Nearly every other firm of Newton & Gordon's size, scale and ambition also sent partners to London to reside. Robert Scott, Sr, had moved there in the late 1730s, and John Pringle joined him in the late 1750s. James Gordon followed them in 1760, as did Thomas Lamar in 1762 and Charles Fergusson in 1763.

[73] Francis Newton to Waddell Cunningham, 4 July 1755, to John Provoost, 2 August 1758, Newton & Gordon to David Barclay, 6 December 1764, to John Provoost, 23 July 1766, to Mackintosh & Hannay, 8 July 1767, to Colt, Baker & Day, 11 October 1798, to William Cole, 16 August 1802, Newton & Gordon letterbooks, vol. I, fos. 165, after 281, vol. III, fo. 353, vol. IV, fos. 33, 105, vol. XIX, fo. 105, vol. XXIII, fo. 392.

into a resilient commercial infrastructure. The conversations with their customers, suppliers, agents and friends provided the Madeira traders with information, created understanding among parties, and helped build global organizations. Personal relationships provided valuable sources of information about the opening of new markets, the successes and failures of other merchants, the tastes of specific communities, local prosecution of infractions of the Navigation Acts, and the like. But the networks served other purposes as well. They helped resolve conflicts. For example, when a correspondent refused to pay the balance of his account, a distributor could draw on someone with whom he had a commercial friendship to apply personal pressure on the defaulter, or to arbitrate the dispute. The networks of commercial relationships also increased the responsiveness and flexibility of the Madeira firms. In hard times, a broad network of potential consumers helped the distributor ride out difficulties in any one market, as was the case with the India market vis-à-vis the American market. And in management crises, such as the dissolution of a firm, it allowed the partners to regroup and recapitalize with greater ease than they might have done, for it provided a pool of potential partners and capital.

The most important personal relationships were with customers, either directly or through the merchants' agents. The correspondence of eighteenth-century Madeira merchants displays a remarkable set of commercial conversations with consumers – about how the wine was made, how it was packaged, shipped and distributed, and how it was stored, displayed and consumed. Through these conversations, consumers were actively involved in the design, assessment and distribution of the product. Consumers' opinions were important in the 'invention' of Madeira wine, when a cheap, simple table wine turned into an expensive, complex and highly processed luxury product.[74]

The history of the fortification of Madeira provides one example of how consumers affected producers. The addition of brandy to Madeira began only in the second quarter of the eighteenth century; not until after considerable discussion with consumers did it become widespread. It may have been an American innovation, for one finds the first highly publicized mention of the practice in the 1743 edition of *Poor Richard's Almanac.* Ten years later, Francis Newton was the first on the island to mention adding brandy as a supplement. Newton's American customers complained that the firm's export wine had arrived acidic, which he attributed to his firm's practice of '*not* putting a bucket or two of brandy in

---

[74] The story about the conversation-influenced introduction of varietals, fortification, agitation, ageing and heating is recounted in detail in Hancock, 'Commerce and conversation', 10–26.

each pipe *as other houses do*. That the brandy 'helped' the wine was clear to most consumers by mid-century: it imparted a smooth taste to rough, sour wines; it moderated naturally sweet wines and prevented their excessive fretting; and it provided a high alcoholic punch. Today, we would say that it ensured microbiological stability, rendering impotent most bacteria and strains of yeast.[75]

Madeira wine distributors adopted the technique of fortifying their wine with brandy in response to customers. There were many palates in British America, and the firms altered their wine formulae to suit these palates. In the West Indies and the southern colonies of North America, wines of a darker hue and sweeter taste were appreciated. To satisfy Caribbean customers, Madeira distributors put less brandy in their export; sometimes, in response to requests from Caribbean planters, they left it out altogether, and sent a quarter-cask of brandy and another of *tinta* along with the wine so that it could be strengthened and coloured to taste. Buyers in Jamaica preferred sweet, dark wines, for instance, while those in Montserrat had a penchant for the scarce, light, very dry green malmsey; both had little brandy. On one occasion, after Newton & Gordon had sent dry, pale, highly brandied wine to a Jamaica doctor, the Creole returned it and requested a redder, sweeter wine with less spirit.[76] In contrast, consumers to the north asked for dryer, paler wines. In response, producers and distributors added one or two gallons more brandy than they put in Caribbean wine. South Carolinians and Virginians preferred extremely pale white wine that had been moderately fortified; Philadelphians requested golden wines with slightly more brandy and body; and New Yorkers wanted an amber, slightly reddish variety that was heavily brandied. Each market demanded its own formula.[77]

The producers did not simply acquiesce with their American consumers. Their correspondence was filled with serious negotiation over body, smoothness, flavour and colour – all of which were affected by the

[75] *Ibid.*

[76] Thomas Murdoch to Pierce Butler, 18 October 1800, Newton & Gordon letterbooks; and Spence, Leacock, & Spence to John Erskine, 26 June 1762, and John Leacock to William Leacock, 10 May 1796, Leacock papers. On colours appropriate for the London market, where 'high coloured wines will never please', see 12 March 1774, Liverpool University Archives; for the Glasgow market, where 'high coloured wines . . . were [also] not so salable', see Andrew Ramsay to Newton & Gordon, 24 September 1759, Cossart & Gordon papers – loose papers, Madeira Wine Company; and for the New York and New England market, see John and William Gordon to Robert Lenox, 11 October 1805, Newton & Gordon letterbooks.

[77] Henry Laurens to Corsley Rogers & Son, 16 May 1755, in Philip M. Hamer, ed., *Papers of Henry Laurens* (Columbia, S.C., 1968), vol. I, p. 248; Thomas Newton to Newton & Gordon, 26 November 1759, Thomas Newton letterbook, Madeira Wine Company Archives; and Baynton & Wharton to Thomas Newton, 2 October 1763, box 2, Cossart & Gordon papers, Liverpool University Archives.

amount of brandy. For New York, for instance, Madeira shippers waged a long campaign for less brandy. By the fourth quarter of the century, New Yorkers came to accept less brandy. If the producers had had their way, they would have sent the wines untouched: as Newton & Gordon informed one New York customer, their 'best wine' was 'excellent only in proportion as it is simple'. In some cases, the education of the consumer worked. But pleasing their customers loomed larger in their minds as time passed. And so, in exasperation but with resignation, Newton & Gordon and most other firms decided that, 'however convinced we may be of the body and essential goodness of our wines', 'we must give up our opinion' and compromise to 'please the palates of our employers'.[78]

It is no surprise that the Madeira wine distributors corresponded with their customers. What is significant is that the correspondence was not limited to the relatively straightforward process of offering and ordering products, of arranging financing and shipping, and of negotiating prices. The correspondence contains full-bodied conversations about the product, the development of the producer and consumer markets in the Americas and Indies, and the role of Madeira among the Americans. The buyers – consumers, retailers and wholesalers – influenced the producers as well as being influenced by them.

At the beginning of the century, the Madeira island merchants were principally wine traders who bought wine from the landowners and growers and, as quickly as possible, put it on board ship, having sold it to the captain or entrusted it to him for delivery to the merchants' customers. The distributors were content to let the customers and consumers consign goods like fish or wheat to the island at their own risk and for their own account, and take away the wine in barter or for cash.[79] Competition among the growing number of island merchants in the 1750s and 1760s altered this mode of doing business. As they struggled over what they always seriously, but incorrectly, viewed as a dwindling market, Madeira's more successful distributors enlisted people and products around the world in their fight, and started trading new products in both directions across the Atlantic and to the east.

With respect to the production and packaging of the wine itself, the distributors mobilized an elaborate procurement network around the

---

[78] Newton & Gordon to John Campbell, 14 April 1798, vol. XVIII, fo. 316, William Johnston to Francis Newton, 22 January 1786, vol. IX, fo. 133, Newton & Gordon letterbooks. The amount and strength of the brandy varied, as did its source. French, Guernsey, Spanish and Portuguese brandies were all used at various times by various firms, although French was always preferred if available and affordable. In 1802, the Newton & Gordon firm used brandy that was 12 to 15 per cent over proof. Thomas Murdoch to George Bridges, 30 April 1802, Newton & Gordon letterbooks.

[79] Blandy, *Bolton Letters*, vol. II, *passim*.

Atlantic. The supply of wine-making and wine-packaging items required commercial relations with merchants around the Baltic, in northern England, the Channel Islands, south-western France, mainland Portugal, southern Spain and North America, at the very least. For instance, once the practice of fortifying with brandy became common, a firm had to have a large stock of the liquor. The overwhelming first choice of all firms was the aged, high-quality brandies that had been distilled, blended and flavoured in the Cognac and Armagnac regions of south-western France. But wars with France often impeded the flow of French brandy, so that supply was unpredictable. Madeira's merchants learned to substitute the brandies of Holland, the Channel Islands, Portugal and Spain. Porto and Lisbon brandies were found to suffice, although Spanish brandy was considered 'trash' and Channel Island stuff much worse. Still, supplies dwindled so badly during the Napoleonic wars that Guernsey shippers, 'trucking' low-quality brandy from Guernsey and Valencia, were able to capture the market, becoming the only enterprisers to distribute the liquor reliably and systematically throughout the Atlantic, at least until the Madeirans began distilling their own brandy in 1794, and the Americans, as neutrals, entered the trucking business the following decade.[80]

For barrels, the distributors had to roam even farther afield to buy wood. In spite of its name, Madeira itself was poorly endowed with construction timber by the eighteenth century. As a result, the distributors had to look elsewhere for packaging materials. Empty pipes were one option, but the cost of cargo space (it appears) made that option unfeasible. Since it would have been much more expensive in freight charges to import empty ready-to-use pipes, they opted to buy staves, hoops and bungs in packs, and employ a cooper to build them on the island. This option was doubly beneficial in that it got round the problem of having to predict in advance the quantity and range of sizes that would be needed. The traditional preference for pipe wood was British oak. But the source of that oak had long since dried up and its prices risen. So Madeira merchants shifted their preference first to Baltic oak, and then as the price of that oak rose in demand for the construction of naval vessels, they turned to Pennsylvania, Virginia and Carolina oak. New Hampshire, New York and Quebec staves were tried from time to time, as were Brazilian and Honduran staves, but these varieties were found to be either

<hr>

[80] Newton & Gordon to Thomas Gordon, 6 December 1792, 20 January 1794, to Evans, Offley & Sealy, 22 March 1794, to Thomas Gordon, 5 December 1794, 27 March 1795, to Evans, Offley & Sealy, 15 March, 10 July 1798, vol. XIV, fo. 462, vol. XV, fos. 346, 366, vol. XVI, fos. 193, 250, vol. XVIII, fo. 271, vol. XIX, fos. 22, 337. The important Guernsey trucking trade which supplied southern Europe and the Caribbean has never been studied.

sappy or thin.[81] Thus, the wood for barrel staves, hoops and bungs came from Canada, New England, Pennsylvania, Virginia and the Baltic states, the iron barrel hoops and the boilers for scalding and seasoning the barrels from western England, the paint for decorating the barrels from Spain, the gesso for fining the must from Portugal, the brandy for fortifying the wine from France, Holland, Iberia and Guernsey: if he was to have enough sound packages to export wine, a merchant in Madeira needed goods from at least five different countries along the Atlantic rim.

Similarly, financing, always the most centralized part of the trade, evolved as enterprise expanded. 'Best and first rate' Madeiras – malmsey, London particular and London Market – were only shipped if the customer paid for them with bills of exchange drawn on a London merchant's house, at thirty, sixty or ninety days' sight or, in situations when the distributor desired 'to serve a friend', sometimes longer. At first, these wines were never shipped 'in truck of any commodity'. But over time, barter trades were tolerated and, as other market centres developed viable financial exchanges and mercantile communities, the necessity of financing through London was relaxed: drawing on Lisbon, New York and Philadelphia houses became more common, stripping London brokerage of its power.[82]

The procurement of ancillary provision goods for resale to island residents, or re-export to customers in southern Europe or the Americas, came to be a permanent feature of the island's trade by the last third of the century. Cloth goods were purchased early on. For example, Madeira distributors entered into the dry goods trade in the first instance to 'serve their customers' – the growers on the island from whom they habitually bought their must each harvest. These merchants consigned the goods to Portuguese shopkeepers, allowing them 4 per cent on the sale, or sold the goods outright, allowing four, five or twelve months to pay. Since non-payment was chronic among the shopkeepers, and the Portuguese judicial system did little to enforce payment, Madeira's merchants began setting up their own shops. After six years of struggling

---

[81] Alexander Gordon to James Gordon, 11 October 1761, Gordon of Letterfourie papers; Newton & Gordon to Thomas Gerry, Sr and Jr, 2 December 1762, to Samuel & John Span, 22 December 1793, and to Lester & Murragh, 14 August 1805, Newton & Gordon letterbooks, vol. III, fo. 74, vol. XV, fo. 296, vol. XIX, fo. 14, vol. XXVII, fo. 27. The shifts in global sources for barrel wood have not been studied, but portions of the story can be pieced together from Robert G. Albion, *Forests and Sea Power: the Timber Problem of the Royal Navy, 1652–1862* (Cambridge, Mass., 1926); H. S. K. Kent, 'The Anglo-Norwegian timber trade in the eighteenth century', *EcHR*, 2nd series, 8 (1955), 62–74; Arthur R. M. Lower, *Great Britain's Woodyard: British America and the Timber Trade, 1763–1867* (Montreal, 1973); and Sven-Erik Åström, 'Britain's timber imports from the Baltic, 1775–1830', *Scandinavian EcHR*, 37 (1989), 57–71.

[82] Newton & Gordon to Willing, Morris & Swanwick, 12 September, 1792, Newton & Gordon letterbooks, vol. XIV, fo. 356.

with dry goods, to cite just one example, Francis Newton 'put up a Huckster's Shop' on the first floor of his own house in 1754 and staffed it with several servants, thereby saving himself the loss of commissions and the breakage or damage to the goods in transit.[83] Cloth goods were usually brought from Britain. Unless they were bought and packed by a long-standing correspondent, employee or relative who was both knowledgeable and trustworthy, the work was risky. Even with reliable help, the likelihood of flawed, spoiled and especially inappropriate goods was high. English-speaking distributors, for example, found it difficult to intuit the textures, colours and patterns attractive to the Portuguese in Madeira and Brazil, and this problem became especially acute after 1783 when Portuguese merchants began sending their own agents to live and work in London.[84]

Frustrated by the perils of the dry goods trade, Madeira distributors turned next to foodstuffs. This served their American customers well enough, by providing an outlet for their grain and fish, and it also provisioned the Madeira inhabitants. The island harvested only a minor wheat crop each year; and Porto Santo and the Azores, where grain crops were larger, did not produce enough to satisfy Madeira's growing demand. In addition, the importation of foodstuffs provided the merchants with currency; 'it was only by importing food' that they could 'at all command cash' for their 'immense payments' to the growers and the government. Throughout the century, the merchants also re-exported American fish and foodstuffs to southern Europe. Cod from Newfoundland and New England, wheat from New England and the middle colonies, and rice from the Carolinas had to be handled with careful attention to multiple sources, long-distance quality control, timing and price, and multiple destinations in southern Europe and Brazil.[85]

[83] Alexander Gordon to James Gordon, 14 February 1761, Letterfourie papers; Francis Newton to George Spence, 23 October 1754, Newton & Gordon letterbooks, vol. I, fos. 10, 126.

[84] On the use of relatives, see Francis Newton to George Spence, 27 October 1753, noting how Mr Loughnan, a brewer in London, supplied his son with clothing goods. Newton & Gordon letterbooks, vol. I, fo. 77. Savvy firms understood this need, and by the end of the century were sending Portuguese representatives to London and New York – people 'who understand the assortment of goods fit for this place & have great advantage over us on this account'. John Leacock, Jr, to William Leacock, 23 January 1801, Leacock & Leacock letterbook 1799–1802, fo. 223, Leacock papers, Casa Branca. For the work of the Londoners, see numerous invoices for goods sent drawn up by Johnston & Jolly and forwarded to Newton & Gordon, box 3, bundle 1764–5, Cossart & Gordon papers, Liverpool University Archives, which state what was sent and from whom they were purchased. See also box 1, bundle 4.

[85] For discussion of the wheat trade, see Newton & Gordon to Robert Lenox, 29 November 1803, and to Robert Maitland, 5 January 1806, Newton & Gordon letterbooks, vol. XXV, fo. 215, vol. XXVII, fo. 239. On rice, see Newton & Gordon to Tunno & Cox, 4 September 1798, to Robert Lenox, 10 May 1803, to Tunno & Cox, 29 July 1805, Newton & Gordon letterbooks.

The case of fish is representative. Dried and salted cod from New England had been a barter good in the trade at least as long as New England's ships had been coming to Madeira for wine – the 1640s.[86] As far as the Madeirans were concerned, the primary American import was cod, and firms like Newton & Gordon continually struggled to maintain a supply.[87] The interruption of shipping lanes during the Seven Years' War, however, and a contraction of cod harvests caused some firms to seek alternative sources of fish. The Gordons began importing herring 'for consumption [that is, purchase] in their shop', constantly devising new schemes to flood Madeira's market with fish from Norway, Sweden or Scotland. In one typical adventure, in 1760, the Gordons joined with Scott, Pringle & Cheap to bring a shipload of red herring from Bergen to Madeira. When it was determined that no more would sell, their ship carried the remainder, together with wine, to the Canaries and South Carolina, where it loaded rice for Lisbon. When such schemes were frustrated by war or the depletion of fish stocks, Madeira distributors opted for smaller and rounder southern European pilchards, which were cheaper still. Depending on their American customers' connections, the firms adopted a pro-cod or pro-herring position, although, when cod stocks ran short, even cod importers turned to herring for a short-term fix.[88]

As competition increased, the Madeirans found they even had to participate more fully in the ownership of shipping. They entered into joint ventures in both cargoes and ships, which ensured provisions and exports, divided risks and shared resources. The Madeirans do not appear to have embraced this opportunity until mid-century. Before then, they were content to service incoming ships, allowing their owners and captains to assume the risks. 'The principle' that guided most firms was to 'very rarely adventure deeply for our own account, whether sending out

[86] Edward Johnson, *Wonder Working Providence, 1628–1651* (New York, 1810), p. 247. According to Johnson, 'Portugal hath had many a mouthful of bread and fish from us in the exchange of their Madeira liquor'. See also Duncan, *Atlantic Islands*, p. 172.

[87] Newton & Gordon to Thomas Gerry, Sr and Jr, 2 December 1762, to William Brown, 2 December 1762, to Thomas Newton, 18 October 1763, to Robert Hooper, 4 November 1763, Cossart & Gordon papers, box 1, bundle 4, box 3, bundle 1764–5, Liverpool University Archives. John Rowe of Boston, Jeremiah Lee of Salem, Robert Hooper and the Daltons of Marblehead jointly consigned about 2,000 quintals of codfish to Newton & Gordon in 1762 and 1763. On cod, see James G. Lydon, 'Fish for gold: the Massachusetts fish trade with Iberia, 1700–1773', *The New England Quarterly*, 54 (1981), 575.

[88] On herring and pilchards, see Alexander Gordon to James Gordon, 8 October 1760, Chambers, Torngren, Bellenden & Co. to James Gordon, 15 September 1762, 2 March, 14 September 1763, Alexander Gordon to James Gordon, 8 July 1766, Letterfourie papers; Orders from Gothenburg, 1764–5, box 3, Cossart & Gordon papers, Liverpool University Archives.

wines or taking in provisions'.[89] But, beginning in the late 1740s, one or two firms 'resolved to buy a small vessel to send to North America', seeing such schemes as 'the only method in the world to push business in America'. Lamar, Hill, Bisset & Co., with its strong Chesapeake and Philadelphia connections, engrossed much of that region's business, for example, by 'holding part of the vessels and being concerned in their cargoes'. By participating as principals, they 'made a great advantage of their grain' which 'turned out to better advantage than if consigned' the normal way. One plan of the Gordons was typical: keeping a vessel of 140 tons constantly sailing between St Kitts and Virginia, and holding it in thirds – the firm taking a third, alongside a Caribbean trader and a Virginian merchant.[90]

After the close of the Seven Years' War, most distributors engaged more fully in the trade to North America by owning shares of not just ships but also their cargoes. Joint cargoes were greatly favoured. John Searle II of Madeira and Thomas Riche of Philadelphia jointly imported twenty pipes of wine into Philadelphia in 1764, and Thomas Newton, the agent of Newton & Gordon in New York, ordered for the firm 'a small quantity of fish to induce a vessel to value on us'. Owning vessels and cargoes was seen as an increasingly reliable way to control the trade. In a matter of decades, the 'entire plan for American correspondences' was rewritten, and flexibly so: firms adventured 'in cargoes of American commodities' on their own account; they took shares in vessels 'according to circumstances'; and they accepted consignments of staple articles like fish, wheat or rice and 'made return', part in first-rate 'London' wines and part in lower quality 'New York' wines.[91]

In 1748, from his first day on the island, Francis Newton started writing 'to potential customers, even when they were committed' to other distributors, 'as groundwork for the future'. In the 1780s, his firm regularly sent 'a favourable sample' or two to prospective customers. And in 1800, James Murdoch gave his visitors engraved cards with his firm's partners' names and addresses printed on them, and sent his London

[89] Newton & Gordon to John Rowe, 13 September 1762, to Thomas & Thomas Gerry, 12 December 1762, and to Thomas Newton, 22 April 1763, Newton & Gordon letterbooks.

[90] Francis Newton to George Spence, 1 April 1749, Newton & Gordon letterbooks, vol. I, fo. 15; and Alexander Gordon to James Gordon, 27 December 1761, Letterfourie papers. Compare the Searles' New York schemes as described in Thomas Newton to Francis Newton, 26 December 1758, 19 February 1759, Thomas Newton letterbook, Madeira Wine Company Archives.

[91] Thomas Riche to John Searle, 9 August 1764, Thomas Riche letterbook, vol. I, HSP; Newton & Gordon to Thomas Gerry, Jr, 23 May 1766, Newton & Gordon letterbooks, vol. IV, fo. 23; Newton & Gordon to Johnston & Jolly, 18 February 1767, to Hugh Moore, 1 April 1783, to Archibald Moncrief, 25 November 1791, and to Samuel Donaldson, 25 September 1794, Newton & Gordon letterbooks, vol. IV, fo. 67, vol. VIII, fo. 18, vol. XIV, fo. 21 and vol. XVI, fo. 96.

partner a list of those Englishmen who had visited their house with 'instructions to be attentive' to their needs upon their return to Britain. From such hints, we learn how aggressive the distributors of Madeira were in marketing their product, adopting many of the techniques emerging in other sectors of the Atlantic consumer market. As a distinctly non-Catholic, non-Latin minority in a Catholic Portuguese province, business was 'the only amusement'; not surprisingly, 'extreme avidity after business' – 'extreme voracity' to some – came to possess the Madeira distributors as the century progressed.[92]

The merchants developed the wines by introducing new varietals and blends. Whereas in 1703 only three grapes were grown and only four different wines made from them, by 1807 thirteen varieties were grown and over twenty kinds of wine were sold. Furthermore, during the same period, they developed or introduced new techniques, such as fortifying, blending, stirring and heating to create a desirable luxury drink.[93]

Simultaneously, they developed, or at least fostered, what may be called a 'wine culture'. They devised a new connoisseur terminology to accompany the new grades. To their customers they sang the praises of new varieties like *sercial* and *boal*, and rare strains like *malvasia*. Certain grades were described as 'opulent', fit only for discerning palates in the metropolis or for men and women who aspired to familiarity with its genteel fashions. After 1780, wines of certain ages were hawked as more suitable for 'intelligent' and 'choice' drinkers.[94] A few merchants adopted the practice towards the end of the century of deploying the testimony of famous men; General Washington's or Lord Nelson's purchase and praise of a wine was used to recommend a pipe of the same lot to future purchasers.[95] At the same time, they priced the varieties as luxury goods, tripling the shipping price of the New York grade between 1750 and 1807, to the point that Madeira was the most expensive wine of the day. Whereas in 1703 it was the cheapest wine in any town or tavern in America, often cheaper than beer, by 1807 it was beyond the reach of many – only 'opulent people' drank it.[96]

To further differentiate the evolving luxury status of their wines, the

---

[92] Francis Newton to John Woodbridge, 8 April 1753, to Thomas Gordon, 25 August 1787, Newton & Gordon letterbooks, vol. I, fo. 23, vol. IX, vol. X, fo. 33; John Leacock to William Leacock, 28 October 1800, Leacock & Leacock letterbook 1799–1802, fo. 206, Leacock papers; Francis Newton to David Campbell, 6 December 1748, Thomas Murdoch to Thomas Gordon, 11 April 1789, Newton & Gordon letterbooks, vol. I, fo. 7, vol. XI, fo. 38.

[93] Hancock, 'Commerce and conversation', 10–12.   [94] *Ibid.*, 26–7.

[95] John Marsden Pintard to Elias Boudinot, 1783, Boudinot papers, American Bible Society; William Johnston to Thomas Gordon, 1783, Newton & Gordon letterbooks.

[96] Unadjusted for inflation, the price rose eightfold. Hancock, 'Commerce and conversation', 27–30. See also Francis Newton to Newton & Gordon, 29 May 1798, loose letters, Madeira Wine Company Archives.

distributors introduced customers to the use of specialized paraphernalia: corkscrews of increasingly intricate and fanciful designs,[97] silver bottle and decanter 'tickets' (labels) etched with the word 'Madeira' to denote the contents,[98] several sizes of crystal decanters also etched with the word 'Madeira',[99] small crystal glasses suitable only for heavily fortified drinks like Madeira,[100] and the like. The merchants graced their own tables with

[97] The corkscrew was probably invented in England during the reign of Charles II, although the French did not lag far behind. The first reference to a corkscrew occurs in 1681, although references to corked bottles precede this reference by six years. The first specimen dates from 1685. On the development of corkscrews, see Bertrand B. Giulian, *Corkscrews of the Eighteenth Century: Artistry in Iron and Steel* (Yardley, Pa., 1995); Robin Butler and Gillian Walkling, *The Book of Wine Antiques* (Woodbridge, Suffolk, 1986), pp. 79–87; Evan Perry, *Corkscrews and Bottle Openers* (Aylesbury, 1980); and Helen McKearin, 'Notes on stopping, bottling and binning', *Journal of Glass Studies*, 13 (1971), 120–7.

[98] Tickets were first hung around the necks of decanters. The first reference to them occurs in 1723, but the first specimen to survive comes from the 1730s. Most specimens that have survived were made of silver; their design is usually symmetrical. On tickets, see Butler and Walkling, *Book of Wine Antiques*, pp. 160–71; Michael Clayton, *The Collector's Dictionary of the Silver and Gold of Great Britain and North America* (London, 1971); Derek Davis, *English Bottles and Decanters, 1650–1800* (New York, 1972); N. M. Penzer, *The Book of the Wine Label* (London, 1947); Raphael A. Weed, 'Silver wine labels', *New York Historical Society Quarterly Bulletin*, 13 (July 1929), 47–67; and Harry J. Powell, *Glass-Making in England* (Cambridge, 1923).

[99] On decanters, see Butler and Walkling, *Book of Wine Antiques*, pp. 132–49; R. J. Charleston, *English Glass and the Glass Used in England, circa 400–1900* (London, 1984), pp. 104–78; G. Bernard Hughes, *English, Scottish and Irish Table Glass, from the Sixth Century to 1820* (London, 1956); John M. Bacon, 'Bottle-decanters and bottles', *Apollo*, 30 (1939), 13–15. On Madeira decanters in America, see Helen McKearin, '18th century advertisements of glass imports into the colonies and the United States, Part II', *Glass Notes*, 15 (December 1955), 15–25; Ivor Nöel Hume, *Archaeology and Wetherburn's Tavern* (Williamsburg, 1969), and *Glass in Colonial Williamsburg's Archaeological Collections* (Williamsburg, 1969); Alfred C. Prime, comp., *The Arts and Crafts in Philadelphia, Maryland and South Carolina, 1721–1785* (Topsfield, 1929) and *The Arts and Crafts . . . 1786–1800* (Topsfield, 1932); *The Arts and Crafts in New York, 1726–1776* (New York, 1938), pp. 96–9; and George F. Dow, *The Arts and Crafts in New England, 1704–1775* (Topsfield, 1927).

[100] Separate 'Madeira' glasses manufactured by glasshouses in Britain, Europe or America do not appear in glass catalogues until the 1830s. By 1677, George Ravenscroft was producing separate claret, sack and brandy glasses. Small glasses were used for Spanish wines, middling glasses for French claret and large glasses for beer. By the middle of the eighteenth century, continental glasshouses were producing glass services, as were English houses after 1780, but these did not include Madeira glasses. Special glasses for port and shrub first appear in the 1780s. If the surviving catalogues of glasshouses are an accurate reflection, 'Madeira glasses' *per se* were not introduced into either England or America until the 1830s and 1840s; although see Newton & Gordon to Thomas Gordon, 6 May 1799, Newton & Gordon letterbooks, vol. XIX, fo. 285, where the firm orders six to eight dozen 'glasses of Madeira wine'. These may have been the smaller, more specialized cordial glasses which had been around since the late seventeenth century or newer variants like port glasses which were used to drink Madeira wine. On the rise of specialized glassware for wine in Britain, see Butler and Walkling, *Book of Wine Antiques*, pp. 191–214; Charleston, *English Glass*, pp. 104–78. On the rise of specialized glassware for wine in America, see Arlene Palmer, *Glass in Early America* (Winterthur, 1993), and 'Glass production in eighteenth-century America: the Wistarburgh enterprise', *Winterthur Portfolio*, 11 (1975), 75–101; and Dwight P. Lanmon, 'The Baltimore glass trade, 1780 to 1820', *Winterthur Portfolio*, 5 (1969), 15–48.

this equipment, and recommended it to visitors and correspondents as the indispensable trappings of informed wine drinkers. By the late-1760s, for instance, island firms were writing to English glass houses to order 'low, round decanters for the table while at dinner' and, to go with them, 'low, heavy glasses for them to hold as little as possible'. They preferred small glasses for drinking Madeira – two-thirds to one-half the size of a common wine glass – for they were more fit 'for seeing [the] wine', and highly appropriate for tasting a large number of different grades, all of which were heavily fortified and highly intoxicating. The idea of tasting was, of course, itself a mark of connoisseurship. During a visit to the island, the distributors introduced house-guests to 'the art and mystery of drinking Madeira' and then sold them the paraphernalia so that they could carry on with the custom after their departure.[101]

Finally, very late in the century, the distributors introduced what one might call 'prestige packaging' into their marketing of the wine. 'From interested motives', they and, even more so, their agents 'chose now and then to give whimsical appellations abroad' to the wine, calling it after the ship that carried it, like the *USS Constitution*, or the family or group that ordered it, like 'The Supreme Court'. The ploy – 'at which a Madeira merchant stares & smiles & knows to mean nothing' – imparted the sense of a limited edition and persuaded 'others that unusual excellence in the liquor accompanies those appellations'.[102] They constructed special pipes, painted them with customers' names, and decorated them with customers' insignia and crests. In this innovation, they took their cue from planters in the Ceded Islands, where the innovation sprang from necessity: correspondents and consumers there specifically requested iron hoops and painted casks (both staves and bungs) 'to keep them free from worm'. The distributors quickly realized that the practice satisfied more than just planters' practical needs – tighter, more attractive casks became 'general fashion'. They cut the surnames of the purchasers into the staves, and their initials into the bung. By specializing the packaging, they enhanced its value: a custom pipe 'pleases the eye, has a neat and attentive appearance to the owners of the liquor, & is of a real service to

---

[101] Newton & Gordon to Johnston & Jolly, 18 February 1767, to Thomas Gordon, 10 December 1783, Newton & Gordon letterbooks, vol. IV, fo. 67, vol. VIII, fo. 150; and John Leacock to William Leacock, 2 November 1794, Leacock & Sons letterbook 1794–7, fo. 6, Leacock papers. In addition to the decanters, carafes and glasses used on a table in Madeira, 'small coloured rubbers' began to be put on the table about 1783 for drinking after dinner 'when the cloth is taken away'.

[102] On naming the wines, see Newton & Gordon to Samuel Vaughan, 2 March 1802, Newton & Gordon letterbooks, vol. XXIII, fo. 115. See also Cossart, *Madeira*, pp. 104–14; Malcolm Bell, Jr, 'The romantic wines of Madeira', *Georgia Historical Quarterly*, 38 (December 1954), 322–36; and André Simon and Elizabeth Craig, *Madeira: Wine, Cakes & Sauce* (London, 1933), pp. 19–28.

the cask'. To further safeguard the interests of the consumer 'against change or improper treatment' shipboard or wharfside, some firms took to stamping 'a private mark on the inside of the bung' that was unique to each customer.[103]

Conclusion

The ways in which a Madeira wine distributor managed his trade in Atlantic wines – personal contacts, interactive conversations with consumers, intensive coordination of expanded enterprise, and aggressive marketing – go much of the way towards understanding the 'revolution in the trade' in the eighteenth century. Of course, these developments in business practice took place in a context: a generally favourable political and economic climate, an increase in demand from a larger population with greater wealth, and significant improvement in transport infrastructure, agricultural transformation and technological change. These factors were all critical in the process of growth.

Yet such factors do not explain *how* the Atlantic economy grew; such factors were primarily conditioning and environmental. The expansion in trade was the work of commercial men and women who created a system piecemeal to ply their trades. Over the course of the eighteenth century, the producers in Madeira simultaneously re-invented their product, and created the marketing and distribution structure to push their luxury product down the Ohio River valley and into the hinterlands of Bengal. The trading system they created was a spider web: decentralized, opportunistic and specific. The Madeira enterprisers, working alone, and in collaboration with other distributors on the island and a whole chain of interested parties around the world, wrought long-term changes in the conduct of the Madeira wine trade. At the same time, they, and other traders like them, built a commercial system in which the gains from trade flowed across imperial boundaries.

[103] Newton & Gordon to Richard Cargill, 23 June 1773, to Thomas Gordon, 15 June 1789, to Edmund Boehm, 20 November 1789, to Evans, Offley & Sealy, 23 September 1797, to Law, Bruce & Co., 30 September 1801, Newton & Gordon letterbooks, vol. V, fo. 234, vol. XII, fos. 86, 172, vol. XVIII, fo. 80, vol. XXII, fo. 280; and Leacock papers, Bill of Lading Book 1791–9, *passim*.

6   Law, credit, the supply of labour, and the organization of sugar production in the colonial Greater Caribbean: a comparison of Brazil and Barbados in the seventeenth century.

Russell R. Menard

One of the many minor mysteries surrounding the history of sugar production in the colonial greater Caribbean concerns differences in the organization of production between the English islands and Brazil.[1] In Brazil, production was dispersed, as much of the cane was grown by small farmers (*lavradores de cana*), some of them tenants, some independent landowners who took their crop to their landlord's mill or to some other big planter's mill for processing.[2] On the islands, by contrast, production was centralized, as most of the cane was tended by slaves owned by a big planter and processed at the planter's own mill. Given the high productivity of gang labour, there would seem to be substantial advantages to the centralized system that prevailed on the islands.[3] It is therefore something of a puzzle why the centralized system did not prevail throughout the region. This chapter, through a focus on Barbados and Brazil in the seventeenth century, attempts a solution to that puzzle.

While it might at first seem odd to compare a small island like Barbados to a colony as large as Brazil, several considerations suggest that the comparison is in fact well grounded. In the middle seventeenth century,

Earlier versions of this chapter were presented to he Early American History Workshop at the University of Minnesota, and to the annual meeting of the Social Science History Association at Washington, D.C., October 1997. I would like to thank Stanley Engerman, David Ryden, Matthew Mulcahy and Stuart B. Schwartz for helpful comments.

[1] For the minor mysteries, see Richard S. Dunn, *Sugar and Slaves: the Rise of the Planter Class in the English West Indies, 1624–1713* (Chapel Hill, N.C., 1973), p. 61. Dunn also presents a useful summary of differences in the organization of production between Brazil and the islands.

[2] On the organization of the Brazilian sugar industry see Stuart B. Schwartz, *Sugar Plantations, and the Formation of Brazilian Society* (Cambridge, 1985).

[3] The centralized system was presumably more efficient because it permitted planters to capture the benefits of the gang system, on which see Robert W. Fogel, *Without Consent or Contract: the Rise and Fall of American Slavery* (New York, 1989), pp. 26–8.

154

Table 6.1. *Estimated population of Barbados, 1640–1700 (in thousands)*

Year	Free	Slave
1640	14.0	
1650	30.0	12.8
1660	26.2	27.1
1670	22.4	40.4
1680	20.5	44.9
1700	15.4	50.1

Source: McCusker and Menard, *Economy of British America*, p. 153.

the period focused on here, Barbados was Brazil's most serious competitor as a sugar producer. Indeed, Barbadian planters were more efficient, perhaps because they followed the centralized system, and were thus able to undersell the Brazilians, and to capture the European markets that Brazilian planters had once dominated.[4] Finally, comparison of the population of Barbados with that of the captaincy of Bahia, the main sugar-producing region of Brazil, reveals that they were roughly the same size during much of the seventeenth century.[5]

It is helpful to begin with the observation that the centralized system was not universal on Barbados throughout its history as a sugar producer. In the middle of the seventeenth century, when sugar monoculture was taking root on the island, some Barbadian sugar estates were organized in the dispersed, Brazilian fashion. Tenant farming was rare on Barbados in the early 1640s. Land was cheap and readily available, especially for those willing to move away from the densely settled west coast into the interior or towards the northern and eastern regions of the island. But, as land prices jumped with the sugar boom and as rich men began to assemble large holdings, recently freed servants who earlier might have acquired a small tract of their own found themselves squeezed out. Many became tenants to big planters, often making sugar for their landlord's mill.

It would be an error to equate tenancy with the dispersed system, since tenants could have grown crops other than sugar – tobacco, indigo, provisions and the like – and small landowners might have grown cane for a big man's mill. Just how many tenants there were, and what proportion of them grew sugar for their landlord's mill, it is impossible to say, but the

---

[4] Dunn, *Sugar and Slaves*, pp. 204–5.
[5] See table 6.1, and Schwartz, *Sugar Plantations in the Formation of Brazilian Society*, p. 88.

practice was common around mid-century. The available evidence will not permit an estimate of the proportion of Barbadian sugar made by the centralized and dispersed methods, but the example of Mt Clapham will suffice to make my point. Mt Clapham plantation, a 510-acre tract in St Michael and Christ Church parishes, acquired by Thomas Noell in 1650 provides a window into the changing organization of the Barbadian sugar industry.[6] Although we should not assume that all tenants were cane farmers, the tenants at Mt Clapham did grow cane on a plantation organized acceding to the dispersed system.

Thomas Noell was a London merchant, who along with his three brothers, Martin, James and Stephen, known locally as the four brethren, ranked among the leading investors in the Barbadian sugar industry. In June 1654, Mt Clapham had a workforce of fifteen servants and twenty-nine slaves, barely enough for a small 100-acre sugar plantation, let alone one of Mt Clapham's size.[7] Noell addressed the labour shortage by recruiting tenants. By June 1654, he had leased out 179 acres to twenty-four tenants for an annual rent of £362 sterling. Ranging in size from 3.5 to 18 acres, often operated by two or three men in a partnership, these tenancies ran for six to nine years at annual rents of £1.5 to £3 sterling per acre. The records do not describe the output of these small leaseholds, but it is likely that the tenants grew cane for Noell's mill as the prices paid for cotton, tobacco, indigo, or provisions could not have supported such rents.

Mt Clapham was not the only Barbadian sugar plantation with insufficient bound labour to operate entirely as a centralized plantation. Indeed, Dunn reports acreage, servants and slaves for four Barbadian plantations between 1640 and 1667, ranging in size between 75 and 360 acres. Only two of them had enough servants and slaves to operate at the optimum level of two acres per worker as centralized plantations.[8] I have supplemented Dunn's list with several additional operations listed in table 6.2. All of those also faced a labour shortage; from this table it appears that most mid-century Barbadian plantations were understaffed. Given the

---

[6] The description of Mt Clapham reported in detail here appears in a deed of sale from Noell to Governor Daniel Searle on 6 June 1654 recorded in recopied deed books, RB 3, 109–13, Barbados Archives, Lazaretto, St Michael. The plantation sold for 228,000 lb of sugar, perhaps £2,700 sterling, a bargain by any standards. Hilary Beckles, *White Servitude and Black Slavery in Barbados, 1627–1715* (Knoxville, 1989), p. 157, provides a brief description of Mt Clapham. Noell had married Thomisin Hilliard, daughter of William Hilliard, and widow of Lancelot Pace, both of them substantial planters, which may explain how he got hold of this tract. Thomisin and Thomas Noell 'are rich' and have 'great sugar works', Lucie Downing to John Winthrop, Jr, 17 December 1648, *Winthrop Papers*, V, p. 291.

[7] The conventional ratio was one worker for every two acres. Dunn, *Sugar and Slaves*, p. 69.

[8] *Ibid.*, p. 68.

Table 6.2. *Acreage and workforce on various Barbados plantations, 1641–4*

	Owner	Acreage	Servants	Slaves
1643	Alexander Lindsay	60	2	4
1643	John Tawyer	70	2	2
1643	Richard Goouse	80	4	0
1643	Edward Lake	40	8	1
1643	Chrstophr Moltrop	250	6	12
1643	Jonathan Hawtayne	100	0	8
1643	Daniel Fletcher	200	5	0
1643	Joseph Pickering	25	5	0
1643	Thomas Dobbs	50	3	0
1642	John Tobin	40	4	0
1641	William Taylor	50	3	0
1641	Owen Williams	30	3	0
1641	Robert Way	60	5	0
1644	Peter Peterson	13	1	1

Source: Recopied deed books, Barbados Archives: RB 3/1, 55–6, 61–3, 66–73, 92–3, 116–17, 122–3, 150–1, 152–3, 154–5; RB 3/1, 546–7.

high and rising price of land on the island, few planters could afford to let much of their estate lie fallow. Thus the temptation to copy Thomas Noell's lead, and lease out some of the extra acreage must have been great. Keeping the entire plantation in cultivation was not the only goal of Barbadian sugar planters that led them to seek out tenants. They were also concerned to make sure that they had enough cane to keep their sugar works operating at full capacity.[9]

The rise of tenancy suggests a considerable contraction of opportunities for ex-servants in the early stages of the sugar boom, but renting offered better prospects than what came next. Neither labour shortages nor tenancy as a solution were unique to Barbados in the early stages of the sugar boom. There is evidence of similar developments on other islands during the conversion to sugar monoculture. Thus, when Christopher Jeaffreson's effort to rebuild his St Kitts' estate in the aftermath of a devastating hurricane in 1681 severely stretched his labour force, he turned to share agreements with tenants in order to acquire

---

[9] This is evident in the papers of Christopher Jeaffreson of St Kitts. John C. Jeaffreson, *A Young Squire of the Seventeenth Century: from the Papers of Christopher Jeaffreson, of Dullingham House, Cambridgeshire* (London, 1878). See also the contracts printed as an appendix to Richard Pares, *Merchants and Planters, EcHR*, Supplement, no. 4 (Cambridge, 1960).

sufficient cane for his sugar mill, and in an effort to keep his land fully cultivated.[10]

The issue of opportunity raises the question of whether tenancy within the context of the dispersed form of plantation organization served as a upward step on an agricultural ladder. For the Mt Clapham tenants, the evidence suggests that it did not – at least none of them appears as a landowner in the deeds registered in the island's court. As the big planters built up their unfree labour force they replaced their tenants with slaves. Mt Clapham had been reorganized as a centralized estate by the mid-1660s.[11] For the island as a whole, it is clear that the centralized plantation dominated sugar production by 1680, although the appearance of some smallholders in the census of that year suggests that remnants of the dispersed system persisted on the island to the end of the seventeenth century.[12] The shift towards the centralized system left ambitious former servants with little choice but to emigrate.[13]

The case of Mt Clapham suggests that we should focus on labour supply to understand why the dispersed system prevailed in Brazil, and the centralized system in Barbados. If my reading of the admittedly scarce evidence is correct, Barbadians flirted with the dispersed system of organizing their plantations in the early stages of the sugar boom, and it was not until the mid-1660s, perhaps not until 1680, that it became clear that the centralized system would prevail. A look at the size of the island's slave population (see table 6.1) suggests why this was the case. Barbados has roughly 166 square miles or 106,000 acres. At a ratio of two acres per worker, island planters owned enough slaves to cultivate only a small portion of the island in 1640, but by 1660, the slave population was sufficient to cultivate about half the island. While planters did not have enough slaves before about 1650 to make much of a dent in the island's available land, potential tenants were available in abundance, in the persons of recently freed indentured servants, who, when out of their time, found it almost impossible to acquire land on the island once the

---

[10] Jeaffreson, *A Young Squire of the Seventeenth Century*; Richard B. Sheridan, *Sugar and Slavery: an Economic History of the British West Indies, 1623–1775* (Kingston, Jamaica, 1994), pp. 153–4. For more detail on this hurricane and the problems it caused Jeaffreson, see Matthew Mulcahy, 'Melancholy and fatal calamities: natural disasters and colonial society in the British greater Caribbean, 1623–1781' (Ph.D. thesis, University of Minnesota, 1999), ch. 3. Mulcahy argues that the frequency of hurricanes in the region quickened the transition to the centralized system, because small farmers with limited resources had great difficulty rebuilding in the aftermath of major storms.

[11] On Mt Clapham in the mid-1660s, see Beckles, *White Servitude and Black Slavery*, p. 157.

[12] On the situation in 1680, see Richard Dunn's analysis of the census of that year, in *Sugar and Slaves*, pp. 84–116.

[13] On emigration from Barbados, see McCusker and Menard, *Economy of British America*, pp. 154–5.

sugar boom had driven land prices up. In consequence, the island was well supplied with young men willing to sign on as tenant farmers making cane for someone else's mill. By the mid-1660s, the demography of the island had undergone a dramatic change. By 1665, there were enough slaves to cultivate about half of the island's arable land, while the supply of recently freed servants had dried up. Faced with these new conditions, planters reorganized their estates according to the centralized system.

The impact of the shift from the dispersed to the centralized system of organization on the economic geography of the island is evident in two detailed maps describing the Barbadian sugar industry produced during the seventeenth century. The earliest of these was drawn by Richard Ligon in 1659 when the dispersed method was still common on the island (fig. 6.1). Ligon felt compelled to list not only the big planters and mill owners, but also hundreds of small farmers, many of whom, if my reading of the evidence is correct, were growing cane for the big planters' mills. Richard Ford, who drew his map in 1674, when the conversion to the centralized system was nearly completed, felt no such compulsion. He was content to list only the mills, although he was careful to distinguish between animal-powered and wind-powered mills.

Barbadian planters, then, flirted with the dispersed style of organizing sugar production when the crop was first cultivated on the island and they did not yet have enough slaves to pursue the alternative, but they quickly purchased the slaves they needed to follow the more efficient centralized system. Why did Brazilians fail to follow their lead and instead stay with the less profitable dispersed system? This decision was not, as is sometimes argued, just one more example of Portuguese backwardness. The outcome was a matter of labour supply and access to capital. Slaves were an expensive investment, and to quickly enter into sugar production on a large scale with plantations organized in a centralized system, a planter needed enormous financial resources, or access to substantial credit. Credit was available to Barbadian planters, at least to those who were in Richard Ligon's apt phrase, 'Well-friended',[14] because of their close connections to the London merchant community, and a legal system that favoured lenders. For Brazilians, by contrast, capital was harder to come by.

Brazil followed what Jacob Price calls the 'Latin rule', which protected the integrity of the plantation as a working unit. Creditors could seize crops but could not use the courts to seize the non-landed accoutrements of the plantation or sugar mills – such as agricultural equipment, livestock or slaves – and thus diminish its productive capacity.[15] In consequence,

<hr>

[14] Ligon, *A True and Exact History of the Island of Barbados* (London, 1657), p. 117.

[15] Jacob M. Price, 'Credit in the slave trade and plantation economies', in Barbara L. Solow, ed., *Slavery and the Rise of the Atlantic System* (Cambridge, 1991), p. 296.

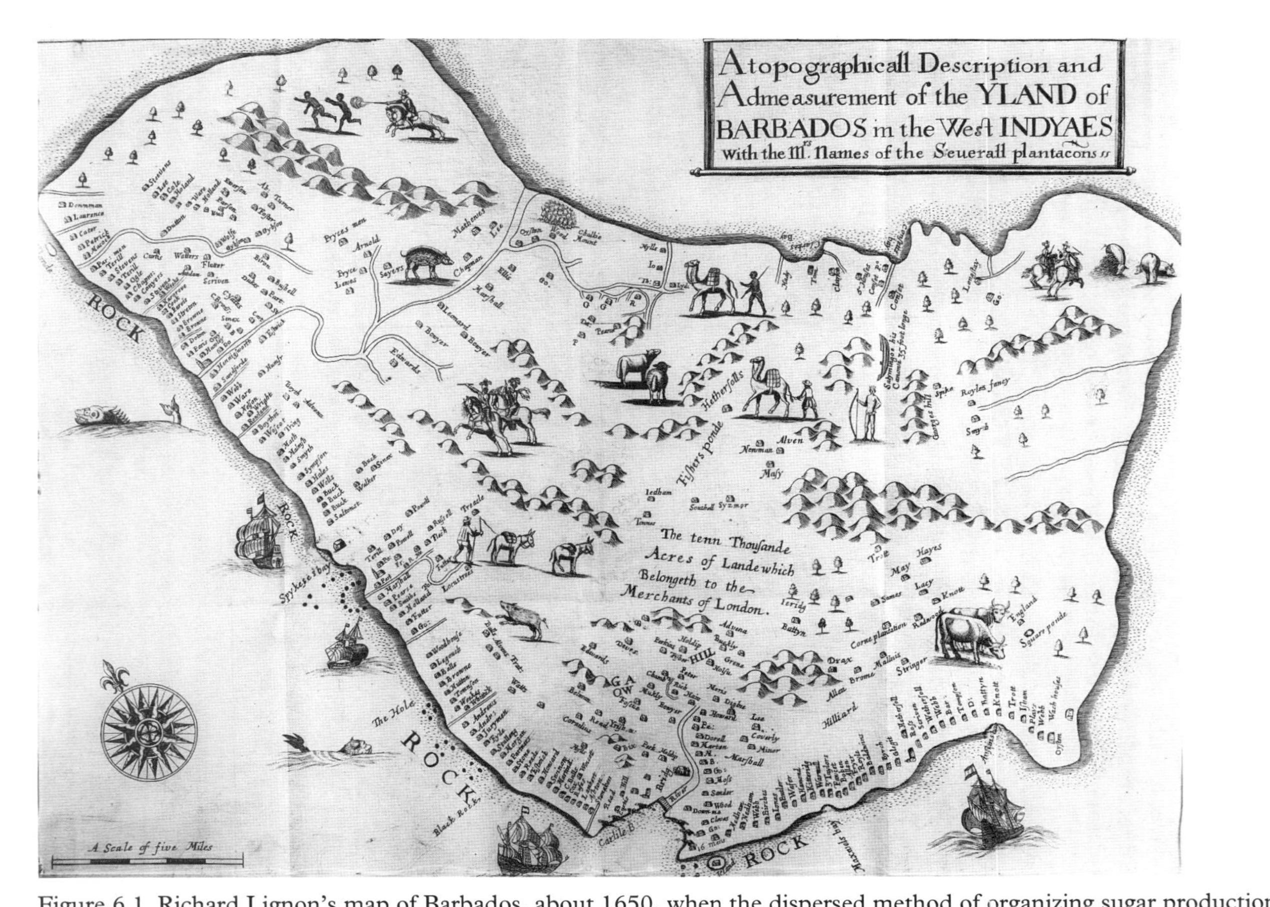

Figure 6.1 Richard Lignon's map of Barbados, about 1650, when the dispersed method of organizing sugar production was still common on the island. (Courtesy of the James Ford Bell Library, University of Minnesota, Minneapolis.)

realizing that it might take a decade or more to collect on a debt, potential creditors were reluctant to lend planters money to buy slaves and tended to charge substantial interest rates when they did so. Price contrasts this to the 'Anglo-Saxon or creditor defense model', which prevailed in Barbados, and in most of British America. There, certain that the courts would back their efforts to collect past due debts, potential lenders were less reluctant, and interest rates tended to be lower.[16]

The difference in the law of credit may lie at the root of the differences in the organization of sugar production. Barbadians, able to get the credit they needed, were able to shift quickly from the dispersed to the more productive centralized system, by rapidly buying the needed slaves. Brazilians were unable to follow the Barbadians and create a centralized system of farming, because their access to the credit needed to buy slaves was restricted by the legal system. Their inability to obtain slaves in sufficient numbers forced them to stick with the dispersed system despite its disadvantages.

I am not arguing that Brazilians were unable to obtain slaves, although as Price notes many of the slaves imported into Brazil may have been diverted away from sugar into other, less protected sectors of the economy. While Brazilian sugar planters were able to get slaves, they could not get them as quickly as could their Barbadian counterparts. Indeed, the most important contrast between Bahia and Barbados is not in the number of slaves but in their distribution. In Bahia, if thirty slaves were making cane for the same mill, those thirty slaves were likely to be distributed among three owners, the mill owner and two *lavradores de cana*, and thus working in units too small to capture the benefits of gang labour. In Barbados, by contrast, all thirty slaves would be owned by the big planter who owned the mill, and who thus would be able to capture the efficiencies of the gang system.

For the issue at hand, speed may have been critical. Brazilians, unable to borrow, were forced to pay for slaves out of current earnings, which meant that it took a long time for a planter to begin operating on the centralized system. In Barbados, on the other hand, the needed slaves could be obtained more quickly. In the 1660s, when Barbadian planters seem to have begun the conversion to centralized sugar production, Barbadian cane farmers were mostly poor tenants, operating on a small scale, and as such easily displaced. The *lavradores de cana* of Bahia, on the other hand, were often substantial producers, on their way to becoming planters in their own right. Their wealth and political influence meant that when Bahian sugar planters reached the point where they could

[16] *Ibid.*

organize along centralized lines, the cane farmers could not be so easily displaced.

This essay could be read as providing yet another object lesson in the failure of populist economics, and of debtor relief legislation. Indeed, it could be argued that the restrictive credit legislation, by inhibiting the shift to the more efficient centralized system, bears the major responsibility for the stagnation of the Bahian sugar industry during the seventeenth century, at a time when the more efficiently organized English sugar islands were booming. With the advantage of hindsight, Bahian mill owners might be persuaded to such an interpretation of their situation. From the perspective of the *lavradores de cana*, it is less clear that the populist economics of the Latin rule failed. For, by inhibiting the development of the centralized system in Bahia, the Latin rule may have kept the *lavradores de cana* from suffering the fate of the cane farmers of Barbados.

7   The revolutionary impact of European demand for tropical goods

Carole Shammas

The history of early modern western Europe is experiencing an identity crisis. More and more frequently, the question crops up as to whether the appropriate unit of analysis is nation state or empire. The years from 1500 onward were a period of extraordinary overseas expansion, but the idea of empire also has added currency because, even within Europe, most states were actually conglomerations of different kingdoms, principalities and provinces, not all of which had entered the state on an equal footing. To contribute further to the unit of analysis confusion, some have suggested that, in regard to many issues, these states operated as regions of an Atlantic world and that such a world is the best conceptual framework. While Great Britain and the topic of a greater British history has occasioned the most spilling of ink on this matter,[1] nearly all western European countries are at risk of being imagined anew or reconfigured as communities.

In keeping with this renewed interest in empire, an impressive number of books and articles on the subject of world trade and colonies have been produced over the past decade. Perhaps inspired or provoked by the great global histories of capitalism by Fernand Braudel and Immanuel Wallerstein, a transnational perspective pervades these works, which trace the expansion of western European sovereigns and the adventurers and trading companies they licensed into the Americas, south-eastern Asia and the subcontinent, and coastal Africa. The technology, goods and labour that Europeans acquired by the conquests and settlements, it is argued, laid the economic foundation for the modern world and European and Anglo-American domination of it.[2] Social and cultural studies have

---

[1] For the most recent listing of the works involved in the greater British history debate, see '*AHR* Forum: the new British history in Atlantic perspective', *American Historical Review*, 104 (1999), 426–500, which includes articles by David Armitage, Jane Ohlmeyer, Ned C. Landsman, Eliga H. Gould and J. G. A. Pocock.

[2] Fernand Braudel, *Civilization and Capitalism, 15ᵗʰ–18ᵗʰ Century*. Vol. I: *The Structures of Everyday Life*; vol. II: *Wheels of Commerce* vol. III: *The Perspective of the World*, tr. Sian Reynolds (New York, 1981–4); Immanuel Wallerstein, *The Modern World System*. Vol. I: *Capitalist Agriculture and the Origins of the European World-Economy in the Sixteenth Century*;

picked up on the way the global exchange of goods characterizes the early modern period, and the terms the 'world of goods' or the 'empire of goods' enjoy considerable popularity.[3]

Not everyone, however, has been happily assimilated into this kind of conceptualization. Many historians of European economic history have been reluctant to integrate empire into their own work. As Patrick O'Brien has commented,

Most of the economic history of Western Europe has been written as if the sources of agrarian improvement, technological progress, capital formation, the accumulation of skills, population growth and internal migration, institutional change and the diffusion of factor and commodity markets which occurred between 1492 and 1789 can be explained almost without reference to shorter or longer cycles of expansion and contraction in the international economy as a whole.[4]

The treatment of consumer demand – 'the world of goods' – is a case in point. The best-known studies proclaiming an early modern 'consumer revolution' focus almost exclusively on European-produced semi-durables and durables,[5] probably because the production of these goods can be linked most easily to nineteenth-century industrialization. Jan de Vries, an expert on the Dutch economy of the golden age, has done some of the most important research on this subject. He argues that European households eager to own the new European manufactures embarked

vol. II: *Mercantilism and the Consolidation of the European World-Economy 1600–1750*; vol. III: *The Second Era of Great Expansion of the Capitalist World Economy 1730–1840s*. John E. Wills recently reviewed twenty-four books in the *AHR* on the history of Asian world trade, all of which had been published between 1987 and 1991. See 'Maritime Asia, 1500–1800: the interactive emergence of European domination', *AHR*, 98 (1993), 83–105. I. K. Steele has drawn attention to the large number of new studies relating to the Atlantic empires, a concept pioneered by the Chaunus, Ralph Davis and Peggy K. Liss, in 'Exploding colonial American history: Amerindian, Atlantic and global perspectives', *Reviews in American History*, 26 (1998), 70–95.

[3] Mary Douglas and Baron Isherwood, *The World of Goods: Towards an Anthropology of Consumption* (New York, 1979); John Brewer and Roy Porter, eds., *Consumption and the World of Goods* (London, 1993); and T. H. Breen, 'An empire of goods: the anglicization of colonial America, 1690–1776', *Journal of British Studies*, 24 (1986), 467–99.

[4] Patrick Karl O'Brien, 'The foundations of European industralization [sic]', in J. C. Pardo, ed., *Economic Effects of the European Expansion* (Stuttgart, 1992), p. 466.

[5] Neil McKendrick, 'Home demand and economic growth: a new view of the role of women and children in the industrial revolution', in Neil McKendrick, ed., *Historical Perspectives: Studies in English Thought and Society in Honour of J. H. Plumb* (London, 1974), pp. 152–210; Joan Thirsk, *Economic Policies and Projects: the Development of a Consumer Society in Early Modern England* (Oxford, 1978); Neil McKendrick, John Brewer and J. H. Plumb, *The Birth of a Consumer Society: the Commercialization of Eighteenth-Century England* (London, 1983); Jan de Vries, 'Between purchasing power and the world of goods: understanding the household economy in early modern Europe', in Brewer and Porter, eds., *Consumption and the World of Goods*, pp. 107–21; and Cary Carson, 'The consumer revolution in colonial British America: why demand?', in Cary Carson, Ronald Hoffman and Peter J. Albert, eds., *Of Consuming Interests: the Style of Life in the Eighteenth Century* (Charlottesville, 1994), pp. 483–697.

upon an 'industrious revolution' of agricultural specialization and intensified regimen of work.[6] The desire for non-European commodities and the specialization and intensification of labour represented by the creation of plantation economies to meet that demand do not get included as part of the process. Other treatments not only exclude non-European imports but also consumer demand. A new, informative history of the Spanish economy from 1700–1900 examines Spain's trade with the Indies, shows the more than thirty-fold growth in the importation of tropical goods such as sugar and chocolate over the course of the eighteenth century but presents no analysis of consumption and concludes that the empire's importance for the peninsular economy has been overestimated.[7] Joel Mokyr's spirited defence of the British industrial revolution as the major transformation in economic history dismisses both those, like Jan de Vries, who tie its origins to consumer demand for early modern manufactures and those, following in the tradition of Eric Williams, who link it to empire and trade in tropical goods.[8]

No more than a passing acquaintance with the dominant paradigms in economic history is necessary to understand why plantation goods get short shrift. First, most economic historians assume that domestic markets, not world markets, are what counts. Second, the shift from artisanal production to factory production remains *the* event most associated with a rise in the rate of economic growth. For these reasons, economic historians, like Patrick O'Brien, who do try to find a place for the empire in economic development, stress the way in which the tropical goods trade stimulated the export of manufactures and the shortcomings of the way that impact has been conceptualized.[9]

As long as the criteria for importance consist of the share of gross domestic product (GDP) claimed by the foreign trade sector and the

---

[6] De Vries, 'Purchasing power and the world of goods'.

[7] David Ringrose, *Spain, Europe, and the 'Spanish Miracle' 1700–1900* (Cambridge, 1996), p. 118.

[8] Joel Mokyr, 'Editor's introduction: the new economic history and the industrial revolution', in Joel Mokyr, ed., *The British Industrial Revolution: an Economic Perspective*, 2nd edn (Boulder, Col., 1999), pp. 58–75.

[9] O'Brien himself seems torn on the issue. In 'Foundations of European Industralization [sic]', after critiquing the insularity of many British economic historians, he notes (pp. 487 and 502) that only the emergence of the British cotton textile industry can be linked closely to transcontinental trade. 'As late as 1841', he writes, '[it] still accounted for only 7 per cent of Britain's gross national product'. So, he concludes, the '"perspective of the world" for Europe is less significant than the "perspective of Europe" for the world'. But, in 'Inseparable connections: trade, economy, fiscal state, and the expansion of empire, 1688–1815', in P. J. Marshall, ed., *The Oxford History of the British Empire: the Eighteenth Century* (Oxford, 1998), p. 75. O'Brien is much more bullish on the economic importance of the empire, as he is in the article written with Stanley L. Engerman, 'Exports and the growth of the British economy from the Glorious Revolution to the Peace of Amiens', in Barbara L. Solow, ed., *Slavery and the Rise of the Atlantic System* (Cambridge, 1991).

direct links between plantation commodities and the emergence of power-driven factory production, no one studying European history is likely to be spending much time contemplating the impact of the demand for consumer goods from tropical climes and the acquisition of large amounts of American, Asian and African subjects and real estate. GDP and even GNP[10] are designed to measure the output of nation states not empires. Domestic markets dominate the economy of most nation states because the majority of services in the past, as today, must be provided locally, and transport costs as well as government policy give an advantage to goods produced internally. Those involved in the export/import side of the economy will nearly always be in the minority. In the period 1500–1800, however, calculating product in terms of nation state economies rather than empires, when most of the world's population was in empires, results in distortions. It means surgically removing the population and output of colonies or tributary principalities from the imperial metropolis yet continuing to internally count sectors, output, revenues and expenditures that would not be there save for the existence of said colonies.

What I would like to explore in this chapter is what early modern economic history might look like if we actually took seriously the notion of an imperial economy instead of one tied to a nation state framework. Such an exercise throws a different light upon certain pivotal events in traditional European economic and political history, just as the histories of the Americas, western and southern Africa, and southern Asia continue to be affected by research on early modern Europe.

The early modern empires

It might be best to begin with some figures. Global, world system and imperial histories are frequently rather vague on the size of the early modern empires in terms of square miles and subjects, numbers that might make it less easy to dismiss overseas dominions. In the two tables that follow I have tried to put together some territorial and population numbers for all western European countries with overseas empires in the late eighteenth century, just prior to the American Revolution.

Table 7.1 provides a percentage breakdown by continent of the total territorial holdings in each of the western European empires.[11] It is often

---

[10] GDP measures the output of those living in a geographical area, usually a nation state. GNP measures the output of all citizens wherever they are living but does not include colonials.

[11] I have included colonies possessed directly by the sovereign or indirectly through a chartered company or proprietor. I have excluded forts with no surrounding colony and lands claimed but not occupied or governed by a colonial authority. Refer to the appendix for information about the areas covered on each continent and the approximate square miles and population of the colonies.

Table 7.1. *Western European Empires: approximate square mile distribution by geographical area* c. *1775 (in percentage of square miles)*

Areas	Empires					
	Spanish	Portuguese	Dutch	British	French	Danish
Europe	3.9	0.9	2.5	11.3	81.8	99.1
Atlantic Isles	0.1	0.1	–	3.9	–	–
Coastal Africa	0.0	9.1	38.0	2.7	0.7	–
Americas	93.7	89.6	22.5	59.3	17.4	0.9
SE Asia	2.4	0.2	37.0	22.8	–	–
Total (sq. miles)	4, 937,994	3,666,777	651,533	788,846	259,627	15,580

Source: see appendix.

remarked that these first colonial empires, in contrast to their counterparts in the nineteenth and early twentieth centuries, involved relatively small amounts of territory. Indeed if represented on a world map, the small islands and coastal enclaves that constitute the empires of all the western Europeans, save the Iberians in the Americas, do not look all that impressive. But then, the square miles of these European countries themselves are not that overwhelming. Consequently, table 7.1 reveals that only in the cases of the French, who had lost much of their empire to the British twelve years earlier, and the Danish, who never became serious colonial players, the real estate in Europe constituted only a tiny portion of the total empire. Spain's is 4 per cent, with most of the remainder in the Americas. Almost 90 per cent of Portugal's square miles were in Brazil and nearly 60 per cent of Britain's were along the Atlantic seaboard of North America and in the Caribbean. Even the Dutch, whose colonies in Surinam and the West Indies are thought of as small, had ten times as much land there as in Europe. France's loss of Canada and Louisiana still left 17 per cent of its land in the New World. Perhaps more surprising is the proportion of real estate occupied in Africa and Asia, continents more associated with the imperialism of later centuries. Spain held North African cities on the Mediterranean but all the other settlements of western European countries were on the sub-Saharan coast. They began as forts but evolved into colonies. Britain had Senegambia, the Dutch held the Cape Province, and the French still occupied islands off the east coast, after having had to cede Senegal to Britain. Portugal, which had the oldest settlements in Africa, had colonies on both the western (Luanda, Bengo and Benguela) and eastern (portions of Mozambique) coasts. In south-eastern Asia, Spain and Portugal had rather modest holdings by 1775, the Philippines and Macao, respectively, but the Dutch held

Table 7.2. *Western European empires: approximate population distribution by geographical area* c. *1775 (in percentage of subjects)*

| | Empires | | | | | |
Areas	Spanish	Portuguese	Dutch	British	French	Danish
Europe	43.9	35.9	18.8	22.7	97.9	97.2
Atlantic Isles	0.7	3.5	–	10.6	–	–
Africa	0.4	32.3	0.5	0.3	0.3	–
Americas	46.6	24.6	1.6	8.4	1.8	2.8
East and South Asia	8.3	3.6	79.1	58.1	–	–
Total no. of subjects	23,904,000	6,956,000	10,625,000	37,931,000	27,570,000	1,029,000

Source: see appendix.

coastal Ceylon and a significant portion of present-day Indonesia, and Britain through the East India Company had control over Bengal, Bombay, Madras and the north Sarkars.

One could quickly protest that much of this land overseas was sparsely settled and could not contribute much to a global economy. Yet, if we measure the importance of an area in the empire by numbers of subjects, those paying a tax, tribute or giving labour services, the pull of the overseas empire is equally compelling. Table 7.2 shows that in all cases except for the colony-poor French (*c.* 1775) and Danish, those subjects living outside Europe far outnumbered those living inside. The Spanish empire's dominant cultural group in terms of numbers was American Indian and *mestizo*, Portugal's was African, whether in Africa or Brazil, the Dutch were heavily Indonesian, and the British, Bengali. No matter that these peoples had little power in that empire or identity with it. They count because, only with difficulty, could they avoid making their economic contribution to it. The numbers give at least some indication as well of the amount of wealth in terms of resources and labour that could be tapped by the metropolitan centres. These subjects constituted nearly 15 per cent of an estimated world population of 750,000,000 *c.* 1775 or one out of every seven persons.

These splotches of imperial colour were not randomly distributed. More than anything else they were the product of the escalating demand for a group of non-European commodities by the Atlantic community. This demand produced an agricultural revolution in the plantations, a revolution so successful that global diets and farming were never to be the same again. This activity also stimulated innovative industrial production in Europe. Both politically supportive and potentially destabilizing was the rise of the commercial sector that financed and managed the production, exchange and distribution of tropical goods. Ultimately, these imperial interests came into conflict with the nation state perspective, producing republican revolutions and a different form of empire.

The demand for tropical goods and the growth of empires

The expansion in empire and trade by western European countries in the first hundred years, 1500 to 1600, continued patterns familiar since at least medieval times. Only the locations changed. The Spanish set up an empire in the Americas through conquests by military adventurers who demanded tributes of gold, silver and labour.[12] Mining of silver took over as the tributes petered out.[13] The Portuguese began their travels to the East Indies in search of traditional luxury products – pepper and spices. Even their Atlantic forays in collaboration with Genoese merchants, which resulted in the establishment of sugar plantations in the Madeiras, Azores, São Tomé, Cape Verde and finally Brazil, had precedents in the medieval Mediterranean.[14]

After 1600, however, the situation altered, as what originally had been subsidiary interests to the Iberians turned into a major focus and attracted the attention of the mercantile communities in other western European countries. The profits to be made from the cultivation and trade of a small group of tropical groceries and one textile – none of which had been popular European consumer goods previously – dominated global affairs for two hundred years. The groceries were tobacco, tea, coffee, chocolate and sugar, in heightened demand as a sweetener for the new caffeine drinks and in its distilled form as an alcoholic beverage, rum. The other major commodity to invade the market was printed cotton from the Asian subcontinent.

Western Europeans appear to have been about the only members of the seventeenth-century world community to whom *all* these goods were exotic. American Indian groups had smoked tobacco and drank choc-

---

[12] On the switch from a military adventurer, tribute-based colonization to a more commercially directed one in the early seventeenth century, see Carole Shammas, 'English commercial development and American colonization 1560–1620', in K. R. Andrews, N. P. Canny and P. E. H. Hair, eds., *The Westward Enterprise: English Activities in Ireland, the Atlantic, and America 1480–1650* (Liverpool, 1978), pp. 151–74.

[13] Dennis O. Flynn and Arturo Giraldez, 'Born with a "silver spoon": the origin of world trade in 1571', *Journal of World History*, 6 (1995), 201–21, draws attention to the importance of Chinese demand for silver currency in the underwriting of the sixteenth-century Spanish empire.

[14] Charles Verlinden, *The Beginnings of Modern Colonization: Eleven Essays with an Introduction*, tr. Yvonne Freccero (Ithaca, 1970).

olate for centuries. Coffee and tea had a venerable history in Africa and Asia where sugar also had been more heavily cultivated than in Europe. Cotton cloth was, arguably, the most important manufactured commodity in world trade prior to 1600. It was simply that that trade was based in Asia and Africa.

A quick look at English foreign trade statistics, which have been written about more extensively than any other, is instructive. From the medieval period to the mid-seventeenth century, England's trade consisted essentially of sending wool and later wool textiles to Europe and the middle east and receiving back goods – wines, linens and spices – that with few exceptions reached no more than the top 10 per cent of the population.[15] It was not that English consumers did not exist; but what they consumed usually had a western European or, even more often, British origination point.

By 1700 much had changed. Re-exports, primarily plantation groceries and Asian textiles, constituted two-thirds of the value of woollen exports and retained imports had spread far beyond the elite of the population. By the 1720s, the official values of wool textiles and re-exports were about equal, and continued to be so throughout the eighteenth century. The situation was unique to this time period, for later, in the nineteenth century, industrial manufactures overwhelmed colonial re-exports.[16]

The statistics are a reflection of a great new consumer demand for these products in Britain, its colonies and its foreign customers. In 1559, groceries, consisting mainly of pepper and spices, represented less than 9 per cent of the total value of imports into England and Wales. By 1772, when groceries included tobacco, sugar products, tea and coffee, the category devoured almost 36 per cent of the total. This figure, moreover, is an under-estimate. Smugglers, whose contributions escape the statistics, supplied many of the consumers, because the government had fixed such heavy duties on these popular products. It is also worth noting that the rise from 9 per cent to over one-third occurred during a period of sharp drops in the price of tobacco, caffeine drinks and sugar.[17]

The gain came from enthusiastic public adoption in the seventeenth and early eighteenth centuries, coupled with the lobbying of trading

---

[15] David Harris Sacks, *The Widening Gate: Bristol and the Atlantic Economy 1450–1700* (Berkeley, 1991) traces the transformation of the overseas merchant community from a trade based on European wines to one primarily concerned with American groceries.

[16] Ralph Davis, 'English foreign trade, 1660–1700', in E. M. Carus-Wilson, ed., *Essays in Economic History*, 2 vols. (London, 1962), II, pp. 257–72, and B. R. Mitchell and Phyllis Deane, comp., *Abstract of British Historical Statistics* (Cambridge, 1962), pp. 279–81 and 293–5.

[17] Carole Shammas, *The Preindustrial Consumer in England and America* (Oxford, 1990), pp. 77–8.

companies, merchants and planters to support the expansion necessary to control the supply of these goods, rather than from any far-sighted government strategy to conquer world trade in the 'new' groceries. As Fernand Braudel has observed with reference to tobacco, the spread of smoking among the world's population can be traced through the record of hastily passed laws prohibiting use in one country after another.[18] In that regard, England, acting in 1604, was one of the earliest to try to discourage use. The same love–hate relationship developed with sugar and the caffeine drinks. The attraction to the substances seemed to be initially of a psycho-physiological nature – people valued them for their energy producing and appetite-appeasing characteristics – but usage also became entrenched through association of the substances with appealing social environments.[19] The profits from grants of monopolies, import duties and excise taxes soon won over government opponents and the western European diet was revolutionized.

High demand also overrode entrenched interests in the case of cotton cloth. The Portuguese, then the Dutch, English and French originally became involved with cotton textiles in order to buy the East Indian 'old' groceries (pepper and spices) and the African slaves needed to produce the 'new'.[20] But when the East Indies trading companies tried selling the cloth in England and Europe in the late seventeenth century, they found they had no trouble unloading the light, bright, washable calicoes on

[18] Braudel, *The Structures of Everyday Life*, pp. 262–3.
[19] On the enthusiasm for the new groceries, generally, and references for further reading, see Shammas, *Preindustrial Consumer*, ch. 6 and pp. 186–8, and James Walvin, *Fruits of Empire: Exotic Produce and British Taste, 1660–1800* (New York, 1997). Sidney Mintz has pioneered work on sugar and its relationship to caffeine drinks. See most recently his 'The changing roles of food in the study of consumption', in Brewer and Porter, eds., *Consumption and the World of Goods*, pp. 261–73. McCusker, *Rum and the American Revolution*; Jordan Goodman, *Tobacco in History: the Cultures of Dependence* (London, 1993); Goodman, 'Excitantia: or, how Enlightenment Europe took to soft drugs', in Jordan Goodman, Paul E. Lovejoy and Andrew Sherratt, eds., *Consuming Habits: Drugs in History and Anthropology* (London, 1995), pp. 126–47 covers smoking. Thanks to Jacob Price we know more about the organization of the trade in tobacco than we do for any other commodity. On coffee, Jurgen Schneider, 'The effects on European markets of imports of overseas agriculture: the production, trade, and consumption of coffee (15th to late 18th century)' in Pardo, *Economic Effects of the European Expansion*, pp. 283–305; Woodruff D. Smith, 'From coffeehouse to parlour', in Goodman *et al.*, *Consuming Habits*, pp. 148–64, and S. D. Smith, 'Accounting for taste: British coffee consumption in historical perspective', *JIH*, 27 (1996), 183–214.
[20] Jonathan I. Israel, *Dutch Primacy in World Trade, 1585–1740* (Oxford, 1989), p. 103; Niels Steensgaard, 'The growth and composition of the long distance trade of England and the Dutch Republic before 1750', in James D. Tracy, ed., *The Rise of Merchant Empires: Long Distance Trade in the Early Modern World, 1350–1750* (Cambridge, 1990), p. 123; Herbert S. Klein, 'Economic aspects of the eighteenth-century Atlantic slave trade', *ibid.*, p. 291; and Philip D. Curtin, *The Rise and Fall of the Plantation Complex* (New York, 1990), p. 211.

consumers whose warmer houses and, in the case of the plantations, warmer climes made the product highly desirable. The Indian calicoes did not just supplement but also competed quite successfully with domestically produced blends and worsteds used in gowns, linings and decorative household furnishings.

So the Asian commercial ventures of the Dutch and English trading companies may have begun as pepper and spice voyages, but both soon shifted the value of their cargoes towards textiles, primarily Indian cottons. By the 1730s, pepper and spices constituted no more than 14 per cent of the worth of the VOC's (Dutch East India Company's) imports and less than 5 per cent of the English Company's. Textiles had risen to 41 per cent of the value of VOC imports, with tea and coffee equalling 32 per cent, while 76 per cent of the value of the English Company's imports consisted of textiles, with 15 per cent in tea and coffee.[21]

Calico's popularity, however, presented an economic problem not encountered with the groceries. In many Western European countries, textiles employed a greater number of workers than any other occupation, aside from agriculture and domestic service. Until mechanization of spinning, Europeans were unable to produce cotton yarn as strong as that found in India, and as a result only made cotton blends. Competition with superior Asian products that also sold at a relatively modest price seemed hopeless. Instead producers and localities threatened by calico launched a campaign against the product. Political pressure produced a complete ban on imported printed cottons in both France and Great Britain, although the East India Company could still sell them in the colonies and other external markets. Much smuggling resulted. Raising tariffs to high levels was common but actually banning a commodity, as was done in this case, and causing the government to lose revenue was unusual.[22]

As far as I can determine, the only non-European good that depended more upon the enthusiasm of governmental authorities than that of the consumer was rice, which in the West was relegated to the almshouse.[23] Generally, the public clamoured for tropical goods, merchants saw them as a means to accumulate great fortunes, and governments grew dependent on the revenues.

While the empire amassed by the Spanish crown in the sixteenth

---

[21] Steensgaard, 'Growth and composition of English and Dutch trade', pp. 116–17.

[22] Braudel, *Civilization and Capitalism*, p. 572, Patrick O'Brien, Trevor Griffiths and Philip Hunt, 'Political components of the industrial revolution: Parliament and the English cotton textile industry, 1660–1774', *EcHR*, 44 (1991), 394–423, and Carole Shammas, 'The decline of textile prices in England and British America prior to industrialization', *EcHR*, 47 (1994), 500–2.

[23] Peter A. Coclanis, *The Shadow of a Dream: Economic Life and Death in the South Carolina Low Country 1670–1920* (New York, 1989), p. 134.

century had little to do with the demand for new groceries and cotton textiles, the holdings of all the others and the eighteenth-century activities of the Spanish themselves make little sense unless one connects them with the history of the cultivation and trade of these goods. Spain, a country usually left out of discussions about consumer revolutions, imported enough cacao *c.* 1775 for every adult in the nation, annually, to place a pound in their cupboard, and enough sugar to place half a pound alongside it on the shelf.[24]

In this period, Portuguese, Dutch, British, French and even the tiny Danish, empires existed primarily because chartered trading companies, independent commercial interests and their planter confederates found the land and labour in foreign parts necessary to profit from consumer demand, and only secondarily for other reasons such as the need to find a market for manufactured goods, a place to dump political/religious dissidents, criminals and the poor, or an outlet for patronage. The growth in the geographic and demographic size of the empires can be attributed to the tendency of western Europeans to monopolize not only the trade and distribution of these goods but also the production by transforming them into plantation crops.

The story of how capital and labour flowed into colonies is becoming better and better documented.[25] The Portuguese developed sugar plantations on a group of tiny Atlantic islands where a couple of hundred thousand people, mostly African slaves, lived. In the late sixteenth century, the centre of production moved to Brazil where land was more plentiful. The other colonial powers centre sugar production in the Caribbean, mostly on islands packed first with indentured European servants and then African slaves.

All colonial powers had planters and merchants operating in the Carribean either on islands or on the North or South American mainland surrounding that sea. Tobacco obtained by English settlers in Virginia from the gardens of Algonkin Indians became the next crop given the plantation treatment.[26] Then cocoa, the preferred caffeine drink of the Spanish, which went form being acquired through the tribute system to become a Venezuelan and Brazilian plantation commodity.

---

[24] Ringrose, *Spain, Europe, and the 'Spanish Miracle'*, pp. 72, 108. In estimating amounts per capita, I assume roughly half the population is adult.

[25] Verlinden, *The Beginnings of Modern Colonization*; Sidney W. Mintz, *Sweetness and Power: the Place of Sugar in Modern History* (New York, 1985); Curtin, *Plantation Complex*; and Robin Blackburn, *The Making of New World Slavery: from the Baroque to the Modern 1492–1800* (London, 1997).

[26] That evolution is documented in McCusker and Menard, *Economy of British America*, ch. 6.

Coffee made the switch around the same time. Originally a commodity traded in the Middle East, the Dutch grew impatient with the price and the quantity available. The VOC turned to Java, their base for their traditional East Indies trade in pepper, spices and silks. To protect themselves and their commerce, the Dutch had already established a major fortified settlement on the island, which was about the size of England with a population, in 1600, of over 3 million. They had also imported a large number of Asian slaves from other islands to do the manual and domestic labour. In about 1700 they introduced coffee bushes, the cultivation of which the Company managed through local Javanese regents. The VOC set the prices it would pay, and the regents delivered the coffee cultivated by what must have been increasingly industrious peasants, encouraged in their industriousness by dramatic drops in the price the Company set on the coffee beans. By the later eighteenth century, coffee produced in Java became the luxury brand, just behind the Yemeni mocha, while the bulk of the beans came to be grown on French, Dutch and Portuguese plantations in the West Indies and South America. There African slaves did the work.[27]

Cotton and tea were 'plantationized' later. The story of how India moved from cotton manufacturer, to just cotton grower and, then, only cotton consumer is a staple of the world-systems narrative. The Portuguese, Dutch, French and English originally established trading forts on the islands and coasts of India. Escalating demand for cotton cloth in Europe, however, increased the number of chartered Company officials and military garrisons in Bengal and coastal India. Europeans took advantage of Hindu–Moslem rivalries just as Indian princes and the Moghul emperors tried to do the same with the competition between western Europeans. Ultimately, the British East India Company acting under crown authority proved the most aggressive, maintaining an army of 30,000 in Bengal alone by 1770.[28] Eventually, British mills began taking over the production of cotton cloth. When this shift took place, the British came to favour cotton from the West Indies and the southern United States where plantation-style production prevailed.

---

[27] John E. Wills, Jr, 'European consumption and Asian production in the seventeenth and eighteenth century', in Brewer and Porter, eds., *Consumption and the World of Goods*, pp. 133–47; Anthony Reid, *Southeast Asia in the Age of Commerce 1450–1680* (New Haven, 1988); M. Hoadley, 'Slavery, bondage, and dependency in pre-colonial Java: the Cirebon-Priangan region, 1700', in Anthony Reid, ed., *Slavery, Bondage, and Dependency in Southeast Asia* (New York, 1983), pp. 90–117; J. Fox, '"For Good and Sufficient Reasons": an examination of early Dutch East India Company ordinances on slaves and slavery', *ibid.*, pp. 246–62; S. Abeyasekere, 'Slaves in Batavia: insights from a slave register', *ibid.*, pp. 286–314.

[28] H. V. Bowen, *Elites, Enterprise and the Making of the British Overseas Empire 1688–1775* (Basingstoke, 1996), p. 30.

When plantations did take root in India, it was with a commodity that had not been important there previously, tea. In the seventeenth century European traders and trading companies seeking tea from the principal supplier, China, had to set up fortified commercial bases in places such as Macao and Java to deal with the Chinese merchants. The Chinese successfully kept control over cultivation of the leaves until the early nineteenth century.[29] It was to pay for the trade with China that Britain developed opium production in India. Ultimately, though, the tea problem was solved in a more direct manner by setting up plantations in Indian highland areas.

Ceylon also became an important tea producing centre, after a blight there destroyed the coffee plantations the Europeans had established. That island, with an eighteenth-century population of over 1 million, first fell to Portugal in the sixteenth century, the Dutch in the seventeenth, and finally the British at the end of the eighteenth. It is a good example of a colonial possession that began its overseas association as a trading centre for western Europeans interested in the old groceries, in this case, cinnamon, and ended up largely as a plantation society producing caffeine crops.

In short, the square miles and the population numbers that appear in tables 7.1 and 7.2 would be unthinkable without the growth in demand for tropical consumer goods. Almost every overseas settlement controlled by western Europeans had a direct or indirect relationship to that demand. Most Atlantic islands were plantation colonies. West Africa was involved in the slave trade to the Americas. Six out of every seven migrants to the Americas prior to the late nineteenth century came from Africa and the vast majority were imported to work on sugar, coffee, tobacco, cacao and cotton plantations. Even in the British thirteen colonies, which attracted the most European migration of all the overseas possessions, 54 per cent of those coming in during the colonial period entered as bound servants, probably three-quarters of whom participated in some aspect of the tropical goods trade. Adding those coming from Africa, an immigration almost exclusively dedicated to plantation work, consumer demand for the new groceries prompted roughly two-thirds of the total Atlantic migration prior to 1776. It is true that much of the population living in New England, the middle colonies and the southern backcountry had come over for religious reasons, to fish, to practise arable husbandry, or, in the case of the woodland Indians, had descended from groups that had been there with their tobacco long before any Europeans had arrived. On the other hand, it is difficult to imagine a

---

[29] Hoe-cheung Mui and Lorna H. Mui, *The Management of Monopoly: a Study of the East India Company's Conduct of its Tea Trade 1784–1833* (Vancouver, 1984), pp. 4–12.

thriving New England post-1640, a south-eastern Pennsylvania and New York City or a British imperial commitment without the sugar islands, tobacco plantations and the slave trade. Perhaps small pietist enclaves, fishing villages, logging camps and fur trading posts dotting the coastline of North America – but over 3 million subjects of the British crown?[30] The Americas without the plantation economies would have been largely Spanish-speaking Indian communities with peninsulars and creoles huddled in mining towns, missions and a few administrative capitals.

The concerns of the East Indies companies and traders, which as reported above, had increasingly focused on Indian textiles, tea and coffee, explain the initial founding of all the south-eastern Asia colonies as well as the 'refreshment' stops in south-eastern Africa: the Dutch Cape colony, the Portuguese settlements in Mozambique, and the French holdings in the Seychelles, Mauritius and Réunion.

The sites for colonies, then, in almost all cases, reflect the demand for tropical goods. The amount of territory occupied, however, frequently exceeded what might be deemed necessary for trade and cultivation. This expansion was more often due to the activities of trading company officials, military leaders, planters and other colonists overseas than part of an imperial design of government officials, company directors or others in the metropolis who often felt political pressure against engaging in potentially costly expansionary projects.[31] Europeans in this period, it is often assumed, were interested in trade not real estate. That cliché may be true of many of the merchants based in the major European ports, but planters, company servants, as they were called, and independent traders in the forts had many reasons to increase the territory and subjects under their control. Planters wanted uncontested rights to land, and traders wanted uncontested rights to commodities. To secure monopolies, the latter offered military protection which was underwritten by the local population. Once in control of both the military and revenue collection,

[30] Using Aaron S. Fogleman's figures, 'From slaves, convicts, and servants to free passengers: the transformation of immigration in the era of the American Revolution', *Journal of American History*, 85 (1998) appendix, 66–76, I assume that the slave migration, the convict migration, and 50 per cent of the eighteenth-century indentured servant migration were involved in some aspect of plantation trade, mostly agricultural labour. On the economic importance of the West Indies trade to New England, see David Richardson, 'Slavery, trade, and economic growth in eighteenth-century New England' in Solow, ed., *Slavery and the Rise of the Atlantic System*, pp. 237–64. See also Blackburn, *Making of New World Slavery*, chs. 9 and 10; Walvin, *Fruits of Empire, passim*.

[31] Bowen in *Elites, Enterprise, and the Making of the British Overseas Empire*, pp. 16–21, emphasizes this point, when critiquing the Cain and Hopkins view of gentlemanly capitalists being the critical factor in imperial designs from the late seventeenth century onwards.

sovereignty soon followed. The Seven Years' War began with land speculators from Virginia, including George Washington, trying to push into the Ohio river valley. The transformation of fortress towns into an empire in India found its greatest support among the Company representatives overseas who had the most to gain.[32] The importance of their role and of those with whom they allied is one more illustration of why one has to count not only subjects at home but also those abroad as well.

Eighteenth-century economic revolutions

Until very recently, when historians have discussed economic revolutions, tropical goods and, to use Philip Curtin's term, the plantation complex have played no part in the discussion or, as in the case of cotton textiles, if they did get included, their tropical origins were obscured. Early modern agricultural revolutions are taken to be changes in grain production through enclosure, mixed husbandry and innovative forms of crop rotation. Even Immanuel Wallerstein in the first of his world-systems volumes, *Capitalist Agriculture and the Origins of the European World Economy in the Sixteenth Century*, focuses more on these developments and their effects on capitalist accumulation than the economic development that arose from plantation agriculture. Yet the former seems to have evolved much more gradually and less revolutionarily than did the establishment of plantations for the growing of sugar, tobacco, coffee and cacao. Debates about the timing of the three century-and-a-half transformation known as the English agricultural revolution still fill the pages of economic history journals, while the title of the most recent assessment of its revolutionary status is 'Too much revolution'.[33] In United States history textbooks, the market revolution had to wait until northern wheat farms become linked to railroads and employ mechanical reapers, not when tobacco, rice and sugar plantations arose in the colonial period or cotton production was transformed in the 1790s, south.[34]

In plantation agriculture, plants indigenous to one area were cultivated in another, with a workforce from a third to produce for a world market, which delivered these highly desirable goods to consumers relatively

---

[32] An example of this process is given in C. A. Bayly, 'The British military–fiscal state and indigenous resistance, India 1750–1820', in Lawrence Stone, ed., *An Imperial State at War* (London, 1994), pp. 322–50.

[33] See Mark Overton, *Agricultural Revolution in England: the Transformation of the Agrarian Economy 1500–1850* (Cambridge, 1996); Robert C. Allen, 'Tracking the agricultural revolution in England', *EcHR*, 52 (1999), 209–35; and Gregory Clark, 'Too much revolution: agriculture in the industrial revolution 1700–1860', in Mokyr, ed., *British Industrial Revolution*, pp. 206–40.

[34] For a typical example, see John M. Murrin *et al.*, *Liberty, Equality, Power: a History of the American People*, 2 vols. (Fort Worth, 1996), I, especially ch. 10.

cheaply. Moreover, this reassignment of the global workforce resulted in a changed work regimen. If any workplace could claim an 'industrious revolution' it was the plantation. By the mid-eighteenth century, this frenzied economic activity had resulted in sugar, the premier plantation crop, overtaking grain as the single most valuable commodity entering world trade.[35] The basic outlines of the system, however, had been put together in Brazil by the Portuguese and west Africans at the end of the sixteenth century.

The rather devastating effects these single-minded enterprises had on communities globally and the slowness in mechanization may explain the curious omission of plantations from the pantheon of economic growth events. Their links to underdevelopment, dependency and political up-heavals have been examined much more closely than their connection to the transformation in agriculture from the sixteenth to the twentieth century. The plantation's scale of production, use of overseers, the mobility of capital and labour, rationalization of work and dedication to world markets all would seem to presage twentieth-century agribusiness much more than did the operations of the mechanized family farm. In the United States today, 77 per cent of farm land is in parcels of 500 acres or more. Moreover, in terms of farm receipts, the traditional cereals and grasses (wheat, barley, oats, hay) make up less than 15 per cent of the total, and, as a category, are less important than the more tropical crops – 'new' groceries, fruits, nuts, vegetables – grown under plantation-like circumstances.[36]

The major controversy over the revolutionary effects of the demand for tropical goods, of course, has concerned its relationship to the industrial revolution not the agricultural. Robin Blackburn in *The Making of New World Slavery* renews this fifty-year debate, which began with Eric Williams's provocative *Capitalism and Slavery*.[37] The research in the intervening years has changed the terms of the debate significantly. First of all, the industrial revolution has been cut down to size and expanded in time. No longer is there the notion of a dramatic take off in economic growth that all at once transformed society. Second, the plantation economy or complex is now viewed less as a feudal remnant and more as one of the more dynamic features of eighteenth-century capitalism. As a

---

[35] Blackburn, *The Making of New World Slavery*, p. 403.

[36] US Bureau of the Census, *Statistical Abstract of the United States, 1994* (Washington, D.C., 1994), pp. 665, 672, 677.

[37] Blackburn, *Making of New World Slavery*, ch. 12. A number of other recent surveys of this material have been made including Solow, ed., *Slavery and the Rise of the Atlantic System*; J. R. Ward, 'The industrial revolution and British imperialism, 1750–1850', *EcHR*, 2nd series, 47 (1994), 44–65; Kenneth Morgan, 'Atlantic trade and British economic growth in the eighteenth century', in Peter Mathias and John A. Davis, eds., *The Nature of Industrialization: International Trade and British Economic Growth from the Eighteenth Century to the Present Day* (Oxford, 1996), pp. 14–33.

result, Blackburn shows rather convincingly the way in which profits from the demand for tropical goods in turn stimulated demand for manufactured goods that was focused on relatively low quality metal-wares and lightweight textiles, two areas in which industrialization first manifested itself. The way the heavy demand in the plantation complex for Indian cottons, which were monopolized by the East India Company, translated itself into an interest in finding a way to manufacture, profitably, cottons in Britain is particularly easy to see. Profits from this global trade also filled the investment capital coffers. While there were many losers in the tropical-goods endeavour, the winners won big, raking in returns impossible to achieve in other ways and furnishing no less than a fifth of Britain's gross fixed capital formation in 1770 and probably much more. The protection of this system had its cost – but it was not borne by the manufacturing sector.

Eighteenth-century political revolutions: the core strikes back

In the histories of Europe and the Americas, republican revolutions rank as the central political events of the eighteenth century. In the American War for Independence and the French Revolution, the rejection of monarchy and the transformation of subjects into citizens followed imperial wars. There is nothing odd about military disasters provoking rebellions, except that these rebellions occurred after victories not losses. Both revolutions began over paying off the debt. The thirteen colonies refused to accept new taxes proposed by the king's ministers and voted in by the British Parliament. The colonists declared independence, and King George III lost over half of his real estate and about two and a half million of his subjects, a number equivalent to the population of Scotland and the north of England combined. During the war, the French monarchy, seeking to liberate the Americans and their trade from the clutches of the British, yet already in debt from earlier imperial wars, borrowed money at high rates, producing a fiscal crisis and a political meltdown. In 1789, revolution broke out at home, the king lost his life, and among other casualties the empire lost its principal colony, Saint-Domingue. The effort to create a whole new empire under Napoleon came to no good end.

It is not simply that fiscal problems within the eighteenth century 'empires of goods' kicked off republican revolutions, but it is also the case that they were instrumental in a particular kind of nation state building. In the colonies, of course, this process is self-evident, but in the western European core countries much less consensus exists as to the relationship between republics, empires and nation states. It is that aspect of the scholarship on empires and the state that I wish to focus upon here.

For those living in the early modern era, empires not nation states constituted the standard global political unit.[38] Kings or generals acting in their name gained subjects through conquest, gifts, or deals with lesser kings and princes. The Spanish followed this path in the early sixteenth century, but otherwise most of the deal making that created the western European empires of the early modern period involved chartered trading companies, merchant guilds or independent licensed traders acting on behalf of a king. In that sense, these empires were different. Still, the political form resembled the imperial model, where a sovereign transferred all or part of his governing powers to others in exchange for revenue and services, much more than a centralized nation state system. The sovereign could, in effect, cut deals with groups and these deals differed as to rights and responsibilities. Different subjects got different deals. They were not necessarily congruent or symmetrical.

Admittedly, republican impulses evident in European countries since at least the seventeenth century complicated these imperial arrangements. The Dutch, for example, did not have a king but a *stadholder* and sovereignty rested in the republic. The British had Parliament. In other western European countries institutions aside from princely ones made claims from time to time. One of the major points of Wallerstein's modern world-systems' theory is that capitalist empires required nation states. Nevertheless, these early modern empires, sometimes referred to as merchant or bluewater or marine empires,[39] lasted for a long time, almost three centuries, without directly confronting the ambiguities of where sovereignty was located.[40] In fact, the movement of war making and plunder to the periphery, the aid of the mercantile community in financing them, and the actual economic benefits to the core (discussed in the previous section) may even have had a stabilizing effect on the monarchy.

At the centre of the imperial booster club in the most successful empire, the British, sat those whose interests lay primarily with the tropical goods trade – the East India Company, the successive trading companies and independent merchants associated with specific plantation commodities, those licensed in the African slave trade, various planter groups in the colonies and absentees in the core. Then there were the commission merchants and the manufacturers supplying the colonial market, the military and a number of people who serviced the navies, the armies and the national debt. Among these are the 'gentlemanly capitalists' that Cain

---

[38] Anthony Pagden, *Lords of all the World: Ideologies of Empire in Spain, Britain and France c. 1500–c.1800* (New Haven, 1995).

[39] See James D. Tracy, ed., *The Political Economy of Merchant Empires* (Cambridge, 1991), pp. 41–116; and Daniel A. Baugh, 'Maritime strength and Atlantic commerce: the uses of "a grand marine empire"' in Stone, ed., *Imperial State at War*, pp. 185–223.

[40] Jack P. Greene, *Peripheries and Center: Constitutional Development in the Extended Polities of the British Empire and the United States, 1607–1788* (Athens, Ga., 1986), ch. 1.

and Hopkins have identified as being so crucial for British imperialism.[41]

In the system, 80–90 per cent of the governmental budget went to the army, a much enhanced navy and a national debt, representing the overruns from past wars.[42] Increasingly these wars were waged to protect overseas trade and plantations rather than to quell uprisings within the British Isles or to acquire more European real estate. In other western European empires as well, including the Spanish by the time of the Bourbons, dominance over world trade came to be equated with world power.

Initially, those making the deals with the sovereign authority were to provide most of the revenues. They furnished their own protection, or collected tributes from local subjects or paid import duties. In some cases, they also loaned money to the government. To buy off those from the landed classes uninvolved in trade, those who liked the English country-side and their place in it but not much else, the direct taxes on real estate, wealth and income rose the least during the eighteenth century. The groceries and textiles coming in from the colonies had higher and higher duties attached to them as they were the 'cause' of much of the naval and military expenditure. Unfortunately, smuggling diminished the practical-ity of depending solely on customs to pay for the military build-up. The trading interests themselves began objecting to imposts that sometimes doubled the cost of a commodity like tobacco or tea. Eventually, the government grew more dependent on excise taxes, taxes on domestic consumption. By the late eighteenth century, the excise tax on beer, the customs duties on sugar and rum, and the land tax all raised about the same amount of money. The metropolitan subjects of the British empire bore a tax burden about twice the level of their French counterparts.[43]

This was a problem, and it caused a backlash against the imperial booster club. As Jacob Price has pointed out in his illuminating article on

[41] P. J. Cain and A. G. Hopkins, *British Imperialism: Innovation and Expansion 1688–1914* (London, 1993); Bowen, *Elites, Enterprise and the Making of the British Overseas Empire*, pts 2 and 3; Nancy F . Koehn, *The Power of Commerce: Economy and Governance in the First British Empire* (Ithaca, 1994); Alison Gilbert Olson, *Making the Empire Work: London and American Interest Groups 1690–1790* (Cambridge, 1992); Jacob M. Price, 'Who cared about the colonies? The impact of the Thirteen Colonies on British society and politics, circa 1714–1775', in Bernard Bailyn and Philip D. Morgan, eds., *Strangers in the Realm: Cultural Margins of the First British Empire* (Chapel Hill, N.C., 1991), pp. 395–436; M. N. Pearson, 'Merchants and states', in James D. Tracy, ed., *Political Economy of Merchant Empires*; Kenneth Morgan, *Bristol and the Atlantic Trade in the Eighteenth Century* (Cambridge, 1993); and David Hancock, *Citizens of the World: London Merchants and the Integration of the British Atlantic Community, 1735–1785* (Cambridge, 1995).

[42] Patrick K. O'Brien, 'The political economy of British taxation, 1660–1815', *EcHR*, 2nd series, 51 (1988), 1–32, and John Brewer, *The Sinews of Power: War Money and the English State 1688–1783* (New York, 1989), chs. 2–4.

[43] Peter Mathias and Patrick K. O'Brien, 'Taxation in England and France 1715–1810', *Journal of European Economic History*, 5 (1976), 601–50.

British America 'Who cared about the colonies?'[44] plenty of people in Britain did, but around 1763 not many in government cared to be associated with them. T. H. Breen has directed our attention to recent research on the growth of British nationalism and its alienating effects in the thirteen colonies.[45] The victories of the Seven Years' War encouraged a British nationalism that incorporated empire. But that moment was fleeting. The sizeable run up in the national debt that resulted from the war gave aid and comfort to the view that it had largely been fought for the benefit of 'negro drivers', colonial land speculators and East India Company nabobs. The booster club at home was shut out of policy, although if the king's ministers had not attempted to change the taxation mix by increasing revenues from colonials, limiting territorial expansion and investigating the East India Company, they well might have had a rebellion at home.

That was not the only problem for the booster club, however. The overseas element had spun out of the control of those in the core supervising the tropical goods trade. The Company servants in India sought improvement of their private fortunes through expansion, even though their actions jeopardized the solvency of the East Indies enterprise. Much of the population in the American colonies by mid-century – whether Scots-Irish backcountry or prolific Yankee farmer – had little connection with the grand plantation trade but a lot of interest in westward expansion. Moreover, some of the home boosters' closest transatlantic associates, the Chesapeake tobacco planters, faced bankruptcy and had lost faith in the system. When pushed, they turned on the boosters themselves with boycotts of British manufactures and then a republican revolution.[46]

The empire forced Europeans and those who identified with them to confront the nation state system. Time after time, even among constituencies who feared rather than embraced republicanism, such as the French nobility and Spanish American creoles, the issue of parity within the empire cropped up.[47] The military–mercantile complex about which Adam Smith and others railed had exerted great influence over revenues, but was ill suited to decide how one part of the empire should relate to the other politically, because everyone's deal differed and, increasingly, many

<hr>

[44] In Bailyn and Morgan, eds., *Strangers in the Realm*, pp. 395–436.

[45] This is T. H. Breen's point in 'Ideology and nationalism on the eve of the American Revolution: revisions *once more* in need of revising', *Journal of American History*, 84 (1997), as he reviews the work of Linda Colley, *Britons: Forging the Nation 1707–1837* (New Haven, 1992), Kathleen Wilson, *The Sense of the People: Politics, Culture and Imperialism in England, 1715–1785* (Cambridge, 1995), and others on British nationalism.

[46] Bowen, *Elites, Enterprise and the Making of the British Overseas Empire*, pp. 183–93, and T. H. Breen, *Tobacco Culture: the Mentality of the Great Tidewater Planters on the Eve of the Revolution* (Princeton, 1986).

[47] Lester D. Langley, *The Americas in the Age of Revolution 1750–1850* (New Haven, 1996), chs. 7 and 8.

of those in the metropolis and in the colonies fell outside the system. Proclaiming a republic was one solution that clearly struck a blow for nation state and created problems for empire.

Empires, in fact, flourished. After the revolutions and independence movements in the Americas, western European imperial powers hardly lost their appetite for dominion. France had its Napoleon, Holland, Spain and Portugal held on to what they could, and, as C. A. Bayly has pointed out, the British continued to expand into India, substituted Australia for the Chesapeake as a dumping ground for convicts, and plucked choice colonies in Africa and Asia from the losers of the Napoleonic wars.[48] A great deal has been written recently about this second imperial period,[49] making clear that it was not free trade nor the shift from west to east that should garner our attention. Most see, as they tally the political repercussions, a turn to the right politically. Yet the most salient difference from what went before has played little role in the discussion. The old boosters, the chartered trading companies, the slave traders, the sugar planters and tobacco merchants were more and more marginalized. The kind of continuity in capitalists suggested by Cain and Hopkins seems not to be there, even though interest in expanding business abroad was. Many in the commercial community got what they wanted from treaties rather than colonies. A whole new cast of characters, unconnected or hostile to the tropical goods trade, emerged, and their enthusiasm indicates the need the social structure of European nations had for empire. In Britain, for example, the Tory politicians, the evangelicals, Anglican and otherwise, and the civil servants had more interest in defining the political relationship than the old boosters ever had. While they created many varieties of imperial structures – colonies, dominions, commonwealths, protectorates – these all shared one characteristic – they clearly were not part of the nation state. Confusion over the difference between empire and nation disappeared. Yet the norm was becoming the nation state, and no matter how many new imperial entities were created they had an anachronistic, doomed quality.[50] As the new colonial boosters fell in quite comfortably with the interests of church, aristocracy and monarchy, so did the politics of the European regimes the process also manufactured.

[48] C. A. Bayly, *Imperial Meridian: the British Empire and the World 1780–1830* (London, 1989).

[49] In addition to Bayly, see P. J . Marshall, ed., 'Britain without America – a second empire?', in Marshall, *Oxford History of the British Empire: Eighteenth Century*, pp. 576–96; Eliga Gould, 'American Independence and Britain's counter-revolution', *Past and Present*, 154 (1997), 107–41, and the many works mentioned in his notes.

[50] As Eliga Gould mentions, even the great historian of the second British Empire, J. R. Seeley, sensed this problem. Eliga H. Gould, 'A virtual nation: Greater Britain and the imperial legacy of the American Revolution', *Amerian Historical Review*, 104 (1999) 486.

APPENDIX: AREAS AND POPULATIONS INCLUDED IN TABLES 7.1 AND
7.2 WITH SOURCES

Areas and populations (first number is square miles, second is millions in
population)

1 Spanish empire: Europe = Spain 192,089 and 10.5; Atlantic is-
   lands = Canaries 2,796 and 0.17; Africa = Ceuta, Melilla and Oran in
   North Africa 18 and 0.1; Americas = Mexico including one-fourth of
   Texas, one-sixth of Arizona, New Mexico, one-fourth California and
   Louisiana (1,504,700 and 5.150); central America, except Belize and
   Mosquito Coast (174,900 and 0.875); Puerto Rico, Cuba, Hispaniola,
   Trinidad (67,000 and 0.384), all of South America, except the
   Guyanas, Brazil and the unoccupied bottom half of Argentina
   (2,880,300 and 4.725) totalling 4,626,900 and 11.134; east and south
   Asia = Philippines including Guam and North Marianas 116,191 and
   2.0.
2 Portuguese empire: Europe = Portugal 34,500 and 2.50; Atlantic
   islands = Azores, Madeira, Cape Verde, São Tomé, Principe 3,117 and
   0.245; Africa = Luanda, Bengo and Benguela districts of Angola and
   Mozambique up to the southern shore of Delagoa Bay 334,980 and
   2.250; Americas = Brazil 3,287,000 and 1.711; east and south
   Asia = Goa, Macao and East Timor 7,180 and 0.250.
3 Dutch empire: Europe = United Provinces 16,163 and 2.0; Africa
   = Cape Province 247,638 and 0.050; Americas = Netherlands Antilles
   (Curaçao, Aruba Boanire, St Eustatius, St Martin and Saba), Guiana
   (Essequibo, Demerara, Berbice) and Surinam 146,466 and 0.175; east
   and south Asia = coastal Ceylon (12,500 and 0.8), Malaccas (800 and
   0.009), and about one-third of present day Indonesia including all of
   Java, Barat, Selatan and Lampung areas in Sumatra, western and
   southern enclaves in Borneo, about one-third the area of Celebes, the
   Moluccas, and one-fifth of West New Guinea. (228,000 and 7.6)
   totalling 241,266 and 8.4.
4 British empire: Europe = Great Britain 88,803 and 8.6; Atlantic islands = Ireland and St Helena 30,935 and 4.003; Africa = Senegambia
   21,127 and 0.100; Americas = Atlantic Canada (77,537 and 0.137),
   thirteen colonies (present state boundaries except Georgia is one-fifth
   present size, Virginia includes West Virginia, Pennsylvania is three-
   quarters, New York one-half, Massachusetts includes one-fifth of
   Maine, New Hampshire is three-quarters, and Vermont is one-half
   totalling 373,670 and 2.5), Florida (6000 or one-tenth current size and
   0.005), West Indies including Bermuda (10,629 and 0.505), Belize
   and Mosquito Coast (25,867 and 0.025), American Indians in settled

British America (0.1) 467,836 and 3.172; east and south Asia = Bengal including Bihar (157,000 and 20), Northern Sarkars (20,060 and 1.5); Madras city and Chingleput district (3,020 and 0.412); and Isle of Bombay (18 and 0.144) totalling 180,098 and 22.056.

5 French empire: Europe = France 212,355 and 27.0; Americas = Saint-Domingue, Martinique, Guadeloupe, St Lucia, St Martin and French Guiana 45,339 and 0.487; Africa = Seychelles, Mauritius and Réunion 1,933 and 0.083.

6 Danish empire: Europe = Denmark 15,444 and 1.0; Americas = Danish West Indies: St John, St Thomas, St Croix (136 and 0.029)

SOURCES (*PASSIM* UNLESS OTHERWISE NOTED)

Colin McEvedy and Richard Jones, *Atlas of World Population History* (New York, 1978); William R. Shepherd, *Historical Atlas* (New York: 1956); *Encyclopaedia Britannica: 1992 Book of the Year* (Chicago, 1992); David P. Henige, comp., *Colonial Governors form the Fifteenth Century to the Present* (Madison, 1970); Robert Montgomery Martin, *History of the Colonies of the British Empire* (London, 1967 reprint of 1843 edn); Lester J. Cappon *et al.*, *Atlas of Early American History: the Revolutionary Era 1760–1790* (Princeton, 1976); D. K. Fieldhouse, *The Colonial Empires: A Comparative Survey from the Eighteenth Century* (New York, 1965), p. 158; McCusker and Menard, *Economy of British America*, pp. 112, 154; Robert V. Wells, *The Population of the British Colonies in America before 1776: a Survey of Census Data* (Princeton, 1975); Philip D. Curtin, *The Atlantic Slave Trade: a Census* (Madison, 1969); T. J. Ade Ajayi and Michael Crowder, eds., *Historical Atlas of Africa* (Cambridge, 1985), map 37; Great Britain, Foreign Office, *Peace Handbooks: Portuguese Possessions* (London, 1920); Sugata Bose, *The New Cambridge History of India: Peasant Labour and Colonial Capital, Rural Bengal since 1770*, III: 2 (Cambridge, 1993), p. 14; Dauril Alden, 'Population of Brazil in the late eighteenth century', *Hispanic American Historical Review*, 43 (1963), 173–205; John Thornton, 'The slave trade in eighteenth century Angola: effects on the demographic structures', *Canadian Journal of African Studies* 14 (1980), 417–28; Adna Ferrin Weber, *The Growth of Cities in the Nineteenth Century: a Study in Statistics* (New York, 1894), p. 450; Jan de Vries and Ad Der Woude, *The First Modern Economy: Success, Failure, and Perseverance of the Dutch Economy 1500–1815* (Cambridge, 1997), p. 432; and Anthony Reid, ed., *Southeast Asia in the Early Modern Era* (Ithaca, 1993), p. 3.

8 The business of distilling in the Old World and the New World during the seventeenth and eighteenth centuries: the rise of a new enterprise and its connection with colonial America

John J. McCusker

Five hundred years intervened between the introduction of the process of alcoholic distillation into Europe and the development of the alcoholic beverage distilling industry there. The distilling of spirits in the West dates from roughly 1150. Even though beer and wine had been known and drunk widely for several millennia before the first European tasted distilled spirits, a clear preference for distilled spirits emerged rapidly, no doubt because of their greater potency. Yet the widespread realization of that preference and the establishment of an industry to serve it were initially thwarted by the considerably higher price for spirits than for beer and wine. Distilled alcoholic beverages became products of mass consumption only after 1650.

Two developments in the middle years of the seventeenth century combined to lower the cost of spirits sufficiently for people to afford to substitute them for wine and beer. First, improvements in the distilling apparatus were implemented that greatly increased the scale on which distilling could be conducted. Second, sugar and sugar byproducts emerged as new, cheap base materials to be distilled in the larger, more efficient apparatus. Much of this change had its roots in the New World where sugar planters had learned by the late sixteenth century to distil rum from sugar-cane juice and sugar-cane molasses. The consequent

I have benefited from the opportunity to respond to critical comments offered at the presentation of these ideas to the Tenth International Economic History Congress, Leuven, Belgium, to the University of Minnesota Center for Early Modern History, to the School of Modern History, Queen's University, Belfast, and to the École des Hautes Études en Sciences Sociales, Paris. An early version of this chapter was distributed as part of the proceedings of the Tenth International Economic History Congress, Session B-14: 'Distilling and its implications for the Atlantic world of the seventeenth and eighteenth centuries', in Erik Aerts, Louis M. Cullen and Richard G. Wilson eds., *Production, Marketing and Consumption of Alcoholic Beverages since the Late Middle Ages* (Leuven, 1990), pp. 7–19.

dependence of the distilling industry of the Atlantic littoral upon these products from the western hemisphere considerably influenced the course of European expansion into the New World.

Changes in the technology of distilling helped to transform the production and marketing of alcoholic beverages. The most important effects of changes in technology are internal economies of scale – the production of a commodity more cheaply on a larger scale than on a smaller scale. Newer technology allows for an increase in production that is somewhat greater than any related increase in the cost of production. The result is a lower cost per unit. In less technical terms, things become 'cheaper by the dozen'.

Canny producers will take advantage of technological changes by passing on most of the lower cost to their customers in the form of a lower price per unit, expecting to benefit from increased consumption. Innovators expect lower profits per unit to be offset by an increase in the number of units sold. Changes in technology, by lowering the factor costs of production, have been the chief source of economies of scale over the past three hundred years.[1]

Obviously crucial to the sellers' success in reaping the advantages of new technology is expanded demand (measured by a product's elasticity of demand). Given a lower price, demand can expand more or less easily, depending on the nature of the commodity and on market conditions. Thus, cheaper shoes will much more readily translate into increased shoe consumption than cheaper aircraft carriers will translate into a demand for more aircraft carriers. There is even a limit for basic commodities such as foodstuffs beyond which further price reductions will not provoke a much greater consumption. As potatoes become cheaper, consumption of them does not necessarily increase at the same rate.

Differences in demand are influenced by the substitution effect, whereby a newer, relatively lower price for one commodity induces people to consume it as an alternative to what they had been consuming previously.[2]

---

[1] Although the attention paid to changing technology as a cause of economic growth has heightened considerably over the past fifty years, some might not agree with this assessment. Some who will agree include David S. Landes, *The Unbound Prometheus: Technological Change and Industrial Development in Western Europe from 1750 to the Present* (Cambridge, 1970); and Nathan Rosenberg, *Exploring the Black Box: Technology, Economics, and History* (Cambridge, 1994). The key works on the subject by economists are W. E. G. Salter, *Productivity and Technological Change*, 2nd edn (Cambridge, 1966); Jacob Schmookler, *Invention and Economic Growth* (Cambridge, Mass., 1966); and Joel Mokyr, *The Lever of Riches: Technological Creativity and Economic Progress* (New York, 1990). Important for the distinctions that he developed therein is Vernon W. Ruttan's article: 'Usher and Schumpeter on invention, innovation and technological change', *Quarterly Journal of Economics*, 73 (1959), 596–606. Compare Mokyr, *The Lever of Riches*, pp. 9–11.

[2] A particularly apposite example of this process is described in Andrew B. Appleby, 'Grain prices and subsistence crises in England and France, 1590–1740', *JEcH*, 39 (1979), 865–87.

One group of commodities for which there is a high marginal rate of substitution is alcoholic beverages. In general, over the long term, people's drinking preferences will shift toward the beverage that offers the highest alcoholic content per unit of cost. Alcoholic beverage consumption is thus more capable than other commodities of benefiting from changes in technology and resulting economies of scale.

There are three broad categories of alcoholic beverages: beers made from fermented grains; wines made from fermented fruits; and spirits made from anything fermented.[3] The fermentation process is basically a controlled chemical decomposition of organic material during which alcohol is produced. It is the alcoholic content of these beverages and the inebriating effects of the alcohol on the imbiber, that set them off from the other liquids people drink. Beers produced naturally will contain no more than about 7 per cent alcohol by weight and wines no more than about twice that amount. What distinguishes distilled spirits from beer and wine is the spirits' much higher alcoholic content. The distillation process acts, in effect, to extract and to concentrate the alcohol from the fermented base materials. Spirits can be anything up to 100 per cent alcohol.

Although the distillation of spirits was originally undertaken in Europe in twelfth-century Italy, the scale of production remained small until the late sixteenth and early seventeenth centuries, when major technological innovations began a transformation that had implications for the entire Atlantic world.[4] Those innovations introduced scale economies into

---

[3] Much basic information about alcoholic beverages is conveniently and authoritatively assembled in Harold J. Grossman, *Grossman's Guide to Wines, Beers, and Spirits*, ed. Harriet Lembeck, 7th rev. edn (New York, 1983). On the subject of wine, examine also the works of André L. Simon, especially *The History of the Wine Trade in England*, 3 vols. (London, 1906–9); Roger Dion, *Histoire de la vigne et du vin en France des origines au XIXe siècle* (Paris, 1959); Georges Durand, *Vin, vigne et vignerons en Lyonnais et Beaujolais (XVIe–XVIIIe siècles)* (Lyons, 1979); Marcel Lachiver, *Vins, vignes et vignerons. Histoire du vignoble français* (Paris, 1988); Tim Unwin, *Wine and the Vine: an Historical Geography of Viticulture and the Wine Trade* (London, 1991); *The Origins and Ancient History of Wine*, ed. Patrick E. McGovern, Stuart J. Fleming and Solomon H. Katz (Luxemburg, 1995); Patrick E. McGovern *et al.*, 'Neolithic resinated wine', *Nature: International Weekly Journal of Science* (6 June 1996), 480–1; and John Noble Wilford, 'In the annals of winemaking, 5000 BC was quite a year', *New York Times*, 6 June 1996. Concerning beer, see Peter Mathias, *The Brewing Industry in England, 1700–1830* (Cambridge, 1959). Compare Stanley Baron, *Brewed in America: a History of Beer and Ale in the United States* (Boston, 1962); and A. Hallema and J. A. Emmens, *Het Bier en Zijn Brouwers. De Geschiedenis van Onze Oudste Volksdrank* (Amsterdam, 1968).

[4] The standard work on European distillation is R. J. Forbes, *Short History of the Art of Distillation [from the Beginnings] up to the Death of Cellier Blumenthal [1840]* (Leiden, 1948). See also R. J. Forbes, *Studies in Ancient Technology*, III, 3rd edn (Leiden, 1993), *passim*. Compare A. J. V. Underwood, 'The historical development of distilling plant', *Transactions of the Institution of Chemical Engineers*, 13 (1935), 34–62. Both Forbes's and Underwood's works are based almost exclusively on technical treatises and, probably for that reason, they do not pay as much attention to beverage distilling as they do to chemical

distilling; they, in turn, were one of two factors that helped lower the price of spirits to levels that created a mass market and a major industry.[5]

The physicians of Salerno who were the first in Europe to distil alcohol were not looking for something new to drink. Their investigations seem mostly to have been conducted as experiments in 'pure science'; they seem to have been interested in the decomposition of matter and its reformation. The equipment they used was that of the laboratory. Their still was probably a small glass bulb with a long tapered neck much like the retort that continues to be used in chemistry laboratories today. However primitive the equipment or chimerical the initial research,

apparatus and scientific applications. While they are fine analyses of the art and science of distillation, they are less successful as studies of the business of distilling alcohol. Forbes's discussion (pp. 32, 87–9) of the earliest references to the European distilling of alcohol can, nevertheless, be considered definitive. See also Lynn White, Jr, 'Technological assessment from the stance of a medieval historian', *AHR*, 79 (1974), 3–4; and McCusker, *Rum and the American Revolution*, I, pp. 55–7, 85–6, n. 133. There is a more recent, more accessible version of a key text to which Forbes refers: *Mappae Clavicula: A Little Key to the World of Medieval Techniques*, trans. and ed. Cyril Stanley Smith and John G. Hawthorne, *Transactions of the American Philosophical Society*, n.s., LXIV, pt 4 (Philadelphia, 1974). Compare René De Herdt *et al.*, *In en om de alambiek. Jenever en alcoholstokerijen* (Ghent, 1981).

Joseph Needham, *Science and Civilisation in China*, in progress (Cambridge, 1954 to date), V, pt 4, pp. 55–162, has demonstrated that the Chinese were distilling alcohol in the seventh century AD and that Chinese distillation techniques made their way to Europe in the twelfth century, as one of a cluster of transmissions that included the magnetic compass, the stern-post rudder and the windmill. See also Pierre Gentelle, 'Alcools et eaux-de-vie en Chine. Notes de géographie et d'histoire', in *Eaux-de-vie et spiritueux. [Actes du] Colloque de Bordeaux-Cognac, Octobre 1982*, ed. A. Heutz de Lemps *et al.* (Paris, 1985), pp. 381–408. There is a fragmentary account of the introduction of Indian sugar-making techniques into China that dates from the ninth century. Although it mentions the use of molasses to make an alcoholic beverage, it appears only to have been a fermented and not a distilled beverage. Fonds Pelliot Chinois, no. 3303, Bibliothèque Nationale de France, Paris; Ji Xianlin, 'Yi zhang youguan yindu zhitang fa zhaunru Zhongguo de Dunhuang canjuan', *Li Shih Yen Chiu*, 20 no. 1 (1982), 124–36 (esp. 134). For help with interpreting this document, I am grateful to Bak See Lau. I wish also to record my thanks to Dr Joan L. Oates of Girton College, Cambridge, for conversations and suggestions that encouraged me to look again at the early history of distilling.

[5] The history of the consumption of alcoholic beverages and of the related beverage distilling industry between the twelfth and eighteenth centuries has been understood somewhat differently by others. See e.g. Forbes, *Art of Distillation*, pp. 94–8, 101–7, 187–92. See also Forbes, 'Food and drink', in *A History of Technology*, ed. Charles Singer *et al.*, 8 vols. (Oxford, 1954–84), II, pp. 141–4, III, pp. 10–12. Compare Fernand Braudel, *Civilisation matérielle, économie et capitalisme, XVe–XVIIIe siècle*, 3 vols. (Paris, 1979), I, pp. 206–13; and Unwin, *Wine and the Vine*, pp. 236–42. Very significantly, there has been little appreciation of the relationship between the introduction of molasses and syrup as base materials and the rapid increase in the size and efficiency of the distilling apparatus as the two factors causative of the considerable relative increase in the consumption of spirits and decline in the consumption of wines and beers. Thus, e.g. Forbes, *Art of Distillation*, pp. 104–6, had difficulty reconciling the growth of commercial distilling in The Netherlands, a country that produced neither wine nor major crops of cereals and that began to tax imported wines and restricted the distilling of cereals. The answer to this quandary – for both the Dutch distillers and Forbes – was found in syrup, domestic and imported (see below).

someone quickly discovered that there was a considerable market for the end product, a market well beyond the merely medicinal. As early as the thirteenth century apothecaries in major European cities had become dispensers of distilled spirits and they dispensed them to more than just those who were under a physician's care. Nevertheless, even well into the seventeenth century, a knowledgeable person such as Samuel Pepys would accept only somewhat quizzically the offer of 'strong water made of Juniper' as a prescription for settling his temporary indisposition.[6] The year was 1663. Within a decade or two everyone in London would recognize that Pepys had been offered gin.

In its fundamentals, the process of distilling has changed little from the twelfth to the twenty-first century. The distiller pours a fermented liquid substance, called the base material, into a container and brings it to a boil over a fire. The heat drives off some of the liquid in the form of gases. These gases are collected and cooled, thereby returning them to a liquid form called the distillate. Fermented base materials yield alcohol as part of that distillate. Alcohol vaporizes at a lower temperature (66° C) than most other substances, including water. By controlling the temperature of the boil and by redistilling the first distillate, a distiller can refine it into purer and purer alcohol. But making a potable beverage requires that some of the qualities of the base materials be retained, and so the distillation must stop short of absolute alcohol. Those congeners or impurities, if you will, in the form of esters, aldehydes, acids and oils, interact and develop in the ageing process and, sometimes with the help of added agents, give various distilled spirits their distinctive smells and tastes.[7]

---

[6] Having been ill for several days, probably as a result of mild food poisoning, Pepys went 'to the office . . . and there Sir J[ohn] Mennes and Sir W[illiam] Batten did advise me to take some Juniper water, and Sir W. Batten sent to his Lady for some for me, strong water made of Juniper'. Entry dated 10 October 1663 in *The Diary of Samuel Pepys*, ed. Robert Latham and William Matthews, 11 vols. (London, 1970–83), IV, p. 329. His colleagues were, respectively, the Comptroller of the Navy and the Surveyor of the Navy. Earlier in the century, the ship's stores for an English fishing vessel included 'aqui vitæ' as one of the medicines; the daily ration of a gallon of beer each was, of course, part of the crew's food and drink. E[dward] S[harpe], *Britaines Busse. Or a Computation Aswell of the Charge of a Busse or Herring-Fishing Ship. As Also of the Gaine and Profit Thereby . . .* (London, 1615), sig. C_1r, sig. C_2r. See table 8.1.

John Chartres tries to argue for a somewhat earlier establishment of 'aqua vitae as a beverage', the late sixteenth century. Note, however, that the 1601 reference he quotes as 'proof of the transition of spirits into a beverage' sounds very much like an apothecary's remedy for Pepys's aliment, counselling the 'Benefit [aqua vitæ provides] . . . for cold Stomacks'. Chartres, 'No English Calvados? English distillers and the cider industry in the seventeenth and eighteenth centuries', in *English Rural Society, 1500–1800: Essays in Honour of Joan Thirsk*, ed. John Chartres and David Hey (Cambridge, 1990), p. 315.

[7] There are numerous seventeenth- and eighteenth-century treatises on distilling. One of many is George Smith's, *A Compleat Body of Distilling, Explaining the Mysteries of That*

The still, too, has remained remarkably unaltered. Although nineteenth- and twentieth-century technology introduced new types of stills – notably in the early nineteenth century, the 'patent still' – the pot still continues to be used widely in the spirits industry even in the twenty-first century. The modern pot still is simply an enlarged version of the medieval still. It has two essential parts: the first is the cucurbit or boiling pot which holds the base materials to be distilled; the second is the alembic where the vapours are condensed in the cap and neck (fig. 8.1). While modern pot stills are many times larger than medieval stills, their essential configuration has altered little.

The first of the two decisive changes in the distilling industry was that very increase in size, an increase the beginnings of which we can date to the last part of the sixteenth century. It happened through major alterations in the fabric and fabrication of the vessel itself, through improvements in the methods used to recondense the vapours, and through modifications in the entire distilling facility. The use of bigger, more efficient stills, probably starting in The Netherlands, then in Great Britain, elsewhere in Europe and, later, in European colonies in the New World signalled the emergence of commercial distilling.[8]

The quantum jump in the size of the cucurbit or boiling pot from a small laboratory-scale apparatus to a huge industrial still depended upon several related developments. The vessel began to be fashioned of metal, usually copper, rather than made of glass or ceramic as had been and continued to

Science, in a Most Easy and Familiar Manner . . . (London, 1725), which was popular enough to be reissued in 1731, 1738, 1749 and 1766. It is singled out here not only because of its apparent popularity but also because the third edition (1738) included the frontispiece used as figure 8.1. Compare Denis Diderot and Jean d'Alembert, *Encyclopédie, ou Dictionnaire Raisonné des Sciences, des Arts et des Métiers*, 35 vols. (Paris, 1751–80), IV, s.v. 'Distillation'; and Francesco Griselini and Marco Fassadoni, eds., *Dizionario delle Arti de' Mestiere*, 18 vols. (Venice [1768–78]), V, pp. 200–30. Compare also the several essays on the modern industry in A. H. Rose, ed., *Alcoholic Beverages*, Economic Microbiology, vol. I (London, 1977), especially the one by M. Lehtonen and H. Suomalainen on 'Rum', pp. 595–633.

[8] While much of the evidence adduced in this chapter is English in start, the development of the industry seems to have had its origin in The Netherlands, just as Forbes, *Art of Distillation*, argues by implication. Certainly for English and Scottish distillers, the exchange of personnel and techniques with their European counterparts was a constant interaction over the centuries. See, for instance, the occasion, *c.* 1787, when John Haig and Company, distillers of Cannonmills, Edinburgh, brought over from Schiedam two Dutch distillers, presumably to have their advice and suggestions, but only to find that the two of them carried back and introduced at Schiedam one of Haig's own innovations. 'Memorial of Mr. James Haig, respecting the Scotch Distillery', London, 6 May 1799, in [GB, Parl., Commons], *[Second] Report Respecting the Distilleries in Scotland* . . ., p. 294. For additional indications of the importance of the Dutch in the distilling industry, see Iseabal Ann Glen, 'An economic history of the distilling industry in Scotland, 1750–1914', 2 vols. (Ph.D. thesis, University of Strathclyde, 1969), pp. 136–7, 160, See also n. 5, above, and nn. 11, 26, 30, 42 and pp. 209–10 below.

Figure 8.1 A small English distillery of the eighteenth century, as pictured in the frontispiece of George Smith, *A Compleat Body of Distilling, Explaining the Mysteries of That Science, in a Most Easy and Familiar Manner . . .* , 3rd edn (London, 1738). Drawn and engraved by Pierre Fourdrinier (fl. 1720–58).

The cucurbit was installed above the furnace marked 'A'. Presuming this to have been the still Smith referred to in his text (preface and p. 85), its volume was about 50 gallons and its charge about 30 gallons (see the appendix). Mounted on top of the cucurbit was the alembic or still head that, in this picture, was held in place by 'a piece of wood ['R'] to prevent [it] flying of[f]'. The alembic carried the vapour into 'the worm within the worm-tub mark'd with prick'd lines' ('Q' and 'B'). There seems to have been no provision for any continuous renewal of the water in the worm-tub, but 'the pump' ('C') was positioned just to the left. (Photograph courtesy of the British Library.)

be the case in laboratories.[9] Considerations of weight, strength and heat conductivity made copper the preferred substance. Very large glass or ceramic stills were either too fragile or weighed too much or both, and metals other than copper could not be worked as easily, did not conduct heat as quickly or as evenly, or reacted chemically with the substances being distilled. Copper vessels were employed in commercial distilleries by the end of the sixteenth century and grew to such an extent that cucurbits measuring almost 5,000 gallons (nearly 18,000 litres) were in use well before the 1750s.[10] By the end of the eighteenth century the largest had doubled in size.[11]

[9] The alcoholic beverage distillers' manuals of the seventeeth and eighteenth centuries (such as Smith, *Compleat Body of Distilling*) all speak of copper stills. While Forbes, *Art of Distillation*, pp. 140, 150 and 193, did mention this development, he paid much more attention to contemporary preference for glass and ceramic stills and to objections to the use of metal apparatus, again a reflection of his implicit bias towards scientific research and laboratory equipment (*ibid.*, pp. 76, 120, 124, 145, 193, 203, 231).

The copper manufacturing industry of Europe reached the sophistication necessary to fabricate such stills only late in the sixteenth century – and in Great Britain only after the 1680s. See Henry Hamilton, *The English Brass and Copper Industries to 1800* (London, 1926); and G. Hammersley, 'The effect of technical change in the British copper industry between the sixteenth and the eighteenth centuries', *Journal of European Economic History*, 20 (1991), 155–73. Compare R. F. Tylecote, *A History of Metallurgy* (London, 1976), pp. 93–6, 128–31; the essays in Hermann Kellenbenz, ed., *Schwerpunkte der Kupferproduktion und des Kupferhandels in Europa, 1500–1650*, Kölner Kolloquium zur Internationalen Sozial- und Wirtschaftsgeschichte, Band III (Cologne and Vienna, 1977), especially Kellenbenz, 'Europäisches Kupfer, Ende 15. bis Mitte 17. Jahrhunderts: Ergebnisse eines Kolloquiums' (*ibid.*, pp. 290–351); Joan Day, 'Copper, zinc and brass production', in *The Industrial Revolution in Metals*, ed. Joan Day and R. F. Tylecote (London, 1991), pp. 131–99, citing, among other sources, John Morton, 'The rise of the modern copper and brass industry in Britain, 1690–1750' (Ph.D. thesis, University of Birmingham, 1985); and Roger Burt, 'The transformation of the non-ferrous metals industries in the seventeenth and eighteenth centuries', *EcHR*, 2nd series, 48 (1995), 23–45. Morton argues that the minor flourishing of the copper industry in England between 1560 and 1660 had no connection with the modern industry which developed only after the 1680s based on newly discovered sources of copper ore and a new technology for smelting that ore using coal. His exposition not only supports one aspect of the argument developed in this chapter but also neatly parallels it.

A major collection of the papers of a London coppersmith, William Forbes and Company, 1752–94, survives in the Forbes of Callendar Muniments, GD 171, Falkirk District Archives, Falkirk, Scotland (formerly in the Scottish Record Office, Edinburgh). As part of its business, the firm fabricated and supplied equipment for sugar refiners and distillers in Great Britain, the colonies and elsewhere (see e.g. the appendix).

[10] Charles Leadbetter, *The Royal Gauger; or Gauging Made Perfectly Easy, As Practised by the Officers of His Majesty's Revenue of Excise*, revised by Samuel Clark, 6th edn (London, 1766), pp. 146–7, and plate VI, opp. p. 152, illustrated and discussed a still in London, *c.* 1740, with a capacity of 4,700 gallons (17,800 litres) – see the appendix.

[11] In 1803, a report to the House of Commons showed that the twenty-two capital distillers of England operated a total of sixty-three stills with a combined capacity of 211,130 gallons (almost 800,000 litres). The largest stills were in excess of 11,000 gallons (41,600 litres). They averaged 3,350 gallons (12,700 litres). PRO, 30/8/296, fo. 231v.

Richard Bush, of Richard Bush and Company, Wandsworth New Distillery, reported in 1787 that one of the large, new distilleries in Scotland had four stills in operation, with a total capacity of 7,500 gallons (28,400 litres), an average of 1,875 gallons (7,100

Big copper pot stills required a considerable installation to support them. The small laboratory cucurbit of an earlier era sat on a small frame over a limited fire, but more sizeable ones had to be mounted in place over a large, fixed furnace constructed of brick and iron.[12] Optimum use of the grander still and furnace was achieved only with regular, frequent distillations. To continue recharging the cucurbit, one had to have available adequate supplies of base materials. Everything necessary thus no longer fitted into a corner of a room. The barrels of base material required to provide a regular charge for a substantial still and the barrels of accumulated distillate could fill several rooms. The distillery came to occupy a whole building, eventually a complex of buildings. The threat of fire from a high-temperature furnace burning continually required that these buildings be made of brick or stone and, usually, that they be set apart from other structures.[13] The relentless demand for water, the need for satisfac-

litres) each. Bush, in London, to William Pitt, in London, 23 November 1787, PRO, 30/8/296, fo. 178r. The wash still of the new distillery at Aberdeen completed in September 1794 had a capacity of 2,650 gallons (10,000 litres). (John Sinclair, *The Statistical Account of Scotland. Drawn Up from the Communications of the Ministers of the Different Parishes*, 21 vols. (Edinburgh, 1791–9), XIX, p. 22 ff.) The three wash stills at use in the late 1790s at the Stein distillery at Kilbagie measured 1,288 gallons (4,900 litres), 2,188 gallons (8,300 litres), and 2,388 gallons (9,000 litres). (*[Second] Report Respecting the Distilleries in Scotland . . .* , p. 443). For this distillery, see also nn. 15, 23, 25, 27, below.

Examples of eighteenth-century French and Dutch commercial stills can be found in the following: [Jacques-François] Demachy, *L'art du distilateur liquoriste* [Académie des Sciences, Paris], *Description des Arts et Métiers* (Paris, 1775), esp. plate 2; and Pieter Jan Dobbelaar, *De branderijen in Holland tot het begin der negentiende eeuw* (Rotterdam, 1930), pp. 117–18, and, especially, the plate opposite p. 226 showing one of five buildings housing the fifteen stills of the large 'De Papegaay' distillery at Delft (*c.* 1790). This distillery is also the subject of commentary in Philip Andreas Nemnich, *Original-Beiträge zur eigentlichen Kentniß von Holland*, vols. II–IV of *Tagebuch einer der Kultur und Industrie gewidmeten Reise*, 2 vols. (Tübingen, 1809), I, p. 148. Contrast Forbes, *Art of Distillation*, who reproduced Dobbelaar's plate (p. 191) but, mistakenly, called it a 'small' distillery (p. 190). For a collection of accounts and papers from a Dutch distillery, see A. J. H. Rozemond, *Inventaris van het Oud-Archief der Distileerderij en Likeurstokerij 'De Graauwe Hengst' Daniel Visser en Zonen te Schiedam, anno 1714* (Schiedam, 1961). G. Gregory, *A Dictionary of Arts & Sciences*, 2 vols. (London, 1806–7), I, pp. 536–7, discussed the roughly 300 distilleries in Weesp, near Amsterdam, the stills of which, in 1774, measured 'usually from three to five hundred gallons each' (1,100 to 1,900 litres). Compare the very much smaller still pictured in fig. 8.1. See also n. 13, below, and the appendix.

[12] For considerations of the use of fuel, see n. 13, below, and the appendix.

[13] A 1774 advertisement for the leasing of Daniel Roberdeau's distillery in the town of Alexandria, Virginia, included the most complete description of an early American distillery yet found. On a plot measuring about one and one third acres (5,400 square metres), there were four major buildings plus a mill house, six covered outdoor cisterns (most likely sunk below ground level but 'fixed above the highest tide water'), and a wood yard. Two buildings were of stone: the distillery proper measured 71 feet by 39 feet (260 square metres); and a three-storey grain storehouse, 50 feet square (230 square metres). There were also two wooden frame buildings, a molasses storehouse and a cooper's shop, both of smaller dimensions than the stone structures. The distillery housed two large stills

tory drainage of effluent, and a facility for transporting large casks of raw materials and finished product influenced their location; in most places distilleries were situated on or near a river, canal or bay.[14]

Large stills needed an equivalent cooling capability to recondense the vapours created in the boiling. The small laboratory cucurbit was adequately cooled by the small still head or alembic. Air circulating naturally around the alembic was sufficient to keep the temperature low enough to turn the vapour back into a liquid. As cucurbits grew in size, this simple method of cooling no longer worked well, and a series of improvements in the alembic was introduced, culminating in the invention of the continuously water-cooled counter-flow worm condenser, which cooled the vapour much more efficiently (compare the more primitive worm condenser pictured in fig. 8.1). Slowly adopted after the end of the sixteenth century, the continuously water-cooled counter-flow worm condenser constituted a major technological innovation in distilling.[15]

(2,500 gallons or 9,500 l. each), a smaller one (600 gallons; 2,300 litres), twenty cisterns each one the size of the big stills, and the worms, worm-tubs, and pumps necessary to service three stills. 'All these pumps are worked by a horse, in an adjoining mill house of large diameter'. The lease included rights to a contract to supply annually 300 cord of ash wood to be used for fuel. The whole facility was located on the waterfront alongside the public wharf (at the south-west corner of the modern Wolfe and Union Streets) (John Pinkney's *Virginia Gazette* [Williamsburg], 1 December 1774). Compare a similar, though less detailed advertisement for the sale of a distillery located in Port-au-Prince 'près le Fort Sainte-Claire, au bord de la mer,' in *Les Affiches Américaines* (Port-au-Prince), 23 November 1768.

[14] The same imperatives that suggested to Roberdeau the wisdom of locating his distillery on the waterfront in Alexandria and to the owners of the Port-au-Prince distillery to locate their distillery 'au bord de la mer' (n. 13, above) – the ease of access to transport, the regular supplies of water for cooling, and the facility for draining effluents – were also at work elsewhere. Local authorities were especially concerned about the drainage of such effluents and some undertook to control it by regulations that remind one of much more modern environmental concerns. See e.g. Glen, 'Economic history of the distilling industry, Scotland', pp. 42, 325–6; and Christopher R. Eck, 'The spirits of Massachusetts: distillers and distilling in seventeenth- and eighteenth-century Boston (MA thesis, University of Massachusetts at Boston, 1993), pp. 51–3, 61–2. I am very grateful to Mr Eck for allowing me to read his thesis while it was still a work in progress. Compare the Pennsylvania regulation mentioned in *The Pennsylvania Gazette* (Philadelphia), 10 March 1763. The high biological oxygen demand of the 'pot ale' that was drained off after distillation damaged the ecological balance of smaller rivers and streams (North of Scotland College of Agriculture), *Draff for Animal Feeding: a Report Made to Pot Still Malt Distillers Association of Scotland* (Aberdeen, 1969), p. 27).

[15] Forbes, *Art of Distillation*, pp. 61, 83–4, 89, 120, 124, 130, 146, 150, 153, 179–82, 207, 217, 222, 224, 232, 240–1, 254–9; Forbes, 'Food and drink', in *History of Technology*, ed. Singer *et al.*, III, 12. See also the stills pictured in fig. 5 in the plate in Ambrose Cooper, *The Complete Distiller . . .* , 2nd edn (London, 1760).

The need for large quantities of water to cool the larger worm condensers prompted distillers to be among the earliest businesses interested in the industrial application of the steam engine to power their pumps (Mathias, *Brewing Industry in England*, p. 82 and n. 2). Compare Carroll W. Pursell, Jr, *Early Stationary Steam Engines in America: a Study in the Migration of Technology* (Washington, D.C., 1969), *passim*. Cooke and Company of

Organizational and managerial changes in the distilling industry complemented these changes in technology. The production of potable spirits required at least two successive distillations, as has been mentioned: one to produce the raw alcohol (or 'wash'); a second to redistil – or 'rectify' – the spirit into 'low wines' that could then be turned into a drinkable beverage, coloured and flavoured to taste. In an earlier period and in smaller-scale circumstances down into more modern times, one distiller performed all of these operations himself using his one small still. As the industry developed it became clear that certain efficiencies were possible if a larger still were used solely and continuously to produce the raw alcohol and one or more smaller stills were employed for redistilling. Early in the eighteenth century, if not before, one can find distilleries organized on this basis and the configuration quickly became standard for middle-level and larger installations.

By 1750, in London at least, a further development had occurred.[16] Some distillers had begun to concentrate on fabricating just the raw spirit which they then sold to smaller specialized distillers, called 'rectifiers', who

London was one of the very first (for this firm see n. 24, below); the Stein distillery at Kilbagie had the first one in Scotland (for this firm see n. 27, below). Compare the horse-powered pumps at Daniel Roberdeau's Alexandria, Virginia, distillery (n. 13, above). By contrast, on the island of Antigua, a place lacking a regular water supply, slaves carried water on their heads to cool the stills. This was the report of Lord Adam Gordon, who visited the island in May and June 1764, as recorded in his 'Journal of an Officer [of the 66th Regiment] who travelled over a part of the West Indies and of North America', 1764–5, BL, King's MS 213, fo. 7v, and as printed in Newton D. Mereness, ed., *Travels in the American Colonies* (New York, 1916), p. 375. See also the lengthy description of the device that Colonel James Bruce installed at his plantation on Dominica as reported by Joseph Senhouse after his visit to 'Castle Bruce' on 20 June 1776. There one could marvel at 'a very simple & ingenious contrivance [constructed] upon the principle of the Persian Wheel, made use of in order to raise a Stream of Water . . . to run into the Worm Tubs'. James C. Brandow, 'The Senhouse papers', *Journal of the Barbados Museum and Historical Society*, 37 (1985), 282. Joseph Senhouse's volume of memoirs from which Brandow extracted this passage is part of the Records of the Family of Senhouse of Netherhall (Maryport), 1762–1831, Cumbria County Council, Archives Department, Record Office, The Castle, Carlisle. A selling point of the 'distil-house' advertised for lease by Abraham Barker and Giles Hosier of Tiverton, Rhode Island, and Caleb Carpenter of Newport in *The Newport Mercury*, 11 April 1774, was that 'the worms are supplied from a constant spring'.

16 *An Impartial Enquiry into the Present State of the British Distillery; Plainly Demonstrating the Evil Consequences of Imposing Any Additional Duties on British Spirits* (London, 1736), pp. 7, 22, stated that the number of distillers in London was 'inconsiderable' in 1689 but that it had grown to roughly 1,500 by the mid-1730s. The author's reference would appear to have been to [Thomas Wilson], *Distilled Spirituous Liquors the Bane of the Nation . . .*, 2nd rev. edn (London, 1736), p. 7, where Wilson states that during the reign of King William III 'there was not one distiller where there is now twenty'. This and other evidence casts doubt on a statement made in a petition in 1621 that 200 distillers were at work there (Wallace Notestein, Frances Helen Relf and Hartley Simpson, eds., *Commons Debates, 1621*, 7 vols. (New Haven, Conn., and London, 1935), IV, p. 108, V, p. 259, VII, p. 77). My doubt is shared by Chartres, 'No English Calvados?', p. 315. He also thought that the small demand in England for spirits before the last quarter of the seventeenth century had been met primarily by imported French brandy (*ibid.*, pp. 316–17 and *passim*).

made the final product for sale directly or indirectly to the consumer. This development resulted in a consolidation of the major, primary distilleries ('capital offices')[17] and a consequent reduction of their number, a development encouraged by government policy.[18] The number of primary London distilleries, twenty-eight in 1736,[19] had grown to thirty by 1750.[20] In addition, there were about ten others located elsewhere in England. Then the consolidation set in, hastened by the prohibition on the distilling of grains between 1756 and 1760 during the Seven Years' War. In the latter year there were only twelve primary distilleries operating in London – and none elsewhere in England.[21] By the 1780s the eight capital houses had garnered the business in London all to themselves.[22] In their petition to Parliament in December 1783, 'the Corn Distillers in and about the City of London' stated that London distillers 'comprize, in Importance and Extent of their Manufactories, upwards of 11/12ths of the whole Distillery of England', based on their having contributed £310,000 out of the £335,000 paid into the Excise for the fiscal year ending that July.[23] It was those capital houses that supplied the numerous smaller secondary distillers – perhaps as many as 1,500 – with the low wines that they, in turn, used to make 'gin' and the other 'turbulent liquors' for their customers – the phrase is John Milton's from his *Samson Agonistes* (1671).

[17] According to the author of *The Corn Distillery, Stated to the Consideration of the Landed Interest of England* (London, 1783), p. 14.

[18] From the 1670s there had been a conscious and persistent government policy of promoting large-scale distilleries through preferential fiscal policies adopted in order to police them more efficiently for compliance with the Excise. Peter Mathias, 'Agriculture and the brewing and distilling industries in the eighteenth century', *EcHR*, 2nd series, 5 (1952), 251. See nn. 23, 24, below.

[19] *Impartial Enquiry into the Present State of the British Distillery*, pp. 7–8.

[20] *The Corn Distillery, Stated*, p. 14.

[21] *Ibid*, p. 17. Compare *The True State of the British Malt-Distillery. Being a Defense of Mr. M[a]wb[e]y's Queries* (London, 1760). Sir Joseph Mawbey (1730–98), MP, was a distiller in Vauxhall, London. See [Thomas] Mortimer, *The Universal Director; or, The Nobleman and Gentleman's True Guide to . . . London and Westminster, and Their Environs* (London, 1763), p. 31.

[22] See the return, dated 26 May 1788, to an order for information about the 'stocks of spirits of the corn distillers in and about London' over the years 1782–7, in *JHC*, XLIII, 505–6. By 1803 the number of capital houses in England was back at twenty-two. See n. 11, above.

[23] The fiscal year ended on 5 July 1783 [G.B., Parl., Commons], *Second Report from the Committee, Appointed to Enquire into the Illicit Practices Used in Defrauding the Revenue* ([London], 1784), p. 27; *JHC*, XXXIX, 835–6. In 1799 John Stein testified that 'in England the Distillers are not Twelve in Number, and those chiefly in London' but 'in Scotland the distillery is in a thousand hands'. 'First Memorial of John Stein, Esquire, respecting the Scotch Distillery', London, 24 April 1799, in *[Second] Report Respecting the Distilleries in Scotland . . .*, pp. 278–9. I wonder if the division of labour between primary and secondary distillers was not the reality behind the report by Hugo Arnot – *The History of Edinburgh, from the Earliest Accounts to the Present Time* (Edinburgh, 1779), p. 335 n. – that in 1779 there were in the city of Edinburgh eight licensed distilleries and over 400 unlicensed distilleries.

All of these considerations required not only a substantial physical plant but also the support of regular returns from sales commensurate with an investment of some size. One gets a sense of the scale of such a business from the late eighteenth-century 'memorandum book' of John Cooke and Company, malt distillers, of Bow Bridge, Stratford-le-Bow, Essex.[24] (Apparently the distillery was located in or near the modern Cook's Road just at Bow Bridge over the River Lea in the East End of London.) Between 1760 and 1790 Cooke and Company produced on average about 500,000 gallons (1,893,000 litres) of spirits per year. In the two years, 1768 and 1769, it distilled annually 433,000 gallons (1,639,000 litres). If we estimate that Cooke sold his spirits for 7s. a gallon, his gross returns would have been £151,550.[25] Base materials cost

[24] The Memorandum Book of Messrs. John Cooke and Co., 1761–93, entitled 'Observations, upon Brewing, Fermentation, and Distillation', is BL, Add. MS 39,683. It is identified as belonging to John Cooke and Co. from several internal references (see e.g. fo. 68r). Compare Mathias, *Brewing Industry in England*, p. 68. The firm can be traced in any of the London city directories of the era. Thus, for instance, Mortimer, *Universal Director*, p. 30; or [William Lowndes], *A London Directory or Alphabetical Arrangement* . . . , [34th edn] (London, [1795]), p. 39. According to the Excise accounts, the company was the second largest distiller in London. As one of the eight firms that signed a 1783 petition to Parliament, it was then called Cooke, Wilbie, Sayer and Smith – attesting by the change in its name to the consolidation of the industry underway in the second half of the eighteenth century discussed above. For the petition, see n. 23, above.

[25] During the late 1760s and early 1770s rum sold at wholesale in London from 7s. to 9s. per gallon (McCusker, *Rum and the American Revolution*, II, pp. 1065–75). Given some contemporary evidence that rum and gin sold at roughly the same price – Henry Atton and Henry Hurst Holland, *The King's Customs*, 2 vols. (London, 1908–10), I, p. 343 – an estimated price of gin at the lower end of the range seems quite reasonable. To lend perspective to this number, according to the most careful of modern estimates, the 'average full-time money earnings' of all adult workers in Great Britain in the 1770s were less than 7s. 6d. a week. Charles Feinstein, *Conjectures and Contrivances: Economic Growth and the Standard of Living in Britain during the Industrial Revolution*, University of Oxford Discussion Papers in Economic and Social History, 9 (Oxford, 1996), p. 12.

The calculation of Cooke and Company's gross earnings does not take into account any returns from their related hog feeding business. The company's 'memorandum book' (cited in n. 24, above) shows that in September 1766 it sold 183 hogs; and in May 1767, another 324 hogs.

The fattening of livestock on distillers' dregs was – and still is – a major offshoot of the distilling (and brewing) industry. According to *The Corn Distillery, Stated*, p. 43, in the early 1750s, 'the whole Distillery of England fatted more than 100,000 hogs annually'; the number afterwards fell to 30,000 annually (*ibid.*, p. 44). The Stein distillery at Kilbagie fed 7,000 cattle and 2,000 hogs annually in the 1790s. Sinclair, *Statistical Account of Scotland*, XIV, p. 625. Compare Glen, 'Economic history of the distilling industry, Scotland', pp. 165–6, 168. William Malcolm, James Malcolm and Jacob Malcolm, *General View of the Agriculture of the County of Surrey, with Observations on the Means of Its Improvement* (London, 1794), pp. 31–7, explained in some considerable detail the economics of the fattening of hogs in London distilleries. See also William Stevenson, *General View of the Agriculture of Surrey* (London, 1809), pp. 537–8; G. E. Fussell and Constance Goodman, 'Eighteenth-century traffic in livestock', *Economic History*, 3 (February 1936), 232–4; and Mathias, 'Agriculture and the brewing and distilling', 249–57. (Whereas Mathias has argued that brewers began livestock keeping because of growing difficulties in the industry, it seems clear to me from the records I

him about £32,960; expenses, calculated in the memorandum book at 4.6d. a gallon, came to £8,300; and Excise duties amounted to £69,000. Thus Cooke and Company would have netted about £41,000. Cooke figured his capital investment at £40,000,[26] giving him in each of those years a return on capital in excess of 100 per cent.[27] Certainly one of London's 'capital houses' turned in a tidy profit in the late 1760s.

In summary, then, by 1650 the art of distilling had emerged from the mists of alchemy and become an industry. In the seventeenth century the combination of the large copper pot still and the worm condenser set alcoholic beverage distilling apart from what had gone before. Significantly bigger yields from one sequence of boiling in larger stills, combined with the more efficient recondensation of the escaping vapours, greatly increased productivity and permitted significant scale economies for the industry. The refinements continued and, over the eighteenth century, distillers multiplied their output by 100 per cent according to one very authoritative contemporary statement. In 1783, in a report to the House of Commons, the Commissioners of Excise in Scotland, estimated that

have seen that they – and the distillers – had been doing so right along. Compare n. 42, below.) The Admiralty, itself a major player in the London food market where it contracted for provisions for the Royal Navy, heard an estimate in 1740 that 90 per cent of the bacon made and consumed in the city was town-fed by distillers (PRO, Letter from the Victualling Board to the Admiralty Secretary, London, 2 July 1740, Adm 110/12, fos. 142–3). For the numbers of 'distillery cows' in eighteenth-century Copenhagen, see Poul Thestrup, *The Standard of Living in Copenhagen, 1730–1800: Some Methods of Measurement*, Københavns Universitet Institut for Økonomisk Historie, 5 (Copenhagen, 1971), pp. 45–6. Dutch distillers fattened pigs herded into The Netherlands from neighbouring Westphalia ('Memorial of Mr. E. G. J. Crookeens [of Bremen], respecting the Distillation of Spirits, & c. in Holland', London, 26 April 1799, in [*Second*] *Report Respecting the Distilleries in Scotland . . .* , p. 318). The spent distillers' grains – 'dross' or 'draff' – are still used as animal feed. *Draff for Animal Feeding, passim.*

26 By adjusting it for inflation on the basis of a commodity price index, we can estimate the modern equivalent of £40,000 sterling in 1768 at about £3,100,000 ($4,800,000) in the year 2000. A 1736 calculation of the number of London distillers and the value of their 'utensils', talked of 1,500 smaller-scale distillers (probably rectifiers) each of whom had an average of just over £250 worth of equipment. The larger operators were '28 [distillers] whose utensils are valued' at £5,000 each (roughly £550,000 ($870,000) in 2000. *An Impartial Enquiry into the Present State of the British Distillery; Plainly Demonstrating the Evil Consequences of Imposing Any Additional Duties on British Spirits* (London, 1736), pp. 7–8. See also the startup costs for a brewery (£2,000 to £10,000) and a distillery (£500 to £5,000) as discussed in R. Campbell, *The London Tradesman. Being a Compendious View of All of the Trades, Professions, Arts . . . Now Practiced in the Cities of London and Westminster* (London, 1747), pp. 332–3 (see also pp. 264–8).

27 Compare the analysis of profitability in the industry offered by Chartres, 'No English Calvados?' p. 327, who arrives at somewhat similar figures. See also the story of the 'great' distillery established in the 1770s by James Stein at Kilbagie, the first large-scale distillery in Scotland. It, too, was said to have cost £40,000 to establish; it employed 300 workers. Sinclair, *Statistical Account of Scotland*, XIV, pp. 623–6; Glen, 'Economic history of the distilling industry, Scotland', pp. 37–9, 122–90; Vivian Eve Dietz, 'Before the age of capital: manufacturing interests and the British state, 1780–1800' (Ph.D. thesis, Princeton University, 1991), p. 202.

between 1705 and then, 'in consequence of the great Improvements made in the Arts of Fermentation and Distillation . . . many Distillers now bring from their Wash near double these Quantities of Low Wines and Spirits'.[28] Such improvement in output, combined with the concurrent decline in the cost of the base materials (about which more later), allowed distillers to charge very much lower prices. Lower prices, in turn, provoked an increased demand for spirits, a demand intensified as the price of spirits continued to fall relative to those of beer and wine.[29]

As a result, commercial distilling began to grow and spread, especially on the continent of Europe – less so in France, more so in the Germanys and The Netherlands – and especially in Great Britain. The increase in the number of distillers and distilleries resulted in the establishment of distillers' guilds in London, in Paris, and in the Dutch distilling centres of Rotterdam and Schiedam, all within a very few years of each other, in the middle third of the seventeenth century.[30] Learned

[28] 'Report, by the Commissioners of Excise in Scotland, to the Committee of the House of Commons, appointed in the Year 1783, to enquire into the Illicit Practices then used in defrauding the Revenue . . . ', as printed in [GB, Parl., Commons], *Report Respecting the Scotch Distillery Duties* ([London], 1798), p. 401. Compare *Second Report from the Committee, Appointed to Enquire into the Illicit Practices Used in Defrauding the Revenue*, p. 5: 'the Proportion of Low Wines and Spirits now produced from a given Quantity of Wash, much exceeds the Quantity formerly produced'.

[29] The consequent decrease in per capita consumption of wine and beer is best documented in the British and Dutch experiences. See André L. Simon, *Bottlescrew Days: Wine Drinking in England during the Eighteenth Century* (London, 1926), p. 67; Mathias, *Brewing Industry in England*, p. 375 and *passim*; and Chartres, 'No English Calvados?', pp. 319–23 (especially fig. 5). See also Forbes, *Art of Distillation*, pp. 96, 195 and *passim*; and the report from the committee on the petition of the Corporation of Brewers and Maltsters of Dublin, 10 November 1773, in [Ireland, Parl., House of Commons], *The Journals of the House of Commons of the Kingdom of Ireland, 1613–1776*, 19 vols. (Dublin, 1753–76), XVI, pp. 182–3.

On the decline of the Dutch brewing industry after the middle of the seventeenth century, see Richard W. Unger, 'Brewing in the Netherlands and the Baltic grain trade', in ed. W. G. Heeres *et al.*, *From Dunkirk to Danzig: Shipping and Trade in the North Sea and the Baltic, 1350–1850: Essays in Honour of J. A. Faber on the Occasion of His Retirement as Professor of Economic and Social History at the University of Amsterdam*, Nederlandsch Economisch-Historisch Archief, series III, no. 4 (Amsterdam, 1988), pp. 429–47; and Richard John Yntema, 'The brewing industry in Holland, 1300–1800: a study in industrial development' (Ph.D. thesis, University of Chicago, 1992). Compare E. M. A. Timmer, *De Generale Brouwers van Holland: Een Bijdrage tot de Geschiedenis der Brouwnering in Holland in de 17de, 18de en 19de eeuw* (Haarlem, 1918), pp. 1–24 and *passim*. See also Hallema and Emmens, *Bier en Zijn Brouwers*. For the earlier period, see Richard W. Unger, 'Technical change in the brewing industry in Germany, the Low Countries, and England in the late Middle Ages', *Journal of European Economic History*, 21 (1992), 281–313; and Unger, 'The scale of Dutch brewing, 1350–1600', *Research in Economic History*, 15 (1995), 261–92. We have almost no price data for these commodities before the seventeenth century. Statements about price behaviour are inferred from the observed effects.

[30] Forbes, *Art of Distillation*, pp. 102, 106–7; André L. Simon, *The History of the Wine Trade in England*, 3 vols. (London, 1906–9), III, 371–2. See also [London, Company of Distillers], *The Distiller of London: Compiled and Set Forth by the Special License and Command of the King's Most Excellent Majesty for the Sole Use of the Company of Distillers of London . . .* (London, 1639); [London, Corporation], *Analytical Index to the Series of*

treatises appeared at the same time, published in several languages, passed about, discussed and translated.[31] In 1641, the Scottish Parliament prohibited the importation of 'strong waters' and then, in 1644, passed its first excise tax on whisky.[32] Over those decades, the consumption of distilled beverages – brandy, gin, whisky, genever and rum – increased spectacularly (see table 8.1).[33] The middle of the

Records Known as the Remembrancia Preserved Among the Archives of the City of London [edited by William Henry Overall and H. C. Overall] (London, 1878), pp. 111–12. Compare, for The Netherlands, J. van Riemsdijk, *Het brandersbedrijf te Schiedam in de 17de en 18de eeuw* (Schiedam [1916]), p. 7; and Dobbelaar, *Branderijen in Holland*, *passim*. The archives of the Distillers' Company of the City of London from the 1630s on are in Guildhall Library, London. See Michael Berlin, *The Worshipful Company of Distillers: A Short History* (Chichester, 1996).

[31] See, for instance, the numerous iterations of the many works by John French: *The Art of Distillation* (London, 1651), of which three more editions appeared before 1667; and French, *The London-Distiller: Exactly and Truly Shewing the Way (in Words at Length, and not in Mysterious Characters and Figures) to Draw All Sorts of Spirits and Strong-Waters* (London, 1652), which appeared in tandem with the second and subsequent editions of the previous work. French also undertook to finish the translation and publish Johann Rudolf Glauber's *Furni novi philosophici, oder, Beschreibung einer Newerfunden Distilir-Kunst*, 5 vols. (Amsterdam, 1646–9), as *A Description of New Philosophical Furnaces, or, A New Art of Distilling, Divided into Five Parts* (London, 1651). The translation had been begun by Cheney Culpeper and Samuel Hartlib. See 'The Letters of Sir Cheney Culpeper (1641–1657)', ed. M[ichael] J. Braddick and M[ark] Greengrass, in *Seventeenth-Century Political and Financial Papers*, Royal Historical Society, Camden, 5th series, no. 7, *Camden Miscellany*, vol. XXXIII (London, 1996), pp. 310, n. 48, 352, n. 10 and *passim*. That the circle of people around Hartlib, of whom Culpeper was one, took such interest in distilling is further demonstration of the point.

[32] [Scotland, Laws and Statutes], *The Acts of the Parliament of Scotland*, [ed. Thomas Thomson and Cosmo Nelson Innes], 12 vols. (Edinburgh, 1814–75), V, p. 418, VI, pp. 76, 238. It was only 'during the eighteenth century [that] distilling in Scotland began to make the transition from a peasant activity to a specialized industry with a commercial scale of operations'. Glen, 'Economic history of the distilling industry, Scotland', p. 4.

[33] Note two observations proposed by the data in table 8.1. First, the roughly thirty-fold increase in consumption by mariners between 1615 and the 1770s was considerably outpaced by the nearly hundredfold increase in consumption by the British civilian population. Second, for the white North American population, consumption figures suggesting that soldiers and sailors drank from three to five times as much as the total civilian population make better sense when we remember that the ratio of adult males to the total population was also roughly one to five. In other words, adult males probably drank spirits at about the same rate in peace and in war – and they probably accounted for most of the consumption of spirits.

However rapid the acceptance of distilled spirits by Europeans, African consumers learned about them perhaps even more quickly – so much so that by the 1660s the Fetu people of what is now central Ghana had cultivated discerning palates for them. According to the Hamburg-born Lutheran pastor and missionary Wilhelm Johann Müller, who lived among them as an employee of the Danish African Company at the company's fort at Frederiksborg from 1662 to 1669, the Fetu insisted exclusively on French brandy. They despised grain alcohol, calling it 'stinkibus' (*Stinck-Buchs*), and they rejected rum out of hand. 'A brandy made in Barbados in the West Indies (called Kill Divell by the English) has also been brought here for sale. But the Blacks would not put it in their mouths.' Wilhelm Johann Müller, *Die Africanische auf der Guineischen Gold- Cust gelegene Landschafft Fetu, Wahrhafftig und Fleissig auß Eigener Acht-jähriger Erfahrung . . .* , [3rd edn] (Hamburg, 1676), p. 173 (my translation).

Table 8.1. *Estimates of annual per capita consumption of spirits, 1600–1800*

Date	Spirit	Consuming population	Estimates	
			gallons	litres
1615	'Aquavitæ'	Ration of medicinal spirits on board an English fishing boat	0.75	2.84
Mid-1650s	English gin	Inhabitants of England	0.02	0.06
Mid-1680s	English gin	Inhabitants of England	0.11	0.42
1724	Rum	Inhabitants of the Bermuda Islands	3.00	11.40
1736	Brændevin	Ration for Danish sailors	3.32	12.56
1740s	English gin	Inhabitants of England	1.40	5.30
1750	Rum	Inhabitants of Kingston, Jamaica	21.43	81.12
1760s–1770s	Rum	Ration for British soldiers in the Caribbean	22.75	86.12
1770	Rum	White inhabitants of British North America	4.20	15.90
1770s	Rum	Ration for British sailors in North America	15.21	57.57
1774	Rum	Inhabitants of Massachusetts	8.00	30.32
1770s–1780s	Rum/whiskey	Ration for soldiers in the United States Army	11.41	43.18
1770s–1780s	Rum	Ration for sailors in the United States Navy	22.81	86.35
c. 1780	Spirits	Inhabitants of Scotland	2.41	9.11
1794	Brændevin	Ration for Danish sailors	5.80	21.95

Sources and notes: The 1615 provisioning list for outfitting a fishing boat, as set out in E[dward] S[harpe], *Britaines Busse. Or a Computation Aswell of the Charge of a Busse or Herring-Fishing Ship. As Also of the Gaine and Profit Thereby* . . . (London, 1615), sig. C₂r, allowed the crew 3 quarts (0.75 gallons, 2.81 litres) of 'aquavitæ' a year as medicine.

In England and Wales, per capita annual consumption of spirits rose from 0.015 gallons (0.061 litres) in the mid-1650s to 0.11 gallons (0.41 litres) in the mid-1680s, a sevenfold increase. By the 1740 it was at 1.4 gallons (5.3 litres), almost a hundredfold increase over a century. These annual consumption figures are estimates developed from data in the volume Excise Statistics and Memoranda, England, 1662–1805, HM Customs and Excise, Departmental Archives, London, by John Chartres, 'No English Calvados? English distillers and the cider industry in the seventeenth and eighteenth centuries', in *English Rural Society, 1500–1800: Essays in Honour of Joan Thirsk*, ed. John Chartres and David Hey (Cambridge, 1990), pp. 316–18. Compare the table in T. S. Ashton, *An Economic History of England: the 18th Century* (London [1995]), p. 243. For these data and their collection consult Selma E. Fine, 'Production and excise in England, 1643–1825' (Ph.D. thesis, Radcliffe College, Harvard University, 1937), pp. 164–71, 241–4, appendix C (after p. 259), and *passim*. The Excise figures are reduced to per capita numbers using the population estmates in E. A. Wrigley and R. S. Schofield, *The Population History of England, 1541–1871: a Reconstruction* (Cambridge, Mass.,

1981), pp. 533–4. Peter Mathias, *The Brewing Industry in England, 1700–1830* (Cambridge, 1959), pp. 375, 542–3, argued that the quantity consumed per capita was to fall off later in the eighteenth century. See, however, the estimate for Scotland, below.

In the 'Account of the Revenue', dated Bermuda, 21 May 1724, the islands' population was 'computed' at '10000 Soles' and the annual importation of rum estimated for revenue purposes at 30,000 gallons annually (CO 37/11, fo. 101r).

The ration of 'brændevin' per sailor on Danish war ships nearly doubled over the eighteenth century from 3.3 gallons (12.61 litres) per year in 1736 to 5.8 gallons (22 litres) in 1794. Poul Thestrup, *The Standard of Living in Copenhagen, 1730–1800: Some Methods of Measurement,* Københavns Universitet Institut for Økonomisk Historie, 5 (Copenhagen, 1971), pp. 35, 155.

There is 'supposed to be vended in Kingston for the Consumption of the Inhabitants Negros and transient People' 300,000 gallons of rum per year according to the Jamaican author of 'An inquiry into the causes of the present scarcity of money and the bad consequences of it to this island' (1750), BL, Add. MS 30,163, fo. 48v. The author estimated that the population of Kingston consisted in '1000 Families of 4 to a Family Transient people included' and 10,000 blacks (*ibid.*, fo. 48r).

The ration of rum allowed sailors on Royal Navy ships victualled in the Caribbean in the 1760s and 1770s was 22.8 gallons (86.11 litres) per year [GB, Parliament, House of Commons], *Report from the Select Committee to Whom It Was Referred to Consider and Examine the Accounts of Extraordinary Services Incurred and Paid, and Not Provided for by Parliament, Which Have Been Laid before the House of Commons in the Years 1776, 1777, and 1778,* HC, Sessional Papers to 1801, Reports, vol. V, no. 36 (London, 1778), appendix no. 20 [p. 7], and appendix no. 21. For soldiers in the British Army in North America during the American Revolutionary War, the ration was 15.2 gallons (57.6 litres) per year. *Ibid.*, appendix no. 8, appendix no. 55 [p. 3].

See McCusker, *Rum and the American Revolution*, I, pp. 476–7, for an estimate that, by 1770, the European-American inhabitants of the colonies drank an average of 4.2 gallons (15.9 litres) of rum per year.

[James Swan], *National Arithmetic: or, Observations on the Finances of the Commonwealth of Massachusetts . . .* (Boston, [1786]), p. 3, n., estimated that, in 1774, the 200,000 inhabitants of the colony drank 60 per cent of the 25,454 hogsheads (2,700,000 gallons) of rum distilled in the province each year. It was, he feared, 'a quantity sufficient to destroy the constitution, and reduce the inhabitants to the most enervated state'.

Discussions of the ration of rum or whiskey for soldiers in the Continental Army of the United States can be found in several parts of the *Papers of Robert Morris, 1781–1784*, edited by E. James Ferguson *et al.*, 9 vols. (Pittsburgh, 1973–99). The official ration was one gill per day. See, for instance, the contract with Comfort Sands and Company, 6 December 1781, *ibid.*, III, 442–348. I am grateful to Elizabeth M. Nuxoll and Mary A. Gallagher for their help with this matter.

The official ration for sailor in the Continental Navy was half-a-pint a day, twice that of the Army [United States, Continental Congress], *Journals of the Continental Congress, 1774–1789*, ed. Worthington Chauncey Ford *et al.*, 34 vols. (Washington, D.C., 1904–37), III, 383.

In his parliamentary testimony in 1799, John Stein, the leading Scottish distiller of the last quarter of the eighteenth century, estimated that 3,500,000 gallons of all spirits were consumed in Scotland *c.* 1780. 'First memorial of John Stein, Esquire, respecting the Scotch Distillery', London, 24 April 1799, in [GB, Parl., Commons], *[Second] Report Respecting the Distilleries in Scotland . . .* ([London, 1799]), pp. 279, 284. For Stein, see Iseabal Ann Glen, 'An economic history of the distilling industry in Scotland, 1750–1914', 2 vols. (Ph.D. thesis, University of Strathclyde, 1969), *passim*. There were an estimated 1,451,000 people in Scotland in 1780. McCusker, *Rum and the American Revolution*, p. 552.

seventeenth century marked a turning point in the history of the distilling of alcoholic beverages.[34]

The full flowering of commercial distilling in the years around and after 1650 could not have been attained without a second innovation: the discovery of an abundant, inexpensive base material in sugar and its byproducts, particularly molasses – 'the mother liquor' – and syrup.[35] The subsequent development of a commercial distilling industry involved the European colonies in the New World in ways that were to affect their own history considerably – and that of the whole Atlantic world.

As we have seen, the common spirits distilled in Europe up to the seventeenth century had been made from either wine or grain. French, Spanish and some German distillers turned wine into brandy. The high cost of all but the worst of wines limited the source of this base material and made their brandy expensive, kept their operations small, and thereby inhibited them from taking advantage of increased scale and associated economies.[36] The distillers of The Netherlands, Germany, and, later, Britain, used grains, mixing various flavouring agents with the fermented base material and producing grain spirits of several types. They, too, had their problems. During the seventeenth and eighteenth centuries, especially after about 1740, the growing population of Europe put ever

[34] A point happily concurred in by Louis M. Cullen, *The Brandy Trade under the* Ancien Régime: *Regional Specialisation in the Charente* (Cambridge, 1998), p. 1 and *passim*. See also nn. 36, 46, 47, below. Distilling was not the only industrial activity to grow and develop during this era. One historian has indeed called it the period of 'the first industrial revolution'. See J. U. Nef, 'The progress of technology and the growth of large-scale industry in Great Britain, 1540–1640', *EcHR*, 5 (1934), 3–24. Peter Mathias, *The First Industrial Nation: an Economic History of Britain, 1700–1914*, 2nd edn (London, 1983), p. 1, while not accepting Nef's viewpoint, did find that an 'industrial transformation occurred in urban brewing in London during the seventeenth century'. Mathias's own work on the brewing industry, upon which he obviously based that assessment, was precisely the kind of study that Nef expected would demonstrate his hypothesis.

[35] 'Molasses may be considered to be the mother liquor which is left after the crystallisation of cane-syrup'. W[illiam] J. Evans, *The Sugar-Planters' Manual: Being a Treatise on the Art of Obtaining Sugar from the Sugar-Cane* (London, 1847), p. 35.

[36] After a start early in the seventeenth century, the commercial distilling of brandy in France grew only slowly for several decades. Lachiver, *Vins, vignes et vignerons*, p. 267, cites 1655–60 as the date for 'le dévelopement de la distillation' of 'l'eau-de-vie'. He associates its introduction with the activities in France of Dutch merchants and distillers (*ibid.*, pp. 261–5). Compare Braudel, *Civilisation matérielle, économie et capitalisme*, I, 206–3; Cullen, *Brandy Trade*, p. 1 and *passim*. See also n. 47 below.

The high price of brandy was the result of a demand that consistently outran supply. Robert Delamain, *Histoire du Cognac* (Paris, 1935), pp. 15–18. Compare Simon, *Bottle-screw Days*, p. 32; Forbes, *Art of Distillation*, p. 206; Fernand P. Braudel and Frank C. Spooner, 'Prices in Europe from 1450 to 1750', in *The Economy of Expanding Europe in the Sixteenth and Seventeenth Centuries*, ed. E. E. Rich and C. H. Wilson, vol. IV of *The Cambridge Economic History of Europe* (Cambridge, 1967), pp. 407–13; and Braudel, *Civilisation matérielle, économie et capitalisme*, I, pp. 208–9.

more pressure on existing grain resources.[37] During periods of dearth citizens objected that brewing and distilling made matters worse by driving up the cost of flour, bread and other foods even higher and causing, in whole or in part, grain shortages and famine. This antipathy surfaced increasingly frequently in the form of regulations prohibiting the brewing of beer and the distilling of alcohol from grain.[38] Distillers and brewers began to compete fiercely over grain supplies.[39] As a result of all these obstacles, distillers of both grain and wine were on the lookout for an alternative base material.[40] They found it in sugar.

[37] For the history of English grain output and prices over this period, see the essays and data in *The Agrarian History of England and Wales*, ed. H. P. R. Finberg and Joan Thirsk, in progress (Cambridge, 1967 to date), V, pt ii, and VI. Most particularly see the grain price series compiled, for 1640–1750, by Peter J. Bowden and, for 1750–1850, by Arthur H. John.

[38] Forbes, *Art of Distillation*, pp. 96–7, 102–5, 161, 189, 191. Very important in this regard is [Wilhelm Naudé, Gustav von Schmoller, and August Karl Friederich Skalweit], *Die Getreidehandelspolitik . . .* , Acta Borussica: Denkmäler der Preußischen Staatsverwaltung im 18. Jahrhundert, 4 vols. (Berlin, 1896–1931). For one instance of grain riots caused by resentment over the continued use of grain in distilling during a time of shortages – Scotland in 1740 – see A. J. S. Gibson and T. C. Smout, *Prices, Food and Wages in Scotland, 1550–1780* (Cambridge, 1995), p. 172. See also n. 39, below. In 1713, 'by reason of the present scarcity of corn and grain', the colony of Massachusetts temporarily forbade the distilling of imported molasses so 'that it may be used for brewing', thus alleviating, indirectly, pressure on the grain supply. [Massachusetts (Colony), Laws and Statutes], *The Acts and Resolves, Public and Private, of the Province of the Massachusetts Bay*, ed. Abner Cheney Goodell *et al.*, 21 vols. (Boston, 1869–1922), I, pp. 724–5.

[39] For the tensions this caused between English farmers and English brewers and distillers, see [Michael Comburne], *An Enquiry into the Prices of Wheat, Malt, and Occasionally of Other Provisions; of Land and Cattle, & c. As Sold in England, from the Year 1000 to the Year 1765* (London, 1768), pp. 66–9, 82–4, and 92–9. For the use of British grain by Dutch distillers, see David John Ormrod, 'Anglo-Dutch Commerce, 1700–1760' (Ph.D. thesis, University of Cambridge, 1973), pp. 204–45; and Ormrod, *English Grain Exports and the Structure of Agrarian Capitalism, 1700–1760*, Occasional Papers in Economic and Social History, 12 (Hull, 1985), *passim*.

[40] In Great Britain the growth in the consumption of imported West Indian rum is linked by many to the restrictions on grain distilling there in the last half of the eighteenth century; that ban had the added effect of stimulating local distillation of syrup, imported molasses, and inexpensive sugars. On the prohibition of grain distilling, see Donald Grove Barnes, *A History of the English Corn Laws from 1660–1846* (London, 1930), pp. 23–48; T. S. Ashton, *Economic Fluctuations in England, 1700–1800* (Oxford, 1959), pp. 36, 153. On the increased importation of rum, see McCusker, *Rum and the American Revolution*, II, pp. 939–82. On the use by London distillers of syrups, molasses and cheap sugars, see the letters from the London firm of Lascelles and Maxwell to Thomas Stevenson of Barbados, 5 February 1757, 24 February 1758, and 15 February 1760, among others, in Lascelles and Maxwell Letterbooks, VII (1756–9), fos. 49, 183, VIII (1760–3), fo. 30, Wilkinson and Gaviller Ltd papers, 1740–72, as extracted in Rhodes House Library, Oxford, Richard Pares Papers. See also Richard Pares, 'The London sugar market, 1740–1769', *EcHR*, 2nd series, 9 (1956), 262; Lowell Joseph Ragatz, *The Fall of the Planter Class in the British Caribbean, 1763–1833: a Study in Social and Economic History* (New York and London, 1928), pp. 290, 317–19. By January 1758 word had reached the West Indies that British distillers had begun to import syrup from

The production of table sugar from raw sugar-cane juice involves a series of stages during which progressively greater quantities of liquid are purged from the crystallizing sugar.[41] All the fluid forms of sugar, ranging from freshly crushed cane juice itself through to the liquid drained from the last refining, could be fermented and distilled. The initial boiling of the cane juice resulted in both a raw brown sugar called muscovado and a liquid byproduct called molasses. Distilled on the spot or shipped elsewhere to be distilled, molasses yielded rum. Raw sugar, exported from the western hemisphere to European refiners who reboiled it and recrystallized it, produced not only a refined white sugar but also another liquid byproduct called various names but most generally syrup.[42] The early

Hamburg. See Scottish Record Office, Edinburgh, Walter Tullideph, at Antigua, to Henry Hancock (sugar refiner), at Edinburgh, 19 January 1758, Walter Tullideph letterbook (1734–44), Ogilvy of Inverquharity Muniments, GD 205/53/8. I wish to express my thanks to Richard B. Sheridan for allowing me to use his transcripts as a guide to these materials. I have, of course, consistently checked them against the originals. I am grateful to Sir Francis Ogilvy for permission to consult this collection and to make reference to this letter.

[41] The standard work on sugar is still Edmund O. von Lippmann, *Geschichte des Zuckers seit den ältesten Zeiten bis zum Beginn der Rübenzucker-Fabrikation. Ein Beitrag zur Kulturgeschichte* (2nd edn, Berlin, 1929). The best that can be said about Noel Deerr's *The History of Sugar*, 2 vols. (London, 1949–50) is that it faithfully renders much of Lippmann's study into English. See also J. J. Reesse, *De Suikerhandel van Amsterdam van het begin der 17de eeuw tot 1894. Ein Bijdrage tot de Handelsgeschiedenis des Vaderlands*, 2 vols. (Haarlem and 's-Gravenhage, 1908–11); Sidney Mintz, *Sweetness and Power: the Place of Sugar in Modern History* (New York, 1985); J. H. Galloway, *The Sugar Cane Industry: an Historical Geography from Its Origins to 1914* (Cambridge, 1989); Jean Meyer, *Histoire du sucre* (Paris, 1989); and McCusker, *Rum and the American Revolution*. For an especially elegant discussion of the linkage of sugar to the consumption of tea, see Woodruff D. Smith, 'Complications of the commonplace: tea, sugar, and imperialism', *JIH*, 23 (1992), 259–78.

[42] Contemporaries recognized a clear distinction in the character of molasses, the West Indian byproduct of sugar manufacture, and the character of syrup, the industrial byproduct of sugar refining. According to A. Blom, in *Vervolg van den Surinaamschen Landman* (Paramaribo), No. 5 (15 January 1802), p. 71, 'die malassie . . . is dunder en wateriger als de Hollandsche syroop' – it was thinner and more watery. Compare Friedrich Wilhelm [von] Taube, *Historische und Politische Abschilderung der Engländischen Manufacturen, Handlung, Schifffahrt und Colonien . . .* (Vienna, 1774), pp. 251–2, n. In Great Britain, the synonym for syrup was and is 'treacle'; confusingly, English speakers sometimes called syrup 'molasses' or 'melasses'. Like real sugar-cane molasses, syrup could be and can be used by itself as a form of sweetener. J. Massie, *A State of the British Sugar Colony Trade . . .* (London, 1759), p. 24; J. C. Drummond and Anne Wilbraham, *The Englishman's Food: a History of Five Centuries of English Diet*, 2nd rev. edn (London, 1957), p. 209; Mintz, *Sweetness and Power*, p. 232, n. 10. Syrup is what Chartres ('No English Calvados?', *passim*) refers to as 'spent molasses'. In the 1630s the use of syrup – 'the refuse or dross of Sugar' – as a base for distilling was still novel enough to be a cause of concern. It was thought 'fitt only for hoggs treacle'. See the complaint, 1638 (?), in PRO, SP 16/408, fo. 41r, para [2], no. 25, and as calendared in [GB, PRO], *Calendar of State Papers, Domestic Series, of the Reign of Charles I*, ed. John Bruce, William Douglas Hamilton and Sophia Crawford Lomas, 23 vols. (London, 1858–97), XIII, 1638–9, p. 252. Compare n. 25, above.

As early as 1585, the weekly Amsterdam business newspaper – the *Cours van der Comenschappen* – regularly listed the prices of four varieties of syrup, one local and three

modern European sugar refining industry, from limited beginnings at Antwerp using sugar from Portuguese Brazil, expanded rapidly starting in the middle of the seventeenth century, based especially in Amsterdam, Hamburg and London, as first the English and then the French established colonies in the Caribbean.[43]

The availability of ever increasing quantities of syrup from European sugar refineries offered commercial distillers an inexpensive supplement or alternative to wines and grains. European distillers made of it what they would because, as all recognized, 'the spirit distilled from melasses or treacle is very pure . . . [and] entirely colourless when first extracted'. This gave distillers the opportunity to flavour and colour it and to give it the character 'as nearly as possible . . . of foreign spirits'.[44] Dutch distillers used syrup, mixed with the juniper berry, to make still more *genever* (Dutch gin).[45] Englishmen distilled syrup to make 'English brandy' and more English gin.[46] German distillers coloured and flavoured the product

imported, including one from England, 'Ciroop van Engelant'. For this publication, see John J. McCusker and Cora Gravesteijn, *The Beginnings of Commercial and Financial Journalism: the Commodity Price Currents, Exchange Rate Currents, and Money Currents of Early Modern Europe*, Nederlandsch Economisch–Historisch Archief, series III, no. 11 (Amsterdam, 1991), pp. 43–83. The existence of a regular market in Amsterdam for English syrup suggests a stronger demand for it in The Netherlands than in England, a suggestion that further supports the idea that the Dutch were ahead of the rest of Europe in the development of distilling (compare n. 50, below).

[43] McCusker, *Rum and the American Revolution*, I, pp. 36–55. See also T. C. Smout, 'The early Scottish sugar houses, 1660–1720', *EcHR*, 2nd series, 14 (1961), 240–52; and Robert Louis Stein, *The French Sugar Business in the Eighteenth Century* (Baton Rouge, La., 1988), pp. 135–51. Concerning the increased consumption of sugar, see the studies cited n. 41, above.

[44] Gregory, *Dictionary of Arts and Sciences*, I, p. 536.

[45] For the Dutch distilling of gin, see the 'Memorial of Mr. E. G. J. Crookeens [of Bremen], respecting the Distillation of Spirits, & c. in Holland', London, 26 April 1799, in [*Second*] *Report Respecting the Distilleries in Scotland . . .* , pp. 308–18; Van Riemsdijk, *Brandersbedrijf te Schiedam*; and Dobbelaar, *Branderijen in Holland*. Compare C[ornelis] Visser, *Verkeersindustrieën te Rotterdam in de tweede helft der achttiende eeuw*, Rotterdamsche Bijdragen voor Economische Geschiedenis, II (Rotterdam, 1927), pp. 91–123.

[46] Peter Shaw, *Three Essays in Artificial Philosophy, or Universal Chemistry* (London, 1731), pp. 123–6, discussed the history of the distillation of syrup. Contemporaries considered his 'Essay on the Business of Distillation' authoritative enough to copy parts of it wholesale. See Ephraim Chambers, *A Supplement to Mr. Chambers's Cyclopedia: or, Universal Dictionary of Arts and Sciences*, [ed. George Lewis Scott], 2 vols. (London, 1753), s.v. 'Rum'; Cooper, *Complete Distiller*, 2nd edn, pp. 80–2; and *Encyclopedia Britannica* [ed. William Smellie], [1st edn], 3 vols. (Edinburgh, 1771), s.v. 'Rum'. The whole process was new enough in the 1670s that distillers felt they had to explain it in some detail. See [Charles Bambridge *et al.*], *The Case of Charles Bambridge, and Other Distillers, with Reference to Their Use of Molasses Made and Manufactured in This Kingdom* ([London (?)], [1679]). The date of this petition, established from internal evidence, is confirmed by reference to *JHC*, IX, 623. See also Charles M. Andrews, *England's Commercial and Colonial Policy*, vol. IV of *The Colonial Period of American History* (New Haven, Conn., 1938), pp. 95, 98–102. The claim was made in 1783 that 'the Gin made by Mr. Bishop in Maidstone', Kent, was 'equal in goodness to Holland Gin' (*The Corn Distillery, Stated*, p. 46).

of their stills and called their product *branntwein* (brandy).[47] Some of them used Danish syrup.[48] By the 1660s an important product of Scottish sugar refining was 'Scottish rum', 'scarce to be decerned . . . from the fynnest of the forraigne Brandie', or so some claimed.[49] Irish distillers observed that syrup, 'a necessary residium' of the refining of sugar, 'would be useless unless distilled'. They used it – in addition to locally grown grain – to make Irish whiskey.[50]

Ironically, in the seventeenth century much of the sugar being refined was English sugar produced in the English West Indies. The lesson came clear only slowly but, by the first decade of the eighteenth century, one contemporary observer could lament that England's re-exportation of its colonial raw sugars to refiners on the continent of Europe cost the nation doubly. Doing so diminished the English sugar refining industry and cost the country not only the potential value-added from manufacturing the refined sugar at home but also the higher Customs revenues from any export of refined sugar. But that was not all. Doing so also cost the nation because of 'the loss of the molasses' or syrup yielded during refining. As matters stood, this syrup was 'of great advantage in the brandy manufacture' by England's competitors and that was especially hurtful because the country then turned around and bought such

[47] For the German distilling of *braantwein*, see Andrzej Klonder, *Napoje Fermentacyjne w Prusach Królewskich w XVI–XVII wieku (Produkcja–Import–Konsumpcja)*, Studia i Materialy y Historii Kultury Materialnej, no. LX (Warsaw, 1989). Compare the 'Memorial of . . . Crookeens, respecting the Distilation of Spirits', London, 26 April 1799, in [*Second*] *Report Respecting the Distilleries in Scotland . . .* , pp. 308–18. Klonder also makes the point that, even though distilling was known in East Prussia in the sixteenth century, it became important there only after the middle of the seventeenth century.

[48] Over the eleven years 1742–54, the Danish West India and Guinea Company shipped from its sugar refinery in Copenhagen something over 1,000,000 litres (260,000 gallons) of syrup to Danzig and nearly 700,000 litres (180,000 gallons) to Königsberg, both in East Prussia. Erik Gøbel, 'Danish Trade to the West Indies and Guinea, 1671–1754', *Scandinavian Economic History Review*, 31 (1983), 34–5.

[49] Smout, 'Early Scottish sugar houses', pp. 241 and after (quotation on p. 252). In the earliest years of Scottish sugar refining, some of the syrup had been exported to distillers on the Continent (compare n. 42, above). By contrast, at the end of the seventeenth century Scotland was exporting 'rum' to England (*ibid.*, pp. 251–3). See also Dietz, 'Before the age of capital', pp. 197–288. Sugar and syrup were very much still in use in Lowland Scotland distilling at the end of the eighteenth century. Glen, 'Economic history of the distilling industry, Scotland', p. 70. Compare Michael S. Moss and John R. Hume, *The Making of Scotch Whisky: a History of the Scotch Whisky Distilling Industry* (Edinburgh, 1981). Moss and Hume would have benefited greatly had they consulted Smout, or Glen, or any of the sources used by either of them.

[50] *An Humble Proposal from the Distillers and Sugar-Bakers of the City of Dublin in Behalf of Themselves and the Rest of the Distillers and Sugar Bakers of the Kingdom of Ireland . . .* ([Dublin (?)], [1715 (?)]), [p. 1]; E[dward] B. McGuire, *Irish Whiskey: A History of Distilling, the Spirit Trade, and Excise Controls in Ireland* (Dublin, [1973]), pp. 106–7. Compare J[ames] Lightbody, *Every Man His Own Gauger . . .* (London, [1695]), pp. 57–60; *Impartial Enquiry into the Present State of the British Distillery*, p. 19.

'brandy' (read: gin) from the very folk 'who refine our sugar' (read: the Dutch).[51]

The situation changed rapidly. In 1736, in the midst of the debate over the 'Gin Act', the British sugar growing and refining industry claimed that a significant part of its production was in the form of syrup used for distilling.[52] Between 1690 and 1770, with the exception of the 1740s, the period of the War of the Austrian Succession, never less than one-eighth and frequently as much as one-fifth of the spirits distilled in England had syrup as the base material.[53] Combined with the advances in distillery technology, it was the availability of syrup that helped establish distilling as an industry across Europe.

The middle of the seventeenth century also witnessed the creation and rapid expansion of a distilling industry in the western hemisphere. Spanish and later Portuguese sugar growers may have turned some of their molasses into spirits beginning as early as the late sixteenth century, but, once the quantities involved became appreciable, the wine and brandy interests at home fought successfully to limit colonial production. Only with the Dutch capture and occupation of Portuguese Brazil between 1630 and 1654 did the potential of sugar for distilling become fully

[51] [Nehemiah Grew], 'The Means of the Most Ample Encrease of the Wealth and Strength of England . . . ', p. 81, Henry E. Huntington Library, San Marino, California. For Grew (1641–1712), see Michael Hunter, *Establishing the New Science: the Experience of the Early Royal Society* (Woodbridge, Suffolk, 1989), pp. 261–78. Compare the June 1713 petition to Parliament from the merchants, sugar refiners and distillers of Liverpool in defense of the distilling industry there. *JHC*, XVII, 392.

[52] *A Collection of Letters Published in the Daily Papers Relating to the British Distillery* (London, 1736), pp. 18–19; *The Case of the Sugar-Trade, with Regard to the Duties Intended to be Laid on All Spirituous Liquors, Sold by Retail* (n. p. (London [?]), [n. d. (1736)]), pp. 1–2; *The Case of the Merchants, and Others, of the City of Bristol, Trading to the British Colonies in America* ([London (?)], 1736). So closely tied were the two commodities that 'a Duty layed . . . upon Melosses spirits . . . was virtually a Tax upon Sugar', in the opinion of Lascelles and Maxwell of London as expressed in a letter to Thomas Applethwaite of Barbados, 13 February 1743/44, Rhodes House Library, Oxford, Lascelles and Maxwell Letterbooks, II (1743–6), fo. 118, Pares Papers.

[53] According to data that Chartres developed from Excise records, in every decade but one between 1690 and 1770, syrup accounted for between 12 per cent and 22 per cent of the spirits distilled in England. Chartres, 'No English Calvados?', p. 329.

   In the mid-1730s, out of the 100,000 hogsheads of sugar annually imported into Great Britain, 60,000 hogsheads were refined. That processing yielded 24,000 hogsheads of syrup ('melasses') of which 14,000 hogsheads were distilled. 'These 14000 Hogsheads of Melasses contain the Substance of 11000 Hogsheads of Sugar, which is almost a ninth part in Quantity, and an eighteenth part in Value, of the whole . . . '. The hogshead of syrup sold on average for £5 sterling (*Collection of Letters Published in the Daily Papers Relating to the British Distillery*, pp. 18–19).

   As the above makes clear, what was called 'molasses' in these discussions was actually syrup (see also n. 42, above). With the singular exception of a few years at the beginning of the eighteenth century, almost no West Indian molasses was imported into Great Britain between 1690 and 1770 (McCusker, *Rum and the American Revolution*, II, pp. 933–4).

realized even in that colony. The British who settled Barbados after 1627 learned most of the techniques of sugar planting and processing from the Brazilian Dutch. Early on the Barbadian settlers turned cane juice into a distilled spirit. They named it rum. British colonists who came afterwards, both to the Caribbean and to North America, brought stills with them, and they quickly put them to work turning molasses into more rum.[54] Although later and to a lesser extent, French, Danish and Dutch West Indian colonists did the same thing.[55] The results were significant

[54] Much of this is dealt with in McCusker, *Rum and the American Revolution*, I, pp. 90–111 and *passim*. For the most recent work on the beginnings of distilling in New England, see Eck, 'Spirits of Massachusetts'. Compare Dean Albertson, 'Puritan liquor in the planting of New England', *New England Quarterly*, 23 (1950), 477–90. See also Henderson Delisle Carter, 'The history of the rum enterprise in Barbados, 1640–1815' (M.Phil. thesis, University of the West Indies, Cave Hill, Barbados, 1992); and Alain Heutz de Lemps, *Histoire du Rhum* (Paris, 1997).

    Early on the Virginia Company of London had sought to promote just such activity in its colony. In 1621 it sent out Joseph Finch, an apothecary, and instructed the colony's governor, Francis Wyatt, to encourage Finch to produce an exportable spirit. 'Wee desire you not to forgett' to employ 'your Apothecaries in distilling of hott waters out of your Lees of beere . . . and good quantities of a[ll] sorts to send us by all ships'. [Virginia Company of London], *The Records of the Virginia Company of London*, ed. Susan Myra Kingsbury, 4 vols. (Washington, D.C., 1906–35), III, pp. 468–82 (quotation, p. 476). Archaeological evidence exists that suggests that Finch (or a successor of his) tried to do precisely what the company ordered. At the site in Jamestown known as structure 110, tentatively identified as a 'brewhouse', modern investigators have found an alembic among other items in the fill. Audrey J. Horning, '"By our industry and plantation of comodious merchandize": early manufacturing at Jamestown', *Colonial Williamsburg Foundation Research Review*, 6 (1995/6), 20.

[55] For the earliest references to rum in Brazil (in the second quarter of the seventeenth century) and for its subsequent history there, see José C. Curto, 'Alcohol and slaves: the Luso-Brazilian alcohol commerce at Mpinda, Luanda, and Benguila during the Atlantic slave trade, *c.* 1480–1830 and its impact on the societies of west-central Africa' (Ph.D. thesis, University of California, Los Angeles, 1996). I am very grateful to the author for permitting me to read several chapters of his dissertation while he was still working on it. Compare Stuart B. Schwartz, *Sugar Plantations in the Formation of Brazilian Society: Bahia, 1550–1835* (Cambridge, 1985), especially pp. 160–3, 541, n. 107; and Luis da Camara Cascudo, *Prelúdio da Cachaça [Etnografia, História e Sociologia da Aguardente no Brasil]* (Belo Horizonte, 1986). By the late 1750s there were seventy-one distilleries in and around Salvador alone; it was then Brazil's largest city. They catered mostly to a local clientele. José Antônio Caldas, *Noticia geral de toda esta capatania de Bahia desde o seu descobrimento até o pres[en]te anno de 1759* (Salvador, Brazil, 1951), pp. 445–8. Compare Dauril Alden, 'Price movements in Brazil before, during and after the gold boom, with special reference to the Salvador market, 1670–1769', in *Essays on the Price History of Eighteenth-Century Latin America*, ed. Lyman L. Johnson and Enrique Tandeter (Albuquerque, N.M., 1990), p. 355 and n. 84, p. 370. Nevertheless, as Joseph C. Miller, *Way of Death: Merchant Capitalism and the Angolan Slave Trade, 1730–1830* (Madison, Wis., 1988), pp. 464–7, pointed out, a fairly high proportion of Brazilian rum was produced for the African slave trade.

    For rum in New Spain, see José Jesús Hernández Palomo, *El aguardiente de caña en México (1724–1810)*, Publicaciones de la Escuela de Estudios Hispano-Americanos de Sevilla, 113 (Seville, 1974); and Teresa Lozano Armendares, *El chinguirito vindicado: El Contrabando de aguardiente de caña y la política colonial*, Instituto de Investigaciones

and had far-reaching economic, social and political consequences. One of them had a particular impact on the British colonies that were to become the United States of America.

Integral to the commercial distilling industry of the European colonies on the continent and in the islands was the trade connecting them. The British North Americans carried food, draught animals and timber products to the Caribbean and received back the produce of the sugar plantations, including rum and molasses. It was a mutually beneficial commerce upon which both came to depend and from which each drew strength. Central to that trade was rum, distilled in the plantations of the West Indies and in the cities of North America and consumed in increasing quantities in both places.[56] One estimate indicates that British North Americans of European ancestry, by the eve of the revolutionary war, consumed over 4 gallons (almost 16 litres) of rum per person per year (see table 8.1). That rate was nearly double the modern consumption in the United States of all distilled spirits.[57] Yet only part of the rum

Históricas, Serie Historia Novohispana, 51 (Mexico City, 1995). See also José Méndez, *Succinta, y General Noticia que dà el Licenciado D. Joseph Mendez . . . : De la Falsa Calumnia que se le Imputò en la Fabrica de Agua Ardiente, que se le Aprehendiò á Bernabela de la Cruz, y Contreras, y Sentencia que en Ella se Pronunciò . . .* (Mexico City, 1725).

[56] Still the standard book on the trade is Richard Pares, *Yankees and Creoles: the Trade between North America and the West Indies before the American Revolution* (London, 1956). See also Frank Wesley Pitman, *The Development of the British West Indies, 1700–1763* (New Haven, 1917). Distillers in the continental colonies also used as a base material the syrup – 'the faces [feces] or dreggs' – from the sugar refineries established there. See, e.g., the Massachusetts Act of October 1713, in [Mass. (Colony), Laws and Statutes], *Acts and Resolves* [ed. Goodell *et al.*], I, p. 725.

[57] In 1990 the per capita annual consumption of all distilled spirits by residents of the United States was 2.2 gallons (8.3 litres) [United States, Department of Commerce, Bureau of the Census], *Statistical Abstract of the United States*, 112th edn (Washington, D.C., 1992), p. 133. See also W. J. Rorabaugh, *The Alcoholic Republic: an American Tradition* (New York, 1979); and Mark Edward Lender and James Kirby Martin, *Drinking in America: A History* (New York, 1987). The drinking of rum punch was an important ritual across society, even among the more genteel members of society. See Peter Thompson, '"The Friendly Glass": drink and gentility in Colonial Philadelphia', *Pennsylvania Magazine of History and Biography*, 113 (October 1989), 549–73; Xiaoxing Li, 'Liquor and ordinaries in seventeenth-century Maryland' (Ph.D. thesis., Johns Hopkins University, 1991); David W. Conroy, *In Public Houses: Drink and the Revolution of Authority in Colonial Massachusetts* (Chapel Hill, N.C., 1995). Lest we rush to the wrong conclusion – perhaps encouraged to do so by the residual influences of an early twentieth-century 'temperance movement' and modern concerns about 'substance abuse' – drinking and public drunkenness were not at such levels in at least two colonies in the seventeenth century to attract the concern of the authorities. This is the conclusion of Karen R. Stubaus, '"The Good Creatures": drinking law and custom in seventeenth-Century Massachusetts and Virginia' (Ph.D. thesis, Rutgers University, 1984). Compare McCusker, *Rum and the American Revolution*, I, pp. 477–9. For an intelligent and informative social anthropology of alcoholic beverage consumption that transcends time and place, see Peter Pope, 'Fish into wine: the historical anthropology of demand for alcohol in seventeenth-century Newfoundland', *Histoire Sociale/Social History*, 27 (1994), 261–78.

consumed in the continental colonies was British in origin – and that provoked a defining confrontation.

The lessons of the early Dutch and British successes in the distilling industry at home and of the British success in the colonies were not lost upon other Europeans. The French, in particular, recognized the impact that the distilling of French West Indian syrup and molasses into French rum could have upon sales of French brandy. French fears were compounded after the beginning of the Second Hundred Years War between Britain and France (1689–1815) when the English Parliament enacted prohibitive duties upon the importation of French wine and brandy that all but excluded them from the English market.[58] Already in 1689 the Englishman William Stout, merchant of Lancaster, could celebrate the 'abundance of stills [that] were set up for extracting good and strong spirrits from mault, melosses, fruit and other materials', good English spirits that were to be drunk 'instead of French brandy'.[59] In reaction to the loss of their English market, the powerful French brandy lobby was able to persuade the government to ban the distilling of anything other than wine, not only in France and but also in the French colonies. There would no longer be any French rum.[60] The echoes of that decision sounded across the next century.

The French prohibition against the distillation of anything but wine

[58] There had been an earlier period of high, prohibitive taxes during the last years 1677–86. See A. D. Francis, *The Wine Trade* (London, 1972), pp. 73–97 and *passim*, and the works cited in n. 5, above. John Vincent Nye, 'Guerre, commerce, guerre commerciale: l'économie politique des échanges franco-anglais réexaminée', trans. Pierre-Emmanuel Dauzat, *Annales: Economies-Sociétés-Civilisations*, 47 (1992), 620–1, also notes the long-term effects of these laws on both countries. In contrast to the argument offered herein, Nye asserts a consequent increase in the English consumption of locally brewed beer and Portuguese wines. As a matter of fact per capita consumption of beer in Great Britain continued to decline over the eighteenth century and into the nineteenth century. See Mathias, *Brewing Industry in England*, p. 375 and *passim*; Chartres, 'No English Calvados?', pp. 320–4 and *passim*. On 10 November 1773 the Master of the Corporation of Brewers and Malsters of Dublin supported the general testimony about the decline of beer consumption and with it the Irish brewing industry by pointing out that whereas there had been seventy brewers at work in the city in 1739 there were in 1773 not above thirty. *Journals of the House of Commons . . . of Ireland*, XVI, 182.

[59] *The Autobiography of William Stout of Lancaster, 1665–1752*, ed. J. D. Marshall (Manchester, 1967), p. 94.

[60] McCusker, *Rum and the American Revolution*, I, pp. 320–1. Compare Théophile Malvezin, *Histoire du commerce de Bordeaux depuis les origines jusqu'à nos jours*, 4 vols. (Bordeaux, 1892), III, pp. 105–9. The developments triggered by the prohibitive duties on imports were reinforced and advanced by the promotion of English distilling through the ending of limitations on domestic distilling by the Act of 2 William and Mary, session 2, c. 9 (1691). In this regard see [London, Company of Distillers], *The Case of the Company of Distillers of London, in Reference to a Bill, Entituled, A Bill for Encouraging the Distilling Brandy from Corn* ([London, 1690]).

wrought considerable consequences. On the one hand, the elimination of other sorts of spirits from the French domestic market increased the demand for brandy. That raised its price. Higher domestic demand and higher brandy prices shrank foreign sales still more. Diminished brandy exports reinforced the original decision and hardened the position of French brandy interests. On the other hand, the creation of a monopoly for brandy in France worked to lower the price of other distilled spirits in other countries, limiting even more the ability of French brandy to compete in those markets. The interdiction in France of the distillation of sugar refinery syrup decreased demand and that lowered the price at which syrup could be sold domestically. Diminished returns from the sale of their syrup cut into the profits of French sugar refiners. As the Intendant du Commerce, Jean-François Tolozan, wrote a century later, 'on peut regarder la défense de les distiller comme une sorte d'impôt établi sur nos Raffineries'.[61] To offset their losses French refiners sought export markets for their syrup.[62] They found them to the north, particularly in The Netherlands and Germany, where Dutch and German distillers added imported French syrup to their stocks of base materials. The increase in the supply of base materials lowered costs for German and Dutch distillers allowing them to charge less for their spirits.[63]

[61] [Jean-François de Tolozan], *Mémoire sur le commerce de la France et des colonies* (Paris, 1789), p. 59. For Tolozan (1722–*c.* 1800), see [France, Bureau du Commerce], *Conseil de commerce et Bureau du commerce (1700–1791): Inventaire analytique des procès-verbaux*, ed. Pierre Bonnassieux and Eugène Lelong (Paris, 1900), pp. lx–lxi. Tolozan thanked a French businessman for help with the essay. According to one authority, 'le négociant de qui on parle dans l'avertisement se nommait Béchet'. Antoine Alexandre Barbier, *Dictionnaire des ouvrages anonymes*, 3rd edn, 4 vols. (Paris, 1872–9), III, p. 166. I have not been able to identify M. Béchet.

[62] See the discussion of a projected regulation designed to encourage the exportation of French syrup, dated 9 December 1717, Série F^{12} 62, fo. 164, AN.

[63] A separate price for French syrup – 'Franse Siroop', 'Fransche Sirop' – began to be quoted regularly in the weekly Amsterdam and Hamburg business newspapers soon after the turn of the eighteenth century, at Hamburg by 1714, at Amsterdam by 1722. See e.g. the *Prys Courant, Hamburg*, 13 July 1714, and the *Cours van Koopmanschappen tot Amsterdam*, 16 November 1722. For these newspapers, see McCusker and Gravesteijn, *Beginnings of Commercial and Financial Journalism*, pp. 43–83, 223–46. Reesse, *Suikerhandel van Amsterdam*, I, pp. 77–90 and *passim*, discussed this trade in syrup. See also Jacques Savary des Bruslons and Philémon-Louis Savary, *Dictionnaire universel de commerce*, new edn, 3 vols. [in 4] (Geneva, 1742), II, p. 1288; [Henri-Louis] Duhamel du Monceau, *Art de rafiner le sucre* [Académie des Sciences, Paris], *Description des Arts et Métiers* (Paris, 1764), pp. 63–4; Johann Beckmann, *Anleitung zur Technologie, oder zur Kentniß der Handwerke, Fabriken und Manufacturen . . .* (Göttingen, 1777), p. 339; [Joseph François Charpentier de Cossigny de Palma], *Mémoire sur la fabrication des eaux-de-vie de sucre et particulièrement sur celle de la guildive et du tafia* (L'Isle de France, 1781), p. 43; and Paul M. Bondois, 'L'industrie sucrière française au XVIIIe siècle. La fabrication et les rivalités entre les raffineries', *Revue d'Historie Économique et Sociale*, 19 (1931), 332, n. 79.

To make a long story short, the stop to the distilling of sugar spirits in France raised the price of French brandy and lowered the price of Dutch gin and German brandy, limiting the market for the former and increasing the market for the latter. Encore Tolozan: 'En avilissant les melasses en France, par la défense des les distiller, on a mis les Distillateurs étrangers en état de donner leurs eaux-de-vie à très-bon marché . . .'[64]

Equally harmed were French sugar interests in the Caribbean. The ban on distilling in the French colonies meant that almost none of the molasses produced in the French West Indies could be sold anywhere within the French domain. Few have appreciated that, after a somewhat slower start than the British colonies, by the time of the American Revolution the French sugar islands had completely outdistanced them. One French colony alone, Saint-Domingue (modern Haïti), produced more sugar than all of the British islands combined.[65] Every hogshead of French sugar yielded its proportionate quantity of French molasses for which there was almost no French market. As one English observer noted,

Savary des Bruslons and Savary, *Dictionnaire universel de commerce*, III [appendix], p. 29, indicate – in a report that reflected conditions before 1720 – that the sugar refinery at Marseilles sold its syrup to Naples and Malta, in addition to The Netherlands. Compare the petition, dated to 1764 or slightly later, presented to the Parlement de Bordeaux, that noted that 'la plupart des propriétaires des vignobles de Bergerac et de Sainte-Foy, dont les vins n'étaient propre que pour la Hollande, mixoinnaient en effet ces vins ou les faisaient avec du sucre ou du sirop pour les rendre plus doux et qu'ils se hâtaient de les envoyer ainsi mixtionnées en Hollande'. As quoted in J.-L. Riol, *Le vignoble de Gaillac depuis ses origines jusqu'à nos jours et l'emploi de ses vins à Bordeaux*, 2nd rev. edn (Paris, 1913), p. 152, citing the Archives municipales de Bordeaux, and Série C. 1617, Archives de la Région Aquitaine et du Département de la Gironde, Bordeaux. At the end of the seventeenth century, responding to the flood of imported French syrup, Dutch sugar refiners tried to stem the tide through an enactment of a high import duty but the attempt was short lived and ineffective, such was the demand. Reesse, *Suikerhandel van Amsterdam*, I, pp. 84–90. See also in this regard Paul M. Bondois, 'Colbert et la question des sucres. La rivalité commerciale franco-hollandaise', *Revue d'Histoire Économique et Sociale*, 11 (1923), 12–61.

[64] [Tolozan], *Mémoire sur le commerce*, pp. 59–60. To appreciate the magnitude of the problem – and the forgone opportunity – created by the profusion of French syrup, understand that when, during 1790, the refiners of Orléans converted 11, 258 metric tons of raw muscovado sugar into 6,363 tons of refined sugar, the processing generated an additional 2,937 metric tons of syrup, nearly 600,000 gallons, over 2,200,000 litres 'Etat des manufactures Orléanaises' (1790), Série F^{12} 562, pp. 86–7, AN, and as cited in Stein, *French Sugar Business*, p. 131. The Orléans refineries produced one-quarter of all the sugar refined in France according to [Tolozan], *Mémoire sur le commerce*, pp. 48–9. If French distillers used that 2,400,000 gallons of syrup to produce some form of cheap spirits and sold it at the London price of 7s. per gallon, their product would have been worth £820,000 (£63,000,000 in the year 2000 [$97,000,000]).

[65] McCusker, *Rum and the American Revolution*, I, pp. 307–22 and *passim*. For the importance of the sugar industry to the economy of eighteenth-century France, at home and abroad, see François Crouzet, *De la supériorité de l'Angleterre sur la France: L'Économique et l'imaginaire, XVIIe–XXe siècle* (Paris, 1985), pp. 28, 281 and *passim*.

molasses 'was of no Value or Estimation among the French . . . they never esteemed [it] more than Dung; for they used to throw it all away'.[66] French planters and plantation officials estimated the loss at from one-fifth to one-third the value of their islands' output.[67]

Fortunately for the French sugar planters their North American neighbours mitigated that loss. The British colonists in North America had a nearly insatiable appetite for molasses. While the population of the continental colonies multiplied more than eightfold between 1700 and 1770, per capita consumption of all West Indian produce went up at an even faster rate. One estimate has it that, over the five years between 1768 and 1772, the British North Americans bought more than half of all the molasses produced on Saint-Domingue.[68] The French West Indies would have been swamped in a sea of molasses had it not been for the British colonists in North America.[69]

Not only did the French West Indies have hardly any outlet within their empire for their molasses, but they also had no easy access to food supplies, draught animals and timber products. In a way parallel to the provisioning trade that grew up after 1630 between the British in North America and their British cousins in the West Indies, so also after about 1660 did a similar trade develop between the French in the West Indies and those same British North Americans. Initially the business was conducted by way of West Indian merchants acting as middlemen in the ports of the British sugar islands but, by the second decade of the eighteenth century, it had been rerouted so that most of it was carried on

[66] [Frayer Hall], 'To the Author of the Daily Post-Boy', *The Daily Post-Boy* (London), 6 March 1731/32.

[67] AN-CAOM, Mémoire from Charles de Courbon, comte de Blénac, Gouverneur Général des Îles d'Amérique [Saint-Pierre, Martinique], 4 March 1687, Fonds des Colonies, C^{8B} 1, nos. 86 [fo.1v]; AN-CAOM, Charles de Thubières de Levy de Pestel de Grimoard, marquis de Caylus, Gouverneur Général des Îles du Vent to the Secrétaire d'État à la Marine, Saint-Pierre, Martinique, 6 October 1749, C8A 58, fos. 266 ff., and [Jean Baptiste DuBuc], *Précis pour les Grands Propriétaires des Colonies Françaises de l'Amérique, contre les Divers Écrits des Négocians des Villes Maritimes du Royaume* (Paris, 1787), p. 5.

[68] That constituted more than three-quarters of the quantity exported from the colony. McCusker, *Rum and the American Revolution*, I, pp. 302–35 and *passim*. Compare Richard Pares, *Merchants and Planters*, Supplement No. 4 to *EcHR* (Cambridge, 1960), p. 24.

[69] As the figures quoted suggest, and as the text cited makes clear, the French planters were not ignorant of the options available to them but simply frustrated by their inability to realize them. Their frustration boiled up repeatedly and became an increasing cause of tension between the French colonists and the mother country because the stakes were considerable. Gabriel Debien, the doyen of twentieth-century historians of the French West Indies, summed up the planters' plight perfectly in *Une plantation de Saint-Domingue. La sucrerie Galbaud du Fort (1690–1802)* ([Cairo, 1941]), p. 75: 'sans tafia point de numéraire', no rum, no money.

directly. In the simplest of terms, it involved the exchange of molasses for food and other supplies.[70]

Nevertheless, however much this trade served the purposes of the colonists, neither metropolis was comfortable with the thought of an international commerce between them, especially once the wars of empire had begun. During the eighteenth century both the British West Indian interests and the French West Indian interests sought intervention from their respective central governments to protect and, if possible, to expand their sales of molasses and rum. The production of sugar had, by itself, been adequate in the seventeenth century to yield a high rate of return on investments in the islands, but that had changed. By early in the next century the sale of the sugar alone was no longer enough. Sugar prices had levelled off while the costs of production continued to rise. The pressure to maintain profitability by diminishing costs and increasing income pushed the British and French planters into a variety of expedients. One way to increase income was to maximize the return from the sale of the byproducts of sugar production. Joseph Massie, a mid-eighteenth-century polemicist, spelled out the interdependence of sugar, molasses and rum precisely: 'for as those Three Commodities are all produced from the Sugar-Cane, the more Money the Sugar-Planters receive from the Two latter, the cheaper [i.e., the more profitably] will they be able to sell the former'.[71] The British planters were more successful in this pursuit; the French planters were less so.[72]

---

[70] Pitman, *Development of the British West Indies*, pp. 189–241. See also Charles M. Andrews, 'Anglo-French commercial rivalry: the western phase', *AHR*, 20 (1915), 539–56, 761–80; Richard Pares, *War and Trade in the West Indies, 1739–1763* (Oxford, 1936).

   According to William Burke, who worked as secretary and registrar in the government of Guadeloupe during the British occupation of that French island in the course of the Seven Years' War, 'the inhabitants of Guadeloupe continue to carry on a greater trade, than any English island does, with North America'. They use that trade to 'dispose of their molasses, as they have not yet fallen into the method of making rum, which the policy of France did not suffer her islands to make, lest that spirit should interfere with the brandies of France'. [William Burke], *An Examination of the Commercial Principles of the Late Negotiation between Great Britain and France in MDCCLXI. In Which the System of that Negotiation with Regard to Our Colonies and Commerce Is Considered*, 2nd edn (London, 1762), p. 43. Compare Massie, *State of the British Sugar-Colony Trade*, p. 25.

[71] Massie, *State of the British Sugar-Colony Trade*, p. 23.

[72] Given the very nature of 'le système exclusif', the efforts of French planters to increase trade with the North Americans could only involve extra-legal subterfuges that, at best, were limited in their effectiveness. Their attempts to get French West Indian rum reintroduced into the trade of the French empire were somewhat more successful, but only late in the eighteenth century. The story of the former efforts occupies much of the history of each French West Indian colony throughout that century. See, in general, Jean Tarrade, *Le commerce colonial de la France à la fin de l'Ancien Régime. L'évolution du régime de 'l'Exclusif' de 1763 à 1789*, 2 vols. (Paris, 1972). The story of the latter efforts has yet to be told adequately but see Guy Josa, *Les industries du sucre et du rhum à la Martinique*

In all of this the British West Indians recognized another opportunity. They could improve their own competitive position within world sugar markets by disrupting French trade with the British North Americans. British West Indian sugar planters realized that such commerce harmed them in two ways. The addition of the French demand to their own tended to increase the price of the provisions sold them by the North Americans. The addition of the French supply to their own tended to decrease the price of the sugar, molasses and rum that the British planters sold to the North Americans. To reverse this situation – to reserve to themselves the trade with North America – would diminish their costs and raise their income. Moreover anything that they could do to hinder the French West Indians harmed a strategic enemy as well. By 1720 the British West Indian planters had succeeded in stifling the indirect commerce between the North Americans and the French West Indies by way of British island ports. After 1720 they strove to end the direct trade. The passage of the Molasses Act in 1733 was the first of several apparent successes in that effort.[73]

During the same period the British North Americans came increasingly to identify their prosperity with the trade between themselves and the West Indies, French as well as British. The West Indian trade earned significant credits in the current account of the balance of payments of the continental colonies. Without those credits the colonists could not purchase abroad all the goods and services they required. The trade also introduced into the colonies the processing of commodities that put to work domestic investment capital and local labour and yielded considerable returns for both. In 1770 there were more than 25 sugar refineries and 140 rum distilleries in the North American colonies, a high propor-

(1639–1931) (Paris, 1931), and McCusker, *Rum and the American Revolution*, I, pp. 303–35. See also contemporary contributions to the continuing debate such as that by [Jean-Baptiste] Gastumeau, 'Mémoire, pour le Corps-de-Ville de la Rochelle, sur la Fabrication & le Commerce des Eaux-de-vie de Sirops, connues dans les Isles à Sucre, sous les noms de Taffia & Guildives', *Journal de Commerce* (Brussels), August 1759, pp. 57–112. For Gastumeau (fl. 1732–63), a merchant of La Rochelle and a member of that city's Chambre de Commerce, and for more on the debate, see Emile Garnault, *Le commerce rochelais au XVIIIe siècle*, 5 vols. (Paris and La Rochelle, 1887–1900), *passim*, but especially, I, pp. 203–12, IV, pp. 238–56. Compare Cullen, *Brandy Trade*, p. 142. The permission the Conseil d'Etat granted on 12 June 1752 for a limited use of French colonial rum in the French slave trade was almost insignificant, especially given the depressed state of the French slave trade. [Auguste Chambon] *Le commerce de l'Amérique par Marseille*, 2 vols. (Avignon, 1764), I, pp. 399–403; Robert Louis Stein, *The French Slave Trade in the Eighteenth Century: an Old Regime Business* (Madison, Wis., 1979), pp. 25–34.

[73] Malachy Postlethwayt, *Britain's Commercial Interest Explained and Improved . . .* , 2 vols. (London, 1757), I, pp. 485–6, 491, 493, 495–9. See also Pitman, *Development of the British West Indies*, pp. 242–70; and Richard B. Sheridan, *Sugar and Slavery: an Economic History of the British West Indies, 1623–1775*, 2nd edn (Kingston, Jamaica, 1994), *passim*.

tion of both in New England alone – all of them dependent on West Indian produce and, therefore, the West Indian trade.[74]

The economies of the British colonies in the West Indies and in North America had developed over the decades in ways that made them progressively more reliant upon the distilling industry. They had been founded during the time when distilling itself became established as an industry; they had all contributed to that establishment; and all had benefited from it. Just as their dependence on rum and the rum trade grew, so also did their mutual awareness that the best purposes of each group were not compatible, were, indeed, antithetical. The sugar producers of the British West Indies could survive only if they could increase returns from their crops. They wanted the price of molasses to go up. The rum distilling industry of North America and the whole trade connected with it required that the cost of molasses be kept as low as possible.[75] Any increase in costs translated immediately into an increased price for rum and so directly into a decline in consumption. For an industry dependent on economies of scale and subject to high marginal rates of substitution, increased costs threatened disaster.

The British West Indians won their battle but lost the war. In an empire increasingly convinced that the economy should be manipulated in the best interests of the most powerful business groups, the sugar lobby proved stronger than the North Americans.[76] The Molasses Act of 1733 offered the West Indians relief but frightened the North Americans. It was neither enforced nor obeyed during its thirty-year life.[77] Its reformulation as the Sugar Act of 1764 again promised relief to the sugar planters but so alarmed the North Americans that it is recognized as one

---

[74] On these subjects, see McCusker and Menard, *Economy of British America, 1607–1789.* See also John J. McCusker and Barbara Bartz Petchenik, 'Economic activity', in *Atlas of Early American History: the Revolutionary Era, 1760–1790,* ed. Lester J. Cappon, Barbara Bartz Petchenik and John Hamilton Long (Princeton, N.J., 1976), pp. 26–7, 103–4.

[75] Or, to quote John Winthrop, first governor of Massachusetts Bay colony, 'it being the common rule that most men walked by in all their commerce, to buy as cheap as they could, and to sell as dear' (1640). *Winthrop's Journal: 'History of New England', 1630–1649,* ed. James Kendall Hosmer, 2 vols. (New York, 1908), II, p. 20.

[76] 'The trade in [sugar, cocoa, coffee and tea] and the production of cacao, coffee and sugar in the European colonies as well as the processing of cocoa and the refining of raw sugar in Europe were extremely important in the development of capitalism.' Werner Sombart, *Luxus und Kapitalismus* (Munich and Leipzig, 1913), p. 117 (my translation). See more generally in this regard, John J. McCusker, *Mercantilism and the Economic History of the Early Modern Atlantic World* (Cambridge, forthcoming).

[77] The most significant thing that one can say about the Molasses Act is that 'no serious attempt was ever made to enforce the payment of the duty on melasses'. *Observations on the Application Which the West India Planters Intend to Make . . .* (London, 1786), p. 4. Compare George Louis Beer, *British Colonial Policy, 1754–1765* (New York, 1907), pp. 230, 244 and *passim*; Arthur Meier Schlesinger, *The Colonial Merchants and the American Revolution, 1763–1776,* Columbia University Studies in History, Economics and Public Law, 78, no. 182 (New York, 1918), p. 41 and *passim*.

of the causes of the American Revolution.[78] Only at great cost did the North Americans extricate themselves from the extraordinary threat to their economy implicit in the Sugar Act. Part of that cost they paid in learning the lesson that Parliament would no longer guarantee to them their rights and liberties as Englishmen. Part of that cost they paid in fighting the American Revolutionary War.[79]

In sum, then, the establishment and expansion of the distilling industry in the Atlantic world after the middle of the seventeenth century can be seen to have had far reaching economic, social and geopolitical consequences. As the costs of spirits fell, relative to the older more traditional alcoholic beverages, people shifted from beer and wine to brandy, gin and rum. The rivalry for markets and for supplies of base materials for the distilling industry added to the tensions otherwise existing between Great Britain and France during the eighteenth century. It induced the government of Great Britain to take measures that further alienated its otherwise loyal subjects in British North America, thus helping change the face of the globe.

Other ramifications, not explored here, are also significant. The increasing consumption of these much more intoxicating and addictive beverages created immense social problems in societies as far apart as the streets of London, the forests of the native North Americans and the steppes of central Asia.[80] The continued success of the sugar plantations hinged on their ability to supplement their income from the sale of sugar

[78] See the remarkably prescient letter from the governor of Massachusetts, Francis Bernard, at Boston, to Richard Jackson at London, 7 January 1764, in Bernard, *Select Letters on the Trade and Government of America* . . . (London, 1774), pp. 9–11. He feared that the act was yet another 'case of the man [who] killed the goose who laid him golden eggs'. Among his specific concerns was the possibility that diminished demand by the North Americans for French West Indian molasses would encourage French planters to distil it into rum themselves.

[79] For an elaboration of all these arguments, see McCusker, *Rum and the American Revolution*, and McCusker and Menard, *Economy of British America*.

[80] There are recent, valuable studies of all three. For the first, see Peter Clark, 'The "Mother Gin" Controversy in the early eighteenth century', *Transactions of the Royal Historical Society*, 5th series, 38 (1988), 63–84. Compare the implications of the increased consumption of spirits with the changes in diet discussed in Carole Shammas, *The Pre-industrial Consumer in England and America* (Oxford, 1990). See also Chartres, 'No English Calvados?' pp. 322, n. 17, 324: 'as in modern experience, alcohol was revealed as a sensitive indicator of rising real incomes'. For the latter two, see, respectively, Peter C. Mancall, *Deadly Medicine: Indians and Alcohol in Early America* (Ithaca, N.Y., 1995); and David Christian, *'Living Water': Vodka and Russian Society on the Eve of Emancipation* (Oxford, 1990).

The literature on this subject runs broad and deep and its extent can only be hinted at here. Concerning this subject, see the many – but not always reliable – references in Gregory A. Austin, *Alcohol in Western Society from Antiquity to 1800: a Chronological History* (Santa Barbara, Calif., 1985). See also David W. Gutzke, *Alcohol in the British Isles from Roman Times to 1996: an Annotated Bibliography* (Westport, Conn., 1996).

with additional income from the sale of the byproducts of sugar's production. Ever larger sugar crops over the eighteenth century required, among other things, a steadily increasing supply of slaves from Africa. Rum exported from the sugar colonies to buy the slaves helped to keep that nefarious commerce operating.[81] European governments, in part to protect and enhance their colonial empires, extracted ever greater taxes from their citizens, increasingly in the form of excise taxes on the production and consumption of alcoholic spirits.[82] The image evoked is that of the serpent feeding upon its own tail.

APPENDIX: THE CAPACITY OF STILLS IN THE EIGHTEENTH CENTURY

There are distinctions to be made among the absolute volume of a still, how much liquid a distiller placed in it (the 'charge'), and the quantity of spirituous liquor yielded in one distillation. One finds that most discussions of the size of a still referred to its capacity, meaning the size of the charge, and not absolute volume or yield, although there are exceptions to that rule.

Charles Leadbetter, *The Royal Gauger; or Gauging Made Perfectly Easy*, 6th edn, rev. Samuel Clark (London, 1766), pp. 146–7, and plate VI, opp. p. 152, discussed how to measure 'real stills, [that are] actually used in and near London, at this day and have been so for several years last past'. The source of his information and of the accompanying plate could not have been more authoritative. He was Joseph Bosley (1671–1737), a

---

[81] Only in the nineteenth century, when the European importation of cheaper East Indian sugar began to undermine the fragile profitability of slave-based plantation agriculture in the western hemisphere, did the movement to end the African slave trade and slavery, and slavery itself, gain momentum. The French colonies continued to dominate West Indian sugar production up to the end of the 1780s; the British West Indies stayed profitable through and after that same period. See in this regard John J. McCusker, 'The economy of the British West Indies, 1763–1790: growth, stagnation, or decline?', as revised and amended in McCusker, *Essays in the Economic History of the Atlantic World* (New York and London, 1997), pp. 310–30, and the works cited there.

[82] See, for example, the morbid preoccupation of the Austrian and British governments with the revenues generated by their distilling industries. J[an] A. van Houtte, *An Economic History of the Low Countries, 800–1800* (London, 1977), p. 256; McGuire, *Irish Whiskey*, pp. 115, 123; Lee Davison, 'Experiments in the social regulation of industry: gin legislation, 1729–1751', in *Stilling the Grumbling Hive: The Response to Social and Economic Problems in England, 1689–1750*, ed. Lee Davison *et al.* (New York, 1992), pp. 25–48. By the 1760s, taxes on vodka constituted something in excess of 25 per cent of all revenues collected annually by the Russian government. Christian, *'Living Water'*, pp. 382–5.

This pursuit of revenue was more than enough to subvert the old principle that 'the expense of the publick . . . [should be] defrayed without debauching the morals of the people'. The lament is Campbell's in *The London Tradesman*, p. 267. Compare Glen, 'Economic history of the distilling industry, Scotland', p. 50, who – citing Sinclair, *Statistical Account of Scotland*, I, p. 361 – notes the reproach of a Scottish clergyman from Stranraer in 1795: 'people should be of more importance to the state than the revenue from taxation' on spirits. But therein rests another story – as the tale of tobacco in the late twentieth century exhibits all too clearly.

long-term employee of the Excise who spent most of his adult life working with the London distilling industry (*ibid.*, p. ix). At the time of his death he was the 'General Surveyor of the London Distillery' for the Excise. The illustration – and, thus, the still – would have to have dated from before 1737; the plate appeared first in Leadbetter's third edition (1750). As befitted the interests of both men, they were concerned about the absolute volume of a still. The smaller of the two Bosley–Leadbetter stills illustrated in the plate (plate VI) measured some 9.2 feet (2.8 m) high and 12.9 ft (3.9 m) in diameter. Its total volume measured, thus, 7,872 gallons (29,800 litres). Compare the considerably smaller still, measuring 607 gallons (2,300 litres), illustrated and discussed in William Symons, *The Practical Gager: Or, the Young Gager's Assistant*, 4th edn (London, 1777), pp. 233–5. Symons was also a 'Collector of Excise'.

The actual amount of liquid to be distilled – called the 'charge' – was, obviously, something less than the total volume of the cucurbit. This was the case for both larger stills and smaller ones. For purposes of his exposition [Jacques-François] Demachy, *L'art du distillateur liquoriste*, [Académie des Sciences, Paris], *Description des Arts et Métiers* (Paris, 1775), pp. 10–11, discussed a still with a capacity – by which we can presume that he meant its charge – of 123 gallons (466 litres). In his illustration of that still (plate 2, fig. 1), he pictured it as roughly half filled, suggesting this as the usual level of the charge. Because, just as his figure shows, stills narrowed considerably at the top, the total volume of the still must have been something less that twice its charge. If we estimate the charge at 60 per cent of volume, then a charge of 123 gallons would have required a still that measured 205 gallons (780 litres) in volume. George Smith, *A Compleat Body of Distilling, Explaining the Mysteries of That Science, in a Most Easy and Familiar Manner* . . . , 3rd edn (London, 1738), preface and p. 85, set his recipes in terms of charges of 30 gallons (114 litres). At that same ratio, Smith's charge of 30 gallons would have occupied a still with a volume of 50 gallons (190 litres) – which, presumably, was the size of the still that he pictured in his frontispiece (see fig. 8.1 which reproduces his frontispiece). The Bosley-Leadbetter still, with a volume of 7,872 gallons, would similarly have had a capacity of about 4,700 gallons (17,900 litres).

As the example used by Demachy suggests, French brandy distillers seem to have preferred smaller-sized stills to those used by British and Dutch distillers – and, as we will see below, their preference seems to have fallen in the lower of the two ranges in use in British America. Indeed Demachy's may have been larger than usual. Denis Diderot's and Jean d'Alembert's *Encyclopédie, ou Dictionnaire Raisonné des Sciences, des Arts et des Métiers*, 35 vols. (Paris, 1751–80), IV, s.v. 'Distillation', spoke of a still of 40 veltes (80 gallons, 300 litres). Étienne Munier, *Essai d'une méthode générale* . . . , 2 vols. (Paris, 1779), stated that stills ranged in size from 30 to 40 veltes (60 to 80 gallons, 225 to 300 litres).[83] The way in which L. M. Cullen, *The Brandy Trade under the* Ancien Régime: *Regional Specialisation in the Charente* (Cambridge, 1998), pp. 106–7 and *passim*, tells us the French brandy trade was organized – many small distillers operating in the countryside, selling their brandy either on site or at local fairs – concurs neatly with the scale of operations possible given stills of this capacity.

For the size of British, Scottish and Dutch stills, see also the discussions in the text and notes (especially nn. 10–11).

Just as in England, Scotland and The Netherlands (if not France), stills used in North America varied considerably in size; they seem also to have grown in size over the eighteenth century. The New York distillery that Augustus Lucas offered for sale in *The Boston News-Letter*, 7 August 1704, had a 'Still-House' that measured 50 ft by 22 ft (102 square metres); it was the only structure mentioned. In it were

two good Copper Stills, Head and Worms; one of said Stills containing about 140 Gallons [530 litres], the other about 100 Gallons [380 litres]. There is a very good Well, Pumps; all the conveniences and Utensils necessary for said Still-House: And a stout lusty Negro Man, who understands Stilling.

Two decades later William Douglass of Boston wrote Cadwallader Colden in New York that 'our distillers in Boston use . . . very large stills of 600 to 1,000 gallons' (2,300 to 3,800 litres). They were more efficient than smaller stills, he argued, 'requiring less firewood in proportion & [permitting (?)] greater despatch'.[84] Letter dated 31 March 1729 in *The Letters and Papers of Cadwallader Colden [1711–1775]*, ed. Dorothy C. Barck, Collections of the New York Historical Society, vols. L–LVI, LXVII–LXVIII, 9 vols. (New York, 1918–37), VIII, p. 191. Stills advertised for sale in Boston newspapers in the 1720s and 1730s would seem to support William Douglass's point. The stills were either small stills, in the range of 30 to 70 gallons (110 to 260 litres), or very large ones, ranging from 200 to 700 gallons (760 to 2,650 litres).[85] See *The Boston News-Letter*, 9 January 1720/21, 20 March 1720/21, 5 November 1721, 25

[83] For the size of the Parisian velte and the other measures referred to in this discussion, see John J. McCusker, 'Weights and measures in the colonial sugar trade: the gallon and the pound and their international equivalents', as revised and amended in McCusker, *Essays in the Economic History of the Atlantic World*, pp. 76–101.

[84] Compare the statement by Philippe Augier, of the house of Augier, the leading brandy merchants in the town of Cognac, who wrote to a correspondent in Amsterdam that the preference for larger stills was because 'il faut la meme quantité de bois pour une petite [chaudière] que pour une grande chaudière'. See the copy of Philippe Augier's letter to Le Riget, 6 January 1725, letterbook, 1724–6, Augier Archives, Cognac, France, as quoted in Cullen, *Brandy Trade*, p. 106.

[85] This duality seems also to have applied to roughly the same degree in Scotland in the last half of the eighteenth century although, by then, the larger stills were of even greater size. See e.g. Glen, 'Economic history of the distilling industry, Scotland', *passim*.

April 1723, 15 August 1723; *The Weekly News-Letter*, 8 July 1731, 14 August 1731, 7 December 1732, 20 October 1737, 3 April 1740.

None the less, by the last third of the eighteenth century there were indeed some very large stills in operation in North America, reflecting the change of scale that had taken place in London if not the consolidation. Colonial distillers by this evidence seemed to want to do both the primary and the secondary distillation in the same shop. In 1767 Joseph Wharton advertised for sale the biggest one discovered so far as part of 'a large and commodious Distillery . . . near the Swedes Church, in the District of Southwark', Philadelphia. It was one of three and had a capacity of 3,300 gallons (12,500 litres). The other two – no doubt used for rectifying – held 550 gallons (2,100 litres) and 160 gallons (610 litres). (*The Pennsylvania Gazette* (Philadelphia), 19 March 1767). On 8 September 1769 Andrew Black of Boston wrote to James Glassford and Company, in Norfolk, to say that 'There is Scarce any Still used here above 1250 Gallons' (4,700 litres). Letter in Neil Jamieson papers, 1757–89, VIII, no. 2320. But this was only half the size of Daniel Roberdeau's two large stills in Alexandria, Virginia – with a volume of 2,500 gallons (9,500 litres) each (for which see n. 13, above). In 1774 Benjamin Heidrith of New York City offered for sale or lease his 'new distill-house' with a 1,100 gallons (4,160 litres) still and, again, a smaller rectifier. See the advertisement in *The New York Journal; or, the General Advertiser*, 20 October 1774. The 'distill-house' advertised for lease by Abraham Barker and Giles Hosier of Tiverton, Rhode Island, and Caleb Carpenter of Newport in *The Newport Mercury*, 11 April 1774, had 'cisterns and stills, to work off about 100 gallons a day' (380 litres). In the summer of 1775 the London coppersmiths, William Forbes and Company, 'paid £12.8 . . . for enlarging a Ships hatchway to take a 1500 gall[on] Still for Quebeck' (5,700 litres). William Forbes, at London, to J[oseph] F[oster] Barham, at Bedford, 17 November 1775, William Forbes and Company Papers, Business Out Letters, 1775, box 25, item no. 25, Forbes of Callendar Muniments, GD 171, Falkirk District Archives, Falkirk, Scotland (formerly in the Scottish Record Office, Edinburgh).[86] John Galloway of Tulip Hill, Maryland, advertised 'a copper still, containing between 4 and 500 gallons' (1,500 to 1,900 litres) in *The Maryland Gazette* (Annapolis), 21 July 1780. In July 1783 Barnabas Deane of Hartford, Connecticut, asked Jeremiah Wadsworth to purchase in Europe two 800 gallon (3,000 litre) stills and one 400 gallon (1,500 litre) still; they arrived in March 1784. He had earlier

---

[86] London coppersmiths like William Forbes and Company made 'many of the Stills in the Neighbourhood of Lisbon' according to the 'Answers to Questions respecting the Distillation of Spirits in Portugal', dated Lisbon, 1 December 1798, in [*Second*] *Report Respecting the Distilleries in Scotland . . .* , p. 306. They were generally from 140 to 500 gallons in size (530 to 1,900 litres).

tried to get one from a Mr Lathan of Philadelphia who is said to have invented an inexpensive wooden still (Chester McArthur Destler, 'Barnabas Deane and the Barnabas Deane & Company', *Connecticut Historical Society Bulletin*, 35 (January 1970), 15–18). As we should expect, the first stills in use over the Appalachian mountains were relatively small. P. Tardiveau of Danville advertised in *The Kentucky Gazette* (Lexington), 15 December 1787, that he had for sale, among other things, 'some stills between 60 and 80 gallons . . . imported into this district' (225–300 litres). (Given that this was the standard size of French stills (see above) and that Tardiveau seems by his name to have been a French trader, it is possible that the stills themselves were French, perhaps brought up-river from New Orleans.) By contrast, Rhode Islanders were importing much larger stills from Denmark. In 1788 Welcome Arnold of Providence, Rhode Island, obtained from Niels Ryberg of Copenhagen three stills, two large ones of 1,350 gallons (5,100 litres) and one small one of 600 gallons (2,300 litres). See Arnold's letters to Ryberg dated 7 May, 22 May, in Welcome Arnold Letterbook, 1787–91, and Ryberg's letters to Arnold, 25 July, 11 October in Arnold correspondence, 1788–90, both in Arnold-Greene Papers, John Carter Brown Library, Brown University, Providence, R.I. For Arnold's correspondent, see Aa[ge] Rasch, *Niels Ryberg, 1725–1804. Fra bondedreng til handelsfyrste*, Jysk Selskab for Historie, Sprog og Litteratur, 12 (Århus, Denmark, 1964). There is a description and a drawing of a 1,200 gallon (4,500 litre) still, done *c.* 1790 (?), in the hand of Benjamin Vaughan, in the Benjamin Vaughan Papers, 1746–1900, American Philosophical Society, Philadelphia.

Stills used in the West Indies were of a more moderate size, apparently. An advertisement for the sale of the plantation of Dr Neil Campbell in *The Antigua Gazette* (St John's), 11 November 1767, described the still house as having two stills, one of 300 gallons (1,140 litres), the second of 200 gallons (760 litres). The Mount Nesbitt estate on Grenada incorporated two plantations, each with its own distillery. They were described in detail in an 'appraisement' done in February 1774 that was sent in a letter from Hugh Hall Wentworth to Arnold Nesbitt, Grenada, 17 February 1774, as printed in Vere Langford Oliver, ed., *Caribbeana: Miscellaneous Papers Relating to the History, Genealogy, Topography, and Antiquities of the British West Indies*, 6 vols. (London, 1909–19), IV, 370–7. Each had two stills, one of 250 gallons (950 litres) and the other, 300 gallons (1,140 litres) (*ibid.*, pp. 373, 374). A year later, *The Free-Port Gazette; or, the Dominica Chronicle* (Roseau), 6 May 1775, contained an advertisement offering for sale the estate of Joseph Charles Emanuel d'Adhémar. The chevalier d'Adhémar's plantation included a 'Still House' with one still of 300 gallons capacity (1,140 litres).

Part III

Imperial economies

9   France, Britain and the economic growth of colonial North America

Stanley L. Engerman

This chapter will discuss some questions about the comparative settlement patterns and long-term development of the imperial economies of the French and the British in the Americas, and how these related to the differential growth patterns of the European nations. Little will be said, however, about their colonies elsewhere in the eighteenth and nineteenth centuries, including those in Africa and in India, which did not attract large-scale settlements of Europeans, as did the American colonies.[1] In some ways the answers to questions about comparative long-term success are obvious – France lost its largest settlement (Canada) in 1763, and its most prosperous settlement (indeed at that time the world's most prosperous area), Saint-Domingue, after 1791. This loss of Saint-Domingue, and its failure to recover as a sugar producing power after independence, provided a major boost to British colonial power, permitting, among other things, the British to increase sharply their share of Caribbean sugar production.[2] France had sold another of its New World settlements to the

I have benefited from comments on an earlier draft of this paper by Seymour Drescher, David Eltis, and the participants at the Canadian Quantitative Economic History Conference in May 1997. I have drawn upon joint work with Stephen Haber and Kenneth Sokoloff under National Science Foundation Grant SBR-9515222.

[1] For background on British and French colonization in this period, see, in addition to the various works cited below: K. G. Davies, *The North Atlantic World in the Seventeenth Century* (Minneapolis, 1974); D. K. Fieldhouse, *Economics and Empire, 1830–1914* (Ithaca, 1973); C. A. Bayly, *Imperial Meridian: the British Empire and the World, 1780–1830* (London, 1989); P. J. Cain and A. G. Hopkins, *British Imperialism: Innovation and Expansion, 1688–1914* (London, 1993); Robert Aldrich, *Greater France: a History of French Overseas Expansion* (New York, 1996); and Herbert Ingram Priestley, *France Overseas through the Old Regime: a Study of European Expansion* (New York, 1939). For more specific comparisons of the British and French settlements and their subsequent economic performance, see Marc Egnal, *Divergent Paths: How Culture and Institutions Have Shaped North American Growth* (New York, 1996), Marc Egnal, *New World Economies: The Growth of the Thirteen Colonies and Early Canada* (New York, 1998), and W. T. Easterbrook, *North American Patterns of Growth and Development* (Toronto, 1990).

[2] See, on British and French West Indian sugar production, Noel Deerr, *A History of Sugar*, 2 vols. (London, 1949–50), I, pp. 158–207, 228–43; Seymour Drescher, *Econocide: British Slavery in the Era of Abolition* (Pittsburgh, 1977), pp. 46–54, 76–91; and David Watts, *The West Indies: Patterns of Development, Culture and Environmental Change Since 1492* (Cambridge, 1987), pp. 284–304.

United States in 1803, after it had effectively lost control of Louisiana to Spain between 1763 and 1800.[3] France's remaining post-1815 settlements in the Caribbean (which still remain parts of France today) were few in number and smaller in total size compared to the larger number and sizes of the British islands. Britain, on the other hand, had gained colonial possessions from France, including Canada and various islands in the Caribbean, and maintained possession of them for considerable time. Britain, however, did suffer some major colonial losses, particularly that of the thirteen mainland colonies in the late eighteenth century, although it soon regained a strong trading relationship with the United States, and what it had left in its colonial empire in the early nineteenth century greatly exceeded in size and economic importance those remaining colonies of the French.

Yet while this British colonial dominance seems to have been the clear pattern seen in the nineteenth century, after the impact of the French Revolution, the Haitian Revolution and the Napoleonic Wars, this had not always been the obvious, expected outcome. It is interesting to turn back to the 1780s and to ask why the performance of the French colonies, particularly those in the West Indies, did not generate more rapid industrialization in France, and why the mix of sugar and slavery, and coffee and slavery, did not do for France what Eric Williams claimed they had done for England – generate an industrial revolution.[4] In the 1780s, the French West Indian colonies produced more agricultural output than did the British, their growth had been more rapid over the previous half-century, and the share of French colonial trade in all foreign trade was larger than for the British – points that were not unknown to many contemporary observers, and of some concern to many British pamphleteers and policy makers of the time.[5] The writings of such authors as

---

[3] For data on the population of Louisiana under French and Spanish rule, see Gwendolyn Midlo Hall, *Africans in Colonial Louisiana: the Development of Afro-Creole Culture in the Eighteenth Century* (Baton Rouge, 1992), pp. 100, 278–9. For at least the last quarter of the eighteenth century, the slave population of Louisiana exceeded the number free.

[4] See Eric Williams, *Capitalism and Slavery* (Chapel Hill, N.C., 1944). For discussions of this position see Roger Anstey, *The Atlantic Slave Trade and British Abolition, 1760–1810* (London, 1975); Drescher, *Econocide*; and Barbara L. Solow and Stanley L. Engerman, eds., *British Capitalism and Caribbean Slavery: the Legacy of Eric Williams* (Cambridge, 1987).

[5] For Caribbean output data in 1770, see David Eltis, 'The slave economies of the Caribbean: structure, performance, evolution and significance', in Franklin W. Knight, ed., *General History of the Caribbean.* Vol. III: *The Slave Societies of the Caribbean* (Paris, 1998). For data on relative growth of French and British foreign trade, see François Crouzet, *Britain Ascendant: Comparative Studies in Franco-British Economic History* (Cambridge, 1990), pp. 17–25, and the sources cited there. See also, on French colonial trade, Patrick Villiers, 'The slave and colonial trade in France just before the Revolution', in Barbara L. Solow, ed., *Slavery and the Rise of the Atlantic System* (Cambridge, 1991), pp. 210–36; and Jean Tarrade, *Le commerce colonial de la France á la fin de l'Ancien Régime. L'évolution du régime de 'l'Exclusif' de 1763 à 1789,* 2 vols. (Paris, 1972).

Postlethwayt, Anderson and Brougham dealing with the mid-eighteenth and early nineteenth centuries, the examination of the relative costs of French and British West Indian sugar production, and the discussion of this trade in the parliamentary hearings in 1789 and 1790, all indicate concern with the prospects for French economic and political expansion at the expense of the British.[6]

The related argument, concerning the contribution of New World slavery to French industrialization, had been presented by C. L. R. James in *The Black Jacobins* several years before his fellow Trinidadian, Eric Williams, had made the similar argument for England.[7] Indeed, some scholars trace a direct intellectual influence from James to Williams, although the fact that the former had only a few brief pages on this topic and the latter an entire book, may be suggestive of how this comparison looked to scholars in the 1940s and certainly the outcomes do seem different.

While not ignoring the role of cultural factors, nor arguing that everything was due to the differences in climate and crops, it seems quite clear that similar European cultural backgrounds did lead to quite different economic and social patterns in different New World regions from the patterns in Europe, and also that patterns of settlement and social formation varied across the colonies of the European nations in a manner influenced by New World climate and potential for growing various crops.[8] Similar climatic conditions often led to similar social

---

[6] See e.g. the writings of Malachy Postlethwayt, particularly *A Short State of the Progress of the French Trade and Navigation* (London, 1756), preface, pp. 72–86; *Great Britain's True System* (London, 1757), pp. 160–2, 256–71; and *Britain's Commercial Interest Explained and Improved*, 2 vols. (London, 1757), I, pp. 421–548; II, particularly pp. 112–72, 200–29; Adam Anderson, *A Historical and Chronological Deduction of the Origin of Commerce*, 4 vols. (London, 1801), III, pp. 264–5, and Henry Brougham, *An Inquiry into the Colonial Policy of the European Powers*, 2 vols. (Edinburgh, 1803), I, pp. 520–47. See also Arthur Young, *Political Essays Concerning the Present State of the British Empire* (London, 1772), pp. 440–2, as well as the seven volumes of parliamentary hearings on the slave trade in 1789 and 1790, particularly the Report of the Lords of the Committee of Council, presented 25 April 1789, in Lambert, LXX, pp. 311–38, dealing with 'The Advantages which the *French* West India Islands are supposed, at present, to enjoy over the *British* Islands, and the Reasons on which these superior Advantages are found'. For some comments by the French, see also Francis Dorothy Acomb, *Anglophobia in France, 1763–1789: an Essay in the History of Constitutionalism and Nationalism* (Durham, 1950), pp. 9, 59–66.

[7] C. L. R. James, *The Black Jacobins: Toussaint L'Ouverture and the San Domingo Revolution*, 2nd rev. edn (New York, 1963), pp. 46–58.

[8] For a comparison of British North America and Spanish America, see Stanley L. Engerman and Kenneth L. Sokoloff, 'Factor endowments, institutions, and differential paths of growth among New World economies: a view from economic historians of the United States', in Stephen Haber, ed., *How Latin America Fell Behind: Essays on the Economic Histories of Brazil and Mexico, 1800–1914* (Stanford, 1997), pp. 260–304; and an expanded version by Stanley L. Engerman, Stephen H. Haber and Kenneth L. Sokoloff, 'Inequality, institutions, and differential paths of growth among New World economies', (forthcoming). On the causes and implications of the pattern of usage of Indian labour in Latin America, which presented a major contrast between Spanish America and French

and economic structures in the New World, despite the cultural differences that existed among countries in the Old World.

One key starting point to the study of New World settlement patterns was a fact known to contemporaries, but given more attention only when reiterated by David Eltis about two centuries later, that down to *c.* 1820 two to three times as many slave blacks came to the Americas as did free and indentured European whites.[9] These slaves were not randomly distributed across the Americas, but were concentrated in specific regions producing specific crops, despite slavery being legal everywhere in the Americas until the last quarter of the eighteenth century. A second important consideration is that settlers from the same European nation evolved quite different patterns of labour institutions and landholding arrangements dependent upon the specific areas of residence. Thus, for example, the Caribbean colonies of the British, French, Dutch and Spanish were quite different from their colonies on the North American and South American mainlands. The Dutch were unusual among settlers of the Americas as their main concern was not with the West Indies and mainland North America, but, as reflected in immigration and trade, with their East Indian colonies.[10] While the British regarded the West Indian colonies as of greater value than those on the mainland, the large numbers in the thirteen colonies meant that they required considerable political

and British North America, see Susan Kellogg, *Law and the Transformation of Aztec Culture, 1500–1700* (Norman, 1995); Mark A. Burkholder and Lyman L. Johnson, *Colonial Latin America*, 2nd edn (New York, 1994), pp. 98–124; and James Lockhart and Stuart B. Schwartz, *Early Latin America: a History of Colonial Spanish America and Brazil* (Cambridge, 1983), pp. 86–180, 194–201. With regard to the locations of Native Americans at the time of European settlement, see Douglas H. Ubelaker, 'The sources and methodology of Mooney's estimates of North American Indian populations' and the 'epilogue' in William Deneven, ed., *The Native Population of the Americas in 1492* (Madison, 1976), pp. 243–88, 289–92.

[9] See David Eltis, 'Free and coerced transatlantic migrations: some comparisons', *AHR*, 88 (1983), 251–80.

[10] On the relative distribution of emigration from The Netherlands, see Jan Lucassen, 'The Netherlands, the Dutch, and long-distance migration in the late sixteenth to early nineteenth centuries', in Nicholas Canny, ed., *Europeans on the Move: Studies in European Migration, 1500–1800* (Oxford, 1994), pp. 153–91. Lucassen estimates that in the seventeenth and eighteenth centuries the migration from The Netherlands, including the remigration of some immigrants from elsewhere in Europe, was 500,000 permanently to the East Indies, about 15,000 to South America, the Caribbean and West Africa, and to the rest of North America, about 10,000. Dutch imports from Asia in the 1750s were about eight times those from the American colonies. See Niels Steensgaard, 'The growth and composition of the long-distance trade of England and the Dutch Republic before 1750', in James D. Tracy, ed., *The Rise of Merchant Empires: Long-Distance Trade in the Early Modern World* (Cambridge, 1990), pp. 102–52 (see, in particular, pp. 148–51). For the British the imports from Asia were only two-fifths those from America. Clearly the Dutch American colonies played only a minor role relative to their settlements in the East Indies.

attention. The French not only received more output from their West Indian colonies than from the mainland colony prior to 1763, but the limited population in Canada relative to that in the islands meant a greater attention of policy makers to these southern areas. A similar pattern of differential geographic influence on policy (here Spanish) set back Cuban economic expansion by over one century, given Spain's greater interests in its mainland colonies.

That shrewd contemporary observer of colonial empires, Adam Smith, commented in 1776 that 'the progress of the sugar colonies of France has been at least equal, perhaps superior, to that of the greater part of those of England'. He further argued that 'the prosperity of the sugar colonies of France has been entirely owing to the good conduct of the colonists', including 'good management of their slaves', while that of the British colonies has been based, 'in a great measure', on 'the great riches of England, of which a part has overflowed . . . upon these colonies'.[11] Or, to paraphrase, the English colonies were profitable mainly because of the prior achievement of the appropriate economic conditions in England, such as an 'equal and impartial administration of justice'. Some of the businessmen examined by Parliament in 1789 argued that the better financial credit system of the British served to make the slave trade and plantation system more profitable.[12] Smith also cast light on that other historical perennial, the so-called Eric Williams thesis on the exogenous role of the slave trade and slavery in contributing to the British industrial revolution. This raises broader issues of the context in which the opportunities for a successful slave-plantation complex could lead to modern economic growth, unlike the outcome observed in the first, and largest, of the slave trading nations, Portugal.

Also of interest to historians of counterfactuals, Smith argued that had it not been for the British–French political and economic rivalry, France could have 'afforded a market at least eight times more extensive, and on account of the superior frequency of the returns, four and twenty times more advantageous, than that which the British North American colonies ever afforded'.[13] France was considerably richer and about eight times more populous than was North America, and this trade could have benefited both European powers. This argument about the relative importance of different trading areas was to appear also during the eighteenth century in dealing with the prospects for trade with an Africa that did not participate in the transatlantic slave trade, and thus presumably

---

[11] Adam Smith, *An Inquiry into the Nature and Causes of the Wealth of Nations*, 2 vols. (Oxford, 1976), II, pp. 586–8.

[12] *Ibid.*, p. 610; Lambert, LXIX, pp. 77–8.

[13] Smith, *Wealth of Nations*, I, pp. 495–6.

would have had more rapid economic expansion and greater trading potential.[14]

The French–British comparisons are also of interest for examining the relative roles of cultural background and natural resources, since both countries had colonies in the Caribbean as well as colonies on the North American mainland. And, for both, the economic and social patterns that emerged on the mainland differed dramatically from developments on the islands. It was the West Indian islands that had at first been regarded as the richest and more productive colonies of settlement (as, indeed at first, they were), but it was the mainland areas that were ultimately to provide more economic output and prosperity.

However dissimilar the political systems and the internal economies of metropolitan France and Britain, both had similar sets of policies regarding their colonial and external markets, the system described as mercantilism.[15] The international restrictions on trade probably did more to harm the French colonies, since it was widely believed at the time that, because of its greater land fertility, as well as (at least prior to the 1780s, when the increased slave imports into Saint-Domingue may have changed things) better care and treatment of slave labour, that French-produced sugar was cheaper than that produced by the British.[16] The relation posited, by Smith, between the better treatment of slaves and the higher output from slave labour can be seen as an early variation of the emerging free labour ideology, as it later figured in the parliamentary debates on abolition and emancipation.[17]

With regard to emigration, neither nation had major restrictions on the

[14] See, for example, some of the testimony before Parliament in 1789, including Equiano (Gustavus Vassa), in Lambert, LXIX, pp. 98–9. See also Postlethwayt, *Britain's Commercial Interest*, II, pp. 200–73, and the brief comments of Wilberforce and others quoted in Klaus E. Knorr, *British Colonial Theories, 1570–1850* (Toronto, 1944), pp. 377–9. For a nineteenth-century example of this argument, see R. J. Gavin, 'Palmerston's policy towards East and West Africa, 1836–1865' (unpublished Ph.D. thesis, Cambridge University, 1958).

[15] On English mercantilism, see, in particular, Lawrence A. Harper, *The English Navigation Laws: a Seventeenth-Century Experiment in Social Engineering* (New York, 1939), while for the French, see Charles Woolsey Cole, *Colbert and a Century of French Mercantilism*, 2 vols. (New York, 1939); Charles Woolsey Cole, *French Mercantilism, 1683–1700* (New York, 1943); and Stewart L. Mims, *Colbert's West India Policy* (New Haven, 1912).

[16] See, for example, Smith, *Wealth of Nations*, II, pp. 586–7. The claim of lower French West Indian than British West Indian sugar prices was a steady theme in the pamphlet literature and parliamentary discussions of the second half of the eighteenth century in Britain. See also the sources cited in nn. 6 and 14 above. It is possible, however, that the very large growth in the Saint-Domingue slave population between 1770 and 1790 may have effected the treatment accorded to the slaves by the French.

[17] See Smith, *Wealth of Nations*, I, pp. 98–9, 387–90; II, p. 587. On the emerging free labour ideology of the late eighteenth century, see David Brion Davis, *The Problem of Slavery in the Age of Revolution 1770–1823* (Ithaca, 1975), pp. 343–85.

outflow of population, although, unlike the British, the French did attempt (after 1627) to limit migration so that 'only native-born French Catholics were to be sent to Canada', at least as permanent settlers, thus restricting the permanent inmigration of Huguenots and Jews.[18] Unlike the French, the British opened their colonies to a more multireligious and multinational population, including Protestant dissidents, a pattern resembling that of the nation then considered the most tolerant in Europe, the Dutch.[19] The French, however, did more than did the British to provide encouragements and subsidies to new, non-slave settlers. Also, while both British and French allowed for slaves to be imported, only the French provided subsidies to encourage the slave trade, first granting financial aid for each slave delivered and, later, also subsidies based on the tonnage of vessels.[20] In general, while only a limited number of direct state operations in regard to migration were undertaken by the French, more financial aids were provided for both slave and free inmigration by the French than the British.

A comparison of the demographic experience of Britain and France, and their North American colonies, poses other interesting questions. In regard to the European metropolises, the years after 1600 saw the onset of higher rates of population growth in Britain than elsewhere in Western Europe, with the rates of population growth for France being similar to those of the other western European nations.[21] It was in emigration, however, that the French experience was unique among the colonizing

[18] See Cole, *Colbert*, I, pp. 177–9; Leslie Choquette, 'Recruitment of French emigrants to Canada, 1600–1760', in Ida Altman and James Horn, eds., *'To Make America': European Emigration in the Early Modern Period* (Berkeley, 1991), pp. 131–71; and Choquette, 'Frenchmen into peasants: modernity and tradition in the peopling of French North America', *Proceedings of the American Antiquarian Society*, 104 (1994), 27–49. On Richelieu's colonization policies, see also Franklin Charles Palm, *The Economic Policies of Richelieu* (Urbana, 1922), pp. 108–24.

[19] According to the estimates of the American Council of Learned Societies, concerning the European basis of the American white population in 1790, the shares of different European nations in the thirteen mainland colonies were: British Isles, 78.9 per cent; Germany, 8.7 per cent (mainly in Pennsylvania, but also disproportionately in Maryland and Tennessee and Kentucky); The Netherlands 3.4 per cent (mainly in New York and New Jersey); France, 1.7 per cent (mainly New York and South Carolina, primarily from the Huguenot migration) Sweden, 0.7 per cent (mainly in Delaware) and others, primarily in New England, 6.6 per cent. Immigration to the thirteen colonies was more open, and attracted more different groups, than for the other major areas of settlement. See the material presented in US Bureau of the Census, *Historical Statistics of the United States, Colonial Times to 1970, Bicentennial Edition*, 2 vols. (Washington, D.C., 1975), II, pp. 1152, 1168.

[20] See James A. Rawley, *The Trans-Atlantic Slave Trade: a History* (New York, 1981), pp. 105–47; Robert Louis Stein, *The French Slave Trade in the Eighteenth Century: an Old Regime Business* (Madison, Wis., 1979), pp. 38–42; and Cole, *Colbert*, II, pp. 117–31.

[21] See the data conveniently put together in Angus Maddison, *Dynamic Forces in Capitalist Development: a Long Run Comparative View* (Oxford, 1991), pp. 9, 62, 223–7.

nations, with considerably fewer colonial migrants than the other major countries in absolute numbers. And, since France had by far the largest population of the colonizing nations of Europe, it had a considerably lower rate of outflow to the Americas.[22]

Down to the end of the eighteenth century, French transatlantic emigration was less than one-tenth that of the British, with many fewer arrivals as either free migrants or indentured servants. An important question is why, even before the major slowing down in the growth of the French population in the nineteenth century, and the Revolution's changes in French land-tenure systems, emigration was so low. Some emigrants from France went to elsewhere in Europe, mainly to Spain. The Huguenot *émigrés* moved primarily within Protestant Europe, with only limited numbers going to British America.[23] Nevertheless, it is doubtful that these intra-European flows were sufficient to alter the basic comparisons of differences in migration patterns. Even the external movement from France in the 1790s had relatively little impact, since many of the *émigrés* (who were fewer relative to population than the American loyalists who went to Canada) during the French Revolution soon returned to France, where they were even given compensation for their property losses.[24]

Fortunately for those enjoying scholarly debate, several different scenarios are proposed by historians to deal with British–French emigration

[22] See David Eltis, 'Slavery and freedom in the early modern world', in Stanley L. Engerman, ed., *Terms of Labor: Slavery, Serfdom and Free Labor* (Stanford, 1999) pp. 25–49. There were fewer migrants to the Americas from The Netherlands than from France, but the major stream of Dutch migration went to the East Indies. Relative to the 1700 population the overall cumulative outflow from France to the Americas was equal to 0.3 per cent of the population, for the Spanish and British about 8 per cent, and for Portugal, over 25 per cent.

[23] See Leslie Page Moch, *Moving Europeans: Migration in Western Europe Since 1650* (Bloomington, 1992), pp. 28–9, 83–8; Peter N. Moogk, 'Reluctant exiles: emigrants from France in Canada before 1760', *WMQ*, 3rd series, 46 (1989), 463–505; and Peter N. Moogk, 'Manon's fellow exiles: emigration from France to North America before 1763', in Canny, *Europeans*, pp. 236–60. On the Huguenots, see Jon Butler, *The Huguenots in America: A Refugee People in a New World Society* (Cambridge, Mass., 1983), pp. 24–7, 46–9. Butler (p. 49) estimates that the Huguenot migration to America was 'about 1,500 persons and certainly no more than 2,000 persons'.

[24] On the *émigrés* from the French Revolution, see François Furet and Mona Ozouf, eds., *A Critical Dictionary of the French Revolution* (Cambridge, Mass., 1989), pp. 324–36, who place the numbers at 150,000–160,000, or about 0.6 per cent of the French population. See also Donald Greer, *The Incidence of Emigration During the French Revolution* (Cambridge, Mass., 1951) who estimates the number of *émigrés* to be about 130,000 (p. 20). The number of loyalists leaving the United States after the Revolution is estimated to have been between 60,000 and 80,000, with almost 50,000 going to Canada. See Jack P. Greene and J. R. Pole, eds., *The Encyclopedia of the American Revolution* (Cambridge, Mass., 1991), pp. 259, 497. For an interesting comparison of the numbers of French *émigrés* and American loyalists, and of their losses, see Robert R. Palmer, *The Age of the Democratic Revolution I: the Challenge* (Princeton, 1959), pp. 185–90.

differences, differences and debates which have continued from the seventeenth and eighteenth into the nineteenth and twentieth centuries. Were large-scale British outflows necessary to avert a crises of overpopulation? Were French incomes believed adequate (and were they actually so) so that only a very limited outflow was desired or needed? Given the relatively small differences in population densities between France and the United Kingdom, why should these have led to such dramatic differences in transatlantic migration rates? Were the limited numbers departing France a symptom of a peasant-oriented and, in some sense, a backward, French economy? Were the French more community oriented and less willing to move, while the British were more individualistic and thus without deep roots? And were the causes of the low rates of emigration from France in the nineteenth and twentieth centuries the same as those explaining the limited movement in the colonial era?[25]

The relatively limited numbers leaving France compared to the British did not, however, influence the patterns of economic development that emerged in the West Indies. In the Caribbean, similarities between British and French colonies were quite apparent (as they were also with the Caribbean colonies of the Danes and the Dutch). The colonies of both France and Britain presented deadly mortality regimes, for whites as well as blacks; both began as tobacco colonies using white labour, shifting in about one-half century to become slave-based colonies with plantations producing primarily sugar (and in the case of French Saint-Domingue also coffee); and both had populations of about 90 per cent black slaves.[26] While Britain began the process of settlement earlier, it was the French colonies that soon were growing most rapidly. By 1700 the French West Indian population was about one-half that of the British, by 1780, 85 to 90 per cent, and in 1790, after the rapid expansion of Saint-Domingue, the French colonies had a larger population, with more slaves but fewer whites.[27]

Over the course of the seventeenth and eighteenth centuries the share of British migrants going to the West Indies declined, as did their absolute numbers. There were, however, substantial increases in the numbers

---

[25] These explanations are discussed briefly in Egnal, *Divergent Paths*, pp. 70–2.

[26] For a brief summary of relevant data on settlement patterns in the Caribbean, see Stanley L. Engerman, 'Europe, the Lesser Antilles, and economic expansion, 1600–1800', in Robert L. Paquette and Stanley L. Engerman, eds., *The Lesser Antilles in the Age of European Expansion* (Gainesville, 1996), pp. 147–64. See also Watts, *West Indies*, and Bonham C. Richardson, *The Caribbean in the Wider World, 1492–1992: a Regional Geography* (Cambridge, 1992).

[27] See the data on Caribbean populations in McCusker, *Rum and the American Revolution*; and Stanley L. Engerman and Barry W. Higman, 'The demographic structure of the Caribbean slave societies in the eighteenth and nineteenth centuries', in Knight, ed., *History of the Caribbean*.

Table 9.1A. *Estimated populations, major British and French Caribbean island colonies, 1680–1780 (in thousands)*

	English colonies			French colonies		
Year	White	Black	Total	White	Black	Total
1680	42	76	118	15	21	36
1690	37	98	135	18	37	54
1700	33	115	148	19	54	73
1710	30	148	178	21	75	97
1720	35	176	212	24	120	144
1730	37	221	258	31	174	204
1740	34	250	285	37	228	264
1750	35	295	330	38	290	328
1760	37	341	379	43	333	377
1770	45	434	479	42	393	435
1780	48	489	537	56	438	494

Source: John J. McCusker, *Rum and the American Revolution*, p. 712.

Table 9.1B. *Estimated populations, British and French Caribbean colonies, 1780 and 1790 (in thousands)*

	British colonies		French colonies	
	Slaves	Total	Slaves	Total
1780	515	595	436	507
1790	561	664	662	749

Source: Stanley L. Engerman and B. W. Higman, 'The demographic structure of the Caribbean slave societies in the eighteenth and nineteenth centuries' in Franklin W. Knight, ed., *General History of the Caribbean*, vol. III: *The Slave Societies of the Caribbean* (Paris, 1998), pp. 45–104.

going to the southern and middle Atlantic states on the mainland.[28] New England attracted relatively few immigrants, its rapid population growth being based upon its high rate of natural increase, aided by the initial importance of family migration and the relatively low rates of mortality. Within the Caribbean the magnitude of both white and black migrants

[28] See Henry A. Gemery, 'Emigration from the British Isles, 1630–1700: inferences from colonial populations', *Research in Economic History*, 5 (1980), 179–231; 'European Emigration to North America, 1700–1820: numbers and quasi-numbers', *Perspectives in American History*, new series, 1 (1984), 283–342; and David W. Galenson, *White Servitude in Colonial America: an Economic Analysis* (Cambridge, 1981).

exceeded the numbers alive there as late as the early nineteenth century, the demographic loss resulting from the particular outcome of the effect of climate upon mortality directly as well as indirectly via crop mix.[29] The growth in population numbers and in sugar production on the French islands were noted by some contemporaries, many of whom thought them more productive than the British islands.[30]

The optimism of the French planters in Saint-Domingue can be seen in the sharp rises in slave prices in the 1770s and 1780s, and the substantial increases in the numbers of slaves imported from Africa then, indicative of their belief in a viable economic and political future.[31] Obviously these economic advances could not continue once the French Revolution and the Haitian Revolution began, but one can perhaps ask why a dramatic impact on industrial development could not have occurred earlier, since these revolutions occurred after the conventional dating of the start of the British industrial revolution, and why some rapid economic recovery to the earlier trajectories was not possible. The French economy bounced back relatively soon after the end of the French Revolution and Napoleonic wars (despite the substantial military deaths as a result of these and the Haitian Revolution), and growth in the nineteenth century was relatively rapid by historical standards.[32] Where the French did suffer, however, was the failure of Haiti to remain a trading partner of any substantial size (and with only a modest compensation paid, in 1825, by Haiti to the French). The British, on the other hand, soon were trading with their former colonies, now the United States, and thus continued to

[29] For data on this, with discussions of the implications, see, in particular Philip D. Curtin, *The Atlantic Slave Trade: a Census* (Madison, Wis., 1969); Eltis, 'Free and coerced transatlantic migrations'; and Robert William Fogel, *Without Consent or Contract: the Rise and Fall of American Slavery* (New York, 1989), pp. 114–53.

[30] Brougham, in *Colonial Policy*, states that 'in every view the French American colonies were much more essential to the mother country than the English' (I: 540). The basis of this claim were the relative sizes of the slave and free populations, the 'produce exported', the tons of shipping and numbers of seamen, and the value of imports. Brougham further argues that 'the proportion which the French colony trade bore to the whole French trade, was also much greater than that which the British colony trade bore to the whole British trade [47.8 per cent versus 19.3 percent]', Brougham, *Colonial Policy*, I, pp. 538–40. This differential is in accord with the late eighteenth-century ratios computed from Patrick Villiers, 'Slave and colonial trade', pp. 211, 213; Tarrade, *Commerce Colonial*, II, pp. 739–41; Paul Butel, 'France, the Antilles, and Europe in the seventeenth and eighteenth centuries: renewals of foreign trade', in Tracy, ed., *Rise*, pp. 153–73; and Phyllis Deane and W. A. Cole, *British Economic Growth, 1688–1959* (Cambridge, 1962), pp. 86–8. The French lead by this measure did not develop until after the 1770s.

[31] The data on slave prices in Saint-Domingue are drawn from plantation records kindly provided by Herbert S. Klein and David Geggus. For estimated slave prices between 1753 and 1785, see Tarrade, *Commerce Colonial*, I, 140–1. Data on slave imports can be found in Curtin, *Atlantic Slave Trade*, pp. 75–84, and Stein, *French Slave Trade*, pp. 205–11.

[32] See Crouzet, *Britain Ascendant*, pp. 371–84, and Maddison, *Dynamic Forces*, p. 49.

Table 9.2. *Caribbean populations, 1750*

	White	Slave	Free persons of colour	Total
British[a]				
Barbados	16,772	63,410	235	80,417
St Kitts	2,783	21,782	109	24,674
Nevis	1,118	8,299	81	9,498
Antigua	3,435	31,123	305	34,863
Montserrat	1,430	8,767	86	10,283
Virgin Islands	1,184	6,062	59	7,305
	26,722	139,443	875	167,040
Jamaica	12,000	127,881	2,119	142,000
Dominica	1,718	5,769	300	7,787
St Lucia	2,524	9,764	506	12,794
St Vincent	2,104	7,184	230	9,518
Grenada	1,285	12,000	455	13,740
Tobago	238	3,082	82	3,402
Trinidad[b]	126	310	295	731
Demerara and Essequibo	380	4,185	34	4,599
Berbice[c]	346	3,802	31	4,179
	8,721	46,096	1,933	56,750
British Honduras	50	114	6	170
Cayman Islands	70	100	–	170
Bahamas	1,265	1,145	76	2,486
Anguilla	350	1,962	38	2,350
Barbuda	40	150	–	190
	1,775	3,471	120	5,366
	49,218	316,891	5,047	371,156
French				
Martinique	12,068	65,905	1,413	79,386
Guadeloupe[d]	8,848	45,238	1,036	55,122
Saint-Domingue	12,799	164,859	4,732	182,390
French Guiana	706	5,471	71	6,248
St Martin	102	185	–	287
	34,523	281,658	7,252	323,433
Dutch				
Surinam	2,133	51,096	598	53,827
Curaçao	3,964	12,804	2,776	19,544
St Eustatius	420	1,200	–	1,620
Saba	155	130	–	285
St Martin	639	3,518	–	4,157
	7,311	68,748	3,374	79,433

Table 9.2. (*cont.*)

	White	Slave	Free persons of colour	Total
Danish				
St Croix	1,323	8,897	–	10,220
St John	212	2,031	–	2,243
St Thomas	315	3,949	138	4,402
	1,850	14,877	138	16,865
Spanish				
Puerto Rico[e]	17,572	5,037	22,274	44,883
Cuba[e]	116,947	28,760	24,293	170,000
Santo Domingo[f]	30,863	8,900	30,862	70,625
	165,382	42,697	77,429	285,508
Swedish				
St Bartholomew	170	54	–	224
Total	258,454	724,925	93,240	1,076,619

Note: The specific years are generally those closest to 1750, but there is a spread of about thirty years in these entries. Thus the totals and broad patterns are useful for suggestive purposes only and do not represent the totals at any specific time period. For purposes of consistency of comparison over time with other estimates, the placements by nationality reflect the ownership for the greatest part of the period, not necessarily the ownership at the date to which the table applies. Changes in ownership among nations are described in the source, pp. 45, 65–66. There are numerous estimates for many areas, often drawn from the same source with modifications and errors in transcription. Secondary sources which examined the primary materials are cited for ease in location of data. While these estimates are to be regarded only as approximations, in very few cases would alternative choices influence basic patterns.

[a] For several of the British islands the census closest to 1750 listed only blacks, with no breakdown between slaves and free persons of colour. Various procedures were used to estimate this division, either interpolation between years for each such ratios were given, use of the ratio for the closest year known, or extrapolation on the basis of other islands or other years. If no allocations were made, and all blacks were treated as slaves, the total slave population of the British Caribbean would be increased by only 1.3 per cent.

[b] Plus 2,082 Amerindians. Between 1782 and 1784 the non-Amerindian population of Trinidad increased from 731 to 5,012. There is a 1777 population estimate of 3,432, which includes the Amerindian population.

[c] Plus 244 Amerindian slaves.

[d] Includes Marie-Galante. The estimated number of free persons of colour is based upon the ratio of free persons of colour to total non-slave population on Martinique.

[e] The breakdown of the free population into free persons of colour and whites is based upon the first available census with such data.

[f] Free population allocated according to that given for 1766 (see McCusker, *Rum and the American Revolution*, pp. 606, 769, n.119 and sources cited there.).

Source: As for table 9.1B.

benefit from trade with the New World, if not necessarily with their New World colonies.[33]

The New World settlements of the British and French were not, of course, restricted to the Caribbean. Both had mainland colonies, with high rates of natural population increase, based on high fertility rates, despite the initial sexual imbalance in the pattern of migration.[34] While the explanations for high fertility may differ – in one case the high fertility being influenced, at least in part, by the role of the Catholic religion, as well as by land availability, in the other more definitely by the availability of abundant land – it is clear that the rates of childbearing and patterns of marriage were to become more similar to each other in the mainland colonies of French and British than they were for each colony in comparison with its home country. The direct comparison of France and French Canada in the seventeenth century by the demographer Massimo Livi-Bacci points to the importance of the earlier age of female marriage and the greater frequency of remarriage in Canada, in helping to explain the higher fertility there.[35] A sharp decline in marriage age for females in the British mainland colonies was earlier pointed to by Malthus, and this pattern has been demonstrated in subsequent studies by scholars.

The major difference between the mainland settlement patterns of the British and the French was in the initial numbers of immigrants. The total net migration to French Canada was only about 10,000–20,000 individuals, with French Canada being most unusual for New World settlements because of its high rate of return migration.[36] Indeed, it is

[33] See US Bureau of the Census, *Historical Statistics*, II, pp. 1176–8; and B. R. Mitchell and Phyllis Deane, *Abstract of British Historical Statistics* (Cambridge, 1962), pp. 309–11. For an early argument that the loss of the colonies would not mean a loss in American trade with England, see John Lord Sheffield, *Observations on the Commerce of the American States* (new edn, much enlarged) (London, 1784), pp. 134–9, 187–92. Export data for Saint-Domingue and Haiti are in Robert I. Rotberg, *Haiti: the Politics of Squalor* (Boston, 1971), pp. 28–40, 68–72, 86, 381–9. See pp. 66–7, 77–8, 397–8 on the indemnity paid to France as a result of the ending of slavery.

[34] For overviews on demographic patterns for the United States and Canada in the colonial period, see J. Potter, 'The growth of population in America, 1700–1860', in D. V. Glass and D. E. C. Eversley, eds., *Population in History: Essays in Historical Demography* (London, 1965), pp. 631–88; McCusker and Menard, *Economy of British America*, particularly pp. 258–76; Jacques Henripin, *La Population canadienne au début du XVIIIe siècle. Nuptialité–fecondité–mortalité infantile* (Paris, 1954); and Hubert Charbonneau *et al.*, *Naissance d'une population. Les Français établis au Canada au XVIIe siècle* (Montreal, 1987).

[35] For a comparison of French Canada and France, see Massimo Livi-Bacci, *A Concise History of World Population* (Cambridge, Mass., 1992), pp. 56–60.

[36] The traditional figures are presented in Henripin, *La Population canadienne*, pp. 12–13; and Charbonneau *et al.*, *Naissance*, pp. 5–22. Some recent estimates suggest the number of migrants may have been somewhat higher. See the discussions of gross (and net) migration in Choquette, 'Frenchmen into peasants', and Moogk, 'Reluctant exiles'. Choquette raises the estimated gross migration to 67,000, based on a net migration figure of 20,000. The rate of return migration from French Canada was quite unusual for settlements in the New World.

probable that the movement of white and black loyalists to Canada during and after the American Revolution, estimated at almost 50,000, exceeded the total net migration from France to Canada before 1800.[37] These migrations, and the high birth rate and relatively low death rate once settled in Canada, led to a total population in New France of 65,000 in 1763, and, after the British conquest, of 192,000 in Upper and Lower Canada in 1790.[38]

The immigration of whites into the British mainland colonies between 1650 and 1780 totalled about 436,000, leading to a white population of 2,200,000 in 1780. In the New England and middle Atlantic states, a total of roughly 133,000 white immigrants led to a population in 1780 of over 1,330,000.[39] The sex ratio of migrants to Canada differed from that of the British to New England and the middle Atlantic states, as did the total numbers migrating. The ratio of net to gross migration was considerably lower for those going to Canada than it was to the northern British colonies, perhaps reflecting the more limited family migration to Canada, perhaps the perceived sense of more limited opportunities in Canada. Clearly, the British migration to the North American mainland, particularly that to its northern colonies, was more family oriented and included relatively more women than did the French. The size of the population of the British thirteen colonies was significantly greater than that of New France, a factor that was no doubt of some help in the conquest of the French mainland colony by the British in 1763.

With regard to labour force institutions, the French and British mainland patterns resembled each other. Labour shortages relative to land availability and the constraints introduced by the new disease environments led to the need (or desire) to attract labour across the Atlantic.[40] Unlike Spain and Portugal, France and Britain relied upon the use of

---

[37] See above, n. 23. It is estimated that about 3,000 black loyalists went to Nova Scotia, and in 1791 over 1,000 left Nova Scotia for Sierra Leone. See Graham Russell Hodges, ed., *The Black Loyalist Directory: African Americans in Exile After the Revolution* (New York, 1996), pp. xi–li.

[38] See William L. Marr and Donald G. Patterson, *Canada: an Economic History* (Toronto, 1980), pp. 151, 155, 169. These estimates exclude Nova Scotia and Newfoundland. See also Jacques Henripin and Yves Peron, 'The demographic transition of the Province of Quebec', in D.V. Glass and Roger Revelle, eds., *Population and Social Change* (New York, 1972), pp. 213–31.

[39] Calculated from Galenson, *White Servitude*, pp. 216–17; and US Bureau of the Census, *Historical Statistics*, II, p. 1168. See also the two essays by Gemery cited in n. 27 above.

[40] For death rates in Canada, see the estimates of Henripin and Peron, 'Demographic transition', reproduced in Marr and Patterson, *Canada*, pp. 156, 159. For estimates for the northern and southern mainland colonies in the seventeenth and eighteenth centuries, see Robert W. Fogel *et al.*, 'The economies of mortality in North America, 1650–1910: a description of a research project', *Historical Methods*, 11 (1978), 76–8. While above that of the northern colonies, the Canadian death rate was below that of the southern colonies.

indentured labour to provide white workers for their colonies on the mainland and in the Caribbean, with the contractual terms being relatively similar in terms of years and working arrangements.[41] Both sent convicts to the Americas, although, as with indentured servants, the French sent fewer overall, with the numbers declining over the eighteenth century. The French basically ended this movement after only a limited number of years of trial in the eighteenth century.[42] Both Britain and France provided for land settlement by a free population, and neither had an initially large amount of wage labour in the early settlement process. More important, both permitted slavery, although after early relative or relatively unsuccessful attempts to enslave Indians in large numbers, the slaves were almost exclusively black Africans. As elsewhere in western Europe at this time it was considered inappropriate to enslave not only one's own nationals but also the citizens of other European countries.[43] Slavery of Africans in the New World began with the slave trades of the Spanish and Portuguese, but over time the British and French areas expanded and together they ultimately received about one-half of all the slaves taken to the Americas from Africa, almost all going to the Caribbean with only a relatively small number going to the southern mainland colonies.[44]

The French and British Caribbean were also similar to each other in terms of demographic patterns and economic structure. Correspondingly, relatively few slaves were taken to the mainland areas north of Maryland, whether under British or French control. Rough estimates of total slave imports into the northern British colonies between 1650 and 1780

---

[41] See Galenson, *White Servitude*; H. Clare Pentland, *Labour and Capital in Canada, 1650–1860* (Toronto, 1981), pp. 8–13; and Christian Huetz de Lemps, 'Indentured servants bound for the French Antilles in the seventeenth and eighteenth centuries', in Altman and Horn, *'To Make America'*, pp. 172–203.

[42] See A. Roger Ekirch, *Bound for America: the Transportation of British Convicts to the Colonies, 1718–1775* (Oxford, 1987), on the transport of British convicts to the colonies, and Pentland, *Labour and Capital*, pp. 13–21, on convict labour in Canada. On convict labour in French Louisiana, see Hall, *Africans in Colonial Louisiana*, pp. 5–9, while for general discussions of convict migration from France, see Gordon Wright, *Between the Guillotine and Liberty: Two Centuries of the Crime Problem in France* (New York, 1983), pp. 28–31, 44–7, 92–5, and Leslie Choquette, *Frenchmen into Peasants: Modernity and Tradition in the Peopling of French Canada* (Cambridge, Mass., 1997), pp. 101, 273–6.

[43] On the enslavement of Indians, see Almon Wheeler Lauber, *Indian Slavery in Colonial Times within the Present Limits of the United States* (New York, 1913). On slavery in Canada, see Robin W. Winks, *The Blacks in Canada: a History* (Montreal, 1971), pp. 1–113; Pentland, *Labour and Capital*, pp. 1–8; and William Renwick Riddell, 'The slave in Canada', *Journal of Negro History*, 5 (1920), 261–377. For the argument on limits to who could be enslaved see David Eltis, 'Europeans and the rise and fall of African slavery in the Americas: an interpretation', *AHR*, 98 (1993), 1399–1423; and Orlando Patterson, *Slavery and Social Death: a Comparative Study* (Cambridge, Mass., 1982).

[44] Curtin, *Atlantic Slave Trade*, p. 216.

were of under 5,000, compared with almost 220,000 to the southern colonies.[45] When the process of gradual emancipation of slaves began in the northern United States after 1777, it is estimated that there were only about 50,000 blacks in these states.[46] French, and then British, Canada had legal slavery, but there were relatively few slaves. It is estimated that in 1759, just before the French lost Canada to Britain, there were probably no more than 1,500 Negro slaves, with perhaps double that number of Indian slaves.[47] Although Canada technically was covered under the British Slave Emancipation Act of 1833 no compensation was paid there, slavery having been basically ended earlier by actions at the provincial level. British-settled Upper Canada introduced in 1793 legislation similar to that of various New England states a little earlier: no slave was to be freed and all children born after the Act were legally free, but would work for their mothers' masters until they reached age 25. Lower Canada provided for the ending of slavery by a mechanism that would be more widely practised later, in colonies in Africa and Asia. A court decision in 1798 not to enforce the return of slave runaways meant that the slave system could no longer be successfully maintained.[48]

Canada and the northern United States provided for the ending of slavery over roughly similar periods at the end of the eighteenth century and start of the nineteenth century, whereas the southern United States and the British and French West Indies maintained slavery longer, until 1834 in the British West Indies, and 1848 in the French West Indies (both ending with compensation to slave-owners), and slavery did not end in the southern United States until 1865. One explanation for these differences in the timing of emancipation was suggested by Adam Smith, who commented that the Quaker freeing of slaves in Pennsylvania demonstrated only that they could not have been very important to them.[49] Or, as can be alternatively worded, the demand curve for morality was, like most demand curves, downward sloping.

The institutional arrangements regarding the other primary factor of production, land, were not initially as straightforward. Neither the British nor the French had the problem of settlement that confronted the earlier Spanish settlers, who located themselves in areas of relatively high population density (even after the numerous Indian deaths accompanying

---

[45] Compiled from Galenson, *White Servitude*, pp. 216–17.
[46] US Bureau of the Census, *Historical Statistics*, II, p. 1168.
[47] See Marcel Trudel, *L'Esclavage au Canada français* (Ottawa, 1960), pp. 42–5. See also Winks, *Blacks in Canada*, pp. 9–10, 486–7.
[48] On this, see Winks, *Blacks in Canada*, pp. 96–113.
[49] Smith, *Wealth of Nations*, II, p. 388. Smith was perhaps unfair to the Quakers since when they began the attack on slavery they undoubtedly had a larger number of slaves than they had in the 1770s.

settlement), in areas which had had quite extensively developed resident societies. The east coast of mainland North America was rather sparsely settled by Indians, and although there were frequent conflicts between settlers and Indians, with later forced movements of Indians to the west, the long-term problems of control differed from those in Spanish America. In Canada and the mid-west, the fur trade required extensive commercial contacts between Indians and Europeans. The nature of the fur trade also meant that the European populations were often geographically dispersed, providing one of the several links in the writings of the Canadian economic historian Harold Innis, demonstrating an important connection between natural resources and the nature of economic change.[50] The agricultural economies of the northern mainland colonies were somewhat similar to each other, with a focus on grains and livestock, and with their production generally based upon family farms.[51]

The adjustment to family farms for production often meant some variation in the original plan of settlement, leading to differences between the pattern of concentration of land ownership and the size of the actual producing unit. In some cases, such as the northern United States, change came relatively rapidly in response to the crop requirements. Pennsylvania, for example, replaced its initial system of large-sized grants by one providing for smaller units, after it became clear that the former was not well adapted to local needs.[52] The pattern of large land grants set by the Dutch in New York was modified throughout the period of settlement, first by the Dutch and then by the British.[53] Alternatively, it took the colony of Georgia, which was initially settled as a non-slave

[50] Harold A. Innis, *The Fur Trade in Canada: an Introduction to Canadian Economic History* (New Haven, 1930). See also the several essays on this theme in Innis, *Staples, Markets, and Cultural Change: Selected Essays* (Montreal, 1995).

[51] Even where serfdom was used to provide a coerced labour force for grain production in Russia, the actual units of production resembled more the smaller farms used to produce grains elsewhere than they did the gang labour systems typical in the production of sugar, coffee, cotton and other staples by slave labour. See Peter Kolchin, *Unfree Labor: American Slavery and Russian Serfdom* (Cambridge, Mass., 1987).

[52] See, for example, James T. Lemon, *The Best Poor Man's Country: a Geographical Study of Early Southeastern Pennsylvania* (Baltimore, 1972); and Gary B. Nash, *Quakers and Politics: Pennsylvania, 1681–1726* (Princeton, 1968), particularly pp. 48–126.

[53] On the pattern of land distribution and use during the early period of Dutch settlement, see Oliver A. Rink, *Holland on the Hudson: an Economic and Social History of Dutch New York* (Ithaca, 1986), pp. 94–116; Van Cleaf Bachman, *Peltries or Plantations: the Economic Policies of the Dutch West India Company in New Netherland, 1623–1639* (Baltimore, 1969), pp. 74–139; and US Bureau of the Census, *Historical Statistics*, II, p. 1168. In 1664 the estimated population of Dutch New York was about 12 per cent black, while that of Dutch Surinam, in 1684, was about 84 per cent slave. Johannes Menne Postma, *The Dutch in the Atlantic Slave Trade, 1600–1815* (Cambridge, 1990), p. 185. In Surinam, as with the other sugar producers, the large plantation was the basic unit of residence and of production.

colony, several decades to adjust its labour force institutions, and to permit slavery.[54] Another case of rapid institutional change in response to natural conditions can be seen in the comparison of the British settlement on Providence Island with that of a similar group of English Puritans in Massachusetts Bay. First settled in 1630, in one decade Providence Island's population was more than one-half slave, quite unlike the planned pattern, and also different from the pattern of white family farm settlement with few slaves in New England.[55]

New France, however, had begun with a seignorial system based on large-scale land grants, which it maintained until (and after) Canada was lost to the British. A seignorial system was apparently never introduced into the French West Indian islands, where settlement patterns resembled more those on British islands. The British continued the seignorial arrangement in Canada, albeit with modifications, until its compensated ending in 1854.[56] Throughout, however, the pattern of ownership size did not accord with the dictates of grain production. This difference was not unusual since similar differences had existed in Argentina in the wheat boom of the 1880s and 1890s, as well as in the postbellum South, where tenants rented land from the still large landholders.[57] In these cases, whatever may have been the cultural or political factors underlying the initial land distribution set by Europeans, they were subject to changes with economic developments. The initial distribution of land did not determine what would be the optimum or, at least, the most frequent size of producing units.

Recent studies of economic growth on the mainland and in the Caribbean suggest that whatever the differences in institutions regarding

---

[54] See, most recently, Betty Wood, *Slavery in Colonial Georgia, 1730–1775* (Athens, Ga., 1984).

[55] See Karen O. Kupperman, *Providence Island, 1630–1641: the Other Puritan Colony* (Cambridge, 1993).

[56] On the overall history of the Canadian seignorial system, see William Bennett Munro, *The Seignorial System in Canada: a Study in French Colonial Policy* (New York, 1907). See also W. J. Eccles, *France in America* (New York, 1972), pp. 79–81, 223–8. For a discussion of 'the economic burden of the seignorial system in New France', see Morris Altman, 'Seignorial tenure in New France, 1688–1739: an essay on income distribution and retarded economic development', *Historical Reflections*, 10 (1983), 335–75; and Altman, 'Note on the economic burden of the seignorial system in New France, 1688–1739', *Historical Reflections*, 14 (1987), 135–42. On the nature of the initial French plans for Canadian settlement and their changes over time in adapting to New World conditions, see also Sigmund Diamond, 'An experiment in "feudalism": French Canada in the seventeenth century', *WMQ*, 3rd series, 18 (1961), 3–34.

[57] For a recent discussion on the pattern of landholding and agriculture production in Canada and Argentina, see Jeremy Adelman, *Frontier Development: Land, Labour, and Capital on the Wheatlands of Argentina and Canada, 1890–1914* (Oxford, 1994), pp. 17–97, while on the United States South see, Robert Tracy McKenzie, *One South or Many? Plantation Belt and Upcountry in Civil War-Era Tennessee* (Cambridge, 1994).

Table 9.3. *Estimated plantation output of the British and French Caribbean, 1770 (values in thousands of pounds sterling, fob Caribbean)*

	British	French	Saint-Domingue
Sugar	1553	1816	1280
Molasses	8	275	202
Rum	899	317	192
Coffee	109	957	614
Indigo	10	289	289
Cotton	76	125	82
Cacao	14	40	18
Total	2669	3819	2677

Source: David Eltis, 'The slave economies of the Caribbean: structure, performance, evolution and significance', in Franklin Knight, ed., *General History of the Caribbean.* Vol. III: *The Slave Societies of the Caribbean* (Paris, 1998), pp. 105–37.

labour and land, the settled areas did have roughly similar rates of growth of per capita income. For the mainland colonies, the growth rates estimated by Morris Altman for Canada are similar to those for the thirteen colonies, while based on population, trade, or sugar production statistics the same is true for the Caribbean settlements.[58] If anything, the French West Indies were growing more rapidly than were the British West Indies throughout the eighteenth century prior to 1790.[59] Comparing the mainland to the West Indian colonies of the two colonial powers, there were relatively similar economic structures, each having a large share of the labour force in agriculture, although the crops grown did differ, as did the legal status of the labour force, and also the role of their trading relations. At this time, to the metropolitan powers, the West Indian islands were regarded as more important in providing economic rewards than the mainland areas. And, on the mainland, the southern colonies were considered more rewarding to the British than those to the north, whose crops overlapped those of the home country to a much greater extent than did those of the areas to the south.[60] This overlapping of production was

[58] See Morris Altman, 'Economic growth in Canada, 1695–1739: estimates and analysis', *WMQ*, 3rd series, 45 (1988), 683–711; Egnal, *Divergent Paths*, pp. 3–7; McCusker and Menard, *Economy of British America*, particularly pp. 258–76; and Edwin J. Perkins, *The Economy of Colonial America*, 2nd edn (New York, 1988), particularly pp. 228–34. Estimates of Caribbean population growth are in Engerman and Higman, 'Demographic structure', as well as McCusker, *The Rum Trade*. Sugar production estimates are in Deerr, *History of Sugar*, and Watts, *West Indies*.

[59] See for example, the estimates of relative output of the French and British Caribbean in 1770, in Eltis, 'Slave economies'.

[60] For this comparison see, among others, Young, *Political Essays*, pp. 328–60.

often pointed to by contemporaries as one reason for limiting settlement in northern areas; another reason for limited northern settlement was provided by a French writer on economic topics, the duc de Sully at the end of the sixteenth century, in arguing against the plans of Richelieu for settling Canada since 'great wealth was never derived from places beyond forty degrees [of north latitude]'.[61] This point, or at least one similar to it, about the relation of growth to climate has also been made more recently by the World Bank, pointing to the high levels of income in countries having temperate climates, with warmer areas today, unlike perhaps in the past, having lower incomes.[62]

An important eighteenth-century discussion of the impact of climate, crop characteristics and potential economic development was seen in the political settlement leading up to the Treaty of Paris in 1763. The French were willing to end the Seven Years' War by giving the British either the island of Guadeloupe (with an area of 619 square miles, and a population of about 80,000) or French Canada (the area of Lower Canada being approximately 200,000 square miles, with a population of over 65,000).[63] The value of exports of these two areas differed even more dramatically than did the populations, and no matter how obvious the choice would seem to us now it was equally an obvious choice at that time, at least on current economic (as contrasted with military) grounds. Although other arguments were provided, such as the costs of Canada's defence needs, and the value of Canada as a needed source of food supplies for the French West Indies, a major reason for the British choosing Canada was not relative profitability but the argument made by British West Indian planters, who feared competition from another sugar producing island. An interesting contemporary cost-benefit evaluation of Canada was provided by Voltaire in *Candide*. Voltaire wrote that these 'two nations are fighting over a few acres of snow on the borders of Canada', and he considered both the English and the French to be 'mad', since 'they spend more money on this glorious war than the whole of Canada is worth'.[64]

[61] Cole, *Colbert*, I, p. 42.

[62] Andrew M. Kamarck, *The Tropics and Economic Development: a Provocative Inquiry into the Poverty of Nations* (Baltimore, 1976).

[63] For a British West Indian discussion of this episode, see Lowell Joseph Ragatz, *The Fall of the Planter Class in the British Caribbean, 1763–1833: a Study in Social and Economic History* (Washington, D.C., 1928), pp. 111–13; and Frank Wesley Pitman, *The Development of the British West Indies, 1700–1763* (New Haven, 1917), pp. 335–60; and for a description from the French perspective, see Eccles, *France in America*, pp. 215–20. Estimates of areas and population are from McCusker, *Rum and the American Revolution*, pp. 545, 586, 671.

[64] Voltaire, *Candide: or Optimism* (Harmondsworth, 1947), p. 110. See the discussion in Lokke, *France and the Colonial Question: a Study of Contemporary French Opinion, 1763–1801* (New York, 1932), pp. 15–18, 40–5.

What all this suggests is that the perceptions of relative importance at the time of settlement, and the imposition of the initial set of economic institutions, did not necessarily predict what would ultimately happen, either politically or economically. While the French empire shrank in the Americas and elsewhere between 1763 and 1815, as the result of internal revolution in Haiti and military losses to the British elsewhere, the British empire did not remain undiminished. It is probable that the overall loss in population in the British empire from American independence exceeded the demographic losses suffered in the French losses of their colonies, and it might also have been that the British economic loss was also initially greater.[65] The major difference was that the French West Indian trade never recovered, but within about two decades United States–British trading relations again reached pre-revolutionary war levels. Loss of empire was less costly to the British than to the French, although in the French case it was not that the loss meant a diversion in trading patterns but rather the economic decline of its former colony and its more limited production and trade.

To return to the initial questions about the relative roles of culture and resources, it is useful to consider that there are differences in per capita incomes and economic structures across, as well as within, continents, and that international differences are generally considerably greater than those within countries. In some cases, however, relative intranational geographic equality is long standing; in others, such as the narrowing of regional differences between French and English Canada, and the northern and southern states of the United States, the convergence has only recently occurred. The causes of this remain debated. Is the present convergence due to the development of new technologies that have permitted long-delayed reductions in the impact of climate and other natural resources, reducing, but not completely eliminating the importance of climate and resources, and possibly influencing only certain sectors of the economy? Or was it, rather, the result of intra-regional changes that were due to convergences in cultural patterns of behaviour and belief?[66] In the United States South, for example, the post-World War II narrowing of its income gap has been attributed, in part, to the developments in the technology of air conditioning, while developments

---

[65] The loss referred to is the decline in empire population with the loss of political control over the particular colonies.

[66] The precise meaning of culture is, as always rather uncertain. Is it meant to refer to the development and persistence of specific patterns of behaviour (e.g. patterns of land distribution), or is it, rather, the openness to flexibility and adaptation to whatever might seem economically desirable in response to changing external constraints? A willingness to adjust to different climate and resource conditions provides a cultural context for economic development, but this is not the usual sense of the argument.

in hydroelectric transmission apparently have had a significant impact on Quebec's economic growth. Thus, to raise a broader question about economic change, while climate and resources may influence original patterns of settlement, and the ensuing economic growth patterns, the changing nature of technical development possibly points to some limits on their long-run effects, whether or not significant cultural changes are believed to have taken place.[67]

[67] See Egnal, *Divergent Paths*, pp. 159–99. It has been argued that many agricultural innovations regarding seeds and planting methods are intended to reduce the impact of climate and soil upon production. On air-conditioning's role in southern economic development, see Walter Y. Oi, 'The welfare implications of invention', in Timothy F. Bresnahan and Robert J. Gordon, eds., *The Economics of New Goods* (Chicago, 1997), pp. 109–41; and Gail Cooper, *Air-Conditioning America: Engineers and the Controlled Environment, 1900–1960* (Baltimore, 1998). For a description of the impact of hydroelectricity in Canada, see W. T. Easterbrook and Hugh G. J. Aitken, *Canadian Economic History* (Toronto, 1965), pp. 524–30. For an earlier example of an innovation that significantly altered the impact of climate, see Lynn White, 'Technology assessment from the stance of a medieval historian', *AHR*, 79 (1974), 1–13.

10 Merchants and bankers as patriots or speculators? Foreign commerce and monetary policy in wartime, 1793–1815

Patrick K. O'Brien

Merchants, credit and overseas trade

After protracted debate few historians now 'represent' foreign commerce as the *primus mobile* behind the development of power and prosperity in Great Britain between 1688 and 1815.[1] Many will observe, however, that over the long eighteenth century the British economy succeeded in securing extraordinary shares of world trade in manufactures and in shipping, banking, insurance and other mercantile services.[2] They might also agree that the rapid enlargement of the island's commerce with the rest of the world actively promoted the long-term development of its industry and towns, extended the state's fiscal base, increased stability and security for the realm, and promoted the nation's imperial and economic ambitions in Africa, Asia and the Americas.[3]

Foreign trade with Europe and trans-oceanic commerce with more distant continents had, however, to be organized and financed.[4] And the multifaceted connections between merchants and their role in extension of credit, on the one hand, and long-term growth in volume, range and organizational complexity of British connections with the rest of the international economy on the other, have been analysed in depth and sophistication by Jacob Price.[5] Aristocrats had long been alive to the material gains and power that would accrue to them from commitment

---

[1] Kenneth Morgan, 'Atlantic trade and British economic growth in the eighteenth century', in Peter Mathias and John A. Davis, eds., *The Nature of Industrialisation: International Trade and British Economic Growth from the Eighteenth Century to the Present Day* (Oxford, 1996), pp. 14–33.

[2] Joel Mokyr, editor's introduction in Joel Mokyr, ed., *The British Industrial Revolution* (Boulder, Colo., 1993), pp. 69–78.

[3] P. K. O'Brien, 'Inseparable connections: trade, economy and fiscal state and the expansion of empire, 1688–1815', in P. J. Marshall, ed., *The Oxford History of the British Empire*, II (Oxford, 1998), pp. 54–77.

[4] Jacob M. Price, *Capital and Credit in British Overseas Trade: the View from the Chesapeake, 1700–76* (Cambridge, Mass., 1980).

[5] Jacob M. Price, *Overseas Trade and Traders.*

250

to maritime trade and empire. Nevertheless, merchants supplied most of the capital and credit and managed Britain's increasing involvement in global trade. Indeed, their role in organizing, coordinating and sustaining commerce between the metropolitan centre and the ports, towns, naval bases, forts, settlements, mines, plantations, farms and fisheries of Britain's far-flung networks for international trade can hardly be overstated. By linking producers and consumers in Europe, Africa, Asia and the Americas into an embryo world economy, merchants can be represented as precursors of modern multinational corporations. Equally, the differences between then and now are marked. With the conspicuous exception of the East India Company, but also of the South Sea, Hudson's Bay, Royal African and Levant companies, corporate organizations based in London played little part in the management of Britain's global trade. After 1688, when Parliament became less inclined to renew trade monopolies, and interlopers illegally entered commerce with Asia, corporate forms of organization for the conduct of global trade faded away. Merchants operated in partnerships, kin groups and a variety of associations, formed and reformed for particular voyages and ventures. They collected, gathered and processed information, drew upon their talents, education, experience and reputations, connected their partners to their relatives and religious and business networks located in distant ports, all in order to operate together, and with greater chances of success, in what was an incredibly uncertain environment for international business.[6]

That environment contained familiar hazards associated with traversing seas and oceans, dealing with extreme climatic conditions and coping with new diseases. For all such risks the sciences, medicines and transport technologies of the eighteenth century continued to provide palliatives but not solutions. Meanwhile, the coordination of markets across space, time and cultures embodied economic and political uncertainties that even the most astute business acumen could only circumscribe. Alien consumers with peculiar tastes, the slow diffusion of commercial intelligence, competition from fellow countrymen and enemy rivals, and above all the unpredictable occurrence of war, called for levels of skill, flexibility and foresight in the management of global and imperial trade that exceeded the expertise required to operate within established intra-European or domestic trades by a wide margin.

The finance and professional skills required to engage in servicing the international economy had been accumulating among communities of merchants in London, Bristol and other port cities well before 1688. By

---

[6] Jacob M. Price, 'What did merchants do? Reflections on British overseas trade, 1660–1790', *JEcH*, 49 (1989), 267–84.

the time of the Glorious Revolution, London's merchants, shippers, warehousemen and financiers more or less ran Britain's transcontinental trades. The capital's hegemony over western ports diminished over the eighteenth century as Londoners made economic space for the prosperity of Bristol and for the rise of Glasgow and Liverpool, as well as other smaller and more specialized British and Irish coastal towns involved with oceanic trade and empire.

Keen competition kept London's merchants alive to possibilities for recruiting new skills, to opportunities for investment, and wherever feasible, to the relocation of their operations outside the expensive confines of the metropolis. Throughout the period London dominated the 'outports' by a large, if decreasing, margin. In scale and scope the capital's communities of merchants reinvigorated themselves decade after decade by absorbing Dutchmen, Huguenots, Jews and Germans from across the North Sea and the Channel and by attracting ambitious newcomers from all over the British Isles to an already prosperous capital city, with long-established success in European and Mediterranean commerce.[7]

Of all the manifold skills required for successful participation in global trade access to and the management of credit has been recognized by Jacob Price as paramount. Buying and selling upon distant markets in the interiors of far away continents; collecting cargoes, hiring crews and fitting out ships sailing far away from home ports for months on end; storing inventories of crops and raw materials harvested seasonally; warehousing stocks of manufactures, gathered over dispersed locations; delivering untrained slaves for work in gangs on plantations, are all examples of tasks undertaken by merchants which required circuitous chains of credit to lubricate the flows of production, distribution and exchange across the time spans and distances involved in European and transcontinental commerce.

Functionally, the production, transport, distribution and finance of trade are interrelated. Indeed, before the rise of specialist international banks, they were often undertaken as conjoined activities by merchants. With some, but rarely enough, liquid capital at their disposal, merchants organized and acted as guarantors for deferred systems of payments all along the line from sites of production, through networks of transport and distribution to points of sale. In the middle ages Italian merchants, and in the sixteenth and seventeenth centuries their Flemish successors, developed the paper instruments, the contractual rules and the institutions required for long distance trade. Later on London and Britain emulated Amsterdam and The Netherlands in extending the range and sophistica-

---

[7] David Hancock, *Citizens of the World: London Merchants and the Integration of the British Atlantic Economy, 1735–85* (Cambridge, 1995).

tion of the system. As financiers, London's merchants not only augmented the volume and velocity of credit but reallocated purchasing power from those who could afford to wait, but who wished to earn interest, to those who had to be paid quickly in order to produce the commodities and capital goods and to hire the labour and transport they required to engage in oceanic trade.[8]

With substantial capital of their own but borrowing much more on the basis of their reputations, London merchants acquired the skills needed to finance as well as manage the distribution of traded goods around the world. Over time merchants, wholesalers, warehousemen and other middlemen, who specialized in the finance of trade, matured in the metropolis and other port cities into international bankers. By the second half of the eighteenth century, London boasted a variegated system of financial intermediation, rivalled only by Amsterdam. Credit became cheaper and available to sustain the development of established enterprises in agriculture, transport, industry and trade throughout the kingdom, as well as its trading networks overseas.[9]

The whole system evolved, moreover, without serious hindrance from central government and the courts. Punishments for those who could not meet their debts remained severe and probably deterred many would be entrepreneurs from taking more than carefully calculated risks. Nevertheless, rules for the extension of credit were left to the prudence and honour of businessmen. The law confined itself to the protection of creditors from fraud but recognized bills of exchange as assignable and negotiable instruments of credit, as paper promises that could circulate as money.[10] When they appeared, no legal restrictions were placed on the foundations and activities of specialized banks.

In 1694 Britain's embryo credit system was underpinned by the foundation of a private corporation, the Bank of England, which assumed responsibility for managing the government's debt, particularly the arrangements to cover any short-term borrowing required to meet day-to-day expenditures in anticipation of revenues from taxation or from long-term loans. The Bank's notes, issued to government paymasters, became currency and quickly matured to supplement bullion as 'reserve assets' for the nation's and the empire's supply of money and credit. Once established, the Bank extended its responsibilities to assume a role akin to a 'lender of last resort' and granted discount facilities for top class bills of

[8] Jacob M. Price, 'Credit in the slave and plantation economies', in Barbara L. Solow, ed., *Slavery and the Rise of the Atlantic System* (Cambridge, 1991), pp. 293–339.
[9] Larry Neal, *The Rise of Financial Capitalism: International Capital Markets in the Age of Reason* (Cambridge, 1990).
[10] Julian Hoppit, *Risk and Failure in English Business, 1700–1800* (Cambridge, 1987).

short maturity to major London merchants and businessmen. That facility, allowed only to clients of status from the City, tended to be used sparingly. On several occasions of crisis the Bank did, however, discount bills of exchange and thereby helped to restore confidence in the pyramid of paper credit upon which government and mercantile transactions, both domestic and overseas, rested.[11] In short, the most important consequence of the financial revolution from 1694–1713 was to create stable conditions for extension and integration of a national and an international capital market centred on London.

As it developed and improved in efficiency, that market supported ever increasing demands from the government, from internal trade and from global commerce. Fortunately, it was neither unduly trammelled by legal controls imposed on the activities of banks and other institutions supplying money and credit, nor undermined by reckless behaviour on the part of the state. Difficulties certainly emerged, particularly during two long and expensive conflicts with France from 1689 to 1713 and again from 1793 to 1815, when a sustained critique emerged, which accused the government, the Bank of England and the mercantile community of mismanaging the nation's credit and monetary system at a time of grave threats from France to the security of the realm and its economic interests in overseas trade and empire.[12] My chapter will be concerned to represent and to reject that bullionist and Ricardian critique of the monetary policy pursued between 1797 and 1819 as little more than vacuous theory.[13] Against classical political economy it offers a historical defence of ministers of the crown, directors of the Bank and leading merchants and bankers of the day who insisted that the wartime economy could not and should not be placed within the constraints of a convertible currency and that the maintenance and stability of overseas commerce demanded a flexible and expansionary monetary policy.[14]

Monetary policy in peace and war, 1694–1783

Today the provision of loans and credit to support economic activity, including foreign trade, operates within a framework of rules and institutions of Britain's long-established national monetary system, regulated by the Bank of England. Acting on behalf (or at least under firm guidance from the Treasury) the Bank exercises a discernible degree of central

[11] Jacob M. Price, 'The Bank of England's discount activities and the merchants of London, 1694–1773', in *Overseas Trade and Traders*, ch. 8.

[12] F. W. Fetter, *The Development of British Monetary Orthodoxy* (Cambridge, Mass., 1965).

[13] Jacob Viner, *Studies in the Theory of International Trade* (London, 1955).

[14] F. W. Fetter, 'The politics of the Bullion Report', *Economica*, new series, 26 (1959), 99–130.

control over the accessibility, availability and costs of finance extended by individuals, firms and above all by financial intermediaries to the rest of the economy. Between its establishment in 1694 and victory over France at Waterloo, neither the state nor the Bank of England presumed to exercise anything like control over the nation's supply and demand for money and credit. Given the legal and institutional rules within which financial intermediation had developed during the long eighteenth century, it is doubtful whether the government (even acting in concert with the directors of a private corporation (the Bank of England)) could do much more than exercise some influence over variations in the overall supply and costs of loans and credit extended to British agriculture, industry and internal and external trade.[15] Indeed, and before Pitt the Younger suspended the operations of the specie standard in February 1797, the parameters of what would nowadays be referred to as monetary policy had never been legislated for, enunciated or even seriously considered.[16] Ministers of the crown and directors of the Bank abided by rather simple and flexibly interpreted rules established for a fully convertible system of paper currency and credit.[17] Government and the private sector demanded credit that could be extended or contracted in relation to reserves of specie and other liquid assets, but upon a purely *ad hoc* and pragmatic basis.[18]

Clearly borrowing by the state and lending by the Bank of England brought about variations in the nation's money supply. By running deficits or surpluses on its budget, the government created and absorbed reserve currency. Through the expansion or contraction of loans to businessmen the Bank likewise increased or decreased the reserves for the remainder of the financial system. Nevertheless, and although the money supply could be affected by actions taken by central government and the Bank, policy (in the sense of conscious management of the money supply in order to achieve some set of objectives) hardly existed either in peace or war throughout the long eighteenth century.[19] Indeed, and during four major wars (1703–13, 1740–8, 1756–63 and 1776–83), the operations of the monetary system had been conducted within the rules operated for the maintenance of convertibility largely because the Bank of England's specie reserves had never fallen to a low enough level in relation to outstanding liabilities to prompt its directors to initiate any serious contraction of credit to the private sector or even to consider how best to conduct monetary policy in wartime. For decades Britain's balance of

[15] Michael Collins, *Money and Banking in the UK: a History* (London, 1988).
[16] E. Wood, *English Theories of Central Bank Control, 1819–58* (Cambridge, 1939).
[17] J. H. Clapham, *The Bank of England*, 2 vols. (Cambridge, 1944), I, pp. 224–72; II, pp. 1–74.
[18] L. S. Pressnell, *Country Banking in the Industrial Revolution* (Oxford, 1956), pp. 356–65.
[19] Clapham, *The Bank*, I, pp. 224–72; II, pp. 1–74.

payments position seems to have been favourable enough to preclude the need for deflationary credit policies.[20] Between and even during these wars, when the government funded heavy borrowing on the London capital market, the Bank supported demands from the state and the mercantile community with a prudential but flexible concern for the safety of its reserves. But before 1793 Britain's monetary and credit arrangements had never been seriously tested by global warfare, widespread depression, volatile harvests or persistent deficits on the country's balance of payments. Rules guiding the operations of the Bank had worked pretty well. Neither the Treasury nor London and other British merchants had ever been denied the credit required to pursue their respective concerns, even in wartime when the state's demands for long- and short-term loans led to a rapid accumulation of the national debt.[21]

During the period 1793–1815 that situation changed radically – the country faced a series of exceptionally bad harvests, financed heavy military expenditure overseas and defeated a determined attempt by Napoleon at economic blockade. Four years after the outbreak of war with revolutionary France, a run on the Bank's gold reserve compelled the government to suspend specie payments. After February 1797 both statesmen and directors, operating within a completely new and very difficult situation, had to examine the whole problem of regulating a non-convertible currency, with very little by way of precedent or economic theory to guide them.[22]

Although the Treasury and Bank of England did not proceed from any set of precedents or principles towards clearly defined objectives, their relations with each other, with the metropolitan capital market and with London merchants determined the direction and rate of change in the money supply between 1793 and 1815. If policy is redefined as the assumptions or premises of actions taken by central authorities which effectively initiated or constrained increases in the supply of money and credit, then it is plausible to refer to wartime monetary policy implicitly formulated and implemented by the Treasury and the Bank of England, acting for most of the war in complete concert. The government's suspension of specie payments in February 1797 allowed the state and its Bank to pursue an entirely pragmatic policy towards the extension of credit to state and private sector alike. From its inception the very flexibility allowed by a non-convertible currency aroused fear and suspicion which

<hr>

[20] J. K. Horsefield, 'The Bank and its treasure', in T. S. Ashton and R. S. Sayers, eds., *Papers in English Monetary History* (Oxford, 1953), pp. 67–98.

[21] M. C. Lovell, 'The role of the Bank of England as a lender of last resort in the crises of the 18th century', *Explorations in Entrepreneurial History*, 10 (1957), 8–21.

[22] PP 1826 (3). Three reports from the Committee of Secrecy on the Outstanding Demands of the Bank of England and on the Restriction on Payments in Cash, 1797.

quickly matured into sustained criticism, which this chapter proposes to survey and evaluate by asking a meta question: Was the monetary policy pursued from 1797 to 1815 functional for the security of the realm and efficient for the growth and stability of Britain's wartime economy?

The contemporary discussion

I propose to begin by analysing the critique of contemporaries, presented as a sequence of macroeconomic arguments before turning to the widespread condemnation of merchants as speculators. For two reasons critics focused attention upon the rate of exchange: first, because the downward fluctuations in that rate provided evidence of currency depreciation; and secondly because no accurate information was available to them in the form of more familiar indices that are used nowadays to discourse about connections between monetary policy and the country's external economic position. Balance of payment statistics were not recorded, official balance of trade figures were regarded as inaccurate and only impressionistic statements could be made about movements in the nation's gold reserves.

For about half the years of suspended specie payments, from 1797–1819, Britain's rate of exchange stood sufficiently close to par to preclude much adverse comment. Serious public criticism of monetary policy only emerged in 1800–1 and between 1808 and 1815 when the exchange depreciated against foreign currencies by 10 per cent or more. Before 1797 a persistent fall in the exchange rate would eventually have led to a contraction of credit by the Bank of England. After suspension the directors allowed the exchange to find its own level and incurred the criticism of Ricardo and other bullionists for not behaving as if convertibility still prevailed.[23] Most critics regarded any instability in the value of sterling as 'an evil in itself', but Malthus, who realized that the merits of a fixed exchange rate must at least be argued, observed that Britain should not separate itself from the rest of the commercial world

in relation to our measure of value and resorting to an imaginary standard which no foreign nations would acknowledge, which might be subject, not only to all the variations which can be supposed to take place on gold, but to others beyond comparison more sudden and more extensive.[24]

---

[23] David Ricardo, 'Three letters on the price of gold contributed to the *Morning Chronicle*, 1809', in P. Sraffa, ed., *Works and Correspondence of David Ricardo*, 3 vols. (Cambridge, 1951–73), III, pp. 20–1, and E. Cannan, *The Paper Pound of 1797–1821* (London, 1925), pp. 19, 32, 45, 71.

[24] T. R. Malthus, 'Review of the controversy respecting the high price of bullion', *Edinburgh Review*, 17 (1811), 339–45.

Around the turn of the century, the government and its supporters argued that the depreciated exchange encouraged exports, discouraged imports and would automatically correct itself without any contraction of credit.[25] Their opponents (who I will classify as bullionists) agreed that it conferred a 'bounty on exports' but were not confident in any powers of self-correction and insisted that depreciation simply raised the cost of imports.[26] Neither side followed its arguments through. The degree of influence exerted by exchange depreciation on receipts from British commodities sold abroad depended on how far export prices lagged behind the falling rate of exchange. If export prices rose more rapidly than the exchange depreciated no economic advantages could accrue from the policy. Receipts from exports also depended on changes in the volume of goods sold abroad. Unless the volume increased more rapidly than the decline in price (expressed in foreign currency per unit exported) again nothing would be gained from allowing the exchange rate to decline. If we compare available indices of export prices and export volumes with deviations from par in the rate of exchange between 1797 and 1815, it can be observed that export prices lagged well behind the fall in the exchange rate and that exports grew in volume at a faster rate than the exchange depreciated.

Foreign demand seemed elastic enough to more than offset the decline in aggregate receipts of foreign currency from the depreciated exchange. Such statistics do not prove that the decline in the value of sterling led to increased income from exports. There might have been an autonomous shift in demand for British commodities abroad and export prices fell steadily after 1802. But they do support the argument that exchange depreciation perhaps helped to increase receipts from exports and cast doubt on Jacob Viner's assertion that the risks and uncertainties of a floating exchange discouraged British exporters during the war years.[27]

On the import side of the balance of payments the advantages of the floating pound look less felicitous. Exchange depreciation did not induce any decline in imports; in fact the volume of imports increased as the exchange rate declined. British demand for imports was apparently in-elastic, largely because most of the commodities purchased abroad con-sisted of basic foodstuffs, raw materials for domestic industry or military

---

[25] F. Baring, *Observations on the Publication of Walter Boyd* (London, 1801) and J. Atkinson, *Consideration of Thoughts on the Propriety of the Bank of England resuming Specie Payments* (London, 1802).

[26] PP 1810 (3). Report Together with the Minutes of Evidence and Accounts from the Select Committee on the High Price of Gold Bullion, 1810, pp. 82–3. Walter Boyd had made these points to the Prime Minister in a letter dated 9 May 1794, PRO, Pitt Papers, 30/8/115.

[27] Viner, *Studies in the Theory of International Trade.*

supplies purchased on government account. Thus the policy of allowing the exchange to depreciate cannot be defended on the grounds that it corrected adverse movements in the balance of trade.[28]

Wartime monetary policy attracted another line of criticism, namely that fluctuations in the external value of sterling had been aggravated by speculation; and that the instability in the rate of exchange hindered the country's ability to borrow abroad. Certainly the abandonment of the gold standard gave more scope to dealings in currency but it is impossible to gauge the influence that speculators had on fluctuations in the rate of exchange after 1797. Although one 'Continental merchant' examined by the Bullion Committee assumed that the effects must have been of a disequilibriating character, there is no obvious reason to accept his assumption.[29] Factors which caused the adverse balances of trade in 1800, 1801 and again between 1810 and 1812 were short run in character and speculators could reasonably share the anticipation of most British merchants that the exchange would appreciate with the return of good harvests and the reopening of European markets.

A floating exchange did, however, increase risks for foreign investors in British assets. During the war years, inflows of foreign capital mitigated the 'crowding out' of British investment by heavy government borrowing and from time to time met short-run deficits on the balance of payments.[30] Foreign capital also played an important role in helping to finance British military expenditure in Europe.[31] Official correspondence for the period is full of the difficulties encountered by Wellington's commissariat in borrowing money in the Iberian peninsula and of attempts by the Treasury to obtain gold for troops serving abroad.[32] In general, since so many influences other than the volatility of the rate of exchange operated on the decisions of foreign investors to retain or transfer capital into British assets, it seems impossible to gauge the force of this critique. Meanwhile, a marked rise in the rate of interest undoubtedly attracted capital from overseas into London.[33] As early as 1801 the *Monthly Magazine* suggested that the depreciated exchange actually

---

[28] The relevant data for these correlations are tabulated in A. D. Gayer, W. W. Rostow and A. Schwartz, *The Growth and Fluctuations of the British Economy, 1750–1850*, 2 vols. (Oxford, 1953), II, pp. 468–70; A. Imlah, *Economic Elements in the Pax Britannica: Studies in British Foreign Trade in the Nineteenth Century* (Cambridge, Mass., 1958), pp. 94–8; J. Silberling, 'British financial experience, 1790–1830', *Review of Economic and Statistics*, 1 (1919), 282–97.

[29] PP 1810 (3), pp. 74–5, 83–4.   [30] Imlah, *Economic Elements*, p. 36.

[31] BL, papers of J. C. Herries, 1778–1855. Uncatalogued MSS, boxes 10, 11 and 17.

[32] BL, papers of Nicholas Vansittart, Baron Bexley, 1766–1851 and Robert Banks Jenkinson, earl of Liverpool, 1770–1826, Add. MSS 31,231, 38,363 and 38,425.

[33] *Monthly Magazine* (June 1801), 101 and *Memoirs and Correspondence of Viscount Castlereagh* (London, 1850–53), VIII, p. 251.

encouraged foreigners to purchase British funds on advantageous terms, a point repeated by Castlereagh in 1811. Furthermore, Britain was not the only country to allow its rate of exchange to fluctuate. Other European countries and the United States also abandoned convertibility.[34] The security of investment in British assets became relative to risks elsewhere and the unrivalled political safety of London as a financial centre could well have offset any risks attendant on a floating exchange. For many years during the war, other major European financial centres (Amsterdam and Hamburg) came under French occupation and when the French invaded Hamburg in 1807 foreign capital flowed into London.[35] As diplomatic relations between Britain and the United States deteriorated between 1808 and 1812, British capitalists repatriated over £4 million invested in the American national debt.[36] But while trade between Britain and the United States continued, American merchants invested considerable sums in Exchequer bills, despite fluctuations in the rate of exchange.[37] No figures for movements of foreign capital in and out of Britain exist but foreign holdings in the national debt increased from £13.5 million in 1792 to about £16 million in 1814–15.[38] There is, moreover, no observed tendency for the withdrawal of foreign capital invested in the national debt to correlate with fluctuations in the rate of exchange. It seems the evidence remains too slender to make affirmative statements about overall movements on the capital account. Economists expect a floating rate of exchange to discourage foreign lending, but just how serious a handicap it became to borrowing overseas during this unusual period of political instability is impossible to gauge.

Although contemporary commentators linked their attacks on monetary policy to the depreciated rate of exchange, they also referred to other indicators which bore directly on connections between overseas commerce and the price level. For example, Walter Boyd, Henry Thornton and several others asserted that rising prices, seen as a consequence of credit expansion, hindered exports and encouraged imports.[39] Translated into modern terminology, the critical position adopted by Ricardo and his 'bullionist' followers towards government, the Bank and merchants in

<hr>

[34] E. L. Hargreaves, *Restoring Currency Standards* (London, 1926).

[35] *Monthly Magazine* (July 1807), 514.

[36] PP 1819 (3). Two reports from the Committee of Secrecy Appointed to consider the State of the Bank of England with reference to the Expediency of the Resumption of Cash Payments (1819), pp. 164–5.

[37] PP 1812 (3). Minutes of Evidence taken before the Committee of the whole House to whom it was referred to consider Several Petitions relating to the Orders in Council (1812), pp. 464, 469.

[38] PRO 30/8/276: Pitt papers, and PP 1819 (3), appx. 43.

[39] W. Boyd, *Letter to the Right Honourable William Pitt*, 2nd edn (London, 1811); *CDC*, XIX (1811), p. 898.

1809 might be summarized as follows. Britain's balance of payments was adverse because imports had increased. Imports had increased because domestic prices had risen and domestic prices had risen simply because the supply of credit had increased.[40] Modern Ricardians (including François Crouzet) castigated supporters of official monetary policy for failing to see, in the words of Jacob Viner, 'that a very important factor determining the relative demand for and supply of foreign bills was the relative level of prices which in turn was determined largely by the relative amounts of currency'.[41]

None of the contemporary or modern proponents of the view (such as Victor Morgan) that monetary policy raised export prices collected statistics to substantiate the point.[42] In fact prices of exported commodities rose less rapidly than the general index of domestic prices. Only Arthur Young took the trouble to find out about prices abroad and he observed that Britain was not the only country to experience price inflation between 1790 and 1815.[43] On the contrary, modern evidence shows that inflation was widespread among European countries and the United States.[44] Information on the prices of foreign commodities that competed with British exports on world markets is meagre but since the rate of technical progress was probably more rapid in British industry than elsewhere, it is difficult to see how British goods could have been undercut.[45] Receipts from exports may have been higher if prices had risen less rapidly, but there is no evidence that exports suffered seriously from inflation. Given that the uneven distribution of income during the war, which widened as a result of the lag of wages behind prices and high taxation, constrained opportunities to increase sales on the home market that merchants simply had to sell more output overseas.[46]

---

[40] David Ricardo, 'The high price of bullion: a proof of the depreciation of bank notes, 1811', in Sraffa, ed., *Works and Correspondence*, III, pp. 47–128; and P. Hoare, *Reflections on the Possible Existence of National Bankruptcy* (London, 1811).

[41] Viner, *Studies*, p. 146; K. Wu Chi-Yuen, *An Outline of International Price Theories* (London, 1939), pp. 113–16; and François Crouzet, *L'économie britannique et le blocus continental*, 2nd edn (Paris, 1987).

[42] V. Morgan, 'Some aspects of the bank restriction period', *Economic History*, 3 (1939), 221.

[43] Arthur Young, *An Inquiry into the Rise of Prices in Europe During the Last 25 Years* (London, 1815).

[44] Earl J. Hamilton, *War and Prices in Spain, 1651–1800* (Cambridge, Mass., 1947), pp. 165–7; C. E. Labrousse, *Esquise du mouvement des prix et des revenues en france au XVIIIe siècle* (Paris, 1933), I, pp. 98, 105, 141; A. Chabert, *Essai sur les mouvements des revenues et de l'activité economique, 1798–1820* (Paris, 1949), I, pp. 226–37; G. F. Warren and F. A. Pearson, *Wholesale Prices, 1720–1932* (Ithaca, N.Y., 1932), pp. 120–3; E. R. Seligman, *Currency Inflation and Public Debts* (New York, 1921), pp. 25, 31, 35, 39, 57.

[45] Imlah, *Economic Elements*, pp. 94–5.

[46] Joel Mokyr and N. Savin, 'Stagflation in historical perspective: the Napoleonic wars revisited', *Research in Economic History*, 1 (1976), 198–259.

Superficially there appears to be more to the argument that monetary policy pushed up domestic prices and encouraged the import of cheaper substitutes. But comparisons of the indices of domestic wholesale and import prices show that except for years of bad harvests import prices increased more rapidly over the war years. Thus, the otherwise plausible arguments of Boyd, Ricardo, Viner and other bullionists, that the volume of imports increased because as domestic prices rose it was cheaper to purchase overseas, does not receive support from the statistics. Correlations of this kind are always open to the objection that an even slower rise in domestic prices might have depressed the volume of imports still further. Aggregate comparisons are, however, often misleading and a breakdown of the import price index into its component commodities reveals why the volume of imports cannot be represented as highly sensitive to changes in domestic prices. Most imports did not compete with domestic products but consisted of raw materials for British industry and foodstuffs that could not be produced within the country.[47] Thus only a small proportion of retained imports can be regarded as competitive with domestic production. Apart that is from grain imports; and Ricardo in his dispute with Thornton argued that purchases of foreign corn had increased because it was cheaper to purchase it abroad.[48] Thus, it may well be true that the supply of credit exerted some influence on wheat prices; but the principal reason why grain prices had risen was simply because of a run of bad harvests. In years of normal harvest yields, imports of grain became insignificant.[49]

There are other less important examples of imports which can be represented as substitutes for home-produced commodities; but the increased volume of merchandise imported can usually be explained by some deficiency in domestic supply. In general, foreign commodities did not compete on the home market for three reasons. First, price differentials between commodities produced in Britain and in countries overseas remained too narrow to encourage additional imports. Secondly (and to repeat the point), Britain was not the only country to experience inflation in wartime, and cost reducing innovations were surely being introduced more rapidly in Britain than anywhere else in the world economy. Thirdly, duties on imports rose to prohibitive levels during the war years. Probably without forethought the government implemented complementary tariff and monetary policies and inflation probably did little to reduce levels of effective protection afforded to British industry and

---

[47] J. Marshall, *A Digest of All the Accounts* (London, 1833) and *CDC*, I (1803–4), statistical appendix.
[48] Ricardo, 'High price of bullion', pp. 59–63.
[49] T. Tooke and W. Newmarch, *History of Prices, 1792–1837*, 6 vols. (London, 1838), I, pp. 179–88, 213–25, 258–76, 293–300, 319–28.

agriculture. Duties were not, however, sufficiently prohibitive to discourage the purchase of certain luxury items abroad. During the French wars large quantities of wine, spirits and tobacco continued to be imported and, though profitable to the revenue, became an added strain on the balance of payments. For this kind of commodity, domestic substitutes were not available and as luxury foodstuffs, consumed by the higher income groups, their demand remained highly inelastic.[50]

Merchants as investors or speculators?

Monetary policy incurred a great deal of contemporary criticism for promoting 'overtrading' and for encouraging merchants to become 'speculators' during the war. For example, William Huskisson believed there had been 'a departure from the true character of commerce. Merchants anticipating a gain . . . became of course anxious to procure credit to the greatest possible amount'. In his view, the result was 'over trading to a very great extent and that among the variety of recent commercial speculations many had failed and occasioned much individual calamity'. He asked Parliament if they did not 'see the race of old English merchants who could never persuade themselves to go beyond their capitals superseded by a set of mad extravagant speculators who never stopped so long as they could get credit'.[51] No doubt Huskisson had in mind those clerks described contemptuously by Sir Francis Baring as 'not worth a £100, establishing themselves as merchants and receiving . . . accommodation from the Bank'.[52] Malthus also asked 'whether the late unusual facility of obtaining discounts though it has undoubtedly tended to increase the capital of the country may not have given it so unsafe a direction as to subject it to losses which more than counter balance its first gains'; and whether the facility for procuring capital

had not obliged some of the most respectable mercantile capitalists, who, in the ways in which they were in the habit of carrying on their trade, scarcely ever failed of increasing national accumulation, to yield to the competition of a new and very different set of merchants who may be said to gamble in trade – who in the hope of great profits will risk any quantity of capital that they command and in whose hands, therefore, national accumulation is quite uncertain.[53]

With so many eloquent quotations available it is not surprising to find similar views in the histories of the period. The tradition that monetary

[50] P. K. O'Brien, 'The political economy of British taxation, 1660–1815', *EcHR*, 41 (1988), 1–32.
[51] *CDC*, XIX (1811), p. 340 and W. Huskisson, *The Question Concerning Depreciation* (London, 1810), p. 340.   [52] PP 1810 (3), p. 132.
[53] Malthus, 'Depreciation of paper currency', p. 365; J. M. Lauderdale, *The Depreciation of the Paper Currency Proved* (London, 1812), pp. 43–7; and see *CDC*, XIX (1811), pp. 334–6, 340, 346, 418–19, 526, 1050.

policy fostered a new breed of British merchants and encouraged a spirit of 'imprudence', 'adventurous enterprise', 'gambling' and even 'maniacal speculation' became firmly established in Victorian and later histories of commerce during the French wars.[54]

Before re-examining this argument in the historical context of trade in wartime, it is necessary to be clear what is implied by terms like speculation. Contemporaries held that overtrading occurred whenever supply exceeded demand in particular markets for exports or for commodity imports. Prices fell to a point where sales had to be made below cost and merchants incurred losses; many fell bankrupt and involved manufacturers, banks and other credit institutions in their collapse. In brief the argument asserts that easy credit conditions encouraged mercantile investments which resulted ultimately in losses for the economy as a whole.[55]

During the long conflict against France, the government needed to promote increases in national income in order to make more resources available for the war effort and to lighten the burden of taxation on society. On its external accounts the country required a surplus sufficient to pay for expenditure on the armed forces stationed overseas and to finance additional imports of military and naval supplies. If monetary policy stimulated expenditures upon non-essential imports, encouraged reckless investments by merchants and hindered exports, the classical critique holds water. Nevertheless, the role played by monetary policy in facilitating and stimulating overtrading can only be properly appraised in the context of fluctuations and instability in the international economy during those difficult years of global warfare between 1793 and 1815.

War slowed down the flow of British trade with Europe and the Americas at a time when production began to grow more rapidly and when British merchants appropriated a dominant share of the Atlantic carrying trade. Between 1793 and 1815 conditions upon world markets led to an unusually high degree of instability for the domestic economy. British merchants found it difficult to provide the economy with a continuous and smooth supply of imported raw materials and foodstuffs. Industrial production became more erratic, largely because its export markets were alternately closed and reopened through enemy action. In turn this imparted instability to the import of industrial raw materials. Government demands for military supplies also fluctuated with the tides of war. Furthermore, an unusual number of deficient harvests necessi-

[54] H. D. Macleod, *Theory and Practice of Banking* (London, 1855), II, p. 137; A. M. Andreades, *History of the Bank of England* (London, 1909), p. 219; A. E. Feavearyear, *The Pound Sterling* (Oxford, 1931), p. 181.

[55] T. Tooke, *Thoughts and Details in High and Low Prices, 1793–1822*, 2nd edn (London, 1824), pp. 63–5, 69, 73, 79; J. R. McCulloch, *A Treatise on the Practice and Principles of Commerce* (London, 1831), pp. 71–2.

tated sudden purchases of foreign grain which affected the general level of demand and production throughout the economy. In short, the incidence of economic warfare and defective harvests induced fluctuations in the British economy well beyond the amplitude experienced in peacetime, or probably in previous wars during the long eighteenth century.

As our narrative will now argue, the long wars with France made it necessary for the economy to carry much higher levels of inventories. On at least four occasions, interruptions to the flow of exports and imports meant that domestic production could only be carried on (and taxes collected) because merchants and manufacturers had invested heavily in stocks of temporarily unvendible commodities.

For example, strategically induced fluctuations in economic activity began with Napoleon's invasion and conquest of the Italian states in 1798–9, which prompted merchants to import additional quantities of thrown and raw silk in case the French army cut off supplies to the domestic silk industry.[56] When the French occupation of Holland and Italy disrupted trade in the summer of 1799, German and British merchants found themselves holding highly priced quantities of coffee and sugar.[57] At the same time a crisis occurred in Hamburg and over eighty mercantile houses failed but in London the Bank of England and other banks extended credit generously and Liverpool merchants secured credit direct from the government.[58] Although bankruptcy figures for November of that year rose above the monthly average more widespread failures had fortunately been avoided by the liberal extension of credit which enabled merchants to hold stocks until prices recovered.[59]

In the early months of 1801 a dispute with the northern powers arrested exports to the Baltic and merchandise en route for Scandinavia, Russia and Prussia had to be retained at warehouses in Liverpool, Hull and London until summer when the government reached a diplomatic compromise on the rights of neutral shipping. Fortunately British merchants had anticipated the possibility of a closure and had accumulated sufficient stocks of timber, flax and hemp to prevent prices rising too rapidly.[60]

---

[56] *Monthly Magazine* (December 1798), 494; (January 1799), 88 and (April 1799), 259.

[57] *Monthly Magazine* (July 1799), 508; (September 1799), 675; (November 1799), 843; *Commercial Magazine* (September 1799), 137; (November 1799), 217–18; Tooke and Newmarch, *History of Prices*, I, pp. 233–6.

[58] *Monthly Magazine* (October 1799), 762; (November 1799), p. 843; *Commercial Magazine* (November 1799), 217–18; *JHC*, LV, 752.

[59] S. G. Checkland, 'American versus West Indian traders in Liverpool', *JEcH*, 18 (1958), 147–8; *Commercial Magazine* (March 1800), 209.

[60] *Monthly Magazine* (1801), 86, 101, 182, 198, 286, 563, 586; PP 1805 (2). Report from the select committee to whom the 11th Report of the Commissioners of Naval Enquiry was referred (London, 1805), pp. 156–61.

At the Peace of Amiens in 1802 British manufacturers anticipated a high level of European demand and increased production; but the uncertainties of the peace treaty with France compelled merchants to stockpile until the French position became clear.[61] In the event their anticipatory investment avoided almost certain losses from confiscation when war broke out in 1803. Their foresight paid off again in 1804–5, when they purchased raw silk supplies to obviate shortages that could flow from threatened reconquest of Italy by French forces.[62]

From the summer of 1807 to the autumn of 1808, the interruption to trade with Europe and America lead to economic depression and inventory investment on a very considerable scale. Napoleon's announcement of his plans to intensify the economic blockade of the British Isles and the beginnings of the American embargo on all trade with the United Kingdom prompted merchants to replenish their stocks of imported foodstuffs and raw materials.[63] In 1807 cotton brokers increased their purchases in the United States by 40 per cent and wool merchants doubled the normal import of merino wool from Spain.[64] Larking, the Navy's principal timber contractor, wrote to the Navy Board in 1806: 'The ports of the Baltic from which I had to import timber that I have contracted for being shut against me, I have turned my thoughts to other channels.'[65] Alas, too few English businessmen took the threat of economic isolation seriously enough to stockpile on a sufficient scale to obviate a rapid rise in prices which occurred when supplies from Europe and the United States were effectively obstructed from the autumn of 1807 through to the summer of 1808. Apparently the reserves of merino wool satisfied demand, but serious shortages of cotton, flax, hemp, raw silk and timber developed.[66]

For the re-export trades some quantitative notion of the volume of mercantile investment in stocks of colonial produce can be obtained by comparing the quantities imported with the quantities re-exported over the war years. Since there is no reason to expect domestic consumption to have increased significantly in that period the widening differential between the two provides evidence of increased investment in inventories of tropical groceries and tobacco.[67] Another statistical indicator of surplus

---

[61] *Monthly Magazine* (November 1801), 377; (December 1801), 474; (January 1802), 570; (February 1802), 94; (March 1802), 194; (April 1802), 306; (August 1802), 94.

[62] *Monthly Magazine* (September 1804), 421 and (May 1805), 518.

[63] Tooke, *Thoughts and Details*, pp. 69–70.

[64] Tooke and Newmarch, *History of Prices*, I, p. 300; W. B. Crump, *History of the Leeds Woollen Industry, 1780–1820* (Manchester, 1921), pp. 90–4.

[65] R. G. Albion, *Forests and Sea Power* (Cambridge, Mass., 1926), pp. 327, 337.

[66] Crouzet, *L'économie britannique*, I, pp. 394–5, and Tooke and Newmarch, *History of Prices*, I, p. 79.

[67] Relevant data are in B. R. Mitchell, *Abstract of British Historical Statistics* (Cambridge, 1962), pp. 274–337 (esp. p. 281).

stocks includes price data. Unable to market coffee and sugar in Europe British merchants attempted to sell more on the home market, and additional supplies depressed domestic prices. Thus in 1807 and 1808, and despite heavy indirect taxation, prices of colonial produce fell to unusually low levels.[68]

Furthermore, qualitative information that British merchants held enormous stocks of coffee, sugar, tobacco and rum is unusually abundant because of the very active campaign conducted by the West India interest for assistance from the government. Throughout the years 1806, 1807 and 1808 they appealed constantly to Parliament and the Committee of Trade.[69]

Between December 1806 and February 1808, no fewer than three select committees investigated their complaints.[70] One report confirmed that the 'obstacles opposed to the exportation of colonial produce added to its forced accumulation in the market . . . have been the principal causes for their plight'.[71] Parliament and its committees recommended that British distilleries should be compelled to use colonial sugar rather than grain and secondly that naval superiority should be used to restore something like a monopoly of the carrying trade to British shipping.[72] In November 1807 the British government issued an order in council to blockade the mainland of Europe to all neutral ships which had not called at a British port and paid customs dues. By then Continental markets had been more effectively closed and the restraints imposed on foreign shipping only increased stocks of colonial produce held in British warehouses.

There can also be no doubt that Napoleon's continental system seriously affected the cotton industry. In the autumn of 1807 manufacturers and export houses held considerable stocks of cotton cloth. By February of 1808 a deteriorating situation prompted employers and their employees from Lancashire cotton towns to petition Parliament against the orders in council, which had closed American markets to them.[73]

---

[68] Tooke, *Thoughts and Details*, pp. 61, 77.

[69] *JHC*, LVII, 857, 942; LXI, 77; LXII, pp. 668, 674; *Reports of the Historical Manuscripts Commission on the Manuscripts of J. B. Fortescue* (London, 1915), VIII, pp. 162–3, 454–6, 469–72, 489–90; and BL, Add. MSS. Papers of William Eden, Lord Auckland, 1744–1814, vols. 34,454 and 34,457.

[70] PP 1806–7 (2). Report from the Committee Appointed to consider the Expediency of permitting the use of Sugar and Molasses in the Distillery and Brewery (1807); PP 1807 (3). Report from the Committee appointed to take into consideration the Commercial State of the West Indies; PP 1808 (4). Reports from the Committee appointed to Enquire how far it may be practicable to confine the Distilleries of the United Kingdom to the use of Sugar and Molasses.

[71] PP 1808 (4), pp. 3–4.   [72] *CPD*, VIII, pp. 238–9 and IX, pp. 735, 1151–3.

[73] PP 1808 (10). Minutes of Evidence taken at the Bar of the House upon taking into Consideration Petitions etc. respecting the orders in council (1808), pp. 344–5, and *CPD*, X, pp. 742–3, 889, 1056–8, 1236, 1281, 1350–1.

They appealed to the House to sue for peace and workmen wanted their wages regulated.[74] But when George Rose introduced a bill 'to limit the excessive depression of wages on persons employed in weaving cotton', Sir Robert Peel opposed it on the grounds that 'the greatest cause of distress at present felt was not the oppression of the masters but the shutting up of the foreign markets and the fact was the masters were now suffering from this cause still more than the men'.[75]

The West Riding woollen industry and other textile industries seem no less affected by the closing of markets in Europe and the United States. Yorkshire's businessmen also petitioned the government to negotiate a peace, and their more desperate employees smashed machinery.[76] Production in the Scottish linen industry declined and it was not until 1810 that Thomas Leach, the Leicester hosier, succeeded in clearing stock he had accumulated in 1808 and 1809. The Midlands also experienced acute depression.[77] At Christmas 1808 George Broom's stocks of carpets at Kidderminster were worth £20,000 more than they had been the previous year. Silk weavers of Coventry and Spitalfields suffered broadly from unemployment.[78]

From the autumn of 1808 to the spring of 1810 the blockade lifted and an export boom to Europe and to the United States developed. Merchants and manufacturers ran down their stocks, prices rose and production revived again.[79] Productive capacity in the export sector increased and British merchants and shippers assumed almost complete responsibility for the world's carrying trade in colonial produce.[80] The rising prices and depleted stocks of 1808 (together with the continued threat of complete interruption to supplies both from Europe and the United States) encouraged British merchants and manufacturers to import heavily throughout 1809 and the early months of 1810.[81] Imports of cotton, wool, silk, tallow, dyestuffs, timber, flax and hemp all rose well above average.[82] There were

[74] PP 1808 (2). Report of the Committee to whom the Petitions of Cotton Manufacturers and Cotton Weavers were Referred, 1808, pp. 97–134.

[75] *CPD* (1811), XI, pp. 425–7.

[76] PP 1808 (10), pp. 119–24 and H. James, *History of the Worsted Manufacture in England* (London, 1857), p. 368.

[77] D. J. Davies, 'The condition of England during the revolutionary and Napoleonic periods as illustrated by the history of Birmingham between the years 1789–1815' (unpublished manuscript in Birmingham Public Reference Library), pp. 86–7 and 98–100.

[78] PP 1812 (3). Minutes of Evidence taken before the Committee of the Whole House to whom it was referred to consider several petitions relating to the orders in council (1812), pp. 125, 193.

[79] Eli Heckscher, *The Continental System* (Oxford, 1926), pp. 180–2, 236.

[80] PP 1810 (3), pp. 58, 62 and G. Chalmers, *Considerations on Commerce, Bullion, Coin, Circulation and Exchange* (London, 1811), pp. 10, 25, 65.

[81] *CPD*, XIX, p. 942.   [82] Marshall, *Digest of the Accounts*.

possibilities for the direct import of raw cotton from the United States. Before the outbreak of war of 1812, existed for three months in 1809, seven months in 1810 and two months in 1811. During that time British merchants anticipated a more prolonged cessation of supplies and purchased cotton on a considerable scale. The 199,000 bales which came into Liverpool in 1810 turned out to be a record for the decade.[83] In the event direct imports from the United States became impossible from 1811 to 1815, but while prices rose the shortage never became serious enough to disrupt textile production. Large stocks had been built up in 1809–10 and Brazilian cotton provided the industry with an alternative source of supply.[84] In addition, merchants successfully smuggled a considerable quantity of cotton out of the United States and a large part of their purchases came into Liverpool, London and Glasgow through Denmark, Sweden, Spain, the Azores and Florida.[85]

With Wellington's troops in Portugal supplies of merino wool could be procured from Spain through Lisbon, but the shortage of timber became a serious cause of concern. Napoleon succeeded in closing one Baltic port after another. Danzig fell to French troops in May 1807. Memel and Stettin remained closed, while at Riga and St Petersburg the Russian government confiscated timber bound for England.[86] Quantities of Baltic wood continued to reach England in neutral ships. Smuggling helped, and at Danzig French officials connived at illegal exports, but it was much more difficult to import bulky commodities like timber by such methods. In 1809–10 timber shortages remained acute enough for the government to give positive encouragement to the development of an alternative source of supply from Canada.[87] Duties on European timber were successively increased to offset the differential in transport costs. 'With dramatic suddenness the North American timber trade burst into life' and alleviated the shortage.[88] Before 1807 British North America had supplied only a fraction of the kingdom's timber requirements. From 1807 to 1815 Canada provided most of the requirements for shipbuilding and nearly half of British imports of pine timber.[89]

From the spring of 1810 until autumn of 1812 the Napoleonic empire reimposed an even more effective blockade and the United States

<hr>

[83] G. W. Daniels, 'American cotton trade with Liverpool under the embargo and non-intercourse Acts', *AHR* 21 (1915–16), 276–87; T. Baines, *History of the Commerce and Town of Liverpool and the Rise of Manufacturing Industry in the Adjoining Counties* (London, 1852), pp. 735–6.

[84] Daniels, 'American cotton trade', pp. 284–5.

[85] T. Ellison, *The Cotton Trade of Great Britain* (London, 1886), pp. 86–7.

[86] Albion, *Forests and Sea Power*, pp. 336–43.   [87] *The Annual Register* (1809), 698.

[88] BL, Add. MSS of J. B. Fortescue (Dropmore papers), VIII, fos. 212, 353–8.

[89] H. Bliss, *The Timber Trade* (London, 1831) and Anon, *Observations on the Timber Trade* (London, 1821), chs. 7–9.

attempted to force the British government to rescind its orders in council against neutral shipping by closing the American market to British goods and enforcing an embargo on exports to Britain. In these two years several sectors of the domestic economy, dependent on foreign trade, encountered a second and even more severe crisis. At times imported supplies from the Continent and the United States became impossible to procure. Alternative supplies of timber came in from Canada, cotton fibres from Brazil and raw silk from India. Nevertheless, the heavy investment of the previous eighteen months in inventories prevented shortages from developing on the scale previously experienced in 1808 and prices remained more stable.

From the winter of 1812–13 it became possible to import from Europe again and merchants replenished their stocks. During the early months of 1814, anticipating an export boom at the close of the war, they invested heavily in industrial raw materials.[90] Merchants could not, however, import raw cotton directly from the United States until December 1814, but the stocks built up in 1810 together with Brazilian and Indian supplies helped the industry to last out until the British and American governments finally made peace.[91]

During the crisis years of 1810–12, trades in colonial produce once again excited the most voluminous comment.[92] Statements from merchants and observations from pamphleteers, the press and select committees of Parliament that British merchants were holding considerable quantities of colonial produce in warehouses at London, Bristol, Liverpool and Glasgow became abundant.[93] In the spring of 1811 the select committee on commercial credit found

that great distress was felt in a quarter which was much connected with this trade, namely, amongst the importers of produce from the foreign West India Islands, and from South America and the commercial agent for the City Corporation of Liverpool told the Committee how the greater part of the immense product of those places now comes to fill the warehouses and exhaust the capitals of the merchants of this country.[94]

[90] Tooke and Newmarch, *History of Prices*, I, p. 344.
[91] Daniels, 'American cotton trade', pp. 284–6.
[92] PP 1823 (4). Report from the select committee appointed to inquire into the State of the Law related to Goods, Wares, Merchandise intrusted to Merchants, Agents, Factors, etc., pp. 306, 347–8, 352, 369–71.
[93] *Monthly Magazine* (February 1810), 93; (May 1810), 404; (June 1810), 514; (July 1810), 616; (August 1810), 95; (November 1810), 387; (January 1811), 591; (February 1811), 109; (March 1811), 197 and (April 1811), 305. PP 1812 (3), pp. 99, 345, 374, 378, 429, 491–3, 631, 663, 667; PP 1823 (4), pp. 343, 347, 357, 369–70, 376, 385, 407.
[94] PP 1810–11 (2). Report from the select committee appointed to take into consideration the present state of commercial credit (1811), pp. 368–71.

Stocks of unsaleable merchandise were to be found not only in warehouses at British ports but at entrepôt islands off the enemy coast or at collecting points on the mainland of Europe.[95]

Even if 'the enterprising exporter succeeded in getting his merchandise deposited in a place of safety (an entrepôt) and surmounted the first difficulties he had to encounter the still greater difficulties in conveying them to a market of consumption'.[96] At Heligoland, for example, a gentleman told Sir Philip Francis that 'from the beach to the stairs he had walked up to his ankles in salted sugar and coffee'.[97]

Widespread depression afflicted British industries manufacturing for the export trades and they were compelled to reduce production and stockpile on a considerable scale.[98] In its report, the select committee on commercial distress observed that 'the embarrassments and distresses were of an extensive nature' and the committee recommended a programme of government loans to help merchants and manufacturers to

gradually to contract their operation, to call in their means to withhold from immediate sale, articles which at present can fetch only most ruinous prices and to keep up the employment of their machinery and their workmen, though upon a very reduced and limited scale; it will divide and spread the pressure of this distress over a larger space of time and enable them to meet it with consequences less ruinous to themselves and less destructive to the interests of the community.[99]

That distress in the Scottish and Lancashire cotton industries is revealed in petitions to Parliament, memorials to the Treasury and in evidence before select committees of the House.[100] Sir Robert Peel, speaking for Lancashire, observed that 'the greatest manufacturers had reduced the quantity of their work by one third, others by one half and others again had been obliged to discharge their workmen altogether' and James Kay of Bury told Parliament that 'we never had so large a stock'.[101] For the woollen industry military orders mitigated the loss of export markets but the industry still sent representatives to Parliament to complain that the orders in council had led to the accumulation of cloth at the factories and warehouses.[102] Suffering in the hosiery industry led to

---

[95] PP 1812 (3), pp. 239, 277, 297.
[96] J. Atkinson, *A Letter on the High Price of Gold Bullion* (London, 1811), p. 96.
[97] P. Francis, *Reflections on the Abundance of Paper in Circulation* (London, 1810), p. 96.
[98] Gayer *et al.*, *Growth and Fluctuations*, II, pp. 535, 549.   [99] PP 1810–11 (2), p. 371.
[100] PP 1810–11 (2), pp. 367–73; *CPD*, XIX, pp. 1017–19; G. W. Daniels, 'The cotton trade during the Revolutionary and Napoleonic wars', *Transactions of the Manchester Statistical Society* (1915–16), 53–8.
[101] *CPD*, XIX, pp. 254, 344; PP 1812 (3), p. 218.
[102] PP 1810–11 (2), pp. 371–2, and 1812 (3), pp. 218, 330; Crump, *Leeds Woollen Industry*, pp. 119, 126, 141.

outbreaks of Luddism,[103] while representatives from the metallurgical trades located in the Midlands and around Sheffield easily convinced Parliament about the extent of distress in their areas. Thomas Potts, a merchant of Birmingham, told the House of Commons, 'the manufacturers have been keeping their men employed in creating stock; piling that stock upon their shelves; they have got the whole capital engaged in a stock three parts finished'.[104] At Sheffield another merchant observed that 'manufacturers were reduced to very great distress, the mercantile houses having in general good capitals were not reduced to actual distress but I apprehend most of their capitals are lying in stocks'.[105]

After the battle of Leipzig, as several countries became liberated from French control British merchants anticipated the prospects for high profits from 'pent up' European demand and invested heavily in stocks of home produced and colonial commodities. Prices of coffee, sugar and other colonial produce rose rapidly, and industrial production recovered. Heavy shipments of goods left for Baltic markets. At the end of 1813 merchants even exported directly to France. By January 1814 it was apparent that war in Europe would terminate very shortly. More inventory accumulation occurred but when hostilities finally ceased in May 1814 the anticipated demand did not materialize because Europe recovered but slowly from the ravages of this devastating war.[106] With hindsight Tooke observed that 'the disastrous effects of these ill judged and extravagantly extensive speculations began to manifest themselves in the numerous failures which took place at the close of 1817'.[107] Tooke's interpretation has, however, been accepted too uncritically by economists like Hawtrey and Macleod, who noted that export speculations peaked in the spring of 1814 and were followed by a violent revulsion and general depreciation of prices.[108] Even Acworth condemned merchants who 'speculated on the almost unlimited demand among the inhabitants of the continent for those goods from the use of which they had been so long debarred, but Europe was limited in its means of purchase'.[109] What these accounts of 1813–15 do not mention is that the United States market remained closed and that a considerable proportion of those exports sent

[103] PP 1812 (2). Report from the select committee to take into consideration the Several Petitions . . . by Persons Employed in the Framework Knitting Trade (1812), pp. 211–306.

[104] PP 1812 (3), pp. 19–22, 29, 46, 67, 74, 96, and Davies, *Birmingham*, pp. 97–100.

[105] PP 1812 (3), p. 135 and G. H. Lloyd, *The Cutlery Trades* (London, 1913), pp. 339–40.

[106] G. W. Daniels, 'The cotton trade at the close of the Napoleonic wars', *Transactions of the Manchester Statistical Society* (1917–18), 18–19.

[107] Tooke, *Thoughts and Details*, pp. 97–9.

[108] R. Hawtrey, *Currency and Credit* (London, 1923), p. 286 and H. D. Macleod, *Theory and Practice of Banking* (1855), II, p. 181.

[109] A. W. Acworth, *Financial Reconstruction in England, 1815–22* (London, 1925), p. 72.

in desperation to Europe consisted of 'pent up' stocks produced for the American market. As Vansittart (the chancellor of the Exchequer) told Castlereagh the American carrying trade with Europe which had fallen into British hands constituted a further strain on the country's extended resources.[110]

Conclusions: merchants, monetary policy and the economy in wartime

Assertions by contemporaries and historians that the policy initiated by Pitt of allowing the rate of exchange to float between 1797 and 1815 exercised deleterious effects on the British economy and the war effort seem difficult to support. Nor does the evidence required to underpin the bullionist criticism that the inconvertible currency had increased deficits on the balance of trade look convincing. For these years the behaviour of bankers and merchants, operating within the framework of a flexible monetary policy, can only be appraised against the background of political disruption and commercial disorganization which characterized the world economy during a period of European and global warfare.

In that context the official monetary policy can be defended because it enabled financial institutions to support and to share in the enormous risks involved in trading overseas in wartime. As Clive Day observed, at sea 'France . . . sought to destroy the commerce on which the life of England depended by sending out innumerable privateers to prey upon it'.[111] In 1797 nearly a thousand British ships were captured by corsairs and after 1812 the British mercantile marine was further afflicted by 'Yankee marauders'.[112] Although the Admiralty organized convoys from 1797 onwards, nearly 11,000 merchant ships were lost to the enemy between 1793 and 1814, and the average ratio of losses to the total number of ships employed in foreign trade rose to nearly 8 per cent per annum.[113]

Wartime delays in trans-shipment also involved British merchants in increased losses.[114] When orders arrived late exporters could be required by the terms of their contract to repatriate the merchandise. Moreover, British merchants consigned large quantities of goods every year to the great fairs of northern Europe and if they failed to catch this seasonal demand their losses could become very large indeed.[115] At several points

---

[110] BL, Vansittart papers, vol. 31,231, letter dated 26 November 1814.
[111] C. Day, *A History of Commerce* (London, 1925), pp. 342–3.
[112] A. T. Mahan, *Sea Power in its Relations to the War of 1812* (1905), II, pp. 207, 211.
[113] A. Ward *et al.*, eds., *Cambridge Modern History* (1904–6), VIII, pp. 485–6.
[114] C. Wright and C. E. Fayle, *A History of Lloyds* (London, 1928), pp. 188–91.
[115] Arthur Redford, *Manchester Merchants and Foreign Trade* (Manchester, 1934), pp. 7, 32, 45–8.

en route to or from Europe or the Americas, British goods passed through the hands of neutral shipping companies or smuggling organizations of one kind and another and the prospects for safe delivery by such unfamiliar means could certainly be much less than they had been through the normal commercial organizations. Yet merchants had to take risks for often their wares could be bought or sold in no other way. On land risks looked no less serious and examples of the confiscation of British property by enemy actions on the Continent, in the United States and in the ports of the Spanish empire are numerous.[116]

Furthermore, and for several reasons, between 1793 and 1815 the time taken between manufacture and the payment for commodities sold abroad definitely lengthened. First a higher proportion of British trade travelled between more distant markets. Shipping space was usually in short supply because the government commandeered a large number of merchant ships for the navy and prevented foreign ships from filling the gap by rigorous implementation of the Navigation Laws.[117] Delays in transit became a common feature of international trade because convoys took time to assemble and smuggling networks had to be developed or contacted. Merchandise was often transferred between ships or from one entrepôt to another before it reached its final destination. Finally the exploitation of new markets and new sources of supply involved British merchants in the construction of new commercial and distributive organizations.

During the French wars, London's credit institutions took over the financing of an increased share of world trade. Britain's own share of global trade expanded and British merchants also carried a much larger proportion of the produce of the Americas to Europe, as the conquest of enemy colonies in the Caribbean, the opening up of the Spanish and Portuguese empires in South America and the command of the seas enjoyed by the Royal Navy gave British merchants (and shipping) almost a monopoly of the Atlantic carrying trade.[118] Furthermore, the disruption of commercial organization in Europe (occasioned by French occupation of the great commercial marts of Amsterdam and Hamburg) meant that London's credit houses assumed more and more responsibility for the finance of international trade. In the two decades after 1793 the bill on London became the dominant means of settlement in international trade.[119]

[116] Heckscher, *Continental System*, pp. 26, 82–3, 97, 234.
[117] C. E. Fayle, 'Shipowning and marine insurance', in C. Northcote Parkinson, ed., *The Trade Winds* (London, 1948), pp. 34–5; and Mahan, *Sea Power*, p. 229.
[118] PP 1812 (3), pp. 86–7, 93, 133, 327, 354–5, 464, 517, 631; and Ralph W. Hidy, *The House of Barings in American Trade and Finance* (Cambridge, Mass., 1949), pp. 27–30.
[119] PP 1810 (3), pp. 58, 65, 73–5, 82, 85, 98; and G. Chalmers, *A Historical View of the Domestic Economy of Britain and Ireland* (London, 1812), pp. 9, 11, 26–7, 71.

As our chronological narrative of fluctuations in foreign and domestic production suggests, flexible supplies of credit from banks and other financial intermediaries made it possible for merchants and manufacturers to stockpile whenever the enemy successfully interrupted the flow of exports and re-exports to Europe and the Americas; or whenever France or the United States threatened to cut off supplies of foodstuffs and industrial raw materials. Wartime conditions between 1793 and 1815 made it very difficult for merchants to provide the economy with a smooth and continuous supply of raw materials. Demand at home became volatile because of blockades to export markets, and because government demand for military goods was also sporadic in nature. The unusual succession of bad harvests engendered not merely unpredictable changes in the purchase of imported grain, but sudden drops in the general level of demand for industrial commodities. Faced with the prospect of obstruction to supplies of foreign raw materials merchants first hurriedly built up inventories and then attempted to find alternative sources of supply such as Brazil for cotton or Canada for timber, or they organized networks for smuggling.

Although conditions in international commodity markets made it imperative for the economy to hold higher levels of stocks per unit of output, bullionists claimed that the opportunities afforded by easy credit conditions encouraged merchants to overtrade on such a considerable scale that prices fell rapidly and involved them and their bankers and suppliers in losses and even failures. The increased facility for procuring credit must have encouraged some 'unproductive speculation' of the kind condemned by bullionists and historians. Nevertheless, it is another monetarist fallacy to represent unwarranted speculation as primarily responsible for the losses encountered by mercantile banking and credit houses engaged in international commerce between 1793 and 1815. More often than not their difficulties surely came from adverse external conditions and not from foolhardy investments. Monetary policy only permitted, and did not cause, the heavy mercantile build up of commodity stocks and the inventory cycle in imported raw materials that persisted throughout the first half of the nineteenth century – a fact which is not that surprising for times when commercial communications remained undeveloped and transport slow.[120] Some kind of generalized response to rising prices remained for a long time characteristic of competitive firms operating in international commodity markets. Small-scale mercantile enterprises importing independently of each other 'overstocked' markets and made losses because they could not hold commodities for any length

---

[120] R. C. O. Matthews, *A Study in Trade Cycle History* (Oxford, 1954), pp. 25–6.

of time. During the French wars existing deficiencies in the basic organization for the import markets became greatly exacerbated by enemy obstruction to British sources of supply. At times prices of available stocks rose to extraordinary heights. Losses subsequently occurred because the response was over-enthusiastic. Fluctuations in investment in commodity stocks which took place can, however, be largely explained as the anticipation or the reactions of merchants to the closing and reopening of foreign sources of supply in Europe and the United States and we must observe that domestic manufacturers gained by the ready availability and reduced prices of raw materials.

Inventory accumulation in 1800–1, 1807 and in 1809–10 certainly added to wartime strains on the balance of payments. It depleted gold reserves and depreciated the rate of exchange which added to the expense of buying essential supplies from overseas. Nevertheless, the longer-term need of the economy on such occasions was to stockpile in order to avoid serious shortages of essential raw materials. The advantages of having Baltic timber and American cotton available when supplies became unobtainable in 1811 and 1812 offset the disadvantages of the depreciated exchange in 1809 and 1810. Even if the ready availability of credit encouraged some import of 'non-essential' foodstuffs and luxury goods, such commodities formed only a small part of total imports and were already heavily taxed. In any case the argument is really a criticism of relying too heavily on the price mechanism and of not resorting to more direct controls over imports, rather than of credit policy as such. Yet at the time controls were represented as despotism.[121]

Monetary policy also enabled merchants and manufacturers working for the export trades to invest heavily in stocks during the crisis years of 1793, 1797, 1799, 1807–8 and 1810–12. Wartime governments certainly appreciated the advantages credit could play in alleviating or anticipating economic depressions, and on four occasions the Treasury provided loans to tide the private sector over liquidity crises. Their monetarist critics remained unimpressed and countered with the charge that the banking system encouraged overtrading and drew contrasts between 'great old capitalists' and 'visionary speculators'. Apparently the former were 'guided by prudence' while the latter were 'men of adventurous and speculative dispositions whose spirit of enterprise needed to be curbed'.

It may well be that the facility of procuring credit encouraged British merchants to become less cautious, but bullionists overlooked the obvious and central point that the risks of trade had increased enormously after 1793. Operating without the constraints imposed by convertibility,

---

[121] G. Rose, *Observations Respecting the Public Expenditure and the Influence of the Crown* (London, 1810), p. 43.

the encouragement afforded by credit institutions to merchants to brave the uncertain conditions endemic to wartime trade undoubtedly raised the level of the volume of merchandise sold abroad. Perhaps Francis Baring's 'race of old English merchants' were superseded by a 'new and very different set of merchants', 'not guided by the same prudence'. Nevertheless, the expansion of foreign trade in the difficult circumstances of long wars against revolutionary and Napoleonic France did not call for old English merchants, prudence or caution but for adventurous, daring, imagination, a willingness to exploit every opportunity afforded by political and administrative weaknesses on the part of the enemy and the opening of markets in new and untried parts of the world like South America.

Finally, in all these attacks on 'speculators' there is a touch of pious hindsight because successful speculators mature into 'real' English merchants. Contemporaries, economists and historians, who have myopically castigated Pitt's wartime monetary policy for its unsubstantiated macroeconomic disadvantages and for the encouragement it gave to reckless overtrading, downplay the nature of international commerce during the French wars. That protracted and costly conflict (which left Britain as the hegemonic naval, commercial and imperial power for more than a century after Waterloo) could hardly have been financed on the gold standard. Bullionists then and monetarists now remain ideologically opposed to flexibility and discretion for statesmen and bankers.

11 America and the crisis of the British imperial economy, 1803–1807[*]

François Crouzet

During the early years of its war against Napoleon, Britain, after a recession in 1803, was on the upswing of a trade cycle, which peaked in 1806, and was not unprosperous. Its domestic exports (mostly manufactured goods) increased in volume by 24 per cent from 1803 to 1806. On the other hand, its re-exports of foreign and colonial merchandise (mainly produce from British colonies) stagnated, as is shown by table 11.1.

Behind these figures loom serious economic difficulties, which, during those years, were affecting the 'sugar islands' of the Caribbean, the fisheries of Newfoundland, the colonies of British North America, the East India trade, and also the British merchant fleet, so that one can speak of a crisis of the imperial economy. A common factor behind the troubles of those different sectors was competition from American shipping and trade, which in some cases involved an American penetration into the imperial economy. Those economic developments were to have serious consequences for political relations between Britain and the United States.

The British West Indies had reached their peak of prosperity in the years before the American Revolution. They had suffered greatly during the War of American Independence, as the Royal Navy had lost the control of the seas. In the decade which followed 1783, the growth of production appears to have been slow, but profits recovered, and it is 'not proven' that the fall of the planter class had started. The slaves' revolt in Saint–Domingue – or 'the destruction of San Domingo', as British observers called it at the time – brought to the British islands several years of great prosperity. Within a few months the first producer of sugar in the world, which was making as much sugar as all the British West Indies, was eliminated, so that sugar became a scarce commodity and its prices increased fast, to reach a peak in the late 1790s: an index of the average

[*] The author thanks two anonymous referees for their useful comments and suggestions.

278

Table 11.1. *Re-exports from Great Britain*

Year	£ millions Official values	Index 1806 = 100
1802	14.4	158
1803	9.3	102
1804	10.5	115
1805	9.3	102
1806	6.1	100
1807	9.4	103

Source: François Crouzet, *L'économie britannique et le blocus continental*, 2nd edn (Paris, 1987), tables 3 and 5, pp. 885, 887.

yearly price of brown sugar in London rises by 126 per cent from 1785/9 to 1795/9. The profitability of sugar-making increased markedly: according to adjusted estimates, by J. R. Ward, from a sample of plantations, average rates of profit for all the British West Indies rose from 8.5 per cent in 1783/91 to 12.6 per cent in 1792/8. Planters were to remember with nostalgia the happy 1790s.[1]

This prosperity, however, was short lived. The high prices of sugar caused a fast increase of its cultivation and production. First in the 'Old British West Indies':[2] imports of sugar from there in Britain rose from 1,571,000 cwt in 1789 to 3,193,000 cwt in 1806. Secondly, some of the 'Conquered islands' (i.e. colonies of Britain's enemies which the British occupied – mainly Trinidad and Dutch Guiana) had large areas of virgin and fertile land, which were put under cultivation, thanks to an inflow of British capital. Produce from those conquests was admitted in Britain on the same footing as that from the old colonies. The result was a strong increase in British imports of

---

[1] Lowell Joseph Ragatz, *The Fall of the Planter Class in the British Caribbean, 1763–1832* (New York, 1928), pp. vii–viii, 190, 204–6; J. R. Ward, 'The profitability of sugar planting in the British West Indies, 1650–1834', *EcHR*, 31 (1978), 197–8, 204, table 6, 207, table 9, 210–12; McCusker and Menard, *Economy of British America*, pp. 167, 368, 376. See also: *Edinburgh Review*, 11, no. 21, October 1807, 157 ff.; PP, 1807, III, pp. 11, 58; PP, 1808, IV, p. 107. The index of prices (customs duties excluded) is based upon J. Marshall, *A Digest of all the Accounts diffused through more than 600 volumes of Journals, Reports and Papers presented to Parliament since 1799*, part III: *A Statistical Display of the Finances, Navigation and Commerce of the United Kingdom* (London, 1833), p. 178. The pessimistic views of Ragatz – a continuous decline of the British West Indies since 1763 – have been much qualified by later writers, e.g. Seymour Drescher, *Econocide: British Slavery in the Era of Abolition* (Pittsburgh, 1977) and 'Le "déclin" du système esclavagiste britannique et l'abolition de la traite', *Annales ESC*, 31 no. 2 (1976), 414–35.

[2] I.e. the islands which Britain owned before 1793.

Table 11.2. *Imports of sugar in Britain (yearly average in million cwt)*

1790/2	1.8
1793/6	2.2
1798/1801	3.3
1802	4.3

Source: E. B. Schumpeter, *English Overseas Trade Statistics 1697–1808* (Oxford, 1960), table H, pp. 58–9. Current values of sugar imports have been computed by Ralph Davis, *The Industrial Revolution and British Overseas Trade* (Leicester, 1979), table 24, p. 37 (£ million): 1784/6, 2.6; 1794/6, 5.9; 1804/6, 6.9.

Table 11.3. *Re-exports from Britain of raw sugar (including the equivalent of refined sugar exports) (million cwt)*

1790	0.2
1795	0.9
1800	1.6
1802	2.0

Source: From Schumpeter, *English Overseas Trade*, pp. 62, 65, tables 18, 30. Current values of sugar re-exports from Davis, *The Industrial Revolution*, pp. 102–4, tables 49, 50, 51 (£ million): 1784/6, 0.2; 1794/6, 1.3; 1804/6, 0.9. The raw sugar equivalent of refined sugar has been calculated according to the ratio 17 to 10.

sugar, specially from 1798 onwards (they doubled from 1797 to 1802).[3]

As a consequence the working of the sugar market in Britain underwent a complete change. In the eighteenth century, the home market absorbed almost the entire empire's sugar output. But, after 1793, British consumption of sugar did not keep pace with imports,[4] so that most addi-

---

[3] *Edinburgh Review*, 11, no. 21, 146; PP, 1807, III, p. 72; Ragatz, *The Fall*, p. 308; J. Holland Rose, 'British West Indian commerce as a factor in the Napoleonic War', *Cambridge Historical Journal*, 3 (1929), 35; Eric Williams, *Capitalism and Slavery* (Chapel Hill, N.C., 1944), pp. 149–50; Drescher, 'Le déclin', pp. 420, 434, n. 14. Some sugar was also imported from the East Indies and, through 'free ports' in the British West Indies, from foreign colonies.

[4] Consumption suffered in the 1790s from the rise in prices, which was aggravated by that of customs duties (which increased from 15s. per cwt in 1791 to 27s. in 1805). According to Davis, *The Industrial Revolution*, pp. 44–5, table 27, consumption per capita in 1794/6 was 15 per cent lower than in 1784/6, but by 1804/6 it was 20 per cent higher,

tional imports had to be re-exported, and the British market was no longer protected and isolated. However, there was no danger as long as sugar was scarce and its international market a seller's market. Indeed, thanks to increased production in its empire, Britain replaced France as the main supplier of sugar to Continental countries, and for some years its exportable surplus was easily sold off.

However, the high level of sugar prices and planters' profits brought about an increase of production, not only in British colonies, but also in other territories, especially in Brazil and Cuba. Within a few years, the deficit in the world sugar output, which the ruin of Saint-Domingue had opened, was made good, while it is likely that the rise of European consumption was slowed down by the war and the economic difficulties it created. There was soon an overproduction of sugar at the world (or at least the Atlantic) scale, and in 1799 sugar prices collapsed on all markets. Henceforth sharp international competition prevailed and the British West Indies were affected.[5]

This renewed competition was made possible by the tolerant policy of the British government towards trade by neutrals with enemy colonies. Indeed, once the Batavian Republic and Spain were at war with Britain, almost all non-British sugar producing territories – except Brazil – were owned by enemies of England. The latter, which was ruling the seas, might have prevented the transport to Europe of those territories' produce. Indeed, on 6 November 1793, an order in council prescribed the capture and condemnation of all neutral ships trading with the French colonies (the idea was that they would be starved to capitulation). This resulted in the capture of hundreds of American ships (which were taking advantage of the opening of French colonial ports), violent discontent in the United States, and strong remonstrances by the American administration. The British had to retreat: a new order, of 8 January 1794, only prescribed the capture of neutral ships, laden with the produce of enemy colonies, which were sailing *directly* from those colonies towards Europe. American ships were thus implicitly allowed to trade between the French colonies and their own ports. This tolerance was extended to European neutrals by an order of 25 January 1798. This was confirmed in a judgment of 1800, by Sir William Scott, judge of the High Court of Admiralty, and in a report of 1801 by the King's Advocate, Christopher

as consumers returned to their old habits. This is confirmed by B. R. Mitchell, *British Historical Statistics* (Cambridge, 1988), p. 709, which gives yearly figures. See also *Edinburgh Review*, 11, no. 21, 160, and 13, no. 26, 386 ff.

[5] *Edinburgh Review*, 11, no. 21, 155–8; BL, Add. MS 38,737, fos.21–36, memorandum by Huskisson, 27 Sept. 1807; Ragatz, *The Fall*, p. 309. Exports of sugar from Cuba are said to have increased sixfold from 1790 to 1805, i.e. from 200,000 to 1,275,000 cwt.

Robinson, which was officially transmitted to the American minister in London; it laid down the transactions which neutrals were authorized to make, and which included the re-export from their ports of goods which had been imported from enemy countries or their colonies. This jurisprudence interpreted in a tolerant way towards neutrals the old British doctrine which prohibited 'continuous voyages' between enemy countries and their colonies.[6]

This regime lasted up to the peace of Amiens and after it had broken down, it was restored by an order in council of 24 June 1803: it forbade neutral ships to trade directly between enemy countries and their colonies; but neutral ships which were trading between their own country and enemy countries or colonies would not be liable to capture, provided that their cargo was neutral property and did not include any war contraband. There was no mention of re-exports from neutral ports of enemy colonies' produce, which meant that they were authorized by implication; everybody assumed that Robinson's report of 1801 remained authoritative.[7]

Still, a number of British naval vessels were stationed off American ports; they stopped and examined all incoming or outgoing ships, to check that the order of June 1803 had been respected. There was much harassment and a few captures, but no real obstacle to American trade.[8] More serious was the '*Essex* affair'; in May 1805, the ship *Essex* was condemned by the Court of Appeal in Prize Causes for having undertaken a 'continuous voyage' from Barcelona to Havana, via Salem. Many officers of the Royal Navy and of privateers believed then that they might prey freely upon American ships, so that dozens of them were captured during the summer of 1805, but most of them were quickly released, and

---

[6] A. L. Burt, *The United States, Great Britain and British North America from the Revolution to the Establishment of Peace after the War of 1812* (New Haven, 1940), pp. 153, 217–18. On the doctrine of continuous voyages, cf. G. B. Elliott, 'The doctrine of continuous voyages', *American Journal of International Law*, 1 (1907), 61–104; L. H. Woolsey, 'Early cases of the doctrine of continuous voyages', *American Journal of International Law* 4 (1910), 823–47; H. W. Briggs, *The Doctrine of Continuous Voyages* (Baltimore, 1926), pp. 17–21; J. W. Gantenbein, *The Doctrine of Continuous Voyages particularly as applied to Contraband and Blockade* (Portland, 1929); A. Baring, *An Inquiry into the Cause and Consequences of the Orders in Council, and an Examination of the Conduct of Great Britain towards the Neutral Commerce of America* (London, 1808), pp. 35–42; *An Examination of the British doctrine which subjects to Capture a Neutral Trade not open in Time of Peace* (London, 1806), pp. 130–3 (James Madison was the author); PRO, FO 5/51, Monroe and Pinkney to Auckland and Holland, 20 August 1806.

[7] Ch. Robinson, *Reports of Cases argued and determined in the High Court of Admiralty,* vol. V (London, 1806), p. 5; also p. 325, and vol. VI, pp. 79, 420, 430, 440, 461, for examples of this order's enforcement.

[8] R. G. Albion and J. B. Pope, *Sea-Lanes in Wartime: the American Experience. 1775–1942* (New York, 1942), p. 91; R. G. Albion, 'Maritime adventures of New York in the Napoleonic era', in *Essays in Modern History in Honor of Wilbur Cortez Abbott* (Cambridge, Mass., 1941), pp. 330–3.

American trade with enemy countries and colonies was soon resumed, to reach its peak in 1806 and 1807. Indeed, the *Essex* affair had been a false alarm, which did not have serious consequences. The British government had not changed its policy and had not ordered the capture of neutral ships; only a group of judges and lawyers had tried to modify jurisprudence to make it more rigorous towards neutrals.[9]

Thanks to Britain's tolerant policy,[10] neutral countries, in effect mostly the United States, developed from 1794 to 1807 (with a sharp setback in 1802 and 1803 because of the Peace of Amiens)[11] a fast increasing and eventually enormous carrying trade in colonial produce. Their ships sailed to French, Dutch and Spanish colonies – especially Martinique, Guadeloupe, Cuba, Mauritius, Java – where they loaded cargoes of colonial produce; they returned to an American port in order to 'break' or 'interrupt' their voyages and to make them lawful in the eyes of the British. In many cases, this was a 'formal' call: taking advantage of convenient American customs regulations, the cargo was landed and a bond given to pay import duties if the goods were not re-exported within a given period. Actually the cargo was soon re-exported, the bond cancelled and a certificate of drawback granted that duties had been paid according to the law. This document could be used in case of a British visit, as evidence that this was not a 'continuous voyage' between an enemy colony and its mother country, even though, quite often, the same ship was used on both legs of the journey. Thanks to this system of fictitious 'bonded warehousing' and to the trade routes which were generally followed across the Atlantic, the detour to call at an American port was not a cause of serious additional expense or delay.[12] Then American ships sailed to Europe, mainly to Holland, but also to Hamburg and Bremen, to French, Spanish and Italian ports.[13]

[9] Robinson, *Reports*, vol. V, pp. 365, 368–9, 395–6, 399–405; Briggs, pp. 22–7; J. B. MacMaster, *The Life and Times of Stephen Girard Mariner and Merchant*, 2 vols. (Philadelphia, 1918), II, pp. 20–3; A. Steel, 'Anthony Merry and the Anglo-American dispute about impressment, 1803–1806', *Cambridge Historical Journal*, 9 (1949), 347; *An Examination of the British Doctrine*, pp. 76, 130–5; PRO, BT 1/27/1; BT 1/27/17, report by Nicholl, 20 March 1806; FO 83/2204, pp. 333–441; FO 5/47, Mulgrave to Monroe and answer, 9 and 12 August 1805; FO 5/51, Monroe to Fox, 25 February 1806.

[10] It was part of a moderate blockade policy, which was maintained up to the orders in council of November 1807.

[11] When direct relations were resumed between France, Holland, Spain and their colonies, in ships of those countries.

[12] Briggs, *The Doctrine*, p. 18; Burt, *The United States*, p. 219; Baring, *An Inquiry*, pp. 82, 88, 92. After the *Essex* affair, American merchants used various expedients to conform to the new criteria which had been laid down by the British Courts of Admiralty. Cf. PRO, BT 1/27/1; FO 83/2204, p. 341; J. D. Forbes, 'European wars and Boston trade', *New England Quarterly*, 11 (1938), 20.

[13] American exports (including re-exports) to 'Germany' were high in 1798 and 1799 (15 and 18 million dollars), owing to the 'quasi-war' with France. Exports to France were only large in 1805–7 (yearly average: 12.7 million dollars). *Historical Statistics of the United*

Table 11.4. *Re-exports from the United States
(US$ million)*

1792	2	1800	39
1793	2	1801	47
1794	7	1800	36
1795	8	1801	14
1796	26	1802	36
1797	27	1803	53
1798	33	1804	60
1799	46	1805	60

Source: Historical Statistics of the United States, Bicentennial
edn (Washington, D.C., 1976), part 2, series U 187–200, p.
886; also series U 295–316, p. 902, Imports of sugar in the
USA, million cwt: 1792, 0.2; 1796, 0.6; 1801, 1.4; 1803, 0.7;
1804, 1.3; 1805, 1.9; 1806, 2.0; 1807, 2.2.

There was thus a striking growth of imports in the United States (but much of them did not stay long on American soil) and a still sharper one of re-exports from the USA, which had been insignificant before 1793, and which increased thirtyfold from 1792 to 1806 and 1807. From 1797 to 1801, and again in 1805–7, the value of re-exports exceeded that of exports of domestic merchandise, which had increased more slowly, and this carrying trade played a decisive role in the fantastic growth of American sea-borne trade during the period of neutrality. Thanks to this trade, the produce of the French, Dutch and Spanish colonies (except those which were conquered by the British) could, without too much difficulty, reach the markets of Europe, and compete there with produce from the British colonies. According to an estimate of 1807, the total trade in produce from the Caribbean was divided in the ratio 60 per cent for the British, 40 per cent for the Americans.[14]

It happened that the British were at a disadvantage in this competition: sugar from 'enemy' colonies and carried by neutrals could be offered on Continental markets at prices lower than those of 'British' sugars, imported from England. A serious crisis struck therefore British re-exports of sugar and British planters of the West Indies, in the early years of the nineteenth century, and especially in 1806–7.

The two major components of sugar prices in Europe were costs of

States, Bicentennial edn (Washington, D.C., 1976), part 2, Series U 317–34, p. 905.

[14] M. Medford, *Oil without Vinegar and Dignity without Pride; British, American, and West India Interests considered* (London, 1807), p. 40; this estimate seems somewhat too favourable to Britain – at least as far as sugar is concerned (see table 11.5). Still, Drescher, 'Le déclin', 423, states that, by 1806, two-thirds of sugar exports across the Atlantic were under British control.

production in the colonies ('island expences') and transport charges to the Continent. In both respects, British sugars were at a comparative disadvantage. The 'Old British West Indies' had been high-cost producers for much of the eighteenth century relative to the foreign – and especially French – islands, and they remained so:[15] soils were often poorer and more exhausted than in enemy colonies, which also were able to trade freely with the United States and to receive from them supplies more cheaply.[16] As for transport costs, in 1806, according to British sources, American shipowners charged freight at 7s. 6d. per hundredweight of sugar, from the Caribbean to Amsterdam, via an American port. Freight changes for British sugar from a British colony to Amsterdam, via London and the Danish port of Tonningen (as direct exports from England to Holland were dangerous), reached a total of 14s. The difference was said to be larger for sending sugar to a port in the Mediterranean. Moreover, American ships were less in danger than British ships from capture by French privateers and they could be insured at lower premiums.[17] A committee of the House of Commons, which inquired in July 1807 on the situation of the West India trade, estimated that the total cost of carrying one hundredweight of sugar from the Caribbean to Holland was 9s. 11d. for foreign sugars via the United States and 18s. 10d. for British sugars via England, which thus supported an additional charge of 8s. 11d. per hundredweight. However, William Huskisson, then secretary to the Treasury, observed that those estimates had been influenced by the West Indian interest, and he concluded that transport costs from the Caribbean to Europe were 4s. per hundredweight higher for British than for foreign sugars.[18]

Under such circumstances, British sugar planters were bound to suffer, once international competition had become acute – from 1799 onwards – and brought about a fall in re-exports of sugar from Britain (they went almost entirely to the Continent), as it appears in table 11.5.

---

[15] R. P. Thomas, 'The sugar colonies of the old empire: profit or loss for Great Britain?', *EcHR*, 21 (1968), 37; Ward, 'The profitability', 197; J. Meyer, *Histoire du sucre* (Paris, 1989), pp. 150–1.

[16] See below, pp. 290–3, on the restrictions on American trade with the British colonies.

[17] The freight was 10s. from the colonies to London; this fits with Ward's findings from plantation records ('The profitability', 199, table 1): 9s. 6d. per hundredweight for freight from Jamaica to London in 1804/7, and 7s. 6d. from the other British islands. Freight rates on West Indian sugar to London had more than doubled from 1783/92 to 1799/1801; they fell during the Peace of Amiens (but remained above their pre-war level) and rose again afterwards: in 1804/6, they were more than twice those of 1783/92. As for insurance premiums, they rose sharply in the 1790s, but were somewhat lower in 1803/8 (Ward, *ibid.*, 200, table 2). There was also a convoy duty of 2 per cent *ad valorem*, which was increased to 3 per cent in 1803.

[18] PP, 1807, III, pp. 5, 13–14; BL, Add. MS 38,737, fos. 221–6. The cheapness of American freight rates is confirmed by many sources.

Table 11.5. *British imports and re-exports of sugar (million cwt)*

Year	1 Imports in Britain	2 Re-exports Britain	3 Retained imports	4 Re-exports from the USA
1802	4.3	2.0	2.3	0.5
1803	3.2	1.7	1.5	0.2
1804	3.2	1.1	2.1	0.4
1805	3.2	1.1	2.1	1.1
1806	3.8	1.0	2.8	[1.1]
1807	3.6	1.4	2.3	

Source: PRO, Customs 17/24–29; PP, 1807, III, pp. 72–3; 1808, IV, p. 179. Column 2 is the addition of raw sugar re-exports and of refined sugar exports; the latter's equivalent in raw sugar has been calculated according to the ratio 10/17. Column 3 gives an idea of the changes in stocks. Column 4 has its source in a memorandum by George Rose, Vice-president of the Board of Trade, in PRO, FO 95/515; except for the 1806 figure, which comes from PRO, BT 1/40/14.

Both imports and re-exports of sugar reached a high level in 1802, the former because of the increased output in the 'Old' and 'Conquered' West Indies, the latter thanks to the Peace of Amiens which made shipments to the Continent easier. They both fell in 1803, as most of the colonies which the British had occupied during the preceding years had been handed back to England's ex-enemies. However, in 1804 and 1805, imports kept at their level of 1803, but re-exports were 35 per cent lower. In 1806 a sharp deterioration occurred: imports rose almost 20 per cent, but re-exports fell slightly. This decline of British sugar re-exports did not result from the prohibitions of British trade by Napoleon and his allies, which were largely ineffective. The main cause was American competition: re-exports of sugar from the United States increased sharply after a low in 1803; by 1805 and 1806, they were roughly equal to British re-exports.[19] 'Enemy' sugars were offered at low prices on Continental markets, so that stocks of sugar in Britain increased,[20] and prices, which were dependent upon those on international markets, fell. Moreover, since 1805, the sale of rum had become difficult and its prices had sharply fallen from 1802 to 1806.[21] The latent crisis of British sugar production became acute and

[19] Compare columns 2 and 4 of table 11.5.
[20] Quantities of sugar in Customs' warehouses in London and other British ports:

31 December 1804	0.6 million cwt
1805	0.8
1806	1.4

Cf. *Edinburgh Review*, 13, no. 26, 390–2, 394; PP, 1808, IV, pp. 226, 243–5.

Table 11.6. *Index of the average quarterly and yearly prices of 'Jamaica brown' sugar on the London market (customs duties excluded). Average yearly price of 1806 = 100*

| Year | Quarter | | | | Yearly average |
	I	II	III	IV	
1804	130	132	138	138	134
1805	135	127	127	116	126
1806	110	105	95	89	100
1807	81	78	78	76	78

Source: This index has been built up from the price series which had been collected by N. J. Silberling, *British Prices of Thirty Five Commodities, transcribed by Miss Nicholas . . . An exact copy of the Material used by Professor Silberling,* Library of the London School of Economics and Political Science.

increasingly worsened.

After a peak in 1798, sugar prices in London had fallen, irregularly, but sharply up to 1802.[22] They rose again from late in 1802 to the summer of 1804. Then a new fall started and gradually accelerated. The index which is used in table 11.6 displays a fall of 41 per cent from the last quarter of 1804 to the first one of 1807; it continues to fall, though more slowly, during the rest of 1807.

Actually, in 1807, imports of sugar slightly decreased, while re-exports increased 36 per cent,[23] but shipments to the Continent were concentrated from March to July, and during the summer the enforcement of the Continental blockade brought re-exports to a standstill. Most of the year, the sugar market was thus depressed and inactive; despite the fall in retained imports, stocks were heavy and in the last quarter, prices fell to their lowest level of the period 1790–1813. On the other hand, from the summer of 1807 onwards, the Continental blockade succeeded American competition as the major cause of the depression for colonial produce prices – even though American foreign trade reached its zenith in 1807,

[21] MMWIPM, IV, minute of 28 November 1805; PRO, BT 1/35/20. Under the pressure of the West India interest, the government decided later (19 July 1808) that imports of brandy would not be any more allowed under licences to trade with France – in order to stimulate the consumption of rum: Crouzet, *L'économie*, pp. 326–8.

[22] The index calculated from Marshall (see n. 1) of the yearly average price of muscovado sugar in London peaks at 166 in 1798, falls to 84 in 1802 and rises again to 140 in 1804 (1806 = 100).

[23] A new system of export bounties, which was introduced early in 1807, helped this recovery, but the low level at which British sugar prices had fallen and which made them more competitive, was also instrumental.

with values of total exports which were not to be surpassed before 1835.[24]

Since the fall of sugar prices had started, the West Indies planters and merchants, through their spokesmen, the West India Committee, had pressed the government to intervene, to save British planters from an impending ruin; at the end of 1806 ministers admitted that there was a serious crisis and that something had to be done quickly.[25] In July 1807, a parliamentary committee stated that the prices obtained for the sugar crop of 1806 would not pay the costs of cultivation, except on very large plantations making high quality sugar. It had calculated that the average prime cost of British sugar sold on the London market was 35s. or 36s. per hundredweight. However, one had also to take into account depreciation of capital and interest on the mortgage loans which almost all planters had obtained. If the planter was to receive a 'fair profit' on his capital (a net yield of 10 per cent), sugar ought to be sold at an average price (customs duties excluded) of 60s. to 65s. per hundredweight.[26]

In fact, the yearly average price of British sugars on the London market was over 50s. in 1800–1 and 1804–5, but fell to 36s. 6d. in 1802, 43s. 1d. in 1803, 43s. 9d. in 1806 and 34s. 1d. in 1807.[27] The spokesmen of the West India interest proclaimed therefore that, after 1800, the planter's net profit had collapsed from 10 per cent on capital to 2.5 and 1.5 per cent, and had become nil in 1806. Actually, the prime cost of 35s. is an average, and it was reported that real costs were within a range of 28s. to 44s. As the low cost plantations were also making the best sugar, which sold well above the average price, it is likely that such plantations remained profitable. On the other hand, small plantations, especially when their soil was poor and their sugar of low quality, ran into serious difficulties during the years 1806–7; they worked at a loss and their owners had to borrow more money. This was accepted in an article of the *Edinburgh Review*, even though it was hostile to the West

[24] *Edinburgh Review*, 11, no. 21, 160–1; 13, no. 26, 390–2, 396–7; PP, 1808, IV, pp. 25, 168, 226, 243–5; Ragatz, *The Fall*, pp. 306–7; Crouzet, *L'économie*, pp. 271–2; *Historical Statistics*, series U 187–200, p. 886.

[25] MMWIPM, vol. IV, pp. 57–71, 74–8, 100–3; *Historical Manuscripts Commission. Report on the Manuscripts of J. B. Fortescue, Esq. preserved at Dropmore*, ed. W. Fitzpatrick, vol. VIII (London, 1912), pp. 471–4, 489–90.

[26] PP, 1807, III, pp. 3–4, 11, 13, 19–20, 22–4, 37; PP, 1808, IV, pp. 215–20, 226, 241; PRO, BT 1/40/14; BL, Add. MS 38,737/fos. 221–6; MMWIPM, vol. IV, pp. 57–71, 83–90; *Edinburgh Review*, 11, no. 21, 151–2, 154; Ragatz, *The Fall*, pp. 288–90, 306.

[27] This is the 'general average price' of all varieties of raw sugar from British plantations; it was regularly calculated by the secretary of the Grocers Company and published in the *London Gazette*. PP, 1903, LXVIII, p. 162; PP, 1807, III, pp. 84–5; PP, 1808, IV, pp. 183, 247; Lowell Joseph Ragatz, *Statistics for the Study of British Caribbean Economic History* (London, 1928), p. 4.

India interest; it concluded that, even after discounting all exaggerations, a situation of 'extraordinary calamity' had been proved.[28] However, such views have not been confirmed by some recent research; J. R. Ward maintains that 'sugar planting in the British West Indies was profitable throughout the years of slavery'; and his estimates of profit rates on some plantations for the years after 1799, though lower than for the period 1792/8, are by no means disastrous (but few of them cover the years 1806–7).[29]

Late in 1806 and early in 1807, the governors of the British West Indies were sending pessimistic reports. In Grenada, planters were discouraged by prices which were falling for sugar and rising for supplies from Britain or America; they obtained £15 per hogshead of sugar, while the minimum price needed, in order not to fall into debt, was £20. The settlers of Demerara, who admitted that their sugar was not of top quality, stated in January 1807 that they had made no money at all on the large quantities of sugar they had shipped to Britain in 1806. In February the island of Antigua was close to famine because of the depression on the London market: planters could not draw bills on the merchants to whom they had consigned their sugar and were thus unable to pay the foodstuffs which were brought by American ships. As for Jamaica, a report to the colonial assembly at the end of 1807 was to state that, since 1799, 65 plantations had been given up, 32 others had been sold by order of the Court of Chancery, and litigation was in progress about 115 estates; so 212 plantations had been fatally damaged, about one quarter of those in the colony. Early in 1808 the West India interest was to stress that the situation in the sugar islands had been deteriorating for months; the fall in sugar prices had made its cultivation unprofitable, planters were in deep distress and on the brink of ruin. Admittedly, merchants in Britain suffered less, but their commissions fell with sugar prices, and interest on their loans to planters was harder to recover.[30]

It is clear, therefore, that in 1806 and 1807, the British sugar colonies were suffering a serious crisis, and that American competition in the carrying trade across the Atlantic was a significant cause of their difficul-

---

[28] PP, 1807, III, pp. 3–4, 10, 19–20, 22, 36–7, 44, 46, 66–7; F. Ilsley, *A Statement of Facts relating to the Prime Cost of Sugar; with Observations in behalf of West India Planters* (London, 1810), p. 50; *Edinburgh Review*, 11, no. 21, October 1807, 153–4.

[29] Ward, 'The profitability', 208, 210–13. Indeed, the only case which he quotes and which is fully relevant to the present study is the plantation of Grand Bras at Grenada, which had the following profit rates: 1792/5, 18.8 per cent; 1802/8, 4.6 per cent; 1811/13, 4.6 per cent. See also Drescher, 'Le déclin', 424, on the variations in profitability between estates.

[30] PRO, BT 1/33/17; BT 1/34/62; BT 1/35/2 and 20; BT 1/40/14; PP, 1808, IV, pp. 174–5, 215–20; Ragatz, *The Fall*, pp. 307–8; Crouzet, *L'économie*, pp. 323–5.

ties. Other sectors of the imperial economy were also affected by this competition.

Before the American Revolution, Britain's north Atlantic empire had been consistent with mercantilist principles of self-sufficiency: Britain supplied with manufactures the Continental colonies, which sent to the British West Indies the foodstuffs, animals and lumber of which they were short; both groups of dependencies supplied Britain with primary produce, both for its home consumption and for re-export to Europe; and the whole of this increasing and large trade was carried on in British – and colonial – ships.

This triangle of complementarities had been shattered by the independence of the thirteen colonies. After a short-lived 'liberal' period, the British government decided, however, to maintain the traditional mercantilist ideal of imperial autarky and 'to repair the breach in the protectionist wall'. They wanted to deprive the United States of any share in the trade of the British Caribbean colonies and to replace them, as suppliers of the latter, by the possessions Britain retained in North America – Newfoundland, the 'maritime' colonies and Canada. However, those territories being 'underdeveloped' and having small populations it would be some time before they would be able to supply all the needs of the Caribbean islands. Therefore, an order in council of July 1786 (and later an Act of Parliament in 1786) authorized the importation into the islands from the United States of a small number of foodstuffs and other necessities, but only in British ships.[31]

The enforcement of this policy came up against serious difficulties, but had some success: trade between British North America and the British West Indies increased significantly. On the other hand, American exports to the British West Indies, which had been worth $2.2 million in 1771/3 (yearly average), were only $1.4 million in 1785/7 and $1.8 million in 1790/2.[32] Moreover, in 1790/2, 38 per cent of the shipping tonnage entering American ports from the West Indies (British and 'foreign') was

[31] H. T. Manning, *British Colonial Government after the American Revolution, 1782–1820* (New Haven, 1933), pp. 250–2, 262–3; R. L. Schuyler, *The Fall of the Old Colonial System: a Study in British Free Trade, 1770–1870* (London, 1945), pp. 82–97; P. J. Cain and A. G. Hopkins, *British Imperialism: Innovation and Expansion 1688–1914* (London, 1993), p. 97. Salt meat and fish were not among authorized imports from the USA, in order to protect Irish and Newfoundland producers.

[32] G. C. Bjork, 'The weaning of the American economy: independence, market changes, and economic development', *JEcH*, 24 (1964), 552, table 3; James F. Shepherd and Gary M. Walton, 'Economic change after the American Revolution: pre- and post-war comparisons of maritime shipping and trade', *Explorations in Economic History*, 13 (1976), 406, table 3, 411, n. 17. Figures for 1771/3 and 1785/7 are from Bjork, for 1790/2 from Shepherd and Walton.

'foreign owned', and most of it must have been British.[33] However, it is generally admitted that 'the extent of illicit trade was fairly considerable': American ships were admitted into British colonial ports with the connivance of customs officials and the Dutch island of St Eustatius was an entrepôt from which the British islands were illegally supplied. But, as far as reported trade is concerned, in 1790, the British West Indies only took 10 per cent of total American exports, while the 'foreign' (mainly French) West Indies' share was 16 per cent.[34]

However, enforcement of the restrictive policy became impossible when war had started between Britain and France in 1793. Despite British ascendancy at sea, relations between the two groups of colonies became difficult and dangerous, because of French privateers – which captured many ships and seamen from the northern colonies; therefore freight and insurance premiums greatly increased. Trade by British ships between American ports and the Caribbean was likewise affected, though to a lesser degree. The supply of the West Indian islands became irregular and inadequate; this was a serious danger at a time when, following the revolution in Saint-Domingue, slaves' revolts were a real threat. The British government was therefore obliged to give up temporarily the Navigation Acts: it authorized the islands' governors to open their ports, in case of need, to importations from the United States in *American* ships. Governors were ordered to grant such permissions only by special proclamations, which would be valid for short periods. However, those proclamations were periodically repeated, and from 1793 to 1802, the ports of the British West Indies were open, without any interruption, to American ships. The peace of Amiens did not last enough for the Navigation Acts to be again enforced and, of course, after war had started anew in 1803, West Indian ports remained open to American vessels.[35]

This situation created much discontent among British shipowners and

---

[33] Shepherd and Walton, 'Economic change', 415–17, table 6, 419. In 1768/72, the share of foreign (i.e. British) shipping had only been 24 per cent. As in all other overseas trades, the proportion of American-owned shipping was higher in 1790/2 than in 1768/72, the incidence of British restrictions on American trade with the British West Indies is obvious.

[34] Bjork, 'The weaning', 551, 553; Shepherd and Walton, 'Economic change', 407. In 1785, Horatio Nelson wrote, from Antigua: 'To see the American ships and vessels with their colours flying in defiance of the Laws, and by permission of the officer of the Customs, landing and unloading in our ports was too much for a British Officer to submit to' (quoted by Bjork).

[35] Manning, *British Colonial Government*, pp. 266–7; J. Davidson, 'England's commercial policy towards her colonies since the Treaty of Paris (1783–1897)', *Political Science Quarterly*, 14 (1899), 47–8; A. B. Keith, 'Relaxations in the British restrictions on the American trade with the British West Indies, 1783–1802', *Journal of Modern History*, 20 (1948), 1–18; Gerald S. Graham, *Empire of the North Atlantic: the Maritime Struggle for North America* (Toronto, 1950), pp. 223, 234.

among the settlers of the maritime colonies. When the Younger Pitt had
returned to power, in May 1804, his government was sympathetic to those
complaints. After a long and thorough investigation, the Board of Trade
recommended to adopt a more restrictive policy towards America. On 5
September 1804, the Secretary for War and Colonies, Lord Camden,
ordered West Indian governors not to allow the importation from the
United States, except in an emergency, of goods of which the entry from
that country was prohibited by statute, such as fish, salt meat and butter. A
circular of 16 January 1805, strengthened this order: the Navigation Laws
ought to be strictly enforced, confiscation to be ordered in case of fraud,
and only grain and lumber might be imported on American ships.[36]

Those decisions were expected to stimulate the trade of British North
America, but it in fact proved impossible to enforce them literally, without exposing the West Indies to a real threat of famine. In some islands
(including Jamaica), the governors made at first a show of zeal and late in
1804, they closed their ports to American ships. But in the course of the
year 1805, they were obliged to reopen them – some times more widely
than beforehand. All the information which arrived in London early in
1806 indicated that imports from British North America were entirely
inadequate and that the islands needed regular supplies, which could only
come from the United States and on American ships.[37]

The new 'Ministry of All Talents' soon came to such a conclusion.
Moreover, some of its members had sympathy for the United States and
thought that the latter's relations with the British West Indies were
mutually profitable and in no way dangerous for Britain; they considered
as selfish the complaints from the shipping interest, and they were hoping
that cheaper food supplies would alleviate the difficulties under which
sugar planters were then labouring. Lord Grenville, the prime minister,
and Lord Auckland, the president of the Board of Trade, agreed that it
was necessary to put relations between the United States and the colonies
on a legal footing which would be more stable than colonial governors'
proclamations, which were in contradiction with statute law and only
valid for six months. They decided to suspend partly the Navigation Acts,
for the duration of the war, and to authorize the entry of American ships
in colonial ports. These decisions did not change much, but it was hoped

---

[36] *JHC*, LXI, 1806, pp. 716–17; Gerald S. Graham, *Sea Power and British North America,
1783–1820: a Study in British Colonial Policy* (Cambridge, Mass., 1941), pp. 189–90;
Manning, *British Colonial Government*, pp. 268–71; Ragatz, *The Fall*, pp. 297–9; PRO, FO
5/47, Cottrell to Hammond, 2 January 1805. These decisions made more expensive the
supplies of foodstuffs and lumber to British islands; they increased thus the prime cost of
sugar and made the 'sugar crisis' more serious. The West India interest loudly protested.

[37] PRO, BT 1/28/36, 37, 40, 41, 42; DP, VIII, p. 140; Ragatz, *The Fall*, pp. 299–300;
Davidson, 'England's commercial policy', 63.

that opening the ports for a long period would bring more regular and better supplies.[38]

On 8 March 1806, the Board of Trade recommended to the Colonial Office to send instructions to the West Indies' governors, so that they would extend, for the duration of the war (plus six months after the peace), their existing proclamations which opened colonial ports to American ships; the latter might import all kinds of foodstuffs and lumber, except salted beef, pork and butter.[39] In April 1806, the government introduced the American Intercourse Bill; after long debates and despite much opposition from Tory MPs, it was passed in July 1806. The Act 46 Geo. 3, c.111 empowered the king in council to authorize the governors of West Indian colonies to issue, during the duration of the war, proclamations (valid for six months) which would authorize the importation on neutral ships of a number of enumerated goods; those ships would also be allowed to export any kind of merchandise, except sugar, indigo, cotton, coffee and cocoa. On 17 September and 1 October 1806, two orders in council were issued according to the new law.[40]

There is no doubt that those various measures, which were taken between 1793 and 1806 and which opened to American ships the ports of the West Indian colonies, were indispensable to the survival of the latter, as it was demonstrated by an inquiry, which the Board of Trade decided to organize, on 1 September 1806. In his answer – which is typical – the president of Tobago stressed that many articles, which were indispensable to both the white and black populations, could only be obtained from the United States. He added that the statements about supplies from British North America were only made by special interests, which were indifferent to the empire's prosperity and to the fate of their fellow countrymen.[41] Moreover, after Pitt's friends had returned to power in March 1807, they did not enforce the policy they had advocated when in opposition in 1806; their order in council of 1 July 1807 was very similar to its predecessor of 17 September 1806.[42]

Thanks to the opening of British West Indian ports – and to overwhelming comparative advantages – the United States was able to increase its exports to the British Caribbean islands and eventually to secure

---

[38] *CPD*, VI, c. 593–6, 1035, 1037–8.

[39] PRO, BT 5/16, 4–5, 7–14, 33. The exclusion of salt meat and butter could not be strictly enforced.

[40] PRO, BT 5/16, 22–3, 290–2; BT 1/32/59; PC 2/171, 168–70, 209, 212; PC 4/14, 372–4; DP, VIII, pp. 57, 59, 102, 112, 285, 293; *CPD*, VI and VII, *passim*; Ragatz, *The Fall*, pp. 301–2; Manning, *British Colonial Government*, pp. 190–302; Graham, *Sea Power*, pp. 190–4; Davidson, 'England's commercial policy', 192–4.

[41] PRO, BT 5/16, 310–11; BT 1/32/59; BT 1/33/29; BT 1/34/62; BT 1/35/20, 31.

[42] *CPD*, IX, c. 682 ff.; PRO, PC 2/173, 203–5, 225, 466; Graham, *Sea Power*, p. 191.

Table 11.7. *Exports from the United States to the British West Indies*

Fiscal year ending 30 September	$ millions
1790/2[a]	1.9
1793/5[a]	2.2
1796/8[a]	3.9
1799/1801[a]	7.4
1802	6.6
1803	5.7
1804	7.0
1805	5.9
1806	5.6
1807	5.9

Source: J. H. Coatsworth, 'American trade with European colonies in the Caribbean and South America, 1790–1812', *WMQ*, 24 (1967), 262, table A.1. Values *FOB* at current prices. This trade brought to the USA invisible earnings (especially freight), which may have been as high as the value of commodity exports; cf. David Richardson, 'Slavery, trade, and economic growth in eighteenth-century New England', in Barbara L. Solow, ed., *Slavery and the Rise of the Atlantic System* (Cambridge, 1991), p. 257.
[a] Yearly average.

the largest share of their supplying. American ships were well adapted to navigation in the Caribbean seas; as neutrals they were somewhat safe from French privateers; therefore, after 1793, they drove out the small British ships, which had previously been used in the trade between American ports and British islands, and which had higher freight rates and insurance premiums. Moreover, the costs of production and of transport were lower for grain, lumber and fish, from the United States than for similar produce from British North America, which moreover suffered from a fatal distance handicap.[43] The success of the United States in continuing to supply the West Indies was in the order of things.

American exports to the British West Indies increased during the 1790s, slowly at first and faster at the end of the decade, to reach a peak in value at $9.6 million in 1801; they fell because of the peace of Amiens and then recovered to a stable level (the British restrictive measures of 1804/5 may have had some effect).

The British West Indies received up to 35 per cent (in 1798/1801) of

[43] Moreover, because of the Navigation Laws, the fisheries of Newfoundland and Nova Scotia had to pay higher prices for foodstuffs, salt and fishing tackle than their New England competitors.

American exports to the Caribbean and South America and 10 per cent of American total exports, but their share declined afterwards,[44] because of the fast progress of American exports to the Spanish colonies.[45] None the less, one reasonable estimate is that, during the years 1803–5, the British West Indies only received from Britain and its possessions one-third of their imports of foodstuffs – and one-twelfth from British North America. About two-thirds of imported foodstuffs came from the USA, as well as almost all the lumber;[46] 85 per cent of those imports were on American ships. In the case of Jamaica, during the three years starting on 30 September 1803, the value of imports per year was (in Jamaican currency): from the United States in American ships, £983,000; from the United States in British ships, £167,000; and from British North America, £100,000.

The war had thus put an end to the efforts intended to break the relationship between the USA and the British West Indies, the economies of which retained their complementarity. Indeed, from 1793 to 1806, trade between British North America and the British West Indies had decreased.[47] As a result, British North America suffered from stagnation, the worst sufferers being the fisheries of the maritime colonies and of Newfoundland. This might be a serious worry for British opinion, which was used to consider those fisheries as the 'nursery of seamen' *par excellence* and thus a pillar of British naval power (though in reality the nursery was no more). This crisis had emerged during the 1790s and, after a lull during the Peace of Amiens, it grew more serious. Its main cause was the narrowing of markets for British-caught cod. In peacetime, Catholic southern Europe was the major market and large quantities of fish were sent there, either directly from Newfoundland or as re-exports from England. But war broke out with Spain in 1796 and again in 1804, much of Italy was occupied by the French, so that British ships could no longer sail to those two countries; the use of neutral ships and of entrepôts at Lisbon, Gibraltar and Malta were not adequate palliatives, so that the Italian and Spanish markets were largely lost, with only the Portuguese market remaining. Exports of cod from Newfoundland to Spain, Portugal and Italy had been 729,000 cwt per year (average) in 1788–90; by 1804, they had fallen to 335,000 cwt; in 1806, they were higher, but only at

---

[44] With a temporary rise to 43 per cent of the region's trade in 1803 – because of the peace of Amiens.

[45] Coatsworth, 'American trade', 251–2, 263, table A-2.

[46] According to Davidson, 'England's commercial policy', 48, n. 1, the share of the USA in the imports of 1804/6 exceeded 90 per cent for bread, biscuits, flour, rice, live animals and pickled fish; it was 65 per cent for cereals, 54 per cent for salt fish, 49 per cent for salt beef.

[47] PP, 1808, IV, pp. 368–71; Graham, *Sea Power*, p. 180; *Empire*, p. 234. More detailed figures in PP, 1808, X, p. 225; *JHC*, LXIII, pp. 733–5; PRO, BT 1/51/8; Ragatz, *Statistics*, p. 2; Medford, *Oil without Vinegar*, appendix 2.

434,000 cwt. As for exports to the British West Indies, they were restricted by American competition. In 1804–5 they were only 69,000 cwt per year, 11 per cent of Newfoundland's total export of cod. During the same two years, the British West Indies received from the USA 58 per cent of their imports of salt fish. The prices of cod at Newfoundland were falling: in four years, 1801 to 1805, from 25s. per cwt to 14s. 6d., and it was maintained in 1805 that the British fisheries were on the verge of ruin. The situation was no better in Nova Scotia: in 1804 the markets for fish and lumber at Halifax were very depressed, for lack of trade with the West Indies, which was crippled by risks of capture and high insurance premiums.[48]

In contrast to those difficulties, American fisheries were insolently prosperous. Since 1783, New England seamen had unceasingly extended their activity and they had been the major beneficiaries of French fishermen being driven out from the Banks. They were fishing not only on the latter, but also in the St.Lawrence estuary and off Labrador; in 1805, 900 American ships took part in cod fishing. The yearly average of American exports of dry cod rose from 394,000 cwt, during the period 1790–8, to 438,000 cwt in 1799–1808; they peaked in 1807 at 474,000 cwt; one-half was sent to the West Indies, of which a large share was to British colonies.

Under those circumstances, the solution for the operators of British fisheries was to export an increasing share of their catch to the United States; from there, it could take advantage of American neutrality, to be re-exported to Europe or the Caribbean. Indeed, the exports of Newfoundland cod to the USA did increase fast:[49]

1804	44,100 cwt
1805	78,000
1806	116,200
1807	155,100

The British cod fisheries were becoming dependent upon the United

---

[48] PRO, BT 1/28/7; BT 5/16, 135–8; DP, VIII, pp. 116–17; *JHC*, LXIII, pp. 733–5; PP, 1808, X, p. 225; Graham, *Sea Power*, pp. 248–50, appendix D; *Empire*, p. 229; Manning, *British Colonial Government*, p. 270; H. A. Innis, *The Cod Fisheries: the History of an International Economy* (New Haven, 1940), pp. 236–8, 301, 305. On the risks of capture, cf. C. N. Parkinson, ed., *The Trade Winds* (London, 1948), pp. 234–8, 247; Graham, *Empire*, pp. 227–8, 232. The fisheries were not really disturbed by hostilities, despite some French attacks during the 1790s.

[49] Innis, *The Cod Fisheries*, pp. 220–4; Graham, *Sea Power*, p. 252; *Empire*, p. 228. American fishermen were accused of annoying their British rivals and of fishing on the Sabbath; PRO, FO 5/47, Cooke to Hammond, with a dispatch from Gower, 12 January 1805. Total exports of fish from Newfoundland were 661,000 cwt in 1804, 768,000 in 1806.

States, which supplied part of the foodstuffs they needed, and which were the entrepôt from which neutral, i.e. American, ships could introduce cargoes of cod into Spanish and Italian ports. There were thus advantages to that dependency. Indeed, this was a return to the pre-1776 situation, when Atlantic Canada – mainly Newfoundland and Nova Scotia – had become New England's outpost and was integrated into New England's economy by the aggressive commercialism of Yankee merchants. The English and Irish communities on Newfoundland's eastern and southern shores had closer relations with ports in New England than with Britain. On the other hand, Americans had then quite properly fished in Newfoundland waters, which they frequented in large numbers. American independence completely changed the situation, inasmuch as Newfoundland was no longer a summer fishing base for visiting ships and fishermen from England's west country, but was being transformed into a colony of settled communities; fishing was increasingly carried on by resident people and boats, and there was an identifiable native Newfoundland fishery. Its dependency upon the United States – now a competitor and a potential enemy – could not but disturb British politicians, who disliked this dangerous violation of the Navigation Acts (which deprived Britain of an important carrying trade), and the shipping interest. The American penetration into some parts of the empire was bound to have political consequences.[50]

Besides, despite the resort to the American entrepôt, the economy of British North America remained depressed: in the maritime colonies agriculture, fishing, lumbering were badly suffering from American competition. Exports to the West Indies had fallen to a very low level, shipbuilding was at a standstill, the balance of trade was very unfavourable, and specie was getting scarce. Depopulation was starting, as many fishermen, seamen, lumbermen, farmers were attracted by the prosperity of the United States and were emigrating from moribund colonies to New England, at a time when Newfoundland was desperate for new colonists.[51]

Early in 1806, the complaints by the merchants of Newfoundland, the settlers of the maritime colonies and the British businessmen who had connections with them had become so loud that government had to do something. On 8 March 1806 the Board of Trade recommended the payment of a bounty of 2s. per hundredweight on the import into British West Indian ports of fish coming from Newfoundland and the other

---

[50] McCusker and Menard, *Economy of British America*, pp. 113–14. It was mainly their neutral status which allowed Americans to penetrate southern European markets.
[51] Graham, *Sea Power*, pp. 44–54, 183, 251–2; *Empire*, p. 229; N. Atcheson, *American Encroachments on British Rights* (London, 1808), p. xlvii; PP, 1808, X, p. 137.

colonies of British North America. Those payments would be made during the year from 1 June 1806 to 1 June 1807 at the expense of the British Treasury, but colonial assemblies would be asked to repay those advances as soon as possible, to provide for the payment of a bounty of 1s. per hundredweight from 1 June 1807 onwards, and to impose at the same time a duty upon imports of fish from the United States. The Board of Trade also asked the Admiralty to organize regular convoys from Newfoundland and Nova Scotia to the West Indies, in order to protect British ships with cargoes of fish. This plan to stop 'the American invasion' was soon adopted.[52]

However, difficulties arose in its enforcement. Colonial assemblies were reluctant to accept this increase in taxation; most of them were hostile to the extension of the bounty beyond 1 June 1807 and still more to a customs duty upon imports of fish from the United States.[53] However, the Board of Trade, after the change of government in March 1807, stuck to its guns. On 23 May 1807, it decided to continue the payment of bounties up to 1 August 1807, but only in colonies which had provided for their repayment; then an order in council of 1 July 1807 prohibited imports of American fish into the colonies which had not established a duty of 2s. per hundredweight on cod imported in foreign ships.[54]

This policy was not ineffective and the economic situation of British North America improved in 1806. Their exports of fish to the British West Indies markedly increased: from Newfoundland they rose from 82,000 cwt in 1805 to 101,000 cwt in 1806 and 103,000 cwt in 1807; during the latter year, British North America overtook the USA, for the first time, as supplier of fish to the British West Indies. However, some difficulties persisted, as this trade was quite irregular, particularly for lack of return freight.[55] Some statements which were made both in the colonies and in London as to the happy consequences of the new system for the British fisheries are obviously too optimistic. Total exports of cod from Newfoundland did indeed rise from 626,000 cwt in 1805 to 768,000 cwt in 1806, but mainly because of the recovery in exports to Europe (377,000 cwt in 1805, 434,000 in 1806), and of the continuing increase in shipments to the USA (see above). The prosperity of 1806 was

---

[52] PRO, BT 5/16, 4–14, 33, 35–43; BT 1/27/13, 14, 15, 16, 19; Ragatz, *The Fall*, pp. 322–3; Manning, *British Colonial Government*, p. 270.

[53] PRO, BT 1/29/8, 15, 45; BT 1/30/11, 35, 36; BT 1/31/2; BT 1/32/24; BT 1/33/16, 17; BT 1/37, 5, 26, 28, 29, 35; Graham, *Sea Power*, p. 253.

[54] PRO, BT 5/16, 393–4, 427–8; BT 5/17, 191–2, 269; BT 5/18, 231–2; PC 2/173, 203–5; Ragatz, *The Fall*, p. 323.

[55] Innis, *The Cod Fisheries*, pp. 242, 301; *JHC*, LXIII, pp. 733–5; PP, 1808, IV, p. 225. Some colonies only received small quantities of fish from British North America; PRO, BT 1/38/43 and 44; BT 1/40/5 and 9.

Table 11.8. *Britain's East India trade: indices of official values (volume),*
1806 = 100

Year	British exports to Asia	British imports from Asia	Imports in Britain of East India piece goods	Re-exports from Britain of East India piece goods
1802	151	154	–	221
1803	141	169	330	190
1804	91	139	272	200
1805	86	162	277	152
1806	100	100	100	100
1807	97	91	102	61

Source: PRO, Customs, 17/24 to 29.

thus fragile. In 1807, exports to Europe fell to 262,000 cwt. and total
exports to 675,000 cwt, while American exports were reaching a peak.
The crisis of the North American colonies was not over, and this had been
realized by business groups with interests in the fisheries; they also had
realized the permanent handicap from which they suffered *vis-à-vis* the
United States. They remained worried and asked for drastic policies
against American competition and penetration.[56]

British trade with a part of the world far away from America – India – also
suffered from American competition. Britain's East India trade had
grown fast after 1793, to reach a peak around 1800; it slightly decreased
afterwards and then, in 1804, exports to Asia fell sharply, to be followed
by imports from that Continent in 1805 and in the two years which
followed.

The main factor of this recession was the fall in the trade of cottons
(East India piece goods), which were the largest component (by value) of
British imports from Asia, and which were the only article among those
imports to be re-exported on a large scale. Imports of Indian cottons
reached a peak in 1798–9, and though the profits on this trade were said
to be low, large re-exports of East India goods were made during the years
which followed. However, the trade suffered when war with France

[56] PRO, BT 1/29/18, 52, 61; BT 5/16, 233, 301, 313, 393–4, 427–8; DP, VIII, p. 454; PP,
1807, III, pp. 52–4, 63–4, 67; PP, 1808, X, p. 225; Graham, *Sea Power*, pp. 192, 252–3;
Empire, p. 228; Atcheson, *American Encroachments*, pp. xlviii–xlix, liv–lv; Innis, *The Cod
Fisheries*, p. 301. Americans also did some smuggling, introducing tobacco, tea, East
India fabrics into the British colonies, exporting furs, salmon and gypsum (from quarries
near the bay of Fundy; it was used as a fertilizer; legally, those exports ought to have been
in British ships).

resumed in 1803. On 4 July 1804 the directors of the East India Company complained that it had become much more difficult and costly to introduce Indian cottons in France, Holland and Flanders, so that demand at the Company's sales had decreased and prices had sharply fallen,[57] especially for high quality fabrics, which had previously their main market in Paris. Re-exports of cottons collapsed in 1805 and again in 1806 and 1807. The Company therefore instructed its 'servants' in India to reduce the shipments of cottons to London, so that imports of East India goods in Britain collapsed in 1806. The Company's finances felt the effects of this crisis, as the sales of cottons (and also of tea, silk, sugar and drugs) were much lower in 1804–5 than expected, and profits mediocre.[58]

The war and the progress of the cotton industry – not only in Britain, but also on the Continent, were certainly the main factors of this crisis, but American competition also played a part and British business interests considered it as responsible. Since the Jay treaty of 1794, American ships had been admitted in the ports of British India, where they came in increasing numbers. Imports on American ships in those ports rose from 1.7 million rupees per year in 1796–1800, to an average of 4.6 million in 1801–5. Those imports were mostly of bullion and specie, and thus of no inconvenience to the British. As for exports on American ships, they increased in value, during the same period, from 2.3 to 5.1 million rupees.[59] Some of those shipments were intended for the US home market, but Americans also did an important carrying trade in East Indian (as in West Indian) merchandise: they re-exported from their own ports or transported directly from India to Europe – or to foreign colonies – cotton fabrics, tea, spices and so on. They were thus short-circuiting British trade, as all goods exported from India on British ships had to be sent first to London. Besides, as neutrals, they had better opportunities to carry their cargoes to enemy ports. And, as far as freight rates were concerned, the advantage which American ships usually had over their British rivals was increased by the special kind of English ships which were employed in the East India trade: the large and expensive East Indiamen, which were heavily armed and had a numerous crew, so that their freight rates were very high, while Americans used smaller vessels. As early as 1799, Ameri-

---

[57] A rough index of the yearly prices of six lines of silk and cotton piece goods sold at the public sales of the East India Company (1806 = 100) falls from 97 in 1802 to 82 in 1803, 79 in 1804 and 76 in 1805; it recovers in 1806, but falls back to 76 in 1807; calculated from Marshall, *A Digest*, p. 181.

[58] C. H. Hamilton, *The Trade Relations between England and India (1600–1896)* (Calcutta, 1919), pp. 174–7, 258; J. D. Parshad, *Some Aspects of Indian Foreign Trade, 1757–1893* (London, 1932), pp. 95–6; PP, 1812–13, VII, pp. 468, 486; PP, 1808, II, p. 127; *Literary Panorama*, 1, January 1807, pp. 805–17.

[59] 1 rupee = 2s. 6d.

cans and other neutrals were said to carry from India to Europe the same quantities of goods as the ships of the East India Company. And the following figures on the re-exports of pepper are suggestive (millions lb):

Year	From Britain	From USA
1802	5.5	5.4
1803	4.3	3.0
1804	3.2	5.7
1805	1.5	7.6

Undoubtedly, American competition contributed to the difficulties which British trade with India had to face.[60] Those difficulties worsened in 1807, when re-exports of East India goods fell to their lowest level of the decade 1802–12, and when stocks of unsold goods accumulated in the Company's warehouses.[61] As a result, the East India Company, which had much political clout, was to join the other pressure groups which were being hurt by the crisis of the imperial economy and were thus hostile to American trade.

Another branch of the imperial economy – merchant shipping – also met difficulties during the years which followed the end of the peace of Amiens, and once more American competition could be blamed for this crisis. The British merchant fleet had enjoyed a strong expansion from 1788 to 1803, but afterwards its increase slowed down and eventually stopped.

This increase resulted mainly from the progress of shipbuilding, which was very active, to reach a peak from 1800 to 1803; but it markedly slowed down in the years which followed.

The first cause of this recession was the state of war, in which Britain was again from May 1803 onwards, and which prevented British ships from sailing to enemy ports, which, in the years we are considering, were most of the ports of western Europe. The war, both in the 1790s, and in

---

[60] PRO, FO 353/69, contains many data on this problem, including important letters of 1807 and 1808 between Sir Francis Baring and the directors of the East India Company. See also PRO, FO 95/515, 'Observations on the American treaty', by G. Rose, August 1807 (it gives the figures of pepper re-exports; admittedly, all American re-exports of pepper did not come from British India); PRO, FO 5/51, Memorandum of 20 October 1806; PP, 1812–13, VIII, pp. 571–6; C. H. Philips, *The East India Company, 1783–1834* (Manchester, 1940), pp. 106–7, 156. It was also said that the 'savings' (or loot) of the Company's servants were largely transferred to England through American traders.

[61] PP, 1807, III, pp. 52–4, 63–5, 68–9; Crouzet, *L'économie*, p. 328. The value of piece goods sold at the Company sales in London (in thousands of pounds) fell badly: September 1805–September 1806: 2,009; September 1806–September 1807: 978.

Table 11.9. *Tonnage of merchant ships registered in Great Britain, Ireland, Isle of Man, the Channel Islands (000 tons)*

1788	1,279
1792	1,437
1798	1,494
1800	1,699
1802	1,901
1803	1,986
1804	2,077
1805	2,092
1806	2,080
1807	2,097

Source: Mitchell, *British Historical Statistics*, p. 535; JHC, vol. LXII, p. 705, vol. LXIV, p. 551; Parkinson, ed., *The Trade Winds*, p. 72; A. P. Usher, 'The growth of English shipping, 1572–1922', *Quarterly Journal of Economics*, 42 (1928), 467.

Table 11.10. *Tonnage of merchant ships built in Great Britain (000 tons)*

1788–92[a]	61
1793–97[a]	71
1798–1801[a]	97
1802	105
1803	116
1804	80
1805	72
1806	59
1807	58

Source: PP, 1813–14, VIII, p. 7; PRO, Customs 17/24–30; Mitchell, *British Historical Statistics*, p. 419.
[a] Yearly average.

the early 1800s, brought about a stagnation and even a fall in the number of ships flying the British flag which sailed from Britain to foreign ports, while the share of foreign ships which visited British ports markedly increased, as neutral vessels were used to maintain relations with enemy ports. Admittedly, during the war with revolutionary France, ships which were 'displaced' from trade with the Continent could be used on several routes where trade was growing fast, particularly in relations with the enemy colonies which Britain had conquered. Moreover, this was a

long-distance trade, and not a short-distance one, like traffic with western
Europe. Those new opportunities gave employment to an increased
merchant fleet up to the Peace of Amiens. The situation was different after
it had broken down. Britain had returned to their former owners most of
its colonial conquests, and only a small number of the latter were occupied
again during the early years of the Napoleonic war, during which, moreover, there were no large-scale military expeditions overseas, so that few
merchant ships were used as transports. On the sea routes which remained
open to British ships, but where they had no monopoly, in the trade with
allied or neutral countries, they met a strong competition from foreign
ships – Danish, Swedish, Prussian, Hanseatic and American – which had
prime costs and therefore freight rates markedly lower than those which
British shipowners demanded. The average tonnage of British ships
cleared from Britain for countries outside the British Isles, during the five
years 1802–6, was only 917,000 tons, as against 1,040,000 in 1792; on the
other hand, the tonnage of foreign ships clearing from Britain to overseas
ports had risen from 150,000 tons in 1790 to 606,000 in 1805.[62]

Among foreign competitors, American ships were the most dangerous,
as they had comparative advantages as far as both building and operating
were concerned. In the age of wood and sail, the price of ship timber was
the decisive factor in the cost of building ships, and this price was mainly
determined by the cost of transport from forest to shipyard. Britain's
timber resources were inadequate for its needs and it increasingly depended upon imports from the Baltic countries, which bore heavy transport costs and customs duties. As the Royal Navy engrossed the best
timber, merchant ships were often built with poor quality materials, and
therefore not too solid and durable. On the other hand, the United States
had enormous reserves of excellent timber, at a short distance of the many
estuaries along the Atlantic coast, which offered most convenient sites for
establishing shipyards. It has been estimated that American shipbuilders
could obtain timber at prices which were from 50 per cent to 80 per cent
lower than in Britain, although admittedly, many accessories – especially
when they had to be imported – were more expensive than in Britain. But
altogether the prime cost of American ships was from 25 per cent to 50
per cent lower than for British-built ships. Moreover, their quality was
better; admittedly, the age of the clipper ships had not yet arrived, but
some shipbuilders were already designing some slim and fast brigs and
schooners, and the ships they were building for transatlantic voyages were

---

[62] Parkinson, ed., *The Trade Winds*, pp. 83–6; Usher, 'The growth', 469; J. Creswell,
'English shipping at the end of the 18th century', *MM*, 25 (1939), 197–207. In fact most
British ships were used in the coasting trade and the traffic with Ireland. Under one-third
of their number and one-half of total tonnage were engaged in colonial and foreign trade.

both simple and robust, and definitely superior to their British rivals.[63]

As for operating costs, American ships had lighter and handier riggings; their masters and mates were brutal to the crews and this was labour saving: it has been estimated that those ships needed 0.5 to 1.5 seamen less per 100 tons burthen than European ships. So higher productivity (plus cheaper provisions) compensated for the higher wages which were paid to American seamen. Altogether, operating costs may have been roughly the same on American and on British ships, but the former had lower expenses for repairs (as they were better built), lower depreciation costs and insurance premiums.[64]

Consequently, in the 1790s shipowning was very profitable in the United States; the freight earned by a ship in two or three long voyages could repay its building costs, and shipowners immediately ploughed back their profits into the building of new ships. At the same time, the sea-borne trade of the United States enjoyed a very fast growth, thanks to the expansion of exports of American produce, of the carrying trade from and to the colonies of Britain's enemies, of trade with the East Indies, and also of tramping between foreign ports. Like the seventeenth-century Dutch, Americans had become *les rouliers des mers*, the universal carriers of the high seas: they engaged in the coasting trade of the Continent (especially between ports of Britain's enemies), as well as in various and complex triangular voyages.[65]

Consequently, the American merchant fleet grew very fast, with a succession of shipbuilding booms, especially in 1795–6, 1800–1, 1805–6. In 1805, American shipyards built 129,000 tons of ships, while the tonnage built in Britain only was 72,000 tons. The growth of American shipping – absolute and relatively to the British – appears in table 11.11.

This remarkable progress could well worry British public opinion, which remained wedded to the old slogan 'Ships, colonies and commerce', inasmuch as American ships, thanks to their lower freights, were acquiring a dominant position on the sea routes where they were allowed to compete with the British, and from which they eliminated the latter. This development was mentioned earlier in the discussion of the trade in foodstuffs and lumber from the United States to the British West Indies,

---

[63] Crouzet, *L'économie*, pp. 91 ff.; J. C. B. Hutchins, *The American Maritime Industries and Public Policy, 1789–1914: an Economic History* (Cambridge, Mass., 1941), pp. 75–9, 196–9, 200–2, 216–20.

[64] *Ibid.*, pp. 221–3; Parkinson, ed., *The Trade Winds*, pp. 35–6.

[65] See e.g. François Crouzet, *Britain, France and International Commerce: from Louis XIV to Victoria* (Aldershot, 1996), ch. 7, 'Opportunity and risk in Atlantic trade during the French Revolution'; Albion and Pope, *Sea-Lanes in Wartime*, pp. 319, 322–5; MacMaster, *The Life*, II, pp. 5–10, 27–30, 34–5; J. D. Phillipps, *Salem and the Indies. The Story of the Great Commercial Era of the City* (Boston, 1947), pp. 227–47.

Table 11.11. *The American merchant fleet*

Year	000 tons	% of the British fleet
1792	290	20
1800	700	41
1803	949	48
1805	1,140	54
1807	1,268	60

Source: Hutchins, *The American Maritime Industries*, pp. 185–6, 225; Albion and Pope, *Sea-Lanes in Wartime*, pp. 70, 94; and see table 11.9.

after the latter's ports had been opened, under the pressure of war conditions, to American ships. As for British ships which were registered in the West Indian and North American colonies, their numbers and total tonnage had markedly decreased.[66]

However, the most striking change took place on the major sea route between Britain and the United States. In 1790/2, American-owned ships only made up 45 per cent of the tonnage entering ports of the United States from Great Britain and Ireland (136,000 tons). But the share of British ships in that traffic fell sharply in 1793/4 and by 1802, it had become quite small; within the few years which followed, it became almost trifling (table 11.12). American ships, thanks to their lower freights and to their neutrality, had monopolized the important and fast-growing Anglo-American transatlantic trade.[67]

It should be added that British shipping also suffered, in the trade with Northern Europe (despite the preferential duties on goods it imported) from competition by Danish, Swedish, Prussian, Hanseatic ships. Their building costs were lower, as shipyards were close to large forests, and the wages of their seamen were much lower than those of British sailors, who were subject to impressment for service in the Royal Navy, so that their number was reduced and their wages driven up. In 1803–5, trade between Britain and northern Europe was shared almost equally between British and foreign ships.

Altogether, there was a worrying foreign competition on all the routes,

[66] Cf. above; also Atcheson, *American Encroachments*, p. lvi; PP, 1808, IV, pp. 365–6, 376–83.
[67] Shepherd and Walton, 'Economic change', 416, table 6; Parkinson, ed., *The Trade Winds*, p. 203. British shipowners and mercantilist politicians complained that the USA had cunningly established a system of preferential tonnage and customs duties in favour of their ships (see e.g. 'Observations', by G. Rose, in PRO, FO 95/515).

Table 11.12. *Total number of entries and clearances in British ports of ships coming from or going to the United States*

Year	Number of Ships		% of American ships	Tonnage (000 tons)		% of American tonnage
	British	American		British	American	
1802	235	772	77	49	185	79
1803	224	955	81	52	227	81
1804	130	775	86	31	190	86
1805	124	879	88	30	222	88
1806	93	1,097	92	20	287	93
1807	122	1,359	92	27	355	93

Source: PP, 1812, X, p. 5; JHC, vol. LXVII, 1812, p. 761.

where, under the Navigation Laws, British shipping did not have a monopoly. Many shipowners therefore took shelter behind these monopolies and employed their ships on 'protected' routes, such as the coasting and colonial trades; but this created an acute competition among them, specially after the 'conquered colonies' had been returned under the peace of Amiens.[68]

Undoubtedly, during the early years of the Napoleonic war, notably in 1806–7, the British imperial economy underwent a crisis, which had mainly structural causes and was countercyclical relatively to the *konjunktur* in Britain – in contrast with the growth of its national economy, especially the industrial sector. There was, in all troubled sectors, a common and direct factor: American competition. As Lord Sheffield had predicted twenty years earlier, the United States were 'an instrument of imperial disunion'.[69] This competition and the penetration by Americans within the imperial economy was a threat to some British interest groups, a threat which engrossed the attention of British opinion and politicians. On the other hand, there was a complementarity between the British and American economies, indeed a close relationship between the prosperity of Britain and of American sea-borne trade.[70]

The United States was British industry's largest single customer, and Britain had a large surplus in its balance of payments with it. On the other

[68] PRO, Customs 17/25, 26, 27; PP, 1820, II, p. 372; Hutchins, *The American Maritime Industries*, p. 203. Needless to say, a share of British trade had always been carried on foreign ships; it was the increase in that share which was worrying, from a mercantilist point of view.

[69] Quoted by Graham, *Sea Power*, p. 180.

[70] This complementarity has often been stressed; see e.g. Frank Thistlethwaite, *The Anglo-American Connection in the Early Nineteenth Century* (Philadelphia, 1959), ch. 1, pp. 4 ff.

hand, the USA enjoyed a large surplus in their dealings with Continental Europe. There was thus a multilateral – roughly triangular – system of settlements. Most of the proceeds from the sales on the Continent of American exports and re-exports were transferred to London and used to pay the exports to America of British manufactures. The growth of British exports to the USA, during the early years of the nineteenth century, had been made possible by the growing American carrying trade in produce from the colonies of Britain's enemies. This trade both made British industry prosperous and the imperial economy depressed.[71] However, only some merchant bankers were fully aware of this triangular system of settlements, while powerful and well-organized pressure groups suffered from the trouble of the imperial economy. They were to demand drastic measures against American competition, which they made responsible for all their difficulties. This story will be briefly told in the last part of this chapter.

In fact, the offensive against American trade was launched by lawyers and not by businessmen. The hardening of the Court of Admiralty's jurisprudence, in the case of the *Essex* and two other ships in 1805, was the initiative of two top judges, Sir William Grant, Master of the Rolls, and Sir William Scott, judge of the High Court of Admiralty. They were supported by the King's Advocate, Sir John Nicholl, who presented to the government a succession of reports, which were diatribes against neutrals and pressed ministers to be more rigorous against them. The same views prevailed among the lawyers who revolved around Admiralty courts. They all had a financial interest in more prizes and in a more intricate jurisprudence,[72] but they also had an exalted idea of Britain's 'maritime rights' and deplored that government, since 1803, was too lenient towards neutrals, who actually were undermining British naval power.[73]

Public opinion was warned of the danger by a pamphlet published in October 1805: *War in disguise or the Frauds of the Neutral Flags*. The author was James Stephen, a lawyer and member of the 'Evangelical party', a relative of Wilberforce and a friend of Spencer Perceval (and also the great-grandfather of Virginia Woolf). He took a high moral ground and denounced the neutrals' frauds as if they were deadly sins. Neutral

---

[71] Crouzet, *L'économie*, pp. 117, 152–4, 310–11; Baring, *An Inquiry*, pp. 5, 61, 63, 138–43, 147, 153; PP, 1808, X, pp. 17, 23–4, 64, 102; PP, 1812, III, pp. 463–4, 469; PRO, FO 95/4, Memorandum by Sir Francis Baring, 27 July 1805.

[72] This is not a malicious innuendo by this writer; the charge was made against Nicholl and Scott by Lord Bathurst, in a letter to Spencer Perceval, 5 November 1807; BL, Add. MS 49,178, bundle 3, 36/21–2.

[73] Robinson, *Reports*, V, pp. 365, 387–8; PRO, BT 1/27/17; FO 83/2204, letter by Nicholl, 9 October 1805; GD 42/10/3; GD 42/11/1 and 8; GD 42/21/5; Add. MS 34,457/fo.163.

trade was responsible for the crisis which had struck the British West Indies and was thus weakening British naval power. Therefore, neutrals had to be forbidden to trade with enemy colonies. Stephen stated that the United States would complain but would not go to war. And even if it did, it would suffer greatly, while war with America would be far less dangerous for Britain than the status quo, which meant the loss of its naval ascendancy.[74] *War in disguise* had much success, but the 'lawyers' offensive' against American trade, to influence government's policy, needed to be supported by powerful interest groups.

The shipping interest was the first to complain, but its demands did not go very far. In 1802, the Society of Shipowners of Great Britain had been founded in order to oppose any more breaches of the Navigation Laws. It organized a campaign which stressed that shipowners were suffering from crushing taxation and from rising prices (for naval stores, shipstores, labour, insurance premiums), while freight rates were not much above their pre-war levels, because of competition by neutral ships, which monopolized trade with foreign countries. Many British ships were thus unemployed, the rest was sailing at a loss, colonial shipping was almost destroyed. Shipowners demanded that the last strongholds of British sea-power, the last 'nurseries of seamen', i.e. the coasting and colonial trades, be defended. Consequently, American ships had to be excluded from trading with the colonies.[75]

Shipowners fought the American Intercourse Bill of 1806, which was intended to regularize American trade with the West Indies, tooth and nail. In May and June 1806, Parliament was flooded with petitions from many ports of shipbuilding and ship registry, according to which the shipping industry was facing imminent ruin. Early in 1807 a new wave of petitions repeated these jeremiads.[76]

In this struggle, shipowners were joined by what we shall call 'the North American interest', the settlers and merchants of British North America, and the British merchants who were trading with those colonies. The former were fiercely hostile to the United States, both for

[74] J. Stephen, *War in disguise or the Frauds of the Neutral Flags* (London, 1805; re-edited in 1917, from the 3rd edn). This pamphlet was full of factual errors and exaggerations.

[75] Ragatz, *The Fall*, pp. 297–8; Graham, *Sea Power*, pp. 180–2; Atcheson, *American Encroachments*, pp. lviii–lxii; Lord Sheffield, *Strictures on the Necessity of inviolably maintaining the Navigation and Colonial System of Great Britain* (London, 1804); J. Alley, *A Vindication of the Principles and Statements advanced in the Strictures of the Right Hon. Lord Sheffield* (London, 1806); J. Marryat, *Concessions to America the Bane of Britain* (London, 1807), pp. 62–3; *Remarks on the Present State of the British Shipping Interest* (London, 1805, 2nd edn); PP, 1808, IV, pp. 375–6; PRO, BT 1/28/6; BT 5/16, 135.

[76] *JHC*, LXI and LXII, *passim*; *CPD*, VI and VII, *passim*; Atcheson, *American Encroachments*, pp. lvii, lxxxii–lxxxv; PC 4/15, 1–3.

economic reasons and from fear of their neighbour's democratic leanings. Late in 1804, the 'Halifax committee' was established; it made a serious effort of propaganda in Britain, where it found a number of supporters (notably Lord Sheffield). Its main demand was for an adequate 'encouragement' to British North America, which would be the prohibition of trade between the United States and the British West Indies; if this was granted, those colonies – Newfoundland included – would be fully able to supply the West Indies with everything they needed. But the British government turned a deaf ear to this and also to the proposals for improving the situation of the maritime colonies, which an eminent lawyer from Nova Scotia, Richard Uniacke, brought to London in 1806. The main point was to establish four free ports, which would be open to American ships for importing foodstuffs and lumber; those goods would be then re-exported to the British West Indies, but exclusively on British ships, which would recover the carrying trade they had lost since 1793. Moreover, customs duties on American imports in the British West Indies would be imposed and their proceeds used to pay bounties to British ships coming from British North America.[77]

The government's indifference created much discontent among the North American interest, which consequently adopted more extreme positions. In 1806, two 'gentlemen from Halifax' published in London a pamphlet, in which they maintained that Britain had to assert its 'maritime rights'; if a war with the United States broke out, it would be most favourable to British interests, and especially to British North America, which would become the only source of supplies for the West Indies.[78] However, the 'North American interest' was not too influential in London, and a decisive turning point in the campaign against American trade was the rallying of a more powerful lobby, the West India interest; this came relatively late.[79]

Since sugar prices had started to fall, the West India Committee had

---

[77] Graham, *Sea Power*, pp. 184–9; Innis, *The Cod Fisheries*, pp. 239–40; Ragatz, *The Fall*, p. 298; Atcheson, *American Encroachments*, pp. 99–102; G. S. Graham, 'The origin of free ports in British North America', *Canadian Historical Review*, 12 (1941), 27–31; D. C. Harvey, 'Uniacke's memorandum to Windham, 1806', *Canadian Historical Review*, 17 (1936), 41; PRO, BT 1/27/55, 56, 57, Memoranda by Uniacke to the Board of Trade; BT 1/28/38.

[78] *The Present Claims and Complaints of America briefly and fairly considered* (London, 1806), pp. xii–xv. The views of the 'two gentlemen' were close to those of J. Stephen.

[79] Actually shipowners and 'North Americans' were hoping for a war (or a least a deterioration of relations) with the USA, and they saw in the exploitation of the theme of neutral trade with enemy colonies the means to exclude American ships from the British West Indies.

besieged the Government with its complaints and demanded measures which would increase prices. But, up to the beginning of 1807, it had denounced taxation as the cause of the crisis and thus had asked for new fiscal arrangements – no more increase of import duties on sugar, a new system of drawbacks and bounties on sugar re-exports. Also, on 5 December 1806, the West Indians asked that sugar be substituted for cereals in breweries and distilleries. And the frequent discussions they had with ministers during 1806 were only about taxation.[80]

There was a change, however, early in 1807, because the sugar crisis became more acute and because the government of Lord Grenville, after making promises to the West India Committee on 29 December 1806, did not actually accept its demands in fiscal matters. A bounty on the re-export of raw sugar was granted, but was deemed too low; on 17 February 1807, a parliamentary committee, to which the question had been referred, reported that the use of sugar in breweries and distilleries would be useless for planters and harmful to revenue.[81] In fact, the government had also tried to put some restrictions upon the American carrying trade in colonial produce, but through an agreement with the United States and not unilaterally. In the autumn of 1806, long negotiations on the differences between Britain and the USA had taken place in London, between, on one hand, James Monroe and C. Pinkney, and Lord Auckland and Lord Holland on the other, and eventually a treaty had been signed on 31 December 1806. According to its article 11, a transit duty of 2 per cent *ad valorem* (the British had at first asked for 4 per cent) would be levied upon produce of enemy colonies which would be re-exported from the United States. The idea was to restore some parity of costs between the American and British carrying trades, though one can wonder whether such a low transit charge would have been effective. However, President Jefferson was to refuse to send the treaty to the Senate for ratification (because the problem of impressment had not been settled) and he demanded a renegotiation, which was refused by the British. The treaty was not made public after it had been signed, the West Indians were not aware of the government's

---

[80] MMWIPM, III and IV, *passim*, especially IV, pp. 50–90, 103–112; PRO, BT 1/29/14; BT 1/31/27, 52; BT 5/16, 179–81, 194, 196–7, 227–8, 230–1, 235, 443–5, 448–9, 463–4; BL, Add. MS 34,457, fos. 166, 177; DP, VIII, pp. 162–3, 181, 395, 455, 471, 474, 489–90; Ragatz, *The Fall*, pp. 290–1, 296. A memorandum of 14 April 1806 had, however, mentioned neutral commerce as a cause of the sugar crisis, but it did not demand measures against it.

[81] PRO, BT 1/32/8, 31; BT 5/17, 10–12, 29, 56, 59, 103; *CPD*, VIII, c. 840–1, 849–51; MMWIPM, IV, pp. 122–41; *Report from the Committee appointed to consider of the Expediency of permitting the Use of Sugar or Molasses in the Distillery and Brewery, for a time to be limited under the Circumstances now affecting the Trade of the British Colonies in the West Indies*, PP, 1806–7, II (no. 83), pp. 71 ff.

attempt to help them and they moved towards a harder line, as the sugar crisis was worsening.[82]

Early in February 1807, a delegation of the West India Committee represented to ministers that the carrying trade by neutrals inflicted serious injury to the British colonies. On 17 February, the General Assembly of the Committee adopted resolutions, couched in strong terms; they expressed the wish that Britain's ascendancy at sea would be used to interrupt the trade of enemy colonies. Despairing of getting help from the government, the Assembly decided to appeal to Parliament, through a petition which was approved on 26 February; it dwelt at length on the mischief caused by neutral trade, but did not demand explicitly some measures directed against it.[83] Still, such a claim had been made in a memorandum to the Board of Trade from the West India Planters and Merchants of Glasgow, of 28 January. It was thus in February 1807 that the West India interest, which had traditionally been in favour of good relations with the United States – because of the West Indies' dependence upon the latter – took an anti-neutral (anti-American) stand. This was a powerful lobby, and there were few politicians who were not attached to traditional views about the vital importance for Britain of its West Indian colonies.[84]

Not long afterwards, the Ministry of All Talents was replaced by a 'Tory' government, with the duke of Portland as its nominal head; some of the new ministers had, in February 1807, demanded a more rigorous blockade policy and this was encouraging for the West Indians.[85] However, the change of government was followed by a general election, and meanwhile sugar prices were falling. So, when a delegation of the West India Committee was received in June 1807 by the new chancellor of the Exchequer, Spencer Perceval, they stressed that the matter was urgent and they noted that no measure of aid could be effective – and quickly – except one which would prevent the transit of enemy colonial produce to the Continent, under the protection of neutral flags. Then, late in June, the West Indians obtained the appointment by the new House of Commons of a committee 'on the Commercial State of the West Indian

[82] Burt, *The United States*, pp. 227–34; *CPD*, IV, c. 394, 1038; DP, VIII, pp. 36, 63, 87, 288, 302, 445, 458–9, 485; PRO, FO 5/51, Auckland and Holland to Howick, 20 and 31 October, 29 December 1806; Monroe and Pinkney to Auckland and Holland, 20 August 1806; BL, Add. MS 34,456, fo. 610. This negotiation fits into the general framework of the Grenville's government moderate policy, which was conciliatory towards the USA (another aspect is the American Intercourse Act).

[83] However, the petition mentioned that neutral trade could have been banned thanks to Britain's naval superiority.

[84] MMWIPM, IV, pp. 122–50 (especially p. 125); PRO, BT 1/32/42; BT 5/17/73–4; *JHC*, LXII, pp. 281–2; *CPD*, IX, c. 85–100, 140–1.

[85] On 4 February 1807, Perceval and Lord Castlereagh had displayed, in the House of Commons, a violent hostility towards the USA; *CPD*, VIII, c. 630–2, 641–4.

Colonies'. Its report, presented on 24 July 1807, was a great success for
the West India interest. It drew a dark picture of the crisis on the sugar
market and of the planters' distress; if some vigorous remedy was not
used quickly, a large number of planters would be ruined and this would
be a fatal blow to Britain's commercial and maritime power. The report
laid down that the fundamental cause of the crisis was the easy relations
between enemy colonies and Europe, under neutral flags. It concluded
that the only remedy was to act severely against neutral trade and to
restrain as much as possible the exports from enemy colonies, so that the
Continent would be forced to import from Britain the colonial produce it
needed. It was important that a parliamentary committee of inquiry had
taken such a hostile stand towards neutral trade. Moreover, the committee had been conscious of the danger which the policy it recommended
involved, and especially of the risks of war with the United States. It had
examined the question of supplying the West Indies, and its conclusions
were heartening. Trade with the United States was not vital for the West
Indies and not equivalent to the disadvantages they were suffering.
Moreover, some spokesmen of the North American interest had persuaded the committee – despite statements by West India planters – that
the West Indies had nothing to fear in case of war with the United States,
as they could be fully supplied with lumber, grain and fish from British
North America.[86] After the parliamentary recess, the West Indians returned to the charge: on 26 October 1807, they submitted to Spencer
Perceval new resolutions, which stressed the state of 'agony' of the West
India trade. They demanded an immediate blockade of the main ports in
the enemy colonies, plus the prohibition in distilleries of all materials but
sugar.[87]

From February to October 1807, the West Indians had thus vigorously
campaigned in favour of a more rigorous policy towards neutrals and
especially of restrictions upon the American trade with enemy colonies.[88]
They had been supported by other pressure groups: the North American
interest, as just mentioned, and the East India Company. On 14 October
1807, its Chairman, Charles Grant, told the directors that the fall in
re-exports of East India fabrics was caused by the transport of such goods
to Europe on American ships. On 6 November, the Company instructed
the government of Bengal to accept into its ports only neutral ships
arriving directly from their country's ports; such ships would also be

---

[86] MMWIPM, IV, pp. 174–77; BT 1/40/14; PP, 1807, III (no. 65), pp. 1–85; W. F. Galpin,
      The Grain Supply of England during the Napoleonic Period (New York, 1925), pp. 48–9,
      52–3.
[87] MMWIPM, IV, pp. 179–91.
[88] Baring, *An Inquiry*, p. 3, on the violence of the West Indians' campaign.

permitted to clear out only for their own ports; they would be forbidden to engage in India's coasting trade, to sail – even on ballast – for some port in Europe or for China.[89]

In addition, some violent attacks against the United States were published in pamphlets and newspapers. *Concessions to America, the Bane of Britain* has an unequivocal title; it was written by Joseph Marryat, shipowner, West India merchant and MP. He demanded to ban the re-export to Europe, by neutrals, of colonial produce. He admitted that such a decision could cause a war with the United States, but stated that such a war would bring large advantages to Britain, which would get the monopoly of supplying Europe with colonial produce; its North American colonies and its shipping would, moreover, recover their prosperity. On the other hand, the United States had everything to lose: its foreign trade would be annihilated, its agriculture and finances ruined, the country's unity jeopardized. Sir Frederick Morton Eden wrote an *Address on the Maritime Rights of Great Britain*, which is still more violent: he accused the United States of being the willing instrument of Bonaparte's machinations against Britain.[90]

Some interest groups were so angry against American competition that they contemplated deliberately, nay complacently, the prospect of a war with the United States. One can even assume that some people demanded rigorous measures against neutral trade, because they anticipated that war would be the result, so that the competition they were suffering from would be destroyed. During the summer and autumn of 1807, there was a 'war party', which wished for war with the United States. In September, the marquess of Buckingham wrote to Lord Auckland that he had dined with some West India merchants, who were eagerly expecting an American war[91] (which the attack on the American frigate *Chesapeake*, on 22 June, had made more likely).

Naval officers shared that eagerness. On 13 August 1807, Rear-Admiral G. Berkeley wrote to Lord Bathurst, the president of the Board of Trade, to propose a pre-emptive strike: he would sail with his squadron

---

[89] PRO, FO 353/69, Chairman to the Courts, 14 October 1807; Court of Directors to the Government of Bengal, 6 November; Sir F. Baring to the Court, 15 September and 16 December 1807; PRO, BT 1/45/12; PP, 1808, X, pp. 29–30; Philips, *The East India Company*, pp. 156–8.

[90] Marryat, *Concessions to America*; Sir F. M. Eden, *Address on the Maritime Rights of Great Britain* (London, 1807). Early in 1808, the chairman of the Society of Shipowners, N. Atcheson, was to publish another unequivocal pamphlet: *American Encroachments on British Rights* (London, 1808).

[91] BL, Add. MS 34,457, fo. 352; also *Edinburgh Review.*, 12, no. 23, 243, 245; *The Life and Times of Henry Lord Brougham, written by himself*, 3 vols. (London, 1871), I, pp. 282–3: Brougham was observing, at the same time, that the West India and shipping interests were inciting the government to war.

to New York and hold the city under the threat of destruction, in order to influence Anglo-American negotiations; or, preferably, he would destroy the thousands (sic) of ships in the harbour and impose an enormous war contribution on the population. He was also planning to destroy the 1,200 American ships which were fishing in the St Lawrence gulf and off Labrador.[92]

As for ministers, they had accepted some of the views which have been mentioned. In several memoranda, which he wrote during the summer of 1807, George Rose, vice-president of the Board of Trade, stressed that a break with the United States would have no unfortunate consequences for British trade and industry, which indeed would greatly profit of such an occurrence, while America, whose ships covered the seas, was highly vulnerable.[93]

Ministers were engaged in the detailed preparation of the famous orders in council which were to be published on 11 November 1807. The problem of their origins and preparation will not be discussed here.[94] Suffice it to say that the crisis of the imperial economy, which has been described, and the pressure of 'interests' – especially the West Indians – which this crisis had made very hostile to the United States, were instrumental in the adoption of those rigorous measures against neutral trade. However, some different considerations also influenced the British government, which were military, political and economic. There was the necessity to take up the challenge of the continental blockade and to answer Napoleon's recent successes by some arrogant posturing. The British blockade was also both 'mercantile' and 'offensive', designed to encourage Britain's trade on one hand, to hurt its enemies' economies on the other. Indeed, it was to be an effective remedy to the crisis of the imperial economy, thanks to the unrestricted use of British naval power – and also to the unintended cooperation of President Jefferson (whose embargo was decided in anticipation of the November orders) and, later, of President Madison. The empire's economic crisis had resulted from the opening – under the pressure of war – of the closed and protected 'Old colonial system' to American competition. From 1808 onwards, the crisis

---

[92] *Historical Manuscripts Commission. Report on the Manuscripts of Earl Bathurst, preserved at Cirencester Park*, ed. F. Bickley (London, 1923), pp. 63–4.

[93] PRO, FO 95/515. In December 1807, J. Stephen handed over to his friend Spencer Perceval a memorandum with the title: 'Coup d'œil on an American war'; he demonstrated that Britain had nothing to fear from a war with the USA, which, actually, would bring many advantages. On the other hand it would ruin American finances and destroy the popularity of Thomas Jefferson and the Republican party, who were 'sold' to France and hated Britain.

[94] See Crouzet, *Britain, France . . .* , ch. 9.

was overcome. Britain got rid of American competition in the colonial carrying trade and secured a quasi-monopoly of relations between the Old and the New Worlds, while military and political changes on the Continent in 1808–9 reopened several of its markets to British colonial produce and manufactures. The British West Indies prospered, and also the North American colonies, where the timber trade grew mightily, after preferential customs duties had been established. On the other hand, the various developments of 1807 – notably the orders in council – set in motion the process which, after several ups and downs, led to the war of 1812 – a war which had been wished for, as early as 1806, by some British 'interests'.

Part IV

Colonial working societies

12 Emigration and the standard of living: the eighteenth-century Chesapeake

Lois Green Carr

A few years ago, a summer seminar of the National Bureau of Economic Research considered American economic growth and the standard of living from the 1780s to the Civil War. The basic question, of course, was the effect of the costs and benefits of industrialization and urbanization on well-being, part of a long-term debate not only in the history of western Europe and America but in the assessment of present-day outcomes for economic and social policy worldwide. The papers discussed well-being or its absence from evidence on life expectancy, on wages and prices, on labour participation rates, on distribution of income and wealth, on availability and quality of food, housing and consumer goods, and on heights as a measure of nutrition and health.[1] I was struck by the relevance of the issues to an entirely different transformation, that brought about by the giant migration of Europeans and Africans to the New World in the seventeenth and eighteenth centuries. It seemed useful to employ what is known so far about the standard of living in Europe and America to assess the consequences of migration for some of the participants in this great movement of preindustrial populations.

My efforts so far are part of a much larger task for future scholars. This

I wish to thank Jean B. Russo for assistance in obtaining data from the computer files and Jane McWilliams for hand counts of livestock and signs of dairying and sales of dairy products from manuscript inventories. I am grateful to Robert W. Fogel, Jennie Lamont Johnson, Peter H. Lindert, Orlando Ridout V, Sandria Ross, Jean B. Russo and Lorena S. Walsh for permission to make use of their unpublished research. In addition, Russo and Walsh kindly read and criticized various drafts. An earlier and shorter version of this essay was delivered to a pre-conference in June 1993, at Arnheim, The Netherlands, held in preparation for the B4 Session of the Eleventh International Economic History Congress held in September 1994 in Milan, Italy. A severely curtailed version, presented at the congress itself, was published in its proceedings. In August 1995, I gave the 1993 version to the Early American History Workshop at the University of Minnesota. I thank the discussants and audiences at all these presentations and the readers for this volume for helpful comments.

[1] The proceedings are published in Robert E. Gallman and John Joseph Wallis, eds., *American Economic Growth and Standards of Living Before the Civil War* (Chicago, 1992).

chapter and an earlier essay are confined to a small part of the New World, the Chesapeake region of eastern North America, and offer only a small beginning. Furthermore, they do not consider, from the perspective of comparative living standards, the consequences of migration for involuntary emigrants – African slaves or European convict servants. Nor do they discuss the impact of European colonization on the indigenous populations of North America. The sufferings of these peoples, of course, are part of the costs of these population movements and are the subject of much on-going study.

The earlier essay describes the seventeenth-century Chesapeake immigrant experience. This chapter looks at the eighteenth century, confining the discussion to the British migration, although as the century progressed the German immigrant population grew steadily. The first article argues that seventeenth-century British immigrants, who were mostly indentured servants, faced a trade off: they had a shorter life and less physical comfort than in England (mitigated by ample food but far more arduous work) versus better opportunities to improve their station by acquiring land and thereby gaining greater control of their lives.[2] It is argued here that eighteenth-century British immigrants found a different situation. Their life expectancy after arrival was probably greater than it had been in the seventeenth century and physical comfort was closer to the mother-country standard; but for poor servant immigrants, especially those who arrived without education or skills, opportunities to acquire land or otherwise much improve their station declined or disappeared for almost all.

In looking at immigrants to the Chesapeake over the eighteenth century, one is scrutinizing a small part of the population. Immigrants were a majority of adults throughout the seventeenth century, but after 1700, the native born were dominant.[3] The proportion of immigrants among Chesapeake inhabitants fell drastically over the rest of the colonial period. Immigrants continued to arrive from the British Isles and to a much lesser degree from Germany, but the rapid growth rate of the creole population quickly swamped the newcomers. During the period from 16 December 1773 to 7 April 1776, the British government made an effort to count all emigrants from ports in England and Scotland, and in that short period, 3,102 men and women, or 1,034 per year, came to the Chesapeake from those two regions; but in 1770 the total

---

[2] Lois Green Carr, 'Emigration and the standard of living: the seventeenth-century Chesapeake', *JEcH*, 52 (1992), 271–91.

[3] Russell R. Menard, 'Immigrants and their increase: the process of population growth in early colonial Maryland', in Aubrey C. Land, Lois Green Carr and Edward C. Papenfuse, eds., *Law, Society, and Politics in Early Maryland* (Baltimore, 1977), pp. 88–110.

white population of Maryland and Virginia had reached nearly 400,000.[4]

What proportion of these might have been immigrants? David Galenson in his study of English servant immigration has shown that it was very light during the 1740s, probably resulting in a net loss of immigrants in the total Chesapeake population by 1750.[5] Supposing that by 1770, any adult immigrant who had arrived before 1740 had died; that during the years 1774 and 1775, immigrants who left from places other than Britain had come to another 500 per year; that immigration per year had been the same from 1750 to 1770 as it was in 1774 and 1775; and that no immigrant who had arrived over that twenty-year period had died by 1770 (obviously untrue). The proportion that year of immigrant colonists from Europe to total Chesapeake population would then be no more than 7.5 per cent. In reality the proportion must have been considerably less.

Bernard Bailyn has recently published an analysis of the 1773–6 British migration, with revealing results. Of a total of 7,249 people who went to the thirteen colonies that became the United States, 2,238, or 31 per cent, went to Maryland. Of these, 91.5 per cent were English, almost all of them from southern England, especially London. Ninety-six per cent were indentured servants, of whom nearly 76 per cent had trades or crafts or other skills. Similar proportions of the 774 immigrants to Virginia were servants and with some sort of training. The migration represented the transfer of a workforce, mostly from London, to an area with a high demand for labour, especially skilled labour.[6]

Were earlier eighteenth-century migrations to Maryland so predominantly servant? There is no way to know for certain. No similar count and description of immigrants, free as well as servant, is available. The Maryland Naval Office records give the numbers of servants who arrived in ships, but passengers who paid their own way were not saleable cargo and were not reported. However, for the years 1745–75, Abbot Emerson Smith has counted 10,560 servants (not convicts) arriving by the shipload

---

[4] Bernard Bailyn, *Voyagers to the West: a Passage in the Peopling of America on the Eve of the Revolution* (New York, 1986) table 6.1; *Historical Statistics of the United States: Colonial Times to 1970*, 2 vols. (Washington, D.C., 1975), II, p. 1168.

[5] David W. Galenson, *White Servitude in Colonial America: an Economic Analysis* (Cambridge, 1981), table H3.

[6] Bailyn, *Voyagers to the West*, chs. 4–7; tables 4.1, 6.1, 6.4, 6.5, 6.5b. Abbot Emerson Smith, *Colonists in Bondage: White Servitude and Convict Labor in America, 1607–1776* (Chapel Hill, N.C., 1947), p. 325, indicates that one-fifth of the servants who arrived in the port of Annapolis in 1774 and 1775 were convicts. Bailyn studied lists taken in England, not the Naval Office records for Maryland, and his source included only 298 convicts. He did not include them in his total for the number of emigrants in table 4.1, from which I conclude that he excluded convicts from his other tables.

in the port of Annapolis alone.[7] Nothing in the records of Maryland or Virginia suggests that free immigrants came in these numbers. Russell Menard has estimated the seventeenth-century proportion of servants in the immigrating population to be 70 to 85 per cent.[8] Over the eighteenth century, although there was doubtless considerable short-term fluctuation, the proportion may have fallen mostly into the seventeenth-century range. The period from 16 December 1773 to 7 April 1775 produced an extraordinary high, but overall the percentage of servants was probably always very large.

What were the social origins of these servants? David Galenson has studied all the available eighteenth-century lists of servants who emigrated to the Chesapeake, although he does not distinguish between Maryland and Virginia. Like Bailyn, he has found that in 1773–6, a great majority of servants – by Galenson's count 80.5 per cent – arrived with a skill. Such people were not from the bottom of British society. However, on lists that run from 1718 through 1759, he has found that only 44.3 per cent of servants were described as skilled. The others were either listed as labourers or without occupations. Since those without occupations (37 per cent of all) were younger and had lower levels of literacy than those who claimed skills, he judged them to be less productive.[9] Such people may well have been from the very poor of England.

What did the decision to enter the Chesapeake labour market mean for those who came? First of all, was their life expectancy as dismally low as it had been for their seventeenth-century predecessors? Doubtless some died during their seasoning period, but what, if any, improvement in survival there was is unknown. Probably much depended on where an immigrant went. The later-settled interior lands, especially in the Piedmont, were less subject to the ague (malaria) and probably to dysentery, typhoid and other diseases that flourished in brackish waters.[10] Once seasoned, the eighteenth-century immigrants had a life expectancy longer than earlier, but not as long as that of people who stayed in England or of the native born in Maryland and Virginia. Life's lottery still penalized immigrants.[11]

---

[7] Smith, *Colonists in Bondage*, pp. 325–6. Nearly as many again were convict servants.

[8] Russell R. Menard, 'Economy and society in early colonial Maryland', Ph.D. thesis, University of Iowa (1975), p. 162.

[9] Galenson, *White Servitude*, pp. 48, 51–78, and table 6.6; Bailyn, *Voyagers to the West*, table 6.5b.

[10] Carville V. Earle, 'Environment, disease, and mortality in early Virginia', in Thad W. Tate and David L. Ammerman, eds., *The Chesapeake in the Seventeenth Century: Essays in Anglo-American Society and Politics* (Chapel Hill, N.C., 1979), pp. 96–125.

[11] Daniel S. Levy, 'The life expectancies of colonial Maryland legislators', *Historical Methods*, 20 (1987), 18–19; E. A. Wrigley and R. S. Schofield, *The Population History of England, 1541–1871: A Reconstruction* (Cambridge, Mass., 1981), table 7.21.

As for opportunities for marriage and raising a family, there is little eighteenth-century data that distinguishes immigrants from native born. The immigrant lists show that few immigrants were women – 10 per cent over the years 1700–75 – a fact that may have affected opportunities for immigrant men to marry if their origins were held against them. The lists also show that the immigrants were young. In 1759, the mean age at arrival for men was 20 to 21, and during 1773–6 about 24; for women it was about 19 and 23 respectively.[12] Finally, it appears likely that most immigrants came as indentured servants. From this information, it can be inferred that most immigrant men probably waited to marry until their early thirties. Those who arrived as single servants at best could not marry until they had finished four or five years of indenture and undoubtedly had to wait longer in order to create the means for establishing a house-hold. In England, by contrast, mean age at marriage for men dropped across the century from 27.3 to 25.9.[13] Consequently, as in the seventeenth century, most eighteenth-century Chesapeake immigrant men formed families later than they might have had they stayed at home. In addition, possibly the proportion never marrying exceeded that in England, given the drastic shortage of immigrant women. However, there was no shortage of women in the general population. It seems probable that immigrant men who could afford to marry did so.

There is no certain information about how long these marriages lasted. In the general population (as seen in Prince George's county, Maryland), mean length of marriage ran from twenty-two to twenty-five years, a big improvement over the eleven to thirteen years of a century earlier.[14] However, shorter life expectancies for immigrants as opposed to the native born, combined with a later age at marriage than the native born enjoyed, probably shortened the years of unbroken family life in households headed by immigrants. The result must have been fewer children than were born to native-born parents. Still, longer life expectancy for immigrants than earlier allowed more children than had been born to immigrants of the seventeenth century, with beneficial results for family stability. Some of the children must have been older at the father's death than they had been in earlier times and more able to offer assistance to their mothers and siblings. Nevertheless, difficulties must have been great if both parents were immigrants. The children were then unlikely to have kin at hand to help them. Luckily, it seems probable that many children of

---

[12] Galenson, *White Servitude*, tables 2.1 and 2.5. Galenson's figures are for all servants, regardless of destination. Bailyn shows a higher proportion of women for 1774–5 than Galenson does – 16.2 per cent. *Voyagers to the West*, table 5.4.

[13] Wrigley and Schofield, *Population History of England*, table 10.1.

[14] Allan Kulikoff, *Tobacco and Slaves: the Development of Southern Cultures in the Chesapeake, 1680–1800* (Chapel Hill, N.C., 1986), table 20.

immigrant fathers had a native-born mother with a family network that could offer support.

In general, then, eighteenth-century immigrants fared somewhat better than those of the seventeenth century with respect to family formation and nurture of children, if not quite as well as they would have in England; and if they ate as well as seventeenth-century immigrants did, they ate better than did their English counterparts.[15] But did they? Were eighteenth-century immigrants, especially immigrants who arrived as servants, as well nourished as their predecessors?

An important part of the evidence for Chesapeake nutrition comes from increase in height in the eighteenth century. Chesapeake-born soldiers measured in 1760 were more than 3 inches taller, on average, than were British soldiers measured in the late 1770s. Between 1760 and 1779, this discrepancy increased. The Chesapeake-born added another 0.4 inches to their height. Heights among the colonial native born must have been the result of nutritional improvement over that of England, an improvement begun in the seventeenth century but still continuing. In addition, comparison of heights of colonial recruits by place of birth tells that the foreign born living in Maryland and Virginia were taller than those who had remained at home.[16] Immigrants who came as children improved their nutritional status enough to catch up to the native born in some degree.

There is, indeed, no reason to suppose that eighteenth-century immigrants fared more poorly than the native born in diet. Nearly everyone lived in the countryside. In consequence, Chesapeake householders raised most of their own food and both staples of their diet, maize and meat. Those who worked as farm hands needed about 4,000 calories a day; in craft occupations, they may have needed somewhat less. Everything indicates that people had adequate nourishment. About four and a half cups of maize per day per adult male, with proportional amounts for women and children, was considered an entitlement for every inhabitant. Eighteenth-century planters' account books show that even slaves received this ration.[17] To avert pellagra, planters supplemented corn with beans, peas, meat or fish, all of which were widely available. Probate inventories suggest that even the poorest households had sufficient cattle and hogs to supply at least half a pound of meat per adult male per day,

[15] Carr, 'Emigration and the standard of living', 273–80.

[16] Kenneth L. Sokoloff and Georgia C. Villaflor, 'The early achievement of modern stature in America', *Social Science History*, 6 (1982), 453–81.

[17] Lorena S. Walsh, 'Work and resistance in the new republic: the case of the Chesapeake, 1770–1820', in Mary Turner, ed., *Chattel Slaves into Wage Slaves* (Bloomington, Ind., 1995), pp. 98–105; Gregory A. Stiverson and Patrick H. Butler III, eds., 'Virginia in 1732: the travel journal of William Hugh Grove', *Virginia Magazine of History and Biography*, 85 (1977), 18–44.

again with appropriate modifications for women and children. For example, in Anne Arundel county, Maryland, from 1710 to 1722, 86 per cent of inventoried rural estates had cattle, and thereafter until 1777, 91 to 96 per cent did so.[18] From 1710 to 1732, 87 to 88 per cent of estates had swine; thereafter, 90 to 94 per cent did so. I have shown that in the seventeenth century, when livestock care was minimal and reproductive increase very low, a couple starting out with just one sow would have meat enough for man and wife and two small children within five years.[19] Two sows would provide enough within three years and surpluses shortly thereafter, even though the family was growing. Inventories show that nearly every eighteenth-century farm household had a sufficiency of cattle and hogs for families of much larger size without assuming any improvement in the care of the animals and hence in their reproductive increase.

Given such a diet, the calories supplied were at least adequate. The maize alone provided about 3,220 calories for an adult man; the meat added a probable additional 570 to 600 calories. (Colonial Chesapeake cattle and hogs provided much less meat than these animals do today.) The remaining calories needed were not hard to come by – a third of a cup of dried beans or peas would supply enough, or a sweet potato, or a cup and a half of milk, or two cups of cider (the usual drink). All of this food even a poor planter could supply from his own resources.[20]

Did servants share in this diet? There is little reason to suppose that they did not. An underfed servant did not have the energy for heavy labour. One planter's account book shows that purchases of meat for servants that came to a pound a day.[21] Servants who worked beside slaves may have shared the slave diet; but this diet must have been adequate for field labour, although not necessarily to the Englishman's taste.[22] In households wealthy enough to purchase the time of an immigrant servant, there was no reason to stint on nourishment. Once servants became free, if they established households, they grew their own corn and other food crops and could soon supply their own meat and milk.

[18] Anne Arundel county inventory computer file, Historic St Mary's City History Office, Maryland State Archives, Annapolis, Md.

[19] Lois Green Carr, Russell R. Menard and Lorena S. Walsh, *Robert Cole's World: Agriculture and Society in Early Maryland* (Chapel Hill, N.C., 1991), appendix 3.

[20] Carr. 'Emigration and the standard of living', 278–9.

[21] Philip Ludwell Lee Account Book, 1762–75, William R. Perkins Library, Duke University, Durham, N.C. I thank Lorena S. Walsh for this reference.

[22] Pregnant and nursing slave women and slave children may have suffered from insufficient protein. Heights show that the children caught up when better fed, as they reached the age for work, although their heights remained somewhat less than those of whites. Robert W. Fogel, 'Nutrition and the decline of mortality since 1700: some additional preliminary findings', in Stanley L. Engerman and Robert E. Gallman, eds., *Long-Term Factors in American Economic Growth*, National Bureau of Economic Research, Studies in Income and Wealth, 51 (Chicago, 1986), pp. 467–73.

How did this diet compare to what poor immigrants had had in England? Robert Fogel has used calorie distributions by decile for adult men from third world countries today to estimate distributions in England about 1790. Only the top 10 per cent did as well as an eighteenth-century ex-servant could as soon as he had some hogs. In England, at the seventh percentile, English men ate only 2,900 calories worth of food, a diet that allowed only six hours of heavy labour; the bottom 20 per cent had at most 1,900 calories, enough for only one hour of such work.[23] Given that most eighteenth-century Chesapeake immigrants arrived with some skills, they did not come from the hungriest levels of British society – but very few came from the top decile. With respect to food, if Fogel is correct, nearly all improved their lot by their move. In any case, they did not lose.

Can the same be said for the comforts of life – housing, consumer goods and working conditions? With respect to housing, there was surely no improvement over England. In the Chesapeake, post-in-the-ground construction, close to universal in the seventeenth century, was still common and houses were still very small. Gregory Stiverson has studied the housing of 279 Maryland proprietary tenants as recorded in 1767–8. These tenants were not at the bottom of the heap. They had leases for life that gave them equity in their farms and incentive to improve their homes. Yet their houses were framed one-and-a-half-storey structures – probably post-in-the-ground that required frequent repair – with clapboard cladding and clapboard roofs, both hard to seal against wind and rain. Most had wooden or wattle and daub chimneys, and many had dirt floors. In size they averaged from 278 square feet per floor on Zechiah manor to 490 square feet on Chaptico manor. Those on Zechiah usually measured about 19 by 14.6 feet, although some were as small as 12 by 12. Most of these were probably one-room houses with a loft or chamber above, although a few had in addition a separate kitchen with loft. Houses on Chaptico averaged about 20 by 25 feet and were doubtless usually two-room houses with chambers above.[24] Such housing was not confined to manor tenants. The Federal Direct Tax List of 1798 for St Mary's county, Maryland, shows that half the houses in the county were cottages 24 by 16 feet or less, with many as small as 16 by 12 feet.[25] Again wooden chimneys abounded.[26]

[23] Robert W. Fogel, 'Biomedical approaches to the estimation and interpretation of secular trends in equity, morbidity, mortality, and labor productivity in Europe, 1750–1980', unpublished draft (1987); Fogel, 'Second thoughts on the European escape from hunger: famines, chronic malnutrition, and mortality rates', in S. R. Osmani, ed., *Nutrition and Poverty* (Oxford, 1992), pp. 243–86.

[24] Gregory A. Stiverson, *Poverty in a Land of Plenty: Tenancy in Eighteenth-Century Maryland* (Baltimore, 1977), p. 59 and table 3.1.

[25] Cary Carson and Lorena S. Walsh, 'The material life of the Chesapeake housewife', *Winterthur Portfolio*, forthcoming.

[26] Lois Green Carr, unpublished research in Federal Direct Tax of 1798, St Mary's county, Maryland, microfilm, Maryland State Archives, Annapolis, Md.

Orphans' court valuations for landowners of Queen Anne's county, Maryland, give information that concentrates on more middling groups in Maryland society. The poorest of these landowners ($n = 177$) did not live as differently from the proprietary tenants as we might expect. Their houses were wooden, framed or log, and probably of one and a half storeys. They averaged about 360 square feet per floor before 1735 and about 434 square feet from 1760 to 1798. Once more, many had wooden chimneys. However, these houses may have been better sealed and floored than those of tenant farmers. Among richer planters, houses, and especially chimneys, began to be built of brick.[27] Indeed, many handsome brick houses from this period survive today.

Poor immigrants of the eighteenth century probably lived in housing like that of the tenant farmers or poor landowners. People who had come from the English countryside were less protected from the weather and perhaps more crowded together than in the homes they had left behind. However, many came from London, where overcrowding was rampant. They may have found the cottages of the Chesapeake comfortable enough.[28]

What is certain is that for rich and poor alike, Chesapeake housing of the eighteenth century was an improvement over what was common in the seventeenth century. There were fewer one-room structures, more shingled or tiled roofs, more plastered interior walls, more window glass, more houses of brick. There were also much oftener outbuildings for cooking, dairying and preserving meat, activities that earlier had to be carried on in the family living quarters.[29] James P. P. Horn has commented that rich people of the seventeenth-century Chesapeake were little better housed than the humble of English society. Over the eighteenth century, the rich developed mansions, with outbuildings and slave quarters that travellers described as little villages.[30]

[27] Jennie L. Johnson, '"We entered the aforesaid lands and viewed the same": plantation development in Queen Anne's County, Maryland, 1708–1798' (unpublished paper, 1992, table 1); Orlando Ridout V, 'Re-editing the past: a comparison of surviving physical and documentary evidence from Maryland's eastern shore' (unpublished paper presented to the Society of Architectural Historians, 1982).

[28] M. W. Barley, 'Rural building in England', in Joan Thirsk, ed., *The Agrarian History of England and Wales*, V (Cambridge, 1985), ch. 20; Carole Shammas, *The Pre-Industrial Consumer in England and America* (Oxford, 1990), pp. 158–64; M. Dorothy George, *London Life in the Eighteenth Century* (London, 1925; reprint, Chicago, 1984), pp. 73–116.

[29] Johnson, 'Plantation development'; Ridout, 'Re-editing the past'.

[30] James P. P. Horn, 'Adapting to a new world: a comparative study of local society in England and Maryland, 1650–1700', in Lois Green Carr, Philip D. Morgan and Jean B. Russo, eds., *Colonial Chesapeake Society* (Chapel Hill, N.C., 1988), pp. 151–2; Cary Carson, Norman F. Barka, William Kelso, Garry Wheeler Stone and Dell Upton, 'Impermanent architecture in the southern American colonies', *Winterthur Portfolio*, 16 (1981), 161–2; Carson and Walsh, 'The material life', 29–30; Shammas, *The Pre-Industrial Consumer*, pp. 166–9.

Furnishings for these houses also improved over the eighteenth century. In both England and the Chesapeake, probate inventories of moveable property provide the chief information. Horn has described the primitive lifestyles of the seventeenth-century Chesapeake poor compared to those of the Vale of Berkeley and East Kent in England and the failure of wealthier Chesapeake planters to reach the level of their English counterparts.[31] Over the eighteenth century, Chesapeake colonists began to catch up, but for poor planters improvements were modest. In 1663 in St Mary's county, Maryland, Forker Frissel, with an estate in personalty valued at £29 (constant value),[32] had no seats as such – he could sit on his chest – and no table. Many households were equally poorly equipped. Over the second half of the seventeenth century about two-thirds of those with a total estate value in personalty under £50 had no chair – that is, a single seat with a back – or no table, although the proportion without either of these basic conveniences was smaller. Over the ten years after 1685, chairs per household at this wealth level came to 1.1 and tables to 0.5.[33] By contrast, in 1765, John Price and his wife, with a personal estate of £35 (constant value), could work or eat at a table, and each could sit in a chair as well. In general, by the 1760s among decedent planters of St. Mary's with less than £50 of moveable wealth, there were 2.4 chairs and 1.2 tables per household.[34] However, in this lowest wealth group, a third were still without tables and 45 per cent without chairs.[35]

[31] James Horn, 'Domestic standards of living in England and the Chesapeake, 1650–1700', in Anton J. Schuurman and Lorena S. Walsh, eds., *Material Culture: Consumption, Life-Style, Standard of Living, 1500–1900*, Proceedings, Eleventh International Economic History Congress, B4 (Milan, Italy, September 1994), pp. 71–82; Horn, 'Adapting to a new world'.

[32] Constant value was established through use of a commodity price index described in P. M. G. Harris, 'Inflation and deflation in Early America, 1634–1860: patterns of change in the British American economy', *Social Science History*, 20 (1996), 487–98.

[33] Testamentary Proceedings 1D: 67, MS, Maryland State Archives, Annapolis, Md.; Horn, 'Adapting to a new world', table 4; Sandria Ross, unpublished research from St Mary's county, Md., inventories, 1685–95, 1725–9, 1762–5, in History Office of Historic St Mary's City, Maryland State Archives. Unless otherwise specified, all manuscripts cited are at the Maryland State Archives.

[34] Inventories 88: 81–2, MS; Ross, unpublished research.

[35] For explanations of wealth groups and discussion of bias and representativeness of inventories, see Lois Green Carr and Lorena S. Walsh, 'Inventories and the analysis of wealth and consumption patterns in St Mary's county, Maryland, 1658–1777', *Historical Methods*, 13 (1980), appendix; Lois Green Carr, 'Diversification in the colonial Chesapeake: Somerset county, Maryland, in comparative perspective', in Carr *et al.*, *Colonial Chesapeake Society*, appendix 1; Lois Green Carr and Lorena S. Walsh, 'Economic diversification and labor organization in the Chesapeake, 1650–1820', in Stephen Innes, ed., *Work and Labor in Early America* (Chapel Hill, N.C., 1988), p. 149, n. 9. The commodity price index discussed by Carr and Walsh in *Historical Methods* (1980) is somewhat different from the one used in later publications listed here and in the present paper.

Faster progress appeared in York county, Virginia. There, from the 1720s on, rural inventories of moveables valued at less than £50 averaged 2.5 to 4 chairs and a table.[36] Yet over the period 1710–77 more than a third of all such households still lacked one or both of these items; and in Anne Arundel county, Maryland, over the same period nearly three-fifths lacked chairs and more than half lacked tables (see table 12.1).

The £50 wealth level in moveables was a watershed. At higher levels, the percentage owning such equipment rose sharply. In addition, of course, more decedents had more of this basic household furniture (see table 12.1). And as time went by, there came greater elaboration in fine woods and fashionable manufacture of such equipment.[37]

Comparisons with eighteenth-century England are complicated by the disappearance after the 1720s of inventories sufficient for quantitative analysis. James Horn and Lorna Weatherill have both made excellent studies, but only Weatherill has taken her work as late as 1725 and both have tabulated percentages of households with particular items, but not mean items per household. In addition Weatherill did not include chairs. Nevertheless, it is apparent that in the Chesapeake, the inventoried poor – defined as people who left estates valued at £50 or less – did not entirely catch up to the English standard of the late seventeenth century. According to Horn, 72 per cent of poor householders in the Vale of Berkeley had chairs from 1660 through 1699 and about 83 per cent had tables. Weatherill's figure for tables, counted from a variety of English locations over the years 1675 through 1725, is 85 per cent. Only in eighteenth-century Annapolis, Maryland, and Williamsburg and Yorktown, Virginia – both Annapolis and Williamsburg were colonial capitals – did the percentage of inventoried households at this wealth level meet the English standard of an earlier time. Richer households were closer to equivalent English households, but only the richest equalled the richest of Weatherill's groups (see table 12.1). Of course, no class of Chesapeake planters had the enormous wealth and its trappings enjoyed by the English aristocracy.

Historians have been interested in tracing not only the acquisition of such basics as chairs or tables but also in following the elaboration of household living standards and the emergence of standards of gentility.

---

[36] Lorena S. Walsh, 'Urban and rural residents compared', Final Report, National Endowment for the Humanities grant, 'Urbanization in the tidewater south. Part II: the growth and development of Williamsburg and Yorktown' (1988), table 5.

[37] Lois Green Carr and Lorena S. Walsh, 'Changing lifestyles and consumer behavior in the colonial Chesapeake', in Cary Carson, Ronald Hoffman and Peter J. Albert, eds., *Of Consuming Interests: the Style of Life in the Eighteenth Century* (Charlottesville, Va., 1994), pp. 62–8, 102–4; Kevin M. Sweeney, 'High-style vernacular: lifestyles of the colonial elite', *ibid.*, pp. 40–9.

Table 12.1. *Chairs and tables in Chesapeake and English inventories,
householders only, seventeenth and eighteenth centuries*

Place, date and wealth in pounds sterling	*n* estates	*n* with chairs	% *n*	*n* with tables	% *n*
A. *By percentage*					
St Mary's County, Md. 1660–99					
0–49	149	42	28	47	32
50–99	98	52	53	52	53
100–249	67	55	82	59	88
250+	58	55	95	52	90
Vale of Berkeley 1660–99					
0– 49	192	138	72	173	90
50–99	103	89	86	98	95
100–249	111	96	86	108	97
250+	74	73	99	71	96
England 1675–1725					
0– 50	1286	–	–	1078	85
51–100	628	–	–	565	90
101–250	627	–	–	583	93
251–500	234	–	–	220	94
500+	127	–	–	121	95
York county, Va. 1710–76					
Urban					
0–49	36	31	86	28	78
50–94	24	21	88	22	92
95–225	35	29	83	32	91
225–490	30	29	97	30	100
491+	32	26	81	29	91
Rural					
0–49	140	85	61	86	61
50–94	86	71	83	71	83
95–225	130	112	86	107	82
226–490	111	93	84	91	82
491+	79	76	96	77	97
All					
0–49	176	116	66	114	65
50–94	110	92	84	93	85
95–225	165	141	85	139	84
226–490	141	122	87	121	86
491+	111	102	92	106	95

Table 12.1. (*cont.*)

Place, date and wealth in pounds sterling	*n* estates	*n* with chairs	% *n*	*n* with tables	% *n*
Anne Arundel county, Md. 1710–76					
Urban					
0–49	53	43	81	45	85
50–94	24	22	92	1	87
95–225	40	38	95	37	92
226–490	31	28	90	29	94
491+	46	42	91	44	96
Rural					
0–49	242	81	33	98	40
50–94	137	79	58	78	57
95–225	227	168	74	148	65
226–490	204	184	90	181	89
491+	198	193	97	190	96
All					
0–49	295	124	42	143	48
50–94	161	101	63	99	61
95–225	267	206	77	185	69
226–490	235	212	90	210	89
491+	244	235	96	234	96

B. *By items per household*

Wealth in pounds	1723–32	1733–44	1745–54	1755–67	1768–76
York county, Va.					
Chairs per household					
Urban					
0–49	3.11	5.46	4.50	8.00	3.50
50–225	8.89	16.33	13.08	3.75	16.53
226+	31.25	23.86	28.50	29.61	32.37
Rural					
0–49	4.17	2.53	2.85	3.57	4.13
50–225	5.91	6.31	7.21	6.28	7.48
226+	17.86	20.79	16.36	12.76	22.21
Tables per household					
Urban					
0–49	0.67	1.36	1.38	1.57	1.40
50–225	3.22	3.80	4.08	4.00	4.07
226+	7.75	7.00	8.75	6.67	9.00
Rural					
0–49	0.74	0.94	0.72	1.19	1.25
50–225	1.25	1.27	1.45	1.44	1.56
226+	2.77	3.97	3.54	2.71	5.58

Table 12.1. (*cont.*)

Place, date and wealth in pounds sterling	*n* estates	*n* with chairs	% *n*	*n* with tables	% *n*
B. *By items per household* (cont.)					
Wealth in pounds	1685–95	1725–29	1762–65		
St Mary's County, Md.					
Chairs per household					
0– 50	1.10	1.60	3.20		
51–135	4.00	3.50	4.80		
136–490	11.00	12.00	9.50		
491+	22.50	38.80	15.00		
Tables per household					
0– 50	0.50	0.60	1.20		
51–135	1.20	0.90	1.90		
136–490	4.10	2.30	3.10		
491+	6.80	7.00	3.70		

Source: Horn, 'Adapting to a new world', tables 4 and 5; Weatherill, *Consumer Behaviour*, Table 5.1; Walsh, 'Urban and rural residents compared' (1988); Anne Arundel county inventory computer files; York county inventory computer files; Ross, unpublished research.

Note: Chesapeake inventories have been reduced to constant value by commodity price indexes made for Maryland and Virginia. Work in probate records has provided convincing evidence that seventeenth-century appraisers made an effort to use sterling. Eighteenth-century Chesapeake prices are in local currencies (Harris, 'Inflation and deflation in early America', 469–505). Horn and Weatherill did not attempt to standardize inventory values. However, Weatherill found no systematic changes in values of English inventoried goods over the period she covered (1675–1725), which includes Horn's (Weatherill, *Consumer Behaviour*, 109). Horn did not deflate the St Mary's county values for 1660–99, but from 1665, our Maryland index showed little difference from the base period, which was 1700–9.

One might suppose that Weatherill's numbers distort the difference between England and St Mary's county in the percentages of estates with tables because she covers fifteen years in which Maryland currency was declining in value with respect to sterling, and hence her wealth classes are not entirely parallel with those that Horn established for seventeenth-century St Mary's county; but her percentages are very close to those of Horn for the seventeenth-century Vale of Berkeley, suggesting that distortions will not seriously affect the contrast between Maryland and England.

Overall, rough comparisons between England and the Chesapeake seem to be allowable.

Lorena Walsh and I have constructed an index of twelve items to measure such change in the Chesapeake. It is described in detail in several publications and is summarized only briefly here. Counted is the presence or absence in every estate of earthenware, china, bed or table linen, table knives, table forks, spices, religious books, secular books, wigs, watches or clocks, pictures and silver plate. Scores run from 0 to 12. Over the eighteenth century, this index rose for every wealth group in every location we studied. Tabulation by item showed the same story and demonstrated that some items that began as luxuries, such as table forks or tea (not indexed), had become commonplace by the time of the American Revolution.[38] Lorna Weatherill's work suggests that similar changes had begun in England by 1675 and continued over the eighteenth century, although with great variation in timing and location, and she does not break down this information by wealth. The proportion of inventories showing earthenware, china, books, clocks, pictures, table linen and knives and forks increased up to 1725 and she uses a variety of evidence to argue that, at falling levels of wealth, increases in amounts of standard items and the appearance of new products can be followed until at least the 1760s.[39] It seems reasonable to conclude that, with a lag in timing and probably in quantity and elaboration, colonial Chesapeake consumers were enjoying improvements similar, if not equal, to those of England in the standard of material life as seen in household goods.

Still, the question remains: did eighteenth-century Chesapeake immigrants, especially those who were poor, suffer a substantial fall in the material standard of living? Unfortunately, the evidence on hand for identifying seventeenth-century immigrants is not available for the eighteenth century. Until 1683, Lord Baltimore granted land in return for transport of settlers, leaving a paper trail of names of newcomers, both servant and free. Once the proprietor substituted payment of money or tobacco for headrights – as proofs of transport were called – the paper trail in Maryland vanished. In Virginia, headrights did not disappear, but in 1699 the governor and council authorized the sale of land warrants, as in Maryland. Consequently, recording of headrights declined drastically.[40] Historians must be satisfied with what they can learn about the population in general and assume that poor or middling or gentlemen planters lived in ways not affected by their status as native born or immigrant.

---

[38] Carr and Walsh, 'Changing lifestyles', in Carson *et al.*, *Of Consuming Interests*, pp. 69–104.

[39] Lorna Weatherill, *Consumer Behaviour and Material Culture in Britain, 1660–1760* (London, 1988), ch. 2 and table 2.1.

[40] John Kilty, *Landholder's Assistant and Land Office Guide* (Baltimore, Md., 1808), pp. 124–6; Nell Marion Nugent, *Cavaliers and Pioneers: Abstracts of Virginia Land Patents and Grants, 1695–1732* (Richmond, Va., 1979), pp. vii–viii.

Once again, in judging the immigrant experience, much depends on the backgrounds of the immigrants. Poor men without skills who left the crowded tenements of London may not have suffered great loss as servants or householders in the Chesapeake; but former poor inhabitants of rural or small-town England may have lived less comfortably than they had in the homes they left. English people from middling groups or the gentry may have noticed a decline, but probably less of one, and not nearly what similar seventeenth-century immigrants had experienced.

What of working conditions, the third area in what I have called the comforts of life? Early in the eighteenth century, immigrant servants and other poor newcomers from Britain must have found some conditions similar to those of the seventeenth century. Farm work was harder and more monotonous than in England.[41] But as virgin forest and its giant root systems disappeared, planters could plough their land, with results that helped make farm work somewhat less exhausting and at the same time more varied.

First, ploughing partly substituted animal for human power in preparing the soil. It also made ridging for corn and tobacco faster. Hence more corn could be grown, enabling planters to pen and feed at least some of their livestock instead of depending heavily on letting animals find their food on the open range. Regular penning of livestock made dairying more productive and produced manure that could be spread on the corn fields to increase yields.[42] Second, ploughing made possible extensive cultivation of English grains. Grain culture required carts, and together ploughs and carts required blacksmiths, wheelwrights and carpenters to make and maintain plough shares, traces, harnesses and carts. Farm life became much more varied as planters and servants paid more attention to training oxen and horses for ploughing and hauling, sowed and reaped grain as well as planted and cut tobacco and corn, and added by-employments in crafts to their activities.[43]

Chesapeake housewives also acquired a more varied routine. As families grew in size and longevity with the advent of a native-born population, there was more labour available for home industry, with results that show in inventories. Increases in butter pots and quantities of butter in inventories that do not show equipment for a dairy suggest that more women than earlier specialized in dairying and sold dairy products to

<hr>

[41] Carr, 'Emigration and the standard of living', 281–2.

[42] Lois Green Carr and Russell R. Menard, 'Land, labor, and economies of scale in early Maryland: some limits to growth in the Chesapeake system of husbandry', *JEcH*, 40 (1989), 407–18.

[43] Carr, 'Diversification'; Jean B. Russo, 'Self-sufficiency and local exchange: free craftsmen in the rural Chesapeake economy', in Carr *et al.*, eds., *Colonial Chesapeake Society*, pp. 389–432.

neighbours.[44] More important was the appearance of spinning and weaving. By the mid-eighteenth century, the great majority of inventoried households had spinning wheels and many had looms.[45]

All these new activities must have made work less monotonous than earlier for both men and women, although to some degree at the expense of leisure; but other changes were not so favourable, at least for field servants. They were increasingly likely to work beside slaves, a fact that probably downgraded their status. Moreover, as planters acquired slaves, masters lengthened the work year, requiring Saturday work and eliminating most holidays. These conditions were extended to white servants and labourers. On the other hand, men with skills were in demand, and it may be that the majority of poor immigrants escaped regular labour in the fields.[46] In addition there is evidence that in the Britain from which they had come men and women were working harder than in earlier times.[47]

An important consequence of the diversification of the local Chesapeake economy was increased neighbourhood exchange, which had effects upon planters' incomes and hence returns us to the subject of consumer goods. Account books of wealthy planters show that they put out spinning and weaving to poor women, who thus augmented the family income. These same books show payments to poor planter-craftsmen for various jobs. Furthermore, the inventories of people with craft tools also show debts receivable. There can be no doubt that the multiplication of activities on the agricultural landscape provided a hedge against fluctuations in prices for planters' crops, strengthening local economies.[48] These changes encouraged increased participation in the acquisition of goods and, in all but the poorest wealth groups, accompanying changes in manners and social ritual that the eighteenth century called gentility. In a study of Chesapeake consumer behaviour that Lorena Walsh and I have made, regressions in most cases have shown diversification of economic activity as the most important variable, apart from overall wealth, in determining both the kinds of household goods families had and the value of their consumer durables.[49]

---

[44] Inventories 88–91, MSS.   [45] Carr, 'Diversification', 373.

[46] Carr and Walsh, 'Economic diversification', 157–9, 163–6.

[47] Jan De Vries, 'Between purchasing power and the world of goods: understanding the household economy in early modern Europe', in John Brewer and Roy Porter, eds., *Consumption and the World of Goods* (London, 1993), p. 114.

[48] Carr, 'Diversification', 372–82; Carr and Walsh, 'Economic diversification', 144–9; Russo, 'Self-sufficiency and local exchange'.

[49] Carr and Walsh, 'Changing lifestyles', 118–23 and tables A1–A4. The dependent variables were amenities scores and value of consumer durables. The independent variables were: total estate value, overall and by wealth class; life cycle stages, overall and by time period; diversification index; immigrant status and native-born generation; urban–rural location; size of bound labour force; education; and time.

Jan De Vries has recently offered the idea that over the long term in early modern Europe and England, household by-employments, especially of women and children, produced a similar effect. Home industries, he argues, and putting out systems – the latter not much part of the Chesapeake economy – both produced goods for sale and created income that could purchase other goods. This was an 'industrious revolution' that long preceded the industrial revolution and had 'demand-side features'. By-employments and the labour of women and children created a redeployment of family resources, sacrificing leisure and 'offering to the market more goods, more labour, and more intensive labour' in return for income that could purchase improvements in the material standard of living.[50]

De Vries tackles several possible objections to the idea of an industrious revolution. He concedes that such changes may have originated in part as a response to pressure of population on the land or to periods of falling real wages and underemployment. Such circumstances required more intensive labour and production for the market to maintain an achieved standard of living, not one that improved. But, he argues, once household production for the market was established, the advent of more prosperous times did not change the habits of industry, and a preference for market goods over leisure and home-made products – a change in tastes – remained.[51]

Economic diversification in the Chesapeake may have something to contribute to the argument, although the processes that brought diversification about were not the same as those of early modern England. At first settlement, an agriculture based on the hoe rather than the plough did not encourage crafts, and the shortage of women and children reduced the pool of labour. Farm building on undeveloped land was the source of wealth, and until farms were well established it was most cost effective to put all labour that could be spared from clearing land, building housing

[50] De Vries, 'Purchasing power', 107–21.

[51] *Ibid.*, pp. 115–16. De Vries also addresses the argument of Herman Freudenberger and Gaylord Cummins (supported by Robert W. Fogel's recent work), who suggest that chronic malnutrition underlay the so-called leisure that preceded the appearance of home industries. 'Health, work, and leisure before the Industrial Revolution', *Explorations in Economic History*, 13 (1976), 1–12; Fogel, 'European escape from hunger', pp. 243–86. By this proposition, the industrious revolution was a response to the need for food, not to the desire for inessential goods. De Vries doubts that for most of the working population in the early modern period, caloric intake was normally as low as Fogel has estimated ('Purchasing power', 115). However, Fogel shows energy requirements for crafts such as carpentry or for sitting and sewing (and hence, presumably, for spinning) much lower than for most agricultural work ('Biomedical approaches', table 1). In the context of the overall argument, the proposition that craft work and home industry did not require as many calories as agricultural labour needs exploration.

and fencing, and growing food into raising tobacco. Planters exported tobacco to England in return for needed manufactures. However, English merchants were willing to risk only necessities and 'coarse goods such as are useful for the country' that were certain to sell. Eighteenth-century merchants, trading to a colony with a still growing and more balanced population and a diversifying economy with farms established, found a developing market for quality products and inessentials that improved the comforts of life.[52] As in England, households began to trade possible increases in leisure for goods. However, we may not be dealing here with a change in tastes, but with demographic and developmental shifts that allowed a return to English habits.

On the whole, then, eighteenth-century British immigrants did not suffer the severe decline in life's comforts and changes in habits that seventeenth-century immigrants had. True, for most the housing was inferior to that of England in permanence and size, and many, especially among the poor, sacrificed some household conveniences. But the big loss for these later immigrants lay elsewhere – in decreasing opportunities to acquire land and participate in local decision-making, the aspects I have called control of one's life.[53]

In the present, and probable future, absence of eighteenth-century career studies of immigrants – except for the handful who served in the Maryland assembly[54] – the argument once more must fall back on what was happening in the general population. At the beginning of the century, depending on the area, two-thirds to three-fourths of Maryland householders owned their land. By 1782–3, this figure was reduced to half. With the growth of population, land prices rose to levels not attainable for

---

[52] Carr, 'Diversification', 350–5; Carr and Walsh, 'Economic diversification', 145–9; Carr and Walsh, 'Changing lifestyles', 104–5, 106 (quote), 107–11, 118–23.

[53] There is disagreement among historians of the Chesapeake over the amount of opportunity for the poor to rise in the seventeenth century. Russell R. Menard has demonstrated that servants who had arrived in Maryland before the 1670s, if they survived their freedom for at least ten years, usually acquired land before they died. 'From servant to freeholder: status mobility and property accumulation in seventeenth-century Maryland', *WMQ*, 30 (1973), 37–64. Edmund S. Morgan has argued more generally for an absence of opportunity for the poor in Virginia. *American Slavery and American Freedom: the Ordeal of Colonial Virginia* (New York, 1975), ch. 11. James P. P. Horn emphasizes the 'if' in Menard's argument; upward mobility for ex-servants depended upon how long they lived. Horn also argues that prospects for the poor in Virginia were less bright than in Maryland. *Adapting to a New World: English Society in the Seventeenth-century Chesapeake* (Chapel Hill, N.C., 1994), pp. 151–60. However, no one has yet tested Menard's thesis with a systematic study of the careers of ex-servants in seventeenth-century Virginia.

[54] Edward C. Papenfuse, Alan F. Day, David W. Jordan and Gregory A. Stiverson, eds., *A Biographical Dictionary of the Maryland Legislature, 1635–1789*, 2 vols. (Baltimore, 1979, 1985).

the poor at the same time that larger families meant that more children could not receive land by inheritance if the holdings were to be large enough to be viable. Those left out had to move downward to tenancy or leave.[55]

Furthermore, upward mobility through marriage declined and for poor immigrants probably disappeared. In the seventeenth-century immigrant society, many a newcomer got his start by marrying a young widow, usually also an immigrant without kin to help her. She brought the estate of her dead husband to the union. Two-thirds of the personal property usually belonged to her children, and her share of the land, if any, would usually go to them at her death. But the children were likely to be young. Mother and stepfather could keep the entire estate intact and improve it until the children came of age. The stepfather could progress up the economic ladder with his wife's share of the assets and the profits from those of the minor children. Such men, if they lived long enough, had opportunities to acquire land. By contrast, eighteenth-century immigrants found a predominantly native-born society with established kin networks to help the widow, who often had children of age, or soon to be of age, to take up their inheritances. In addition, husbands who left wills began to restrict the widow's legacy to her widowhood; if she married, she lost the property to her children immediately.[56] Given all these circumstances, widows had less incentive to remarry, and particularly less incentive for marriage to a poor struggling immigrant; and all poor men had less to gain from such a union.

As early as the beginning of the eighteenth century, opportunity for poor immigrants in the older settled regions was minimal. Tenancy, which once had been a step along the way to ownership of land, was becoming a poor man's fate. Those determined to succeed had to move to more distant frontiers.[57] Nothing suggests that in later years, opportunities at the bottom improved. And immigrants who arrived with nothing must have been at the bottom of the ladder.

---

[55] Menard, 'Economy and society in early colonial Maryland', p. 425; Stiverson, *Poverty in a Land of Plenty*, table 1-A; Earle, *Evolution of a Tidewater Settlement Society*, pp. 209, 210; Paul G. E. Clemens, *The Atlantic Economy and Colonial Maryland's Eastern Shore: From Tobacco to Grain* (Ithaca, N.Y., 1980), p. 231; Somerset county land price file, History Office, Historic St Mary's City Commission, Maryland State Archives; Lois Green Carr and Russell R. Menard, 'Procedures for estimating per capita wealth in St Mary's county Maryland, 1660, 1709, 1755, and 1774', available in typescript from the Omohundro Institute of Early American History and Culture and on the Institute's website; and Lois Green Carr, 'Inheritance in the colonial Chesapeake', in Ronald Hoffman and Peter J. Albert, eds., *Women in the Age of the American Revolution* (Charlottesville, Va., 1989), pp. 162–8, 186–94.

[56] Carr, 'Inheritance', 155–97.   [57] Menard, 'Economy and society', 425–7.

The story of William Roberts, who came to Maryland in 1756, can illustrate the poor immigrant's difficulties.[58] It is supplied in several letters he wrote to relatives on leaving for America and after his arrival. He came as an indentured servant; his parents were not well off enough to help him, although his mother had a well-to-do brother. As a servant, William had no complaints about his food, but he felt the discomfort of clothing much inferior to what he had been used to; he wrote his mother that he 'had but to Sharts for a year and as Courss as [the] apron you ware When you Scower pewter'. Nevertheless, he was full of hope after a few years as a freeman. By 1767 he wanted 'to go to house keep in' and set up a plantation.[59]

Roberts asked his uncle for help. The young man needed about £37 (Maryland current money, undeflated) for the purchase of two horses, two cows and two sows, corn and meat for a year, and for rent (£8) of land.[60] He also asked that his uncle supply him with some household furnishings: a bed tick with sheets and blankets, a 4-gallon and an 8-gallon pot, a dozen pewter plates, four dishes of different sizes, a 1.5 gallon basin, six knives and forks, a pint and a quart pewter pot, six pewter spoons, two candlesticks, a gridiron, a box iron with heaters and a frying pan. In addition, he wanted tools: a broad axe, a narrow axe, a handsaw, an adze, a drawing knife, two augers, a gouge and a half a dozen 'gimblets' of all sizes to help him make a plough. He expected to buy feathers for his mattress, a bedstead, chairs and probably a table.[61]

The household goods were far more elaborate than a seventeenth-century ex-servant would have expected to start with, and probably more than many of Roberts's contemporaries expected for a beginning. He had surely been used to living with such equipment at home and saw it about him in the houses where he boarded. Perhaps he also had his eye on a wife who would demand it. The livestock were what he needed for pulling his plough and supplying him with milk and meat. Had he asked for money to buy land rather than rent it, he would have needed at least £25 (Maryland current money, undeflated) for the minimum size required for

<hr>

[58] James P. P. Horn, 'The letters of William Roberts of All Hallows parish, Anne Arundel county, Maryland, 1756–1759', *Maryland Historical Magazine*, 74 (1979), 117–32.

[59] *Ibid.*, 124–5.

[60] In his letter to his uncle, Roberts valued the items he wanted in hard currency and converted the final sum to sterling. I have converted Roberts's overall figure from sterling to Maryland current money, which was by law used by appraisers in valuing inventories and commonly used in paying for land. I have converted his rent from hard currency to the same kind of money. The necessary exchange rates are laid out in John J. McCusker, *Money and Exchange in Europe and America, 1660–1775* (Chapel Hill, N.C., 1978), pp. 199, 203. In constant value, the total request came to about £28.

[61] Horn, 'The Letters of William Roberts', 125–7.

a plantation, 50 acres.[62] Clearly he feared that such a request would be unsuccessful. He must have hoped instead as a tenant to save enough to acquire land eventually.

Unfortunately, the uncle did not come through with money or equipment. Roberts tried briefly to rent a farm with a partner, but a dry summer left him in debt, with prospects gone. After two years of vainly writing his uncle, he gave up, and nothing certain is known about his later career. James Horn, who edited and published these letters, has judged that Roberts was the poor tenant farmer of the same name who lived in the same area – southern Anne Arundel county – and appears on a census of 1776 and a tax list of 1783. By 1776 he was married with three children; by 1783, he had seven children and a taxable estate of £28 (undeflated). In the 1790 federal census he had ten children. That he ever acquired land is doubtful. Even though his children probably worked in the fields, raising their own food and making possible larger tobacco crops, the price of land would have been too high unless he pulled up stakes and moved to the frontier.[63]

If he had done so he would not necessarily have improved his opportunities. Allen Kulikoff has examined the prospects for poor migrants to

---

[62] This estimate for the price of a 50-acre plantation is based on Anne Arundel county land prices, 1760–70, collected from the land records for Historic St Mary's City and Historic Annapolis under NEH grant RS20199–81–1955. The price files are in the History Office, Historic St Mary's City, Maryland State Archives, Annapolis, Md. I selected land from All Hallows parish, where Roberts was living, and from Westminster parish, where lower land prices indicate that the land and its occupants were poorer. In All Hallows parish, 22 per cent of tracts ($N = 75$) sold for less than £1.00 per acre; in Westminster, 83 per cent sold below £1.00 ($N = 75$). (Since most of these prices were in Maryland current money, I converted the others to this money, and since Roberts used hard currency or sterling, I have converted his calculations to the same current money. The inventory values in this paper are also in Maryand current money, which by law was used in appraisals.) It is unlikely that Roberts could have found a small farm in All Hallows that he could have afforded. In Westminster the mean price was 13.2s. per acre, which would bring the price of a 50-acre plantation to £33; but Roberts might have found land at a price below the mean. The mean of land sold for less than £1.00 per acre was 8s. per acre, or £20 for 50 acres. On the other hand, some of the lower price sales may have been of unimproved land. (Deeds are not a good source for determining how much improvement was part of the price.) Roberts would have wanted to buy rather than build a house. On the assumption that he would have needed a bargain, but had to have a house, I have selected £25 (current money, undeflated) as an estimate of what he would have had to pay. In constant value, this would be about £19. In sterling, it would be about the same, using the exchange rate established in McCusker, *Money and Exchange*, pp. 199, 203. For All Hallows, these prices differ from those offered by Carville V. Earle, *The Evolution of a Tidewater Settlement System: All Hallow's Parish, Maryland, 1650–1783*, the University of Chicago Department of Geography, Research Paper No. 170 (Chicago, 1975), p. 210 because in 1973, McCusker's collection of exchange rates was not yet completed.

[63] Horn, 'The letters of William Roberts', 119–23, 128–9.

the southside counties of Virginia not settled before the eighteenth century and found that many who moved to undeveloped areas arrived as squatters who could not accumulate enough capital to patent their land. There were as yet no roads and poor planters could not get a tobacco crop to market. As roads were built and population grew, better-heeled men arrived who could take up the land. Squatters then had to move on and begin again. Their standard of living was probably lower than what life as tenants offered them in the tidewater.[64]

On the other hand, men who could afford to survey and patent land could make a success in the southside. While Roberts found it beyond his capacities to pay the 8s. per acre[65] that house and land even in the poorer parts of southern Maryland brought in the 1770s, perhaps he could have afforded the costs of taking up frontier land. However, life in the newly settled southside of Virginia was certainly less comfortable for everyone than it was in the tidewater. Inventories show that for every southside wealth group amenities were much less available than for equivalent groups in the tidewater counties.[66]

Men without land usually could not vote and, in the older counties, had little opportunity to hold office in their communities. This had not always been so. Early in the eighteenth century, tenants in Prince George's county, Maryland, had served on juries and in other local offices, but by the 1730s, this participation was limited to freeholders; by the 1770s, with a much larger population to choose from, sheriffs in Prince George's, at least, were confining jury service to the more substantial planters.[67] Immigrants who did not achieve a middling position must have shared in this loss of political status. Certainly Horn judges that Roberts did not enjoy it.

The final question is why people left eighteenth-century England to come to Maryland? Why were so many poor men willing to face the risk of early death and some privation without the lure of land? Historians generally agree that real wages rose in England over the first half of the century, seemingly a disincentive to migration; but underemployment was a problem, and after mid-century, real wages began to fall in southern

<hr>

[64] Kulikoff, *Tobacco and Slaves,* pp. 143–52.   [65] See note 62 for this price calculation.

[66] Southside, York, Anne Arundel, St Mary's, and Somerset inventory computer files, Historic St Mary's City Commission, Maryland State Archives, Annapolis, Md. See Carr and Walsh, 'Inventories', 84 for a description of how we measured the appearance of amenities.

[67] Lois Green Carr, 'County government in Maryland, 1689–1709', Ph.D. thesis, Harvard University (1968), printed in Harold Hyman and Stuart Bruchey, eds., *American Legal and Constitutional History,* A Garland Series of Outstanding Dissertations (New York, 1987), pp. 604–9, 655–8; Kulikoff, *Tobacco and Slaves,* pp. 281–3.

England, the source of most of this migration.[68] Were opportunities to work in themselves enough to beckon young men to Maryland?

Conditions in Maryland lend themselves to this idea. In England vagrants were sent to the workhouse. In the Chesapeake no need was felt for such institutions until the end of the colonial period.[69] Instructions of 1699 to the royal governor of Maryland called for 'construction of public worke houses in Convenient places for the Imploying of poore & indigent people', but the assembly judged such expenditure of public funds 'all together Needless. None need Stand still for want of Imploymt. The Province wants workmen, workmen want not work'.[70] When a similar instruction arrived in 1706, the assembly again refused to cooperate, 'there being no such thing as beggars going from doore to doore for want of employment'.[71] At mid-century the situation was little changed. For example, in Talbot county over the twenty years from 1739 to 1759, there were only twenty petitions to the county court for poor relief that did not specify people as old, sick or very young.[72]

After mid-century, opportunities in Maryland for employment of poor men began to decline and poor relief became a bigger problem.[73] Beginning in 1768, the assembly began to authorize counties to raise taxes to establish almshouses and two were in operation by 1773. With these Acts came powers for the county justices to commit vagrants, punish them for resistance and put them to work.[74] This is not to say that unemployment was a severe problem or that almshouses were filled with able-bodied

---

[68] On economic growth and living standards, see E. L. Jones, 'Agriculture and economic growth in England, 1660–1750', *JEcH*, 25 (1985), 1–18; A. H. John, 'Agricultural productivity and economic growth in England, 1700–1760', *ibid.*, 19–33; Peter H. Lindert, 'Unequal living standards', in Roderick C. Floud and D. N. McCloskey, eds., *The Economic History of Britain since 1700*, 2nd edn, 2 vols. (Cambridge, 1994), I, pp. 357–86; L. D. Schwarz, 'The standard of living in the long run: London, 1700–1860', *EcHR*, 2nd series, 38 (1985), 24–41; F. W. Botham and E. H. Hunt, 'Wages in Britain during the Industrial Revolution', *ibid.*, 40 (1987), 380–99. On unemployment, see Bailyn, *Voyagers to the West*, ch. 8; K. D. M. Snell, *Annals of the Laboring Poor: Social Change and Agrarian England, 1660–1900* (Cambridge, 1985), pp. 1–86 and ch. 5. On origins of Maryland servants, see Bailyn, *Voyagers to the West*, table 6.4; Galenson, *White Servitude*, p. 51 and tables 6.1 and 6.6.

[69] In Maryland, the first legislation authorizing counties to establish and run almshouses and raise taxes to pay for them was passed in 1768. The Act applied to Frederick, Anne Arundel, Worcester and Charles counties, and almshouses in Frederick and Anne Arundel were functioning by 1773. William Kilty, ed., *The Laws of Maryland*, 2 vols. (Annapolis, Md., 1799), I: Acts 1768, c. 29; Acts 1770, c. 7; Acts 1771, c. 18; Acts 1773, c. 9. St Mary's county and Baltimore county received legislative authorization in 1773 and Talbot county in 1774, but the revolution postponed action in Talbot. *Ibid.*, Acts 1773, c. 18, c. 30; Acts 1774, c. 16; II: Acts 1785, c. 15.

[70] William Hand Browne *et al.*, eds., *Archives of Maryland*, 72 vols. (Baltimore, 1883–1972), XXII, pp. 373, 381 (quote).

[71] *Ibid.*, XXVI, p. 117.   [72] Unpublished research of Jean B. Russo.

[73] Kulikoff, *Tobacco and Slaves*, pp. 298–9.   [74] See references in note 69.

poor; but the appearance of such institutions suggests that young immigrants starting out with nothing after paying for their transport with service were having increasing difficulty making their way.

One might suppose that these changes would discourage emigration to Maryland; on the other hand, falling real wages in southern England counties and in London – the areas from which nearly all the immigrants to Maryland came – could have increased incentives to make the move.[75] In any case, the glimpse Bailyn offers for the motives of those who participated in the great migration of 1773–6 suggests that hope, not despair, was the driving force. Customs officials recording departures were supposed to inquire 'for what reason they leave the country'. The answers of those who left from England, as more than 90 per cent of those who went to Maryland did, and paid their own way indicate positive rather than negative motivation – plans for the future, not escape from difficulties. Unfortunately, the designation 'indentured servant' stood in for an answer for those who went as servants, and this was the status of 96 per cent of all who came to Maryland. Still, Bailyn's profile of departing servants, borne out by that of Galenson for the same period, show them as three-quarters or more skilled. Such men might well share the optimism of better-off emigrants that there would be demand for their labour and a better future than in England, whether or not the reality included ownership of land.[76]

That there was indeed a demand for labour – the more skilled the better – is clear, but the outcome for any particular individual often is not. William Roberts had some education – he could read and write a legible hand – but he complained that he lacked a trade. He believed that with a trade, he might have escaped his life in 'plantasion' work, 'lookin over slaves and makein corn, wheat and tobacco' and suffering 'the heate and sun from daybreak tell [sic] dark'. His letters show an immigrant who arrived full of hope and suffered disappointment. But if he was the William Roberts who appeared in All Hallows parish in 1776, he was by then a householder and master of a family.[77] In the end was he satisfied with his choice? We will never know for certain. What is certain is the need for historians to know much more of the actual experiences of eighteenth-century immigrants, before their departure as well as after their arrival. Until we do, we can not fully judge the wisdom of the fateful decision to risk a new life in the Chesapeake.

[75] See references in note 68.

[76] Bailyn, *Voyagers to the West*, pp. 189 (quote), 190–203, 270 and table 5.24; Galenson, *White Servitude*, table 6.6.

[77] Horn, ed., 'Letters of William Roberts', 119, 125 (quote), 128 (quote). Bailyn offers evidence of opportunity or lack of it in England for the 1773–6 emigrants in *Voyagers to the West*, ch. 8.

13 After tobacco: the slave labour pattern on a large Chesapeake grain-and-livestock plantation in the early nineteenth century

Richard S. Dunn

The early modern Atlantic economic system depicted by the previous essayists in this volume – in which labourers from Africa cultivated sugar, rice and tobacco crops in America that were marketed in Europe – developed in unexpected and unusual ways in one important region of the Atlantic world. In Virginia and Maryland, market forces created a plantation system at the close of the eighteenth century with a surplus of agricultural labourers. Elsewhere in America, labour shortages were endemic, especially in the sugar plantations on the Caribbean islands where the work gangs could only be sustained through massive and continuous importation of new labourers.[1] Why a surplus developed in the Chesapeake by 1800 is well understood, but the management practices of the leading planters with the largest number of labourers during the first two decades of the nineteenth century have been little examined. This chapter endeavours to throw some fresh light on the post-revolutionary Chesapeake agricultural labour pattern.

From the 1620s to the 1770s, tobacco had of course been the Virginia and Maryland mainstay. As Jacob Price has demonstrated in his masterly series of books and articles on the transatlantic tobacco trade, this staple crop was marketed skilfully and profitably by English and Scottish entrepreneurs, with much of the Chesapeake production re-exported from Britain to France and other European venues. From the beginning, the colonial tobacco planters required a large and dependable supply of unskilled manual workers for their labour-intensive crop. At first they relied upon British indentured servants, but in the 1680s they began to

---

[1] I have discussed the problem of labour shortages throughout pre-revolutionary British America in 'Servants and slaves: the recruitment and employment of labor', in Jack P. Greene and J. R. Pole, eds., *Colonial British America* (Baltimore, 1984), pp. 157–94. I have discussed the special problems created by labour shortages on the British Caribbean sugar plantations in '"Dreadful idlers" in the cane fields: the slave labor pattern on a Jamaican sugar estate, 1762–1831', *JIH*, 17 (1987), 795–822; and in 'Sugar production and slave women in Jamaica', in Ira Berlin and Philip D. Morgan, eds., *Cultivation and Culture: Labor and the Shaping of Slave Life in the Americas* (Charlottesville, 1993), pp. 49–72.

344

import their workers from Africa, and from the 1720s onward most of their field labourers were black slaves. Thus the transatlantic tobacco trade and the transatlantic slave trade went hand in hand in the Chesapeake, just as sugar and slavery went hand in hand in the Caribbean. Furthermore – again as in the West Indies – the most aggressive planters very quickly acquired a high percentage of these new workers and assembled them into large labour gangs. By 1755 some 165,000 African American slaves lived in Virginia and Maryland – 37 per cent of the total Chesapeake population – and these captive labourers were very unevenly distributed. Ten per cent of the white householders possessed half the slaves, and the biggest tobacco planters commandeered a hundred or more slaves apiece. The crops that these black workers produced enabled their elite white masters to found family dynasties, to build great houses and to dominate Chesapeake politics and society.[2]

The crucial difference between the Chesapeake and the Caribbean was that imported slaves survived and multiplied in Virginia and Maryland whereas they died and had to be replaced in the island colonies. Well before the American Revolution the leading planters in Virginia and Maryland had as many tobacco workers as they wanted, and they stopped the slave trade from Africa. But the black population continued to increase naturally. By 1782 – despite the flight of thousands of slaves during the revolutionary war – the number of slaves in the Chesapeake had nearly doubled since 1755. There were now about 300,000 African American slaves, constituting 39 per cent of the total population. And by this time, the traditional Chesapeake staple was in deep trouble. Since tobacco exhausted the soil, many planters in Maryland and some in Virginia had converted to grain production before the war. During the war the tobacco planters were unable to export their crop to Britain, and after the war they lost most of their foreign markets, thanks to British commercial policy, the French Revolution and the European wars of the 1790s. By 1802, American tobacco exports to Britain were only 25 per cent of what they had been in 1773.[3]

The leading Chesapeake planters had few options as they searched for alternatives to tobacco culture and for new ways to employ their large

[2] For background on the Chesapeake tobacco economy, see Jacob M. Price, *Tobacco in Atlantic Trade*, chs. 1–4; McCusker and Menard, *Economy of British America*, chs. 6, 10–11; Allan Kulikoff, *Tobacco and Slaves: the Development of Southern Cultures in the Chesapeake, 1680–1800* (Chapel Hill, N.C., 1986); Philip D. Morgan, *Slave Counterpoint: Black Culture in the Eighteenth-Century Chesapeake and Lowcountry* (Chapel Hill, N.C., 1998), chs. 1–4; Ira Berlin, *Many Thousands Gone: the First Two Centuries of Slavery in North America* (Cambridge, Mass., 1998), chs. 1, 5, 10; Rhys Isaac, *The Transformation of Virginia, 1740–1790* (Chapel Hill, 1982); and T. H. Breen, *Tobacco Culture: the Mentality of the Great Tidewater Planters on the Eve of the Revolution* (Princeton, 1985).
[3] Price, *Tobacco in Atlantic Trade*, ch. 3, appendix A.

black workforce. They could not switch to cotton, which was just beginning to be profitable in Carolina and Georgia around 1800, because Virginia and Maryland were too far north for commercial cotton production. And they had some difficulty in selling off their surplus slaves, because the slave market in the lower South did not develop fully until the 1830s. To be sure, many thousand Chesapeake slaves were exported to the west and south between 1780 and 1810, but more whites than blacks migrated out of the region in these three decades, with the result that the black population continued to grow faster than the white population. By 1810 there were 64,000 free blacks and 504,000 slaves in Virginia and Maryland, or 42 per cent of the Chesapeake total. These slaves were distributed more widely than in the colonial era. For the first time, over half of the white householders in Virginia were slave owners. But the system remained hierarchical, and most slaves were attached to large plantations. By 1810, the biggest planters in the region had mainly settled on grain and livestock farming – a style of mixed agriculture that demanded considerably less intensive labour than tobacco. Wheat, in particular, was a much more seasonal crop than tobacco: it required only two or three months of labour per year. In the northern states, grain and livestock had long been the standard cash crops on small family farms, but in Virginia and Maryland the largest slave-operated production units were now also raising wheat and corn and cattle and hogs.[4]

It was a rule of thumb in all slave-based plantation societies that labourers be kept hard at work and fully occupied year round. Idle or underemployed slaves were dangerous slaves. Thus it is instructive to explore how the Chesapeake planters – especially those with the largest numbers of slaves – organized their steadily swelling black labour forces for effective production and full employment. Fortunately, the surviving records of John Tayloe III (1771–1828), the owner of Mount Airy plantation in the northern neck of tidewater Virginia, reveal in rich detail how one particularly entrepreneurial planter conducted his agricultural operations. John Tayloe was among the largest slaveholders in the Chesapeake and he kept the most informative records yet discovered for any early nineteenth-century Virginia plantation.[5] He inventoried his

---

[4] See Jacob M. Price, *France and the Chesapeake: a History of the French Tobacco Monopoly, 1674–1791, and of Its Relationship to the British and American Tobacco Trades*, 2 vols. (Ann Arbor, 1973), pp. 682–734; and Richard S. Dunn, 'Black society in the Chesapeake, 1776–1810', in Ira Berlin and Ronald Hoffman, eds., *Slavery and Freedom in the Age of the American Revolution* (Charlottesville, Va., 1983), pp. 49–82.

[5] The records of the Virginia Tayloes, which are fullest for the nineteenth century, are principally preserved in the Tayloe papers, MSS 1 T2118, held by the Virginia Historical Society, Richmond, hereafter cited as Tayloe. This splendid family archive of 28,000

slave gang every year from 1808 onwards, recording each person by name, age and occupation, and identifying the mothers of all the young children. By correlating one list with another, we can reconstruct the individual careers – and to some extent the family histories – of the many hundred African Americans who lived and laboured at Mount Airy. By means of these annual inventories one can also observe the constantly shifting occupational structure of Tayloe's labour force.[6] In addition, Tayloe kept an elaborate series of work logs detailing the daily assignments of his craft workers and the weekly assignments of his field workers, as well as a series of shop books for his artisans. Only a broken set of these records survive, the most instructive volumes dating from 1805 to 1819, but collectively they recapture the seasonal and annual rhythm of labour at Mount Airy, and measure the productivity of his workers.[7]

The Tayloes had built a very large labour force during the course of the eighteenth century. They staked out their plantation at Mount Airy about 1680, which proved to be an optimal time, because it was just when the slave traders were beginning to sell imported Africans on the Rappahannock river in sizeable numbers. William Tayloe possessed twenty-one slaves when he died in 1710, and his son John – the chief architect of the family fortune – enlarged this labour gang fifteen-fold. At the time of his death in 1747, John Tayloe I held 167 slaves at Mount Airy and another 161 on other plantations in Virginia and Maryland. His son John Tayloe II continued to expand, building the Mount Airy slave force up to about 250 when he died in 1779. And in the fourth generation John III became the largest slave-owner in the history of the Tayloe family, holding 355

documents has been microfilmed: see the *Records of Ante-Bellum Southern Plantations from the Revolution through the Civil War, Series M*, reels 1–57. I wish to thank the Virginia Historical Society for permitting me to cite these records, and Mrs H. Gwynne Tayloe and her son H. Gwynne Tayloe for generously showing me their house and grounds at Mount Airy.

[6] Tayloe very probably began to inventory his Mount Airy slaves annually in 1792, when he took over management of the estate, but his one surviving inventory book starts in 1808, and the first complete inventory is dated 1 January 1809. When Tayloe died in 1828, his son William Henry Tayloe inherited Mount Airy and three of the farm quarters, and continued the annual inventories; altogether, sixty-eight of these lists are preserved among the Tayloe papers, spanning the years 1808–65. A total of 648 slaves appear on John III's lists, and an additional 328 are recorded on William Henry's lists. See Tayloe a 13, d 538, d 3453, d 13424, d 13450, d 23707.

[7] The fullest work logs – tracing the activities of both craft and farm labourers – are dated 1 January to 7 December 1805 (Tayloe a 8); 9 January to 4 September 1811 and 10 February to 31 December 1812 (Tayloe a 10); and 1 January 1813 to 16 March 1814 (Tayloe a 11). There are also more fragmentary day books and minute books for 1795–6, 1797, 1806–7, 1811, 1814 and 1815–27, as well as a blacksmith book for 1793–4, spinning books for 1805–6, 1806–7 and 1816–19, a mill book for 1810–13, and a shoemakers' book for 1816–17. See Tayloe a 9, a 11, a 12, and the uncatalogued papers in boxes 1–3.

slaves at Mount Airy and another 350 on additional properties in Virginia and Maryland at his death in 1828.

John Tayloe II was growing both tobacco and wheat at Mount Airy in the 1770s, but by the 1790s his son had switched mainly to grain and livestock production, although he still cultivated some tobacco. After 1800, no tobacco was grown on the estate. In 1792, when John Tayloe III entered his majority and assumed the management of Mount Airy, he placed the following advertisement in the local newspapers: 'For sale. 200 Virginia born men, women, and children, all ages and descriptions.' Prospective buyers were directed to Tayloe's agents in the town of Fredericksburg, near Mount Airy, for fuller particulars.[8] Records of any actual sales are lost, but the tax lists for Tayloe's personal property indicate that the slave population at Mount Airy was reduced from about 340 in 1792 to about 260 in 1794.[9] Probably young Tayloe was paying off his father's debts as well as pruning his work force for efficient grain production. But after he married and began to raise a large family, he sold relatively few slaves and instead opened up new work sites to be staffed with his surplus labourers. By 1815 he had seven sons and five daughters to provide for. John Tayloe III was a patrician planter par excellence, and also the premier horse breeder in Virginia. Not content with living all year round in the handsome Palladian mansion that his father had constructed in the 1750s on a commanding site inland from the Rappahannock river, John III built the elegant Octagon (now maintained by the American Institute of Architects) as his town house in the new city of Washington, where he spent the winter social season. At the time of his death he owned twenty-three farms in Virginia and Maryland, as well as three ironworks, a schooner on the Rappahannock and another on the Potomac, a hotel in Washington, and some 700 slaves.[10]

The centre of Tayloe's domain was his 'Mount Airy Department', as he called it. Here he operated eight farm quarters on 8,000 acres in three adjacent counties along both sides of the Rappahannock, as well as a congeries of craft shops on the 1,700-acre home plantation. Mount Airy itself (where the Tayloes still live today) is situated in Richmond county. The eight farm quarters were called Old House, Doctors Hall, Forkland,

---

[8] Tayloe advertised his sale in the *Virginia Gazette and General Advertiser* (Richmond), the *Virginia Herald and Fredericksburg Advertiser* (Fredericksburg), the *Virginia Chronicle and Norfolk and Portsmouth General Advertiser* (Norfolk), the *Virginia Gazette and Alexandria Advertiser* (Alexandria), the *Maryland Gazette* (Annapolis), and perhaps in other newspapers during September to November 1792. I owe these newspaper references to Michael L. Nicholls and Michael Mullin.

[9] See the personal property tax lists for Richmond, Essex and King George counties in the 1790s in the Library of Virginia, Richmond. Tayloe's total slave force can only be approximated from these lists, since they do not include non-taxable negroes under age 12.

[10] For John Tayloe III's will, dated December 1827, see Tayloe d 539–43.

Marshfield and Menokin in Richmond county, Gwinfield in Essex county across the Rappahannock, and Hopyard and Oakenbrow in King George county upriver from Richmond county. In 1809, there were 276 slaves living on the farm quarters and 105 slaves living on the home plantation, for a total population of 381. Of these, 142 were farm labourers, 59 were craft workers, 34 were domestics, 21 were non-working old people and invalids, and 125 were non-working young children. The slaves were valued collectively at £22,700 (or $75,590) – for an average of nearly £60 ($200) per person, young and old. The total estate was appraised at over £98,000 ($326,000), but John Tayloe objected to this figure. 'I wish the above Valuation could be realized', he noted in his inventory book in 1808. 'Its certainly much too great.'[11] However that may be, Tayloe operated an extensive agricultural enterprise, staffed by 235 slave workers.

The most conspicuous feature of Tayloe's employment pattern is the very large number of slave domestics and slave artisans at Mount Airy – about 40 per cent of the total workforce. In 1809, sixteen of the Mount Airy slaves were house servants waiting on the Tayloe family, five were coachmen and grooms, four were gardeners, and one was a jockey. In addition, eight other domestics kept house for the overseers who supervised the farm quarters. Meanwhile the artisans were employed in crafts that promoted economic self-sufficiency. Using cotton grown and ginned on the estate, and wool sheared from Mount Airy sheep, the fifteen spinners and weavers made coarse cloth for slave apparel and fine cloth for household linen. The four shoemakers tanned and dressed leather from Mount Airy cattle to make coarse shoes for the slaves and custom shoes for their white clients, as well as harnesses for the horses, mules and oxen. The nine smiths and joiners built and repaired wagons, ploughs and hoes, and shod horses, while the fifteen carpenters and masons moved about the estate erecting and repairing buildings.

But the key players in this scenario were the agricultural labourers on the eight Rappahannock farm quarters, who numbered 142 in 1809. Tayloe derived most of his profits from their exertions. These workers annually produced some 8,000–11,000 bushels of wheat and 4,000–6,000 barrels of corn.[12] Tayloe paid between 7 and 8 per cent of the wheat and corn harvested to his seven overseers, used about 15 per cent of the wheat to seed the next year's crop, and retained nearly 2,000 barrels of

[11] Tayloe's 9,700 acres were valued at over £52,000 (just under $174,000), or more than twice the valuation of his slaves. His house and outbuildings were valued at £14,000 ($46,620). See the inventories for 1808 and 1809 in his inventory book spanning the years 1808–27, Tayloe d 538.

[12] For wheat and corn production at Mount Airy in 1802, 1806, 1808, 1809, 1811, 1812 and 1816–17, see Tayloe a 10, a 11, d 369–403, and uncatalogued papers, box 3.

corn to feed his slaves and stock. But this still left him a handsome surplus. In an average year, Tayloe's schooner – named *The Federalist* to betoken the party allegiance of its owner – made four or five trips to Baltimore or Alexandria. This vessel, manned by four slave sailors, annually transported about 7,000 bushels of Mount Airy wheat and 2,500 barrels of Mount Airy corn for sale. Tayloe could expect to receive $8,000 to $9,000 for his wheat and another $8,000 to $9,000 for his corn. Livestock production was also important at Mount Airy. The field hands tended some 350 cattle, 350 sheep and 400 pigs, valued collectively at approximately $8,000. The cows produced milk for the estate; the heifers were sold; the sheep produced over a thousand pounds of wool per annum;[13] and a third of the pigs were butchered every year for consumption on the estate.[14]

Five work logs dated 1805, 1811–12 and 1813–14 show the actual jobs performed each day of the year by the Mount Airy craft workers, and each week of the year by the Rappahannock farm gangs. These logs document admirably the cyclical character of the agricultural year, as the calendar slowly revolved through the seasons, each with its appropriate and interlocking set of tasks. It is easy to romanticize the seasonal rhythms of plantation life and work, and easy also to conclude that John Tayloe III with his dozens of domestic servants and artisans had more slaves than he knew what to do with, and that he stretched part-time employment into year-round employment by maintaining a benevolent and leisurely pace of work. To be sure, Tayloe considered himself to be a benevolent and well-intentioned master. But close inspection of his records demonstrates that he worked his slaves hard and manipulated their lives very freely.

Throughout the year the Mount Airy artisans and field hands generally laboured at separate tasks, except for a week in June and another in July, when the artisans joined in the grain harvest. But the work assignments of the artisans and farm labourers were always closely coordinated. During the coldest six weeks of the year from mid-December to the end of January, when the previous season's crops had all been harvested and the winter wheat was in the ground, the field workers and jobbers shucked and beat corn, cut and hauled timber to the saw mill for fence rails and posts, and cut ice from Rappahannock creek. The carpenters meanwhile operated the saw mill, while the smiths and joiners repaired ploughs, wagons and harnesses for spring ploughing. In February the field hands worked with the carpenters and joiners in putting up fencing, with the jobbers in clearing and manuring the fields for ploughing, and with the sailors in

---

[13] See the May 1814 memorandum on sheep shearing in Tayloe's minute book for 1814, Tayloe a 12.

[14] For hog killing in 1811, see Tayloe, uncatalogued papers, box 2.

loading the previous year's surplus corn on to *The Federalist* for shipment and sale. In March the field gangs planted oats, in April corn, and in May cotton and peas, while the smiths and joiners repaired their tools. In mid-April, just before the Tayloe family arrived for the summer from their city house in Washington, seventy labourers from the five closest Rappahannock farms came to Mount Airy to dress up the mansion lawn.

In late May, while the field workers began to weed the corn, the smiths, joiners and carpenters were making and mending rakes, cradles and scythes for the coming harvest. In mid-June the wagoner went to Kinsale, a nearby town, to fetch five barrels of whiskey, and Tayloe also laid out extra rations of bacon, pork and herring for his harvesters.[15] The wheat crop was harvested in one frenzied week during mid-June or late June. Parallel gangs were deployed on the eight quarters to cut, rake, bind and stack the grain. This was a complex operation involving the synchronized labour of close to 200 slave workers. Interestingly, the most skilled harvest work was not done by the regular field hands, but by the artisans. Every year Tayloe paid about fifty of his craft workers $1 each on average for their work as harvesters, and recruited a few free blacks to join them at $3 each. Sometimes he also hired slaves from neighbouring planters as supplementary cutters and rakers.[16] Most of the regular field hands assisted in the harvest, but except for extra food and drink they were not paid bonuses for their work.[17] Twenty to twenty-five blacksmiths, jobbers, carpenters, masons, joiners, shoemakers and sailors cut the grain with scythes, while twenty-five young male artisans and female spinners, weavers and housemaids raked and bound the wheat into sheaves.[18] Twenty-three cradle scythes were stored at Mount Airy for use on the nearby wheat fields at Forkland, Old House, Doctors Hall, Menokin and Marshfield, while the twenty-two cradle scythes used at more distant Gwinfield, Hopyard and Oakenbrow were stored at those quarters.[19]

On the evening of 18 June 1801, John Tayloe III sat down to write a letter, protesting to his correspondent that he was 'just from my harvest

[15] For the whiskey, see the entry for 18 June in the 1805 work log, Tayloe a 8; for the extra rations, see the 1807 day book in Tayloe uncatalogued papers, box 3.

[16] In 1806, Tayloe paid £7 to hire two slave cradlers for eleven days, and 10s. to hire one slave raker for four days (Tayloe uncatalogued papers, box 3). The cradlers cost more than twice as much *per diem* as the raker, demonstrating that skilled wheat cutters were especially prized.

[17] On 24 June 1812, however, it was noted that Fork Tom, a twenty-nine-year-old field hand on this quarter, cut wheat occasionally during the harvest week, and cut 'very well' (Tayloe, a 10). Tom later became the foreman of the Forkland field gang.

[18] There is a list of forty-one harvest hands, dated 24 June 1811, in Tayloe a 10; a list of fifty-four hands, dated 24 June 1812, also in Tayloe a 10; and a list of forty-four hands, dated 25 June 1813, in Tayloe a 11. Only the 1812 list includes the artisans deployed at Gwinfield, Hopyard and Oakenbrow.

[19] See the lists of farm implements in the 1809 inventory, Tayloe d 538.

field and fatigued to death'.[20] Tayloe was not fatigued from handling a cradle scythe or a rake; he was worn out from riding through his fields to supervise the pace of harvest work. No doubt the men and women who did the real work were also pretty tired. In June 1805, a 33–year-old blacksmith named Lewis and a 20–year-old joiner named James each cut the ripe wheat by hand with cradle scythes for eight straight working days, first harvesting the fields at Forkland, then moving on to Old House, and finishing up at Menokin. Both of these men were not only tough but durable; Lewis continued to work as a smith at Mount Airy until he died in 1832 at age sixty, while James continued to work as a joiner on the estate right up to his death in 1852 at age sixty-seven.

In July the seasonal pressure continued, as almost all hands joined for a second week to harvest the oats crop. During the next few weeks the field gangs worked mainly in the corn fields, ridging and hoeing the plants. The Mount Airy farm labourers spent a lot of their time hoeing. Two hundred hoes were inventoried on the eight farm quarters in 1809: 102 weeding hoes, 84 ridging hoes, and 14 grubbing hoes.[21] In August the field hands turned from hoeing the corn to cutting the hay and threshing the wheat. The jobbers helped with the hay, the carpenters made grain barrels, and the smiths and joiners worked as before on ploughs and wagons. In September the wagoner and sailors helped the field hands to load *The Federalist* with wheat for the market. Now it was time to gather the corn leaves as fodder, and to start the long process of seeding the winter wheat for next year's crop. With the autumn racing season approaching, the smiths set to work on shoeing Tayloe's racehorses. Shortly after the races, the Tayloes departed for Washington, and the craft workers could now make necessary repairs on the mansion house – as in 1805, when the carpenters, joiners, jobbers and masons worked for a month reshingling the mansion roof under the supervision of a hired white builder.[22] In October the spinners joined the field hands at picking cotton, and from mid-November to mid-December, after the wheat fields were seeded, the field hands harvested the corn and hauled the stalks to the mill. Just before and after Christmas, the slackest work period of the year, the masons, carpenters and jobbers were sent to repair the Richmond county courthouse.

It is impressive to see how John Tayloe, his estate manager and his seven overseers synchronized the individual labours of 235 slave workers to keep an elaborate enterprise in continuous motion. Occasionally, a major crisis

[20] John Tayloe III to John Rose, 18 June 1801, John Tayloe letter book, 1801, Tayloe d 170.
[21] Tayloe d 538.
[22] The carpenters worked uninterruptedly on this shingling project from 26 October to 4 December 1805. The joiners collaborated with them for fourteen days during this period, the jobbers put in twelve days, and the masons put in five days. See Tayloe a 8.

flared up. In 1801 the overseer at Forkland quarter – a man named Cannady – suddenly disappeared in the middle of the wheat harvest, leaving thirty slave workers unsupervised. Tayloe was outraged by Cannady's negligence, and he reacted decisively. In a letter bristling with haughty disdain, he told the man that he was fired, and that his pay was stopped; thus Cannady would not receive his share of the Forkland wheat crop, which probably amounted to about 60 bushels, worth $75. 'Your conduct', Tayloe wrote,

has been so extraordinary in absenting yourself, particularly in the midst of harvest, that I have no further use for you as an overseer. You will therefore prepare yourself to leave the plantation tomorrow. My Waggon will be ready to convey your furniture etc. any distance within 10 miles.[23]

Tayloe's wagoner was a twenty-seven-year-old slave named Barnaby, who would labour at Mount Airy until he died in 1825 at age fifty-one. Barnaby carted all manner of heavy goods during the course of the year – ice, coal and wood in the winter, fence rails and manure in the spring, harvest whiskey in the summer, stone and bricks in the autumn. Hauling away the overseer's furniture would be a comparatively light task for him, and perhaps an amusing one. Overseers were rarely popular with the slave labourers in the old south.

There were not many slack times for the Mount Airy slaves. Tayloe and his managerial staff kept the workers continually busy by constantly shifting their job assignments. One of the most striking features of the Mount Airy work logs is that they reveal the multitude of tasks performed by each individual agricultural and craft worker during the course of the year. In 1805 the smiths, joiners, masons and jobbers were each given thirty to forty different assignments, and the field workers had an even greater variety of jobs. At Old House quarter and at Doctors Hall quarter, the field hands laboured at more than fifty separate tasks during the course of the year, and seldom worked for more than two or three days on any given assignment before being switched to a new job. From the slaves' perspective, the labour routine at Mount Airy was surely taxing. They were required to work six days a week throughout the year. In 1805, the jobbers worked a total of 300 days, the smiths, masons and joiners a total of 303 days, and the field hands a total of 306 days. Apart from Sundays, the field hands had only seven days of released time: Easter Monday, one free Saturday in July, and a five-day Christmas break from 25 to 29 December.

In other respects, also, Tayloe's field workers seem to have been pressed quite hard. Lorena S. Walsh has recently provided a yardstick for

---

²³ John Tayloe to Overseer Cannady, 17 June 1801, John Tayloe letterbook, 1801 (Tayloe d 170).

measuring the per capita productivity of Chesapeake farm labourers in the early nineteenth century, and by her reckoning the Mount Airy slaves were producing at the very top of the scale. According to Walsh, the planters in the lower Rappahannock region (the neighbourhood of Mount Airy) obtained a notable long-term rise in corn and wheat output per labourer starting in the 1730s. Whereas their labourers produced 10 barrels of corn on average in the early eighteenth century, productivity rose to 15 barrels per labourer in the 1760s, and continued rising to over 30 barrels by the 1810s. At Mount Airy, John Tayloe III was doing better than this. In 1809, for example, his total corn crop was 5,303 barrels, and when 422 barrels are deducted as the overseers' share, his net crop amounted to 4,881 barrels.[24] In this year Tayloe employed 143 field hands, of whom – if we apply Walsh's methodology – the 57 men and 40 women may be construed as full shares, while the 24 boys and 22 girls who were under nineteen years of age may be construed as half shares, for a total of 120 shares. Tayloe's farm workers thus produced nearly 42 barrels of corn per labourer in 1809. And the same pattern is found in wheat production. In the lower Rappahannock region, Walsh tells us that planters obtained about 20 bushels of wheat per labourer in the 1760s and improved this to nearly 50 bushels per labourer in the 1810s. But again, Tayloe's field hands surpassed this performance. In 1811, the net wheat crop at Mount Airy amounted to 8,010 bushels. The eight farm gangs were now smaller than in 1809 because a number of slaves had been moved to new work sites, and they totalled $102\frac{1}{2}$ shares. By this measure Tayloe's farm workers produced over 78 bushels per labourer in 1811.[25]

The field hands at Mount Airy put about 60 per cent of their labour into corn and wheat production. For example, in 1805 the field hands at Old House quarter worked for 128 days on the corn crop, 54 days on the wheat crop and 124 days on all other tasks. In the same year, the hands at Doctors Hall quarter worked 130 days on corn, 65 days on wheat, and 111 days on all other tasks.[26] The corn crop was obviously much more labour intensive than the wheat crop, and required attention every month of the year except September and October. Corn tasks included ploughing, manuring, planting, replanting, weeding, thinning, ridging, hoeing, harvesting, carting, husking, shelling, measuring, beating and storing the

---

[24] For particulars on the 1809 corn crop, see Tayloe d 369–403.

[25] See Lorena S. Walsh, 'Plantation management in the Chesapeake, 1620–1820', *JEcH*, 49 (1989), 398–9. I have followed the procedure Walsh outlines in note 1 of her article in calculating the crop outputs per labourer at Mount Airy. Productivity calculations can be made for the Mount Airy corn crops in 1802, 1808 and 1809, and for the wheat crops in 1802, 1805 and 1811. See n. 12 above.

[26] See Tayloe a 8.

grain. After harvest, the hands on each quarter also had to deliver several hundred barrels of surplus corn to *The Federalist* for shipment and sale. They also had to gather the corn shucks, cut the cornstalks and cart them to the mill. Labour on the wheat crop was much more concentrated, but the field hands spent about four weeks seeding the wheat fields, a task that stretched with interruptions from early September to mid-November. The other crops – oats, hay, cotton and peas – required far less attention. In 1805 the Old House hands spent twenty-three days cultivating and harvesting the oats crop and eight days on the hay crop; at Doctors Hall they spent fourteen days tending oats and sixteen days on hay. In addition, Tayloe's Rappahannock farm gangs spent about a month every year repairing or rebuilding the fences that were designed to keep the cattle, sheep and pigs out of the grain fields. This was cold work, done mostly in January and February. And it was heavy work, for the slaves had to cut fence rails, haul logs to the saw mill, dismantle the old fencing, and set up new posts and rails.

In comparison with the field hands, the artisans at Mount Airy had considerably more specialized job assignments. The seven jobbers were semi-agricultural workers, who collaborated closely all year with the farm hands. They spent over half of their time cutting ditches and cutting fence rails. In May they sheared the sheep, and in December and January they cut ice. The four joiners, by contrast, spent nearly half of their time – 126 days in 1805 – constructing or repairing the forty farm wagons, carts, and tumbrils on the estate, or making wheels for these vehicles. In 1805 they also put in sixty-six days making and repairing ploughs and plough stocks, and twenty-one days making or repairing doors and gates. On four days they made coffins. The three masons spent about half their time raising stone for their building projects and cutting wood for their brick kiln and lime kiln. In 1805 they built three chimneys, which took fifty-two days, and they put in nineteen days plastering and whitewashing. The twelve carpenters are harder to track through the records, because they were more perambulatory than the other artisans. Every few months they would be off, sometimes to make repairs at the Tayloes' town house in Washington, other times to do carpentry in the Tayloes' outlying plantations and ironworks in Virginia and Maryland. In 1805, when they were resident at Mount Airy, the carpenters spent a lot of their time making and repairing cradle scythes, and coopering 2,000 to 3,000 barrels for shipping the plantation corn.

The labour routine of the four shoemakers is particularly well documented. They spent 95 per cent of their time making shoes – though this included such ancillary tasks as dressing hides, cutting tan bark, tanning leather, cleaning the tan vats and constructing lasts. In 1809 their workshop was equipped with (among other items) two hammers, four rasps, two awls, four knives, two pairs of pinchers and a hundred lasts.[27] The shoemakers appear to have been quite accomplished craftsmen. During a four-month period in 1812 they turned out 231 pairs of shoes. At this pace, each of the four cobblers produced 172 pairs of shoes per annum, or more than one shoe per working day.[28] Furthermore, their work must have been of pretty high quality. A shoemakers' shop book for 1816–17 indicates that most of the leading planters in Richmond county ordered shoes from them. Three members of the Carter family from nearby Sabine Hall ordered twenty-two pairs of Mount Airy shoes. All in all, Tayloe's slave shoemakers made 142 pairs of shoes for white customers during this two-year period.[29] But this was not their chief employment. The 1805 work log shows that the shoemakers in this year spent 110 days making coarse shoes for the field workers, 48 days making custom shoes for the Tayloes' white neighbours, 36 days making shoes for the slave artisans and domestics, and 17 days making shoes for the Tayloe children. On 19 June, 'Joe made a pr. of shoes for Master Edward'.[30] Joe was a thirty-eight-year-old African American who would continue to make shoes at Mount Airy until he died in 1829, age sixty-two. Master Edward was John Tayloe III's fourth son, Edward Thornton Tayloe – future student at Harvard College – who was two years old at the time.

The five blacksmiths were also active in the shoe business. They spent much of their time – fifty-nine days in 1805 – shoeing the farm horses and mules on the estate, as well as Tayloe's seven carriage horses, his six riding horses and ponies and his four racehorses. Tayloe's prize thoroughbred was Top Gallant, valued in 1809 at £600 ($2,000) – six times the price placed on his most highly skilled slaves.[31] But the chief task of the blacksmiths at Mount Airy was making and repairing ploughs, on which they spent ninety-six days in 1805, or the equivalent of four months during the course of the year. Ploughing was a key element in Tayloe's system of cultivation; during the ploughing season his farm hands on each quarter would run up to ten ploughs simultaneously. Accordingly, Mount Airy was well stocked with these implements. In 1809 nearly 200 ploughs in seven different designs were listed in the farm quarter inventories. There were seventy-eight half share ploughs, fifty-six bar share ploughs, twenty-five skimmer ploughs, twelve trowel ploughs,

<hr>

[27] The 1809 inventory lists the tools kept in all of the craft shops at Mount Airy; see Tayloe d 538.

[28] See the shoemakers' account in the work log for 1811–12 (Tayloe a 10).

[29] The 1816–17 shoemakers' shop book is in Tayloe uncatalogued papers, box 3.

[30] See Tayloe a 8.

[31] The other three race horses – P.M. General, Pavilian and Marcia – were valued at £200 ($666), £300 ($1,000) and £150 ($500) in 1809 (Tayloe d 538).

eight carry ploughs, eight 'small' ploughs and seven new ground ploughs. And Tayloe had eighty-seven oxen, sixty-four mules and twenty-eight horses to power these ploughs. Here, of course, was a fundamental contrast with the Caribbean sugar production system, where no draught animals or labour-saving tools were utilized, and where all of the field work was done by hand. The only agricultural implements listed in the early nineteenth-century sugar estate inventories were hoes for planting and weeding the young cane, and sharp curved knives called bills for cutting the ripe cane during crop time.

A particularly interesting set of Mount Airy artisans were the cloth-workers: thirteen spinners, two weavers and two ginners in 1809.[32] Before the American Revolution, the Tayloes had imported their cloth from England, but in the 1770s John Tayloe II set up a spinning and weaving shop for the local manufacture of woollen, cotton and linen textiles, and his son continued to manufacture some or all of the textiles needed for slave clothing at Mount Airy. Fourteen of the seventeen clothworkers in 1809 were female, and slave women were still spinning yarn and weaving cloth on the estate right through the Civil War. Two males ginned the cotton to separate lint from seed, and one of the hand loom weavers was a forty-three-year-old man named Israel, but this was essentially a female production unit. A spinning book for 1806–7 lists the productivity of each worker week by week,[33] and indicates that most women produced $1\frac{1}{2}$ lbs of cotton yarn or $5\frac{1}{2}$ lb of woollen yarn per week, with little difference in output between the strongest and feeblest workers. Apparently every spinner aimed at a minimally acceptable work pace. Most of these spinners were young and vigorous; nine of the thirteen in 1809 were in their teens, twenties or thirties. And they were long-lived; the eight who spent their entire careers at Mount Airy died at an average age of sixty-eight. Consequently, Tayloe had a very stable group of clothworkers. Five of the spinners on the 1809 list were still spinning yarn at Mount Airy in the 1830s. During the course of a year these women spent about ten months spinning cotton, one month spinning wool and one month out in the fields picking cotton and harvesting grain.

Because John Tayloe inventoried his Mount Airy slaves annually, we can see how he continually shuffled his labourers to achieve the right mix on each work site. The slave population at Mount Airy was constantly expanding, with two recorded births for every recorded death, so that

---

[32] The Mount Airy ratio between spinners and weavers was (and still is) standard. Laurel Thatcher Ulrich observes that 'in textile-producing areas of Europe, eight to ten spinners kept one weaver supplied with thread'. See Ulrich, 'Wheels, looms, and the gender division of labor in eighteenth-century New England', *WMQ*, 3rd series, 55 (1998), 9.

[33] Tayloe a 9. Fragments of spinning books for 1805–6 and 1816–19 are in Tayloe uncatalogued papers, box 1.

Tayloe generally had a number of surplus labourers at his disposal. As we have seen, he sold about eighty of his Mount Airy slaves in the early 1790s, and he continued to sell slaves thereafter from time to time. In 1816 he dispatched twenty-six men, women and children that he wanted to get rid of for $7,210 – or $277 apiece.[34] But he also brought in new slave workers, and after 1800 his prime objective was to expand operations in order to provide adequate inheritances for his many children. Accordingly he acquired additional work sites where he could employ his surplus labourers. For example, in 1810 he bought an iron furnace at Cloverdale in the Blue Ridge Mountains, 150 miles to the west, and sent twenty-seven slaves from Mount Airy to work there as woodcutters. Twenty-five of these migrants were field hands, most of them in their teens.

Tayloe's practice of moving his workers to where they were most needed was no doubt an efficient policy, but it played havoc with the slaves' family connections. During the last twenty years of Tayloe's life, from 1809 to 1828, 35 per cent of the slaves who lived at Mount Airy in 1809 were either sold or transferred off the estate.[35] Generally, Tayloe kept mothers and young children together, but not always. And he routinely separated boys and girls from their parents when they reached their early teens. Girls were most commonly moved to a new work quarter between the ages of ten and fourteen, and boys between the ages of ten and eighteen. The Mount Airy children began to work regularly in the fields or to train as apprentice artisans at age ten or twelve – and if they looked to be unpromising workers, this was also the best time to sell them.

The slaves who lived at the home plantation and kept in close personal touch with the Tayloes in the big house had considerably greater job security than the field hands on the Rappahannock farm quarters. Tayloe did not keep a work log for his domestics, but these personal retainers were clearly among his favourites. Eight of the men and six of the women who performed domestic service in 1809 worked for the Tayloes for forty years or more. And of the twenty-six house servants, stable hands and gardeners employed at Mount Airy in 1809, twenty-one continued to work either at Mount Airy or at the Octagon in succeeding years. Only four were transferred to other work sites during Tayloe's lifetime, and only one was sold. This was a house servant named Peter, who worked for the Tayloes at Mount Airy during the summer months and at the Octa-

---

[34] Tayloe sold twenty of these slaves in September 1816 to L. Bevan, and the other six to J. Snide. Several of the adults fetched low prices and were described as sickly or diseased. See Tayloe d 414–40.

[35] Of the 381 slaves inventoried in 1809, 133 were sold or transferred to other Tayloe work sites and 70 died between 1809 and 1828, so that only 178 were still living on the estate when Tayloe died.

gon in Washington during the winter months. Hence, Peter would seem to have been a highly favoured person. Yet when he was forty-years-old in 1816, Tayloe sold him for the high price of $500. Peter's wife Elsy, a spinner, had died the year before, leaving five young children. When Tayloe sold Peter, he kept the five orphaned children at Mount Airy, training them all as domestics or craft workers – which suggests that he got rid of Peter in punishment for some sort of misconduct. Tayloe seldom whipped his slaves, but when they ran away or crossed him in some other way, he often responded by selling them.

The craft workers at Mount Airy had even greater job security than the domestics, because they were trained for skilled jobs. Of the twenty-eight shoemakers, blacksmiths, joiners, masons, and carpenters listed in 1809, only two were sent away during Tayloe's lifetime – both of them to Cloverdale in 1810 – and none was sold. The children of these male craft-workers cannot generally be traced, since the inventories only identify the mothers of young children, not the fathers. But in so far as the children of the domestics and artisans at Mount Airy *can* be traced, they very often followed their parents in domestic or craft employment. Three of the younger domestics in 1809 – a housemaid named Franky, a dairymaid named Nancy and a cook named Joice – had children whose careers can be examined. Fourteen of the children born to these three women lived to maturity. Of these, six became domestics, six became artisans and none became field hands in the Mount Airy farm quarters. To be sure, three of the girls from this group were sold. But five of the children of Franky, Nancy and Joice were still living on the estate, all elderly family retainers, when the last Mount Airy slave inventory was taken in 1862.[36]

The situation for the field slaves was very different. For example, thirty-four adults and children lived at Doctors Hall quarter in 1809. Nine of these people – mostly boys and girls in their teens – were moved to Cloverdale in 1810. Three were moved to other work sites, four were sold and five died during Tayloe's lifetime. Consequently, only thirteen were still living at Mount Airy in 1828. Another significant point is that only one of the children at Doctors Hall in 1809 ever became a craft worker at Mount Airy: young Travers, who started his apprenticeship as a joiner in 1814. Otherwise, the children of these field slaves all became farm labourers like their parents. The largest slave family at Doctors Hall in 1809 was Sally and Ampy's. Sally was a twenty-nine-year-old field hand and her husband Ampy was twenty-seven. In 1809 they had five children, and Sally went on to have eight more, the last five born after Ampy died in

[36] See Tayloe d 23707.

1815. Sally bore her thirteenth child in 1826 when she was forty-six years old. Through the Tayloes' slave records, one can trace forty-two of Sally's grandchildren and twenty-four great grandchildren born by 1865. But almost as striking as the huge size of Sally's family is its amazing dispersal. Sally herself lived out her life at Doctors Hall quarter, but of her seventy-nine traceable descendants, only four were living at Mount Airy by the close of the Civil War. Some were of course dead by this time, but more than fifty of Sally's progeny were living in Alabama in 1865, having been sent there – or having been born there – when the Tayloes put hundreds of their Virginia slaves to work on their Alabama cotton plantations from the 1830s onwards.

One further feature of the Mount Airy plantation system needs to be considered: the role of gender in the African American labour pattern. Lois Carr and Lorena Walsh have recently advanced the provocative argument that as Chesapeake farmers improved their wheat and corn outputs and modernized their production techniques during the period 1760–1820, the female labourers were forced into increasingly burdensome work routines. Carr and Walsh contend that the new skilled jobs like ploughing, harrowing and carting were taken up by the slave men, while the unskilled drudge jobs like hoeing, weeding and grubbing were left to the slave women. They point out that at Monticello and Mount Vernon, because Jefferson and Washington employed more men than women as artisans and domestics, the majority of the workers on the outlying farm quarters were women. Furthermore, a work journal kept by Washington's farm manager shows that the Mount Vernon field hands were divided by sex, with the men getting the more responsible and variegated work assignments.[37]

Does the evidence from Mount Airy support Carr and Walsh's argument? Unfortunately it is not easy to tell from John Tayloe's work logs whether the men and women performed separate field tasks. A typical entry for 23 March 1805 reads: 'Old House. Fallowing all the week. Tumbrels Hauling out manure. one cart hauling post & railing for Carpenters, the other hands delivering corn to Fed[eralist], leaveling ditches, Grubing etc'. There were about eight men and sixteen women and children employed on the Old House workforce in 1805. If we can assume that the fallow ploughing was done by men, and that the tumbrils and cart were also operated by men, then the women and children must have been doing most if not all of the ditching and grubbing. The wheat harvest at Mount Airy was conducted pretty much as at Mount Vernon,

---

[37] Lois Green Carr and Lorena S. Walsh, 'Economic diversification and labor organization in the Chesapeake, 1650–1820', in Stephen Innes, ed., *Work and Labor in Early America* (Chapel Hill, N.C., 1988), pp. 175–88.

with men doing all of the mowing and women and adolescent boys doing most of the binding and raking. But Tayloe also employed several strong young men as rakers and binders, so the sexual division of labour at harvest time was by no means complete. And women at Mount Airy had somewhat more variegated employment opportunities than at Mount Vernon or Monticello, because Tayloe employed fourteen female cloth-workers in addition to sixteen female domestics. Nevertheless, women were systematically excluded from all of the most highly skilled and highly valued jobs. And if Tayloe did not consign all of the least desirable chores to his women workers, he did something more striking. He deliberately engineered a male-dominated work force at Mount Airy by importing men and selling women.

For many years the Tayloes had maintained a pronounced male majority at Mount Airy. In 1783, according to the Richmond county tax list for that year, the sex ratio was about 120.[38] By 1809, it had climbed to 131. More important, in 1809 the male workers at Mount Airy outnumbered the female workers by a margin of 146 to 89, a sex ratio of 180.[39] This is quite different from the more normal and equal sex ratios of 95 at Monticello in 1774 and 98 at Mount Vernon in 1786.[40] The reason for the male dominance at Mount Airy is that Tayloe made a regular practice of bringing new male workers on to the estate and getting rid of unwanted girls. Consequently the Mount Airy population pyramid for 1809 shows an unusually small number of women aged fifteen to twenty-four and an unusually large number of boys and men aged ten to forty-four. And Tayloe sustained this pattern at Mount Airy until he died. The inventories show that thirty-four workers were brought to the estate between 1809 and 1828, while 116 slaves left to work at Tayloe's outlying properties. During these twenty years John Tayloe also sold forty-five slaves – three females for every male. The net result of all this movement was that the sex ratio on the estate remained stable, and that Tayloe always had more male than female workers at his disposal. The population pyramid for 1828, the year of Tayloe's death, shows some changes from 1809,

[38] In 1783 the Tayloe properties in Richmond county reported 98 male and 82 female slaves (see the Richmond county Personal Property tax lists, Library of Virginia). I have found no equivalent tabulation by sex for the Tayloe slaves in Essex and King George counties.

[39] There were seventy-six non-working female slaves at Mount Airy in 1809: sixty-four under-age girls and twelve old or invalid women. There were seventy non-working male slaves: sixty-one under-age boys and nine old or invalid men.

[40] For the 1774 inventory of Jefferson's ninety-eight working slaves, see Edwin Morris Betts, ed., *Thomas Jefferson's Farm Book, with Commentary and Relevant Extracts from Other Writings* (Princeton, N.J., 1953), facsimile pp. 5–9. For the 1786 inventory of Washington's 122 working slaves, see Donald Jackson and Dorothy Twohig, eds., *The Diaries of George Washington* (Charlottesville, Va.), vol. IV (1978), pp. 277–83.

with fewer children and more old people than twenty years earlier. But as before, the proportion of teenaged girls and young women is abnormally low and the proportion of prime-aged men is abnormally high. Had Tayloe kept all of his female slaves, the Mount Airy population would have grown at an even more rapid pace. And his male workers would have had a much easier time finding wives. However, from a labour perspective, Tayloe's force was better organized for maximum productivity than Jefferson's or Washington's. In 1828, as in 1809, half the domestics, more than half the farm workers, and three-quarters of the craft workers at Mount Airy were men.

When I first began to examine John Tayloe's operations at Mount Airy, I saw him as an outmoded relic from the past – a leisured gentleman, a fading tidewater aristocrat, absorbed in his horses and his family network, with exhausted farm lands and too many slaves.[41] But the more I study Tayloe's plantation records, the more I am inclined to argue that he made the difficult transition from tobacco culture to mixed agriculture in an aggressively entrepreneurial style. It is, of course, dangerous to generalize from one example, but Tayloe's performance suggests that the Chesapeake plantation system was sufficiently adaptable for an enterprising planter to continue to flourish during the first three or four decades of the new republic – even in the tidewater, where tobacco cultivation had depleted the soil for nearly two centuries. But tidewater agriculture took a turn for the worse in the 1830s and 1840s, with declining yields and falling prices. John Tayloe's sons, who inherited their father's land and slaves in 1828, quickly concluded that they could no longer make adequate profits from Virginia grain and livestock, and plunged into cotton production in Alabama. Starting in the 1830s and continuing into the Civil War, they transferred most of the Mount Airy labourers to new cotton plantations 800 miles away. But that is another chapter in the saga of the Tayloes and their slaves.

To return to John Tayloe III, the employment pattern he established and sustained at Mount Airy clearly demonstrates the flexibility and functionality of his methods. But of course these methods were very damaging, socially and psychologically, for his enslaved labourers. When workers can be moved around like chessmen at the dictate of the master, their utility can be maximized. Tayloe understood this point. Obviously if he had been operating in a wage economy he would have hired many fewer workers. But he found jobs for almost all of his surplus slaves: some as domestics to maintain the seigneurial style of his establishment, some

---

[41] See Richard S. Dunn, 'A tale of two plantations: slave life at Mesopotamia in Jamaica and Mount Airy in Virginia, 1799 to 1828', *WMQ*, 3rd series, 34 (1977), 32–65, esp. 64.

as artisans to make things like farm implements and clothing that otherwise would have to be purchased, some (mostly young field hands) as
manual labourers in newly opened work sites elsewhere in the
Chesapeake. And Tayloe sold those people who did not fit into his
system. A number of slaves ran away, but they were always caught. Not a
single one of the 648 slaves who lived on Mount Airy between 1809 and
1828 escaped permanently during John Tayloe's lifetime. And it must
have been well known in the slave quarters that anyone judged guilty of
misconduct by the master was likely to be sold: surely an efficient method
of social control. Tayloe was a benevolent patriarch by his lights, but he
had few compunctions about slaveholding. Rich as he was, he freed only
one of his African American labourers, his faithful body servant Archy, at
the age of fifty-seven.[42] All of the others remained trapped. It was a system
that worked very well for John Tayloe, but that stifled initiative, thwarted
ambition, and denied personal and family freedom to the hundreds of
people who laboured for him.

[42] Tayloe provided for Archy's manumission and an annual pension of $100 in his will,
dated December 1827 (Tayloe d 539–43).

Index